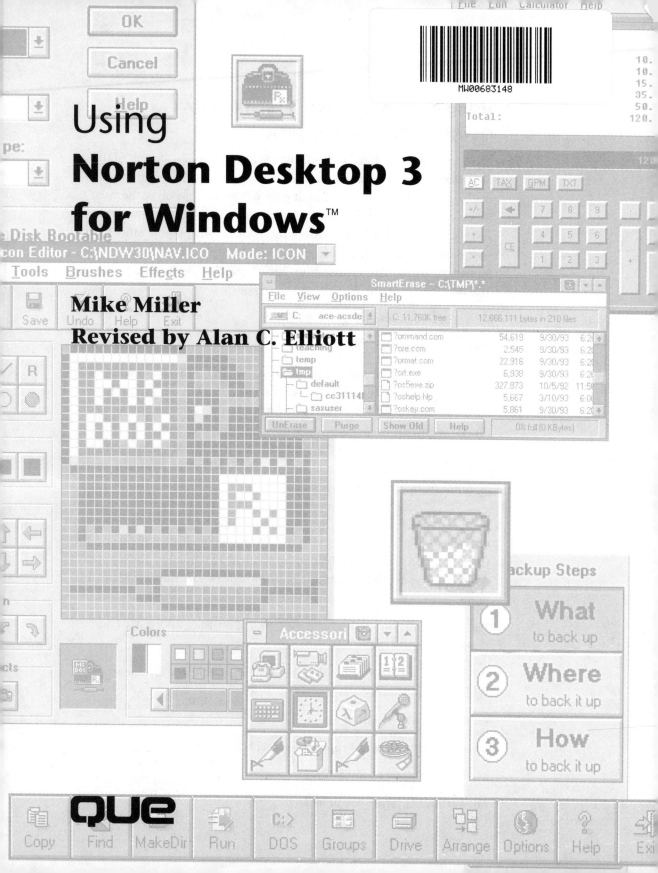

Using Norton Desktop 3 for Windows™

Mike Miller
Revised by Alan C. Elliott

QUE

Using Norton Desktop 3 for Windows

Library of Congress Catalog No.: 93-86749

ISBN: 1-56529-586-2

95 94 93 5 4 3 2 1

Interpretation of the printing code: the rightmost double-digit number is the year of the book's printing; the rightmost single-digit number, the number of the book's printing. For example, a printing code of 93-1 shows that the first printing of the book occurred in 1993.

Screen reproductions in this book were created by using Collage Plus from Inner Media, Inc., Hollis, NH.

Using Norton Desktop 3 for Windows is based on Norton Desktop 3.0 for Windows.

Publisher: David P. Ewing

Director of Publishing Projects: Michael Miller

Managing Editor: Corinne Walls

Marketing Manager: Ray Robinson

Credits

Publishing Manager
Thomas H. Bennett

Acquisitions Editor
Thomas F. Godfrey III

Product Director
Bryan Gambrel

Production Editors
William A. Barton
Susan Ross Moore

Editors
Elsa Bell
Donald R. Eamon
Heather Kaufman
J. Christopher Nelson
Pamela Wampler

Technical Editor
Rowan Trollope

Editorial Assistants
Jill L. Stanley
Michelle Williams

Cover Designer
Jay Corpus

Book Designer
Amy Peppler-Adams

Production Team
Jeff Baker
Angela Bannan
Claudia Bell
Danielle Bird
Katie Bodenmiller
Paula Carroll
Charlotte Clapp
Anne Dickerson
Meshell Dinn
Karen Dodson
Brook Farling
Carla Hall
Bob LaRoche
Beth Lewis
Nanci Sears Perry
Caroline Roop
Marc Shecter
Tina Trettin
Jennifer Willis
Donna Winter
Lillian Yates

Indexers
Michael Hughes
Johnna VanHoose

Composed in *ITC Garamond* and *MCPdigital*
by Que Corporation.

About the Authors

Alan C. Elliott is an assistant director of Academic Computer Services at the University of Texas Southwestern Medical Center in Dallas. He has authored several books, including *Using Norton Utilities 6, Introduction to Microcomputing with Applications, A Daily Dose of the American Dream,* and *PC Programming Techniques*. He also is the coauthor of Que's *Using PROCOMM PLUS* with Walt Bruce and is a coauthor of the 1985 and 1988 editions of the *Directory of Statistical Microcomputing Software*. He is author of the software packages Kwikstat (Data Analysis), PC-CAI (Computer-Assisted Instruction), and Information Please (Data Analysis), published by TexaSoft. His articles have appeared in professional and popular periodicals, including *PC Week, College Microcomputer Journal, Communications in Statistics,* and *American Statistician.*

Mike Miller is the author of more than a dozen best-selling computer books for the Que, Sams, and Alpha imprints, including several books in the ever-expanding OOPS! series. Mike has been working with computers and computer users since the old Kaypro days. When he is not writing, Mike is the Director of Marketing Strategies for Prentice Hall Computer Publishing and collects all sorts of wonderful electronic toys.

Acknowledgments

Using Norton Desktop 3 for Windows is the result of the efforts of several dedicated and talented people. Que Corporation thanks the following people:

Jill L. Stanley and Michelle Williams for their last-minute phenomenal formatting.

Donald R. Eamon and Pamela Wampler for going above and beyond the call of sanity.

Heather Kaufman for her steadfast and timely copy-editing.

J. Christopher Nelson for his sensitivity to tone.

Special thanks to Susan Ross Moore for picking up the torch, on this her first book, when her fellow production editor finally succumbed after working two days overtime with the flu.

Trademark Acknowledgments

Que Corporation has made every effort to supply trademark information about company names, products, and services mentioned in this book. Trademarks indicated below were derived from various sources. Que Corporation cannot attest to the accuracy of this information.

Norton Disk Doctor, Norton Commander, Norton Utilities and UnErase, and Q&A are registered trademarks, and Norton AntiVirus, Norton Backup, Scheduler, Sleeper, Speed Disk, and SuperFind are trademarks of Symantec Corporation.

Trademarks of other products mentioned in this book are held by the companies producing them.

Contents at a Glance

Contents

V Using ScriptMaker 499

30 Learning ScriptMaker Basics 501

31 Creating Simple ScriptMaker Programs 521

32 ScriptMaker Command Reference 535

Introduction

When Microsoft Windows 3.0, the precursor to Windows 3.1, was introduced, critics called it revolutionary. Its graphical user interface (GUI) would change how computer users interact with their programs, as well as how future programs would work. Windows was so easy to use, so intuitive, so perfect an environment that users would throw away all their add-on utilities and self-help books and drift away on a sea of mouse-driven ecstasy.

Those reviews were the predictions. Reality, unfortunately, is sometimes different from expectations. Yes, Windows is far easier to use than are DOS command prompts. Yes, the Windows GUI is a much better environment for most users than are character-based environments such as DOS. Yes, Windows changed the way people use computers. But Windows is far from perfect, and users—never satisfied, of course—soon wanted more. Windows 3.1 fixed some of the shortcomings of version 3.0, but some areas still are awkward to use.

Accustomed to the benefits of the Windows GUI, however, many users wanted even more graphical elements in their interface. Accustomed to Windows' improved ease of use, many users wanted an even easier-to-use environment. Accustomed to using a mouse instead of a keyboard, many users wanted even more mouse compatibility. As is true of most major technological developments, Windows merely whetted the appetites of consumers hungry for a truly easy-to-use computing environment. Enter Symantec's Norton Desktop for Windows.

Notes on Norton Desktop for Windows

Now available in version 3, Norton Desktop for Windows (often shortened to NDW) is a combination of operating environment, user tools, and utility programs that runs "on top of" regular Windows. (This means that you must have Windows installed on your computer to run NDW—and, of course, DOS to run Windows.) NDW fills in the gaps present in the Windows environment. NDW makes Windows more robust and powerful, easier to use, and even more "Windows-like" and mouse-compatible than Windows alone.

In short, Norton Desktop for Windows is the perfect "add-on" program for Microsoft Windows. Although NDW is not a miracle cure for all Windows' real or perceived ills, many users find that NDW makes them more productive in working with their computers. That benefit, in itself, is worth the purchase price of the program.

So what exactly *is* Norton Desktop 3 for Windows? First, NDW is a "shell" program that replaces the normal Windows Program Manager shell. The NDW shell is more easily configurable for different user needs than is the Program Manager. If you prefer a menu-driven environment, you can configure NDW to operate with a variety of custom menus. If you prefer an icon-driven environment, you can configure the NDW workspace to contain as many program and document icons as you can fit on-screen. NDW provides a degree of flexibility that Windows lacks—and that many users prefer.

NDW also is a collection of user tools and utility programs. Software tools are much like regular tools; if you need to accomplish a specific task, having the right tool at hand is always helpful, whether a Phillips screwdriver or an UnErase utility. NDW's tools include individual programs that enable you to customize Windows icons, quickly identify the key combinations that produce special characters, blank the screen if you are not using your computer, optimize the performance of your hard disk, and more. NDW even includes Norton Backup for Windows, Norton AntiVirus, Norton Disk Doctor, and Speed Disk, which are among today's most popular programs for managing and backing up data on your hard disk. In short, NDW is a veritable tool chest of useful tools and utilities.

Version 3 of NDW adds several new features to the mix and addresses a few shortcomings of several existing features retained from earlier versions. Among the new or improved features of version 3 are the following:

- The Day Planner Appointment Calendar, To Do List, Address and Phone Book.
- FileAssist, which improves file management from within applications and provides support for long file descriptions.
- A central configuration routine called Control Center.

- Extensive drag-and-drop capabilities.
- Graphical, configurable toolbars available throughout the program.
- PKZIP 2.0 support and view file capability.
- More than 100 file formats supported in the Norton Viewer.
- Full disk repair through Norton Disk Doctor for Windows.
- Full disk optimization through Speed Disk for Windows.
- Increased support for various backup formats, including tape sharing, support for QIC 40/80 and SCSI devices, and DES encryption.
- Extensive virus protection against more than 2,300 known viruses, plus protection against even unknown viruses.
- Rescue capabilities that use a special Rescue Disk, which stores critical information about your system needed to restore the system after a crash.
- Improved graphical on-line Help, a special Treasure Chest containing tips and shortcuts, and an on-line tutorial.
- Faster program performance.
- More NetWare information, available through System Information.
- A special Visual Basic-like programming language, called ScriptMaker, that enables you to write and compile scripts for the desktop.
- A DOS Fix-It disk containing DOS versions of the Disk Doctor, Speed Disk, UnErase, Format Recover, and DOS Restore to help you recover your files after system crashes.

Norton Desktop for Windows, developed by the Peter Norton Computing Group of Symantec, has a suggested retail price of $179. The program is available through most major software retailers.

Who Should Use Norton Desktop?

Norton Desktop 3 for Windows is an ideal add-on for novice and occasional computer users. Many such users find the Norton Desktop more intuitive and easier to use than the standard Windows desktop. If you are a "reluctant" PC user, NDW's friendlier GUI may make your computing sessions more palatable.

Norton Desktop 3 for Windows also is ideal for experienced and "power" computer users. Its collection of tools and utilities, as well as the customization capabilities of the Norton Desktop, appeal to frequent users who perform a variety of tasks with their PCs. If you use your computer frequently, you are likely to find at least one utility in NDW's tool chest that could some day be a lifesaver—or a file saver.

Note

Symantec specifies that version 3 of NDW be run on a computer with a 386 or higher processor and at least 4M RAM, running DOS 3.3 or a later version and Windows 3.1. You also need about 17M free disk space to load the full program to your hard disk.

The only users who may not find any value in NDW are those who adamantly stick to character-based interfaces. (If you are anti-GUI, therefore, you probably should stick with DOS as your interface.)

Notes on This Book

You need to know, first, what *Using Norton Desktop 3 for Windows* is not. Even though its coverage of NDW version 3 is comprehensive in both scope and depth, this book is not to be considered a replacement for the program's original documentation. This book is not a step-by-step beginning tutorial, although it does show beginners how to use all aspects of the program. Neither is this book a quick reference to common features of the program, though you can find in its pages the information you need to help you perform many everyday operations. Finally, this book is not a collection of power-user secrets, even though it does contain numerous tips to help you get more out of the program. So just what *is* this book?

Using Norton Desktop 3 for Windows is a combination of both entry-level tutorial and comprehensive reference. The book covers all important aspects of NDW and includes as much material aimed at beginning users as it does for power users. In short, if you buy only one book about Norton Desktop 3 for Windows, this book is the one to buy.

This book has several unique features. The first such feature you may notice is the use of **Notes**, **Tips**, **Sidebars**, **Cautions**, and **Warnings**. These items point out information of specific importance that, although not essential to the main text, make you more productive in using Norton Desktop. Tips appear in the margins of the book. Notes, Sidebars, Cautions, and Warnings appear in boxes within—but separate from—the main body of text.

The second unique feature to this book is how its information is presented. You are most likely used to books that present information in a linear, step-by-step fashion. That approach works if you deal with a linear subject. NDW, however, is very much a nonlinear program. Each individual part of the program works independently from all other parts.

Because you do not use NDW in an "A-B-C" fashion, this book does not present information about the program linearly. The book is arranged just as you use NDW—in independent modules. To use Norton Backup, for example, you need not read through the chapters on Shredder and KeyFinder first. This book enables you to go directly to the information you need now, without trudging through information you may not need until tomorrow.

To further assist you in using this book, words and terms used or defined for the first time are printed in *italic typeface*. Words, phrases, and symbols that you type appear in **boldface**. Text that exactly represents the text you see on-screen appears in a `special typeface`. You also can use the book's program icons, which appear in the margins, as a kind of "road map" to the specific features or particular aspects of the program that these icons denote.

Who Should Use This Book?

This book is for you—no matter how you use Norton Desktop for Windows.

- If you are a beginning user, you should find Part I, "Using Norton Desktop Basics," especially useful.
- If you want to use NDW mainly to copy, move, and delete files and disks, Part II, "Managing Files and Directories," contains the information you need.
- If you enjoy personalizing your computing environment or just want the most out of using NDW and Windows, look to Part III, "Designing the Perfect Desktop."
- To use NDW's many tools and utilities most effectively, closely examine Part IV, "Using the Norton Desktop Tools and Utilities." Each chapter in this section is devoted to a single utility.

- Finally, if you are a power user, make sure that you explore NDW's capability to create powerful batch files, as described in Part V, "Using ScriptMaker."

Even if you are only thinking about buying NDW in the future, this book can give you the flavor of the program at only a fraction of the price.

Other Useful Que Books

To get the most you can from this book, you may want to refer to other Que books that explore DOS, Windows, and the application programs you use every day. To learn more about these important, related topics, you can try the following titles:

Using Norton Desktop for DOS

Using Norton Utilities 7

Using MS-DOS 6.2, Special Edition

Using Procomm Plus for Windows

Using Microsoft Windows 3.1, Special Edition

Using Excel Version 5 for Windows, Special Edition

Using Word for Windows Version 6, Special Edition

Using WordPerfect 6 for Windows, Special Edition

Using 1-2-3 Release 4 for Windows

Using Ami Pro 3, Special Edition

Using Quicken 3 for Windows

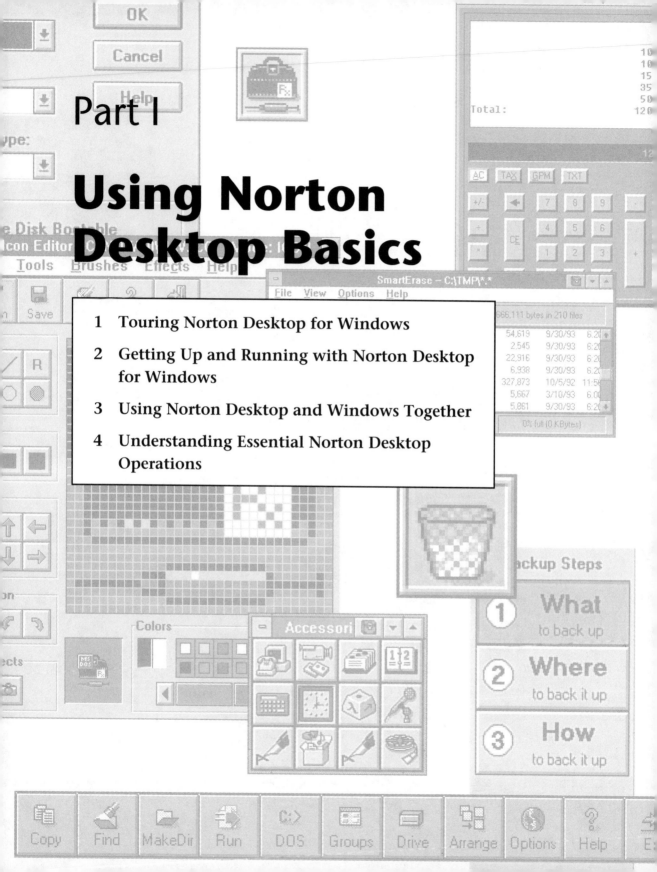

Part I

Using Norton Desktop Basics

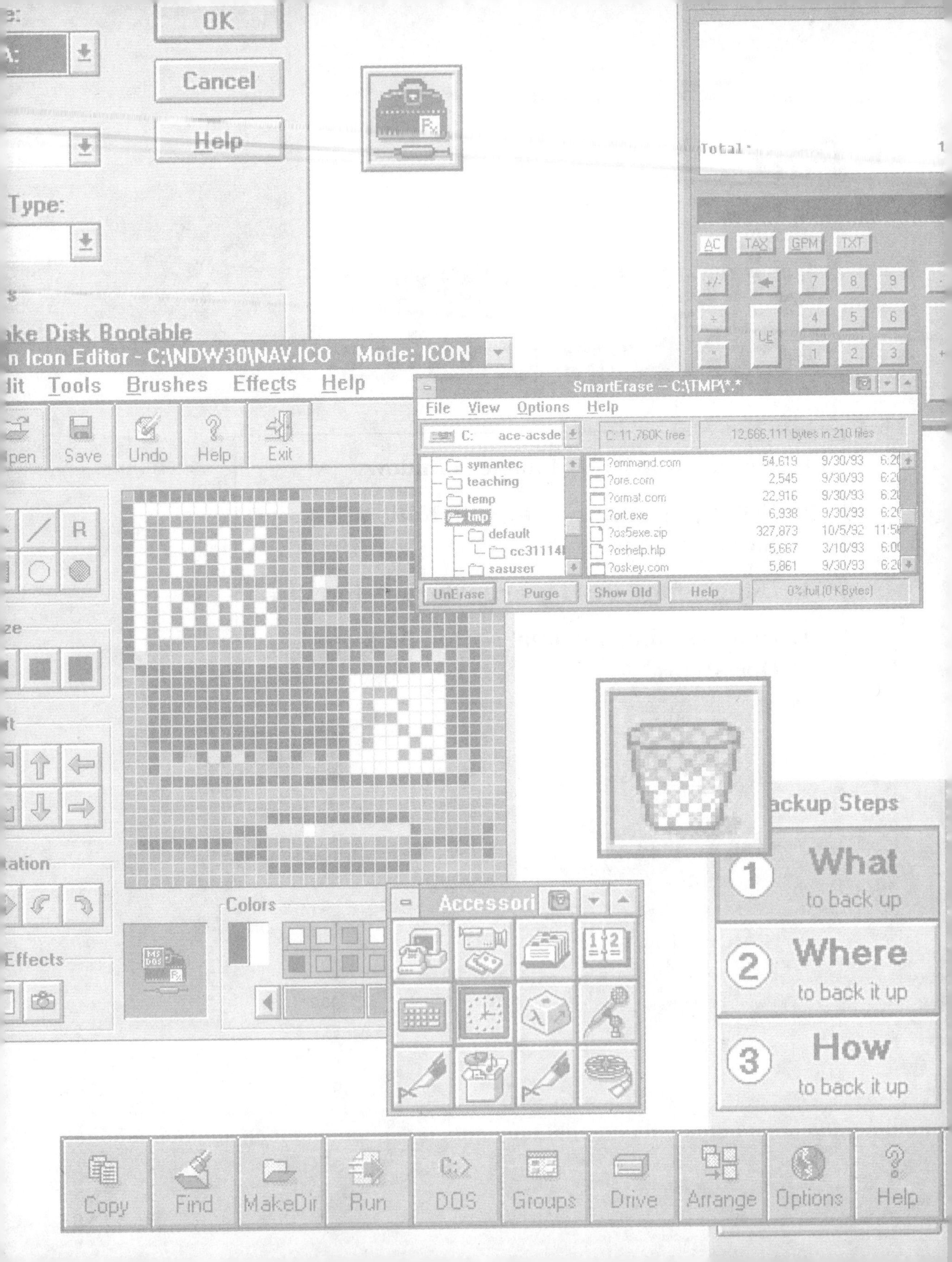
OK
Cancel
Help
Type:
ake Disk Bootable
n Icon Editor - C:\NDW30\NAV.ICO Mode: ICON
dit Tools Brushes Effects Help
pen Save Undo Help Exit
Colors
Effects
SmartErase – C:\TMP*.*
File View Options Help
C: 11,760K free
12,666,111 bytes in 210 files
symantec
teaching
temp
tmp
default
sasuser
UnErase Purge Show Old Help
0% full (0 KBytes)
Total:
AC TAX GPM TXT
Accessori
ackup Steps
1 What to back up
2 Where to back it up
3 How to back it up
Copy Find MakeDir Run DOS Groups Drive Arrange Options Help

Chapter 1

Touring Norton Desktop for Windows

What exactly do you do after you install Norton Desktop 3 for Windows (as described in Appendix A)? This chapter provides a tour to the many features of NDW and guides you to more detailed information located in later chapters of this book.

For more details about the various components of the Norton Desktop, for example, you need to see Chapter 2, "Getting Up and Running with Norton Desktop for Windows." To learn how the Norton Desktop differs from the regular Windows environment, see Chapter 3, "Using Norton Desktop and Windows Together." For more information about how to use the mouse and keyboard to operate Norton Desktop, see Chapter 4, "Understanding Essential Norton Desktop Operations."

If you are already familiar with the information presented in these chapters, you can go directly to Part IV, "Using the Norton Desktop Tools and Utilities," which covers the program's specific features.

In this chapter, you learn to perform the following tasks:

- Make the Desktop work for you
- Create and edit icons
- Manage disks, directories and files
- Increase your productivity in using the Norton Desktop

Making the Desktop Work for You

The Norton Desktop program is a shell that enables you to access all the NDW tools and utilities, as well as all regular Windows and DOS programs. The Norton Desktop program is easier to use than the DOS 5 or 6 shell or the Windows Program Manager. You can use the mouse or the keyboard to access all your Windows and DOS applications.

After you first start the Norton Desktop program, a screen that also is called the *Desktop* appears, similar to that shown in figure 1.1. From the Desktop, you can access all NDW functions, tools, and utilities by using either the Desktop icons or the menu system.

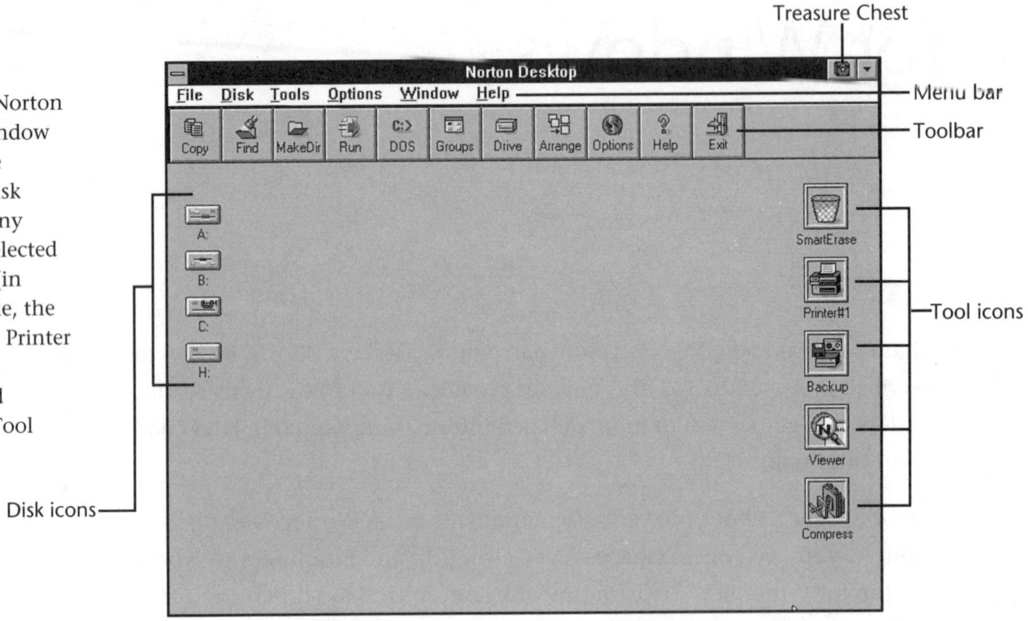

Fig. 1.1
The initial Norton Desktop window displays the available Disk icons and any currently selected Tool icons (in this example, the SmartErase, Printer #1, Backup, Viewer, and Compress Tool icons).

Learning Components of the Norton Desktop

Chapter 2, "Getting Up and Running with Norton Desktop for Windows," details all the components of the Norton Desktop. To begin, however, you need only recognize the menu bar, the Treasure Chest, the Drive icons, the Tool icons, and the Desktop icons, as described in the following list:

- The *menu bar* contains several pull-down menus. Use the mouse to open these menus by clicking the menu name in the menu bar. Then click the command names that appear under the main menu item to choose the menu commands. You also can choose menu commands by pressing F10 to access the menu bar and then by using the right-arrow and left-arrow keys to move the highlight down the menu from item to item. Press Enter to access the selected (highlighted) menu item. See Chapter 2, "Getting Up and Running with Norton Desktop for Windows," for more information.

- The *Treasure Chest* is found throughout the program. After you click it, helpful tips about using that portion of the program appear on-screen. See Chapter 2, "Getting Up and Running with Norton Desktop for Windows," for more information.

- *Drive icons* represent the disk drives present on your system. They are usually located at the far left of the Desktop. Double-clicking a Drive icon displays a drive window (see fig. 1.2). The drive window displays the directories and files present on that disk. Use drive windows to manipulate files and directories. See Chapter 5, "Using the Drive Windows," for more information.

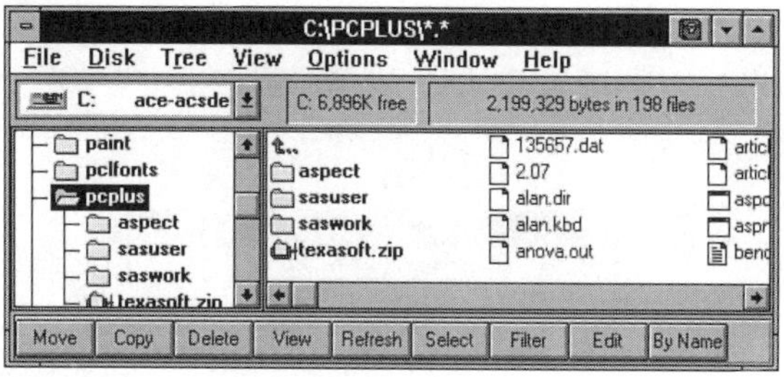

Fig. 1.2
A Norton Desktop drive window, displaying the tree and file panes.

- *Tool icons* are special Norton Desktop icons representing NDW's essential tools, such as SmartErase, Norton Backup, Norton Viewer, Norton AntiVirus, Norton Speed Disk, Norton Disk Doctor, and the Printer function. These tools are normally located down the right side of the Desktop. Access these tools by double-clicking the icon. See Chapter 28, "Using System Information," for more information.

- *Toolbar icons* appear directly below the menu bar and are "shortcut" icons you can use to choose commonly used commands. Access these commands by double-clicking the icon.

- *Desktop icons* are icons you install on the desktop to represent programs and documents. Create Desktop icons by dragging files from drive or group windows onto the Desktop. These icons can be placed anywhere on the Desktop. Access the program represented by the icon by double-clicking the icon.

Launching Programs

Whether you are a DOS or Windows user, you should find the Norton Desktop easy to use. You can start—or *launch*—all your applications from the Desktop by using the mouse or the keyboard.

If you are accustomed to DOS command line operations, you can choose the Run toolbar icon or use the **F**ile **R**un command to start programs. Access this command by opening the **F**ile menu and choosing **R**un. After the Run dialog box appears, enter the necessary DOS command line to launch the program. You also can choose the **F**ile Run **D**OS command to open a DOS window and work directly from the DOS prompt.

If you are accustomed to using the Windows Program Manager, you can start programs from the Norton Quick Access group (see fig. 1.3). You can install this group—which is similar to the Windows Program Manager in that it displays icons that represent program groups—on the Desktop. You also can access the Quick Access group from the **W**indow menu or by clicking the Groups toolbar icon. The benefit of using the Quick Access group is that you can nestle groups within groups and display these groups of icons in any of several styles.

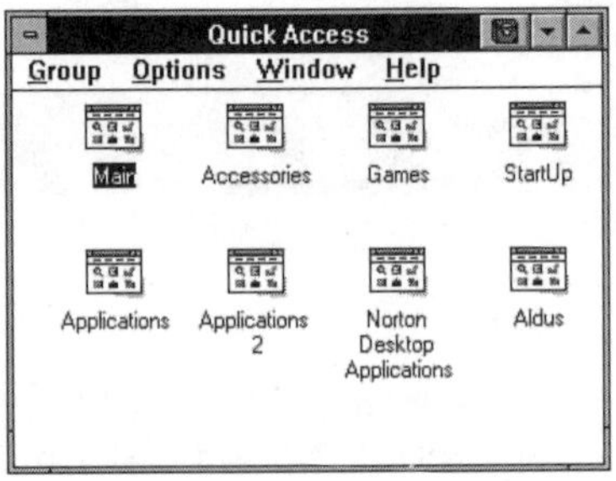

Fig. 1.3
The Norton Quick Access group contains several icons that represent groups of programs.

If you are accustomed to using the Windows File Manager, you can start programs from a Norton drive window. Simply double-click a Drive icon to open a drive window, navigate to the correct directory, and double-click the selected program or data file.

You can even create your own Desktop icons for frequently used programs and permanently install these icons on your Desktop by opening a drive window, selecting the program file, and dragging and dropping the file onto the Desktop. To start the program, just double-click its Desktop icon.

Creating and Editing Icons

Icons are very important to Norton Desktop. NDW's main tools appear on the Desktop as special *Tool icons*; programs can reside on the Desktop as *Desktop icons*; disk drives are pictured as *Drive icons*; and minimized programs appear as standard Windows *Program icons*.

Norton Desktop 3 for Windows enables you to change the appearance of the icons that represent any application. The Icon Editor utility functions as a paint program for icons so that you can edit existing icons or create new icons with point-and-click ease (see fig. 1.4). See Chapter 17, "Using Icon Editor," for more information about editing icons.

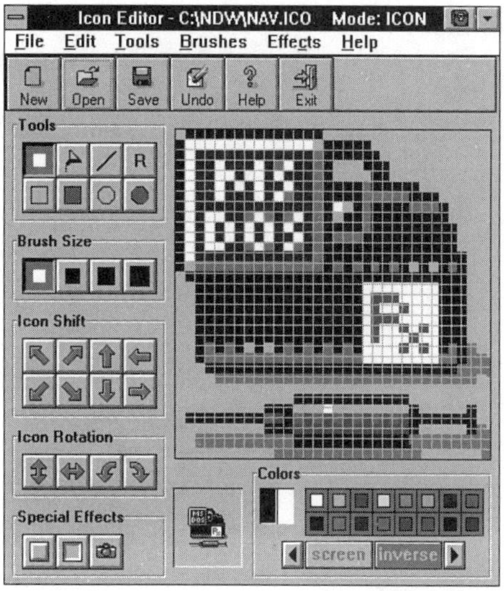

Fig. 1.4
The Norton Icon Editor, showing the AntiVirus Icon being edited.

Customizing the Desktop

You can customize the Norton Desktop itself to your own personal taste. You can determine the Tool icons that NDW displays on the Desktop, what files appear in drive windows, how the files are displayed in drive windows, and dozens of other settings that affect your day-to-day use of NDW. The **O**ptions **C**ustomize menu contains the "Control Center," which is the configuration location for all Desktop commands. See Chapter 11, "Customizing Norton Desktop's Settings," for more information.

You also can completely customize the Norton Desktop menu system by using the menu editor located in the Control Center. If you want a menu item called **P**rograms, for example, you can create it in Norton Desktop. This feature is particularly useful if you use NDW without a mouse; you can add all your favorite programs and commands to the pull-down menus. See Chapter 12, "Creating a Menu-Based Desktop," for more information.

Managing Disks, Directories, and Files

Norton Desktop 3 for Windows provides a painless way to work with files on your floppy disks and hard disks. By using the program's menus and icons, you can format, copy, view, print, and edit files—often with nothing more than a click of your mouse.

Formatting Disks

Formatting floppy disks is as easy as accessing a menu in a Norton Desktop drive window (refer to fig 1.2). The **D**isk menu includes the **F**ormat Diskette command along with commands for other common disk operations. Just choose **D**isk **F**ormat Diskette, insert a disk in the selected drive, and begin the format procedure. See Chapter 6, "Managing Your Disks with Norton Desktop," for more information.

Copying Files

You can copy files in Norton Desktop several ways. The most popular method involves opening one or more drive windows, selecting the files to copy, and then dragging the files from one drive window to that of a different drive or directory.

You also can select the files to copy in a drive window and then click the Copy button in the drive window's button bar. Clicking this button activates a dialog box that enables you to specify where to copy the files. You also can drag selected files from an open drive window to a Drive icon or from the file pane to the tree pane of the same drive window. The Desktop's Copy command, however, operates differently. Clicking the Desktop's Copy toolbar icon displays a dialog box that enables you to type file specifications for files to copy and to specify their destinations. See Chapter 6, "Managing Your Disks with Norton Desktop," for more information.

You also can copy complete disks of the same size and format by choosing the **D**isk **C**opy Diskette command.

Moving Files

Moving files is as easy as copying files: Simply choose the **F**ile **M**ove command from the menu bar of a drive window to display the Move dialog box. If you prefer to use the drag-and-drop method to move a file, just press and hold the Alt key as you drag and drop the file from its current location to its destination; this method moves the file instead of just copying it.

Deleting Files

You can delete a file in any of several ways. Open a drive window, and choose the **F**ile **D**elete command from its menu bar to access the Delete dialog box; this dialog box enables you to select files to delete.

You also can select the files you want to delete and then click the Delete button on the drive window's button bar. (Pressing the Del key also deletes the selected files.)

Another way to delete a file is to use the SmartErase tool. Select a file in a drive window, drag the file from the drive window, and drop the file on the SmartErase Tool icon. NDW deletes the file.

Deleting a file, however, does not actually delete the information from your hard disk. Normal delete or erase commands just tell your hard disk that you no longer use the selected file and that the space occupied by the file is available for use by new files. Until a new file overwrites the disk area occupied by the old file, the old file still exists on your hard disk. (You also can *undelete* the file by using SmartErase, which is discussed in the following section.)

If, for security reasons, you want to completely eliminate from your hard disk the data in any deleted files, you can use NDW's Shredder tool to overwrite the deleted data immediately. Just drag such selected files from a drive window, and drop them onto the Shredder Tool icon instead of onto the SmartErase icon; after they are "shredded," the deleted files can no longer be undeleted. To do this, you must have the Shredder icon available on your Desktop—which you can choose from the Control Center options discussed earlier in "Customizing the Desktop."

Undeleting Files

If you accidentally delete a file you do not want deleted, NDW's SmartErase tool enables you to easily restore any recently deleted files. Double-click the SmartErase Tool icon, or choose the **T**ools **U**nErase command. The UnErase dialog box appears, enabling you to select deleted files and restore them (see fig. 1.5).

Printing Files

If you use Norton Desktop, you need not start an application to print one of that application's file. NDW enables you to print files directly from the Desktop, even if the associated program is not running. Print files by choosing a drive window's **F**ile **P**rint OK command from a drive window or by selecting a file in the drive window and dragging and dropping it onto the Printer Tool icon.

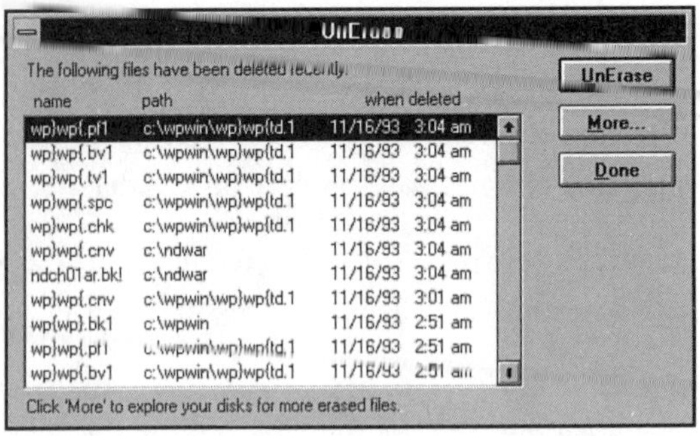

Fig. 1.5
The UnErase dialog box lists those files that have been deleted but that still can be unerased.

Finding Files

If you ever forget the name or directory of an important file, Norton Desktop's SuperFind utility can help you quickly locate the lost file. Choose the Find toolbar icon to access the SuperFind window (see fig. 1.6). SuperFind enables you to search for files by file type, file location, or text contained within the file.

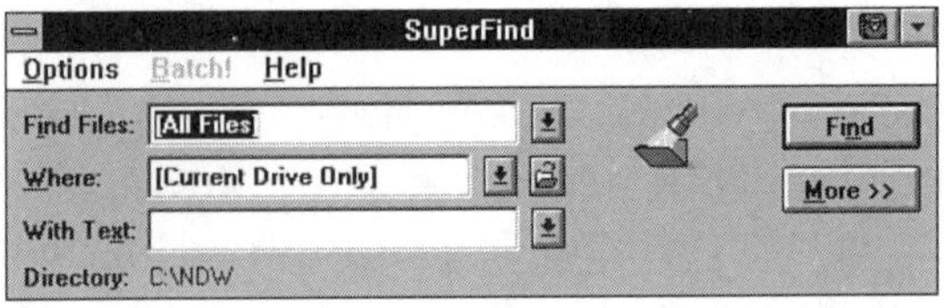

Fig. 1.6
The SuperFind dialog box enables you to specify which files to locate.

Editing Files

Sometimes you need to edit text files quickly—including such system files as AUTOEXEC.BAT or WIN.INI. You no longer need to start your word processor to perform this task, however; you can simply use NDW's new Desktop Editor utility, which functions much like a mini-word processor for ASCII text files. Choose **F**ile **E**dit from a drive window's menu bar to open the Desktop Editor window (see fig. 1.7). You also can choose **T**ools **T**ext Editor from the Desktop's menu bar to access the Desktop Editor.

Viewing File Contents

Sometimes you need to view the contents of a file without running the associated application. NDW provides several ways to view file contents. If a drive window is open, the simplest way to view a file is to click the View button on the drive window's button bar (refer to fig. 1.2). This displays the contents of the selected file in a *drop-down view pane* below the drive window.

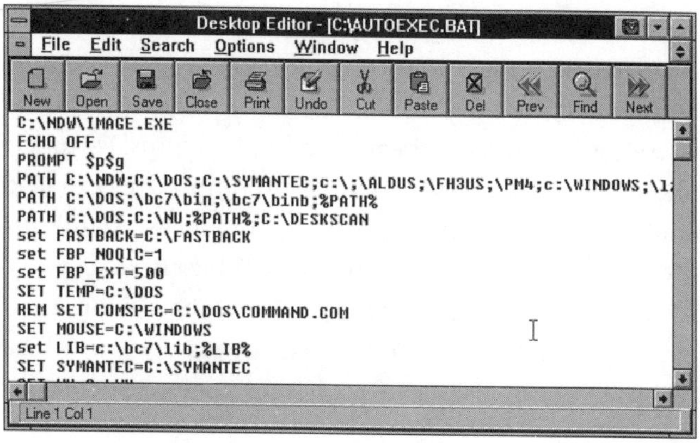

Fig. 1.7
The Desktop Editor window, showing the file AUTOEXEC.BAT being edited.

You also can use the Norton Viewer tool to view the contents of multiple files at one time. Choose the **F**ile **V**iew command from a drive window menu bar, choose the **F**ile **O**pen command (or click the Open icon), and then select the files you want to view from an Open File dialog box. This opens the Norton Viewer window, which displays each file in its native format (see fig. 1.8). Another way to view multiple files is to select the files in a drive window and then drag and drop them onto the Viewer Tool icon.

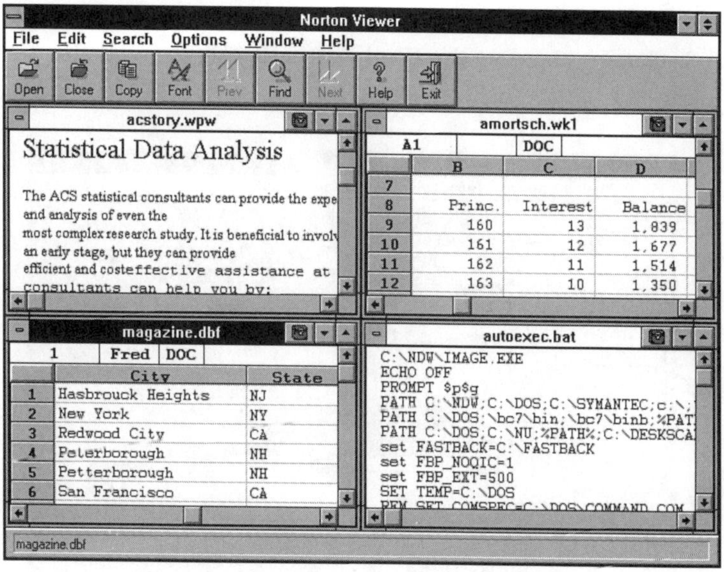

Fig. 1.8
The Norton Viewer window, showing four different files viewed at once, each displayed in its native format.

Protecting Your System from Computer Viruses

Computer viruses can cripple your computer system. If you exchange disks with other computer users or download files from computer bulletin boards or on-line services, you risk contracting a computer virus. Fortunately, NDW now includes the Norton AntiVirus tool. Norton AntiVirus can be configured to run automatically as your system boots up, or you can start it by choosing the **T**ools Norton Anti**V**irus command or by double-clicking the Norton AntiVirus Tool icon (if you added it to your Desktop). Norton AntiVirus scans your system's memory and disks and detects the presence of any harmful virus. AntiVirus can even disinfect your system from many common viruses.

Backing Up and Restoring Your Data

You can avert catastrophe in the event of data loss caused by a computer virus, a damaged disk, or even an accident (such as inadvertently formatting your hard disk), by keeping a backup of your data on separate backup disks or tapes. You then use these backup disks or tapes to restore the lost data to your hard disk.

Among its many tools, NDW includes Norton Backup for Windows (see fig. 1.9). This essential tool enables you to back up your hard disk to floppy disks or tapes quickly and easily. Backup even provides ways to automate your backups and perform different types of backups for different needs. Start Norton Backup by choosing the **T**ools Norton **B**ackup command or by double-clicking the Backup Tool icon.

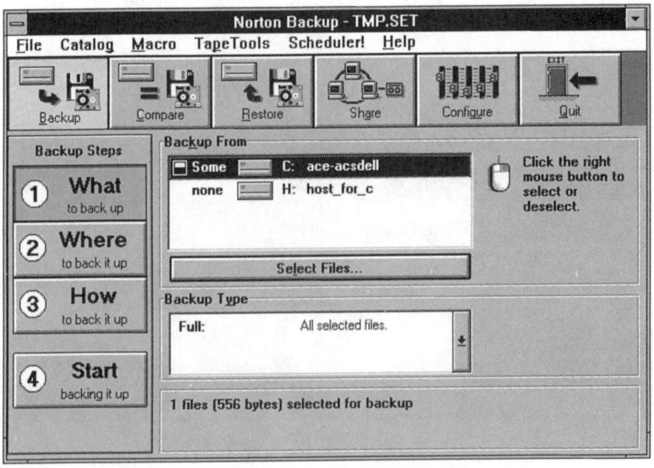

Fig. 1.9
Norton Backup for Windows enables you to back up important hard disk files to disks or tapes.

Norton Backup also enables you to restore data to your hard disk. Of course, the backup is of no use to you if Norton Backup for Windows, Norton Desktop, and Windows itself are missing from your hard disk. In such emergencies, you can use the Norton Emergency Restore disk. This special disk that you create includes a DOS-based version of Norton Backup that enables you to restore files even if Norton Backup for Windows is missing from your hard disk. See Chapter 10, "Restoring Files with Norton Backup and the Fix-It Disk," for more information.

Increasing Your Productivity by Using Norton Desktop

NDW enables you to perform many more tasks than simply starting programs and working with files. Almost every common computer operation is easily achievable with NDW, including some not-so-common—but very useful—operations made possible by Norton Desktop's many tools and utilities.

Using Special Characters in Your Documents

Few users know that you can use characters in your documents other than those characters that appear on the standard keyboard. You can access these special characters, such as ¢, ", and ½, by using special key combinations. You can learn these key combinations with the help of NDW's KeyFinder utility. Simply choose the **T**ools **K**eyFinder command to activate KeyFinder (see fig. 1.10).

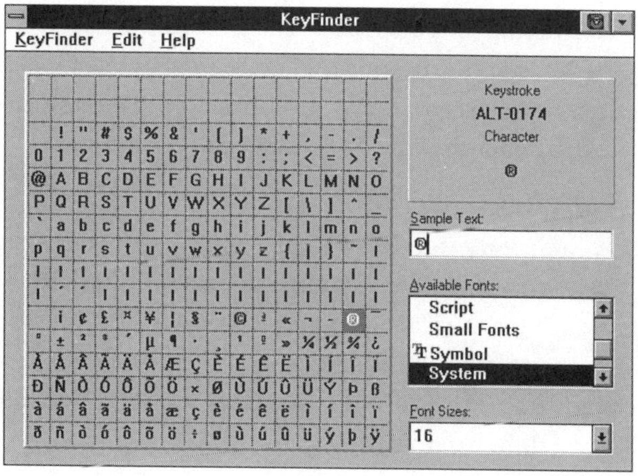

Fig. 1.10
The KeyFinder utility displays the available characters for each font.

Working with Calculators

Norton Desktop includes three separate calculators you can access by using the **T**ools **C**alculator command. These include a simple Tape Calculator, a complex Scientific Calculator, and a Financial Calculator that includes special functions for loan amortization, bond analysis, and other common financial calculations (see fig. 1.11). See Chapter 14, "Using the Calculators," for more information on all these calculators.

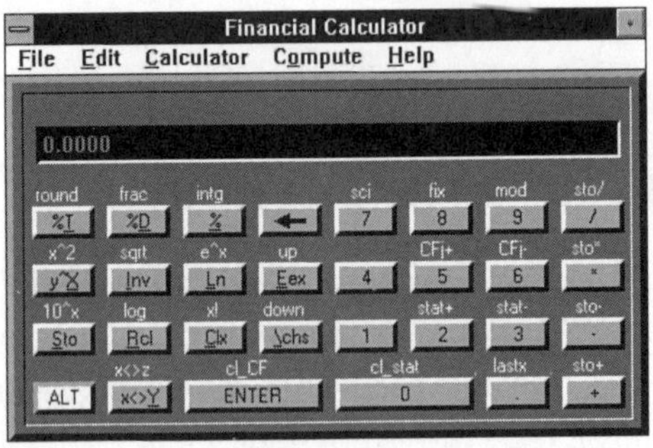

Fig. 1.11
The Desktop Financial Calculator contains all the functions of an actual financial calculator.

Saving Your Screen from Burn-In

As you may know, you can damage your computer monitor by leaving a static program on-screen for extended periods of time. Static images can cause screen *burn-in*, which looks like a ghost image of the original static image. This ghost image, however, is permanently etched onto your screen.

NDW provides a fun and useful utility, called Screen Saver, that prevents screen burn-in. Screen Saver displays lively and entertaining images on-screen if it detects inactivity in your computer. These images replace your static screen image. If you start using your system again (by pressing a key or moving your mouse), Screen Saver returns the normal image to the screen. Activate Screen Saver by choosing the **T**ools **S**creen Saver command.

Analyzing Your System

Occasionally, you may want to know more details about your system's components and performance. NDW includes the System Information utility, which displays such technical data about your system as its microprocessor type and speed, the amount of installed and available memory, and similar technical details. Choose the **T**ools **Sy**stem Information command to open the System Information window (see fig. 1.12).

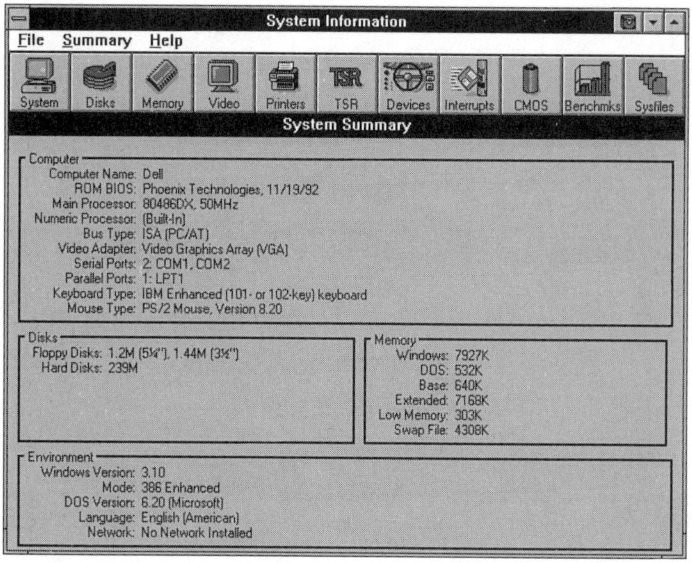

Fig. 1.12
The System Information window enables you to view details about your computer's features and configuration.

NDW also enables you to analyze your hard disk to check for any potential physical or logical defects. Norton Disk Doctor can warn you of pending disk damage before that damage can affect your system and your data (see fig. 1.13). If damage occurs on your drive, the Norton Disk Doctor also can repair the damage and recover seemingly lost data. Access the Norton Disk Doctor by choosing the **T**ools Norton **D**isk Doctor command or by clicking the Backup icon (if you selected it to appear on your Desktop).

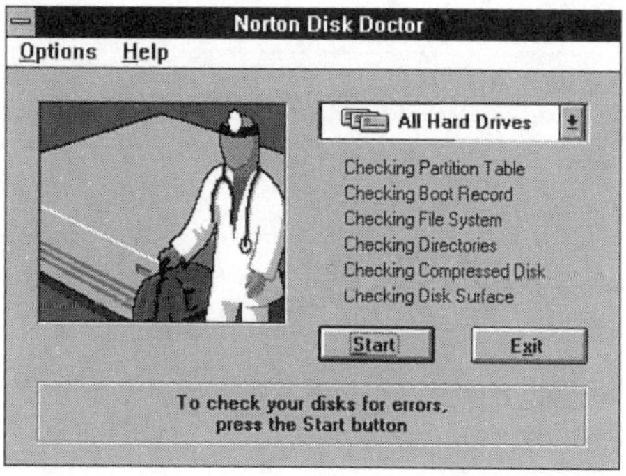

Fig. 1.13
Norton Disk Doctor enables you to diagnose and repair problems on your disk.

Scheduling Events

If you need to be reminded of important events, Norton Desktop can help. The Scheduler utility functions like a timer to alert you at specified dates and times. You also can set Scheduler to activate programs at selected times (see fig. 1.14). Activate Scheduler by choosing the **T**ools Schedu**l**er command.

Fig. 1.14
The Scheduler utility enables you to display messages or schedule future events.

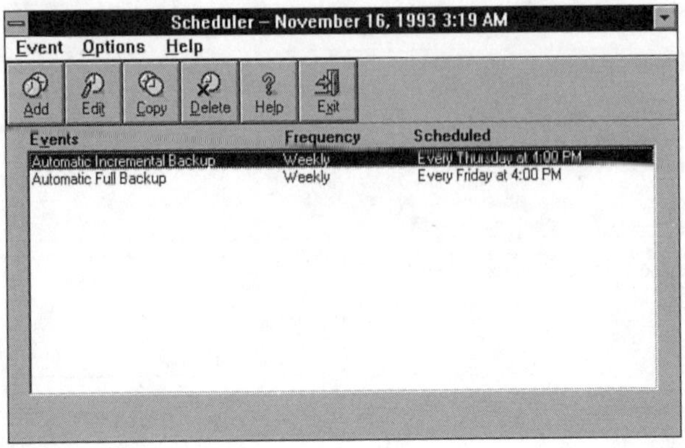

Automating Operations and Procedures

Some tasks become repetitive, even in Windows and Norton Desktop. NDW incorporates a special ScriptMaker utility that enables you to automate common operations easily. You can capture all keystrokes and mouse movements by using a macro recorder and then play them back at the touch of a single key. You also can edit the prerecorded macro, line by line, by using the ScriptMaker's editor. Figure 1.15 shows the ScriptMaker editor. Access the ScriptMaker by choosing **T**ools Scr**i**ptMaker.

Fig. 1.15
The ScriptMaker editor enables you to write macro programs to automate Desktop operations.

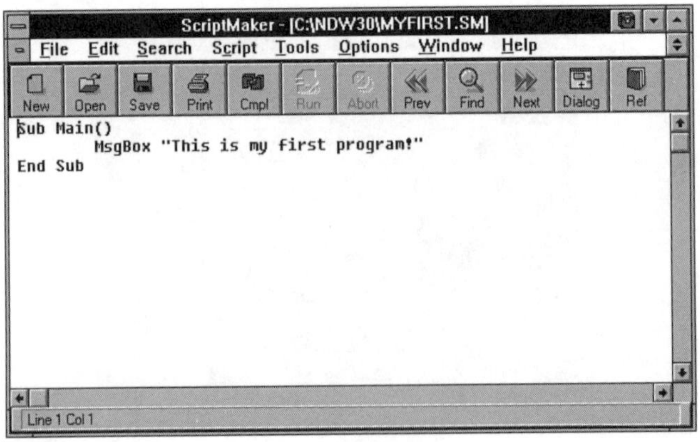

Planning Your Days

Everyone needs some help planning activities, so Norton provides a feature called the Day Planner to help you manage your affairs. Start the Day Planner by choosing the **T**ools **D**ay Planner command. By using this program, you can schedule events and view your calendar by day, week, or month. You can keep separate business and personal phone books, set priorities in a To Do list, and otherwise organize your life. Figure 1.16 shows the Day Planner's main window.

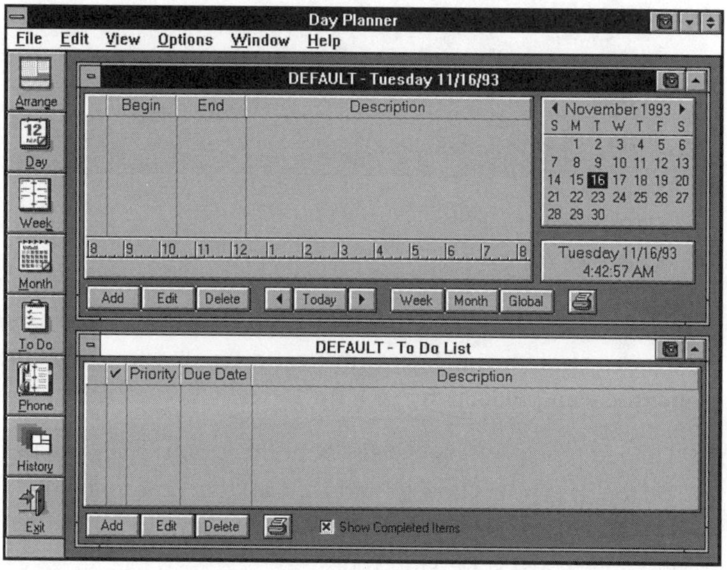

Fig. 1.16
The Day Planner main window enables you to schedule your calendar, manage a phone list and create a To Do list.

Using Speed Disk for Windows

Continued use of your disk can cause your files to become fragmented, which in turn can cause your disk access time to increase. Restructuring your hard disk on a regular basis by using the Norton Speed Disk program is highly advisable. Speed Disk reorganizes your files on disk in an optimum way so that access to the files remains as efficient and fast as possible. Begin Speed Disk by choosing the **T**ools Speed Dis**k** command. The initial Speed Disk window appears, as shown in figure 1.17.

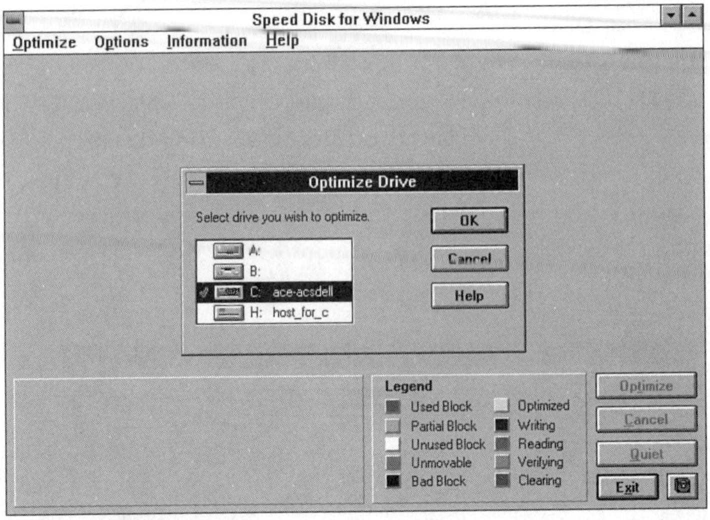

Fig. 1.17
The Norton Speed Disk for Windows initial window enables you to specify what drive to optimize.

Summary

This chapter took you on a quick tour of the Norton Desktop. You saw how the Desktop can work for you, how to manage disks, directories and files, and how to increase your productivity with the Desktop.

The next chapter provides more details about the various components of the Norton Desktop. It explains how to start the Desktop; how to use the Desktop's menus, dialog boxes, controls, and icons; how to use Desktop Groups; and how to access Desktop Tools.

Chapter 2

Getting Up and Running with Norton Desktop for Windows

2

In this chapter, you learn to perform the following tasks:

- Understand the Norton Desktop
- Understand NDW's dialog boxes and controls
- Understand menus, icons, and groups
- Understand NDW tools and utilities
- Understand NDW's Help system
- Use Treasure Chest helps

You just purchased version 3 of Norton Desktop for Windows. You opened the nicely packaged box and carefully removed all the contents. Now what?

This chapter answers that important question. You learn how to start the program and are introduced to all the components that comprise NDW. (For information on NDW installation, see Appendix A, "Installing Norton Desktop 3 for Windows.")

If you are already using NDW comfortably, you may want to skip this chapter. If you are just starting out, however, reading this chapter is essential.

Starting Norton Desktop

Assuming that you chose to have Norton Desktop replace the Windows Program Manager as your Windows shell, Norton Desktop starts whenever you start Windows. To start Norton Desktop, therefore, type **WIN** at the DOS prompt. The Windows start-up screen appears while Windows and NDW load. The Norton Desktop then appears on-screen, as shown in figure 2.1.

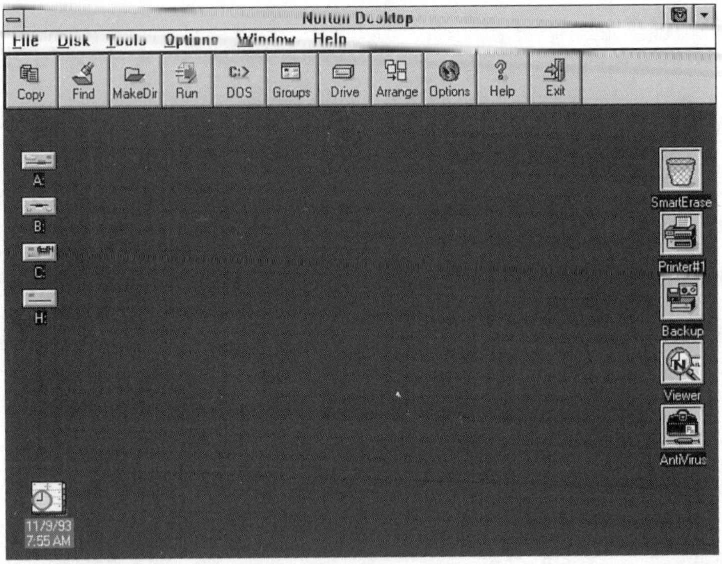

Fig. 2.1
A typical view of version 3 of Norton Desktop for Windows.

Note

Depending on the system setup and the installation options selected, your screen may differ slightly from the screen shown in figure 2.1.

If you see the Windows Program Manager rather than the Norton Desktop, one of the following two things may have happened:

- Windows is running in Real mode. Norton Desktop runs only in Windows Standard or Enhanced modes, not in Real mode. You may need to reconfigure or add more memory to your computer to run Windows in Standard or Enhanced mode. Find out what mode Windows is running in by accessing the **H**elp menu and choosing **A**bout. The About dialog box tells you whether Windows is running in Real, Standard, or Enhanced mode.

- You did not select Norton Desktop as the shell during the NDW installation procedure. Reinstall NDW, and select Norton Desktop as the Windows shell.

Tip
You can edit the Windows SYSTEM.INI file to select Norton Desktop as the permanent shell by changing the line SHELL=PROGMAN.EXE to SHELL=NDW.EXE.

If you didn't configure NDW to run Norton Desktop as the shell, you still can run Norton Desktop by choosing one of the following options:

- Exit Windows; then restart Windows by typing **WIN NDW**. This method starts Windows and loads Norton Desktop.

- From within Windows, open the Norton Desktop group from the Program Manager. Double-click the Norton Desktop icon to run Norton Desktop.

> **Note**
>
> These options do not make Norton Desktop a permanent shell; they make Norton Desktop usable only for the current session.

Exiting Norton Desktop is the same as exiting Windows. Just double-click the Control menu button, click the Exit toolbar icon, or open the **F**ile menu and choose E**x**it Windows. A dialog box asks you to confirm that you want to exit; if you answer OK, both Windows and Norton Desktop close, returning you to the DOS prompt.

> **Warning**
>
> Never turn off your computer with Windows or Norton Desktop running. You can damage important files if you do not exit Windows and Norton Desktop before turning off your PC.

Understanding Windows Basics

To fully understand Norton Desktop, you first must understand Windows. Windows is a graphical, object-oriented, multitasking computing environment. This explanation sounds complicated, but the underlying complexity of Windows actually makes the environment relatively easy to use.

The key to Windows is its use of objects. *Objects* are independent items that perform individual tasks. Windows includes the following types of objects:

- *Windows* are individual areas that hold information or applications.

- *Icons* are pictorial representations of other objects, including applications.

- *Menus* are lists of commands that initiate actions in windows and applications.
- *Pointers* represent a specific screen location and help initiate specific actions.
- *Dialog boxes* are special kinds of windows that enable you to enter data or information that is used to perform a function or direct how a function is performed.

Windows contain specific elements that are uniform from application to application (see fig. 2.2).

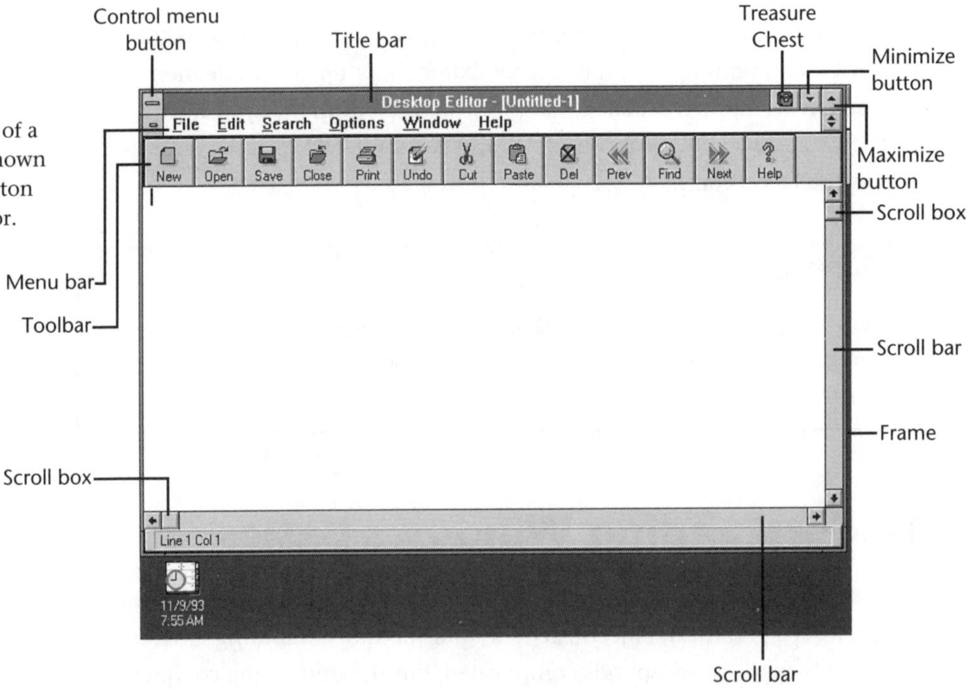

Fig. 2.2
The elements of a window, as shown using the Norton Desktop Editor.

The following table describes the elements shown in figure 2.2.

Feature	Function
Control menu button	Activates the Windows Control menu.
Frame	Surrounds the window space; clicking and dragging the frame resizes the window.

Feature	Function
Treasure Chest	Displays how-to information concerning a Norton tool or task.
Maximize button	Makes the window fill the entire screen.
Menu bar	Displays the various pull-down menus.
Toolbar	Command buttons for commonly used commands.
Minimize button	Reduces the window to an icon.
Scroll bars	Enable you to scroll through a space larger than the current window, either vertically or horizontally.
Scroll box	Enables you to manually move the contents of the window by dragging the scroll box, to see different parts of the document, application, or image inside the window.
Title bar	Displays the name of the current application or document.

You can access these window elements by using either the mouse or the keyboard. The Windows environment was designed specifically for mouse use, particularly for point-and-click and drag-and-drop actions. (Chapter 4, "Understanding Essential Norton Desktop Operations," discusses mouse and keyboard use in depth.)

The three types of NDW windows are as described in the following list:

- *Application windows* hold entire programs, such as Excel or Microsoft Word for Windows.

- *Document windows*, which appear within application windows, hold documents for the current application.

- *Dialog boxes* are a type of window that can appear anywhere in the environment. Dialog boxes either request information from the user or present information to the user.

Norton Desktop uses the same objects in exactly the same way as Windows. In fact, you should find that NDW's more diversified use of many objects makes the program easier to use than Windows.

Understanding the Norton Desktop

The Norton Desktop is just that—a Desktop. Consider this Desktop just as you consider the top surface of an office desk. Initially, you find a clean desktop, no more than an empty surface. On this empty surface, you eventually place the various objects you use every day.

The Norton Desktop is a plain surface on which various software objects are placed in the form of icons. The Desktop also uses pull-down menus, as do most other Windows applications.

If maximized (its normal state), the Norton Desktop shell fills the entire Windows screen. The Desktop shell contains many elements familiar to Windows users and also several elements unique to Norton Desktop.

Figure 2.3 illustrates how the Norton Desktop initially appears on-screen.

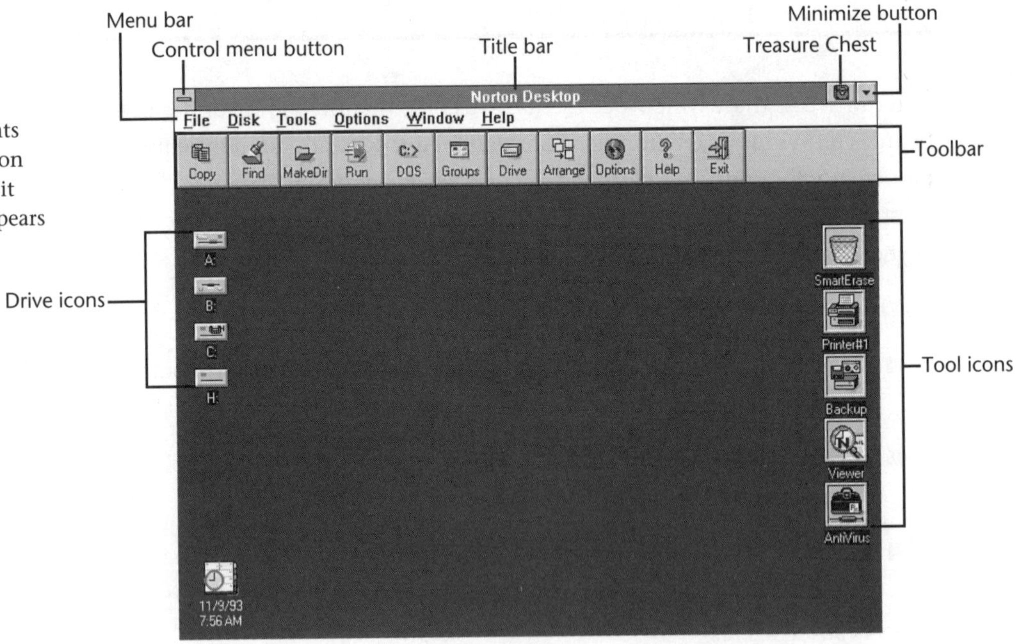

Fig. 2.3 The elements of the Norton Desktop as it initially appears on-screen.

The following table lists those elements of the screen worth noting.

Feature	Function
Title bar	Shows that this screen is the Norton Desktop window.
Treasure Chest	Displays how-to information about a Norton tool or task.

Feature	Function
Control menu button	Displays the Windows Control menu.
Menu bar	Displays the elements of the Norton Desktop main menu; each menu element opens to display additional menu items.
Toolbar	Contains commonly used commands.
Minimize button	Shrinks the Norton Desktop shell to an icon (see fig. 2.4); double-click the icon to maximize the desktop shell.
Drive icons	All drives on the system as identified by NDW.
Tool icons	For NDW's main user tools: SmartErase, Norton Backup, Shredder, Norton Viewer, the Print utility, and Norton AntiVirus.

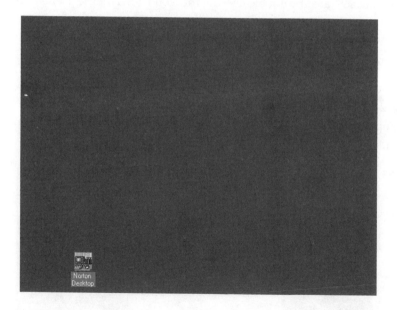

Fig. 2.4
If the Norton Desktop shell is minimized, it appears on the Desktop as an icon.

The various icons reside directly on the Desktop. All your work—applications, documents, utilities, and so on—resides on the Desktop. You can keep a clean Desktop or a messy Desktop; the Desktop can be devoid of icons or cluttered with icons. By using Norton Desktop, you can arrange your computer Desktop in as many ways as you can arrange the top of an office desk.

After you open any Windows application, the application window appears on the Desktop. If you minimize the application to an icon, the application icon appears in the lower-left corner of the Desktop. Subsequent application icons appear to the right of any initial application icons in this corner of the Desktop. If application icons fill up the entire bottom row of the Desktop, a new row of application icons appears, stacked above the first icon row.

Norton Desktop uses several types of icons. In Norton Desktop, you can create program or document icons that appear as raised buttons anywhere on the Desktop. Minimized application icons appear as flat icons in the lower-left corner of the Desktop. Special icons for NDW's main user tools, such as SmartErase, appear as raised buttons with a heavy border in user-selected areas of the Desktop. Raised drive icons appear for each active drive identified for the system. (A full discussion of icons follows later in this chapter.)

Icons are activated by double-clicking the icon with a mouse. Double-clicking a minimized application icon maximizes the application. Double-clicking a Drive icon opens the drive window for that drive. You can move icons anywhere on the Desktop by clicking an icon and dragging it to its new location.

If you double-click the Desktop surface, the Task List dialog box appears (see fig. 2.5). This dialog box enables you to switch to an open application, close an open application, and arrange minimized application icons and open windows.

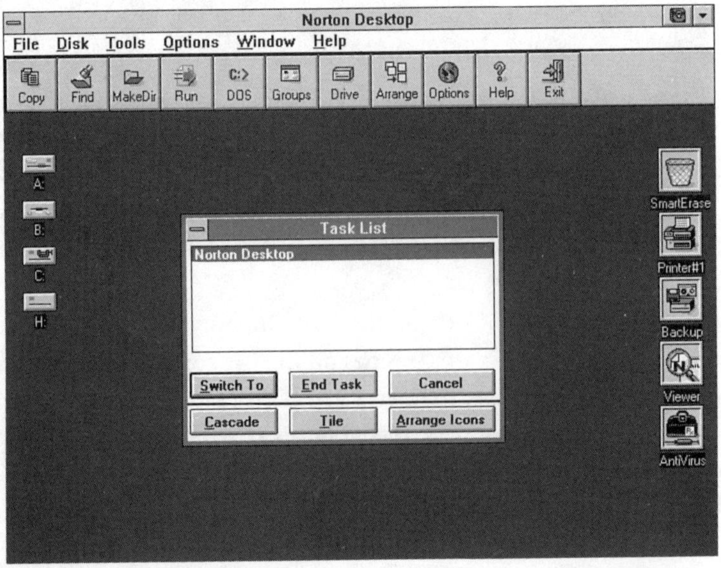

Fig. 2.5
The Task List dialog box enables you to switch to any open application.

Navigating through and operating the Desktop elements works the same as in regular Windows. The easiest way to use Norton Desktop is with a mouse. With a mouse, you can use point-and-click operations to choose icons and options, pull down menus, maximize and minimize windows, scroll through windows, and perform many other tasks.

Tip
The Task List dialog box appears if you double-click the Desktop with the left mouse button. A double-click of the right mouse button displays the Quick Access Group window instead.

If you do not have a mouse, you can use the keyboard to perform many essential Windows operations. Using the keyboard is more awkward than using the mouse, but you may encounter some situations in which you cannot use a mouse, such as if using a portable PC on an airplane; in these situations, knowledge of Windows keyboard operations is essential. (For a complete overview of mouse and keyboard operations, see Chapter 4, "Understanding Essential Norton Desktop Operations.")

Remember that the Norton Desktop is just a shell. You can minimize Norton Desktop just as you can any other application, making it an icon in the lower portion of the total Desktop. Double-clicking the Norton Desktop icon maximizes the shell to fill the entire screen again.

Understanding Norton Desktop Menus

You can access most essential NDW operations through the Norton Desktop menu system. You can customize Norton Desktop's menus, as discussed in Chapter 12, "Creating a Menu-Based Desktop," and Chapter 13, "Creating an Icon-Based Desktop."

Tip
Many file control commands found in the Norton Desktop **F**ile menu in version 2.0 now are located in the individual drive window menus.

Menus in Norton Desktop behave just like regular Windows menus. The main menu bar consists of a series of pull-down menus. You access these pull-down menus by using either the mouse or the keyboard.

Accessing a menu by using the mouse is simple: Just move the pointer to the menu item and click; the menu opens to display more menu commands. Clicking a command activates the command or produces additional menus or dialog boxes.

Accessing a menu by using the keyboard is only slightly more complex: Just press the Alt key in combination with the underlined letter of the menu you want to access. The **F**ile menu has the F underlined, for example; to access the **F**ile menu, press the Alt+F key combination. These key combinations are called keyboard shortcuts. (If you see a notation such as Alt+F, F, press and hold the Alt and then press the F key. Release the key combination, and then press the F key again.)

Menu commands often require additional input and lead to "submenus" or dialog boxes. If you see ellipses (...) after a menu command, a dialog box appears after you choose the command. If you see an arrow (▶) after a menu command, another menu appears after you choose the command.

The Norton Desktop main menu bar contains the menus described in the following table. (Keyboard shortcuts to access the menus are in parentheses.)

Menu	Command Categories
File (Alt+F)	Runs programs and finds files.
Disk (Alt+D)	Performs disk functions such as disk format and copy.
Tools (Alt+T)	Direct access to NDW tools and utilities.
Options (Alt+O)	Configuration and customization options for Norton Desktop and its tools.
Window (Alt+W)	Chooses various window views; direct access to individual program groups.
Help (Alt+H)	Access to the Norton Desktop Help system.

The Windows Control menu—accessed from the Control menu button at the top left of the Desktop or by using the Alt+spacebar keyboard shortcut—also contains commands that enable you to manipulate the Norton Desktop shell and start other applications by using NDW's new Launch List feature.

The following sections explain the contents of each menu as displayed with full menus. If applicable, keyboard shortcuts are presented in parentheses; some commands have two different keyboard shortcuts. Remember that commands followed by ellipses (...) open dialog boxes; commands followed by an arrow (▶) branch to additional menus.

Control Menu

The Control menu appears on all Windows applications (see fig. 2.6). Norton Desktop adds some new commands not present on the standard Windows Control menus. Notice that not all commands are applicable to all applications; in fact, several Control menu commands are inactive (grayed out) in the Norton Desktop shell.

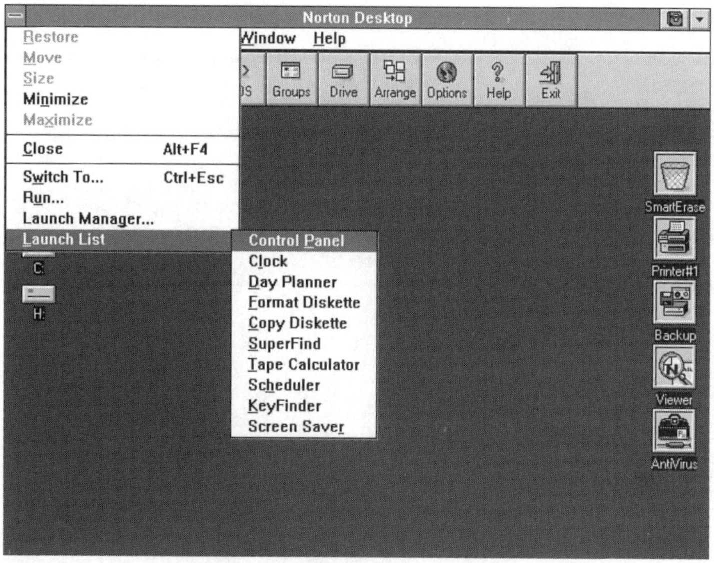

Fig. 2.6
The Desktop Control menu, with the Launch List menu open.

The following table lists the commands on the Control menu.

Command	Function
Restore (Alt+spacebar, R)	Restores an application window to previous size (not applicable with the Norton Desktop shell).
Move (Alt+spacebar, M)	Moves an application window with keyboard arrow keys (not applicable with the Norton Desktop shell).
Size (Alt+spacebar, S)	Changes an application window's size with keyboard arrow keys (not applicable with the Norton Desktop shell).
Mi**n**imize (Alt+spacebar, N)	Shrinks the Norton Desktop to an icon.
Ma**x**imize (Alt+spacebar, X)	Enlarges an application window to full-screen size (not applicable with the Norton Desktop shell).
Close (Alt+spacebar, C; or Alt+F4)	Closes Norton Desktop and exits Windows.
S**w**itch To (Alt+spacebar, W; or Ctrl+Esc)	Displays the Task List dialog box, which enables you to select open applications and arrange icons and windows.
R**u**n (Alt+spacebar, U)	Launches any DOS or Windows program by using command-line options.

(continues)

(continued)

Command	Function
Launch Mana**g**er (Alt+spacebar, G)	Creates a custom Launch List to appear on the Control menu of all applications.
Launch List (Alt+spacebar, L)	Displays a list of commonly used programs for quick launching, as created by the Launch Mana**g**er menu command.

File Menu

The **F**ile menu contains commands to run programs and find files (see fig. 2.7).

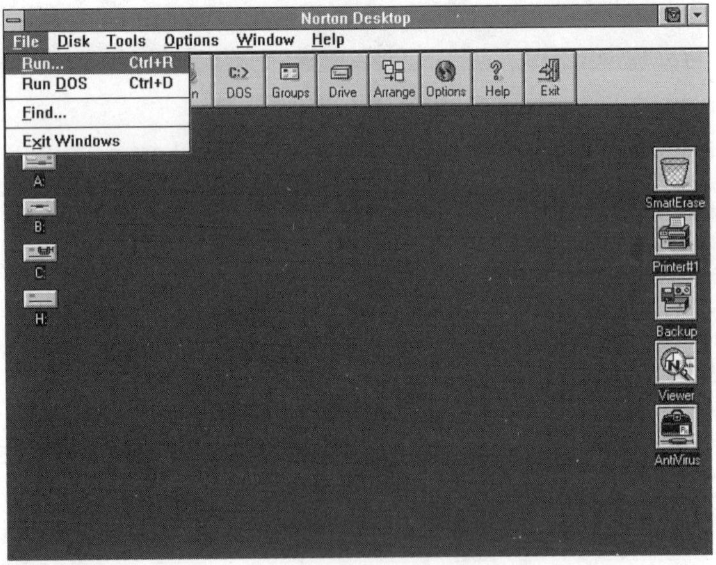

Fig. 2.7
The Norton Desktop **F**ile menu enables you to run programs, find files, and exit the program.

The following table lists the **F**ile menu commands and their functions.

Command	Function
Run (Alt+F, R; or Ctrl+R)	Runs a selected program, document (with associated program), or ScriptMaker file.
Run **D**OS (Alt+F, D; or Ctrl+D)	Opens a DOS window.
Find (Alt+F, F)	Starts the SuperFind utility to find specified text files.
E**x**it Windows (Alt+F, X)	Closes the Norton Desktop shell and exits Windows.

Disk Menu

The **D**isk menu contains all the commands necessary to work with hard disks and floppy disks (see fig. 2.8). In addition to the Windows **D**isk commands found in the File Manager, Norton Desktop adds four new commands—two network commands and two sharing commands.

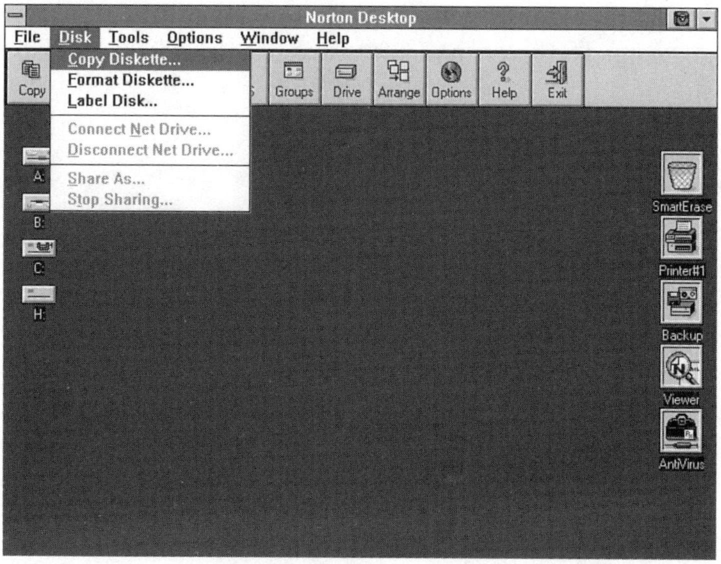

Fig. 2.8 The Desktop **D**isk menu, enabling you to copy, format, label, and manage disks.

The following table lists the commands on the **D**isk menu.

Command	Function
Copy Diskette (Alt+D, C)	Copies the contents of an entire floppy disk to another disk.
Format Diskette (Alt+D, F)	Formats a floppy disk by using NDW's Safe format program.
Label Disk (Alt+D, L)	Assigns a new or different label to a disk.
Connect **N**et Drive (Alt+D, N)	Connects a network drive if system is hooked up to a network.
Disconnect Net Drive (Alt+D, D)	Disconnects a network drive if system is hooked up to a network.
Share As (Alt+D, S)	Shares drives.
S**t**op Sharing (Alt+D, T)	Stops sharing drives.

Tools Menu

The **T**ools menu enables direct menu access to NDW's user tools and utility programs (see fig. 2.9). Choosing these commands starts the appropriate tool or utility. (These tools and utilities are discussed in greater depth later in this chapter, as well as in separate chapters in Part III, "Designing the Perfect Desktop.")

Tools and utilities accessible from the **T**ools menu are as noted in the following list:

- Deskt**o**p Editor (Alt+T, O) (see Chapters 12 and 13)
- Day **P**lanner (Alt+T, P) (see Chapter 15)
- Schedu**l**er (Alt+T, L) (see Chapter 22)
- Sc**r**iptMaker (Alt+T, R) (see Chapters 30 through 32)
- Sp**e**ed Disk (Alt+T, E) (see Chapter 26)
- **U**nErase (Alt+T, U) (see Chapter 25)
- Norton **D**isk Doctor (Alt+T, D) (see Chapter 20)
- Norton **B**ackup (Alt+T, B) (see Chapters 9 and 10)
- Norton Anti**V**irus (Alt+T, V) (see Chapter 19)
- S**h**redder (Alt+T, H) (see Chapter 23)
- **C**alculator (Alt+T, C) (see Chapter 14)
- **I**con Editor (Alt+T, I) (see Chapter 17)
- S**y**stem Information (Alt+T, Y) (see Chapter 28)
- **K**eyFinder (Alt+T, K) (see Chapter 18)
- **S**creen Saver (Alt+T, S) (see Chapter 24)

Options Menu

The **O**ptions menu contains commands that enable you to configure and customize Norton Desktop and various NDW tools and utilities (see fig. 2.10).

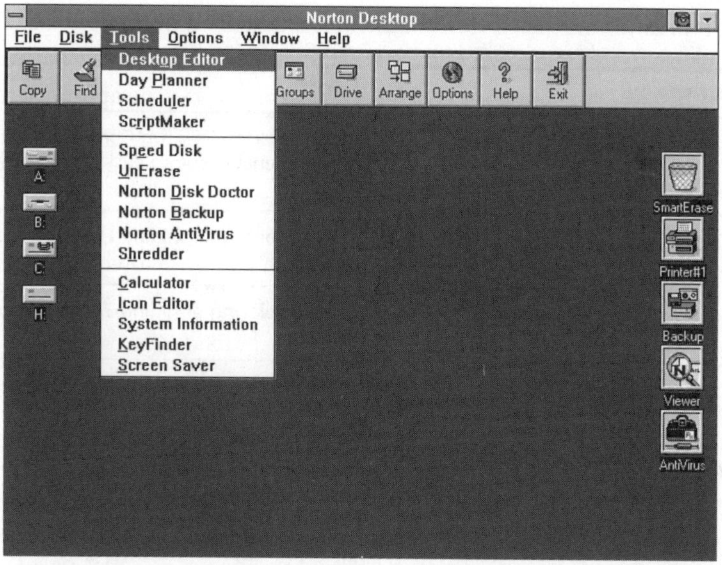

Fig. 2.9
The **T**ools menu gives you direct access to Desktop tools.

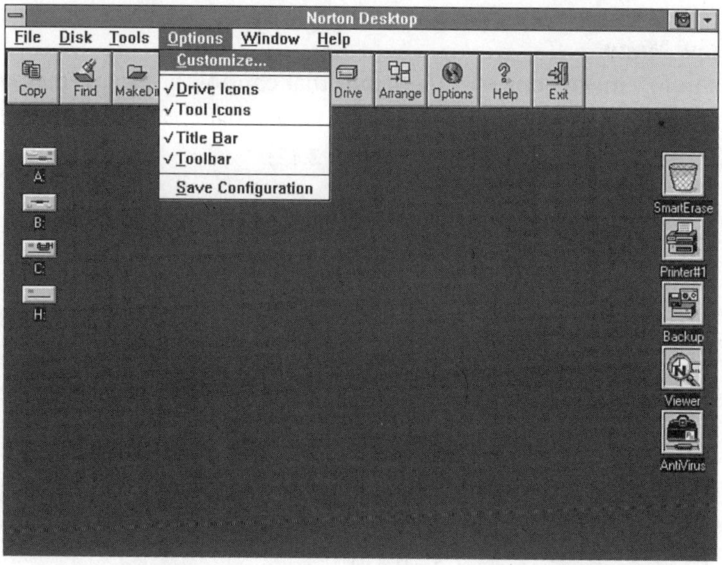

Fig. 2.10
The **O**ptions menu enables you to customize the Desktop to your preferences.

The Commands on the Options menu are as described in the following table.

Command	Function
Customize (Alt+O, C)	Displays the Norton Desktop Control Center dialog box to enable you to customize various options.
Drive Icons (Alt+O, D)	Toggle for displaying or hiding Drive icons on the Desktop.
Tool Icons (Alt+O, I)	Toggle for displaying or hiding Tool icons on the Desktop.
Title Bar (Alt+O, B)	Toggle for displaying or hiding the Desktop title bar.
Toolbar (Alt+O, T)	Toggle for displaying or hiding the Desktop toolbar.
Save Configuration (Alt+C, S)	Saves the current Norton Desktop configuration options.

Window Menu

The **W**indow menu contains commands that control the arrangement of Windows on the Desktop, as well as commands that enable you direct menu access to various program groups (see fig. 2.11).

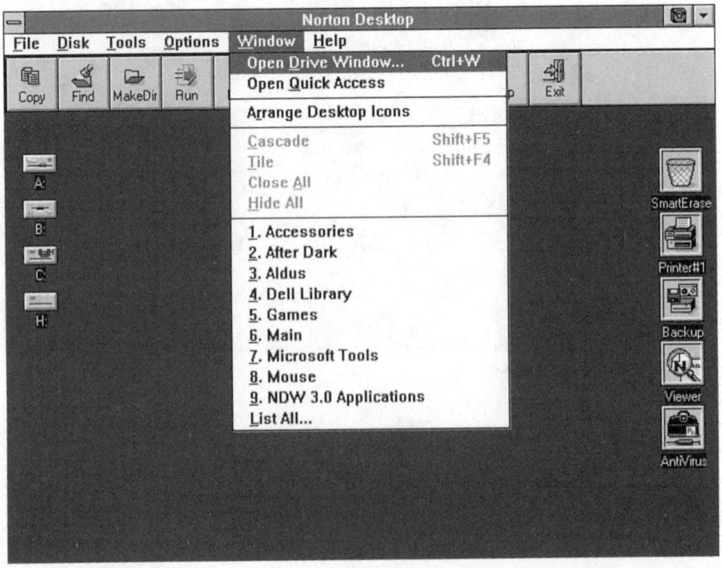

Fig. 2.11
The **W**indow menu enables you to open windows and select how they appear on the Desktop.

Commands on the **W**indow menu are described in the following table.

Command	Function
Open **D**rive Window (Alt+W, D)	Opens a new drive window.
Open **Q**uick Access (Alt+W, Q)	Opens the Norton Desktop Quick Access window.
Arrange Desktop Icons (Alt+W, A)	Aligns all icons on the Norton Desktop.
Cascade (Alt+W, C)	Arranges open windows in a cascading fashion.
Tile (Alt+W, T)	Arranges all open windows in a tiled (nonoverlapping) fashion.
Close **A**ll (Alt+W, A)	Closes all open windows.
Hide/Un**h**ide All (Alt+W, H)	Hides or unhides all open windows.
Program Groups (Alt+W, Number)	Opens a specified program group.
List All... (Alt+W, L)	Displays a list of all available program groups.

Help Menu

The **H**elp menu enables access to individual sections of the NDW Help system (see fig. 2.12).

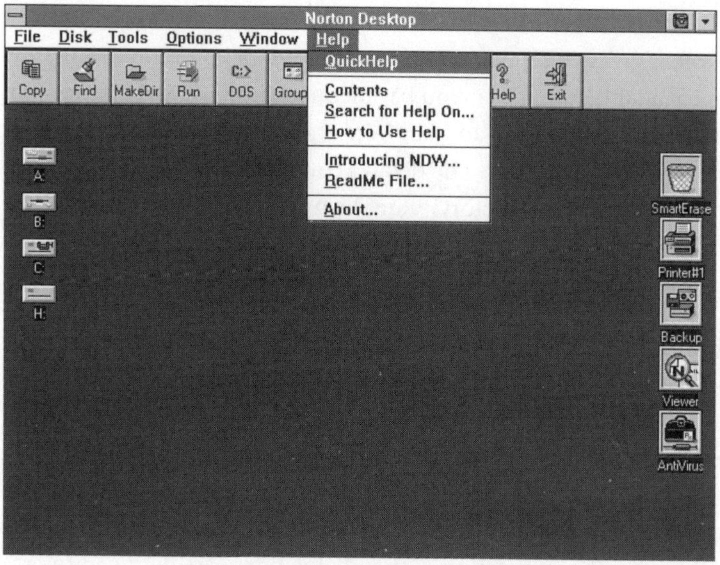

Fig. 2.12
The **H**elp menu gives you access to the Desktop Help system.

Individual sections of the Help system accessible from the Help menu are described in the following table.

Option	Function
QuickHelp (Alt+H, Q)	Provides a Quick Access screen to Desktop Help.
Contents (Alt+H, C)	Displays a table of contents for the Norton Desktop Help system.
Search for Help On (Alt+H, S)	Specifies the topic for which you want to display help.
How to Use Help (Alt+H, H)	Tutorial on how to use Help.
I**n**troducing NDW (Alt+H, N)	Introduction to Norton Desktop for Windows.
ReadMe File (Alt+H, R)	Displays the ReadMe file that lists last-minute changes and instructions for the program.
About (Alt+H, A)	Displays information about NDW and Windows, including version number and program mode.

Toolbar

The Desktop toolbar appears on-screen directly below the menu bar. The option items on this bar—Copy, Find, Run, and so on—can appear as icons only, as names only, as names and icons, or not appear at all, according to your configuration choices. Usually, the items on the toolbar appear as icons and names.

The toolbar gives you quick access to a number of common commands that also are available from the menu bar menus. Rather than opening a pull-down menu and choosing an item from the menu, just click the icon to access the command directly. The default commands on the toolbar are Copy, Find, MakeDir (Make Directory), Run, DOS, Groups, Drive, Arrange, Options, Help, and Exit.

Understanding Norton Desktop Dialog Boxes and Controls

Norton Desktop, as does many Windows applications, makes extensive use of dialog boxes. A dialog box is a special kind of information window. Most dialog boxes are designed to accept information from the user and route that information to the application. Other dialog boxes are designed to provide information about the program to the user. Dialog boxes are so important that you often cannot return to your application until you enter information and/or close the dialog box.

After you use Windows or Norton Desktop for any length of time, you soon become familiar with dialog boxes. Many Windows operations require input in a dialog box. Many Norton Desktop menu commands actually open dialog boxes for additional input. In fact, you should find that working more than five minutes in Windows or Norton Desktop without a dialog box popping up on-screen is unusual.

Dialog boxes are like other windows in that, usually, they can be moved around the screen. (This feature is useful if the default dialog placement covers up information you need in the application window.) Dialog boxes are unlike other windows, however, in that they cannot be sized, maximized, or minimized.

If you see a dialog box, first read any information contained in the box. After you learn what information you need to supply, enter this information. After you are done entering information, close the dialog box. This sounds simple, but dialog boxes ask for information in numerous ways.

Almost all dialog boxes contain buttons that enable you to OK the entry of information, Cancel information input, or seek Help. Many dialog boxes also include a Control menu, accessible from the normal Control menu button.

Dialog boxes can contain a number of other elements, all designed to elicit your input. These elements are variations on buttons and boxes. A button usually requires a singular on or off input; boxes require the entry or selection of text.

You find the following buttons and boxes in dialog boxes:

- *Check boxes* enable you to turn on or off an option, much like a toggle switch. If you select (mark) the check box, the option is enabled. If the check box is deselected (the mark removed), the option is not enabled.

- *Combination boxes* are a blend of text boxes and list boxes that enable you either to choose from the list box or type new information in the text box.

- *Command buttons* include the OK and Cancel buttons. Some command buttons, if activated, open other dialog boxes to enable you to input even more information. Other command buttons just execute commands, such as the command to exit the dialog box.

- *Drop-down list boxes* look like normal text boxes except for the down arrow beside the box. After you choose the down arrow, the box *drops down* to present more information, much like a regular list box.

- *Group boxes* assemble related buttons, much like a mini-dialog box within the dialog box.

- *List boxes* contain lists of information. If the information extends below the size of the box, vertical scroll bars appear so that you can scroll through the entire list. You must select one choice from a list box, either by using the mouse or by scrolling through the list by using the keyboard arrow keys and selecting (highlighting) the entry by pressing the spacebar.

- *Radio buttons* (also called *option buttons*) enable you to choose one—and only one—option from a group of options. After you choose one radio button within the group, the previously selected radio box becomes deselected.

- *Increment arrows* look like little up and down arrows and enable you to cycle through specific information. You also may have the option of typing information directly in the text box next to the increment arrows.

- *Text boxes* are rectangular boxes in which you enter information. Often, a text box appears that contains default information. You then can either accept the default text or type new text.

If you use a mouse, activating the buttons and entering text in the boxes is easy: Just move the pointer to the item and click to activate buttons or choose items from a list box. To enter information in a text box, place the cursor in the box and begin typing.

Working without a mouse is different. Fortunately, dialog boxes almost always become the active window on-screen so that you do not have to worry about moving from window to window. To move between items within a dialog box, just use the Tab key to move forward through the items, and use the Shift+Tab combination to move backward through items. You also can move directly to an item with an underlined letter in its title by typing Alt+*Letter*.

List boxes require that you use the up- and down-arrow keys to scroll through the list. To select or deselect items, press the spacebar. As usual, pressing Enter confirms current selections and closes the dialog box, and pressing the Esc key cancels all input and closes the dialog box.

Although dialog boxes come in all shapes and sizes, several kinds of dialog boxes are common to various parts of the Norton Desktop. The most common—and most important—dialog box appears after you click the Browse open folder icon available with numerous Desktop operations. The Browse dialog boxes, although sometimes sporting unique features necessary for the operation at hand, all serve the same function—they search disks for specific files.

Browse (Open File) dialog boxes, as shown in figure 2.13, contain the common elements described in the following table.

Element	Function
Directories	Shows the drive and directory currently selected. The scrolling list box displays a graphical representation of the directories and subdirectories on the current disk; use to select the directory from which to display files.
File **N**ame text box	Shows the selected file or file selection criteria; can display wild cards, such as *.*, which enable you to view any file on your disk; the list box shows all files in the current directory that match the selection criteria displayed in the File **N**ame text box.
List Files of **T**ype list box	Drop-down list box displays filters to list files of a specified type in the File **N**ame text box.
Drives list box	Drop-down list box displays a graphical representation of the disk drives available on your system.
Command buttons	Browse command buttons: choose OK to confirm the file selection and close the dialog box; choose Cancel to close the dialog box without selecting a file; choose **H**elp to access NDW's Help system.
File Description	A brief description of the file.
File Information	FileAssist information about the file.
Tool Buttons	Give you access to commonly needed file-related commands.

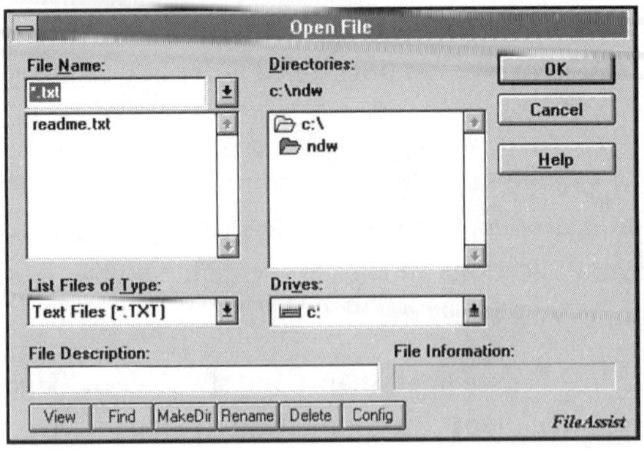

Fig. 2.13
A sample Browse dialog box enables you to search for and select a file name.

The File Description and File Information fields at the bottom of the Browse dialog box contain information about the file if a file description or information has been defined for this file. The buttons at the bottom of the Browse dialog box enable you to access other commands associated with looking for a file. The View button, for example, enables you to View the contents of a file; Find enables you to look for a search string within a file; MakeDir enables you to make a new directory; Rename enables you to rename a file; Delete enables you to delete a file; and Config enables you to set options for FileAssist.

Tip
NDW does not label Browse dialog boxes as such; Browse dialog boxes display the same label as the preceding dialog box. The Browse dialog box accessed from the **O**pen command, for example, is labeled Open File, although it is a Browse dialog box.

To select a file by using the Browse dialog box, select a drive from the Dri**v**es list box, and then scroll through the **D**irectories list box to select a directory or subdirectory. Next, set the search criteria directly in the File **N**ame text box or in the List File of **T**ype list box. Finally, scroll through the File **N**ame list box or use Speed Search to select the file, and then click the OK command button. In this way, you can "browse" through all the disks and directories on your system to find the right file.

Understanding Icons

You have no doubt noticed that the Norton Desktop makes extensive use of icons. Icons are just small pictures that represent larger objects. Norton Desktop uses icons because they are smaller and easier to arrange on-screen than are fully maximized applications. You can place a dozen icons on the Desktop more easily than you can place a dozen open application windows.

Norton Desktop enables you to use icons to represent programs not currently in use, saving valuable screen space for the maximized applications you are currently running.

Icons are used to represent a wide variety of objects. Some of the icons used in Norton Desktop are as described in the following list:

- *Application icons* represent currently running applications; they appear in the lower-left corner of the Desktop after the application is minimized.
- *Desktop icons* represent items that were dragged from another window onto the Norton Desktop; these icons appear as raised 3-D buttons.
- *Document icons* represent currently open documents that are minimized.
- *Drive window icons* represent minimized drive windows.
- *Group icons* represent minimized Quick Access groups.
- *Group item icons* represent applications contained in Quick Access groups.
- *Tool icons* represent NDW's resident tools, such as SmartErase and Shredder; these icons appear as raised 3-D buttons with a thick raised border.

Double-clicking an icon maximizes a minimized application or document, activates a group item or tool, or opens a group or drive window. You also can activate an icon by using the keyboard to highlight the icon and pressing Enter.

You can move an icon anywhere on the Desktop by "grabbing" the icon with the mouse pointer and dragging it to a new location. You even can move an icon between group windows by using the drag-and-drop method.

To create Desktop icons, you just drag an icon from a group window or drive window and drop it on the Desktop. You can create Desktop icons, with their distinctive 3-D appearance, from both applications and documents. (Activating a Desktop document icon starts the associated program with the selected document open.)

Note

Interestingly, NDW's Desktop icons technically are not true icons. Norton's engineers devised a type of control that uses a bit-mapped image (the normal icon artwork) overlaid on another bit-mapped image (the gray raised button image). Although these Desktop "icons" behave like normal icons, they have some special features that regular icons lack, such as having Control menu boxes. Norton's engineers selected this *faux icon* because it uses fewer system resources and offers more flexibility than does a real icon.

You can alter various icon properties by using Norton Desktop. By using Desktop icons, you merely click the icon once to display the Control menu box (see fig. 2.14). The Control menu box enables you to open the associated application or document, change the associated properties for the icon, and close the icon (remove it from the Desktop).

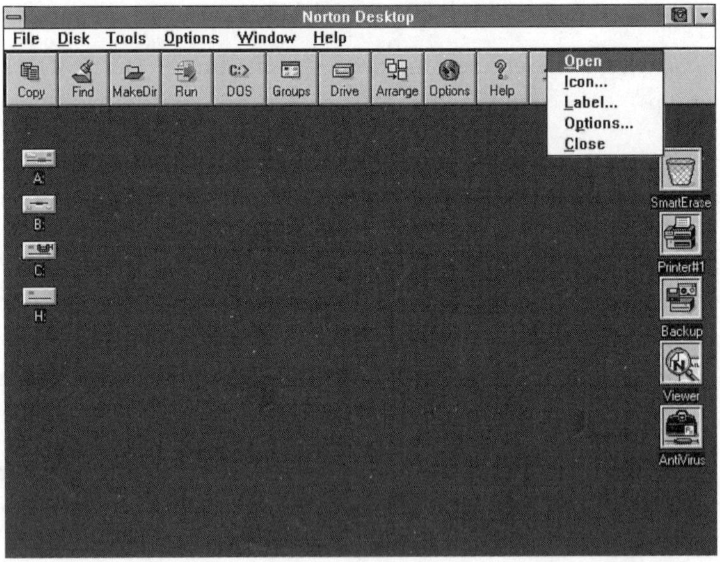

Fig. 2.14
The Control menu box for a sample icon enables you to alter various icon properties.

You can alter properties of icons in program groups by choosing the **I**con and **L**abel commands from the icon Control menu box. The **I**con command displays the Choose Icon dialog box, as shown in figure 2.15, which enables you choose what icon to use. The **L**abel command enables you to choose what label is displayed with the icon.

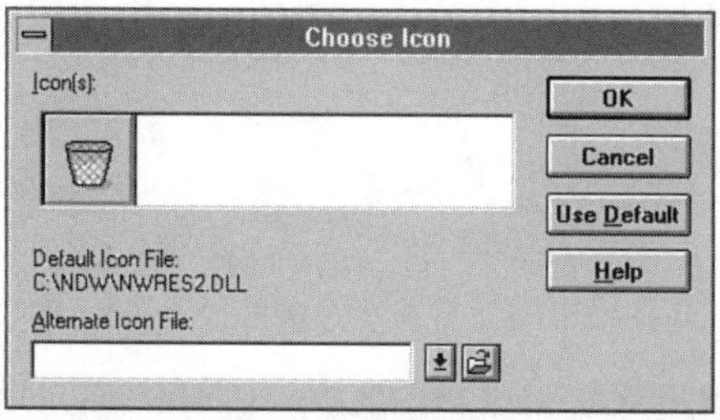

Fig 2.15
The Choose Icon dialog box enables you to select what icon is used on the Desktop.

You can even edit the artwork for the icons or create completely new icons by using NDW's Icon Editor utility, as discussed in Chapter 17, "Using Icon Editor." For more information on customizing Norton Desktop icons, see Chapter 13, "Creating an Icon-Based Desktop."

Understanding Groups

Groups in Norton Desktop are similar to groups in Windows. A group is a collection of icons. In Windows, each icon represents a specific application or utility; in Norton Desktop, icons can represent both individual applications and groups of applications. In Windows, each group is called a Program Group; in Norton Desktop, each group is called a Quick Access Group.

As in Windows, you can display Norton Desktop groups in icon form or enlarged to window size. Norton Desktop enables you to view each group in one of three styles: icon, list, or toolbox. The icon style enables you to arrange the Group item icons in the order you desire, similar to the standard Windows Program Group style (see fig. 2.16). The list style arranges the Group item icons in a vertical row in a scrolling window (see fig. 2.17). The toolbox style groups icons in an icon *toolbox*, showing only the icons and not the text labels (see fig. 2.18).

Tip
If you can determine what each icon represents without reading the text label, use the toolbox style to save a great amount of screen space.

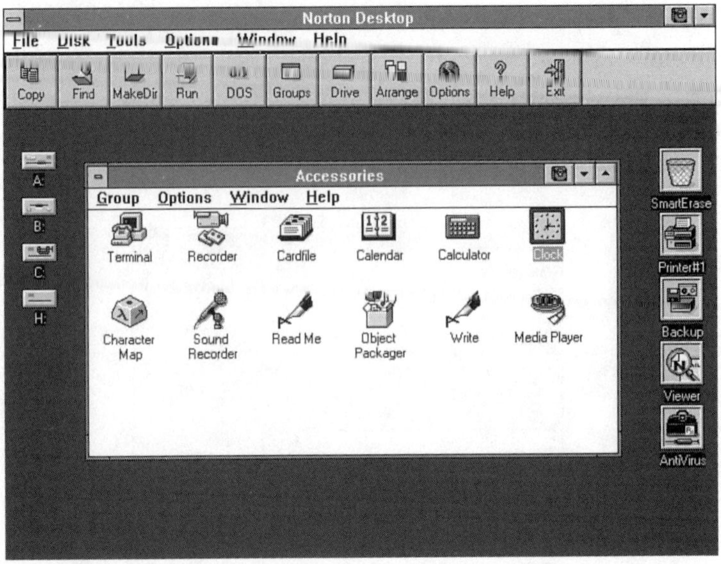

Fig. 2.16
A group displayed in icon style is the default display mode for group windows.

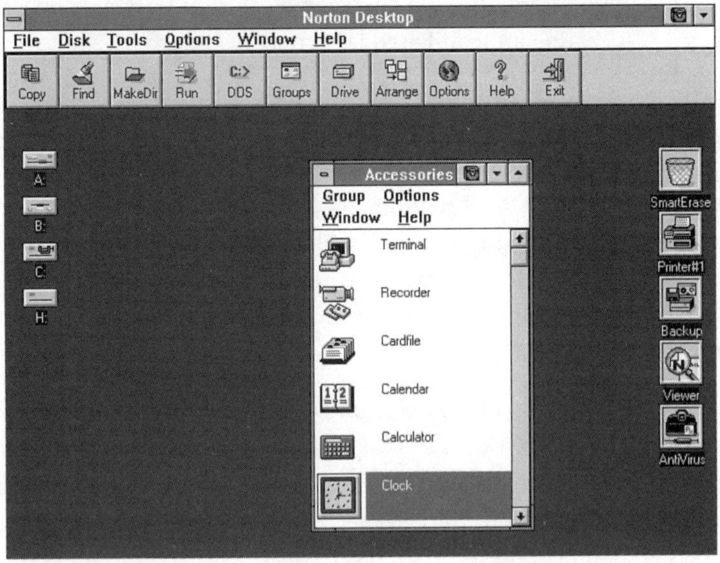

Fig. 2.17
A group displayed in list style shows programs in a vertical list with the name to the right of the icon.

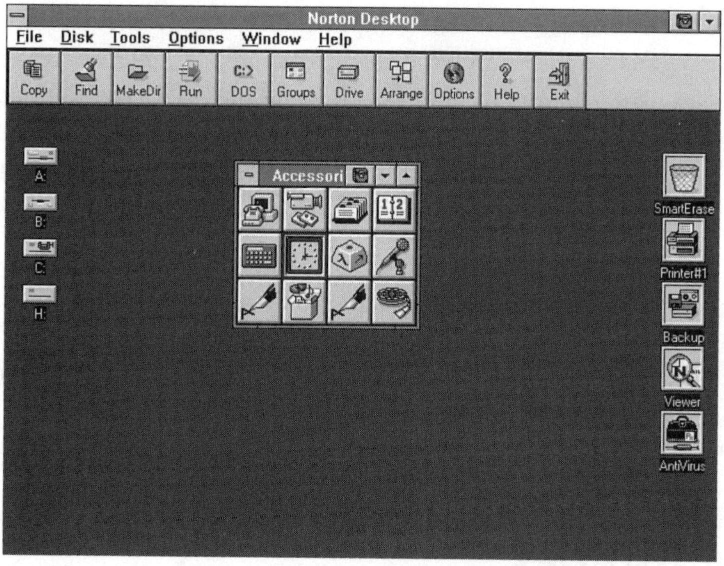

Fig. 2.18
A group displayed in toolbox style is the most compact way to display icons in a group.

You can change the display style for any Quick Access Group by following these steps:

1. Open the Quick Access Group you want, and maximize it to normal window size.
2. Choose the **W**indow **V**iew Group As command. The View As dialog box appears.
3. Choose the View Group As option that you want. To apply this style to all Quick Access Groups, choose the Change All Groups option.
4. Choose OK. The Quick Access Group appears in the style you choose.

Tip
If you change display styles, you may need to resize the Quick Access Group window.
If you change to icon style, you may need to rearrange the group item icons.

NDW's Quick Access Groups operate in much the same way as do the standard Windows Program Groups. Each group contains various icons that represent either applications or additional Quick Access Groups. Clicking an icon opens the application or group.

You can move items from group to group by dragging the icon from one group to another. You also can add items to or delete items from groups by choosing the **F**ile **N**ew or **F**ile **D**elete menu option.

Tip
To open the master Quick Access Group quickly, double-click the Desktop by using the right mouse button.

Because NDW enables you to nest groups within groups, you do not need to clutter the Desktop with a multitude of separate groups. You may create, for example, a master group called Applications and then place groups titled Windows Applications and DOS Applications within the master group. Opening the master group displays the two subgroups; opening the subgroups displays groups or items that represent individual applications.

NDW creates a special group called AutoStart. All applications or documents copied to this group automatically load as you start Windows. This method is convenient for setting up the Desktop so that your favorite programs are ready to use with each new Windows session. For more information on Quick Access Groups, see Chapter 8, "Launching Files with Norton Desktop."

Understanding Norton Desktop Tools and Utilities

Besides the Norton Desktop shell, NDW includes a collection of useful tools and utilities. By using these software programs, you can perform various maintenance and functional tasks that often are overlooked by larger, more expensive application programs.

Many of these programs have roots in Symantec's Norton Utilities software. The Norton Utilities have long provided this kind of functionality for the character-based DOS environment. NDW updates many of the DOS-based utilities for the Windows environment and adds several tools unique to NDW and Windows.

NDW's tools and utilities are run just like you run separate application programs. Most are accessed through Desktop icons or through the Norton Desktop group. The Norton Fix-It disk also contains—among several useful DOS-based utilities—a DOS-based restore program that enables you to restore programs backed up from your hard disk, in case you have a catastrophic hard disk failure.

Each tool and utility performs at least one useful task. Some are tasks you use every day; others are tasks you may never use. A great thing about NDW is knowing that no matter what problem arises, a useful tool is probably no farther away than the click of a mouse button.

You can find detailed information about each tool and utility in Part IV of this book. ScriptMaker is covered in Part V, and Norton Backup is covered in Part II. The following section gives you a brief overview of these useful applications.

Calculators

If the Norton Desktop is analogous to a real desktop, finding a calculator among the other Desktop items makes sense. NDW includes not one, but three on-screen calculators. The Tape Calculator is similar to a normal 10-key calculator, complete with the capability of keeping a running *tape* of transactions and even printing a complete transaction list.

The Scientific Calculator is a more complex program, complete with scientific and statistical operations.

The Financial Calculator contains functions useful in financial or accounting applications. You can use all three calculators with the keyboard's numeric keypad or with the mouse. All the calculators are accessible from the Norton Desktop Applications program group, although you may want to keep them all on the Desktop as permanent icons.

Desktop Editor

NDW's Desktop Editor is just a simple word processor. This utility enables you to edit ASCII text files, making it ideal for editing system files such as AUTOEXEC.BAT and WIN.INI.

Icon Editor

NDW's Icon Editor enables you to create new or edit existing Windows icons. You can edit icons in Windows applications or create icons specifically for use on the Norton Desktop. The program is full-featured and works in the same manner as a paint program. Icon Editor includes a variety of tools you use to "paint" icons. This program is deceptively addicting. Although you may not think that you will ever need or desire to edit icons, many users suddenly realize that they are spending long hours behind the mouse-based paintbrush, creating imaginative and often totally useless icons for all their Windows applications.

KeyFinder

KeyFinder is a simple utility that provides a "map" of available characters you can use in documents. KeyFinder not only displays standard alphabetic and numeric characters, but also displays special characters, such as the bullets, foreign-language characters, registration and trademark characters, and so on, which are accessible only through special key combinations. KeyFinder displays character maps for all fonts available on your system; you can paste these characters directly in your documents.

Norton AntiVirus

This utility is based on Symantec's popular DOS-based program. AntiVirus checks your system for computer viruses that can damage files and even helps repair infected or damaged files.

Norton Backup for Windows

Many users buy NDW just for this application. Norton Backup for Windows is a special Windows-based version of the classic DOS-based Norton Backup program. Norton Backup enables you to back up the data on the hard disk, more conveniently, faster, and by using fewer backup disks than the standard DOS backup command. You can choose from a variety of backup customization options, including the capability of backing up automatically only the files that changed since your last backup. You can even use Norton Backup in conjunction with the Scheduler utility to create timed backups.

If you have hard disk problems, you can use Norton Backup to restore backed-up data. Smart computer users back up their data frequently; this simple procedure ensures against the loss of valuable data files due to hard disk failure, accidental erasure or reformatting, or power loss.

Norton Disk Doctor

Norton Disk Doctor for Windows contains six tests that check the integrity of disks and files. Disk Doctor finds and repairs disk or file problems that may interfere with your ability to store or find data on floppy disks and hard disks.

Norton Rescue Disk

The Norton Rescue disk is a bootable disk that contains a DOS-based subset that contains six DOS-based utilities: Norton Diagnostics, Safe Format, Disk Edit, UnErase, UnFormat, and a DOS version of Norton Disk Doctor. Keep the Rescue disk in a safe place in case you ever need to recover from a hard-disk failure; the disk can function independently from Norton Desktop or any other program on a hard disk.

> **Note**
>
> You must create a Rescue disk during installation or create a Rescue disk by choosing Rescue Disk from the Norton Desktop Applications Group. Always create a Rescue disk and have it available in case it is needed.

Norton Viewer

You can use Norton Viewer—an icon-based tool—to view the contents of selected files. Unlike the viewing capabilities of Norton's drive windows, the Viewer enables you to view multiple files at one time.

Scheduler

You can program the Scheduler utility to remind you of important events or appointments, automatically run programs at preset times, or just display reminder messages on-screen. You can set Scheduler to load as you start Windows, or you can run Scheduler from the Norton Desktop Applications program group if you need to be reminded about specific tasks.

Screen Saver

Screen savers proved to be the most popular add-on programs for the Windows environment. Screen savers prevent screen *burn in* by sending constantly changing images to the monitor if a PC is not actively used. NDW's Screen Saver is a flexible utility that provides several entertaining screen-saving routines. You can set up Screen Saver to run as you load Norton Desktop, and it goes to work after your PC sits unused for a preselected time.

ScriptMaker

ScriptMaker enables you to create powerful self-running files that automate common tasks and operations. You create these files by using ScriptMaker's Dialog Editor and built-in programming language and run the files just as you run other Windows programs. Script making is not for the casual user, but more experienced users find that ScriptMaker can save them the time and drudgery associated with many common tasks.

Shredder

Most users do not realize that "deleting" or "erasing" a file does not remove the file from a disk, but merely eliminates references to the file. The file continues to reside on disk until some new file or data overwrites the file.

Shredder is a security tool that permanently removes erased files from a hard disk. This tool permanently *shreds* deleted data so that no one (including you) can recover or unerase sensitive information.

SmartErase

As the name implies, SmartErase is a smart tool, used to delete files from disks. Unlike the DOS ERASE or DELETE commands, SmartErase enables you easily to recover any files erased accidentally. SmartErase is, by default, installed as an icon on the Norton Desktop.

Speed Disk

Speed Disk enables you to reorganize the files and directories on a hard disk so that the disk operates at optimal efficiency. During normal use, hard disk files become fragmented and take longer and longer to access. Periodically using Speed Disk keeps file access time to a minimum. The Norton Desktop Speed Disk for Windows is similar in operation and capabilities to Speed Disk for DOS, which is available on the Fix-It disk.

SuperFind

SuperFind is a useful utility you can use to search a hard disk for selected files. You can configure SuperFind to search for particular types of files or for files that contain specific text. It is accessed from the Norton Desktop Applications program group or by choosing the **F**ile **F**ind command. You also may want to install this utility permanently as a Desktop icon.

System Information

System Information, after it is activated, lists detailed information about your computer system. Available statistics include information about your disk drives, system memory, microprocessor chip, printer, video card, and other parts of your system. You can even see how your system's performance stacks up against the performance of other PCs.

Understanding Norton Desktop's Help System

NDW has an extensive on-line Help system. By accessing NDW's Help, you can find answers quickly and easily to many operational questions.

NDW offers context-sensitive Help for many operations. Figure 2.19 shows the Norton Desktop Help Contents window.

From this window, you can display information about specific topics.

Context-sensitive Help delivers instructions for specific applications and operations. You access context-sensitive Help by pressing F1. If you are in the KeyFinder utility, for example, pressing F1 activates the Help window for KeyFinder.

All parts of the Help system follow the same operational guidelines. All Help windows feature the same button bar at the top of the window. This Help screen button bar is common to all Windows 3.1 applications.

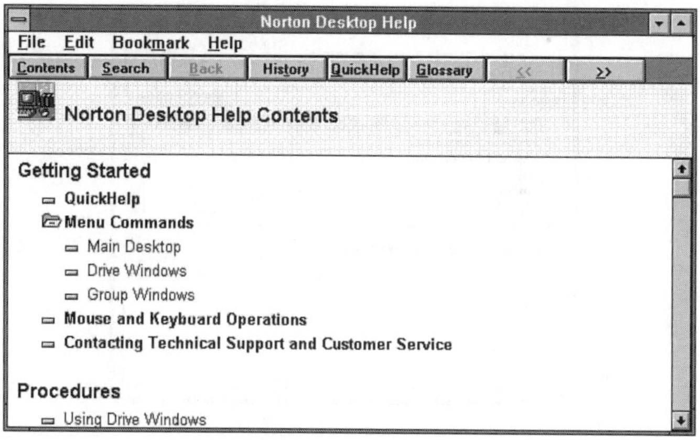

Fig. 2.19
The Norton Desktop Help Contents window enables you to choose the topics you want to view.

The buttons on the Help system button bar are as described in the following table (refer to fig. 2.19).

Button	Function
Contents	Displays all topics available in the current Help system.
Search	Searches for specific Help topics.
Back	Retraces your steps by displaying the previous Help topic selected.
History	Displays a list of all the Help topics you looked at during a session.
QuickHelp	Displays a context-sensitive Help menu on a particular tool.
Glossary	Displays a list of computer terms and terms used in Norton Desktop.
<<	Moves to the preceding topic in this specific Help system.
>>	Moves to the next topic in this specific Help system.

Usually, the fastest way to find help on specific topics is to use the **S**earch command. To search for help, follow these steps:

1. Press F1 to activate the Help system. The initial Help window appears.
2. Choose the Search button. The Search dialog box appears (see fig. 2.20).
3. Type the search word or phrase in the text box. Help topics that match the word or phrase appear in the top list box.

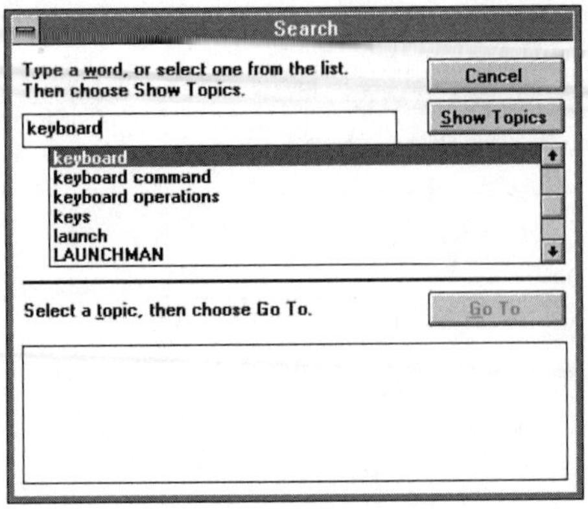

Fig. 2.20
The Search dialog box in the NDW Help system.

4. Scroll through the list box until you find the phrase that best fits the search criteria. With this phrase selected, choose the **S**how Topics button. Topics that include the selected phrase appear in the bottom list box.

5. Scroll through the list box until you find the topic on which you need help. With this topic selected, choose the **G**o To button. A Help window appears, containing information on the selected topic.

NDW's Help system, like the standard Windows Help system, features *hypertext* linking. Hypertext linking provides access to additional information about selected topics or key words. Any green-colored or underlined text has a hypertext link; almost all bit-mapped images in NDW's Help system also have hypertext links.

After you move the pointer to a hypertext link, the shape of the pointer changes to a hand with a pointing finger. The hand-shaped pointer alerts you to the hypertext link to additional information.

The two kinds of hypertext links are the information box and the information link. An information box is a brief dialog box that pops up on-screen if you press the mouse button. Topics with information boxes are indicated by green text with a dotted underline. Most bit-mapped images also have information boxes.

An information link actually takes you to the full Help description of the linked topic. Topics with information links are indicated by green text with a solid underline.

Information boxes only stay on-screen as long as you hold down the mouse button or Enter key. To open an information box by using the mouse, follow these steps:

1. With the Help window open, move the pointer to a linked topic. The pointer changes to resemble a hand shape with a pointing finger.
2. Click the green text. The information box appears (see fig. 2.21).

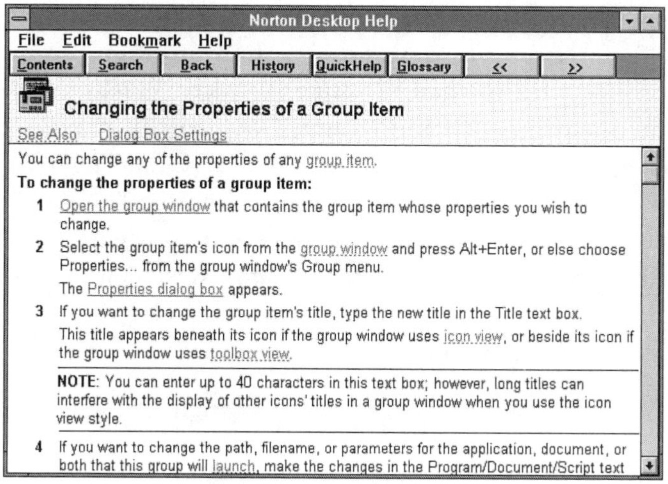

Fig. 2.21
An information box, displaying information on a linked topic.

3. Click anywhere on-screen to close the information box.

To open an information box by using the keyboard, follow these steps:

1. With the Help window open, press Tab to move to the next linked topic. Continue pressing Tab until you reach the topic.
2. Press the Enter key. The information box appears.
3. Press the Enter key again to close the information box.

You can jump to related information links much the same way. To jump to an information link by using the mouse, follow these steps:

1. With the Help window open, move the pointer to the topic with an information link.
2. Click the left mouse button once. The Help window displays the linked topic.

Tip
If you use an information link to jump to a related topic, you can use the **B**ack button to jump back to the original topic.

To jump to a related topic with an information link by using the keyboard, follow these steps:

1. With the Help window open, press Tab to move to the next linked topic. Continue pressing Tab until you reach the topic.

2. Press Enter. The Help window now displays the linked topic.

Using Treasure Chest Helps

In many Norton tools, you find a Treasure Chest icon, usually located at the upper right of a tool window. The Treasure Chest, new to version 3, contains how-to information about a specific task. Figure 2.22 shows the Treasure information box that appears after you click the Desktop Treasure Chest, which tells you how to use the right mouse button to open the top-level Quick Access group. You can scroll the Treasure text window to get other helpful hints. Look for the Treasure Chest in other Desktop tools, and see what helpful treasures are contained in the box.

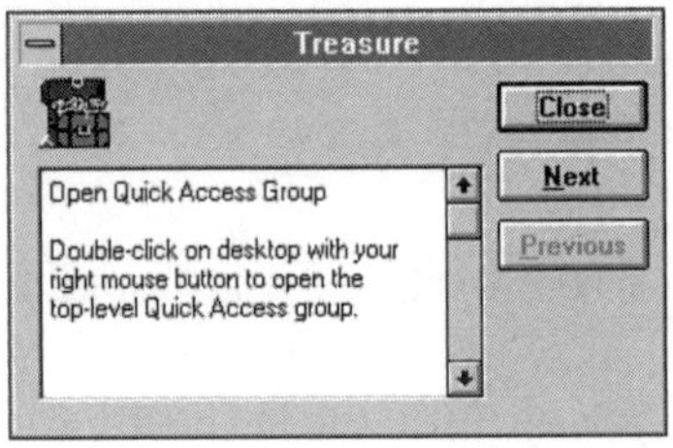

Fig. 2.22
A Treasure Chest information box.

Summary

This chapter presented a comprehensive overview of all the features in version 3 of Norton Desktop for Windows. You learned about Windows Basics, the Norton Desktop, Norton Desktop menus, Norton Desktop dialog boxes and controls, icons, groups, tools and utilities, Desktop's Help system, and Treasure Chest helps.

Chapter 3, "Using Norton Desktop and Windows Together," explains some differences between Norton Desktop and Windows and shows how to perform similar functions in both environments. You learn how to replace the Windows File Manager with the Norton Desktop and use Windows Applications with Norton Desktop.

Chapter 3

Using Norton Desktop and Windows Together

In this chapter, you learn the best ways to use Norton Desktop with Windows, examining the differences in how the two programs perform similar operations and learning how Norton Desktop builds on Windows' common functions.

In this chapter, you learn how to perform the following tasks:

- Use Norton Desktop with Windows
- Replace the Windows Program Manager with Norton Desktop
- Replace the Windows File Manager with Norton Desktop

Replacing the Windows Program Manager with Norton Desktop

If you used Windows prior to installing NDW, you are familiar with the Windows Program Manager. The Program Manager is the default *shell* included with Windows 3.1 that serves as the main operating interface.

Using the Program Manager and Windows Shells

The Program Manager is key to the Windows *graphical user interface* (GUI) (see fig. 3.1). The Program Manager incorporates numerous Program Groups that contain individual applications and utilities. Each Program Group can be enlarged to fill a window or minimized to an icon. Double-clicking a Program Group icon enlarges the group; double-clicking icons within a group starts individual applications.

The Program Manager also includes a *menu bar*. This bar consists of several pull-down menus; each menu, when pulled down, displays additional options. Clicking these menu options activates various Windows operations.

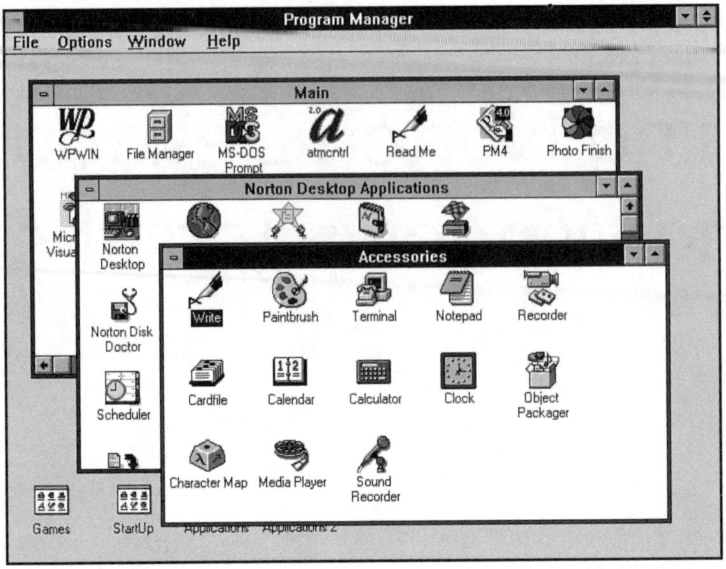

Fig. 3.1
The standard Windows Program Manager shell showing several open windows.

You do not have to stick with the Program Manager as your Windows shell. Although you can run only one shell at a time, you can instruct Windows to install any number of third-party programs as the main Windows shell. In fact, this is just what NDW does during installation; it instructs Windows to load Norton Desktop as the Windows shell in place of the Program Manager.

Every time you load Windows, the SHELL line in the SYSTEM.INI file (usually located in the C:\WINDOWS directory) tells Windows what program to use as the operating shell. If, for example, you want the Program Manager as the shell, the SHELL line in the SYSTEM.INI file must read as follows:

```
SHELL=PROGMAN.EXE
```

Windows loads the executable file PROGMAN.EXE. If you want Norton Desktop as the operating shell, the SHELL line in the SYSTEM.INI file must read as follows:

```
SHELL=NDW.EXE
```

Windows loads the executable file NDW.EXE.

Norton Desktop for Windows automatically changes the SHELL line to `SHELL=NDW.EXE` in the SYSTEM.INI file during installation—if you make that selection at the appropriate prompt.

> **Note**
>
> You can use a text editor, such as NDW's Desktop Editor, to change the SHELL line in the SYSTEM.INI file any time you want to change the Windows operating shell.

Comparing figures 3.1 and 3.2, you can see some of the differences between the Program Manager and Norton Desktop shells. Although both shells use menus, groups, and icons, Norton Desktop expands the Program Manager to add operational functionality to the shell in the form of extra menu items and additional Desktop icons.

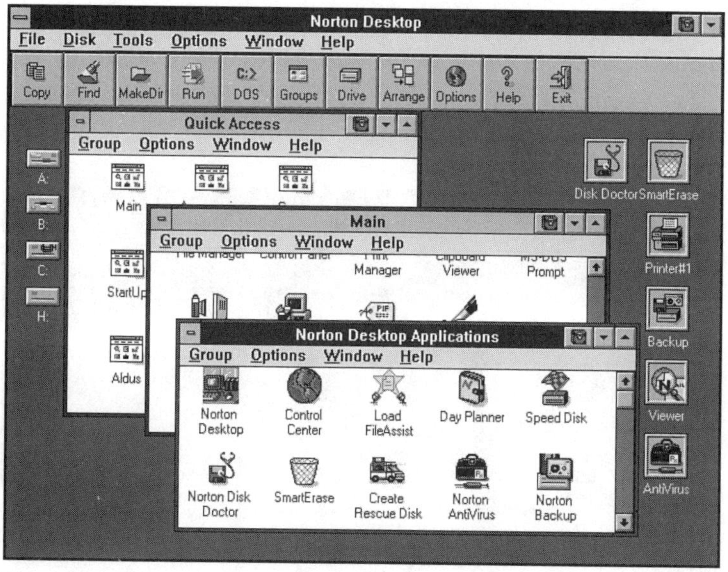

Fig. 3.2 The Norton Desktop shell showing the Quick Access window and two other open windows.

Comparing the Program Manager and Quick Access

The Program Manager compares more to NDW's Quick Access than it does to Norton Desktop as a whole. After you double-click Norton's Groups icon, a collection of Quick Access Groups that is very similar to the Program Manager's Program Groups opens.

NDW's installation program automatically searches for existing Program Groups and creates matching Quick Access Groups for the Norton Desktop Shell. When you first start Norton Desktop, therefore, the same groups are available as under the Program Manager.

Many users are happy using Norton's Quick Access Groups exactly as they used the Program Manager's Program Groups, but by following their lead, you overlook some of the added functionality of NDW.

One major difference between Quick Access and the Program Manager is that with Quick Access you can nest groups within other groups. The main Quick Access Group is itself an example of nested groups. This one group, symbolized by the Groups icon, contains all the other groups that exist on your system. You can go beyond this level and nest other groups within these groups.

Figure 3.3 shows one way you can exploit this group nesting feature. You can see that the Quick Access Group contains icons for various other groups, including an Applications group. The Applications group contains two icons, one for Windows Applications and one for DOS Applications. The Windows Applications group contains several icons, including one for Word Processors. This final group contains icons for individual Windows word processing programs.

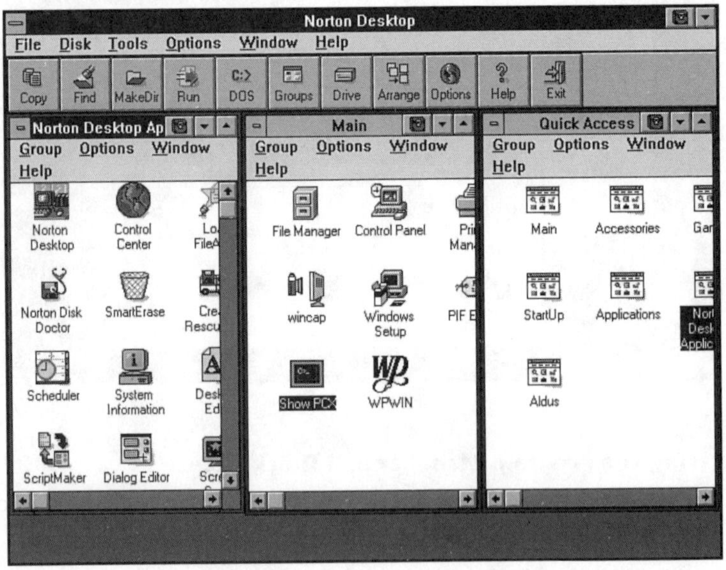

Fig. 3.3
An example of nested groups in a Norton Desktop Quick Access window.

You can display the contents of a Quick Access Group differently from the display of Program Groups. As explained in Chapter 2, "Getting Up and Running with Norton Desktop for Windows," you can display Quick Access Groups as free-form collections of icons (the same Program Groups are displayed), as scrolling lists of icons, or as compact toolboxes. You even can select different display styles for different groups. The Program Manager, in contrast, enables you to display only collections of icons.

Comparing the Program Manager and Norton Desktop Shells

The differences between the Program Manager and Norton Desktop go well beyond the differences between Program Groups and Quick Access Groups. Perhaps the biggest difference is that Norton Desktop is a more complete desktop than the Windows Program Manager.

Only two types of items can occupy the regular Windows desktop: the Program Manager itself and minimized icons representing open groups or applications. Norton Desktop, on the other hand, enables you to display icons representing disk drives; open groups or applications; and unopened groups, applications, and documents. You can position icons on the Norton Desktop for your most-used applications, without having to launch each individual application beforehand. With this feature, you gain ease of use under Norton Desktop.

Norton Desktop also supplements the normal Windows menu system with new menus and options that increase Windows' ease of use. A new pull-down menu, for example, enables direct access to NDW's most-used add-on tools. With the new options on the **F**ile menu of a drive window, you can associate files more easily with applications and change the properties of various desktop objects. With NDW, you also have the option of creating your own custom menu system—something definitely not possible under Windows' Program Manager.

In a nutshell, using Norton Desktop as your Windows shell gives you all the options possible with the Program Manager, plus a great deal more.

Running Program Manager as an Application within Norton Desktop

You may encounter situations in which you still might need to access the Windows Program Manager. (Some program installations, for example, fail to recognize the Norton Desktop shell and require the presence of the Program Manager for correct installation; these instances are rare.) In these cases, you have two options: editing the SYSTEM.INI file to replace Norton Desktop with the Program Manager as your shell or loading the Program Manager as a stand-alone application from within the Norton Desktop environment. Norton Desktop actually simulates the Program Manager so that your application's install program does not need to be aware of NDW.

You can run Program Manager as easily as you run any other application program by using one of the following two methods:

- Choose the **F**ile **R**un command. After the Run dialog box appears, type **PROGMAN.EXE** in the Command Line text box; then choose OK.

- Open the drive window for the drive on which Windows is installed (normally drive C) by double-clicking the appropriate Drive icon. Select the WINDOWS directory from the tree list, and then double-click the file name, PROGMAN.EXE.

Program Manager appears as an open application on your Norton Desktop; you can use it as you normally would or simply leave it open while you install new Windows applications (see fig. 3.4).

Fig. 3.4
The Windows Program Manager as an open application on the Norton Desktop.

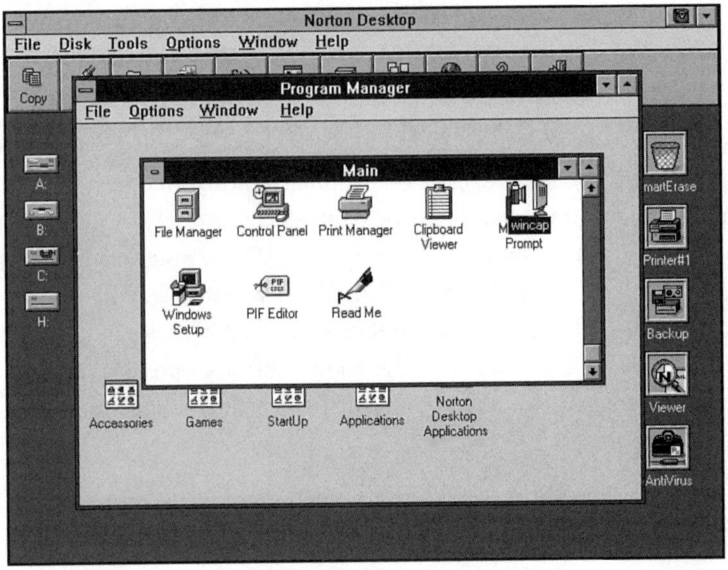

Replacing the Windows File Manager with Norton Desktop

Another significant difference between NDW and regular Windows is in the respective file management systems. Windows 3.0 received strong criticism for its poor implementation of the File Manager; even under Windows 3.1, the improved File Manager is, at best, barely adequate for the needs of most users.

Norton Desktop 3 for Windows, on the other hand, uses a superb file management scheme. Using Norton Desktop's drive windows, file management is extremely flexible and user friendly.

File Management with MS-DOS

File management is an important maintenance task for all PC users. From time to time, you need to copy files, either from one directory to another or from one disk to another. At other times, you may need to erase files or directories or to rename files. You may even have occasion simply to view the contents of particular files.

Without the Windows GUI, you must rely on MS-DOS commands to accomplish these tasks. To copy a file from drive to drive, you must learn the correct syntax to issue a command that looks something like the following:

COPY C:\WINDOWS\TEST.DOC A:

Even if you learn all the DOS commands, you still just cannot accomplish some procedures. No DOS command exists, for example, that enables you to view the contents of a nontext file. The DOS TYPE or PRINT commands do not provide this capability.

Numerous utilities have been introduced to fill the DOS file management holes. Many of these add-on programs—including PC Tools Deluxe and the Norton Commander and Norton Desktop for DOS—replace the DOS command line with a visual representation of all the files on a disk, in the form of a directory tree. Because DOS files are kept in directories that often have branching subdirectories, this concept of a directory tree makes perfect sense. Often the utility shows a directory tree on one-half of the screen and the contents of that directory—the individual files—on the other half of the screen.

In spite of the proliferation of such programs, DOS itself remained command-line bound—that is, until the advent of MS-DOS 5. The releases from Microsoft since version 5 of DOS include the DOS Shell. This character-based shell uses the concept of a directory tree to facilitate file management. Users can select files or directories and then pull down menus to select operations that involve those files. This method is not perfect, but it is better than typing in obscure DOS commands. However, the DOS shell is so limiting that very few users actually use it—most either stick with DOS completely or completely switch to Windows.

File Management with the Windows File Manager

Windows includes a utility called the File Manager. The Windows File Manager, like the MS-DOS Shell, operates on the principle of directory trees and associated files. Because File Manager operates in the mouse-driven graphical environment of Windows, it enables the use of clicking and dragging to facilitate file operations. That is, you can drag or move a file from one directory to another simply by dragging it with the mouse. You also can launch an application by clicking a document file associated with an application.

All this sounds good on paper, but in reality, the original Windows 3.0 File Manager fell short. First, it did not show a directory and its associated files side by side in a split screen. After you started the File Manager, all you saw was a directory tree of the selected disk drive. After you double-clicked a directory, a separate window appeared that contained the contents (files) of that directory. If you wanted to see the contents of another directory, you had to double-click again and open another directory window. If you worked with several directories at one time, your screen could become very crowded and confusing.

With the advent of Windows 3.1, Microsoft has taken steps to improve the File Manager. As you can see in figure 3.5, the Windows 3.1 File Manager now features the expected split-window directory tree/file listing. Some of the operations also have been simplified. But File Manager still lacks viewing capabilities, as well as a customizable button bar for common operations.

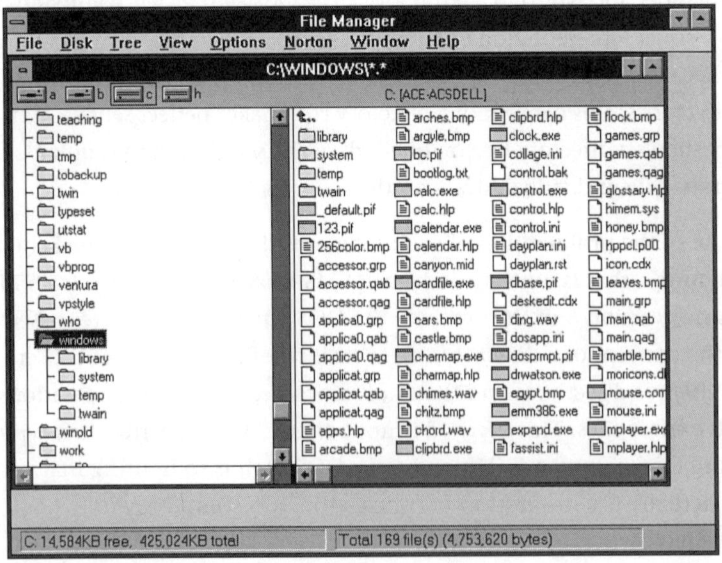

Fig. 3.5
The Windows 3.1 File Manager, showing a split window.

File Management with Norton's Drive Windows

Symantec took a different approach to file management with Norton Desktop for Windows. Instead of designing a utility for file management, NDW embraced the concept of drive management. Norton Desktop, therefore, has no dedicated file manager; instead, the Desktop is populated with individual Drive icons for each active drive on your computer system.

At first glance, a Norton drive window resembles the Windows 3.1 File Manager (see fig. 3.6). The main window is divided into two halves; the left half contains the directory tree for that drive, and the right half contains the files for the selected directory. Each file has an accompanying icon; different types of files have different types of icons. The similarities end there, however.

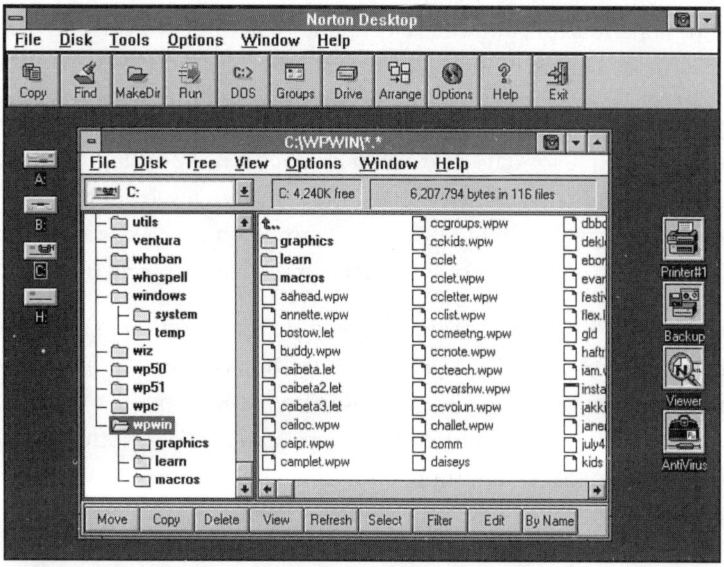

Fig. 3.6
An open Norton Desktop drive window showing a split window.

The first difference is that, with NDW, you can open multiple drive windows simultaneously directly from the Desktop without having to first open the File Manager. If you are copying files from drive C to drive A, for example, you can open both A and C drive windows to drag files between them. If you are on a network, you see Drive icons for all accessible drives on the network. If you have external nondisk storage devices, such as CD-ROM drives, you even see Drive icons for these devices.

The next difference: Each Norton drive window features a button bar at the bottom of the window. This button bar contains up to 13 buttons for common file management operations so that you can easily select a file and then click a button to perform a task. This button bar also is customizable; you can instruct NDW to create buttons for any six operations that appear on the normal Norton Desktop menu system.

Norton's drive windows, like the Windows 3.1 File Manager, also embrace the concept of *drag and drop*. This mouse-oriented operation involves clicking a file in the drive window and then dragging the file to an icon to initiate an operation. You can click a word processing file from the drive window, for example, and drag the file to the NDW printer icon. After you drop the file icon on the printer icon, the file prints. Desktop loads the appropriate program, prints the file, and returns to the Desktop drive window.

NDW also makes selecting multiple files in the drive windows easier. By using the right mouse button, you can select more than one file at a time. This feature facilitates many multiple file operations.

Tip
To see the contents of more than one file at a time, use the separate Norton Viewer tool. Norton Viewer enables you to open multiple files at one time.

In addition, NDW provides a utility that enables you to view the contents of any file in its native format—text-based or graphical. By opting to display the view pane, the contents of any selected file appear in a subwindow that drops down below the existing window panes. Turning on the view pane enables you to browse through a list of files, viewing the contents one file at a time.

In short, Norton's drive windows go several steps beyond the traditional Windows File Manager. Although many operations are similar between the two programs, Norton adds extra functionality. Most users find that file and disk management is much more intuitive and easier under Norton Desktop; indeed, the file management function is one major reason NDW has received such critical acclaim.

Note

You can run the Windows File Manager as an application within Norton Desktop. Simply choose the **F**ile **R**un command, and select the WINFILE.EXE file.

Using Windows Applications with Norton Desktop

All Windows applications run the same way in Norton Desktop as they do in traditional Windows. NDW does add some options, however, that make launching your programs much easier.

You can very easily launch programs from within drive windows. With a drive window open, all you need to do is double-click any application file, and the application promptly launches. You can even double-click any document file, and NDW finds the application associated with that document type and automatically launches the correct application—with the selected document loaded.

You can launch applications from within Norton's Quick Access Groups. Although this process resembles launching programs from the Windows Program Manager, the nested groups help you organize a large number of applications logically and with ease.

You also can create custom menu items that enable you to directly launch your favorite applications. You may create a menu, for example, labeled Applications. After you pull down this menu, you see a list of options that corresponds to the applications on your hard drive.

Finally, you can create Desktop icons for your favorite applications. Simply by dragging an application or data file from a drive window onto the desktop, you create a permanent icon that places your application conveniently on your Desktop. Just double-clicking a Desktop icon automatically launches the associated application.

Remember, too, that NDW adds items to the Control menu that is found on every Windows application. New options—available only if running Norton Desktop—include a Launch Manager, a Launch List, and a **R**un command. By using these options, you can easily switch to other documents, applications, and tools from within any Windows application. Your applications, then, operate just as they always have—but you have more options available for launching the applications.

Summary

This chapter showed you the major differences between Norton Desktop and Windows. You learned how the Desktop interface replaces the Windows interface, compared the Windows Program Manager to the Norton Desktop, and learned how Desktop file management is different from DOS or Windows file management.

Chapter 4, "Understanding Essential Norton Desktop Operations," examines the operations you need to learn to efficiently operate Norton Desktop 3 for Windows. This includes use of the mouse, dragging and dropping, and manipulating files.

Chapter 4

Understanding Essential Norton Desktop Operations

In this chapter, you learn to perform the following tasks:

- Basic mouse operations
- Basic keyboard operations
- How to manipulate files

Using Norton Desktop 3 for Windows is just like using Windows' Program Manager—only more so. Navigating is easier by using a mouse than by using the keyboard, although you also can use the keyboard to make your way around the Desktop. In fact, Norton Desktop enables you to speed operations by assigning keyboard shortcut keys to any menu item.

Norton Desktop makes more extensive use of mouse and keyboard operations than does Windows. To really make NDW fly, you need to learn some special operations, such as using the right mouse button and the intricacies of *drag and drop*, in which you use the mouse pointer pick up a file, drag it to another location on the Desktop, and drop the file onto an icon or another drive.

Using Basic Mouse Operations

You cannot do justice to the sophisticated ease of use of Norton Desktop (or Windows, for that matter) without a mouse. The *graphical user interface* (GUI) environment was designed for *point-and-click* operations; pointing without a pointing device is difficult. A GUI uses the graphical capabilities of your monitor while providing an interface between you and the computer, as opposed to the text-based interface of DOS.

Although this chapter (and this book) discusses using the mouse as a pointing device, pointing devices other than the mouse exist. Some computers use pens, trackballs (particularly laptops), and touchscreens as pointing devices.

Pointing and Clicking

Tip
You can reconfigure the mouse buttons to conform to left-handed operation; if you already did so, just convert all references to the left button in this book to right-button references, and vice versa.

The most common mouse operations are *pointing* and *clicking*. Note that, unless stated otherwise, clicking assumes the use of the left mouse button. (Some operations use the right mouse button; you learn about these operations later in this chapter.)

Pointing and clicking is simple; just move the mouse so that the mouse pointer touches the object you want to select, and then click the left mouse button. Whenever you see an instruction to click the mouse button, single-click it. (Double-clicks are discussed in the following paragraph.) Pointing and clicking is an effective way to select menu items, display command boxes on Desktop icons, and select directories and files in drive windows.

To launch applications, however, you must double-click. A *double-click* involves pointing at an on-screen element with the mouse pointer and then clicking the left mouse button twice in rapid succession. Double-clicking a Desktop icon launches the application; double-clicking a Drive icon opens the drive window; and double-clicking a file in the drive window launches the associated application.

Dragging and Dropping

Dragging is a variation of clicking. You drag by pointing at an object with the mouse pointer and then pressing and holding down the left mouse button. Move the mouse without releasing the mouse button, and drag the object to a new location. After you successfully move the object, release the mouse button.

You can drag icons around the screen to customize the look of the Desktop. You also can drag icons between group windows. You can drag items out of group windows or drive windows and drop them onto the Norton Desktop to create Desktop icons. You can even drag files in a drive window between directories or between drive windows. Dragging and dropping are effective operations in Norton Desktop.

Several specific drag-and-drop operations are important in Norton Desktop. The first operation concerns SmartErase. SmartErase is a special erase utility included with Norton Desktop, which appears as an icon on the Desktop. Use SmartErase to delete a file by dragging and dropping the file from the drive window onto the SmartErase icon. You do not need to use special Delete keys or buttons; the drag-and-drop operation "smart erases" the selected file.

The second drag-and-drop operation enables you to print selected files—without starting the associated application. Just drag and drop the file from the drive window onto the Printer icon. Norton Desktop prints the file in the application format associated with that file type. Again, you do not need to use any Print keys or buttons or even have the associated application running; the drag-and-drop operation prints the file.

Other drag-and-drop operations involve Norton Tool icons. You can back up selected files by dragging and dropping the files from the drive window onto the Norton Backup icon. You can drag and drop files onto the Viewer icon to view the contents of these files. You also can drag and drop files onto the Shredder icon to permanently delete the files from your disk.

Finally, you can *launch* applications automatically, with specific files loaded, by using drag and drop. Dropping an Excel document file called SAMPLE.XLS on top of the Excel program file EXCEL.EXE, for example, launches Excel with the SAMPLE.XLS worksheet open.

To use drag and drop to launch an application with a file loaded, follow these steps:

1. With a drive window open, select the document or file by single-clicking the file name (see fig. 4.1).

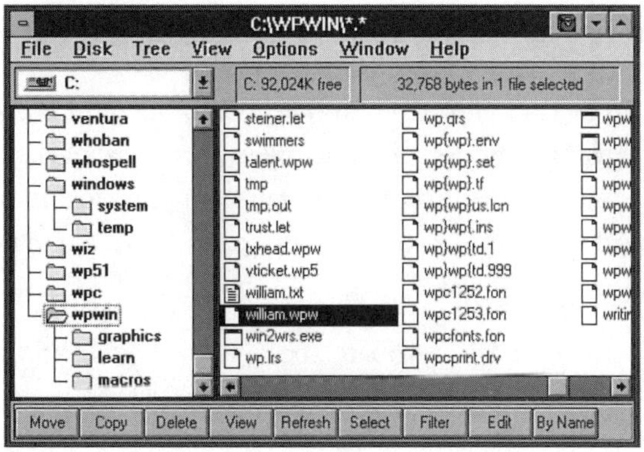

Fig. 4.1
The WordPerfect for Windows document file, WILLIAM.WPW, selected in a Norton Desktop drive window.

2. Press and hold the left mouse button, and drag the file until it is on top of the correct application file (see fig. 4.2).

3. Release the mouse button to drop the document file on top of the program file. The program launches and loads the selected document file.

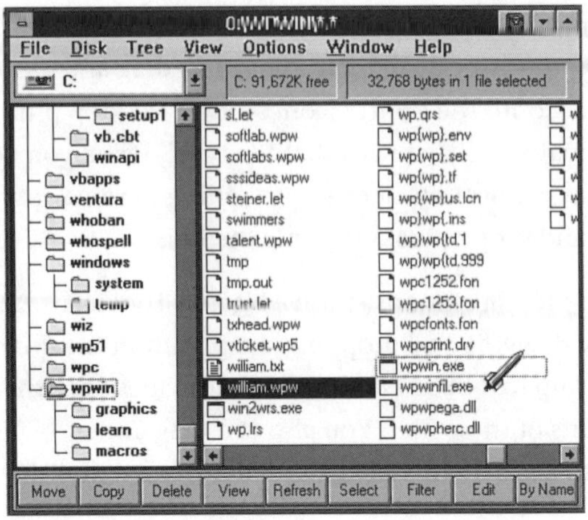

Fig. 4.2
The file WILLIAM.WPW is dragged onto the WPWIN.EXE (WordPerfect for Windows application) file. The mouse pointer becomes a rocket to show that the application is being "launched."

Using the Right Mouse Button

To this point, you used only the left mouse button. The right mouse button also has uses. If you click the right mouse button while pointing to any blank area of the screen, a menu that contains the same options as the menu bar appears. You can use this menu to select any item you usually select from the menu bar, which is handy if the menu bar at the top of the screen is covered by another window.

Tip
You can select the right mouse button's actions by choosing the Default category in the Control Center. See Chapter 11 for more information.

Using Basic Keyboard Operations

You may want to learn Norton Desktop keyboard operations because you absolutely hate using a mouse, you may be using a portable computer in a confined space and have no access to a mouse, or you even may be looking for ways to speed common Norton Desktop operations. No matter the reason, you need to know how to use Norton Desktop with a keyboard only.

If you remember a few basic keyboard strategies, using Norton Desktop without a mouse is not difficult. Notice the following methods:

- Access the menu bar by pressing F10. After the menu bar opens, you can move forward and backward through menu items by using the right- and left-arrow keys. Pull down menus by using the down-arrow key, and select items by pressing Enter.

- Access any underlined item on-screen (menu item or button) by pressing the Alt key, plus the underlined letter. If you want to open the **F**ile menu (with the **F** underlined), for example, press Alt+F.

- Cycle through all items in a dialog box by using the Tab key; cycle backward by using Shift+Tab.
- Select the current item by pressing Enter. Exit a dialog box or menu, without selecting anything, by pressing Esc.
- Get context-sensitive Help at any time by pressing F1.
- Although you cannot use the Desktop icons and Drive icons on the Desktop without a mouse, you still can access all of NDW's tools by opening the **T**ools menu. You also can access all your Program Groups and Quick Access Groups by opening the **W**indow menu.

Manipulating Files

To correctly manage files in Norton Desktop, you must learn how to select files and then how to perform specific file operations, such as copy, move, and delete. All these operations are easy to master.

Tip
If you use the keyboard exclusively, create a customized menu that contains your most-used applications. See Chapter 12, "Creating a Menu-Based Desktop," for details.

Note

If you cannot remember specifics, you always can use the mouse or the keyboard to perform any operation from Norton Desktop's menu system. With the mouse, single-click the menu name to pull down that menu; then single-click the menu option. With the keyboard, press F10 to access the menu bar, use the left- and right-arrow keys to move from item to item, and then press Enter to pull down the selected menu.

Manipulating Files with the Mouse

You must master some special mouse operations to successfully manipulate files in a drive window. In particular, you need to know how to select multiple files and how to move files.

Tip
You also can use the right mouse button to deselect individual files. Click the right mouse button with the pointer on a selected file you want to deselect; the file is now "unselected."

You can select multiple files either by using the mouse alone or by using the mouse and the keyboard together. The key to using the mouse alone is that you use the left mouse button to select single files and the right mouse button to select multiple files.

To select multiple files by using the mouse alone, follow these steps:

1. With the drive window open and the pointer on the first file you want to select, click the left mouse button once.

2. With the pointer on the next file you want to select, click the right mouse button once.

3. Repeat step 2 to select additional files (see fig. 4.3).

After you select all the files you want, you can perform an operation such as delete, move, or print on the selected files.

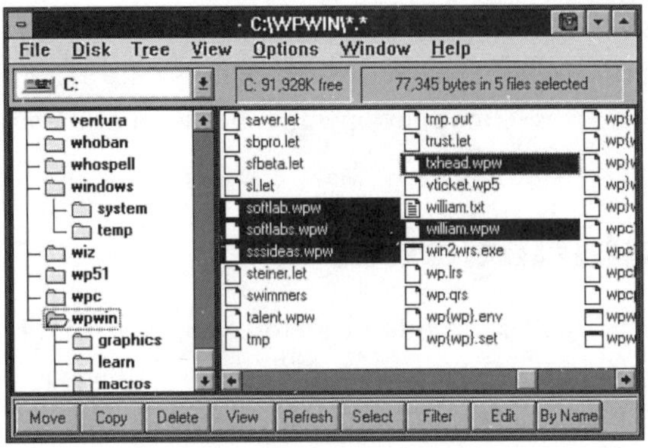

Fig. 4.3
A Norton Desktop drive window showing multiple files selected. Selected files are highlighted.

Tip
To select multiple adjacent files, you do not need to click each individual file. To select several files in a row, just drag the pointer over the adjacent file names while holding the right mouse button.

Many users prefer using the mouse and keyboard together. The key to joint operation is knowing that the Ctrl key enables you to select multiple, nonadjacent files. (The Shift key also enables you to select multiple files, but Shift works only with *adjacent files*—that is, files that are next to one another in the list.)

To select multiple files by using the mouse and the keyboard, follow these steps:

1. With the drive window open and the pointer on the first file you want to select, single-click the left mouse button.

2. Press and hold the Ctrl key.

3. Single-click the left mouse button to select additional files.

4. Release the Ctrl key after you select all the files you want. You can then perform an operation on the selected files.

To drag and drop a group of selected files, you must click and hold the mouse button on one of the selected files to drag the entire group.

Copying files, as previously discussed, involves dragging a copy of selected files to another directory or drive. Deleting files involves selecting the files and then pressing the Del key or choosing **F**ile **D**elete. You can move files by first copying them to a new location and then deleting the original files. Fortunately, NDW has a simpler way to move files.

Moving files in Norton Desktop involves using the mouse and the keyboard together. Pressing and holding the Alt key while dragging files moves the files to a new location instead of simply copying them. To move files, follow these steps:

1. Open a drive window, and select the files you want to move.
2. Press and hold the Alt key.
3. Press and hold the left mouse button while holding the Alt key.
4. Drag the selected files to a new directory or drive.
5. Release the Alt key and the left mouse button after you move the selected files to the new location.

Caution

Remember that moving a file copies the file to a new location and erases it from the old location. Do not use Move if you need to keep a copy of the file in the old location.

Manipulating Files by Using the Keyboard

To manipulate files without using a mouse, you must remember a few essentials. First, always use the up- and down-arrow keys to scroll through a list of items. Second, use the Tab key to move from one pane to another. Third, hold the Shift key to select multiple adjacent items. Fourth, press Shift+F8 to start the process that enables you to select multiple nonadjacent files. And fifth, use the spacebar to select and deselect nonadjacent files.

You can use these operations in any window that displays a file listing. Some common windows of this kind are drive windows and browse dialog boxes. Start by opening the appropriate window; then use the up- and down-arrow keys to scroll through the directory tree in the directory pane. With the directory name selected, press the Tab key to move into the file pane.

To select an individual file, scroll through the list of files until the file you want is selected. You then can perform an operation on the file.

If you need to deal in batch-type operations, you often must select more than one file. NDW enables you to select groups of both adjacent and nonadjacent files.

To select multiple files that are adjacent to one another, follow these steps:

1. Scroll through the list of files until your first file is selected.
2. Press and hold the Shift key.
3. Use the up- and down-arrow keys to scroll through the list until you reach the last file in the desired group; all files in this group are now selected.
4. Release the Shift key. The group of files is ready for the operation you want to perform.

To select multiple files that are not adjacent to one another, follow these steps:

1. Scroll through the list of files until your first file is selected.
2. Press Shift+F8 to begin multiple file selection.
3. Use the up- and down-arrow keys to scroll through the list to find the other files you want to select.
4. Press the spacebar to select each file.
5. Repeat steps 3 and 4 to select additional files.
6. Press Shift+F8 to end multiple file selection. The files are available for the operation you want to perform.

Tip
Use the spacebar to both select and deselect files. Move to a selected file and press the spacebar; the file is deselected.

A faster way to select multiple files is to use the **S**elect command to select all files or all files of a specific type.

To select all files in a directory, follow these steps:

1. Activate the desired pane, and then press Alt+F to open the **F**ile menu.
2. Press S for the **S**elect option.
3. Press A to select **A**ll files. All files are selected, and you can perform an operation on the group of files.

To select a particular type of file, follow these steps:

1. Activate the pane you want, and then press Alt+F to open the **F**ile menu.
2. Press S for the **S**elect option.
3. Press S to select **S**ome files. The Select Some dialog box appears (see fig. 4.4).

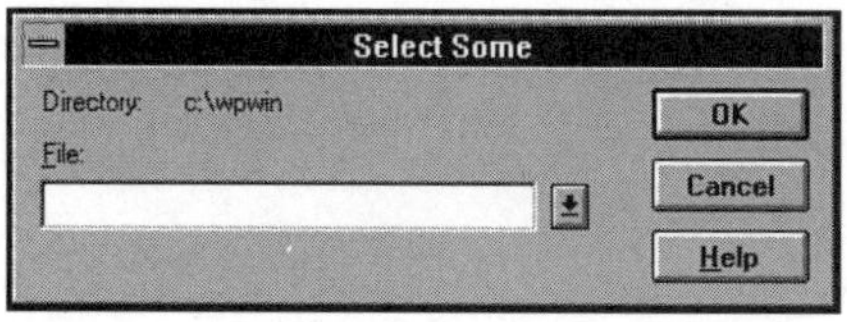

Fig. 4.4
The Norton Desktop Select Some dialog box appears after you choose the **S**ome option from the **S**elect menu.

4. Type the file names you want to select in the text box. You can type complete file names or wild cards. (Use the * wild card, for example, in ***.DOC** to select all files with the extension DOC.)
5. Press Enter to accept the selection. With all files selected, you can perform an operation on the group of files.

Tip
You can easily access the Select Some dialog box by using the mouse; just click the Select button at the bottom of the drive window.

Deselect specific types of files—as easily as you select them—by using the **D**eselect command. Press Alt+F, D to open the **D**eselect option; then select **A**ll, **S**ome, or **I**nvert, just as with the **S**elect command. Notice that the **S**ome option opens a Deselect Some dialog box that functions just like the Select Some dialog box.

After you select the files, performing the correct operation is simple. With the files selected, open the **F**ile menu by pressing Alt+F and then select the operation you want by pressing the underlined letter of the particular menu option. To delete a file, for example, press Alt+F, D.

Tip
To select all files except a particular type, choose **F**ile **S**elect **I**nvert. This option selects all currently deselected files and deselects all currently selected files. Remember that you must start with all the files you do not want to select highlighted.

Summary

This chapter covered the essential keyboard and mouse operations for Norton Desktop. This chapter included basic mouse operations, basic keyboard operations, and manipulating files.

Section II provides a detailed look at drives, windows, managing disks and files, launching files, backing up files, and using Norton Backup. Chapter 5, "Using the Drive Windows," covers understanding drive windows, manipulating multiple drive windows, and using view panes.

Part II

Managing Files and Directories

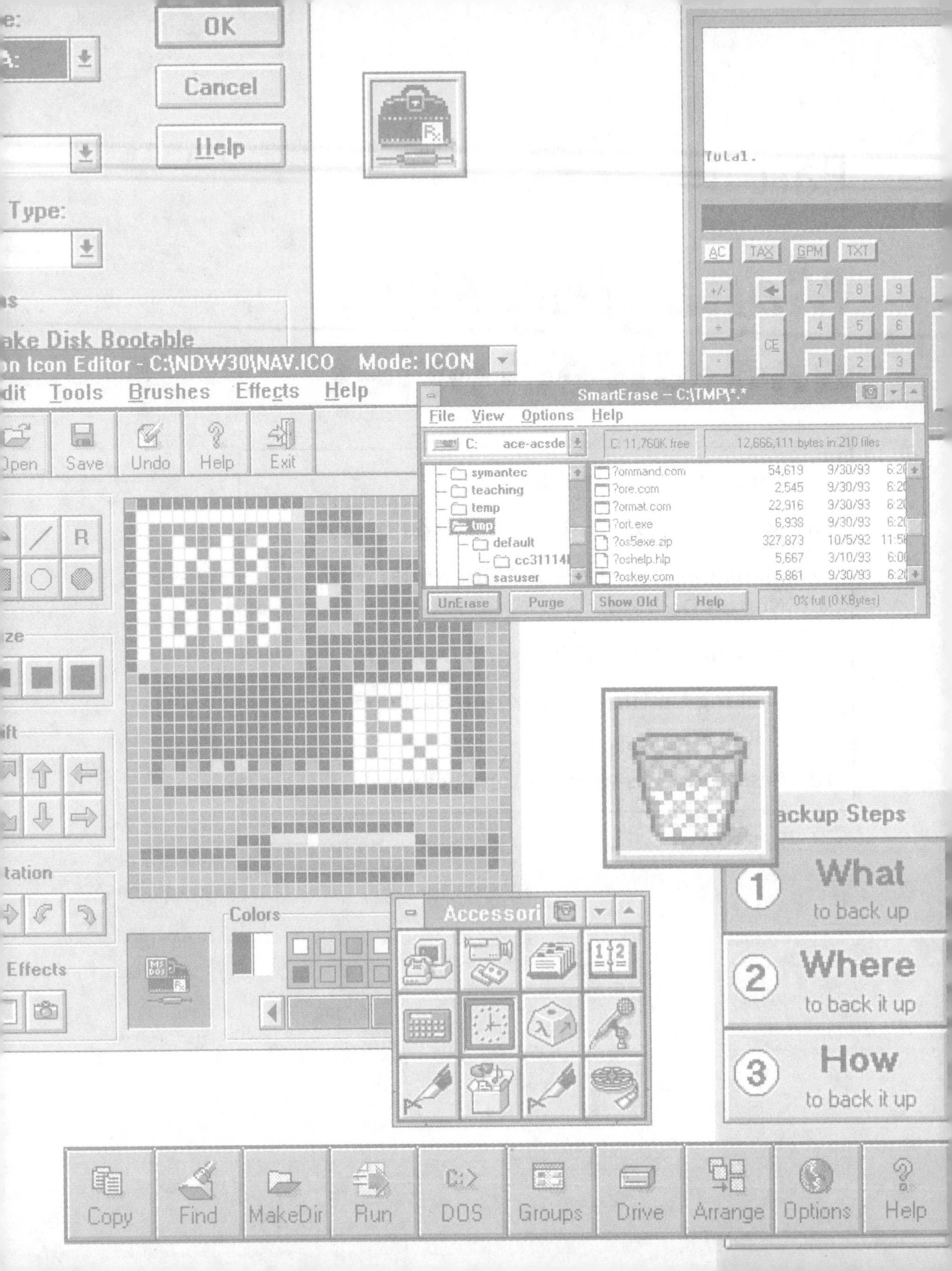

OK
Cancel
Help
Type:
Make Disk Bootable
Icon Editor - C:\NDW30\NAV.ICO Mode: ICON
Edit Tools Brushes Effects Help
Open Save Undo Help Exit
Colors
Effects
Total.
AC TAX GPM TXT
CE
SmartErase – C:\TMP*.*
File View Options Help
C: ace-acsde
C: 11,760K free
12,666,111 bytes in 210 files
symantec
teaching
temp
tmp
default
sasuser
?ommand.com 54,619 9/30/93
?ore.com 2,545 9/30/93
?ormat.com 22,916 9/30/93
?ort.exe 6,938 9/30/93
?os5exe.zip 327,873 10/5/92
?oshelp.hlp 5,667 3/10/93
?oskey.com 5,861 9/30/93
UnErase Purge Show Old Help
0% full (0 KBytes)
Accessori
Backup Steps
1 What to back up
2 Where to back it up
3 How to back it up
Copy Find MakeDir Run DOS Groups Drive Arrange Options Help

Chapter 5

Using the Drive Windows

Your system stores all data in *files*. Files can contain *data*, which is either textual, graphical, sound, or video in nature, or executable *programs*. You can copy files from one part of your system to another; you also can delete files, move files, and rename files. Because all programs and data are contained in files, controlling files is the key to controlling all the software on your system.

Files are arranged on your disk in *directories*. The directory structure resembles that of a tree. Each directory is a branch of the main tree trunk; in the computer world, the main tree trunk is called the *root directory*. Each directory extending from the root directory can branch out to other *subdirectories*; each subdirectory also can branch out to its own subdirectories, and so on.

If you use DOS, you must use obscure single-line commands to manipulate files and directories. Windows' graphical user interface, however, enables you to view and manipulate files graphically by producing a graphical representation of each disk's directory structure. This structure also resembles a tree. In fact, directory structures often are called *directory trees*.

Windows includes a utility called the File Manager, which enables you to manipulate directories and files. The Windows 3.1 File Manager consists of a series of directory windows (see fig. 5.1); you can create a separate window for each drive on your system. Each directory window consists of two parts: The left half displays the directory tree, and the right half shows the files in the current directory. You can move or copy files from one directory to another (or one drive to another) by dragging and dropping; you also can access these and other file operations from the File Manager's pull-down menus.

In this chapter, you learn to perform the following tasks:

- Use and open drive windows
- Understand the drive window menu bar
- Configure drive windows and the button bar
- Customize the button bar
- Use multiple drive windows
- Use the view pane to view files

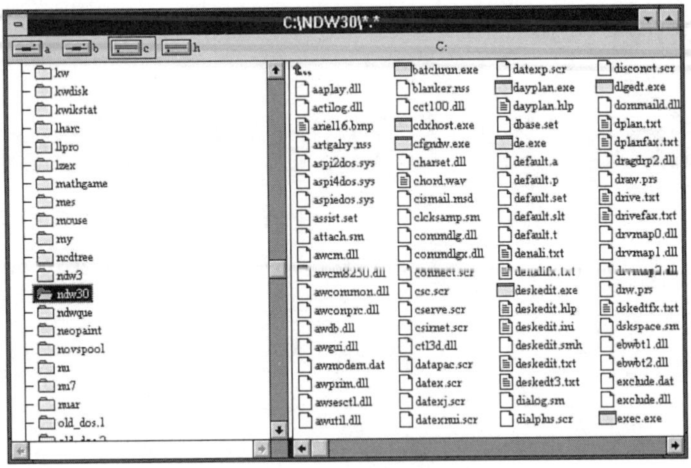

Fig. 5.1
The Windows 3.1 File Manager, showing a directory tree in the left pane and a file list in the right pane.

Although the Windows File Manager is easier to use than DOS-based command operations, it still lacks versatility. As explained in Chapter 3, "Using Norton Desktop and Windows Together," the File Manager may not deliver some features you want in a directory and file management utility: the capability to view the contents of files, the capability to choose multiple files by using only the mouse, the capability to access essential features quickly by using a button bar, or the capability to use Speed Search to locate files or directories. Norton Desktop 3 for Windows, fortunately, supplies a replacement for the File Manager that addresses all these concerns.

Understanding Drive Windows

Norton Desktop 3 for Windows (NDW) offers more features than does the Windows File Manager. The File Manager concentrates on managing files only. NDW embraces a concept called *drive management*, which provides additional capabilities related to the drive. NDW manages files and also provides such features as a file viewer, drag-and-drop capabilities, button bar commands, and additional options for displaying information in the drive window.

Norton's concept of drive management differs slightly from Windows' concept of file management. Windows relies on one central utility in which all file management takes place. Norton recognizes several points in the computing environment at which you need to manipulate files and enables access to drive windows at each point. Norton does not force you to use a central utility; instead, Norton furnishes you with the versatility to access file management wherever appropriate.

Drive windows are available from several locations on the Norton Desktop. The most noticeable are the Drive icons in the upper-left corner of the Desktop. Norton Backup, SmartErase, and other NDW tools and utilities also use drive windows as part of their core operations.

All Norton drive windows share the same appearance. Figure 5.2 shows the parts of a typical drive window, and table 5.1 describes its key features.

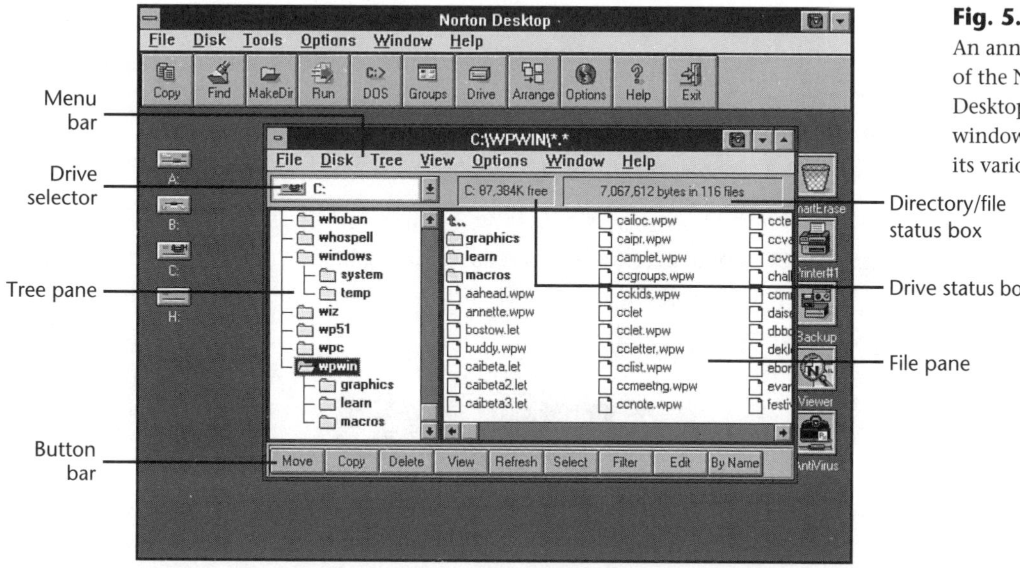

Fig. 5.2
An annotated view of the Norton Desktop drive window, showing its various features.

Table 5.1 Drive Window Features and Functions

Feature	Function
Menu bar	Displays the menus available in the drive window; each menu opens to show additional menu commands.
Drive selector	Shows the current drive and its label, if any, and enables you to choose other drives.
Drive status box	Lists the remaining unused space on the chosen drive.
Directory/file status box	Lists information about the current directory and/or selected files.
Tree pane	Shows the directory tree for the current drive.
File pane	Shows the files in the current directory.
Button bar	Contains user-configurable buttons that provide direct access to common file operations. Buttons may appear as text, as icons, or as text and icons.

Like most windows, you can resize a drive window to make it smaller or larger or maximize the window to fill your screen completely. You also can use the mouse to drag the *pane divider* horizontally to resize the directory and file panes.

Opening Drive Windows

On the default Desktop, no drive window is open. You can easily open one or more drive windows, however, by using any of the following methods:

- Double-click the appropriate Drive icon.
- Choose the **W**indow Open Drive **W**indow command. The Open Drive dialog box appears (see fig. 5.3). Open the **D**rive drop-down list box, and select from the list the appropriate drive; then click the OK button.
- Press Ctrl+W to access the Open Drive dialog box. In the **D**rive drop-down list, press the up and down arrows to select the drive you want; then press Enter.

Fig. 5.3
The Open Drive dialog box enables you to select the drive window to open.

You also can open multiple drive windows, either for different drives or for the same drive (for copying or moving files between directories). This capability enables you to transfer files easily from one drive window to another.

To change the drive represented by a drive window, click the arrow to the right of the **D**rive list box to open its drop-down list, and then select a different drive from that list. You also can move to the **D**rive list box by using either the mouse or the Tab key and then type the letter for the new drive. The directory and file panes change to reflect the contents of the newly selected drive.

Updating Drive Windows

If you use regular Windows or DOS commands to add or delete directories from your disk, Norton Desktop 3 for Windows does not automatically update its drive windows after the directories are added to or deleted. To update the drive window and display the most up-to-date directory and file information, choose **V**iew **R**efresh, click the Refresh button on the button bar, or press F5.

Understanding the Drive Menu Bar

You can access many NDW disk-related operations through the drive window's menu system. Pull-down menus in a drive window resemble regular Desktop menus. In fact, the drive window **H**elp pull-down menu is identical to the Desktop's **H**elp menu.

Norton Desktop's drive window menu bar contains the default menus described in table 5.2. (Keyboard shortcuts to access these menus appear in parentheses following the menu names in the table.)

Table 5.2 Drive Window Menus and Command Functions

Menu	Command Functions
File (Alt+F)	Manipulates and configures files.
Disk (Alt+D)	Manipulates disks and network drives.
T**r**ee (Alt+R)	Provides expansion and contraction options for the directory trees shown in the drive windows.
View (Alt+V)	Provides viewing options for drive windows and the Norton Viewer.
Options (Alt+O)	Provides configuration and customization options for Norton Desktop and its tools.
Window (Alt+W)	Opens another drive window.
Help (Alt+H)	Provides access to the Norton Desktop Help system.

The tables in the following sections explain the contents of each menu. If applicable, keyboard shortcuts appear in parentheses after the command; some commands may have two different keyboard shortcuts. Remember that commands followed by ellipses (...) open dialog boxes and commands followed by a right-pointing arrow▶( ) open additional menus.

File Menu

The **F**ile menu contains all the commands necessary to manipulate files (see fig. 5.4). Norton Desktop adds several commands to those of the standard Windows **F**ile menu.

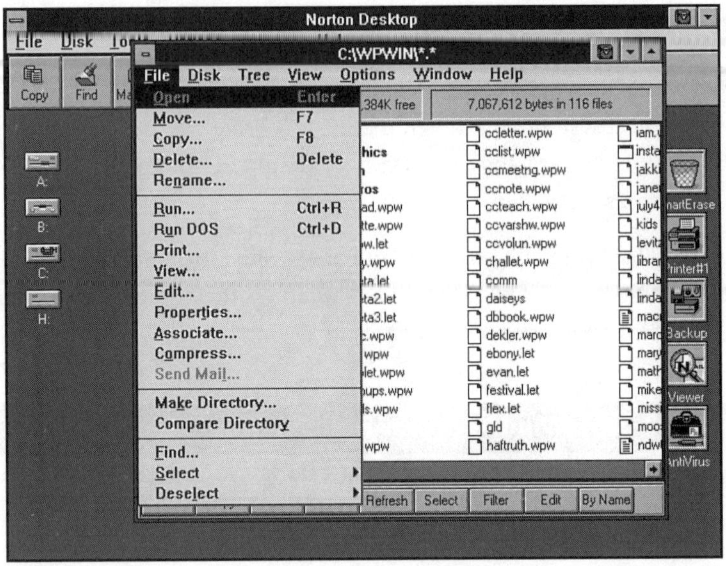

Fig. 5.4
A Desktop drive window with its **F**ile menu open, showing the various commands available on that menu.

Table 5.3 lists the **F**ile menu commands and their functions.

Table 5.3 File Menu Commands and Functions

Command	Function
Open (Alt+F, O; or Enter)	Opens a selected program group.
Move (Alt+F, M; or F7)	Moves selected files to a different directory and/or drive.
Copy (Alt+F, C; or F8)	Copies selected files, group, or objects.
Delete (Alt+F, D; or Del)	Deletes selected files, group, or objects.
Re**n**ame (Alt+F, N)	Renames a file, group, or object.
Run (Alt+F, R; or Ctrl+R)	Runs a selected program, document (with associated program), or Batch Builder file.
R**u**n DOS (Alt+F, U; or Ctrl+D)	Opens a DOS window.
Print (Alt+F, P)	Prints selected file or sets up printer.
View (Alt+F, V)	Views selected file.
Edit (Alt+F, E)	Edits selected file.
Proper**t**ies (Alt+F, T)	Sets file attributes and group object options.
Associate (Alt+F, A)	Associates applications with file extensions.

Command	Function
Co**m**press (Alt+F, O)	Compresses one or more files by using ZIP file format compression.
Send Mai**l** (Alt+F, L)	Sends the file via E-mail.
Ma**k**e Directory (Alt+F, K)	Creates new directories on your disk.
Compare Director**y**	Compares two directories and shows differences in contents.
Find (Alt+F, F)	Starts the SuperFind utility to locate specified text files.
Select (Alt+F, S)	Selects multiple files; the **S**elect menu includes options for **A**ll, **S**ome, and **I**nvert.
Dese**l**ect (Alt+F, L)	Deselects multiple files; the Dese**l**ect menu includes options for **A**ll, **S**ome, and **I**nvert.

*Notice that both **O**pen and Co**m**press use Alt+F, O as their keyboard shortcut and that both Send Mai**l** and Dese**l**ect use Alt+F, L as their keyboard shortcut. In each case, selecting the shortcut toggles the highlight bar between the two options. To activate the highlighted command, press Enter.*

Disk Menu

The **D**isk menu contains all the commands necessary to work with hard and floppy disks (see fig. 5.5). In addition to the normal Windows **D**isk menu commands found in the File Manager, Norton Desktop 3 for Windows adds two commands that enable you to connect with and use disk drives that are on a network just as if they were local disks.

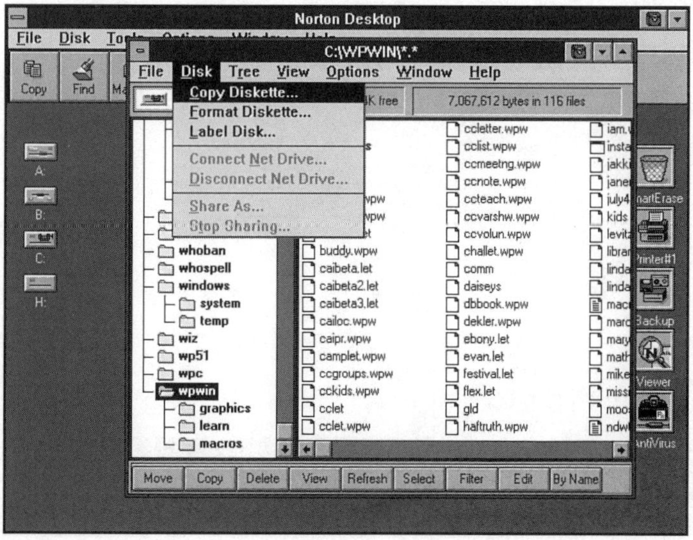

Fig. 5.5
A Norton Desktop drive window with its **D**isk menu open, showing its several available commands.

Table 5.4 lists the commands on the **D**isk menu.

Table 5.4 Disk Menu Commands and Functions

Command	Function
Copy Diskette (Alt+D, C)	Copies the contents of an entire disk to another disk.
Format Diskette (Alt+D, F)	Formats a disk by using NDW's format prog-ram. See the section "Formatting Disks," in Chapter 6.
Label Disk (Alt+D, L)	Assigns a new or different label to a disk.
Connect **N**et Drive (Alt+D, N)	Connects a network drive if system is physically connected to a network.
Disconnect Net Drive	Disconnects a network drive if system (Alt+D, D) is physically connected to a network.
Share As (Alt+D, S)	Similar in function to the DOS SHARE com-mand; enables you to share files on a network.
S**t**op Sharing (Alt+D, T)	Terminates drive sharing as set up by the **S**hare As command.

Tree Menu

The T**r**ee menu contains commands that affect the view of the directory tree in various drive windows (see fig. 5.6).

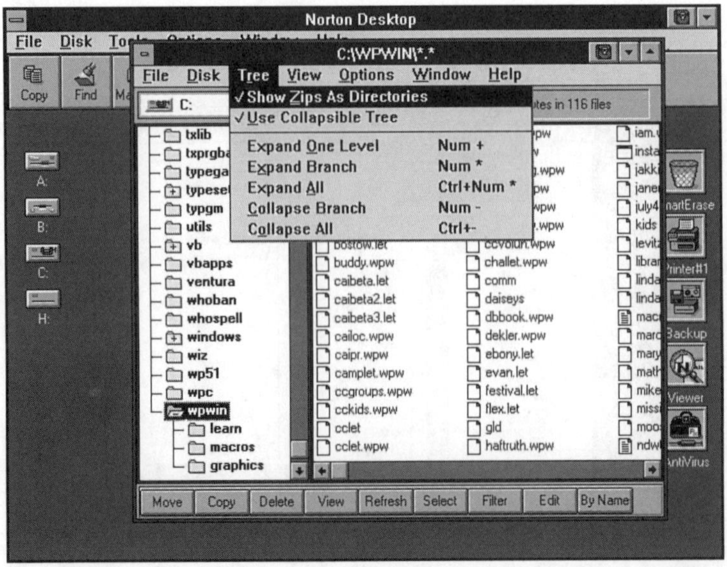

Fig. 5.6
A Desktop drive window with its T**r**ee menu open, showing the commands that affect the view of the window's directory tree.

Table 5.5 lists the commands on the T**r**ee menu.

Table 5.5 Tree Menu Commands and Functions

Command	Function
Show **Z**ips as Directories (Alt+R, Z)	Zipped files are treated as directories, and the files within the zipped files are shown as files.
Use Collapsible Tree (Alt+R, U)	Instructs NDW to use a tree that can be collapsed or expanded.
Expand **O**ne Level (Alt+R, O; or Num +)	Expands the directory tree by one level.
E**x**pand Branch (Alt+R, X; or Num *)	Fully expands the current branch.
Expand **A**ll (Alt+R, A; or Ctrl+Num *)	Fully expands the entire directory tree.
Collapse Branch (Alt+R, C; or Num –)	Collapses the current branch.
Collapse All (Alt+R, O; or Ctrl+ –)	Fully collapses the entire directory tree.

The designation "Num" with any keyboard shortcut means to press the key for the following symbol on the numeric keypad and not on the regular keyboard.

View Menu

The **V**iew menu contains commands that apply specifically to drive window displays (see fig. 5.7).

Table 5.6 describes the commands on the **V**iew menu.

Table 5.6 View Menu Commands and Functions

Command	Function
Tree Pane (Alt+V, T)	Shows or hides the tree pane (activated if checked).
File Pane (Alt+V, F)	Shows or hides the file pane (activated if checked).
View Pane (Alt+V, V)	Shows or hides the view pane (activated if checked).
S**h**ow All Files (Alt+V, E)	Shows all the files on the chosen drive.
Refresh (Alt+V, R; or F5)	Updates the tree display.

(continues)

Table 5.6 Continued

Command	Function
File **D**etails (Alt+V, D)	Selects types of information to display for each file. Options include: **I**con, **S**ize, **D**ate, **T**ime, **A**ttributes, and Di**r**ectory.
File Fi**l**ter (Alt+V, L)	Includes or excludes specified types of files from the display.
Fo**n**t (Alt+V, N)	Selects **F**ont, Font St**y**le, and **S**ize for the text shown in various drive windows.
Sort By (Alt+V, S)	Selects options for sorting the files displayed. Options include sorting by **N**ame, **T**ype, **S**ize, **D**ate, or **U**nsorted, plus in **A**scending or **D**escending order.
Vie**w**er (Alt+V, W)	Shows commands for the view pane: **F**ind, Find **N**ext, Find **P**revious, **G**oto, **O**EM Text, and **C**hange Viewer.

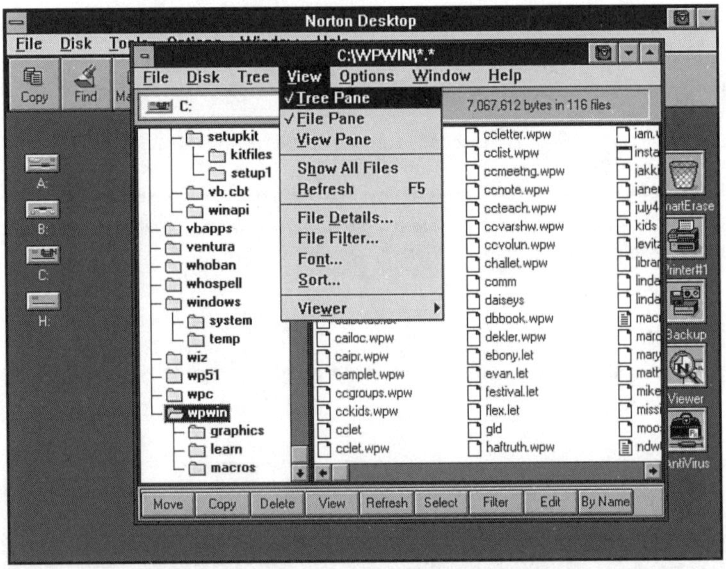

Fig. 5.7
A Desktop drive window **View** pull-down menu open, displaying the commands that affect the window's appearance.

Note

The other drive window menus, **O**ptions, **W**indow, and **H**elp are essentially the same as the menus of the same names on the Norton Desktop. (These menus are described in detail in Chapter 2, "Getting Up and Running with Norton Desktop 3 for Windows.")

Learning About the Drive Window Button Bar

At the bottom of the Drive window is a series of buttons that give you quick access to the most commonly used commands. These buttons access options that are identical to some of those previously described and accessed from the pull-down menus. Eleven default buttons are available on the drive window button bar, as described in table 5.7. (The exact number of buttons that actually appear on-screen depends on the width of the current drive window.)

Table 5.7 Button Bar Buttons and Their Functions

Button	Function
Move	Opens the Move dialog box, which enables you to move files and subdirectories from one directory or disk to another.
Copy	Opens the Copy dialog box, which enables you to copy files and subdirectories from one directory or disk to another.
Delete	Deletes the selected files or directories.
View	Turns the view pane on or off.
Refresh	Refreshes the drive window.
Select	Opens the Select Some dialog box, which enables you to select files that meet specified criteria.
Filter	Opens the Filter dialog box, which enables you to select what types of files to show in the drive window.
Edit	Starts the Desktop Editor with the selected file loaded.
By Name	Sorts files in the drive window by file name.
By Type	Sorts files in the drive window by file extension.
MakeDir	Makes a directory.

Note

Not all buttons appear in all drive windows. Depending on the size of your drive window and your monitor's resolution, one or more of the last buttons may not be visible (refer to fig. 5.2).

Configuring Drive Windows and the Button Bar

NDW is very flexible and configurable. You can customize the drive windows to show data exactly as you want to view it. You can choose the panes and files to show, the details to show about each file, and so on.

Selecting Panes To View

The drive window actually offers three possible panes. You already have seen the directory and file panes; the third pane is called the *view pane*. This pane is a smaller version of the Norton Viewer; it displays the contents of the currently chosen file. Figure 5.8 shows a drive window with an open view pane.

Fig. 5.8
A Desktop drive window showing open tree, file, and view panes.

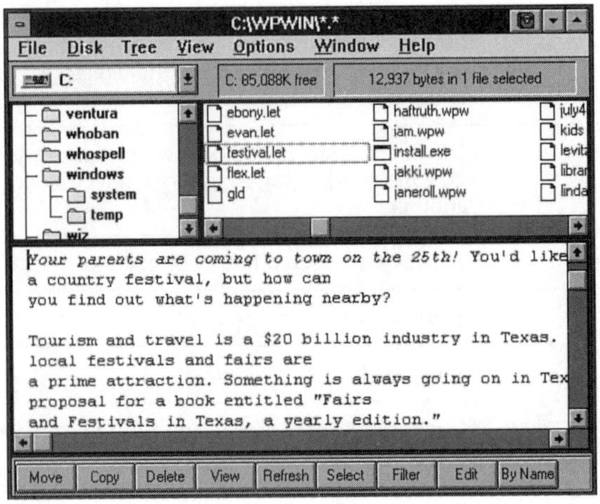

Choose the panes you want to display in a drive window by choosing their corresponding options on the **V**iew menu. Choosing these options places check marks on the menu next to the names of the panes you want displayed. (The directory tree and file pane options are checked on the menu by default.) These options are on and off toggles; choose the option to turn it on, and choose it again to turn it off.

You can display in the drive window a list of all the files on your drive by choosing **V**iew S**h**ow All Files. The directory pane disappears, and the file pane lists all files on the chosen drive, as shown in figure 5.9.

Configuring the File Listing

You can customize the file listing in the file pane in several ways. You can choose the types of files to show and what information to show about each file. You can even choose the order in which the files are listed and the font you want to use for the file information. All these options are accessed through the **V**iew menu.

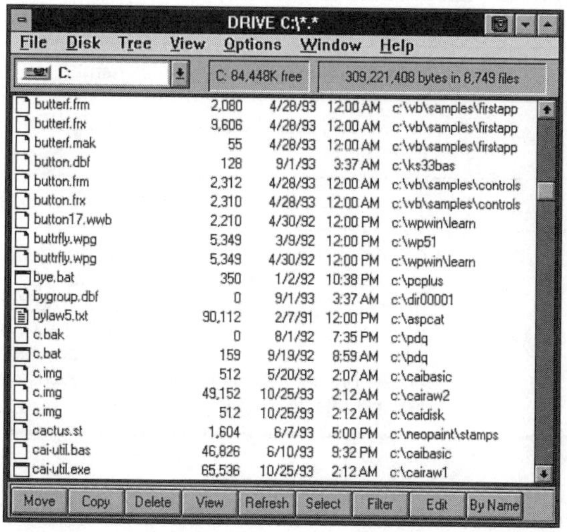

Fig. 5.9
The file listing that results from choosing the **V**iew **Sh**ow All Files drive window command.

Using Viewer File Filters. After you choose the View File Filter command or click the Filter button on the button bar, the Filter dialog box appears (see fig. 5.10). This dialog box enables you to choose what files are shown in the file pane. You can filter files by file type or attributes.

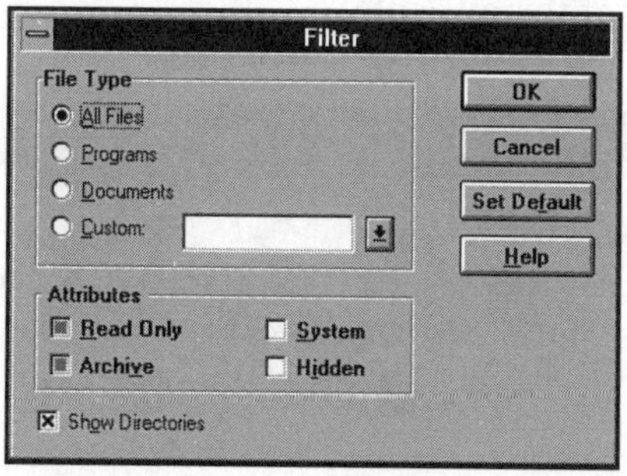

Fig. 5.10
The Desktop Viewer's Filter dialog box enables you to choose which files to display.

Note

Settings made in the Filter dialog box can be designated as the default settings for all subsequently opened drive windows, including those used in other NDW utilities and tools, by selecting the Set De**f**ault button.

Filtering by File Type enables you to show only files with a certain file extension. The filter is in effect for all directories you view in the drive window. The following table describes the available options for this filter.

Option	Function
All Files	Shows all files, regardless of file name.
Programs	Shows only executable files with EXE, COM, or BAT extensions.
Documents	Shows only text files with DOC and TXT extensions.
Custom	Creates a customized file filter; to choose this option, choose the **C**ustom radio button, and type the file extension(s) in the **C**ustom text box. You can choose, for example, to list only 1-2-3 files that use a WK? extension. (*?* is a wild card that matches any character.) You can access previous filters by opening the **C**ustom drop-down list and selecting a filter from the list.

Filtering by file attribute enables you to show only files that either do or do not have the given attribute. Each check box in the Attributes area of the Filter dialog box represents one of three different states, shown by a blank check box, an X in the check box, or a gray square in the check box. A deselected check box (blank box) instructs Norton to list only files without the specified attribute. A selected check box (with an X) instructs Norton to list only files with the attribute. A gray box instructs the program not to take into account the setting of this attribute.

Note

The first time you select a check box in the Filter dialog box, an X appears in the check box; the second time you select the same check box, you place a gray square in the box; the next time you select this check box, the box is deselected and becomes blank—neither an X nor a gray square appears in the check box. (These check boxes are toggles.)

The following table lists the available attributes and their functions.

Attribute	Function
Read Only	Protects files from being edited or erased.
Archi**v**e	Indicates files that have not been backed up since they were last edited.

Attribute	Function
System	Indicates system files.
Hidden	Indicates critical files that are "hidden" from normal use.

The Filter dialog box also enables you to choose whether subdirectories for the current directory appear in the file pane. Select the Show Directories check box to display subdirectories in the file pane.

Tip

To see more files in the file pane, deselect all file detail check boxes except Icon. This setting produces a multiple-column file listing that displays more files than does the standard single-column listing.

Setting Viewer File Details

After you choose the **V**iew File **D**etails command, the File Details dialog box appears (see fig. 5.11). This dialog box enables you to choose exactly what file details are shown for each file in the file pane. These details include file **I**con, **D**ate, **A**ttributes, **S**ize, Time, and D**i**rectory. By using these options, you can display only the file details that you need and avoid cluttering the window with details you do not want to see. A sample file listing showing the chosen details appears at the bottom of the dialog box.

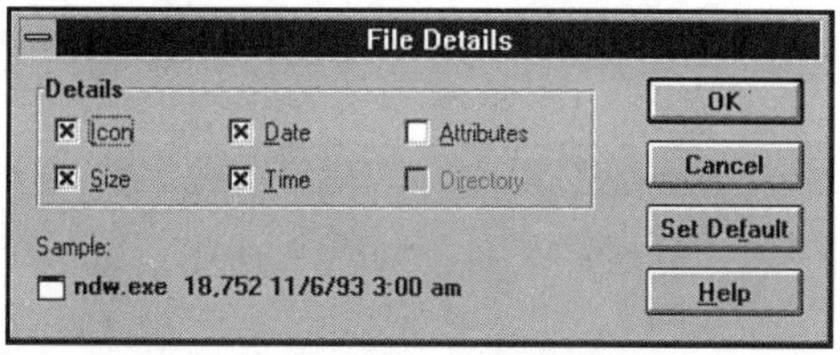

Fig. 5.11
The File Details dialog box, which enables you to specify how much information appears in the file pane.

Choosing Viewer Fonts

You can change the font shown in the drive windows by choosing the **V**iew Fo**n**t command. This command opens the Font dialog box, as shown in figure 5.12. This dialog box enables you to choose among the options listed in the following table.

Option	Function
Font	A list box enables you to choose among all available fonts on your system.
Font Style	A list box enables you to choose how to display the chosen font—in Regular, Italic, Boldface, or Bold Italic style.
Size	A list box enables you to choose among the available type sizes for the selected font.

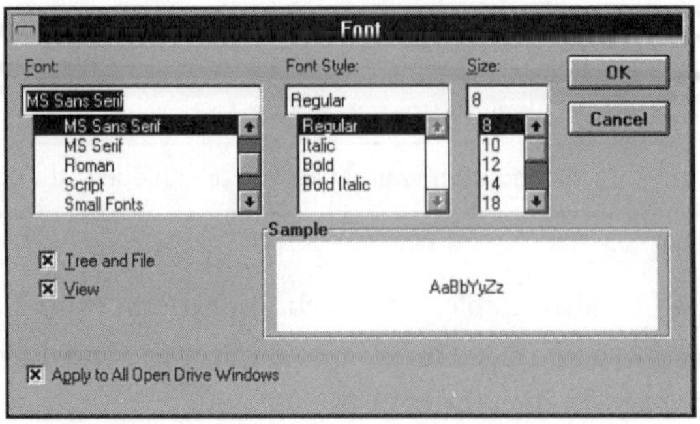

Fig. 5.12
The Viewer's Font dialog box enables you to specify the font to be used for displaying file information.

The check boxes in the Font dialog box enable you to use the selected font in the **T**ree and File pane, in only the **V**iew pane, or in all three panes. You also can choose to apply this selection to all open drive windows by selecting the A**p**ply to All Open Drive Windows check box. The Sample box shows you a sample of the currently selected font.

Choosing Sort Order

You can determine the sort order for files by choosing the **V**iew **S**ort command. After you choose this option, the Sort dialog box appears (see fig. 5.13), listing the available sort options, as described in the following table.

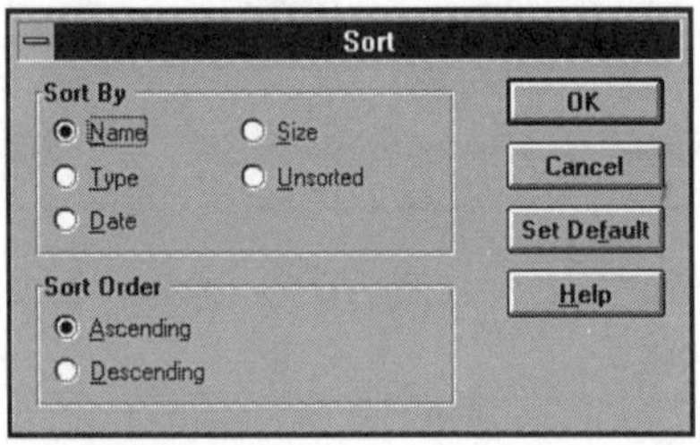

Fig 5.13
The Desktop drive window's Sort dialog box enables you to choose sort options for listing files.

Option	Function
Name	Sorts by file name, in alphanumeric order (symbols first, numbers second, alphabetic characters third).
Type	Sorts by file extensions in alphanumeric order; a secondary sort within each file type is by file name.
Date	Sorts by date and time; places most recent files first.
Size	Sorts by file size; places largest files first.

Option	Function
Unsorted	Does not sort files in any order; lists files in the same order they appear in a DOS DIR listing.
Ascending	Uses an ascending sort.
Descending	Uses a descending sort.

Note

Two buttons on the default button bar enable you to quickly choose the two most popular sort options. The By Name button sorts files in the drive window by file name, and the By Type button sorts files by file extension.

Customizing the Drive Window Button Bar

The drive window's button bar consists of the row of buttons that appears at the bottom of the window. (It also is often called a toolbar and may even appear at the top of the window, depending on your configuration.) These buttons provide direct access to the most common operations performed on files and directories. By default, the button bar accesses several preset operations (described in table 5.7). You can, however, customize each button in a drive window's button bar to represent a different operation.

To customize the drive window button bar, follow these steps:

1. Choose the **O**ptions **C**ustomize command to open the Control Center dialog box, and then select Drive Windows in the **C**ategories list. The Control Center dialog box for drive windows appears (see fig. 5.14).

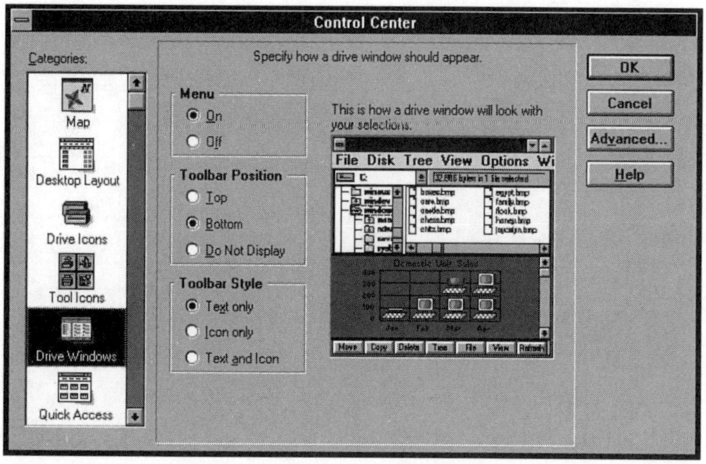

Fig. 5.14
The Control Center (Drive Windows) dialog box enables you to specify options for drive windows.

Three areas containing option buttons now appear in this version of the Control Center dialog box: Menu, Toolbar Position, and Toolbar Styles

2. Choose the option buttons you want from each of these areas: From the Menu area, choose **O**n or O**f**f. From the Toolbar Position area, choose **T**op, **B**ottom, or **D**o Not Display. From the Toolbar Style area, choose Te**x**t Only, **I**con Only, or Text **a**nd Icon.

3. (Optional) Choose the Ad**v**anced button to open the Drive Window - Advanced dialog box. This dialog box enables you to specify the default size of a drive window, select the function of the right hand button to mean **E**xtended Selection or **P**op-Up Menu, choose to Save **T**ree Information Locally (to a local drive) if you use a nonwriteable disk (such as a CD-ROM), and choose to **D**isable Drive Window Launch so that a file cannot be opened from a window drive. Choose OK to return to the Control Center (Drive Window) dialog box.

4. Choose OK to return to the drive window.

You also can customize your drive window by specifying what commands appear on the drive window's button bar. To make these specifications, follow these steps:

1. Choose the **O**ptions **C**ustomize command to access the Control Center dialog box, and then select Toolbars in the **C**ategories list.

2. In the Toolbar Type area, choose the Drive **W**indow option button. The Control Center dialog box for drive window button bars (listed on-screen as "Drive Window Toolbar") appears, as shown in figure 5.15.

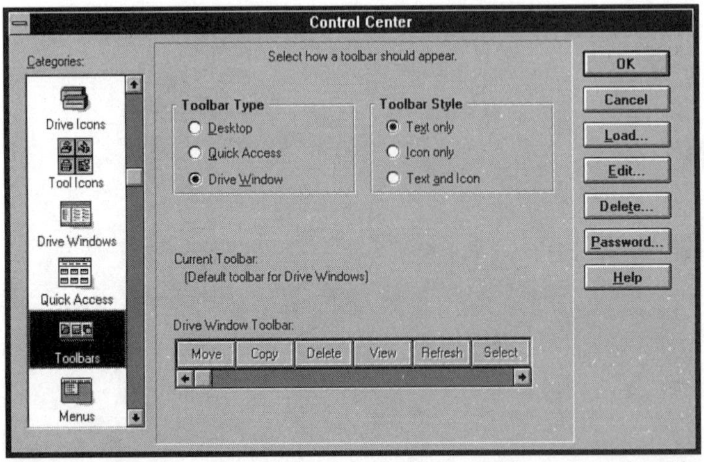

Fig. 5.15
The Control Center (Toolbars) dialog box enables you to specify what commands appear on the drive window button bar.

3. In the Toolbar Style area, choose how you want the button bar to appear in the drive window: as Te**x**t Only, **I**con Only, or Text **a**nd Icon.

   At the bottom of this dialog box is the Drive Window Toolbar button list. You can use the scroll bar to see what commands are currently on the list. The Current Toolbar information line tells you what toolbar file is currently being used to define the commands on the button bar.

4. To load a new toolbar definition file, choose the **L**oad button (one of the command buttons running down the right side of the dialog box). The Toolbars - Load dialog box appears (see fig. 5.16). By default, you can choose between the Default Toolbar for Drive Windows and the Old Button Bar from NDW 2.x. If you save other toolbar definitions, these also appear in the toolbar definition list. You also can choose the **D**irectory button to search for other drive window toolbar definition files.

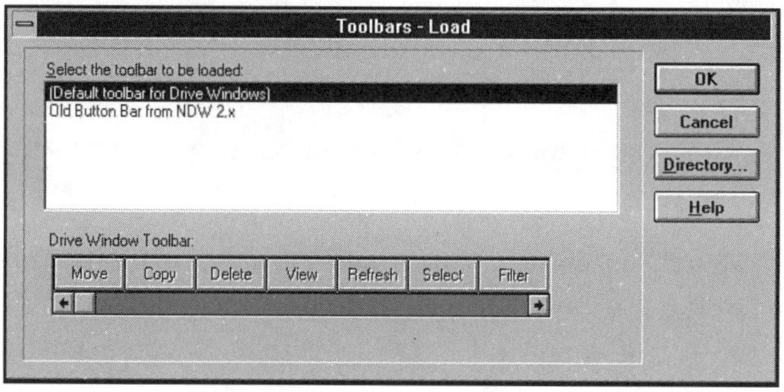

Fig. 5.16
The Toolbars - Load dialog box enables you to load a new toolbar definition file.

5. Select from the Select the Toolbar To Be Loaded list the toolbar definition you want, and then choose OK. (Or choose Cancel if you change your mind.) You return to the Control Center (Toolbars) dialog box.

6. To edit the commands on the button bar, choose the **E**dit button (refer to fig. 5.15). The Toolbars - Edit dialog box appears, as shown in figure 5.17.

7. Select from the Available **C**ommands list the command you want added as a button to the button bar.

8. Choose the **I**nsert button to insert the command at the top of the sample toolbar list, or choose **A**ppend to add the command to the end of the list. You also can first select a current command in the sample

Drive Window Toolbar list, select a command from the Available Commands list, and then choose **I**nsert to insert the new command immediately above the highlighted current command in the sample list.

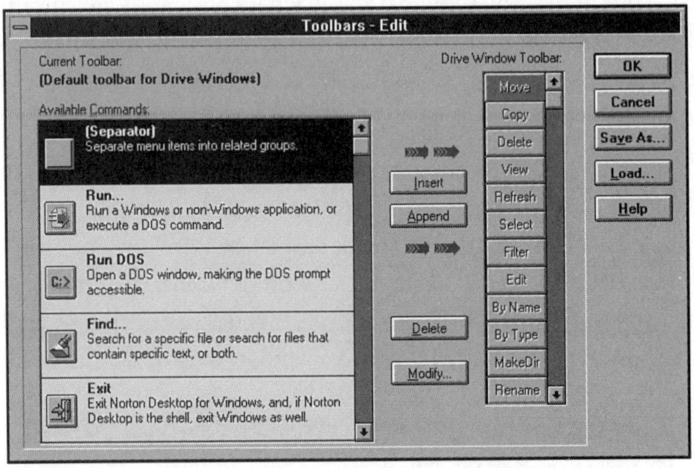

Fig. 5.17
The Toolbars - Edit dialog box enables you to customize the drive window's button bar.

9. To remove a command from the button bar, select a command in the sample Drive Window Toolbar list, and then choose the **D**elete button.

10. To modify the meaning of a button, select a button on the Drive Window Toolbar list, and then choose **M**odify. You can then edit the button label for the command and, if applicable, the command related to the button.

11. To save your new toolbar definition, choose the Sa**v**e As button.

12. Choose OK to confirm your new button bar configuration and close the dialog box.

After making your changes, your new button bar now appears on all open drive windows.

Using Multiple Drive Windows

A key feature of Norton's drive windows is the program's capability to display multiple windows on-screen. You open these additional drive windows the same way you open the first drive window; you can open additional windows for the same drive or for different drives.

Arranging Multiple Drive Windows

If you open a second drive window, the new window appears *cascaded* in front of the first window. Subsequent windows are cascaded in front of the last opened window. Norton enables you to size and arrange multiple drive windows manually, or you can instruct Norton to cascade or *tile* the windows automatically.

To cascade drive windows, choose the **W**indow **C**ascade command from the Desktop. (The current active window appears topmost on the pile.) To tile drive windows, choose the **W**indow **T**ile command from the Desktop.

Tip

To move from one drive window to another by using the keyboard, press Ctrl+Tab. You also can access specific drive windows by opening the **W**indow menu and choosing the window you want.

Selecting Directories and Files

Norton's drive windows enable you to easily select directories and files. If you use a mouse, simply point to the file name and click the left mouse button. To select multiple files, click the right mouse button on each file to select, or click and hold the right button and drag the mouse pointer over a list of files to be selected.

Tip

You also can temporarily hide all open drive windows by choosing the **W**indows Hide **A**ll command. To show hidden windows, choose the **W**indows Show **A**ll command.

If you use the keyboard, remember to press Tab to move the cursor from one pane to another and then press the arrow keys while holding the Shift key. Select multiple files by pressing Shift+F8 before using the spacebar to select files. Press Shift+F8 again after you finish selecting files.

Note

You can quickly move to a directory in the directory pane or to a file in the file pane by using Norton's Speed Search function. After you open a pane, start typing the name of the directory or file you want to find. As soon as you start typing, the Speed Search box appears, as shown in figure 5.18. As you type, the first directory or file that matches the name you are typing is highlighted. Press Enter to accept that selection and close the Speed Search box, or press Esc to close the Speed Search box without making a selection. If the highlighted name is not what you want, keep typing in more letters of the file's name until that file name is highlighted.

Dragging and Dropping Files between Drive Windows

Moving or copying files from one drive window to another is especially easy if you use the drag-and-drop feature; simply select a file, press and hold the left mouse button, drag the file to a new destination, and then release the mouse button, which drops the file at its new location.

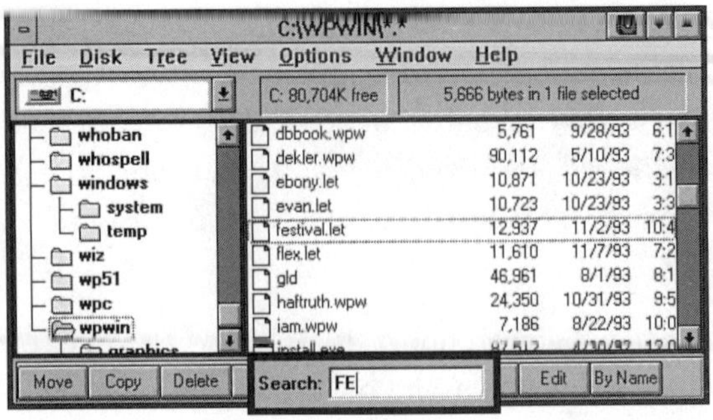

Fig. 5.18
The Speed Search box (at the bottom of the drive window) enables you to quickly find a specific file name within a long list of files.

Tip
Select multiple files by using the right mouse button. After all multiple files are selected, click the left mouse button for dragging and dropping.

You can copy a file by dragging it from the source window and dropping it onto the destination window. To move a file, press and hold the Alt key while performing the drag-and-drop operation. You can drop files onto a particular directory in the directory pane, or you can drop files anywhere in the file pane.

Using the View Pane To View Files

To show (or hide) the view pane, choose the **V**iew **V**iew Pane command. (If the command is checked on the **V**iew menu, the view pane appears on-screen; if the command is not checked, the view pane does not appear.) If the view pane is displayed, the contents of the currently selected file appear in the file panel.

Note

The view pane is similar to the Norton Viewer, which is described in more detail in Chapter 21, "Using Norton Viewer."

The view pane discerns what type of file is selected and picks the correct viewer for that file type. If you want a different viewer for a particular file, choose the **V**iew Vie**w**er **C**hange Viewer command. You now can change the active viewer by using the options in the Set Current Viewer dialog box.

If the current file is larger than the view pane, click the scroll bars to browse through the balance of the file. If you view a text file, you can search for specific text by choosing the **V**iew Vie**w**er **F**ind command. A Find dialog box appears, enabling you to enter a text string for which to search. Similarly, choose the **V**iew Vie**w**er **G**oto command to move to specific cells or fields in spreadsheet and database files.

Note

If viewing a bitmapped graphics file, you can size the graphic to the view pane by double-clicking the left mouse button while the mouse pointer is on the graphic. Double-clicking again restores the graphic to its original size.

Summary

This chapter showed you how to use Norton's drive windows to manipulate directories and files. You learned how to open a drive window, configure a drive window, use multiple windows and use the View Pane.

The next chapter explains how to work with disks by using Norton Desktop's disk management features, which enable you to format disks, label disks, and copy disks.

Chapter 6

Managing Your Disks with Norton Desktop

In this chapter, you learn to perform the following tasks:

- Manage disks
- Format disks
- Label disks
- Copy disks

Your computer system uses data stored on *disks*. A disk is a round piece of metal, glass, or plastic with a magnetized surface. As a disk rotates, a tiny electromagnet called a read/write head reads the data stored on the disk's magnetic surface and converts it into electrical signals your PC recognizes. Conversely, the same read/write head writes information as magnetic pulses onto the spinning disk's magnetic surface.

Learning about Disk Management

To successfully manage your disks, you must know what types of disks are available. The two kinds of disks you use for most of your computing are hard and floppy disks.

A *hard disk* is a nonremovable disk composed of several rigid platters. Hard disks can store large amounts of data—as much as 500 *megabytes* (million bytes) for desktop computers and more than 1 gigabyte (1,000 megabytes) for network computers. The size of hard disk drives is increasing yearly. (You probably have never seen an actual hard disk, as it is enclosed inside your PC's system unit, free from prying eyes—and damaging dust particles.)

A *floppy disk* is a removable disk consisting of a single, plastic platter. Floppy disks come in two sizes, 3 1/2 inches and 5 1/4 inches, and can commonly store up to 1.44 and 1.2 megabytes (M) of information, respectively. Some PCs also contain 2.88M 3 1/2-inch disk drives.

Although some computers come equipped with only one size floppy disk drive, many newer computers contain both floppy disk drive sizes. On a typical dual floppy disk machine, the 5 1/4-inch disk is labeled drive A, and the 3 1/2-inch disk is drive B. (On some PCs, however, these drives are just the opposite.) Hard disks usually are labeled as drive C. If your system has more than one hard disk, however, the additional disks may be labeled drive D, drive E, and so on. (If your computer uses a CD-ROM drive, it is often named drive D.)

You generally use hard disks to store your programs and other essential information. Floppy disks are used to store information that must be moved from one location to another. You also use floppy disks to back up data from hard disks or to store less-often used data. *CD-ROM drives* use removable hard disks, much like music CDs, which are normally used to store large amounts of reference information, including text, graphics, and video clips. *Network drives* are often used to centrally store programs or corporate data.

A blank disk, fresh from the factory, often comes unformatted and, therefore, is unusable. The disk must be *formatted* before it can be used. Formatting prepares a blank disk by encoding on the disk *tracks* to receive data. The very first track on a disk also is encoded with information about the disk's format itself.

Each disk track is divided during formatting into *sectors*. Multiple sectors are called *clusters*. Each track, sector, and cluster is numbered, and a special table—called the *file allocation table*, or *FAT*—is created to serve as a road map to each track, sector, and cluster number. A program uses DOS to read the FAT and locate exactly where on your disk these bits of data are stored.

After a disk is formatted, it is ready for use. You then can assign a *volume label* to the disk. Disk volume labels are particularly useful if you keep many floppy disks; the volume labels help you locate the correct disk in a large number of floppies.

Note

Volume labels are labels that are stored on the disk electronically to identify the disk. They should not be confused with the paper labels that are physically attached to the disk jacket.

You may need to copy information from one disk to another. Chapter 7, "Managing Your Files and Directories with Norton Desktop," shows you how to copy individual files from disk to disk, but you also can copy an entire disk's contents to a disk of like size and capacity. Norton Desktop's **D**isk **C**opy Diskette command enables you to make exact duplicates of 3 1/2-inch and 5 1/4-inch disks. You can access all these operations from the **D**isk menu on the Norton Desktop drive window.

Formatting Disks

Formatting floppy disks in Norton Desktop is very easy. In fact, NDW provides three different methods of disk formatting; each method offers its own tradeoff between speed and safety.

> **Note**
>
> You cannot use Norton Desktop to format a hard disk, a network drive, or a CD-ROM.

Follow these general steps to format a floppy disk:

1. Choose the **D**isk **F**ormat Diskette command. The Format Diskette dialog box appears, as shown in figure 6.1.

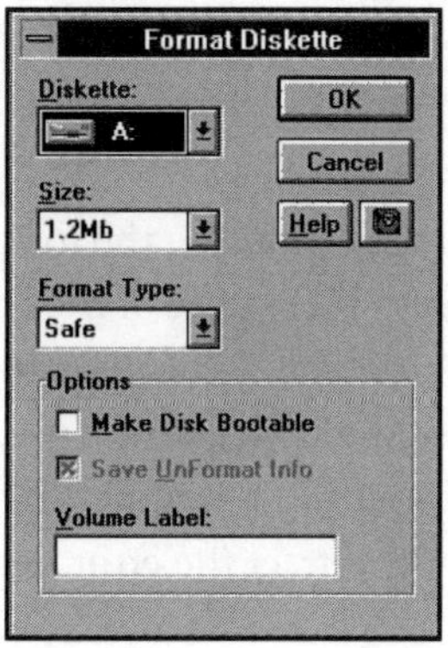

Fig. 6.1
The Format Diskette dialog box enables you to format a floppy disk.

2. Select from the **D**iskette drop-down list box the desired disk drive.

3. Select from the **S**ize drop-down list box the correct storage capacity of the disk to be formatted.

4. Select from the **F**ormat Type drop-down list box the type of formatting you want.

5. To create a bootable disk, select the **M**ake Disk Bootable check box.

6. To assign a label to the disk, type a name in the **V**olume Label text box.

7. Insert the disk to be formatted into the correct drive, and choose OK.

   The formatting begins, and a message box appears, containing a status bar that displays the percentage of the formatting completed. After formatting is complete, you are asked if you want to format another disk.

8. To format another disk, choose **Y**es and repeat steps 2 through 7. To quit formatting, choose **N**o to return to the Format Diskette dialog box.

9. Click the Cancel button to close the dialog box.

Note

You also can access the **F**ormat Diskette dialog box by opening the Norton Desktop group and double-clicking the Format Disk icon. Format also is available on the *Launch List*. (See Chapter 8, "Launching Files with Norton Desktop," for more about the Launch List.)

Several message boxes may appear during the formatting process. If an error occurs, a message box conveys the nature of the error and asks for instructions on how to proceed. Errors can occur if the disk drive door is not completely closed or if you place the wrong disk type in a disk drive (for example, a 360K double-density disk in a 1.2M high-density drive). If an error occurs, take the appropriate action to correct the error, and begin the format again.

Note

If you believe you have a defective disk, end the formatting process and discard the disk. Although the disk may have portions of usable media, the cost of a floppy disk is so inexpensive that using defective disks is not worth the risk of losing valuable data.

If you format a disk that has never been formatted—or one with an otherwise unreadable format—a message box appears asking if you want to proceed with a *Destructive format* (see the following section). Choose **Y**es to confirm this option, and the format operation proceeds.

Learning Types of Disk Formats

The following three format types are available in Norton Desktop:

- *Safe.* A Safe format moves the existing information in the system area of the disk to an unused area elsewhere on the disk. This type of format enables you to easily recover from an accidental disk format by using the UnFormat utility, as discussed in Chapter 29, "Using Norton Fix-It and Rescue Disks."

- *Quick.* A Quick format simply erases the contents of the FAT and the root directory. This formatting method is the quickest of the three. This type of format can be used only on previously formatted disks.

- *Destructive.* A Destructive format not only erases the contents of the FAT and the root directory, but also overwrites all information in the data area of the disk. This formatting method is the slowest, but the most thorough. You must use this method as you initially format a new, blank disk.

Caution

If you format disks by using the Quick format method, and the disk contains a virus, the virus may not be destroyed. The common "Stoned" virus, for example, is not destroyed by a Quick format. Formatting a disk by using the Safe or Destructive format, however, does destroy any viruses on the disk. (You can, of course, scan a disk by using the Norton AntiVirus to confirm that no viruses infect the disk.)

Using Other Formatting Options

The following three options also are available in the Format Diskette dialog box:

- ***M**ake Diskette Bootable.* Selecting the check box for this option instructs Norton Desktop to copy the DOS system files onto the formatted disk, enabling you to boot your computer from the floppy disk. Use this option only on disks that contain programs that are essential for use if your hard disk is inoperable, such as the Norton Fix-It Disk.

- *Save **U**nformat Info.* Selecting the check box for this option instructs Norton Desktop to copy information from a disk's system area into an unused area of the disk. It is selected by default if you use the Quick format method, and you also can select the option with the Safe format method; this option is not available if you choose the Destructive format method.

- ***V**olume Label.* Adding a volume label to any disk is optional. (The volume label is the electronic label stored on the disk, not a paper label.) If you choose to include a volume label on the disk, you can type a label up to eleven characters long in the text box.

Labeling Disks

If you do not choose to apply a volume label to a disk during formatting, you can change or add a label later by using Norton's **D**isk **L**abel Disk command. To create a new disk label or edit an existing disk label, follow these steps:

1. Choose the **D**isk **L**abel Disk command. The Label Disk dialog box appears, as shown in figure 6.2.

Fig. 6.2
The Label Disk dialog box enables you to specify a volume label for the disk.

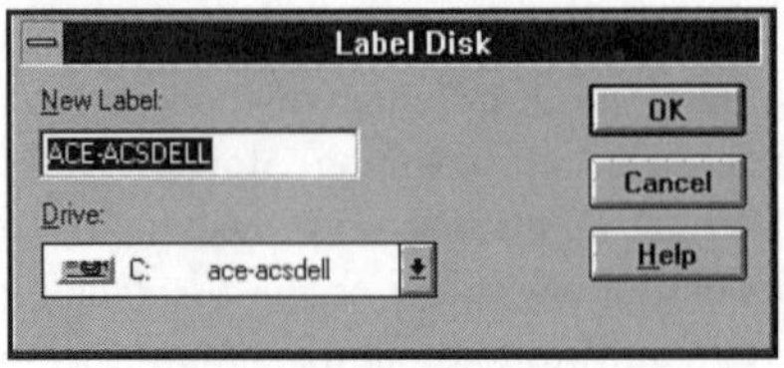

2. Select from the **D**rive drop-down list box the disk drive containing the disk you want to label.

3. Type the new label name in the **N**ew Label text box.

4. Choose OK. The new label is added to the disk, or the existing label is changed.

Labels are useful for identifying the contents of a disk. You may, for example, label a disk that contains copies of your budget files BUDGETS or label a disk containing recipes RECIPES.

Copying Disks

Use Norton's **D**isk **C**opy Diskette command to copy the contents of one disk to another disk of the same size and capacity. This command works similarly to the DOS DISKCOPY command. The Norton Desktop is much faster, however, because it reads all the disk into memory. DOS DISKCOPY, on the other hand, requires you to swap disks many times, because available system memory is generally less than the storage space on a disk.

Note

You cannot use this command to copy files to disks of different sizes or capacities. You can copy a 3 1/2-inch, 1.44M disk to another 3 1/2-inch, 1.44M disk; you cannot, however, copy a 3 1/2-inch, 1.44M disk to a 3 1/2-inch, 720K disk or to any 5 1/4-inch disk.

The drive from which you copy a disk is called the *source drive*, and the drive to which you copy the disk is called the *destination drive*. Usually, the destination drive also is the source drive, unless your system has two identical floppy disk drives. In using a single drive to copy, NDW actually reads information from the source disk into system memory; then, after you switch disks, the program writes the data from memory onto the destination disk. (If you used DOS's DISKCOPY prior to DOS 6.2, you would need to swap disks several times before all the information is copied from the source disk to the destination disk.)

To copy the contents of one source disk onto the same-capacity destination disk by using a single drive, follow these steps:

1. Choose the **D**isk**C**opy Diskette command. The Copy Diskette dialog box appears, as shown in figure 6.3.

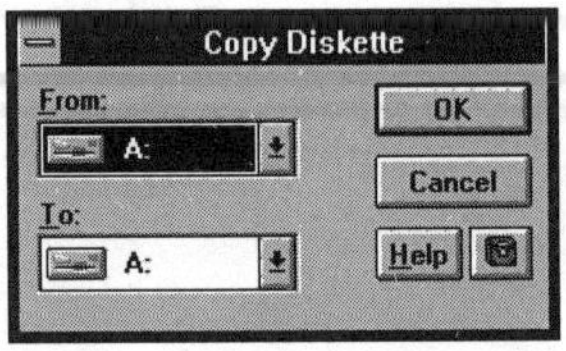

Fig. 6.3
The Copy Diskette dialog box, used to copy information from one floppy disk to another.

2. Select the source drive from the **F**rom drop-down list box.
3. Select the destination drive from the **T**o drop-down list box. (In this example, this drive is the same as the source drive.)
4. Insert the source disk in the drive.
5. Choose OK. NDW begins to read the contents of the source disk into memory.
6. Remove the source disk and insert the destination disk into the drive after NDW prompts you to do so. (The message dialog box that prompts you for the destination disk calls it the "target diskette.")

   After the copy operation is complete, another message dialog box asks if you want to make another copy of the same disk.
7. Choose **Y**es to copy another disk from the same source disk. Choose **N**o to end the copy operation. Repeat steps 2 through 6 to copy another disk.

Note

If the destination disk is unformatted, NDW asks if you want to format the target disk. Choose **Y**es to format the target disk and then begin the copy operation.

If you do have two identical disk drives on your system, such as two 3 1/2-inch high-density drives, follow these steps:

1. Select the **D**isk **C**opy Diskette command. The Copy Diskette dialog box appears.
2. Select the source drive from the **F**rom drop-down list box.
3. Select the destination drive from the **T**o drop-down list box.
4. Insert the source disk in the source drive.

5. Insert the target disk in the target drive.

6. Choose OK to begin the copy process. After the copy operation is complete, a message box appears to ask if you want to make another copy of the same disk.

7. Choose **Y**es to copy another disk from the same source disk. Choose **N**o to end the copy operation. To copy another disk, repeat steps 2 through 6.

Summary

This chapter covered methods used to manage your disks in Norton Desktop 3 for Windows. You learned how to format disks, create volume labels, and copy disks.

The next chapter, "Managing Your Files and Directories with Norton Desktop," explains how to work with individual files and directories. You learn how to copy files and directories, move files and directories, delete files and directories, rename files and directories, print files, view files, edit files, and create icons from files.

Chapter 7

Managing Your Files and Directories with Norton Desktop

In this chapter, you learn to perform the following tasks:

- Manage files and directories
- Copy and move files and directories
- Delete files and directories
- Rename files and directories
- Print, view, and edit files
- Create icons from files

As discussed in Chapter 5, "Using the Drive Windows," all data your computer uses is contained in *files*. Files are arranged in *directories*; your hard disk contains multiple directories, each filled with multiple files. Because the goal of computing is to increase productivity by manipulating data, you must manipulate data efficiently—meaning you need to know all about files and directories and what to do with them.

Norton Desktop 3 for Windows helps you achieve your goal by efficiently handling file and directory management. By using drive windows, icons, and the menu system, you can easily and quickly copy, move, delete, print, edit, and view files, as well as move directories and delete entire directories, including all files in that directory.

Understanding Files and Directories

Chapter 6, "Managing Your Disks with Norton Desktop," explains how disks are organized and formatted. Disks shipped from the factory are either blank (*unformatted*) or contain minimal system data. As you install new programs and create new documents, you add data to the disk. This data must be organized so that both you and your computer system can locate specific data as necessary.

All data is arranged in files. A file can contain executable program code that runs a particular program. A file can contain characters and numbers that comprise a specific document. A file can contain graphics code that displays multicolored, high-resolution pictures. A file can contain multimedia types of information such as sounds, music, or video. In short, a file can contain practically any type of information needed in the day-to-day use of your computer system.

Each program you install includes dozens of small program files necessary for operation. Every memo, letter, and spreadsheet you create comprises a new file. Over several months, you can install or create literally thousands of files on a single hard disk. This proliferation of files means that you must organize your disk to locate specific files more easily. You can accomplish this organization by creating separate directories to hold specific kinds of data.

A directory is much like a file folder; it holds multiple files. As with file folders, you can place directories within other directories. As with file folders, too, each directory can be labeled to help you easily identify its contents. Your initially formatted hard disk contains a single *root directory*. Think of this directory as the file cabinet; all other file folders are contained within this cabinet.

The root directory contains all the basic files needed for your computer to start up and begin operation. Key files located in the root directory include the AUTOEXEC.BAT and CONFIG.SYS files; these two files are consulted to provide the configuration information necessary for your PC to operate correctly each time you turn it on.

As you add new programs to your hard disk, these programs are installed in newly created *subdirectories*. These subdirectories branch off from the root directory, like branches off a tree trunk. (The structure of all subdirectories and directories is often called a *directory tree*.)

Each directory can contain files and subdirectories; these subdirectories also can contain files and other subdirectories, and so on. The entire directory tree structure, therefore, can often be quite complex. Figure 7.1 shows a typical directory tree with several levels of subdirectories.

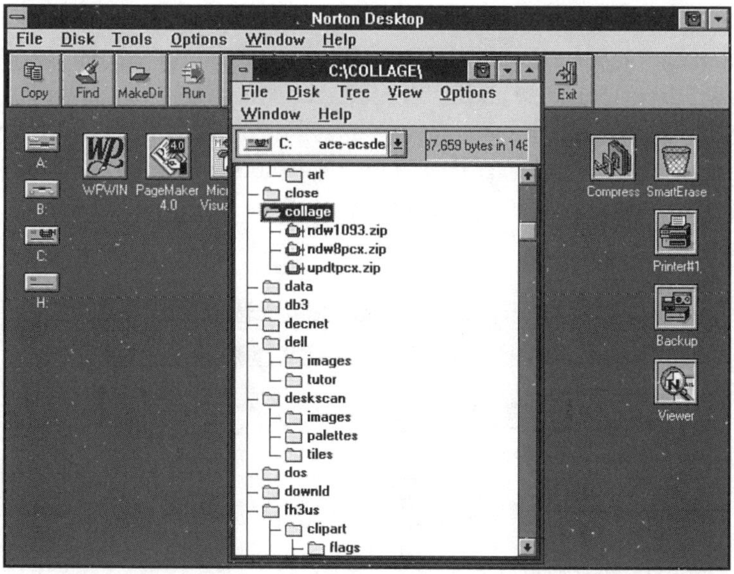

Fig. 7.1
A sample Norton Desktop directory tree, displaying multiple branches.

Note

Although every directory other than the root directory is technically a subdirectory, you usually call the main branches of a directory tree just "directories."

In your everyday computing, you must manipulate files. You may, for example, need to copy a particular file, either to another directory or onto another disk. You may need to move a file to a new location. You may need to rename a file or to delete a file from your disk. You may even need to view, edit, or print the contents of the file.

Before the advent of the Windows graphical user interface, all file manipulation was accomplished by typing commands at the DOS prompt. To copy a file to another drive, for example, you entered a command line such as the following:

COPY C:\AMIPRO\DOCS\FILE1.SAM A:

Each part of the command line is important, and success at such operations requires a mastery of sometimes obscure commands and syntax. If you misplace but one character, the operation fails. If you choose the wrong command, you must deal with sometimes complicated consequences.

In both Windows and Norton Desktop 3 for Windows, file and directory manipulation is much easier and more intuitive. Norton Desktop uses its drive windows to display all the directories and files on individual drives (see fig. 7.2). You can manipulate files and directories directly from within the drive windows, without ever needing to type another obscure command line. (Drive windows are explained in detail in Chapter 5, "Using the Drive Windows.")

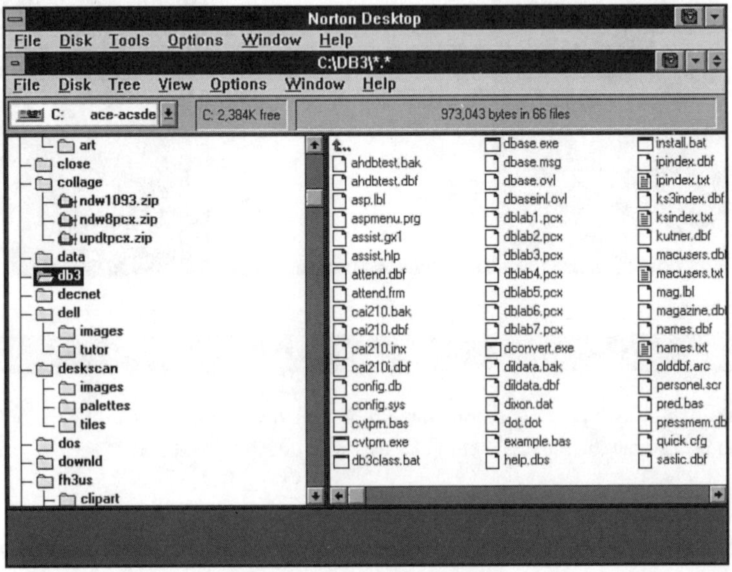

Fig. 7.2
A Norton Desktop drive window showing both a directory tree pane and a file pane.

> **Note**
>
> Drive windows may be sized so that you can see many or fewer directories and files. Figures 7.1 and 7.2 have been sized so that you could clearly see a number of directories and files.

Because directories form a structure resembling a tree, Norton Desktop's drive windows display a directory tree in the tree pane in the left half of the window. You can select a directory in the tree by clicking its name with the mouse or by using the keyboard to select a directory name. All files contained in the currently selected directory appear in the file pane in the right half of the drive window. By selecting these files (either by using the mouse or the keyboard), you can move, copy, rename, delete, view, print, and even edit them.

As is true of many operations in NDW, you often can perform each file or directory operation in several ways. You can use the pull-down menu system, for example, to access file or directory commands. You can use the mouse to drag and drop files from one pane or window to another. You can use the buttons on a drive window's button bar to choose common file operations. You can use icons on the toolbar to access some file commands. You even can use a combination of drive window and menu operations, selecting files in the drive window and then opening a menu to access commands and operations. This chapter discusses the many ways to use Norton Desktop for file and directory management.

Note

See Chapter 5, "Using the Drive Windows," for detailed instructions on how to access and navigate Norton drive windows.

Copying Files and Directories

Perhaps the most common file/directory management operation is the copy operation. *Copying* a file creates an exact duplicate of the selected file in another location; the original file remains in its original location. (This operation differs from the move operation, discussed in the following section, in which the original file actually moves to a new location and no longer exists at its original location.) In Norton Desktop, you can copy or move a single file, a group of files, or entire directories.

You must use the DOS COPY command to copy files from the DOS prompt. The syntax you use for this command is as follows:

COPY *FILENAME DESTINATION*

To copy a file named FILE1 from the root directory of drive C to drive A, for example, you type the following command:

COPY C:\FILE1 A:

Norton Desktop provides the following ways to copy files:

- Select a file or files in the drive window, click the Copy button, and enter a destination.

- Choose the **F**ile **C**opy command and then enter the name of the specific file you want to copy and its destination.
- Use the drive windows to drag and drop files from one location to another between two windows.

Copying Files by Using the Menu System

To copy a file by using the menu system, first open a drive window, and choose the window's File **C**opy command (or click the Copy tool in the Desktop's toolbar). The Copy dialog box appears (see fig. 7.3).

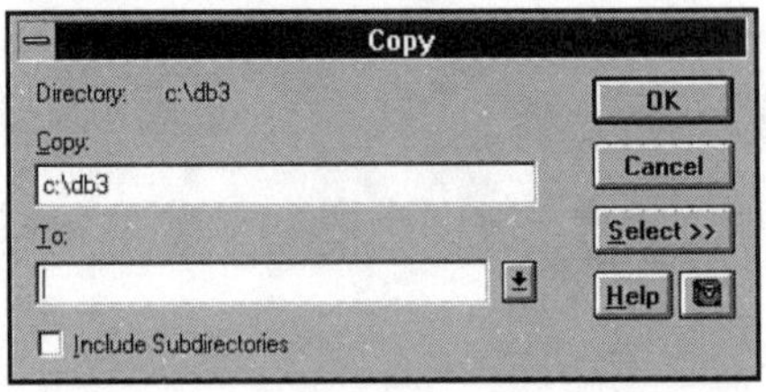

Fig. 7.3
The Copy dialog box enables you to specify which files to copy.

If a Quick Access group option is active on your desktop, choosing the **G**roup **C**opy command displays a special Copy dialog box that enables you to copy groups and group items to other groups (see fig. 7.4).

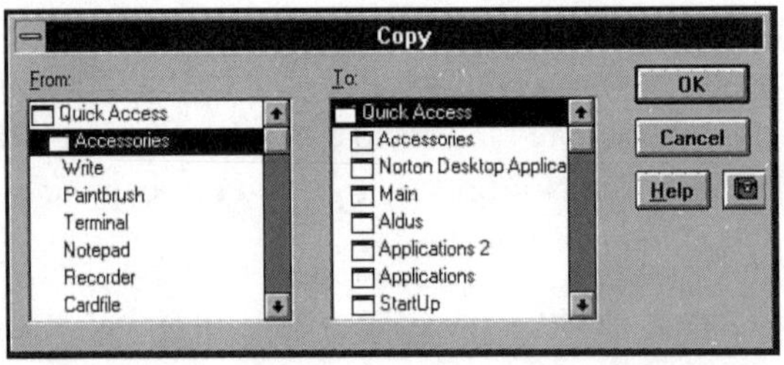

Fig. 7.4
The Copy dialog box, accessed from a Group window, is used to copy groups and group items.

Tip
You also can press F8 to display the Copy dialog box for groups.

The basic Copy dialog box has three parts. Type the name and path of the file you want to copy in the **C**opy text box. Type the drive and path to which you want to copy the file in the **T**o text box. If you are copying an entire directory, select the **I**nclude Subdirectories check box to include the subdirectories located in that directory in the copy operation.

Using Wild Cards

You can use wild cards to copy more than one file at a time. *Wild cards* are characters that represent other possible characters or combinations of characters. The * wild card represents any 1- to 8-character file name or 1- to 3-character extension. The *?* wild card represents any single character in a file name or extension. The following table illustrates some of the possible ways to use wild cards.

File Name	Function
*.DOC	Selects any file with a DOC extension.
FILENAME.*	Selects any file called FILENAME with any extension.
FILE*.DOC	Selects any file name starting with the letters FILE and having a DOC extension.
?ILENAME.DOC	Selects any DOC file with ILENAME as the last 7 characters in the root file name and any other character as the first character.
.	Selects all files.

To copy a file by using the Copy dialog box, follow these steps:

1. Open a drive window, and then choose the Copy button. The Copy dialog box appears (refer to fig. 7.3).

2. Type in the **C**opy text box the name of the file (or, by using wild cards, files) you want to copy. (The name of a file selected in a drive window automatically appears in the **C**opy text box of the Copy dialog box.)

3. Type in the **T**o text box the destination drive or directory. Type **A:**, for example, to copy files to drive A. To copy files to the SAMPLE directory on drive C, type the following line:

   C:\SAMPLE

4. Choose OK to copy the file.

To copy all files in a directory, without copying the directory itself, follow these steps:

1. Open a drive window, and then open the Copy dialog box (as described in step 1 of the preceding steps).

2. Type in the **C**opy text box the path of the directory, followed by the *.* wild card. To copy all files in the SAMPLE directory on drive C, for example, type the following line:

   C:\SAMPLE*.*

3. Type the destination in the **T**o text box.

4. Choose OK to copy the files.

To copy an entire directory, follow these steps:

1. Open a drive window, and then open the Copy dialog box.

2. Type in the **C**opy text box the path of the directory. Do not type the *.* wild card after the directory name. To copy the SAMPLE directory and all its files on drive C, for example, type the following line:

   C:\SAMPLE

3. Type the destination in the **T**o text box.

4. Select the **I**nclude Subdirectories check box to copy all subdirectories in the selected directory.

5. Choose OK to copy the directory and its files.

Tip
If you often copy to the same destination, you can reselect your most recently used destinations, which appear as options in the **T**o drop-down list box. Click the down-arrow button to access the drop-down list.

If you are not sure where you want to copy the selected file, the **S**elect button displays the Copy (File Search) dialog box to reveal more information, as shown in figure 7.5. This version of the dialog box enables you to select the destination drive from a drop-down list box and the destination directory from a scrolling directory tree. This expanded Copy dialog box also includes a bar chart that displays a graphical representation of the free disk space on the selected destination disk.

To use the expanded Copy dialog box to choose a copy destination, follow these steps:

1. Place the cursor in the original Copy dialog box's **T**o text box.

2. Choose the **S**elect button (located to the right of the **T**o text box). The Copy (File Search) dialog box appears.

3. Select the destination drive from the **D**estination drop-down list box.

4. Select the destination directory from the scrolling directory list box.

After you select the drive and directory, the associated path appears in the **T**o text box.

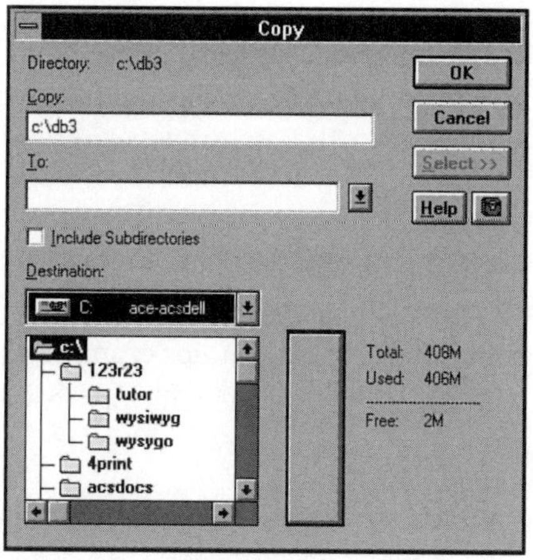

Fig. 7.5
The Copy (File Search) dialog box enables you to locate the exact destination for the files you want to copy.

Copying Files by Using the Drive Window

Using the drive windows for file copying is even easier than using the main menu system. With drive windows open, you simply select the files you want to copy and then click the Copy button or access the **F**ile **C**opy command. The Copy dialog box appears; then you merely enter the name of the destination drive or directory, and choose OK to complete the operation.

Follow these steps to use the drive window to copy a file:

1. Open a drive window by double-clicking the appropriate Drive icon. (To copy a file that resides on drive C, for example, double-click the Drive icon for drive C.) The drive window appears.
2. Scroll through the directory pane until you locate the directory that holds the file or files you want to copy, or use NDW's Speed Search feature to locate a specific file.
3. In the file pane, select the file or files you want to copy.
4. Click the Copy button on the drive window's button bar, or use the window's menu system to choose the **F**ile **C**opy command. The Copy dialog box appears with the selected files listed in the **C**opy text box.

Tip
Remember that you can select multiple files by clicking the right mouse button to select the files.

Tip
Norton Desktop enables you to open multiple windows for the same drive. Just double-click the same Drive icon a second time to open a second window, and so on.

5. Enter the destination in the **To** text box.

6. Choose OK to initiate the copy operation.

Copying Files by Dragging and Dropping

An even easier method for copying files by using drive windows involves *dragging* files from one pane or window and *dropping* them on another pane or window.

The easiest way to use dragging and dropping involves two open drive windows. One window becomes the *source window*, the other the *destination window*. To copy files from drive C to drive A, for example, open drive windows for drives A and C. To copy files from one directory to another directory on drive C, open two drive windows for drive C.

The operation is as simple as selecting the files in the source window and then dragging and dropping them on the file pane or directory name in the destination window. Figure 7.6 shows two drive windows open and ready for a drag-and-drop copy operation.

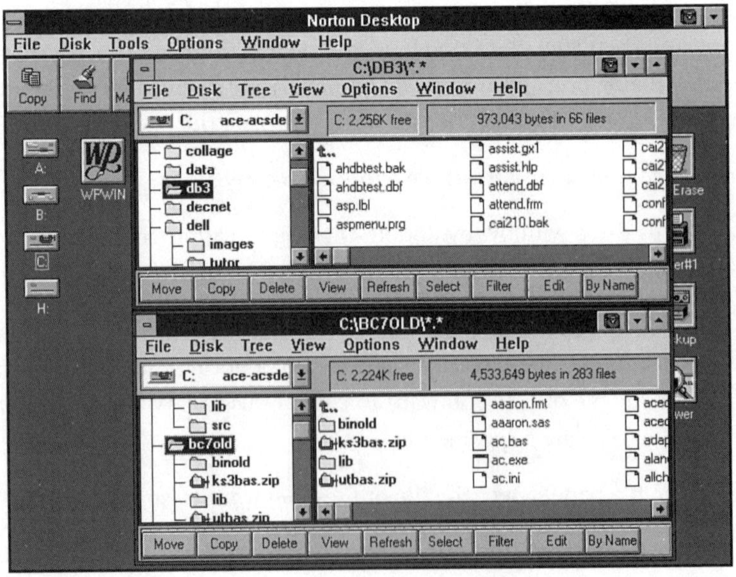

Fig. 7.6
Two drive windows open and ready for a drag-and-drop operation for copying files from one directory to another on the same drive.

Follow these steps to perform drag-and-drop copying from drive window to drive window:

1. Open the drive window for the source file by double-clicking the appropriate Drive icon.

2. Open the drive window for the destination file by double-clicking the appropriate Drive icon.

3. Scroll through the directory pane of the destination drive window until the destination directory is selected.

4. Select in the source window the file or files you want to copy.

5. Drag the files from the source window to the destination window.

6. Drop the files on either the file pane for the destination directory or the directory name itself in the destination directory pane.

Tip
You also can copy files to another drive by dropping the selected files on a Drive icon without actually opening its drive window.

Copies of the selected files now exist in the destination directory of the destination drive.

Copying Directories by Dragging and Dropping

You can use the same drag-and-drop procedure to copy entire directories and subdirectories from one drive to another. Select from the source directory pane the directory you want to copy. (You also must select all subdirectories you want to copy along with the main directory.) Then drag the selected directory and drop it in a new location in the destination window.

Caution

If you do not select subdirectories as you copy the main directory, the subdirectories are not copied.

Moving Files and Directories

DOS versions prior to DOS 6.0 have no command for moving files; you must COPY files to a new location and then ERASE them from their original location.

In Norton Desktop, *moving* files and directories is similar to copying them. The **F**ile **M**ove command not only copies files and directories to new locations, but also deletes them from their original locations.

Moving Files and Directories by Using the Menu System

Choose the **F**ile **M**ove command to access the Move dialog box (see fig. 7.7). The Move dialog box is similar in appearance and function to the Copy dialog box, even to including the option to expand the Move dialog box by choosing the **S**elect button.

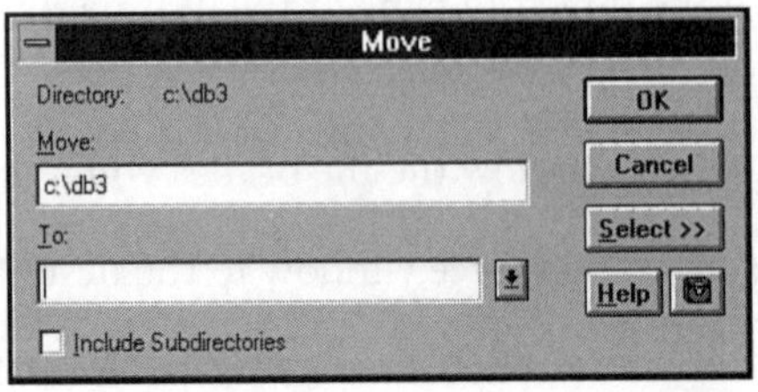

Fig. 7.7
The Move dialog box enables you to specify files or directories to move.

Tip
You also can press F7 to display the Move dialog box. If a drive window is open, the Move dialog box shown in figure 7.7 appears; otherwise, a Move dialog box appears that is similar to the Copy dialog box shown in figure 7.4.

Follow these steps to move files or directories by using the Move dialog box:

1. Open a drive window by clicking the appropriate Drive icon.
2. Open the Move dialog box by choosing **F**ile **M**ove or by pressing F7.
3. Type in the **M**ove text box the name of the file (or files) or the path of the directory you want to move.
4. Type the destination in the **T**o text box, or, if necessary, use the **S**elect button to choose a destination drive and directory.
5. Select the **I**nclude Subdirectories check box to include all subdirectories in a directory move.
6. Choose OK to move the files or directories to their new destination.

Moving Files and Directories by Using the Drive Window

You also can move files and directories by using the drive window. To do so, follow these steps:

1. Open a drive window by clicking the appropriate Drive icon.
2. Select the files or directories you want to move. You can select multiple files by clicking the right mouse button.
3. Click the Move button on the drive window's button bar, or use the window's menu system to choose the **F**ile **M**ove command. The Move dialog box appears.
4. Enter the destination in the **T**o text box. You also can use the **T**o drop-down list to choose a destination from recently accessed directories.
5. Choose OK to move the files or directories to their new destinations.

Moving Files and Directories by Dragging and Dropping

As with copying, you also can move files by using the drag-and-drop operation. This operation is identical to that used for copying files and directories, except that you hold the Alt key while dragging the files.

To use drag-and-drop to move files or directories, follow these steps:

1. Open the source and destination drive windows by clicking the appropriate Drive icons.
2. Select in the source window the files or directories you want to move.
3. Press and hold the Alt key as you drag the files or directories from the source window to the destination window.
4. Still holding the Alt key, drop the files on the tree pane for the destination directory or the directories on the directory name in the destination directory pane.

Deleting Files and Directories

DOS enables you to use the DEL, ERASE, or DELTREE commands to *delete* files. Norton Desktop enables you to delete files by using menus, drive windows, or Tool icons. Although some files and directories can be unerased, you should not delete files or directories you plan to unerase later, because restoring such items may not always be possible.

Deleting Files and Directories by Using the Menu System

Deleting a file, a group of files, or a directory by using the Norton Desktop menu system is similar to copying or moving files. Choose the **F**ile **D**elete command from the menu system to display the Delete dialog box (see fig. 7.8); then enter the name of the file or path of the directory to delete. Use wild cards to delete multiple files and include subdirectories as you delete a directory.

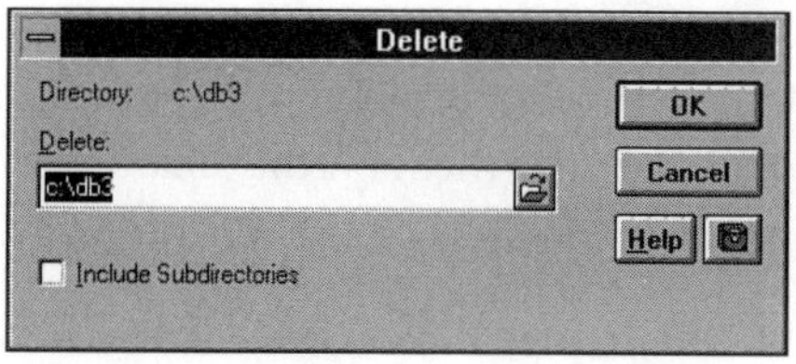

Fig. 7.8
The Delete dialog box enables you to select files or directories to delete.

Tip
You also can display the Delete dialog box by clicking the Delete button in a drive window.

If you are not sure of the name of the file you want to delete, click the folder icon to display the File Search version of the Delete dialog box (see fig. 7.9). This dialog box works like all other File Search dialog boxes, enabling you to scroll through the directory tree to select specific files. Choose OK to exit the File Search dialog box; the Delete dialog box reappears with the files selected in the File Search dialog box displayed in the **D**elete text box.

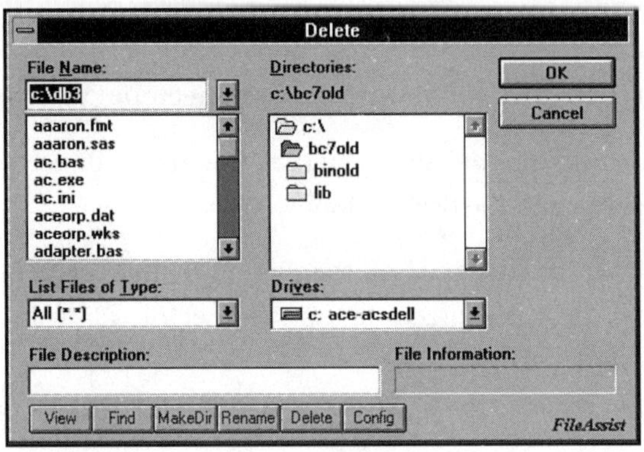

Fig. 7.9
The Delete (File Search) dialog box enables you to delete files and directories.

Deleting Files by Using the Drive Window

You also can select files for deletion in the file pane (or directories in the tree pane) if a drive window is open. After files are selected, the following three options are available for fast deletion by using the Delete dialog box:

- Click the Delete button in the window's button bar.
- Choose the **F**ile **D**elete command.
- Press the F8 key.

Choose any of these options to display the Delete dialog box, with the selected files or directories listed in the **D**elete text box. Choose OK to proceed with the deletion.

Deleting Files with SmartErase

The SmartErase utility (discussed in detail in Chapter 25, "Using SmartErase") provides another method of deletion. Select files or directories in the drive window, and then drag and drop them on the SmartErase Tool icon. The SmartErase operation erases the files.

> **Note**
>
> If SmartErase and SmartCan are enabled, "deleted" files are stored in the buffer SMARTCAN directory for a specified time limit. See Chapter 25, "Using SmartErase," for more details.

Deleting Files by Using Shredder

Finally, to completely overwrite the files marked for deletion, you can use the Shredder tool, as discussed in Chapter 23, "Using Shredder." Select the files to delete in the drive window, and then drag and drop them on the Shredder Tool icon. The Shredder operation totally overwrites the files.

> **Warning**
>
> Files deleted with Shredder *cannot* be unerased. Use this tool only for those sensitive or confidential files that you do not ever want recovered.

Renaming Files and Directories

Sometimes you want to change the name of selected files. You may want to *rename* a DOC file with an ARC extension, for example, to denote an archival status. From the DOS prompt, you must use the DOS REN command. In Norton Desktop, however, you can use the **F**ile Re**n**ame command.

Tip
You can use the Rename dialog box to change the name of a file only; you cannot change the name of a directory.

Renaming Files from the Menu System

To rename a file by using the Norton Desktop menu system, choose the **F**ile Re**n**ame command. This command displays the Rename dialog box, as shown in figure 7.10.

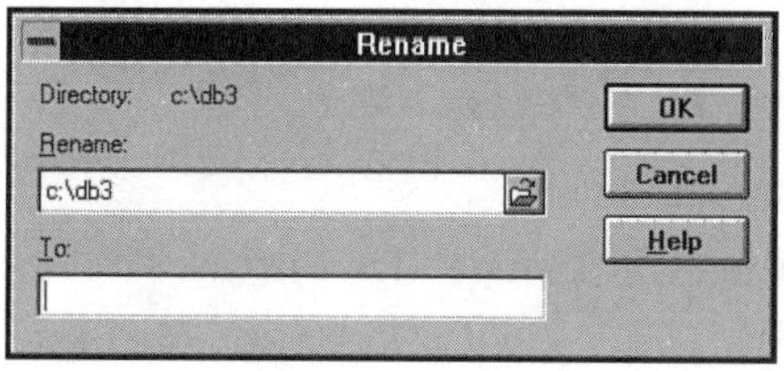

Fig. 7.10
The Desktop's Rename dialog box enables you to rename files.

The Rename dialog box is one of the easier dialog boxes to use. Simply type the file's old name in the **R**ename text box and the file's new name in the **T**o text box. Choose OK to activate the Rename procedure.

Tip

You also can click the folder icon at the right of the **R**ename text box to open a File Selection dialog box; this dialog box can help you identify files for renaming.

Renaming Files from the Drive Window

If a drive window is open, select a file in the file pane, and then choose the **F**ile Re**n**ame command or click the Rename tool on the toolbar. This command displays the Rename dialog box with the selected file already displayed in the **R**ename text box.

Printing Files

You normally *print* files from within specific applications—an Excel worksheet from within Excel, for example, and an Ami Pro document from within Ami Pro. By using Norton Desktop, however, you can initiate document printing without actually running the specific application.

Norton Desktop *associates* files with specific applications. NDW knows, for example, that documents with a SAM extension are Ami Pro documents. Choosing to print a document from Norton Desktop causes NDW to look for the application associated with the file, start the program (in the background), and then initiate printing. After the print job ends, NDW closes the program. You do not need to launch the program and load the document; Norton Desktop does all the work for you.

Note

If a given file type does not have an association, Norton Desktop cannot print the file. You can create associations by using the **F**ile **A**ssociate command. See Chapter 8, "Launching Files with Norton Desktop," for more details.

Printing Files from the Menu System

To print files from the Desktop menu system, follow these steps:

1. Choose the **F**ile **P**rint command to display the Print dialog box, as shown in figure 7.11.

2. Type in the **P**rint text box the name of the file you want to print, or click the folder icon to the right of the text box to display a File Search dialog box to help you find the name of the file to print.

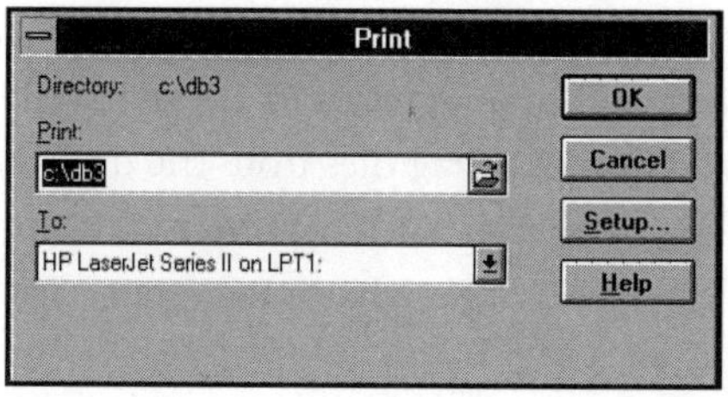

Fig. 7.11
The Print dialog box enables you to specify a file to print.

3. Select the destination printer from the **T**o drop-down list box.
4. If you have special needs for printing the document—such as printing in landscape mode—click the **S**etup button to display the Windows Printer Setup dialog (which is the same as the Control Panel Printer Setup dialog box). This dialog box enables you to set print options for the selected output device. If you have no such special printing needs, skip this step.
5. Choose OK to start the print process.

The associated application is launched, the selected file is loaded, and printing is initiated. The application closes after printing finishes.

> **Caution**
>
> Do not initiate a second print job from the same application until the first printing is finished. Under certain conditions, the second print job may not start.

Printing Files by Using the Printer Tool Icon

You also can use drag-and-drop operations to print files. With the drive window open, you simply select from the file pane one or more files to print; then drag the file and drop it on the Printer Tool icon. Printing begins.

Viewing Files

You can view the contents of selected files by using Norton Viewer or by opening a view pane in a drive window as follows:

- Activate a view pane by clicking the View button on the drive window's button bar. The contents of any selected file are displayed in an active view pane. Refer to Chapter 5, "Using the Drive Windows," for more details.

- Activate Norton Viewer by choosing the **F**ile **V**iew command. Norton Viewer launches, and then you can load specific files into the Viewer for viewing. You also can drag files from the drive window onto the Viewer Tool icon to launch Norton Viewer with the selected files loaded. See Chapter 21, "Using Norton Viewer," for more details.

Editing Files

You edit the contents of ASCII text files by using the Desktop Editor utility, discussed more fully in Chapter 16, "Using Desktop Editor." You can access this utility by using either of the following methods:

- Select a file from a drive window, and click the Edit button on the button bar. Desktop Editor launches with the selected file loaded.

- Choose the **T**ools Desktop **E**ditor command. This command launches Desktop Editor with no files loaded; open files individually to edit them.

Creating Icons from Files

You can create your own Desktop icons for selected files—either programs or documents. Simply open a drive window, select a file, and then drag and drop the file onto the Desktop. This operation creates a Desktop icon that you can double-click to launch a program file or load and launch a document with its associated application.

After you create a Desktop icon, you can change the properties of the icon, such as its label or appearance, by editing the icon. Chapters 8, 13, and 17 discuss icon creation in more detail.

Summary

This chapter covered management of your files and directories. You learned how to use Norton Desktop to copy, move, delete, print, view, and edit files by using icons, drive windows, and NDW's menu system.

Chapter 8, "Launching Files with Norton Desktop," delves into the specifics of launching program files from Norton Desktop. You learn how to launch files by association, launch files from drive windows, create and use a Launch List, use the DOS window to launch files, and use Quick Access to launch files.

Chapter 8

Launching Files with Norton Desktop

8

Under regular Windows, you have only a few ways to start, or *launch*, programs. Most users use the icon-based Program Manager to open files; others launch files directly from the File Manager. In Norton Desktop, however, you can launch programs in any of the following ways:

- Use the Quick Access Group (similar to the Windows Program Manager).
- Use drive windows.
- Use the menu system.
- Use Desktop icons.
- Use drag-and-drop operations.

This flexibility is one of the reasons Norton Desktop is such a popular program. You need only to pick the method that works best with your computing style—and launch away.

In this chapter, you learn to perform the following tasks:

- Launch by association
- Use the drive windows to launch files
- Use the Launch List to launch files
- Use the **R**un command to launch files
- Use the DOS window to launch DOS files
- Use Desktop icons and Quick Access to launch files

Launching by Association

Norton Desktop 3 for Windows (NDW) can launch both program files (those with EXE, COM, and BAT extensions) and individual document files. If you open a document file, Norton Desktop actually launches the associated application with the selected document loaded.

An *association* tells NDW which application to launch after you select a document. Associations connect the file extension of a document type to the file name of the application and starts that application along with its document.

Documents with a SAM extension, for example, are associated with Ami Pro, and documents with an XLS extension are associated with Excel.

Most programs set up associations in the WIN.INI file as you install them in Windows. If no association exists for a given file type (for example, you assigned a nonexistent extension to a WinWord document file), you can create associations by choosing the **F**ile **A**ssociate command.

To create an association, follow these steps:

1. Choose the **F**ile **A**ssociate command. The Associate dialog box appears (see fig. 8.1).

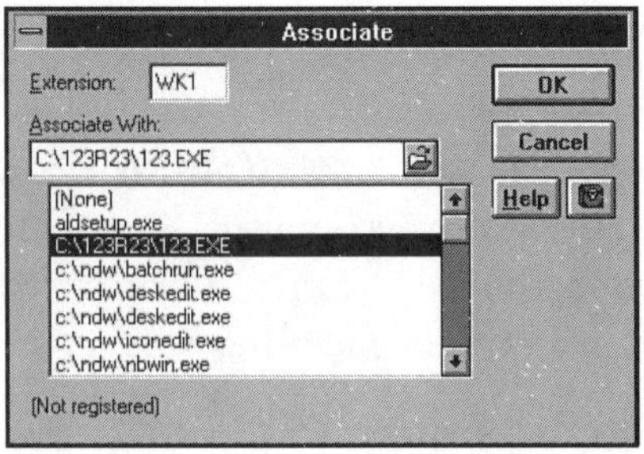

Fig. 8.1
The Associate dialog box enables you to associate an extension with an application.

2. Type in the **E**xtension text box the file extension you want to associate. Type **WK1** in the text box, for example, to associate WK1 files.

Note

If an association already exists for that extension, the name of the associated program file appears in the **A**ssociate With text box.

3. Scroll through the list of program files, and select the appropriate application to display in the **A**ssociate With text box. If you prefer, click the Browse button at the end of the **A**ssociate With text box to search for additional program files.

4. Choose OK to confirm the association.

You are ready to begin after your files are associated.

Using the Drive Windows To Launch Files

The drive windows provide two convenient ways to start files. The following sections show how you can launch files from a file pane or by using drag-and-drop. Figure 8.2 shows a sample drive window.

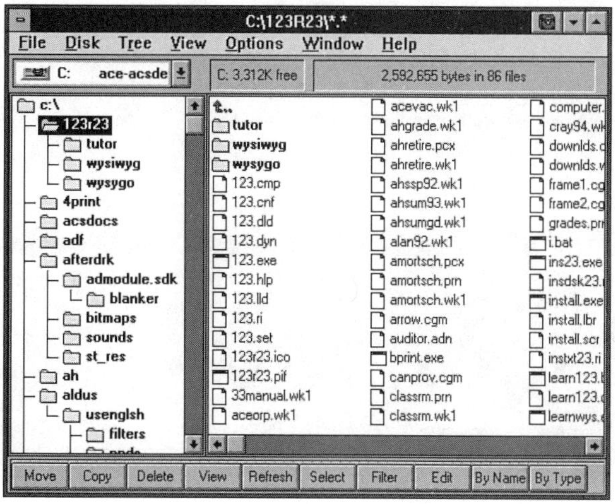

Fig. 8.2
A typical Norton drive window, from which you can launch files by using drag and drop or the file pane.

Launching Files in the File Pane

The most direct way to launch a file in a drive window is to double-click the file name in the file pane. This practice launches the selected file. You also can select the file and then choose the **F**ile **O**pen command to launch a file from the drive window. You can even simply select the file name and press Enter.

Launching Files by Using Drag-and-Drop Operations

If you do not create a file association, you can still use a drag-and-drop operation to launch files. You can use either of two drag-and-drop operations from the drive window: You can drag a file onto the program file name, or you can drag a file onto a program icon. You can, for example, use drag and drop to perform the following operations:

- Select a document file with a WPW (WordPerfect for Windows) extension, and drag and drop this file onto the program file WPWIN.EXE. The program launches, and the document file loads.

■ Drag the file SAMPLE.SAM from the file pane, and drop it on the Ami Pro Desktop icon. The program launches, and the document file loads.

See also the section, "Creating and Editing Desktop Icons," later in this section, for more information on using drag and drop.

Note

After you place it on a program icon, the mouse pointer changes shape to resemble a "launched" rocket ship, as shown in figure 8.3. The associated program launches with the dropped file loaded and becomes the active window.

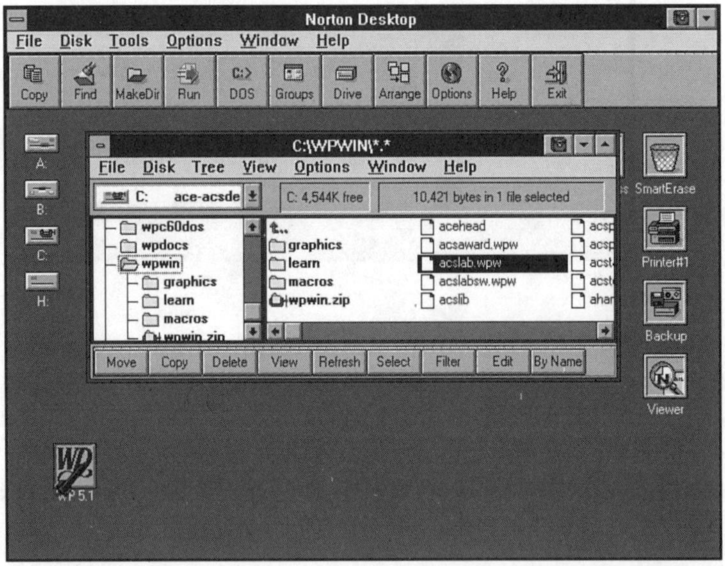

Fig. 8.3
The drag-and-drop method of launching a program with the associated file loaded.

Note

If you drop a document file atop a minimized program icon (that is, an icon for a program that is already running), NDW loads the dropped file into the already launched program.

Using the Launch List To Launch Files

The pull-down Control menu (the button in the top left corner of every application window) offers numerous options. Norton Desktop adds to the options, including an option called the ***Launch List***.

Launching Files from the Launch List

After you choose the Control **L**aunch List command, the Launch List appears (see fig. 8.4). Launch items from the Launch List by choosing the Control **L**aunch List command, and then choosing the utility or tool you want to launch.

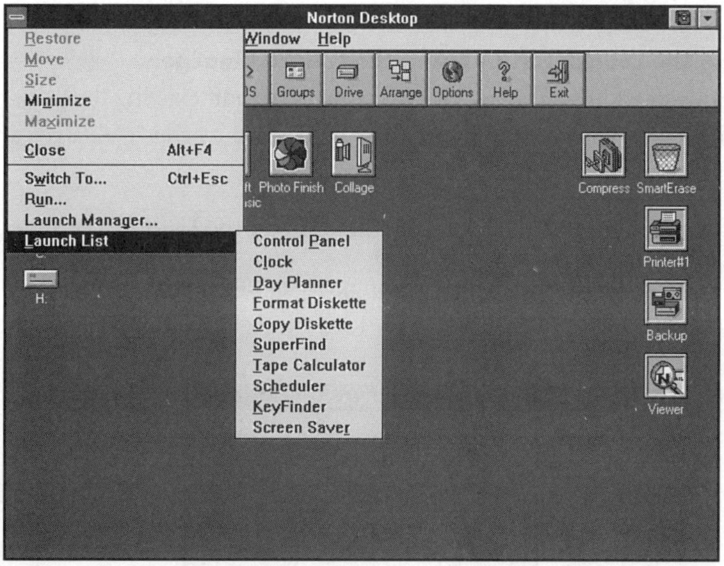

Fig. 8.4
The Control menu's **L**aunch List command enables you to launch any programs that appear on the list.

II Managing Files & Directories

> **Note**
>
> The primary advantage of the Launch List is that you can access it directly from any Windows application by pulling down the Desktop Control menu.

The default Launch List contains commands that enable you to launch the following tools and utilities:

Control **P**anel

C**l**ock

Day Planner

Format Diskette

Copy Diskette

SuperFind

Tape Calculator

Sc**h**eduler

KeyFinder

Screen Save**r**

Editing the Launch List by Using the Launch Manager

You can add additional items to the Launch List, edit existing items, or delete existing items. You edit the Launch List by using the *Launch Mana**g**er*, also accessed from the Control menu.

Follow these steps to add, delete, or edit items on the Launch List:

1. Choose the Control Launch Mana**g**er command. The Launch Manager dialog box appears (see fig. 8.5).

Fig. 8.5 The Launch Manager dialog box enables you to specify which programs appear in the Launch Manager **M**enu Items list.

2. Delete an item by selecting the item in the **M**enu Items list box and then choosing the **D**elete button. (The Delete button is grayed until a menu item is selected.)

   Edit an item by selecting the item in the **M**enu Items list box and then choosing the **E**dit button to display the Edit Launch List Item dialog box. You then can edit the item's text, command line, and shortcut key. (The Edit button is grayed until a menu item is selected.)

Add a new item by choosing the **A**dd button to display the Add Launch List Item dialog box (see fig. 8.6). You can use this dialog box to specify items to add to the Launch List.

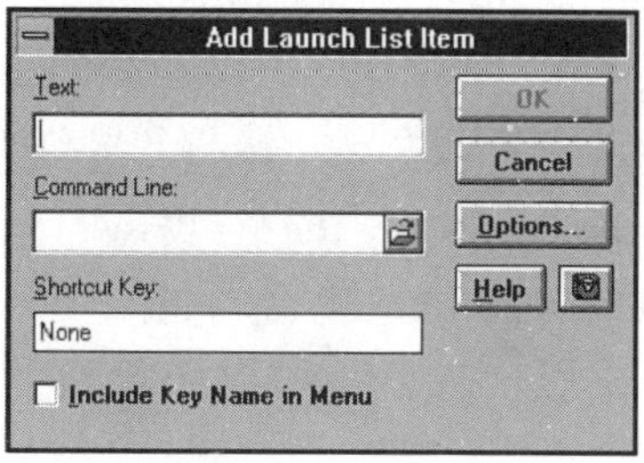

Fig. 8.6
The Add Launch List Item dialog box enables you to specify what programs to add to the Launch list.

You also can select a menu item and then choose the Move **U**p or Move D**o**wn button to move the item in the list, reordering the list as you want.

3. Choose OK to confirm the selections after you make all your changes.

The Edit Launch List Item and the Add Launch List Item dialog boxes are almost identical. Both enable you to enter information for the following options:

- ***T**ext.* The text label that appears on the Launch List.
- ***C**ommand Line.* The path and program name, plus any switches required to launch an application. If you need to locate a program file name on disk, you can choose the Browse icon at the end of the **C**ommand Line text box to display a Browse dialog box.
- ***S**hortcut Key.* The keyboard combination you press to launch the program without directly accessing the Launch List. (This command is optional.)
- ***I**nclude Key Name in Menu.* If you selected a shortcut key, this check box determines whether the key combination appears on the Launch List menu. Select it to add the key combination to the menu name. Deselect it to remove the key combination from the menu.

If you choose the **O**ptions button in the Add Launch List Item dialog box, the Options dialog box appears (see fig. 8.7). Use this dialog box to determine the **S**tartup Directory for the selected program. You also can choose among three **R**un Styles. The run styles determine how the launched program appears onscreen. The three options are to run at normal size, maximized to full-screen size, or minimized to icon size. You also can instruct the program to prompt you for specific program parameters each time you use the program. If you need to locate a program file name on disk, you can choose the Browse icon at the end of the **S**tartup Directory text box to display a Browse dialog box.

Click the Pass**w**ord button to display the Set Password dialog box. Use this dialog box to require a password to run an application—an optional feature. Your password can be up to 20 characters in length and can include any keyboard characters.

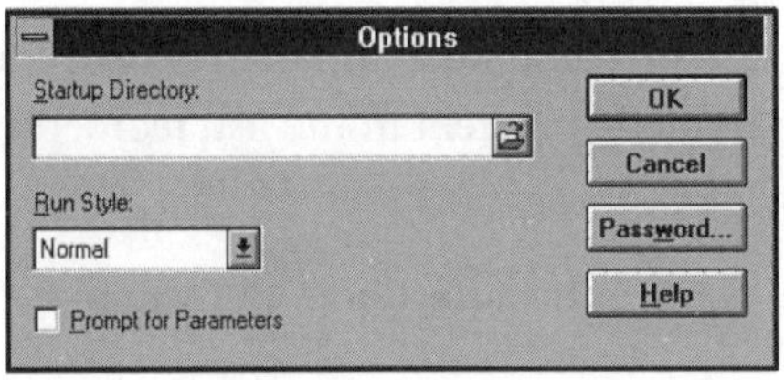

Fig. 8.7
The Options dialog box enables you to choose run options for a program on the Launch List.

Using the Run Command To Launch Files

Another option available on the Control menu, as well as on the NDW **F**ile menu, is the **R**un command. Choose this option (or press Ctrl+R) to display the Run dialog box, which enables you to specify particular Windows or DOS programs to run (see fig. 8.8).

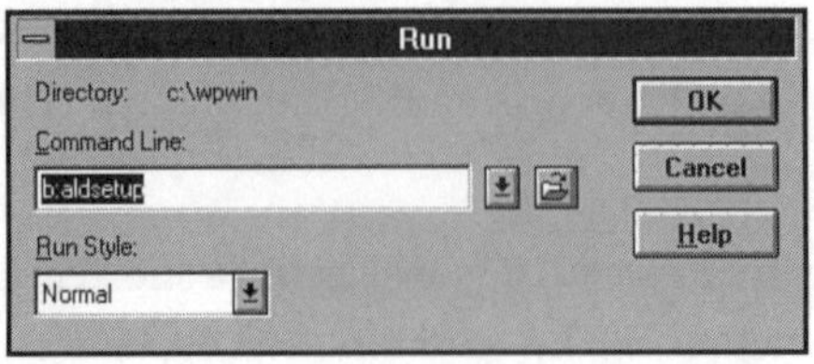

Fig. 8.8
The Run dialog box enables you to specify a program to run.

Launching a file by using the Run dialog box is simple: Enter a **C**ommand Line, select the **R**un Style (normal, maximized, or minimized), and then click the OK button. Click the Browse icon to the right of the **C**ommand Line text box to activate a Browse dialog box and search for files to launch; you also can access the **C**ommand Line drop-down list to display and select recently launched files.

Using the DOS Window To Launch DOS Files

You can either use the **R**un command or launch the program from a DOS window to launch a DOS application. Open a DOS Command window by clicking the DOS Toolbar icon or by choosing the **F**ile R**u**n DOS command. The DOS Command window opens with the familiar DOS prompt. View DOS as a window by typing Alt+Enter (see fig. 8.9). Launch any DOS application in the DOS Command window by typing the correct command at the DOS prompt.

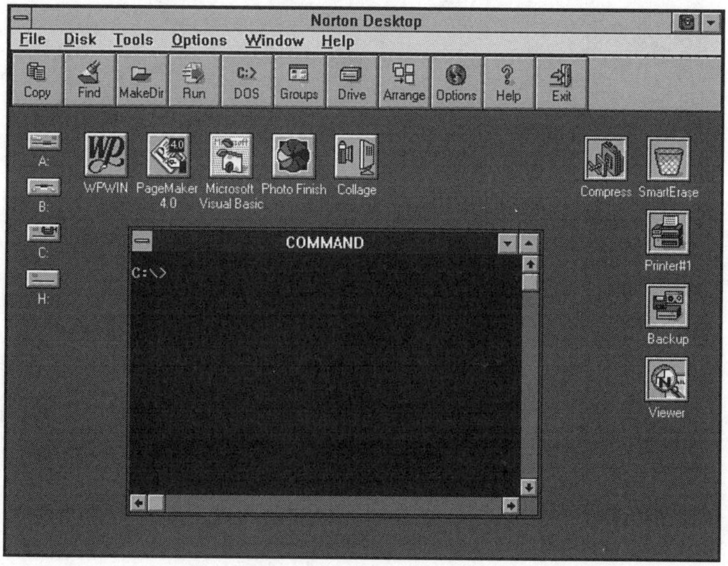

Fig. 8.9
An open DOS Command window, ready for you to launch a DOS application from its DOS prompt.

Caution

Do not attempt to run Windows applications from the DOS Command window. Notice, too, that not every DOS program can run while Windows is running. Programs that need exclusive use of system resources (such as Symantec's Norton Utilities programs or the DOS CHKDSK command) cannot start under Windows.

Using Desktop Icons To Launch Files

The most "Norton-like" of all launch operations involves using Desktop icons created as you drag files from the drive window and drop them permanently on the Desktop. Many users prefer this icon-based mode of operation; Chapter 13, "Creating an Icon-Based Desktop," details the procedures for creating an icon-based Desktop.

Launching Files from Desktop Icons

If a Desktop icon is present on your Desktop, double-click the icon to launch the associated file or document. See figure 8.10 for some samples of Desktop icons.

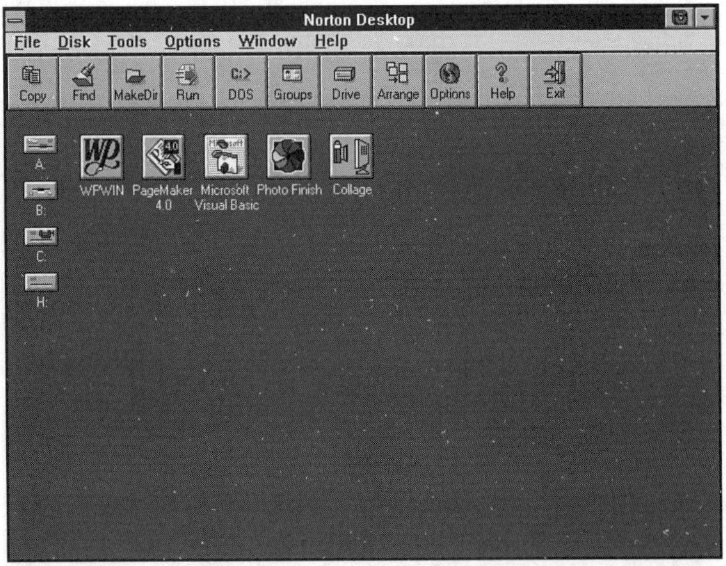

Fig. 8.10 Some sample Norton Desktop icons for popular applications, including WordPerfect for Windows, Pagemaker, and Microsoft Visual Basic.

You can create Desktop icons for programs or for documents. As with all launching activities in Norton Desktop, launching a document actually launches the associated application with the selected document loaded. You may want to create a general WordPerfect Desktop icon, for example, as well as a separate icon for your monthly budget spreadsheet document. Double-clicking the Budget icon launches WordPerfect and loads your monthly report. You can even customize the icon with different artwork and a special title.

Creating and Editing Desktop Icons

Create a new Desktop icon by selecting a file in the drive or group window, dragging it from the window, and dropping it on the Desktop. After you drop it on the Desktop, you can customize the properties of the icon.

As you single-click a Desktop icon, you display its Control menu box (see fig. 8.11). This box contains three commands: **O**pen, **P**roperties, and **C**lose. **O**pen acts like a double-click and launches the associated file. Choosing **C**lose removes the icon from the Desktop. Choosing **P**roperties displays the Properties dialog box.

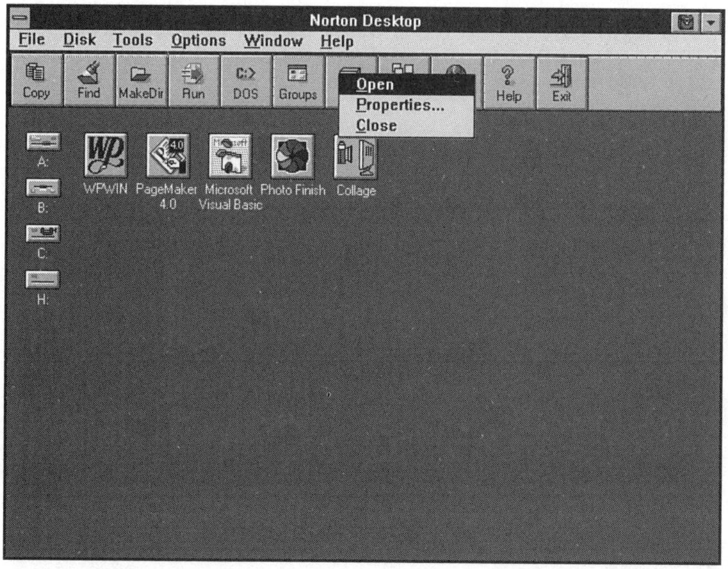

Fig. 8.11
A Desktop icon's Control menu box enables you to manage your Desktop icons through its three commands.

The **C**ategories icon list of the Properties dialog box enables you to choose what aspect of the icon property to manage. Select the General category of the Properties dialog box to customize your Desktop icons (see fig. 8.12). First, you can change the title of the icon by editing the text in the **T**itle text box. As you first drop an icon on the Desktop, the title is the same as the file name. You probably want to enter more appropriate titles for all your Desktop icons.

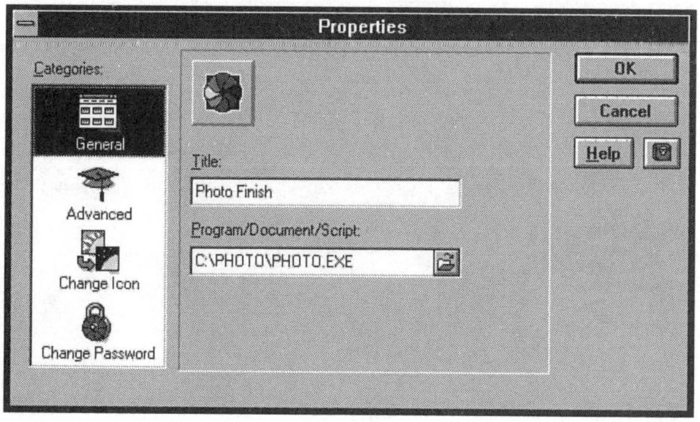

Fig. 8.12
The Properties dialog box with the General category option selected.

You also can edit the command line that executes the program by editing the text in the **P**rogram/Document/Script text box. You may need to add command line switches, for example, to initiate certain program functions.

If you need to change the start-up directory or add a shortcut key for the Desktop icon, click the Advanced category option to display the Advanced options of the Properties dialog box (see fig. 8.13). You also can choose in this dialog box whether to launch the program in normal, maximized, or minimized form.

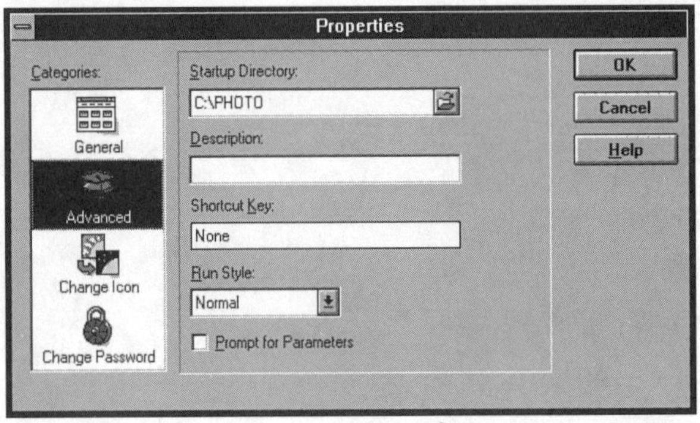

Fig. 8.13
The Properties dialog box with the Advanced category option selected.

By choosing the Change Icon category, you can choose a different icon to appear on your Desktop in place of the original icon. After you click the Change Icon category, the Properties dialog box changes to display the Change Icons options (see fig. 8.14). From this box, you can browse through directories to choose a new icon file to examine. The list of icons in the chosen file is shown in the **I**con(s) list box. Select a new icon from the list box by clicking the icon in the box. To revert back to the default icon, choose the Use **D**efault button. Choose OK to exit the Change Icon dialog box.

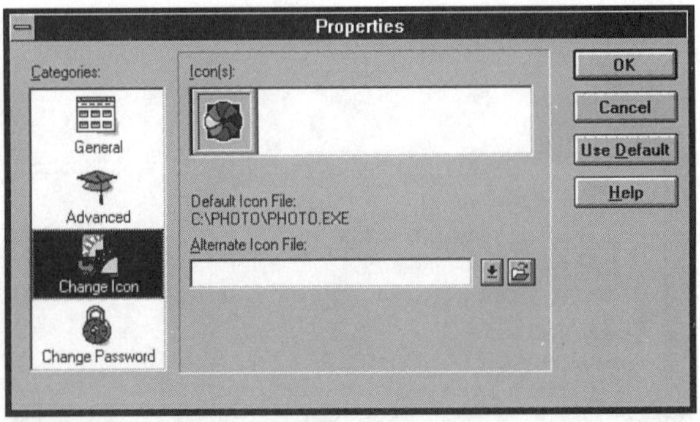

Fig. 8.14
The Properties dialog box with the Change Icons category option selected.

From the **C**ategory list, you also can choose Change Password to display the Password dialog box and set up password protection for the icon's use. After all the options are set, choose OK to close the Properties dialog box. You now have a totally customized Desktop icon that automatically launches a document or application.

Using Quick Access To Launch Files

Norton Desktop includes a feature known as Quick Access. Quick Access serves as a replacement for the Windows Program Manager file and program management system and is similar in many ways to the Program Manager. Both contain iconic representations of applications and utilities. Both enable you to launch programs by double-clicking icons. The similarities end there.

Understanding Quick Access

Quick Access is a system that consists of an unlimited number of group windows. The main group window is called the Quick Access Group. Figure 8.15 shows a Desktop Quick Access Group. This group, like the Windows Program Manager, contains other groups available on your system. Unlike the Program Manager, however, groups can exist in group windows outside the Quick Access Group. You can place group windows directly on your Desktop and access them from the **W**indows menu.

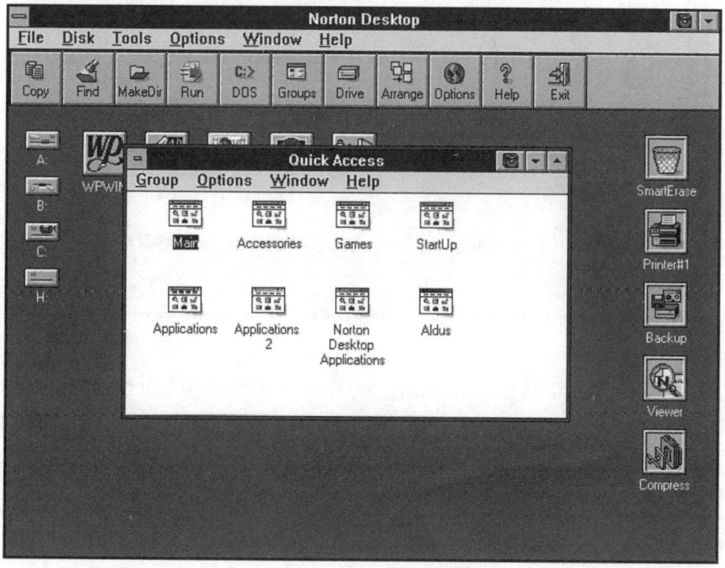

Fig. 8.15
A Norton Desktop Quick Access Group displays program group icons similar in appearance to those of the Windows Program Manager.

Norton Desktop's group windows are much more versatile than regular Windows program groups. Group windows enable you to **V**iew groups in one of three ways: Icon, List, or Toolbox style. They also enable you to nest groups within groups—keeping file folders within other file folders, so to speak.

The Quick Access Group consists of other groups that exist on your system. You can think of the Quick Access Group as the "root directory" of all program groups. At the time NDW is installed, it automatically looks for any existing Windows program groups (or access groups from a previous version of NDW) and creates group windows for each group. You then can arrange the groups in whatever order you want.

Configuring Quick Access

You can configure universal options for all group windows, individual options for specific group windows, and individual options for the icons within each group. To configure Quick Access, choose the **O**ptions **C**ustomize command to access the Control Center dialog box and then select the Quick Access category command to display the Control Center (Quick Access) dialog box (see fig. 8.16).

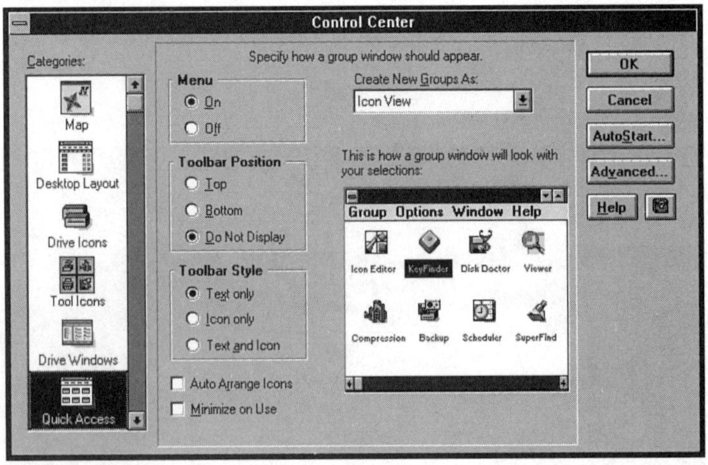

Fig. 8.16
The Control Center dialog box's Quick Access mode enables you to choose Group icon options.

This dialog box enables you to control the settings described in the following table.

Setting	Function
Menu	Choose **O**n or O**f**f to specify if the Group menu is displayed.

Setting	Function
Toolbar Position	Choose **T**op, **B**ottom, or **D**o not Display to specify where or how the toolbar appears.
Toolbar Style	Choose Te**x**t Only, **I**con Only, or Text **a**nd Icon to specify how the toolbar is displayed.
Create New **G**roups As	Determines the type of view (Icon, List, or Toolbox) that new groups inherit; does not affect any existing groups.
Auto A**r**range Icons	Aligns all the icons in Quick Access groups whenever you add or move an item from a group.
Minimize on Use	Causes all groups to minimize to icon form as icons within the group are opened.

You also can instruct Norton Desktop to automatically load Quick Access as Windows loads. (This is the recommended setting, because it gives you access to all other program groups from one window.) Choose the Auto**S**tart button from the Control Center's Quick Access dialog box. Then choose the Load Quick Access option from the dialog box that appears; Quick Access now loads automatically whenever you start up Windows.

Choose the Ad**v**anced button to display the Advanced dialog box, and select the **N**ame for your topmost group, a Shortcut **K**ey, and Hori**z**ontal or **V**ertical grid spacing, which determine how far apart group icons appear in the group window. If you change the icons used to represent any of your groups and you want to change them back to their default icons, choose **R**eset Icons. Make sure that you choose the **S**ave Configuration option from the **O**ptions pull-down menu to save all the changes you have made.

Each group window can have its own distinctive view. To change the view for any group, follow these steps:

1. Open the group window. (For example, double-click a group icon in the Quick Access window.)

2. Choose the **O**ptions **V**iew Group As command. The View Group As dialog box appears, as shown in figure 8.17.

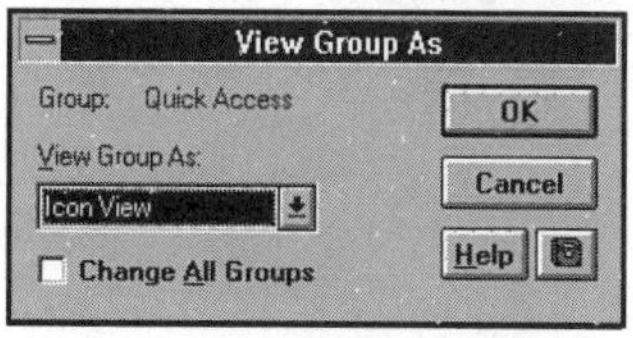

Fig. 8.17
The View Group As dialog box enables you to choose a view type for the group.

II Managing Files & Directories

3. Use the **View Group As** list box to choose among Icon, List, or Toolbox views.

4. Optionally, choose the Change **All** Groups option to make this view apply to all groups.

5. Choose OK to confirm the selection.

Figure 8.18 shows three groups displayed in each of the three available viewing styles. The left window is the Icon view, the middle is the List view, and the right window is the Toolbox view.

Fig. 8.18
Three Quick Access group windows, displayed in Icon, List, and Toolbox views.

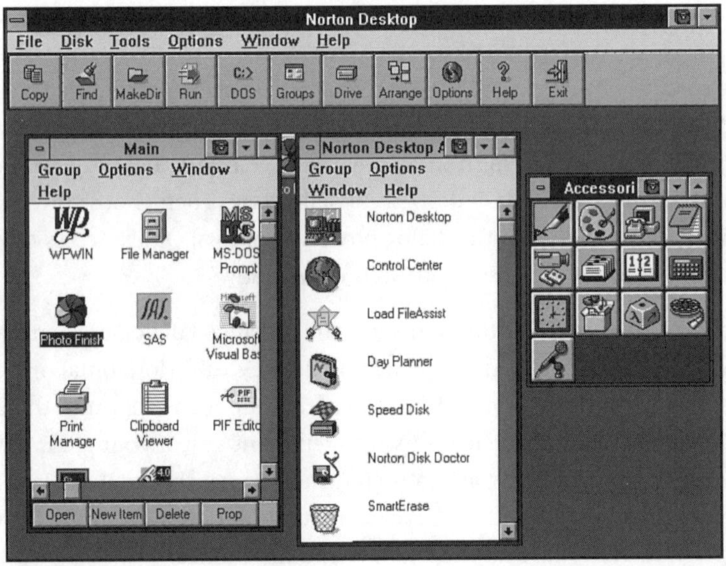

Each group window can be sized individually, just as you can any window. If you have more icons than window space, vertical and/or horizontal scroll bars appear so that you can scroll to additional icons.

Caution

The Toolbox view does not display scroll bars if you have more icons than window space. You must enlarge the group window to display all the Tool icons in this view.

You can change the properties of any icon within a group, including the title, command line, and icon art. Select the icon, and choose the **G**roup Proper**t**ies command from the group's **W**indow pull-down menu. After the Properties dialog box appears, make the necessary changes.

> **Note**
>
> The Properties options are the same for Groups as they are for individual icons.

Running Quick Access Under Norton Desktop

Running Quick Access under Norton Desktop is easy. Just make sure that you configured your Desktop so that the toolbar is visible; then click the Groups icon, and the Quick Access Group appears.

> **Tip**
> You can open the Quick Access Group instantly by double-clicking the right mouse button anywhere on the Desktop.

Opening Groups and Group Items

Opening a program or group window by using Quick Access is just like opening a program or program group in Windows. Position your mouse pointer on the group, and then double-click.

If you are using the keyboard, you cannot easily move from one group to another on the Desktop. You can, however, go directly to any group by using the menu system. Open the **W**indow menu, select the group you want to open, and then press Enter.

Creating New Groups and Group Items

Add both new groups and new items to existing groups by using the **G**roup New **G**roup command. Choosing this command accesses the New Group dialog box.

Follow these steps to create a new group:

1. Choose the **G**roup New **G**roup command. The New Group dialog box appears (see fig. 8.19).
2. In the Group **F**ile Name text box, type an eight-character name (no extension) to describe the new group, or click the Browse icon to locate a current group file.
3. In the **T**itle text box, type the title of the new group.
4. Click the Change Icon category button, and edit the Icon dialog box to assign a customized icon to this group.

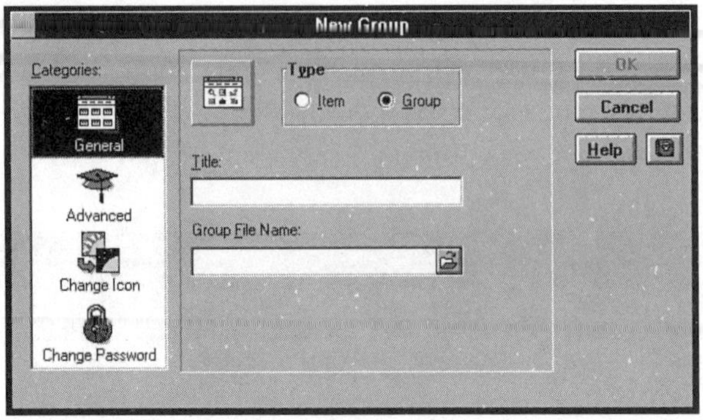

Fig. 8.19
The New Group dialog box enables you to add a new group.

5. Choose OK to create the new group.

Follow these steps to add a new item to an existing group:

1. Open the group to which you want to add an item.
2. Choose the **G**roup New **I**tem command. (If you are in the New Group dialog box, choose the **I**tem option button.) The New Item dialog box appears (see fig. 8.20).

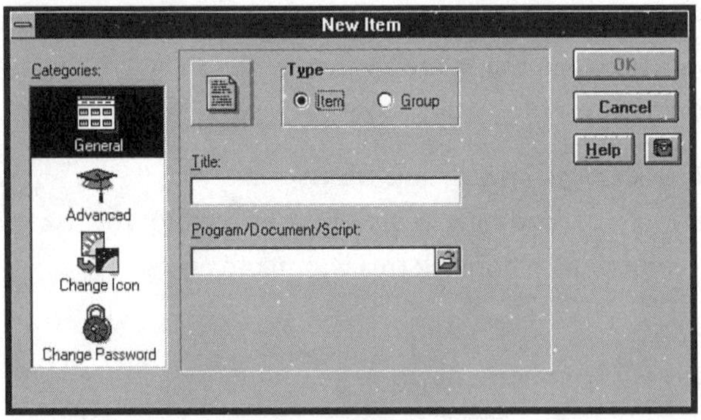

Fig. 8.20
The New Item dialog box enables you to add a new Item to a group.

3. If you know the path and file name of the item you want to add, enter it in the **P**rogram/Document/Script text box. Otherwise, click the Browse icon to search for the item.
4. In the **T**itle text box, type a title for the new item.
5. Click the Change Icon category, and use the Icon dialog box to assign a customized icon to this item.

6. Choose OK to add the new item to the group window.

To delete items or entire groups, select the item and choose the **F**ile **D**elete command. A group must be minimized for you to delete it this way.

Tip
You can add items to groups by selecting them in a drive window and then dragging and dropping them in the open group window.

Moving Items from Group to Group

Just as you can drag and drop items from drive windows into group windows, you also can drag and drop items from group window to group window. Begin with both group windows open, and then select the item to move, drag it out of the source group, and drop it in the destination group. This item is now located only in the new group.

Nest groups within groups in the same manner. Select a closed group from the main Quick Access Group, and drag and drop it on any other open group. After you nest a group, you can access the nested group only if the parent group is open. (This practice is a great way to eliminate group proliferation.)

Creating a Start-Up or AutoStart Group

The Start-Up, or AutoStart, group is a special group. Any items in the Start-Up/AutoStart group automatically load as Windows starts up. The Start-Up/AutoStart group provides an ideal way to make sure that the applications and utilities you use commonly are always loaded and ready. You may want to assign Scheduler, a calculator, and your most-used word processor and spreadsheet to the Start-Up group.

Tip
You can drop items on a minimized group item to add them to the group.

Note

AutoStart is NDW's version of Windows 3.1's Start-Up group. Both function in exactly the same manner; the one on your system depends on whether you installed Windows 3.1 first or NDW first.

Caution

Putting too many programs in the AutoStart Group significantly slows down the machine's start-up time.

Summary

This chapter showed you the many ways you can launch files in Norton Desktop. You learned how to associate files and how to use the drive windows, the Launch List, the **R**un command, the DOS window, Desktop icons, and Quick Access to launch files. You also learned about using the AutoStart or Start-Up group to launch specific files automatically as you load Windows.

Chapter 9, "Backing Up Files with Norton Backup for Windows," shows you how to configure Norton Backup, back up files, use advanced backup options, and automate your backups.

Chapter 9

Backing Up Files with Norton Backup for Windows

No other computing operation is more important than *backing up* the data on your hard disk. If you ever experience a hard disk error or accidentally erase important data, your backup copies of this data may be your only source for restoring the lost information.

Norton Backup for Windows enables you to back up all or part of your hard disk quickly and easily. You can even customize and automate your backup procedure—and you can do it all without ever leaving Windows and Norton Desktop for Windows.

In this chapter, you learn to perform the following tasks:

- Understand backups and Norton Backup for Windows
- Start Norton Backup for Windows
- Configure Norton Backup
- Back up files by using Norton Backup
- Automate your backups

Understanding Backups and Norton Backup for Windows

Norton Backup for Windows is the Windows version of the popular Norton Backup program. Its inclusion as part of Norton Desktop 3 for Windows in many cases more than justifies the entire purchase price of NDW. The original Norton Backup (for DOS) gained its popularity because it simplified the tedious task of backing up data.

The importance of keeping backups of significant data cannot be overstated. If your files are important enough to create and store on your hard disk, they are important enough for you to keep archived copies in a safe place. The concept of backing up data this way is not new. People often keep copies of important papers in a different location than the originals, in case the originals are stolen or damaged by fire. Backing up computer data serves a similar purpose.

Backing up data, however, is different from simply copying data. Backups are created in a file format that conserves disk space and is, therefore, unreadable by regular programs. That data must be *restored* to its original format before it can be used again. Norton Backup both backs up and restores data.

You can back up data without resorting to a program such as Norton Backup. DOS includes a BACKUP command that *archives* in a *compressed* format the data from hard disks. The DOS BACKUP command, however, is neither flexible nor user-friendly, and you cannot create automated backups by using the BACKUP command.

Norton Backup for Windows, however, is extremely user-friendly, flexible, and automatable. By using standard Windows operations, you can easily back up all or some of the data on your hard disk—even while you perform tasks in other open windows. Norton Backup also is faster than the standard DOS BACKUP command, which is important to all busy computer users, and compresses data to such an extent that fewer disks are needed per backup.

As Norton Backup backs up your files, it creates a *catalog* containing information about this backed-up data. As you restore backed-up data, Norton Backup—or the utility on the Fix-It disk—seeks out the backup catalog to help the program retrieve selected files from the backup disks. The catalog includes important information about the backed-up data, including name, size, and attributes of backed-up files and directories; the directory structure of the backed-up data; the total number of files; the total size of the backup; the name of the setup file used; and the date the backup was made. Two backup catalogs are created for each backup, one on the hard disk and one on the last backed-up disk.

If a restore is attempted and the backup catalog is missing, Norton Backup attempts to reconstruct the source data and its structure from the partial catalogs that Norton Backup creates on each disk. Each partial catalog contains information about the data on that particular disk.

The key to successful backups is dedication. You must set a backup schedule and stick to the schedule. Whether you back up once a day, once a week, or once a month, make sure that you regularly use Norton Backup to protect yourself against the possibility of catastrophic data loss.

Starting Norton Backup for Windows

You can start Norton Backup for Windows in any of several ways. As part of the normal NDW installation, Norton Backup is installed as a Tool icon. You can start Norton Backup this way by simply double-clicking the Norton Backup Tool icon located on the Desktop.

Note

You can choose whether the Norton Backup Tool icon appears on your Desktop by choosing the **O**ptions **C**ustomize command and then selecting the Tool Icons category. The Control Center dialog box that appears enables you to select the NDW utilities that appear as Tool icons on the Desktop (including Norton Backup).

You also can choose the **T**ools Norton **B**ackup command to start Norton Backup from the menu.

Before you can use Norton Backup to back up your data, however, you must first configure the program for your system. Norton Backup then relies on these configuration settings to perform its backup chores.

Configuring Norton Backup

Norton Backup's configuration and compatibility tests are important because they analyze the components of your system. These tests also determine the fastest and most reliable way to back up data from your hard disk. Without performing these tests, Norton Backup cannot efficiently use your computer's drives to perform the backup. If you attempt to perform a backup without having performed the configuration, a warning message tells you that you must set the configuration before proceeding with the backup.

Using Initial Configuration and Compatibility Testing

Before you begin the configuration and compatibility tests, you need two blank disks in the same format as your backup disks. If you plan to use high-density 5 1/4-inch disks for backup storage, for example, you need two blank 5 1/4-inch high-density disks.

> **Note**
>
> These disks do not need to be blank—but they must not contain any important files, because they are formatted as part of the backup process. They do not even need to be currently formatted; Norton Backup automatically formats unformatted disks. Because Norton Backup writes over any information present on these disks, therefore, make sure that they do not contain important information.

Follow these steps to configure Norton Backup for your system:

1. Choose the **T**ools Norton **B**ackup command, or click the Backup Tool icon on the Desktop. The initial Norton Backup window appears (see fig 9.1).

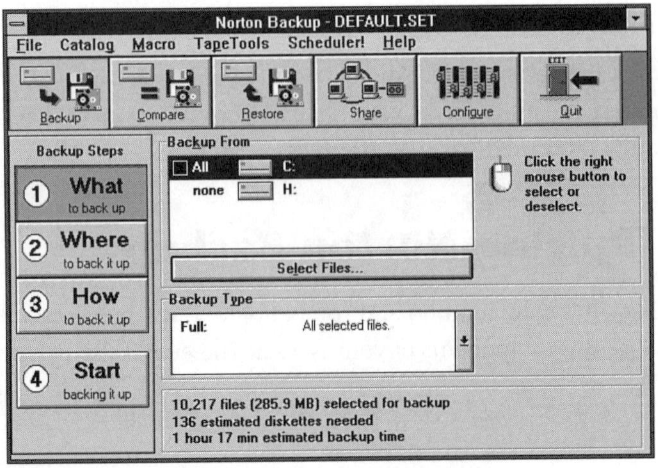

Fig. 9.1
The initial window that appears after you begin the Norton Backup program.

2. Choose the Configure button from the button bar at the top of the Norton Backup window. A second window, titled Norton Backup DEFAULT.SET, appears. This dialog box enables you to set configuration options (see fig. 9.2).

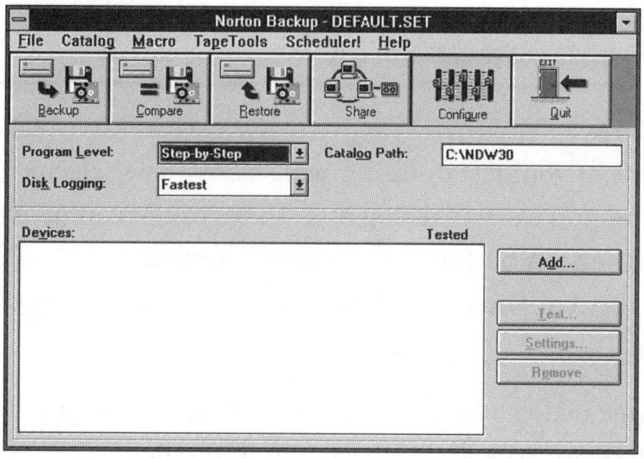

Fig. 9.2
The Norton Backup DEFAULT.SET window, showing configuration options.

3. Choose the Add button to display the Add Devices dialog box (see fig. 9.3). The Add Devices dialog box lists those devices available to you for your backups (disk drives, tape drives, and hard drive paths on your system).

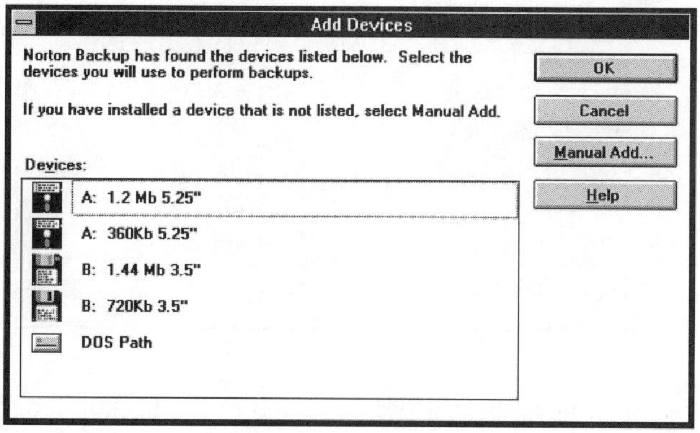

Fig. 9.3
The Add Devices dialog box enables you to choose which devices to use for your backups.

4. Select from the Devices list the drive and disk type you intend to use for your backup, and then choose OK.

   A Compatibility Test dialog box appears, telling you that the program is about to perform a compatibility test on the selected device (see fig. 9.4).

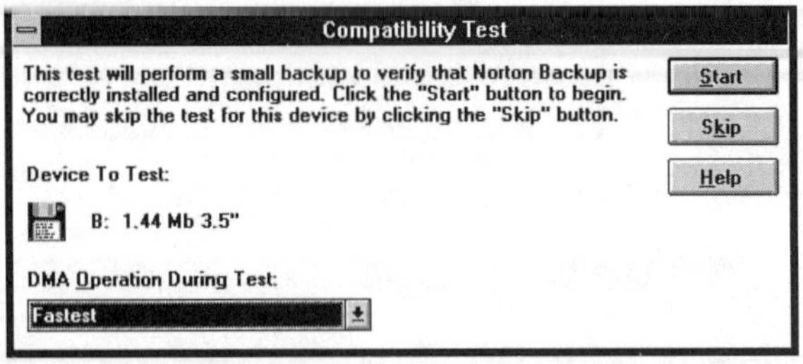

Fig. 9.4
The Compatibility Test dialog box enables you to begin a backup test on a selected device.

5. Place one of your test disks in the disk drive you selected in the Devices list of the Add Devices dialog box. To begin the compatibility test, choose the **S**tart button. If you skip the test, you can use the device for backup, but you run the risk that the backup settings may not be optimal.

   A message dialog box appears warning you that you cannot use the selected disk drives while a backup is in progress.

6. Choose OK to acknowledge the warning in the message dialog box. Norton Backup begins the compatibility test. The Backup Progress dialog box appears (see fig. 9.5).

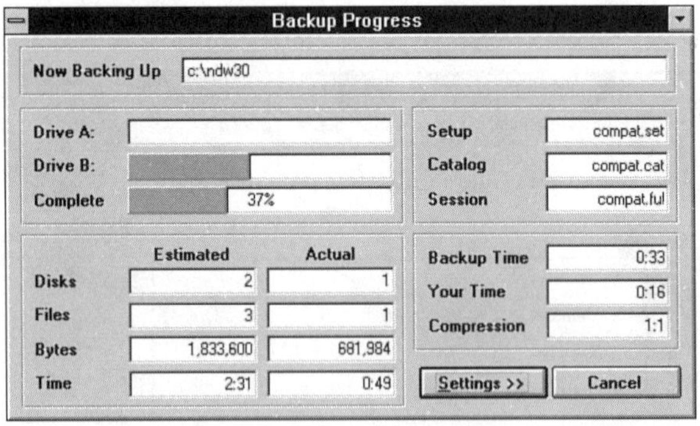

Fig. 9.5
The Backup Progress dialog box, showing the progress of the compatibility test.

Notice the progress bars at the upper left of the Backup Progress dialog box. These boxes show you the progress of the backup. At the lower left of the dialog box are two sets of progress statistics called Estimated and Actual. The Estimated numbers show you estimates of how many disks the backup may take, how many files and bytes can be backed up, and how long the backup may take. The Actual statistics tell you the actual status of the backup.

Other information in the dialog box tells you the name of your setup file for this backup, the catalog file, and the session name. These files contain information about the files being backed up. In this case, the compatibility backup test information is stored in the files COMPAT.SET, COMPAT.CAT, and COMPAT.FUL.

The Backup Time box tells you how much time is spent copying files to tape or disk, and Your Time tells you the amount of time spent waiting for you to place your disk in the drive. The Compression information tells you what amount of compression is being used to store your backed up files to disk.

After a period, another message dialog box appears, prompting you to insert the second test disk. (Although the disk light on the drive stays on, you can remove the first disk and insert the next disk. The drive light remains on to save time so that the drive need not come back up to speed after the motor slows down.)

7. Remove the first disk, and insert the second disk in the drive; the backup continues. The test uses only two disks. After a few seconds, the backup is complete, and the progress screen disappears.

After the backup portion of the test is complete, Norton Backup compares the test backup data with the original data on your hard disk. Another message dialog box appears, prompting you to reinsert the first disk.

8. Remove the second disk, reinsert the first test disk, and then choose OK.

Norton Backup begins data comparison. The Compare Progress dialog box appears. This dialog box is virtually identical to the Backup Progress Box. After a brief period, another message dialog box appears, prompting you to reinsert the second test disk.

9. Remove the first test disk, and reinsert the second disk. The Compare Progress box continues to report the compare progress until the Complete progress bar reaches 100 percent.

After this data comparison test is complete, a message dialog box appears, announcing that all the comparison tests are complete.

10. Choose OK to acknowledge the message. You return to the Norton Backup - DEFAULT.SET window, showing the device tested and a check mark in the Tested column of the Devices list (see fig 9.6).

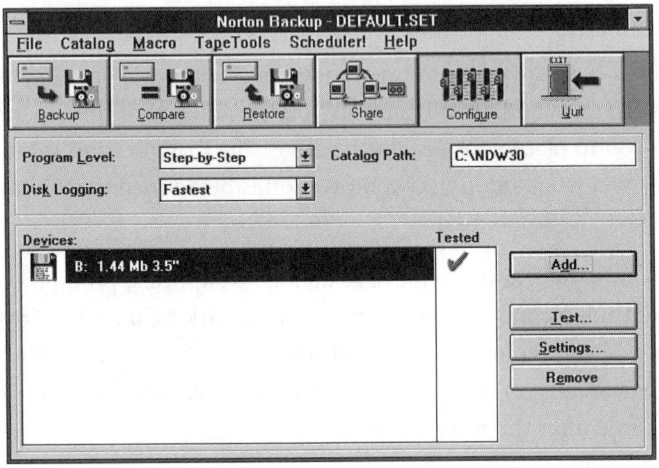

Fig. 9.6
The Norton Backup - DEFAULT.SET window, showing devices selected and tested for backup.

11. Choose the **B**ackup button after you complete the configuration procedure to return to the initial Norton Backup window (refer to fig. 9.1).

The Configuration window offers several other configuration options. The Program **L**evel option is discussed in the following section, "Selecting Norton Backup Program Levels." The Dis**k** Logging options, for example, enable you to choose either the Fastest backup method or the Most Compatible method. Both options are set during the configuration process; you can change them later, if necessary. The **T**est button enables you to retest a device already on the De**v**ices list. The **S**ettings button enables you to choose between fastest and most compatible backup settings for an individual device. The **R**emove button enables you to remove a device from the Devices list.

> **Warning**
>
> If Norton Backup configures your Dis**k** Logging as Most Compatible, *do not* change these settings to Fastest. Doing so could jeopardize the integrity of your backups so that they are not totally accurate.

Selecting Norton Backup Program Levels

The Program **L**evel drop-down list box of the Norton Backup - DEFAULT.SET window offers three distinct program levels from which to choose. Each level displays a slightly different window containing a different number of options. The three program levels are as described in the following list:

- *Step-by-Step.* This level is the easiest to use; it is the default level for Norton Backup for Windows. Fewer options exist here than at other levels, and all options are presented as simple check boxes. This level is recommended mainly for casual users.
- *Advanced.* This level is the most flexible and most powerful to use. All Norton Backup options are available at this level, and you can choose from both manual and automatic file selection methods. This level is the most complex of the three and is recommended for serious users only.
- *Preset.* This level uses an extremely simple interface and is intended for individual users in a workgroup situation in which a group leader or manager creates setup files for all group users. This level makes no options available.

Choose the user level you want for your backups by following these steps:

1. Choose the Config**u**re button from the initial Norton Backup window to display the Norton Desktop - DEFAULT.SET dialog box (refer to fig. 9.2).
2. Click the down arrow next to the Program **L**evel drop-down list box to display the Program **L**evel list, and select from the list the level you want to use.
3. Choose the **B**ackup button in the button bar to return to the initial Norton Backup window.

The following section assumes you selected the Step-by-Step user level in these steps.

Note

This book does not go into detail about the Preset user level, because options for users at this level are designed to be set up by a network group manager or leader.

Backing Up Files by Using Norton Backup

You can set several options for your backup operation. (These options are discussed later in this chapter. See the section "Backup Types.") If you simply want a normal backup, however, follow these steps:

1. From the Norton Desktop, begin Norton Backup for Windows.
2. Make sure that the **B**ackup button (the first button on the button bar) is selected (refer to fig 9.1). If it is not, choose the **B**ackup button now. Notice at the left of the Norton Backup - DEFAULT.SET window the four buttons labeled `What`, `Where`, `How`, and `Start`.
3. Choose the What To Back Up button (1).
4. Select from the Bac**k**up From box, the drive that holds your data.
5. Choose the Se**l**ect Files option below the Bac**k**up From box. The Select Backup Files - DEFAULT.SET window appears, enabling you to select from the window the files you want to back up (see fig. 9.7).

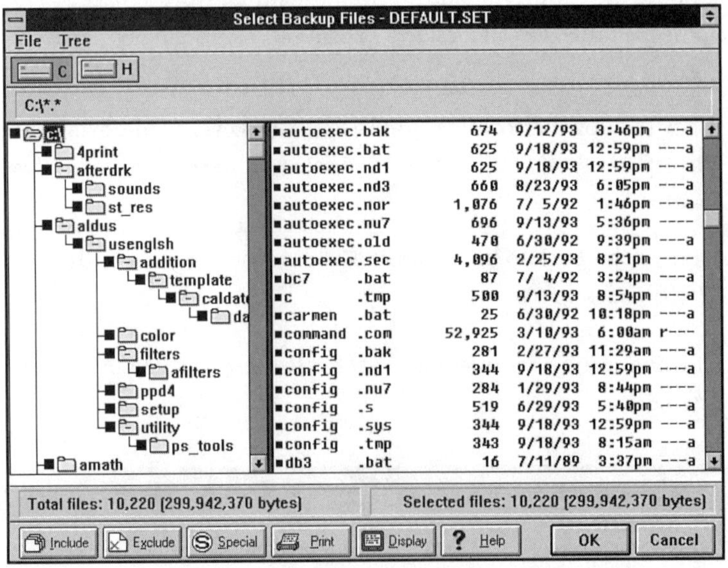

Fig. 9.7
The Select Backup Files window shows files that have been selected for backup.

Because this example runs a full backup, however, you do not need to select any files at this time. They are all selected by default. (Refer to the section "Individual Files for Backup," later in this chapter, for information about selecting files for backup.)

6. Click OK to continue with the backup. The main Norton Backup - DEFAULT.SET window reappears.

7. Choose the Where To Back It Up button (2). The window changes in appearance, as shown in figure 9.8.

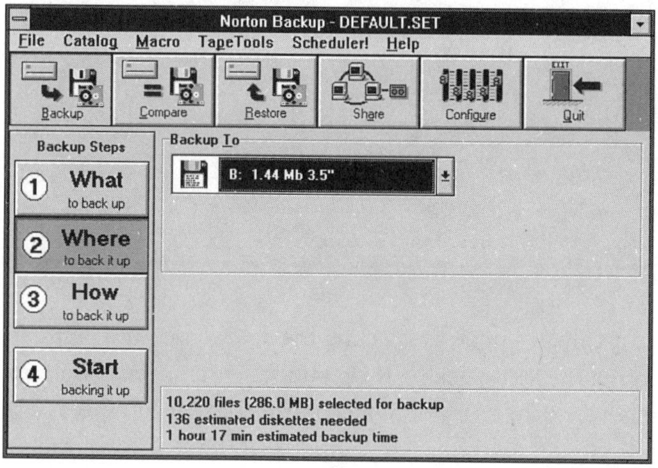

Fig. 9.8
The main Norton Backup window, displaying the Backup **T**o list box.

8. From the Backup **T**o drop-down list box, select the drive that is to receive your backup data.

9. Choose the How To Back It Up button (3) from the Norton Backup - DEFAULT.SET window. The window changes appearance again, as shown in figure 9.9. Four backup option buttons are displayed: S**p**eed, Safet**y**, Defau**l**t, and Cus**t**omize. (See the section "Other Basic Backup Options," later in this chapter for a description of these options.)

10. For this backup, choose the Defau**l**t option.

11. Choose the Start Backing It Up button (4) to begin the backup (refer to fig. 9.9).

Note

You can back up data to floppy disk drives or to any storage device that uses a DOS path. These devices include network drives, Bernoulli cartridges, or any tape drives that can be configured as a DOS device. You can even back up data from one part of your hard disk to another part of your hard disk. If you added a DOS Path option earlier during configuration and then choose the DOS path in the Backup **T**o box, the Path combination box appears. Simply type or select the path to which you want to back up your data.

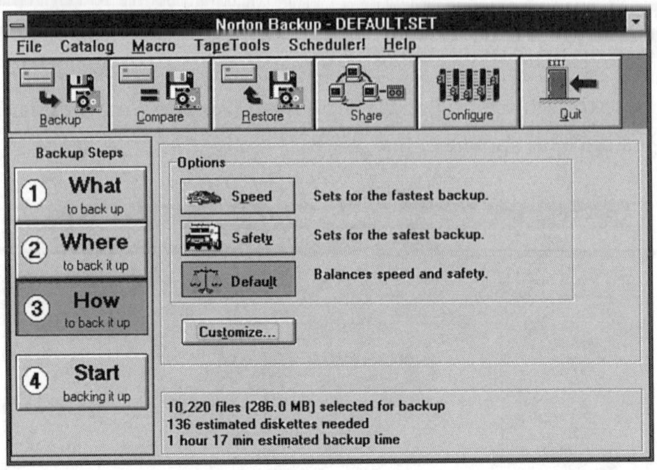

Fig. 9.9
The How To Back It Up version of the main Norton Backup window.

Most backups are as simple as selecting the data source and destination and then choosing the Start Backing It Up button. Other backup options also are available, however, to give you more control over backup speed, efficiency, and file selection. If you consider yourself a Norton Backup power user, or simply want to know more about backup options, the following sections are for you.

Setup Files

All the main options for a given backup are stored in *setup files*. These setup files contain information used by the program to perform certain kinds of backups, such as instructions to backup all database files, all spreadsheet files, or all word processing files. You use predefined setup files by choosing the Norton Backup window's **F**ile **O**pen Setup command to instruct Norton Backup to initiate common backup processes. You can create your own setup files or use one of six predefined setup files. All setup files end with the SET extension.

Setup files contain the following settings:

- The Backup **F**rom drive.
- The Backup **T**o drive.
- Individual files or file types to back up.
- The type of backup to perform.
- Other setup options.

Essentially, a setup file saves all the settings displayed in the Norton Backup window to a SET file. Then, if you want to do the same or a similar backup, you can use the saved SET file to reset the options instead of needing to choose all the settings manually.

The following table lists Norton Backup's six predefined setup files.

Setup File	Function
ASSIST.SET	Works with the Automated Backups to perform a full backup of drive C on day one and incremental backups on the remaining days of the week. (See the section "Automating Your Backups," later in this chapter, for information.)
DBASE.SET	Selects dBASE and Q&A files on drive C.
FULL.SET	Selects all files on drive C.
DEFAULT.SET	Selects all files on drive C; this is the Norton Backup default.
SPRDSHT.SET	Selects 1-2-3 and Excel files on drive C.
WORDPROC.SET	Selects WordPerfect, Microsoft Word, Ami Pro, JustWrite, and text files on drive C.

You can easily create new setup files of your own. Follow these steps to create a new setup file:

1. Begin Norton Backup from the Desktop.
2. Choose the settings you want for all the backup options—What, Where, and How—available from the Norton Backup window (refer to fig. 9.1).

   Optionally, if you do not want to back up all files, select specific files or file types to back up by using the Se**l**ect Files option.
3. After you choose your settings, open the Norton Backup **F**ile menu, and choose the Save Setup **A**s command. The Save Setup File dialog box appears.
4. Type a new file name in the File **N**ame text box.
5. Type a file description in the **D**escription text box. (This step is optional.)
6. Choose OK to save the new setup file. You return to the Norton Backup window.

Follow these steps to edit an existing setup file:

1. Open a current setup file by choosing **F**ile **O**pen Setup in the Norton Backup window.

2. Select the setup file you want to edit from the Open Setup File dialog box.

3. Make the necessary changes to any Norton Backup What, Where, or How settings (refer to fig 9.1).

4. After you make all your changes in the settings for the setup file, choose the **F**ile **S**ave Setup command. The Save Setup File dialog box appears.

5. Click OK to save the settings under the current file name.

Using a setup file—especially one of your own creation—is the easiest way to implement a specific backup operation in Norton Backup. All you need do is start Norton Backup, select the setup file that governs the type of backup you want to run, and choose the Start Backing It Up button. Norton Backup does the rest.

Backup Types

Norton Backup can perform five different types of backups. (These are not the same as the setup file options described in the preceding section.) Each backup type backs up specific types of files, as described in the following table.

Backup Type	Function
Full	Consists of all files you select on the main Norton Backup screen; restoring a Full backup requires the set of Full backup disks.
Incremental	Consists only of those files in your selected set that have changed or are new since your last Full or Incremental backup; restoring an Incremental backup requires both the set of Full backup disks and all sets of Incremental backup disks.
Differential	Consists only of those files in your selected set that have changed or are new since your last Full backup; restoring a Differential backup requires the set of Full backup disks and the most recent set of Differential backup disks.
Full Copy	Performs a Full backup but does not mark the files as backed up; useful only to transfer files to another computer without disturbing your normal backup cycle.

Backup Type	Function
Incremental Copy	Performs an Incremental backup but does not mark the files as backed up; useful only to transfer files to another computer without disturbing your normal backup cycle.

Warning

If you perform Incremental backups, you must retain disks from all Incremental sessions. If you are missing a set of Incremental backup disks, you cannot restore all the information backed up from your hard drive. For this reason, many users prefer to perform Differential backups.

Recommended Backup Strategy

A good backup strategy involves using a combination of Full and Differential backups. Because a Full backup of your entire hard disk is time consuming, many users prefer to perform Full backups only occasionally. Differential backups, then, can be used between Full backups to archive any files changed since the last Full backup. Follow these steps to use a good backup strategy:

1. DAY 1: Perform a Full backup of all files on your hard disk. Store these disks in a safe place, preferably in a different location than your computer.

2. DAYS 2 through 7: Perform Differential backups daily.

Repeat this procedure weekly so that each week you have one Full backup, with daily Differential backups on the remaining days. This procedure provides you with the maximum protection with the minimum amount of effort.

Alternatively, you can perform Incremental backups on days 2 through 7. You must remember to keep separate sets of Incremental disks for each day; in case you have to restore the data, you need all six sets of Incremental backup disks. Conversely, with Differential backups, you can reuse the backup disks, because each Differential backup contains all the data changed since the last Full backup.

Individual Files for Backup

Thus far, this chapter has covered backing up your entire hard disk. You may find, however, that you want to back up only particular types of files, or files in particular directories, or even just specific files. Norton Backup makes this task relatively easy by using a variation of the Norton Desktop drive window called the Select Backup Files window.

Tip
Back up small groups of files by dragging the selected files or a directory subtree from a drive window and dropping them on the Desktop Backup icon. Norton Backup then starts and backs up the selected files.

Access the Select Backup Files window by choosing the Se**l**ect Files command in the main Norton Backup window. The Select Backup Files window appears initially in full-screen size, but it can be minimized to a smaller window that takes up less screen space (refer to fig. 9.7).

The following table explains the main parts of the Select Backup Files window.

Window Elements	Function
Drive Icons	Represent all recognized drives that can be backed up.
File Filter Information Line	Displays the current directory and file filter information.
Tree Pane	Displays a directory tree listing.
File Pane	Displays all files—along with complete file information—or the currently selected directory.
File Summary Line	Displays information about the total number of files on the current drive, the amount of space they occupy, the number of files currently selected for backup, and how much space the selected files occupy.
Button Bar	Contains buttons that perform specific functions related to file selection.

Use this window to select the files you want to back up. Select the directories and files for backup for each specific drive, one drive at a time. Select and deselect directories and files by single-clicking the right mouse button or double-clicking the left mouse button.

Tip
Select the file name and choose the **F**ile **V**iew command to view the contents of a selected file by using the Norton Viewer.

Choose the **F**ile Select **A**ll command to select for backup all directories and files on the selected drive. Alternatively, select the appropriate Drive icon by single-clicking the right mouse button or double-clicking the left mouse button.

Follow these steps to select specific directories and the files included in those directories:

1. Move the mouse pointer to the directory name.
2. Choose the selected directory name by single-clicking the right mouse button or double-clicking the left mouse button.

Follow these steps to select specific files within directories:

1. Move the mouse pointer to the file name.
2. Single-click the right mouse button or double-click the right mouse button to select the file.

To deselect directories or files, repeat the preceding steps for clicking the selected file or directory. After a selected file or directory is deselected, the black box beside the name disappears and the file name appears in red.

Access additional operations by using the button bar at the bottom of the window. Many of these operations, discussed in more detail in the following section of this chapter, are available only if you choose the Advanced level.

Note

The buttons for Advanced operations do not appear on the button bar if you have the Basic user level selected.

The following table outlines the operations you can access by using the button bar:

Button	Operation
Include	Selects paths and file types to include for backup; available only with the Advanced user level.
Exclude	Selects paths and file types to exclude from backup; available only with the Advanced user level.
Special	Sets up conditions under which Norton Backup includes or excludes certain types of files, such as copy protected files, System files; available only with the Advanced user level.
Print	Prints a file listing for the selected drive.

(continues)

Tip

If a directory or file is selected, a black box appears next to the directory or file name.

Tip

Select all subdirectories under a main directory by collapsing the main directory (clicking the – on the directory icon) and then selecting the main directory for backup. Expand the main directory (click the +), and all subdirectories, as well as the main directory, are selected.

Tip

Select multiple directories or files by dragging the pointer across sequential directories or files while holding down the right mouse button.

(continued)

Button	Operation
Display	Selects options for the directory and file pane displays.
Help	Displays the Norton Desktop Help system.

Choose OK to return to the main Norton Backup window after you select specific directories and files to include or exclude from your backup.

Other Basic Backup Options

If you choose the Where To Back It Up button (2) from the main Norton Backup window, the currently selected backup device is displayed (refer to fig. 9.8). Select another backup device by clicking the drop-down box and choosing another device.

If you choose the How To Back It Up button (3) from the basic Norton Backup window, the How version of the Norton Backup window appears (refer to fig. 9.9). From this dialog box, you can choose among three basic options: S**p**eed, Safet**y** or Defau**l**t. You also can choose the Cus**t**omize option to choose specific options.

If you choose the Cus**t**omize option, information about the selected backup options is displayed. Figure 9.10 shows the backup options used for the S**p**eed option. Figure 9.11 shows the backup options for the Safet**y** option and figure 9.12 shows the Defau**l**t options. If you choose the **S**ettings options, additional option choices are displayed. Additional setting options include settings for three categories, General, Safeguards, and Security. Figure 9.13 shows the General options category selected.

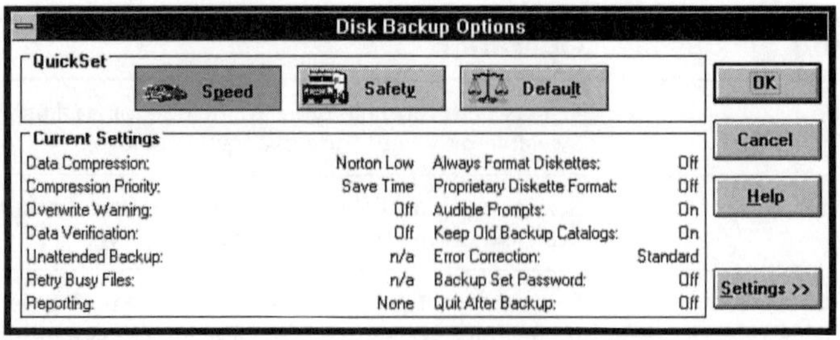

Fig. 9.10
Norton Backup's How To Back It Up Speed Backup Options.

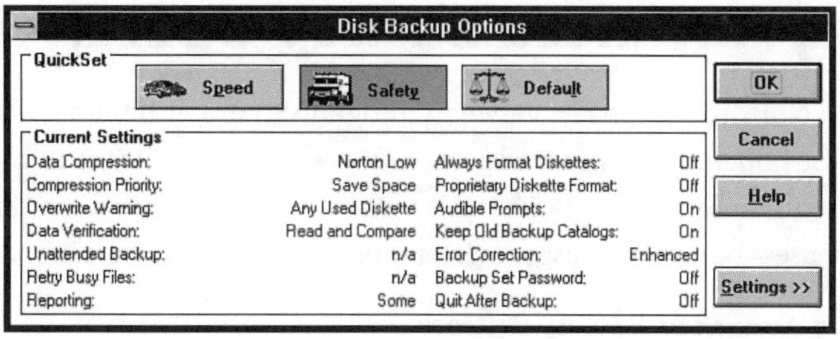

Fig. 9.11
Norton Backup's How To Back It Up Safety Backup Options.

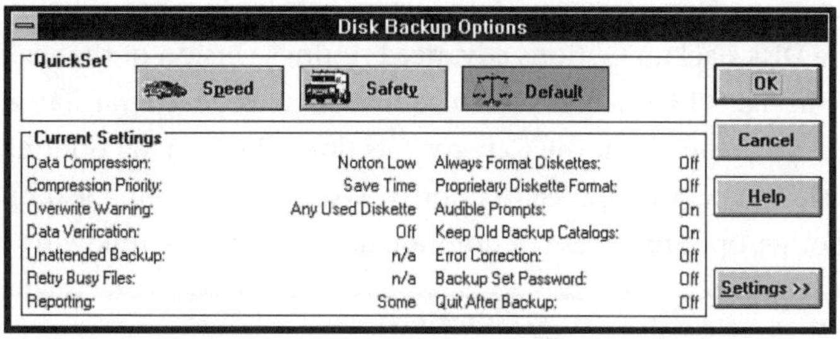

Fig. 9.12
Norton Backup's How To Back It Up Default Backup Options.

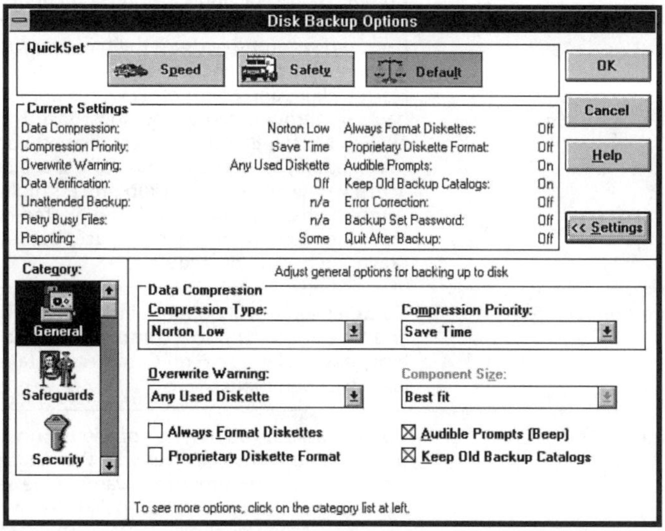

Fig 9.13
Norton Backup Default Backup options plus additional backup option choices.

Using Advanced Backup Operations

Although Norton Backup is a very easy program to use, it has enough control over various operations that it appeals to power users who want to totally customize their data backups. The following operations—not necessary for everyday use—help power users master all aspects of Norton Backup.

Selecting Advanced Backup Options

Selecting the Settings option on the Disk Backup Options dialog box enables you to fine-tune Norton Backup for your specific backup needs (refer to fig. 9.12). The Disk Backup Options advanced settings version of the dialog box, as shown in fig. 9.13, enables you to choose advanced General, Safeguards, and Security options from the Cate**g**ory section. The General options include **C**ompression Type, Co**m**pression Priority, **O**verwrite Warning, Component Si**z**e and other options. These options are described in the following table.

Option	Function
Compression Type	The Data Compression box enables you to choose **C**ompression Type and Co**m**pression Priority. Compression causes the backup to use fewer backup disks and speeds up the backup process; Compression types include Off, Norton Low, Norton High, and Microsoft Low. No Compression backs up through normal methods; Save Time enables Norton Backup to select the best compression method; Norton Low saves disk space but may actually slow down the backup process, unless your computer has a very fast CPU; and Norton High saves the most amount of disk space, but slows down the backup procedure.
Co**m**pression Priority	Co**m**pression Priority options include Save Time and Save Space. The Low compressions take less time, but the Norton High Compression takes up less space on disks.
Overwrite Warning	During backup, you may use previously unused disks or used disks. The Overwrite Warning specifies what kinds of disks produce a warning message. Types of warnings are Any Used Diskette, which alerts you if the target disk contains any data of any type; DOS-Formatted Diskette, which alerts you if the target disk has been formatted; Backup Diskettes, which alerts you if the target disk contains data from a previous session of Norton Backup; and Off, which does not alert you at all, no matter what is—or is not—on the disk.

Option	Function
Component Size	Sets the size of the backup groups created if backing up to a nondisk device; useful if you are backing up to a network drive backup that is then copied to individual disks; choose from Best Fit, which enables Norton Backup to size the data to the actual backup media, or from 360K, 720K, 1.2M, or 1.44M options; active only if you selected Backup to DOS Path in the Backup window.
Always Format Diskettes	Automatically formats all disks inserted for destination backups; a safeguard against inadvertently using a disk formatted on another drive with misaligned heads; slows down the backup process.
Proprietary Diskette Format	If selected, this option creates backup disks by using a proprietary, non-DOS formatting, which is faster and more efficient than regular DOS formatting, but prohibits using normal DOS commands on the data.
Audible Prompts (Beep)	Sounds beep if alert boxes instruct you to take action, such as inserting backup disks.
Keep Old Backup Catalogs	Keeps catalogs, normally deleted at the next full backup, for all old backups on your hard disk; useful only to perform backups from several different sets of backup disks.

The Safeguards Backup options enable you to choose the type of Data Verification to use—Off, Sample Only, or Read and Compare—and the type of Error Correction to use—Off, Standard, or Enhanced. In both cases, Off produces the fastest backup, and the other options provide more safety by performing slower backups. Data Verification compares data from the source disk to data on the destination disks; choose to turn Off verification (for the greatest speed), to Sample Only selected data (a good compromise between safety and speed), or to Read and Compare all backup data (the slowest but safest method).

Error Correction places error correction information on each backup disk, increasing the capability to successfully restore backed up data; it slows down the backup process, however, and also may use more backup disks (more than 10 percent more disk space than normal).

The Security Backup options enable you to choose password protection for your backup. With password protection, your backup disks cannot be reloaded onto a machine unless the password is first entered. This prevents unauthorized use of your backups.

Tip
For the most efficient and reliable operation, turn on the Norton Low Compression, Prompt Before Overwriting Used Diskettes, Use Standard Error Correction on Diskettes, and **A**udible Prompts (Beep) options.

The Automation Backup options enable you to choose options related to unattended backup operation. You can choose for U**n**attended Backup to be set to off or at a 1-, 5-, 15-, or 60-second delay. You also can choose to have Norton Backup **Q**uit After Backup and choose from several **B**usy File retry options.

The Report Backup options enable you to choose what kind of report is created to describe a backup. The Report options settings are Include Backup **O**ptions, Include Processed F**i**les, Include **E**rror messages, **I**nclude Backup Statistics, and **A**ppend Each Report to the Previous Report.

Including and Excluding Types of Files To Backup

If you select the **I**nclude, E**x**clude, or **S**pecial buttons from the Select Backup Files window (refer to fig. 9.7), several additional options enable you to make more specifications in your backup strategy.

The Include/Exclude List is useful if you need to select specific types of files to include or exclude from the backup. You may want to exclude, for example, all files with a BAK extension in the C:\ directory or any subdirectory.

Choosing either the **I**nclude or E**x**clude buttons displays the Include/Exclude Files dialog box (see fig. 9.14). You can use this dialog box to specify path and file name filters that include or exclude types of files from your backup.

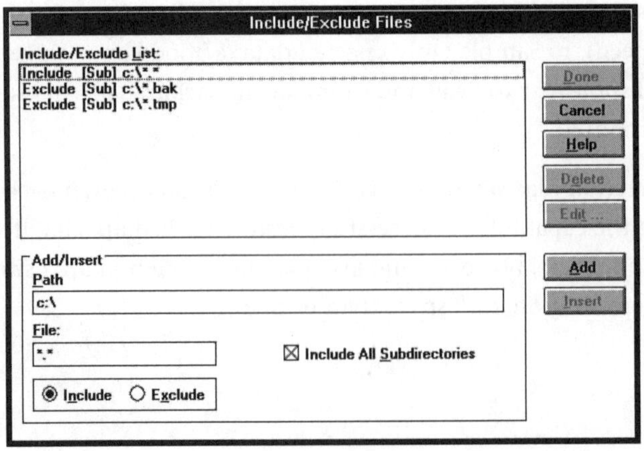

Fig. 9.14
The Include/Exclude Files dialog box enables you to select which files to back up.

You can add lines to the Include/Exclude list to include or exclude several different types of files. To do so, follow these steps:

1. Choose to **A**dd a new specification. The dialog box shown in figure 9.15 appears.

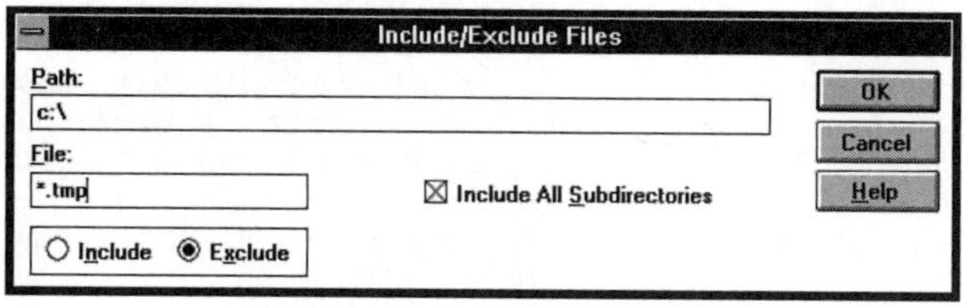

Fig. 9.15
Specify in this version of the Include/Exclude Files dialog box the path and file specification of files to include or exclude.

2. Type in the **P**ath text box the path of the files to include or exclude.
3. Type in the **F**ile text box the file name or file filter by using wild cards. (For example, enter ***.TMP**.)
4. Choose whether to I**n**clude or E**x**clude this type of file by selecting the appropriate option button.
5. Choose whether to Include All **S**ubdirectories under the selected path by selecting or deselecting that check box.
6. Click OK. The new line appears in the Include/Exclude **L**ist of the original Include/Exclude Files dialog box (refer to fig. 9.14).

Tip
Delete lines from the Include/Exclude **L**ist by selecting the line and choosing the D**e**lete button.

Clicking the **S**pecial button on the button bar activates the Special Selections dialog box (see fig. 9.16). Various special options are available from this dialog box; they enable you to further determine what types of files to include in the backup, such as files created during a certain time period.

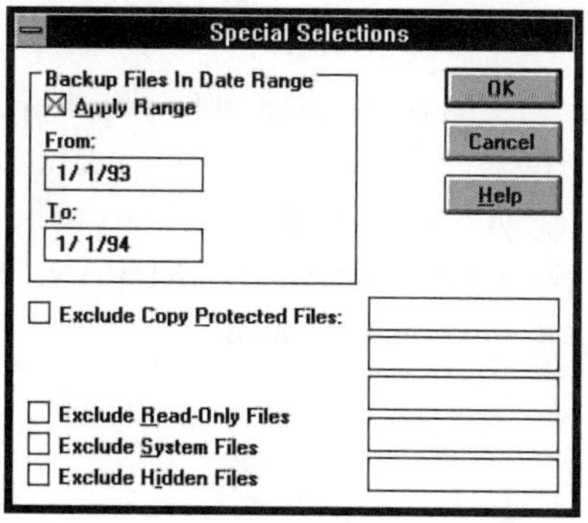

Fig. 9.16
The Special Selections dialog box enables you to specify additional backup file options.

The following table describes the special options.

Option	Function
Apply Range	Selects a date range for files you want to include in the backup. You must select the **A**pply Range check box and then enter dates in the **F**rom and **T**o text boxes.
Exclude Copy **P**rotected Files	Selects up to five copy-protected files to exclude from the backup; type file names in the text boxes to the right of the option.
Exclude **R**ead-Only Files	Excludes Read-Only files that can only be read, not written, to.
Exclude **S**ystem Files	Excludes System files that are essential, generally Hidden files DOS needs to operate.
Exclude H**i**dden Files	Excludes non-System Hidden files kept from general view.

Select the options you want from the Special Selections dialog box; then choose OK.

Using Norton Backup with Command Line Options

You can attach special command line options to the command used to start up Norton Backup. These switches enable various options and scenarios to run after Norton Backup starts up.

Note

Command line options apply only if you start Norton Backup by using the **F**ile **R**un command on the menu system, from a Desktop, Group, or Tool icon, or from the Scheduler utility.

To start Norton Backup by using command line options, simply add the appropriate switches to the end of the normal Norton Backup command. If, for example, you normally type **NBWIN.EXE** to start Norton Backup from the **F**ile **R**un command, you would instead type **NBWIN.EXE /ti** to start Norton backup with an incremental backup.

The following table lists the command line options available to you.

Option	Function
@	Runs the macro associated with a setup file.
/a	Starts a backup immediately after Norton Backup loads.
/tf	Starts a Full backup.
/ti	Starts an Incremental backup.
/td	Starts a Differential backup.
/tc	Starts a Full Copy backup.
/to	Starts an Incremental Copy backup.

The @ and /a switches are mutually exclusive.

Tip

You can edit the command line for a Norton Backup icon. Display the icon's Properties dialog box and edit the NBWIN.EXE command in the **Pro**gram/Document/Script text box to include the command line options.

You also can start Norton Backup and automatically access a specific setup file. Type the name of the setup file after the NBWIN.EXE command. To start the ASSIST.SET setup file, for example, type **NBWIN.EXE ASSIST.SET /a**. (The /a switch starts the backup automatically after loading.)

Note

Entering a command by using the **F**ile **R**un command is really counter to the icon style of Norton Backup. If you plan to use one of these options regularly, therefore, you may want to create an icon that carries out the desired option. See Chapter 8, "Launching Files with Norton Desktop," for more information.

Automating Your Backups

Automate your backups with Norton Backup for Windows by using the Norton Scheduler. (Use of the Scheduler is described in detail in Chapter 22, "Using Scheduler.")

Scheduling a Norton Backup

You can use the Desktop Scheduler to select a time for backup to be performed on a regular basis. To schedule a weekly scan of your disks, for example, choose the Scheduler! option from the main Norton Backup window's menu bar. This accesses the Scheduler dialog box. In the Scheduler, you can choose to **A**dd an event and then specify the event as a Norton Backup (NBWIN.EXE), weekly, and at a specific time. You then see an entry similar to the one shown in the Scheduler dialog box in figure 9.17.

Follow these steps to schedule a weekly backup:

1. Choose the Scheduler! option from the Norton Backup menu bar (refer to fig. 9.1). The Scheduler dialog box appears (see fig. 9.17).
2. Specify a description, specify the program NBWIN.EXE as the command to run, and specify a Frequency, Day of Week, and time in the Scheduler dialog box.

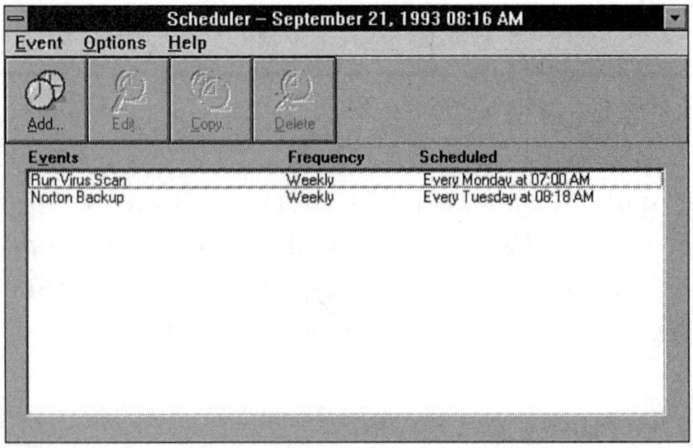

Fig. 9.17
Using the Norton Desktop Scheduler to schedule a weekly backup.

3. Minimize the Scheduler. You return to the Norton Backup dialog box.

Using Norton Backup Macros

A macro is a series of keystrokes that have been recorded by Norton Backup. You can play back these keystrokes with a simple command, thereby automating the keystrokes that perform the backup procedure.

To record a macro, follow these steps:

1. Choose the **M**acro Re**c**ord command from the main Norton Backup window (refer to fig. 9.1). From this point on, all keystrokes are recorded.
2. Choose the desired steps for the procedure. You must use keystrokes rather than mouse clicks to record your choices. (The mouse pointer is not visible while you are recording.)

3. Press F7 to stop recording after you finish the procedure.
4. Choose the **F**ile **S**ave command to save the macro in the current setup file.

> **Note**
>
> Macros are associated with specific setup files and with specific user levels. Before you record or play back a macro, make sure that you selected the correct setup file and user level.

Summary

This chapter explained how to use Norton Backup for Windows to back up your data. You learned the essential features of backing up your hard disk, how to configure Norton Backup, how to back up files, how to select and use advanced backup options, and how to automate backups.

When you need those backed up files, the Norton Backup program provides you with a Restore procedure. The next chapter discusses how to restore backed up files by using both Norton Backup for Windows and the Norton DOS-based Restore program on the Fix-It disk.

Chapter 10

Restoring Files with Norton Backup

Now that you know how to back up your files, as described in Chapter 9, "Backing Up Files with Norton Backup for Windows," you also must know how to restore that data if necessary. By using Norton Backup, the Fix-It Disk, and the Rescue disk, you can restore data just as easily as you can back up data.

In this chapter, you learn to perform the following tasks:

- Understand file restoration
- Respond to an emergency
- Use Norton Backup for Windows to restore data
- Use the Norton Fix-It Disk to restore data

Understanding File Restoration

As Norton Backup backs up your data, it creates a list of all the backed-up files and places this list in a *catalog file*. If you need to restore data, you simply select from this catalog file the files you want to restore. You can have multiple catalog files from multiple backups. If you combine Full backups with Incremental or Differential backups, for example, you have catalog files for each of these backups. Norton Backup creates two copies of each catalog: one on the hard disk and one on the last backup disk. Norton Backup also creates partial catalogs on each floppy disk of your backup disk set.

Norton Backup enables you to restore an entire set of backup disks or only selected files or directories from the backup set. You can search through the catalog to determine which files to restore, or you can simply use Norton Backup to restore all the backed-up data. The capability to restore selected files is useful if you accidentally delete a single file but have a recent copy of the file on your backup disks. You can simply restore the specific file without needlessly restoring to your hard disk all the backed-up data.

Responding to an Emergency

Tip
You cannot restore data you have not backed up. Always remember to construct a workable backup program—and then stick to that program.

If you do experience a disk disaster, the main thing to remember is not to panic. If you used Norton Backup for Windows, you have a set of backup disks containing relatively recent data—so all is not lost.

You may encounter two major types of emergencies. The first type involves losing only some of the data on your hard disk; in this case, you still can start Norton Backup for Windows and selectively restore missing data to your hard disk. The second type of emergency involves your entire hard disk; you cannot start Norton Backup for Windows, Norton Desktop, Windows, or even DOS. In this case, you must use the Norton Rescue Disk and the Fix-It Disk to restore all the data to your hard disk.

If You Can Still Start Norton Backup for Windows

If you can access Windows and Norton Desktop for Windows, you also can start Norton Backup for Windows. After you access Norton Backup, you can search for the correct catalog file on the hard disk. After you select the correct catalog file, you can select the specific files you want to restore. If only some of your data is missing, you need not restore the entire disk; just select those files that are missing or damaged.

Note

If Norton Backup cannot locate the catalog file on the hard disk (if that section of the hard disk is damaged, for example), insert the last backup disk. Norton Backup can access the catalog file on this disk, and you can select the files to restore. If for some reason the catalog file on the backup disk is unusable, Norton Backup can attempt to restore the data. Norton Backup can reconstruct a catalog file from the data on the other backup disks in your backup set, because partial catalog files are stored on each backup disk.

If You Must Use the Fix-It Disk or Rescue Disk

If your entire hard disk is damaged or has accidentally been reformatted or otherwise damaged so that no data exists, you must use the emergency restore programs on the Rescue and the Fix-It Disks. (The Rescue disk is primarily an emergency boot disk, and the Fix-It disk is a disk that contains emergency restoration programs.) Simply insert the Rescue disk into your floppy disk drive, and reboot your computer. Refer to Chapter 29, "Using Norton Fix-It and Rescue Disks," for information on running the Rescue program to recover your hard disk's missing data. If you still cannot access Norton Desktop, use the Fix-It program to completely restore your entire hard disk. The program uses catalog information to restore the disk or, if the catalog is missing, reconstructs a catalog from the data on the backup disks. See the section "Using the Norton Fix-It Disk To Restore Data," later in this chapter, for more information.

Warning

Before you restore data to your hard disk, you should use Symantec's DOS-based Norton Disk Doctor to check the physical status of your hard disk. The DOS Norton Disk Doctor also is included on the Rescue Disk.

Using Norton Backup for Windows To Restore Data

Not only can you back up data by using Norton Backup for Windows, you also can use this program to *restore* the data you back up. Access the Norton Backup for Windows Restore utility by choosing the **R**estore button in the main Norton Backup window. This activates the Rescue window.

Like the Norton Backup window, the Restore window contains four options: What, Where, How, and Start. The initial Norton Backup Restore window is shown in figure 10.1. Notice that this is the Restore window because the **R**estore icon is currently chosen on the icon bar at the top of the window.

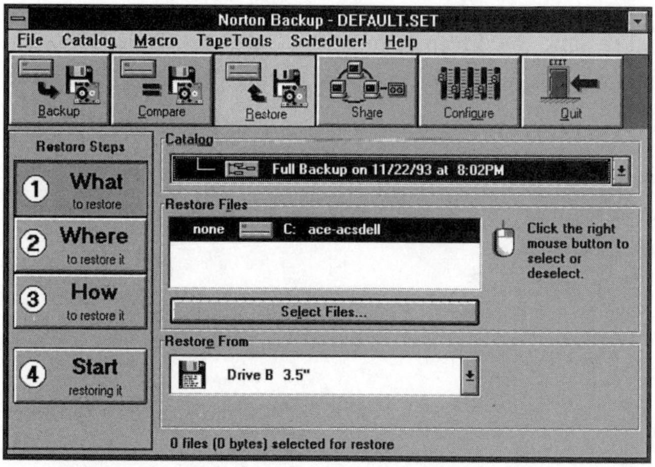

Fig. 10.1 The Norton Backup Restore window with the What To Restore option displayed.

The following sections describe the four stages of file restoration.

Using What To Restore

The Norton Backup Restore window's What To Restore screen contains several preliminary options that enable you to identify the files you want to restore (refer to fig. 10.1).

This window incorporates four features, or areas, as described in the following table.

Feature	Function
Restore Steps	Contains the four steps to use to restore files to your hard disk.
Catal**o**g	A drop-down list that contains all known backup catalogs.
Restore F**i**les	Contains information about the files to be restored. Use the Se**l**ect files button below this list to select the files to restore.
Restor**e** From	Selects the drive on which the backup disks are located.

Follow these steps to define what files to restore:

1. Select a backup catalog from the Catal**o**g list in the Norton Backup Restore window (What To Restore). This tells the Norton Restore utility what files are available to be restored.

2. Select the correct drive name from which you intend to restore the files if the Restor**e** From option is incorrect.

3. Choose the Se**l**ect Files button. This opens the Select Restore Files window, as shown in figure 10.2. This window consists of two panes.

   The left pane is a directory tree. It lists the directories on your hard disk. Directories that contain files to be restored appear in this pane as open file folders.

   The right pane contains a list of files from that directory that are available for restoration. Initially, none of the files are selected to be restored.

> **Note**
>
> The Select Restore Files window operates in much the same way as does the Select Backup Files window, discussed in Chapter 9, "Backing Up Files with Norton Backup for Windows."

4. Select from the file pane the files you want to restore by highlighting the file name and pressing the spacebar or by clicking the file name with the right mouse button.

5. After making your selections, click OK to return to the main Restore window.

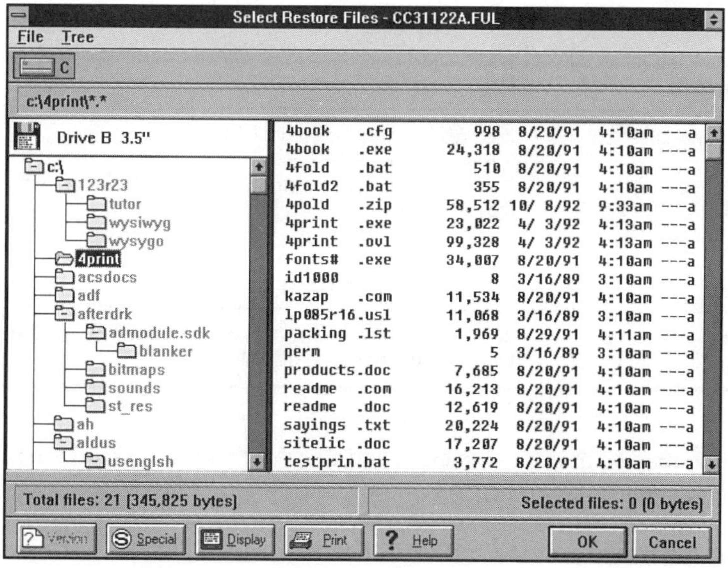

Fig. 10.2
Use the Select Restore Files window to choose what files to restore.

Using the Where To Restore It Window

Click the Where To Restore It (2) button to display that version of the Norton Backup Restore window, as shown in figure 10.3. Choose the restore destination from the Restore **T**o drop-down list box. The most common option is to restore files to their Original Locations. The different options available in this list box are described in the following table.

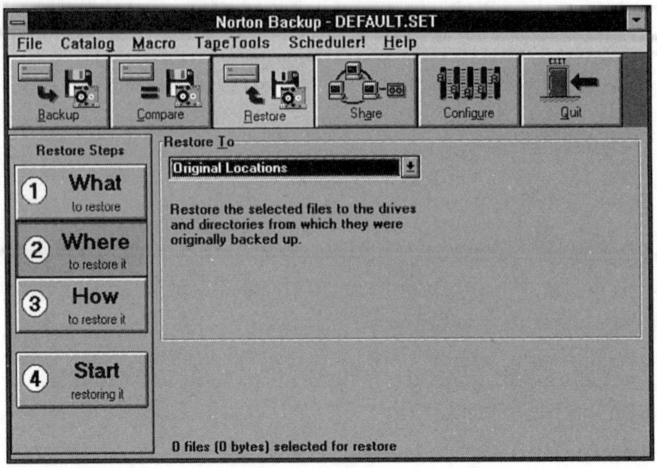

Fig. 10.3
The Where To Restore It window enables you to select where the restored files are placed.

Option	Function
Original Locations	Restores files to their original locations.
Alternate Drives	Restores files to a different drive than the one from which they were backed up.
Alternate Directories	Restores files to a different directory than the one from which they were backed up.
Single Directory	Restores all files to a single specified directory, no matter what was their original directory.

You also may be prompted to enter additional information during the restore operation, depending on which options you choose.

Using the How To Restore It Window

Click the How To Restore It (3) button to display that version of the Norton Backup Restore window, as shown in figure 10.4. This window enables you to specify the speed and safety options for restoring files. Three basic options are available, plus a Customize option. These options are virtually the same as the speed and safety options described for Norton Backup in Chapter 9, "Backing Up Files with Norton Backup for Windows."

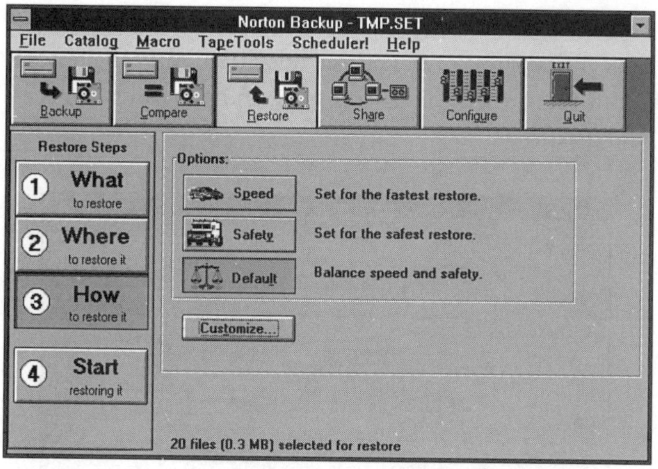

Fig. 10.4
Use the How To Restore It window to specify safety and speed options.

The Speed option enables you to restore files by using the fastest possible speed. The Safety option restores your files by using maximum verification. The Default option uses a balance between speed and safety. The Customize option enables you to choose the degree of speed and safety you want. After you choose the Customize button, the Disk Restore Options dialog box appears, as shown in figure 10.5. From this dialog box, you can set any or all the speed and safety restore options.

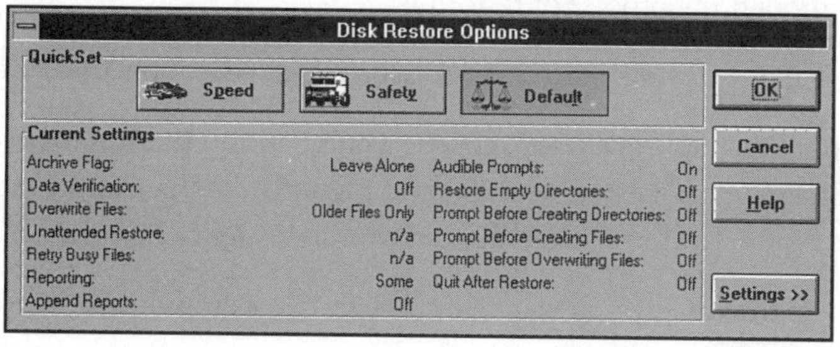

Fig. 10.5
Use the Disk Restore Options dialog box to specify detailed speed and safety options.

Starting the Restore Process

After you choose the What, Where, and How options you want, you can begin the restore procedure by choosing the Start Restoring It (4) button. After the restore begins, a Restore Progress dialog box appears, similar to that shown in figure 10.6. This dialog box tells you what is currently being restored; it also tells you which disk is being used and provides other information about the progress of the restore operation. After the restoration is complete, your files are completely restored, and you can now access them on your hard disk.

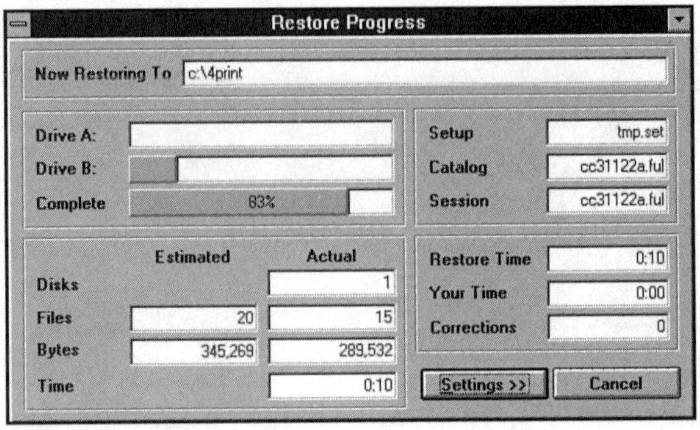

Fig. 10.6
The Restore Progress dialog box shows the progress of your restore operation as files are copied from the backup disks onto your hard disk.

Restoring Files by Using Norton Backup for Windows: An Overview

Up to this point, you have learned how to set up and perform a restore by using the What, Where, How, and Start options. This section takes you step by step through the process of restoring files.

To restore files by using Norton Backup for Windows, follow these steps:

1. From the Norton Desktop, choose **T**ools, Norton **B**ackup to access the initial Norton Backup window, and then choose the **R**estore icon to access the Norton Backup Restore window (refer to fig. 10.1).

2. Select the catalog you want from the Catalo**g** drop-down list box of the Norton Backup What To Restore window.

3. Select the disk drive that holds your backed-up data from the Restor**e** From drop-down list box.

4. Choose the Se**l**ect Files button to display the Select Restore Files window (refer to fig. 10.2).

5. Select from the Select Restore Files window the directories and files you want to restore. Click OK after your selection is complete.

Tip
Choose to restore all files and directories from the Select Restore Files window by opening the window's **F**ile menu and choosing the Select **A**ll command (refer to fig. 10.2).

6. Click the Where To Restore It button to access the Norton Backup Where To Restore It window, and select from the Restore **T**o drop-down list box a destination for the files to be restored (refer to fig. 10.3).

7. If necessary, click the How To Restore It button to access the How To Restore It window to change the option for efficiency—by speed, safety, or a balance between the two (the Default). (You probably do not need to change this from the Default option, however, because the difference between speed and safety is actually not that noticeable.)

8. Click the Start Restoring It button to begin restoring the files.

9. Insert the correct backup disks in the floppy disk drive after you are prompted to do so. Norton Backup displays an on-screen message after the restoration is finished, telling you that the restore is complete.

10. Choose OK to end the restore procedure.

Tip
You usually want to restore files to their Original Locations. Only in very special cases do you select one of the other Restore To options.

Using the Norton Fix-It Disk To Restore Data

On rare occasions, your Windows program may become damaged. This could occur if your disk becomes too fragmented, if a program accidentally overwrites some important file, if the magnetic image of an important file becomes unusable—or any number of possibilities. Some of these problems can be prevented by regular use of Speed Disk and Norton Disk Doctor, but the savvy computer user knows that, in the long run, some problems are inevitable—no matter what the precautions. To help you recover from such in-the-long-run problems, Norton has provided a handy safety net of programs in the form of the Norton Fix-It disk.

If you cannot access Norton Backup for Windows, you must use the Norton Fix-It Disk before restoring files to your hard disk (including all the Norton files). The Fix-It Disk contains a special DOS-based Emergency Restore program that works with the backup files you created by using Norton Backup for Windows.

Norton Emergency Restore works similarly to the Restore function in Norton Backup for Windows: Insert your backup disks, and select the catalog file you want to restore; optionally, select specific files to restore, select various options, and then start the restoration process.

Configuring Norton Emergency Restore

Before you can use Norton Emergency Restore, you must first install the program from the Fix-It Disk to your hard disk. Follow these steps to complete the installation:

1. If you cannot boot your computer, use the Rescue disk to boot your computer and restore elements of your DOS system required to make your disk operate. (See Chapter 29, "Using Norton Fix-It and Rescue Disks," for details about using the Rescue disk.)

2. Insert the Fix-It Disk in the appropriate floppy disk drive.

3. Log to the correct floppy disk drive at the DOS prompt. If, for example, the Fix-It Disk is in drive A, type **A:**, and then press Enter.

4. Type **NRINST** at the DOS prompt (usually `A:\>`), and press Enter.

The Install program installs Norton Emergency Restore to your hard disk (see fig. 10.7).

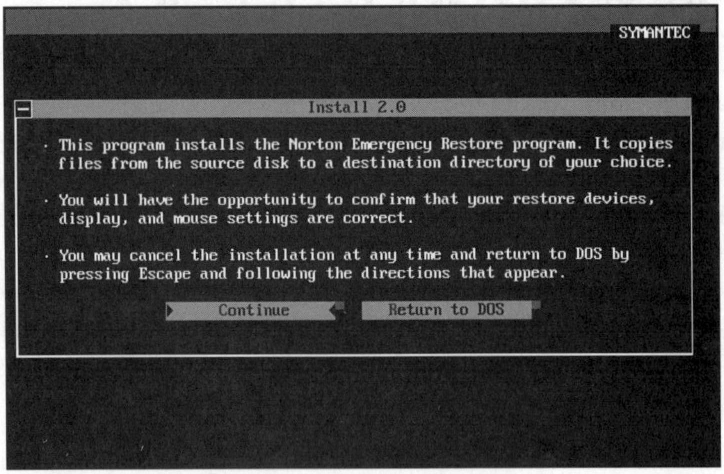

Fig. 10.7
The Norton Install program installs Norton Emergency Restore to your hard disk.

To start Norton Emergency Restore, follow these steps:

1. At the DOS prompt, log to your hard disk drive.

2. Change to the NRESTORE directory by typing **CD\NRESTORE** and pressing Enter.

3. Type **NRESTORE**, and press Enter.

The main Norton Emergency Restore screen has three options you can use to Configure the program, begin the Restore procedure, or Quit the program.

If you choose the Configure option, the Configure dialog box appears. In this box, you can choose Video and Mouse options and Restore Devices options.

To configure Norton Emergency Restore for your particular system, choose Restore Devices. The Restore Devices dialog box appears. You can use the options in this dialog box to configure floppy disk drives A and B manually, or you can select Auto Config so that the program configures itself.

After you choose OK to leave this screen, or if you select Restore from the main screen, the Catalog Options screen appears. From this screen, you can choose among the options described in the following table.

Option	Function
No Catalog	Restores all files from the set of backup disks. Use this option if the catalog file is damaged or missing or if you want to restore the entire hard disk.
Retrieve	Retrieves the catalog file and then enables you to select specific files to restore.
Rebuild	Builds a new catalog file from the partial catalog files on each backup disk and then enables you to select specific files to restore. Use this option if the catalog file is damaged or missing and you need to restore only specific files.

You exit this screen after you choose any option, and the main Norton Restore screen appears. This screen closely resembles the same screen in Norton Backup for Windows and contains the options described in the following table.

Option	Function
Backup Set Catalog	Displays a list of catalog files from which to select for restoration.
Restore From	Selects the drive from which to restore files.
Restore To	Selects where to restore files; choose from Original Locations, Other Drives, Other Directories, and Single Directory.

(continues)

(continued)

Option	Function
Restore Files	Enables you to select files from a list of specific files to restore.
Select Files	Displays the Edit Include/Exclude List, with which you can select certain file types or file locations to include or exclude from the restoration process.

Restoring Files by Using the Fix-It Disk

Even though Norton Emergency Restore offers many options, the restoration process itself is relatively simple. Just follow these steps to restore your files:

1. Install Norton Emergency Restore from the Fix-It Disk to your hard disk.

2. Start Norton Emergency Restore by typing **NRESTORE** and pressing Enter (see fig. 10.8).

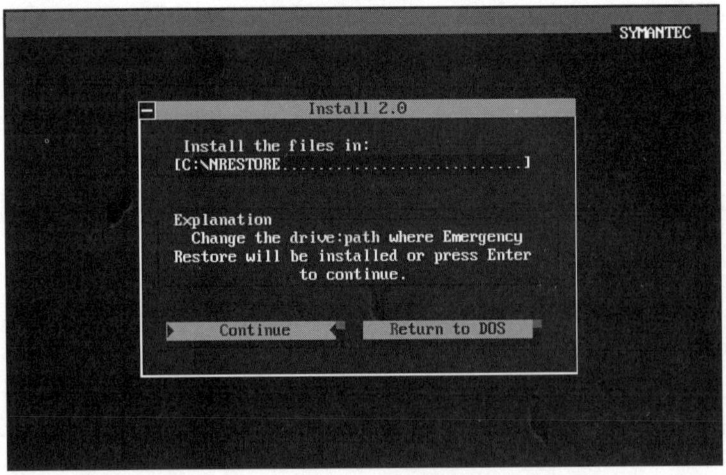

Fig. 10.8
Start Norton Emergency Restore by typing the NRESTORE command.

3. Choose Configure from the main screen.

4. Choose the relevant options from the Configure screen, and then choose OK to return to the main screen.

5. Choose Restore from the main screen.

6. Select No Catalog from the Catalog Options screen to restore all files.

7. Select the correct Backup Set Catalog from the Norton Restore screen.

8. Select the correct drive to Restore From.
9. Select to Restore to Original Locations.
10. Select the Start Restore option.
11. Insert disks, as prompted, until the restoration is complete.

By following this procedure, you can quickly recover from a disaster that affects your entire hard disk drive. To restore only specific files, simply select the appropriate options from the Norton Restore screen.

Tip
If you need to restore only selected files, you may be more comfortable using Norton Backup for Windows rather than Norton Emergency Restore.

Summary

In this chapter, you learned how file restoration works, how to respond to an emergency, how to use Norton Backup for Windows to restore data, and how to use the Fix-It disk to restore data. Added to what you learned in Chapter 9, "Backing Up Files with Norton Backup for Windows," this information gives you a better understanding of why and how to back up and restore data from your hard disk.

This chapter concludes Section II, in which you learned the many ways to manipulate disks, directories, and files by using Norton Desktop 3 for Windows. Section III shows you how to configure the perfect Desktop by using the NDW tools and utilities, whether that be icon-based, menu-based, or a combination.

In the next chapter, "Customizing Norton Desktop's Settings," you learn how to configure the Desktop to your preferences; how to configure Drive icons, network drives, drive windows, Quick Access, and menus; and how to save configuration changes.

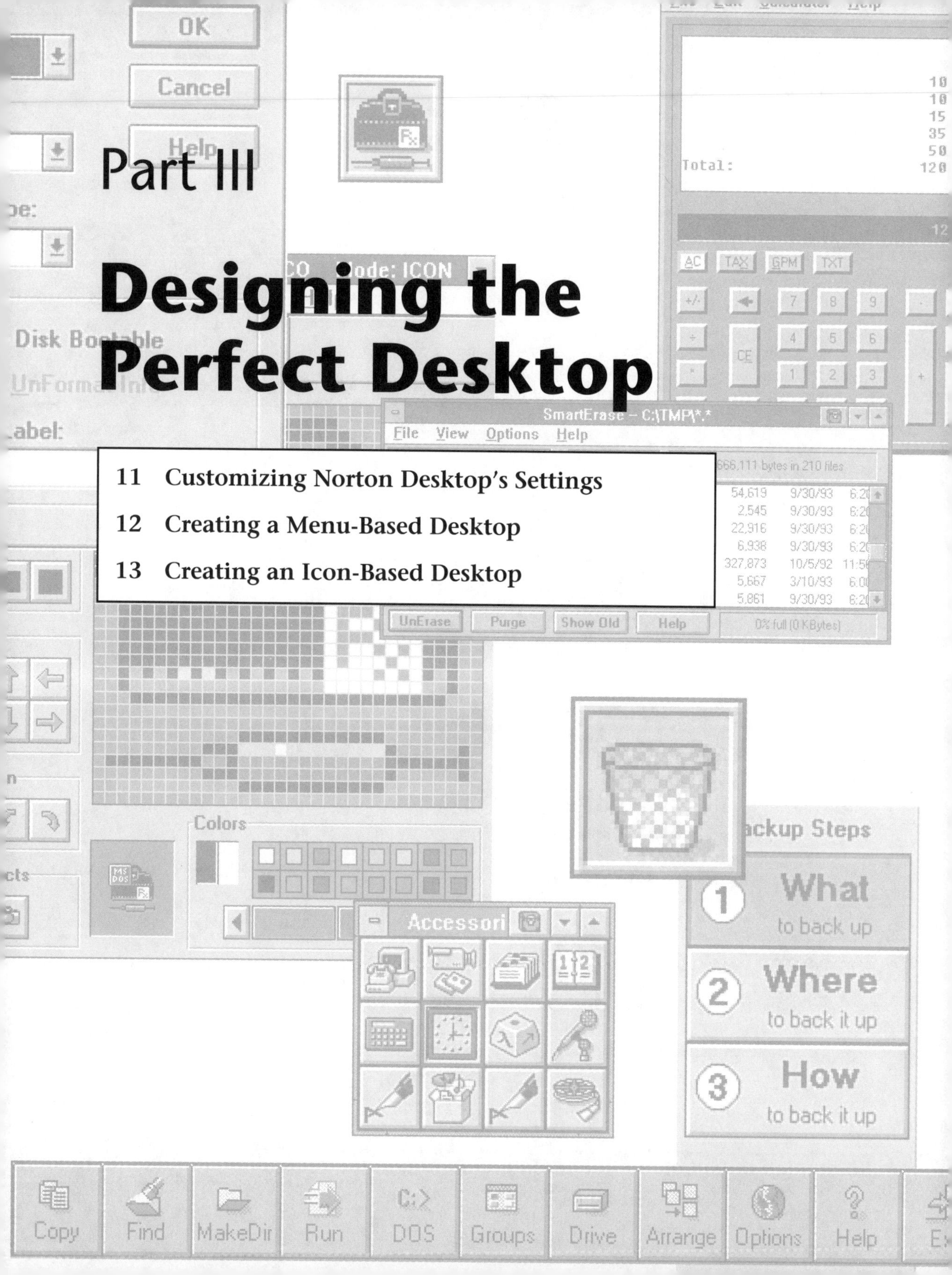

Part III

Designing the Perfect Desktop

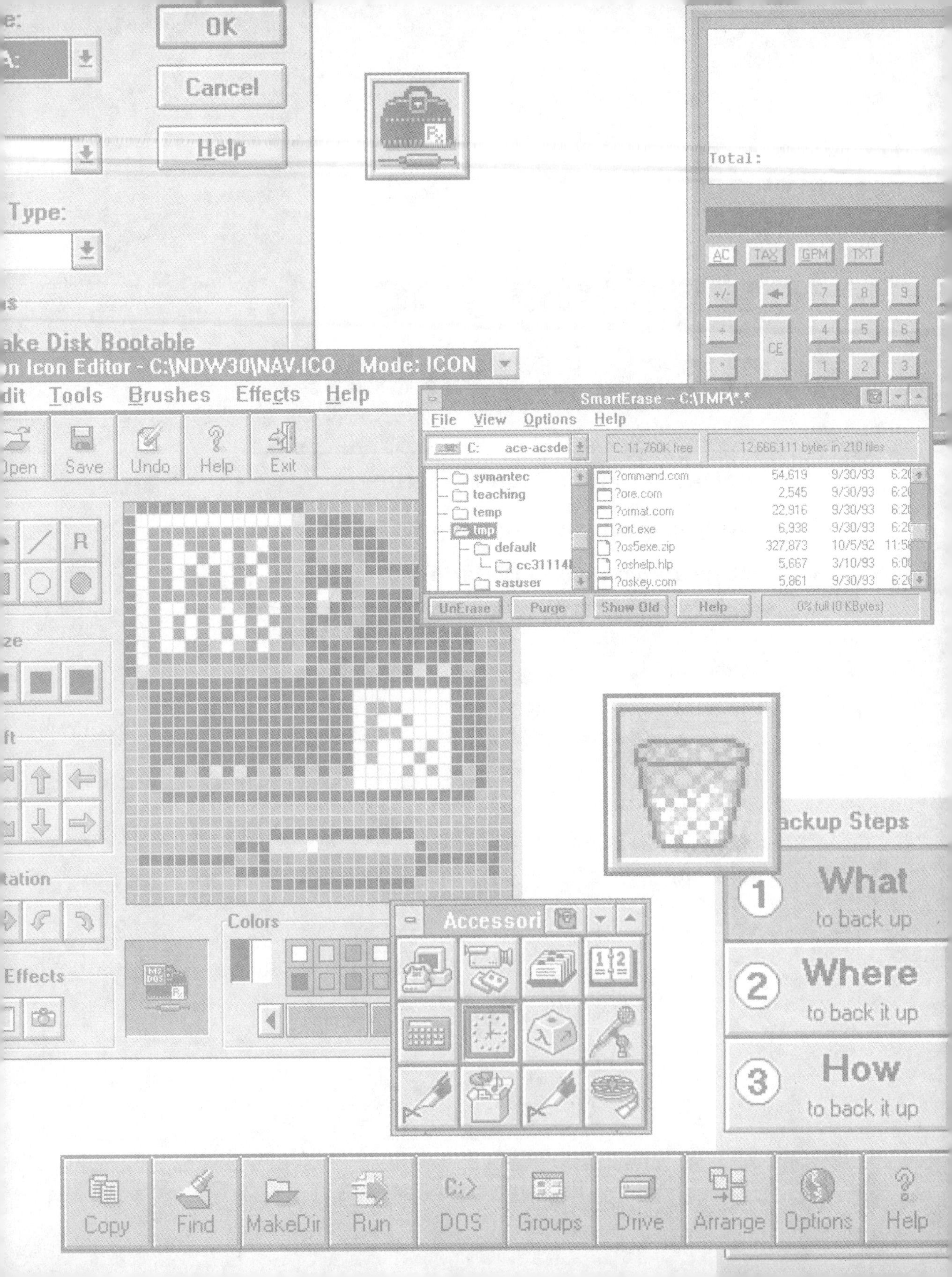
OK
Cancel
Help
Type:
ake Disk Bootable
on Icon Editor - C:\NDW30\NAV.ICO Mode: ICON
dit Tools Brushes Effects Help
Open Save Undo Help Exit
R
ze
ft
tation
Colors
Effects
Total:
AC TAX GPM TXT
CE
SmartErase - C:\TMP*.*
File View Options Help
C: ace-acsde
C: 11,760K free
12,666,111 bytes in 210 files
symantec
teaching
temp
tmp
default
cc31114
sasuser
?ommand.com 54,619 9/30/93
?ore.com 2,545 9/30/93
?ormat.com 22,916 9/30/93
?ort.exe 6,938 9/30/93
?os5exe.zip 327,873 10/5/92
?oshelp.hlp 5,667 3/10/93
?oskey.com 5,861 9/30/93
UnErase Purge Show Old Help
0% full (0 KBytes)
Accessori
ackup Steps
1 What to back up
2 Where to back it up
3 How to back it up
Copy Find MakeDir Run DOS Groups Drive Arrange Options Help

Chapter 11

Customizing Norton Desktop's Settings

The preceding chapters in this book show you Norton Desktop's many features. You learned about the numerous tools and utilities and how to perform essential operations by using the Norton Desktop environment. In short, you learned everything you need to know to be a productive user of Norton Desktop for Windows.

In this chapter, you learn to perform the following tasks:

- Configure Norton Desktop preferences
- Choose Desktop settings by menu

Most computer programs give you tools to accomplish everyday tasks, make you more productive, and make you more efficient. Norton Desktop, however, is not like most programs. Norton Desktop not only enables you to be productive, it enables you to be creative and individualistic.

Norton Desktop provides numerous options that enable you to customize the program to your own individual needs and style. Take the time to read all three chapters in this section to learn how to make Norton Desktop fit the way you want to compute. You learn how to configure Norton Desktop so that it feels right to you. You learn how to customize menus, settings, and icons to create a truly custom environment. In short, you learn how to be *you* in Norton Desktop.

Configuring Norton Desktop Preferences

You may want to configure certain options for the operation of the entire desktop. Virtually all the configuring options for all programs are found in the Desktop's Control Center. From the Control Center, you can select program options and preview how those changes affect the look of your Desktop. Click the Control Center icon or choose the **O**ptions **C**ustomize command to display the initial Control Center (Map) dialog box (see fig. 11.1).

Fig. 11.1
The Control Center (Map) dialog box is a menu for the customization of the Desktop.

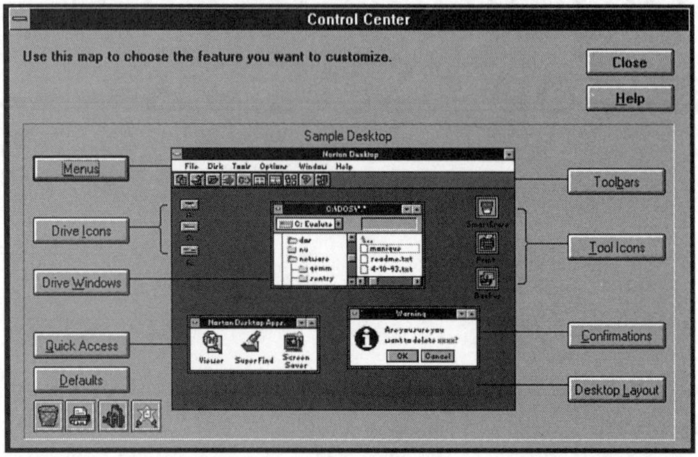

Using the Control Center

The Control Center (Map) dialog box enables you to graphically choose what part of your Desktop to configure. Each major feature of the Desktop is displayed, and a button also is displayed for that feature. Click the button related to the feature you want to configure. The following sections describe the specific items you can configure for each of these features.

Configuring Desktop Layout

The Control Center (Desktop Layout) dialog box enables you to select which items appear on your Desktop (see fig. 11.2). From this dialog box, you can choose a Title, turn the Menu bar off and on, turn the Toolbar off and on, and select the Drive icon positions.

The **B**ackground button enables you to select a wallpaper for your Desktop, and the **S**pacing option enables you to choose the amount of spacing between icons on the Desktop, which helps you keep your Desktop looking organized and planned rather than haphazard. Click the **H**elp or Treasure Chest icons to display Help information and tips about using the Control Center. After you make your selection, choose OK to exit the Control Center.

At the left of the Control Center (Desktop Layout) dialog box is a list of categories. From this category list, you can choose what parts of the program to configure. To select choices for the drive window, for example, click Drive

Windows in the **C**ategories list. The Control Center (Drive Windows) dialog box appears.

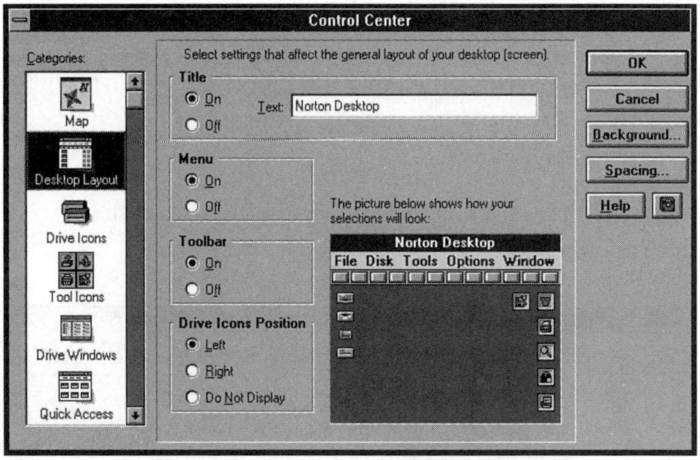

Fig. 11.2
The Control Center (Desktop Layout) dialog box enables you to choose what components appear on the Desktop.

Configuring the Drive Icons

By default, Norton Desktop displays all hard and floppy drives on your system as Drive icons and places them in the top left corner of your screen. To change the Drive Icon options, choose the Drive Icons icon from the **C**ategories list. From the Control Center (Drive Icons) dialog box, you can elect to display only hard drives, only floppy drives, or even no drives at all (see fig. 11.3). In the **D**rives list box, you can select what individual drives to display. You can even change the placement of the icons on the Desktop. The R**e**fresh button causes the program to check for all currently accessible drives. The Treasure Chest displays helpful hints about using this dialog box. The picture at the lower right corner of the dialog box shows you what the Desktop looks like with your current drive selections.

Options in this dialog box enable you to select whether to display Drive icons; which specific drives and drive types to display; whether to enable access to selected drives; and whether to place the drives on the left or right of the screen, as described in the following list:

- If you do not want to show Drive icons on the Desktop, select the Do **N**ot Display option button in the Drive Icons Position box.
- To move the Drive icons to the right of the screen, select the **R**ight placement option. Select **L**eft to display the icons at the left position.

- To show only icons for local hard drives, make sure that only the All **H**ard Drives Drive Types check box is selected. Select the All **F**loppy Drives check box to display floppy drives. Select the All **N**etwork Drives check box to display all network drives.
- To select only specific drives to display, deselect all Drive Types options and select individual drives in the **D**rives box. A check appears to the left of all selected drives.
- After you finish selecting options, choose OK to save the new configuration.

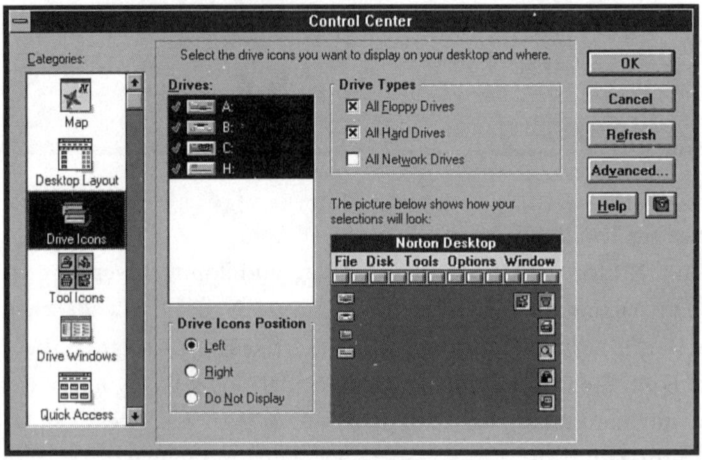

Fig. 11.3
The Control Center - (Drive Icons) dialog box enables you to choose the placement of Drive icons.

Configuring Tool Icons

After you choose the Tool Icons icon in the **C**ategories list, the Control Center (Tool Icons) dialog box appears, as shown in figure 11.4. This dialog box enables you to select which Desktop icons are displayed. A picture of the Desktop shows you what it looks like with the current selections.

The Tool Icons that you can choose to display are described in table 11.1.

Table 11.1 Tool Icons Options

Option	Description
Protection	
Speed Dis**k**	Optimizes the arrangement of files on your disk for maximum access speed.

Option	Description
Protection	
Smart**E**rase	Unerase tool.
Disk Doctor	Diagnoses and fixes problems on your disk drive.
Norton **B**ackup	Hard disk backup tool.
Norton **A**ntiVirus	Checks and protects against viruses.
Shredder	Permanently wipes out files.
File Management	
Viewer	Norton Viewer.
C**o**mpression	ZIP file compression.
Productivity	
Mail	Sends and receives E-mail.
Printers Installed List	Selection of printers.

Select the **H**elp and Treasure Chest icons to display additional information and tips about using toolbars. After you finish selecting options, choose OK to save the new configuration.

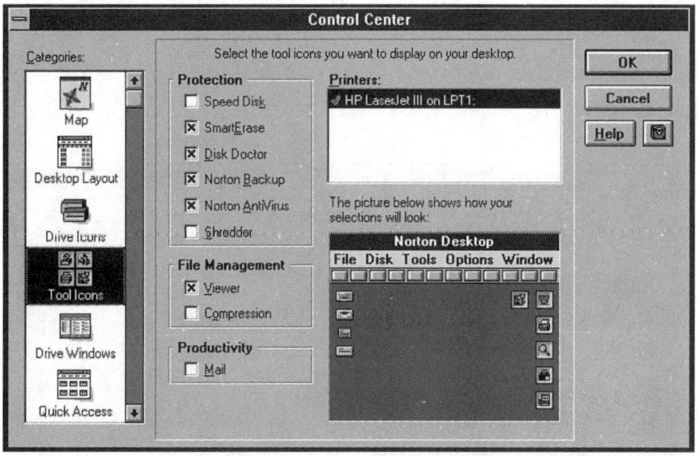

Fig. 11.4
The Control Center (Tool Icons) dialog box enables you to choose which Tool icons appear on the Desktop.

Configuring the Drive Window

The Control Center (Drive Windows) dialog box enables you to select options for how a Desktop drive window appears on-screen (see fig. 11.5). In this dialog box, you can choose to have the menu bar on or off; choose the toolbar position and whether it appears; and whether the toolbar contains textual tool buttons, graphical tool buttons, or textual and graphical tool buttons. (The graphical toolbar is a new feature of version 3 of Norton Desktop for Windows.)

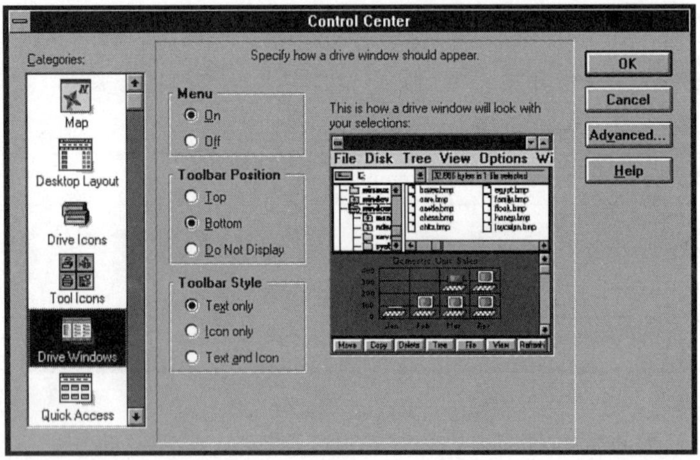

Fig. 11.5
The Control Center (Drive Windows) dialog box enables you to choose how a drive window appears on the Desktop.

After you choose the Ad**v**anced option, the Drive Window - Advanced dialog box appears, as shown in figure 11.6. This window contains a sample drive window that you can resize and position to set up the size and position of new drive windows that are opened on your Desktop. To reset the window back to its original size, select the **R**eset button.

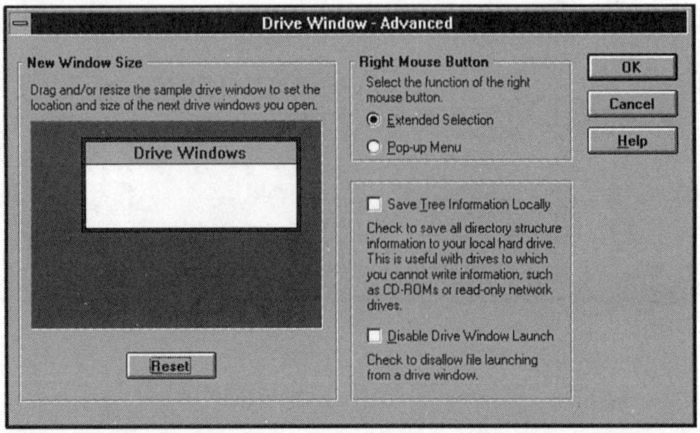

Fig. 11.6
The Drive Window - Advanced dialog box enables you to set the initial size of a drive window.

The Right Mouse Button options of the Drive Window - Advanced dialog box enable you to select the function of a right mouse button click. You can choose for this button click to mean **E**xtended Selection or to display the **P**op-Up Menu. **E**xtended Selection enables you to use the right mouse button to select multiple files from the drive window's file list. The pop-up menu contains drive window command options. The Save **T**ree Information Locally option should be used if you have a disk that cannot be used to save directory tree information, such as a CD-ROM drive. The **D**isable Drive Window Launch option enables you to prevent file launching from a drive window. After you size the sample window and set any other Advanced options, click OK to return to the Control Center (Drive Windows) dialog box.

Configuring the Quick Access Window

After you choose the Quick Access category in the Control Center, the Control Center (Quick Access) dialog box appears, as shown in figure 11.7. This dialog box enables you to choose options about how the Quick Access window appears on your Desktop.

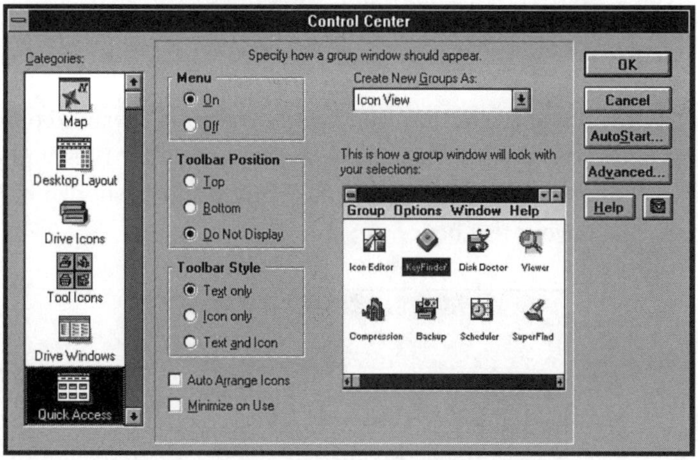

Fig. 11.7
The Control Center (Quick Access) dialog box enables you to choose how your Quick Access windows are displayed.

In Chapter 8, "Launching Files with Norton Desktop," you learn how to work with Quick Access and how to determine which of the three views (Icon View, File View, or Toolbox View) to use. Quick Access, however, has some additional configuration options.

In the Menu area, you can choose **O**n or O**f**f to make the main Group menu visible or not. The toolbar Position area controls the location of the toolbar on the group. These options include **T**op, **B**ottom, or **D**o Not Display. If you choose to make the toolbar visible, you can choose the style of the Toolbar from the Toolbar Style area. You can select from Te**x**t Only, **I**con Only, or Text **a**nd Icon. These options are similar to the Control Center (Drive Windows) Toolbar Style options.

If you select the Auto A**r**range Icons check box, icons within group windows are automatically rearranged whenever the group window is resized. If you select the **M**inimize on Use check box, the group window automatically appears as an icon whenever one of the items is opened.

In the Control Center (Quick Access) dialog box, you also can select which view to use for new groups you create. Open the Create New **G**roups As drop-down list box, and select from Icon View, List View, or Toolbox.

Choose the Auto**S**tart button to select the group you want to start upon running Windows. You will probably choose to use the Windows' StartUp group as the AutoStart group.

Note

You can select only one group to activate upon starting Windows.

By selecting the Ad**v**anced button, you can choose more advanced options from the Quick Access - Advanced dialog box (see fig. 11.8). These options include specifying the name of your topmost group and the horizontal and vertical spacing of your text boxes.

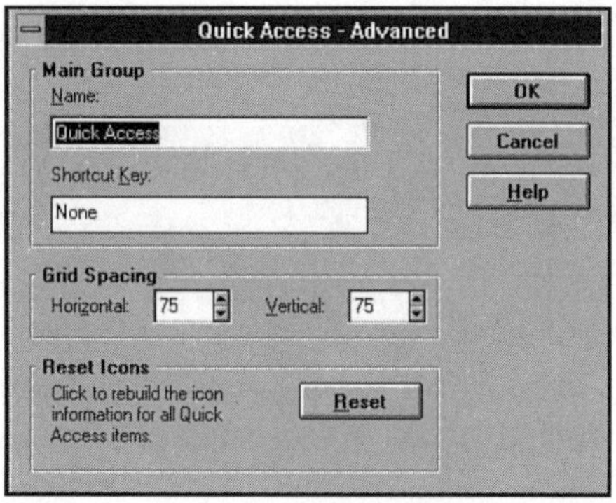

Fig. 11.8
The Quick Access - Advanced dialog box enables you to change the name of your topmost group.

If you do not like the name Quick Access, you can change the name of the main Quick Access Group by entering new text into the **N**ame text box. You can even use the Shortcut **K**ey text box to assign a shortcut key to access the Quick Access menu.

You can select the Horizontal and **V**ertical spacing between group item icons by using the corresponding increment arrows in the Grid Spacing area. The spacing is measured in pixels; 75 pixels is the default spacing.

Finally, you can choose to entirely rebuild the icons of the Quick Access group with their original options by selecting the **R**eset button from the Reset Icons area.

Configuring Toolbars

The Toolbar contains a number of icons that give you instant access to often needed commands. After you choose the Toolbars icon from the Category list, the Control Center (Toolbars) dialog box appears (see fig. 11.9).

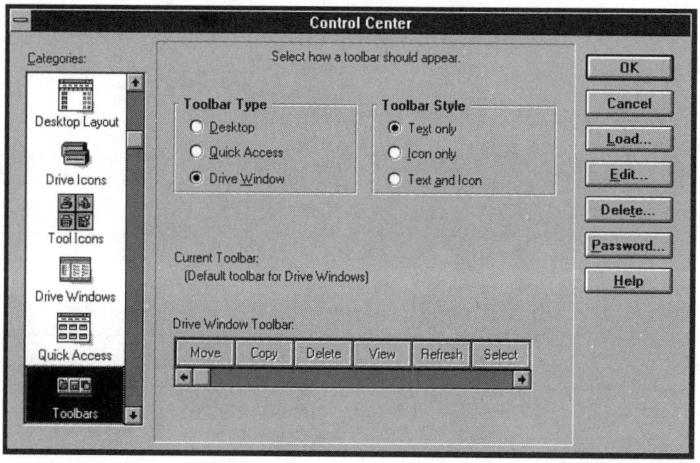

Fig. 11.9
The Control Center (Toolbars) dialog box enables you to choose how your toolbars look on the Desktop.

Three types of Toolbars can be configured in this dialog box: **D**esktop, **Q**uick Access, and Drive **W**indow. You can choose a Toolbar Style for each Toolbar Type. The default toolbars are described in table 11.2.

Table 11.2 Default Toolbars

Tool/Button	Function
Desktop Toolbar (Default Style: Text and Icon)	
Copy	Copies files.
Find	SuperFind.
MakeDir	Makes a directory.

(continues)

III Designing the Perfect Desktop

Table 11.2 Continued

Tool/Button	Function
Desktop Toolbar (Default Style: Text and Icon)	
Run	Runs a DOS or Windows program.
DOS	Displays a DOS window.
Groups	Displays the Quick Access window.
Drive	Opens a drive window.
Arrange	Arranges Desktop icons.
Options	Displays the Control Center.
Help	Displays the Help menu.
Exit	Exits Windows.
Quick Access Toolbar (Default Style: Text only)	
Open	Opens a Quick Access Group.
New Item	Creates a new Quick Access Group.
Delete	Deletes a directory or files.
Prop	Changes the properties of a file or group items.
Run	Runs a DOS or Windows program.
Arrange	Arrange icons on the Desktop.
Drive Window Toolbar (Default Style: Text only)	
Move	Moves files.
Copy	Copies files.
Delete	Deletes files.
View	Views contents of files with Viewer.
Refresh	Rescans directories.
Select	Selects files to display.
Filter	Defines a filter for displaying file names.
Edit	Edits a file.
By Name	Sorts by file names.

Tool/Button	Function
By Type	Sorts file names by type.
MakeDir	Makes a directory.
Rename	Renames a file.

In the Toolbar Style box, you can choose to display the toolbar in one of three ways: Te**x**t Only, **I**con Only, or Text **a**nd Icon.

By choosing the **E**dit button to access the Toolbars - Edit dialog box, you can select from a list of icons which icons appear in the toolbar (see fig. 11.10).

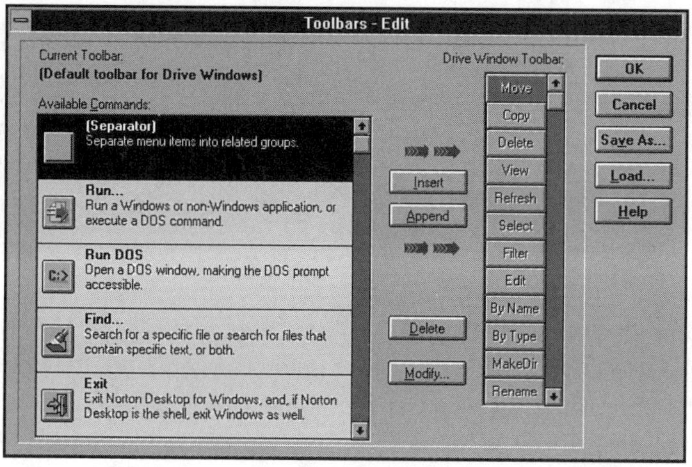

Fig. 11.10
The Toolbars - Edit dialog box enables you to customize the toolbar commands.

The Toolbars - Edit dialog box enables you to select other icons to appear in the Toolbar. To add a new tool (for example, Print) to the beginning of the Toolbar, follow these steps:

1. Choose the Print command from the Available **C**ommands list.
2. Choose the **I**nsert button to insert the Print icon into the sample toolbar.
3. Choose OK to return to the Control Center (Toolbars) dialog box. The Print command now appears in the sample toolbar.
4. Choose OK to exit the Control Center.

Selecting Menu Options

After you select the Menus option in the **C**ategories list, the Control Center (Menus) dialog box appears, as shown in figure 11.11. This dialog box enables you to create customized menus for your Desktop. The steps for customizing your menus are discussed in detail in Chapter 12, "Creating a Menu-Based Desktop."

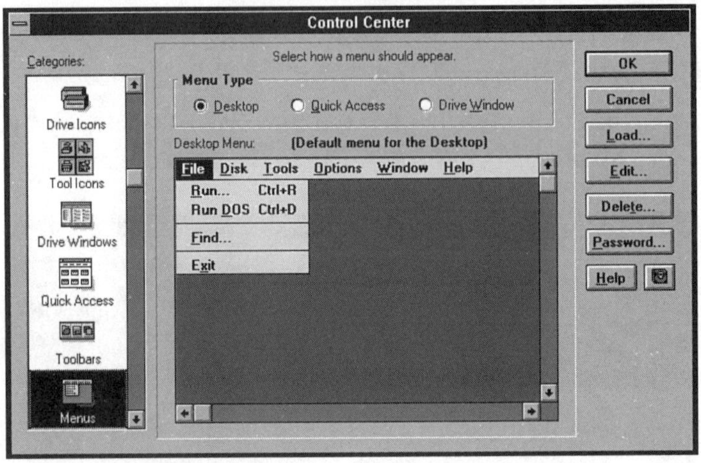

Fig. 11.11
The Control Center (Menus) dialog box enables you to customize your Desktop menus.

Selecting Confirmation Options

After you select the Confirmations icon in the **C**ategories list, the Control Center (Confirmations) dialog box appears, as shown in figure 11.12. This dialog box enables you to choose when you want the program to display a confirmation notice before carrying out a command. For example, after you highlight a file name and choose **D**elete, the message `Are you sure you want to delete the file?` appears, and you must answer OK before the file is actually deleted. If you deselect the **D**elete File check box in the Control Center (Confirmations) dialog box, the file is deleted without the program displaying the confirmation notice.

The commands for which you can select to use a confirmation notice or not include the following:

Exit Norton Desktop

Mouse Operation (any action you specify with the mouse, such as deleting or launching a file)

Unassociated Print (a print request using a file that is not associated with an application)

Delete File

Delete **S**ubdirectory

Replace File

Move **G**roup

If you choose the **A**dvanced button in the Control Center (Confirmations) dialog box, the Confirmation - Advanced dialog box appears (see fig. 11.13). In this dialog box, you can specify when the program prompts you for a file name, even if you have a file name highlighted in a drive window. The options are **E**dit File, **V**iew File, **P**rint File, and **D**elete File.

After you select the advanced confirmations you want, choose OK to return to the Control Center (Confirmations) dialog box, and then choose OK again to exit the Control Center.

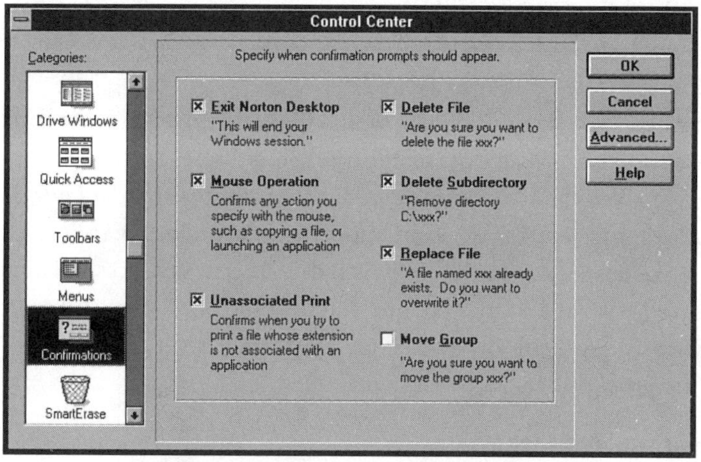

Fig. 11.12
The Control Center (Confirmations) dialog box enables you to choose when a confirmation question is asked.

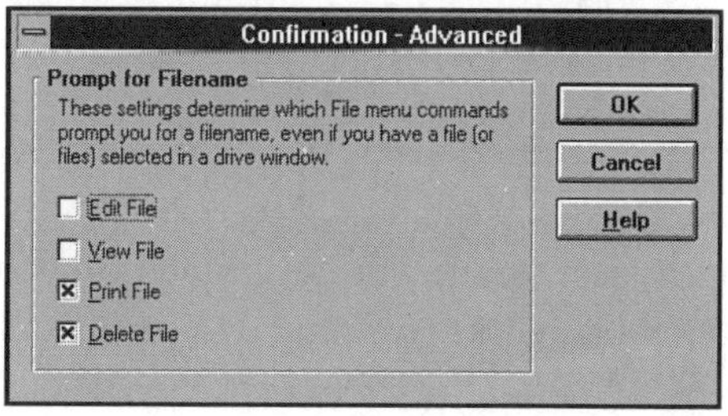

Fig. 11.13
The Confirmation - Advanced dialog box enables you to choose when you are prompted for a file name.

Configuring SmartErase

After you choose the SmartErase icon in the **C**ategories list, the Control Center (SmartErase) dialog box appears (see fig. 11.14). The use of SmartErase is covered in detail in Chapter 25, "Using SmartErase."

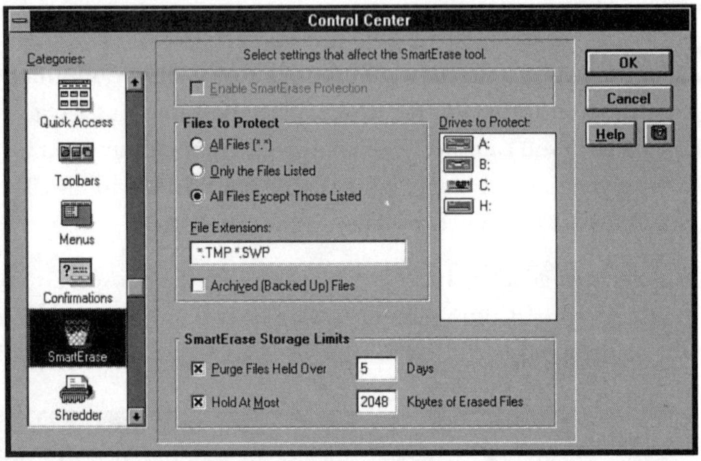

Fig. 11.14 The Control Center (SmartErase) dialog box enables you to choose files to protect and the storage limits of SmartErase.

In this dialog box, you can choose which files and drives to protect after they are erased and can set up storage limits for SmartErase. The **F**ile Extension text box enables you to enter file specifications for files that are not protected if the All Files **E**xcept Those Listed option is chosen. The SmartErase Storage Limits box enables you to choose how many days to save files before they are purged and enables you to set a limit to how much disk space is used in protecting erased files. The **D**rives to Protect list enables you to choose which drives are protected.

Configuring Shredder

After you choose the Shredder icon in the **C**ategories list, the Control Center (Shredder) dialog box appears (see fig. 11.15). Shredder is a program that permanently erases files; it is covered in detail in Chapter 23, "Using Shredder."

In the Control Center (Shredder) dialog box, you can specify whether to use the US **G**overnment Shredding standard. You also can specify a Special **O**ver-Write Pattern and a **R**epeat Count. The government shredding standard overwrites the information on a disk according to Department of Defense (DOD) specifications. These call for a 1/0 pattern (a pattern of 1s and 0s) to be written to the disk three times, a random number to be written to the disk, and the last number written to the disk to be read back from the disk for verification (DOD 5220.22-M). The government adopted these specifications because a single erasure of magnetic information may not be enough. A faint "fingerprint" may remain on a disk after a single erasure. The Use Special **O**ver-Write Pattern and **R**epeat Count options enable you to specify some other pattern and number of overwrites.

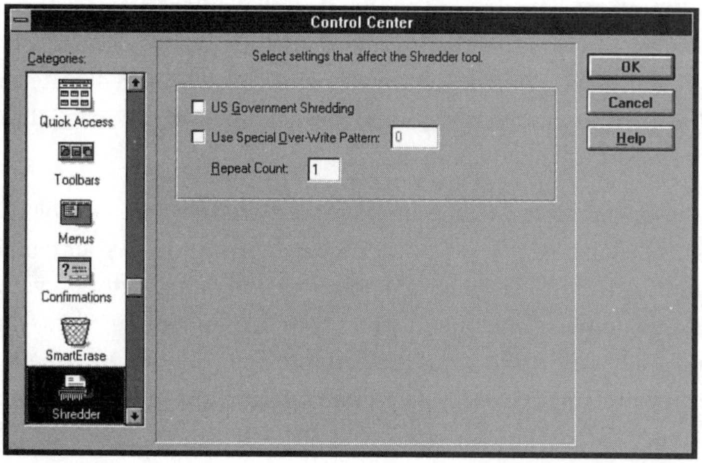

Fig. 11.15
The Control Center (Shredder) dialog box enables you to choose how files are shredded.

Configuring Compression

File Compression enables you to shrink the amount of disk space required to store a file. Several methods of compression exist, giving you an opportunity to choose which method you prefer (see fig. 11.16). In the Storage Method box, you can choose for the program to Automatically Select **B**est Method or choose to always use the H**i**ghest Compression, Super **F**ast, or **N**o Compression options. The H**i**ghest Compression option offers the best file size reduction, but takes more time than does the Super **F**ast option.

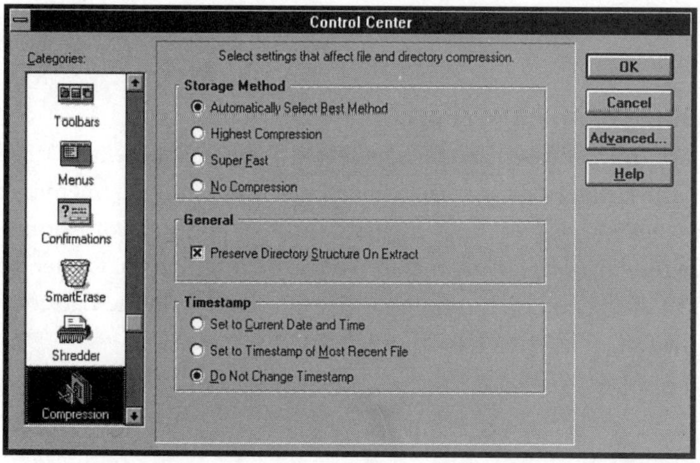

Fig. 11.16
The Control Center (Compression) dialog box enables you to choose a method for compressing files.

If a number of files are compressed, they are placed in a file with a ZIP extension. In the General box, you can choose to have the files compressed so that their full path names are retained. This may help you replace files to the correct directory after the files are uncompressed (unzipped).

In the Timestamp box, you can choose the following options for the compressed files' date and timestamps (the dates and times associated with files when you display a directory of the file names): Set to **C**urrent Date and Time (the time they are compressed), Set to Timestamp of **M**ost Recent File (in the list), or **D**o Not Change Timestamp.

The Ad**v**anced button activates the Compression - Advanced dialog box. From this dialog box, you can select the directory in which your temporary files are stored. Storing all your temporary files in one directory is very efficient. Large numbers of temporary files scattered throughout your hard drive can drastically slow down your disk performance. You can use SuperFind to locate all your temporary files. (For more information, see Chapter 27, "Using SuperFind.")

Configuring FileAssist

After you choose the FileAssist option in the **C**ategories list, the Control Center (FileAssist) dialog box appears, as shown in figure 11.17. In this dialog box, you can select what information is displayed in FileAssist dialog boxes. In the Options box, you can choose to include **F**ile Description/Information, how many **R**ecently Opened Files to list, whether to enable **S**peed Search and S**m**art Fill, and whether to display the dialog box by using a 3-D **L**ook and Feel. You also can choose the **O**verride Application-Level Settings option if you want to override FileAssist settings you may have previously adjusted in specific applications and instead use the settings you specify here. Select the **E**nable FileAssist check box to enable FileAssist dialog boxes for use in your applications.

Configuring Program Defaults

In the Control Center (Defaults) dialog box, you can choose the **D**efault Viewer, the Default **E**ditor, select which objects have pop-up menus, and choose whether to save your configuration each time you exit Norton Desktop (not always recommended). You access the Control Center (Defaults) dialog box by choosing the Defaults icon from the **C**ategories list in the Control Center (see fig. 11.18).

Choose the **A**dvanced button to display additional default options (see fig. 11.19). In the Defaults - Advanced dialog box, you can choose what items appear on Desktop Control menus: Launch **L**ist, **T**ask List, Launch **M**anager, and **R**un. You can select the Hide **S**criptMaker Icon check box to hide this icon while ScriptMaker is running. Selecting the File Manager E**x**tensions on Main Desktop Menu check box enables third party applications that attach menus to the Windows File Manager to attach them to the main Norton Desktop menu bar. By selecting the **L**oad Quick Access check box, you can enable Quick Access to group windows after you start Norton Desktop.

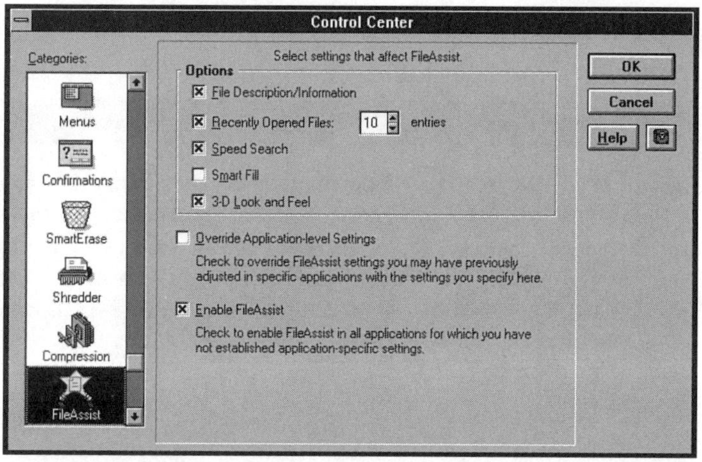

Fig. 11.17
The Control Center (FileAssist) dialog box enables you to select what information is available in FileAssist dialog boxes.

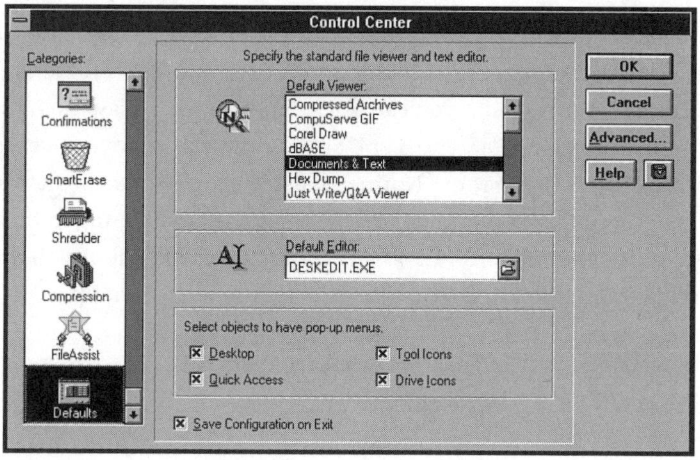

Fig. 11.18
The Control Center (Defaults) dialog box enables you to choose program defaults.

III

Designing the Perfect Desktop

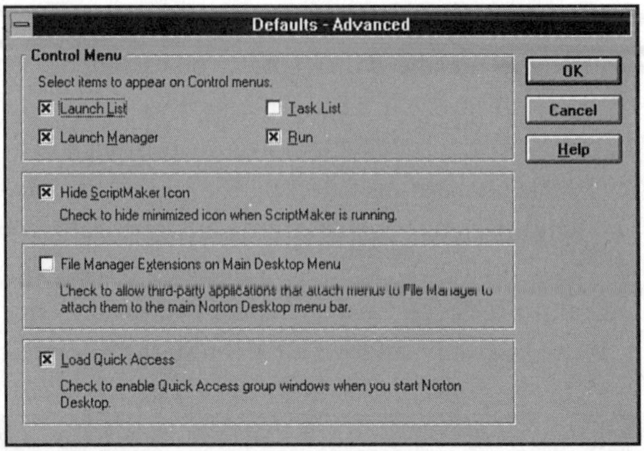

Fig. 11.19
The Defaults - Advanced dialog box enables you to choose additional default options.

Note

You may want to deselect the **S**ave Configuration on Exit check box in the Control Center (Defaults) dialog box if you are creating an icon-based custom Desktop. In this case, you arrange the items on the Desktop to your liking and then save that particular configuration. You do not want to save on exit, as the Desktop may not be correctly arranged at that time. See Chapter 13, "Creating an Icon-Based Desktop," for more details.

Choosing Desktop Settings by Menu

Besides using the Control Center to select Desktop options, you also can choose a limited number of program options from the **O**ptions menu (see fig. 11.20). From this menu, you can select whether to display the **Dr**ive Icons, Tool **I**cons, Title **B**ar, and **T**oolbar. You also can choose to save your current Desktop configuration. Normally, using the **S**ave Configuration option to save your Desktop is preferable to using the **S**ave Configuration on Exit option shown in figure 11.18. This eliminates the possibility that you may accidentally save some temporary changes in your Desktop.

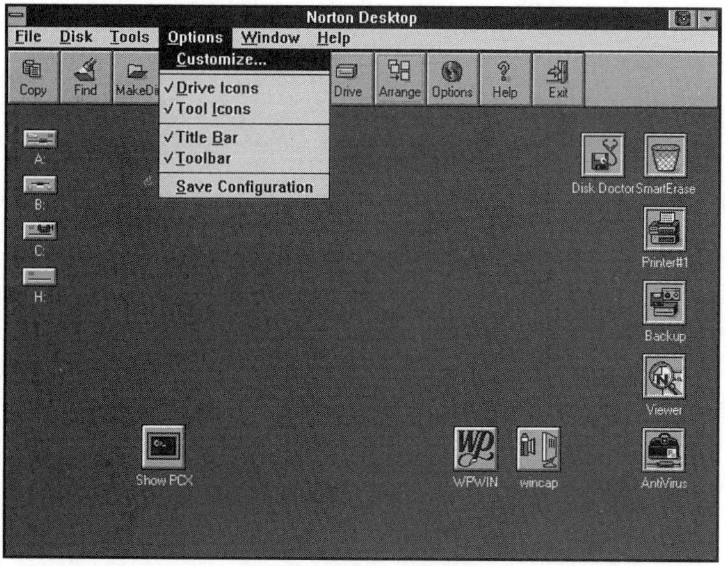

Fig. 11.20
The **Options** pull-down menu also enables you to customize the Norton Desktop.

Summary

This chapter showed you dozens of ways to customize your Desktop for your personal preferences by using the Control Center. You learned how to configure your Desktop Layout, Drive Icons, Tool Icons, Drive Windows, Quick Access, Toolbars, Menus, Confirmations, SmartErase, Shredder, Compression, FileAssist, and Defaults.

Chapter 12, "Creating a Menu-Based Desktop," shows you how to further customize Norton Desktop for a menu-based Desktop.

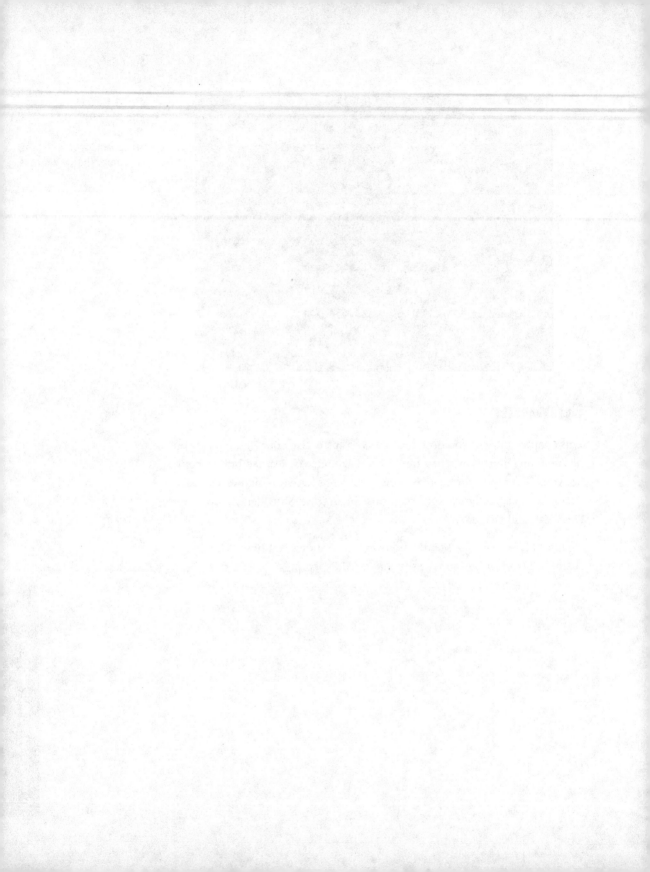

Chapter 12

Creating a Menu-Based Desktop

Menus and icons are the two most popular options that graphics-based computer programs offer users for accessing functions. Although command lines also are useful, most Windows users tend toward menus or icons.

If you prefer the instant access to functions that an icon offers, see Chapter 13, "Creating an Icon-Based Desktop," for a detailed discussion of the Norton Desktop 3 for Windows icon-based desktop.

NDW also offers a menu-based desktop for those who prefer to use pull-down menus. Menus offer access to various menu commands and options through a series of cascading menus, as well as direct shortcut-key access to commonly used commands.

In this chapter, you learn to perform the following tasks:

- Understand Norton Desktop menus
- Modify the menu structure
- Load new menus
- Customize menus
- Create new menus for your computing needs

Understanding Norton Desktop Menus

The menu bar is the collection of pull-down menus located at the top of every Windows screen. Each application has its own unique menu bar, although certain menus and commands, such as the placement of the **F**ile menu and the commands on the **W**indow menu, are semi-standardized for all Windows applications.

Each menu, after it is opened, displays a "submenu" of commands. These commands (referred to as menu items) choose various operations and options necessary for the given application and are often grouped within a menu, with different groups separated by *separator lines*. Menu items often cascade into additional menus, or, after being chosen, branch to related dialog boxes. Figure 12.1 shows the default Norton Desktop 3 for Windows menu bar.

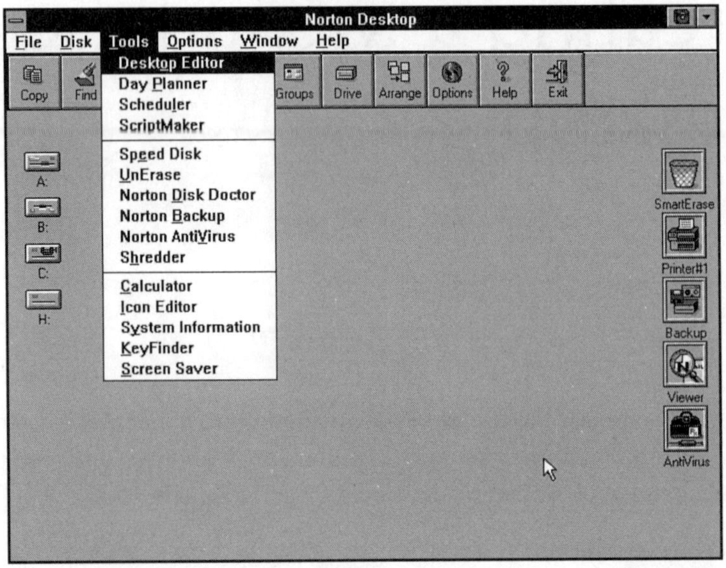

Fig. 12.1
The default Norton Desktop menu bar with the **T**ools menu open.

Certain commands also have associated shortcut keys that enable access to the command without having to pull down the menu. You can pull down a menu by pressing Alt plus the underlined letter on the menu (for example, Alt+F opens the **F**ile menu). You also can access the menu bar by pressing F10 and then using the right- and left-arrow keys to move from menu to menu. After you press Enter, you open the currently selected menu.

Norton Desktop permits the use of multiple menu systems. You can change menus in Norton Desktop as easily as you load new applications. You can even create custom menus and menu bars to personalize your computing environment for your own particular needs.

Modifying the Menu Structure

The entire menu structure of your Desktop can be changed by using the Control Center (Menus) dialog box. After you choose **O**ptions **C**ustomize to access the Control Center dialog box and then select Menus, the Control Center (Menus) dialog box for the Desktop menu appears, as shown in figure 12.2.

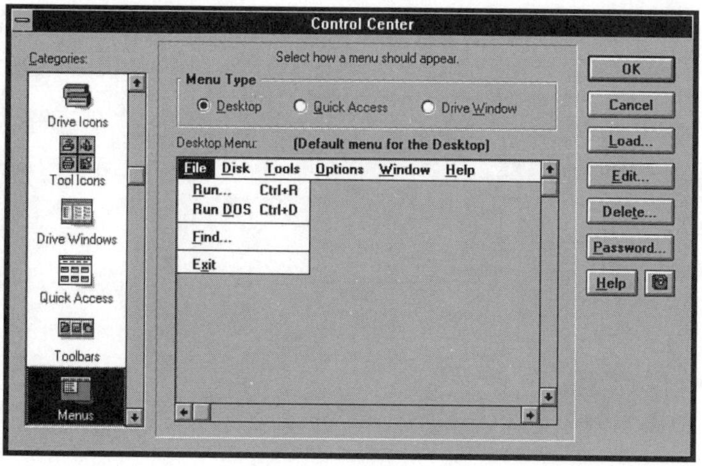

Fig. 12.2
The Control Center (Menus) options screen, showing the default Desktop menu bar.

This screen enables you to modify the menu structure for three types of Desktop menus. Use the Menu Type options to choose which menu to edit. Figure 12.3 shows the Menus option screen for **Q**uick Access, and figure 12.4 shows the Menus option screen for Drive **W**indows. Notice that the menus for each type are different. You can customize the menus for any or all of the three menu types. The following sections describe menu editing techniques that are the same for all three menu types.

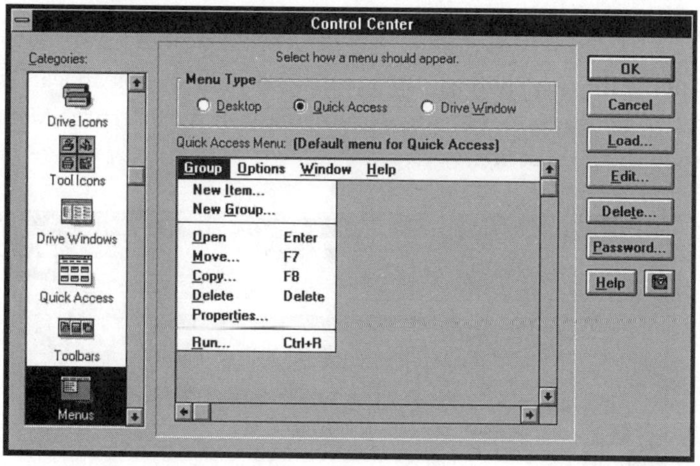

Fig. 12.3
The Control Center (Menus) options screen, showing the default Quick Access menu.

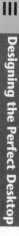

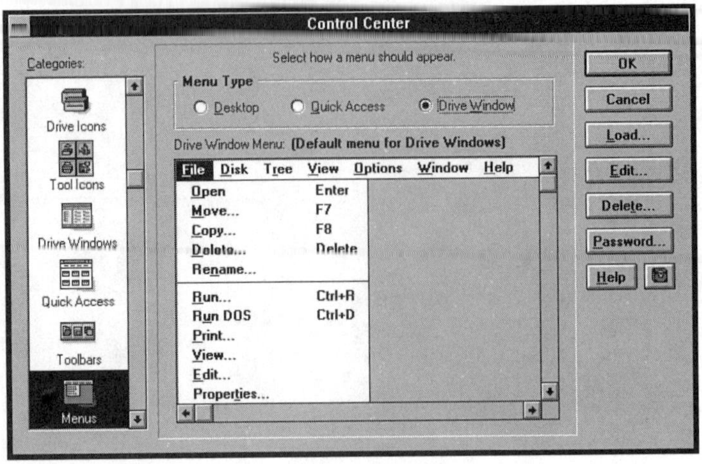

Fig 12.4
The Control Center (Menus) options screen, showing the default Drive **W**indow menu.

Loading New Menus

Loading a new menu is easy. Menu systems are stored in menu files with MNU extensions. Choose the Control Center (Menus) **L**oad button to load MNU files into Norton Desktop.

To load a new menu, follow these steps:

1. Choose in the Control Center (Menus) dialog box which menu type you want to modify: **D**esktop, **Q**uick Access, or Drive **W**indow.
2. Choose the **L**oad button. The Menus - Load dialog box appears (see fig. 12.5). All current menu options appear in the **S**elect the Menu To Be Loaded list box.

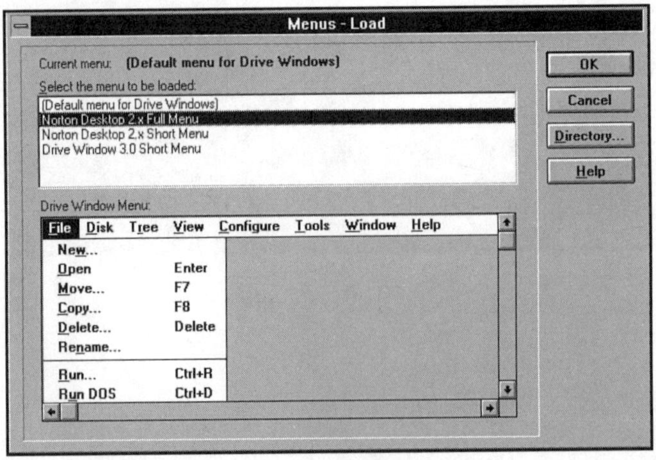

Fig. 12.5
The Menus - Load dialog box enables you to load a predefined menu file.

3. Select the menu you want from the current list, or choose the **D**irectory button to select from another directory. After you first load Norton Desktop for Windows, the default menus are selected. Notice that the menu options include Norton Desktop 2.x Full Menu and Short Menu options. If you want to use the full or short menus that were present in the 2.x version of Norton Desktop, you can choose one of these options. Also shown in figure 12.5 is a Drive Window Short Menu option for Norton Desktop version 3.

4. After you select the new menu, choose OK to close the dialog box and load the menu.

Norton Desktop 2.0 came with two predefined menus: Full and Short. The Short and Full menus feature the same menu titles on the menu bar but have different menu items on each menu. NDW 3 also has a Short Menu option for the Desktop and drive windows. As you may expect, Full has more items than Short. Table 12.1 compares the Short and Full menus for the Norton 3 Desktop and drive windows. Quick Access menus have no short version.

Table 12.1 Item Comparison of the Short and Full Menus

Menu Item	In Short Menu?
Desktop Menu Comparison	
***F**ile Menu*	
Run	Y
R**u**n DOS	N
Find	Y
E**x**it	Y
***D**isk Menu*	
Copy Diskette	Y
Format Diskette	Y
Label Disk	N
Connect **N**et Drive	N

(continues)

Table 12.1 Continued

Menu Item	In Short Menu?
Desktop Menu Comparison	
Disconnect Net Drive	N
Share as	N
S**t**op Sharing	N
***T**ools Menu*	
Deskt**o**p Editor	Y
Day **P**lanner	Y
Schedu**l**er	Y
Sc**r**iptMaker	N
Sp**e**ed Disk	Y
Unerase	Y
Norton **D**isk Doctor	Y
Norton **B**ackup	Y
Norton Anti**V**irus	Y
S**h**redder	N
Calculator	Y
Icon Editor	Y
S**y**stem Information	N
Key Finder	Y
Screen Saver	Y
***O**ptions Menu*	
Customize	Y
Drive Icons	Y
Tool **I**cons	Y

Menu Item	In Short Menu?
Title **B**ar	Y
Toolbar	Y
Save Configuration	Y
W*indow Menu*	
Open **D**rive Window	Y
Open **Q**uick Access	Y
A**r**range Desktop Icons	Y
Cascade	Y
Tile	Y
Close **A**ll	Y
Hide All	Y
H*elp Menu*	
Quick Help	Y
Contents	Y
Search for Help on	Y
How to use Help	Y
About	Y
Drive Window Menu Comparison	
F*ile Menu*	
Open	Y
Move	Y
Copy	Y
Delete	Y
Re**n**ame	Y
Run	Y

(continues)

Table 12.1 Continued

Menu Item	In Short Menu?
Drive Window Menu Comparison	
R**u**n DOS	N
Print	Y
View	Y
Edit	N
Proper**t**ies	Y
Associate	N
C**o**mpress	N
Send Mai**l**	N
Ma**k**e Directory	Y
Compare Director**y**	Y
Find	Y
Select	N
Dese**l**ect	N
***D**isk Menu*	
Copy Diskette	Y
Format Diskette	Y
Label Disk	N
Connect **N**et Drive	N
Disconnect Net Drive	N
Share as	N
S**t**op Sharing	N
*T**r**ee Menu*	
Show **Z**ips as Directories	N
Use Collapsible Trees	Y
Expand **O**ne Level	Y

Menu Item	In Short Menu?
E**x**pand Branch	Y
Expand **A**ll	Y
Collapse Branch	Y
C**o**llapse All	Y
***V**iew Menu*	
Tree Pane	Y
File Pane	Y
View Pane	Y
S**h**ow All	N
Refresh	Y
File **D**etails	Y
File Fi**l**ter	Y
Fo**n**t	Y
Sort	Y
Vie**w**er	N
***O**ptions Menu*	
Customize	Y
Toolbar	Y
***W**indow Menu*	
Open **D**rive Window	Y
***H**elp Menu*	
Quick Help	Y
Contents	Y
Search for Help on	Y
How to use Help	Y
About	Y

Use the Load Menu dialog box not only to change between NDW's two pre-defined menus, but also to load any custom menus you create. Creating a custom menu is simple, as explained in the following section.

Customizing Menus

In Norton Desktop, you can edit existing menu bars by adding or deleting menu items. You also can create completely new menu bars with menu titles and menu items of your choice. You do all your editing and creating in the Menus - Edit dialog box.

Learning the Menus - Edit Dialog Box

Access the Menus - Edit dialog box by first selecting a menu type in the Control Center (Menus) dialog box and then choosing the **E**dit button (see fig. 12.6).

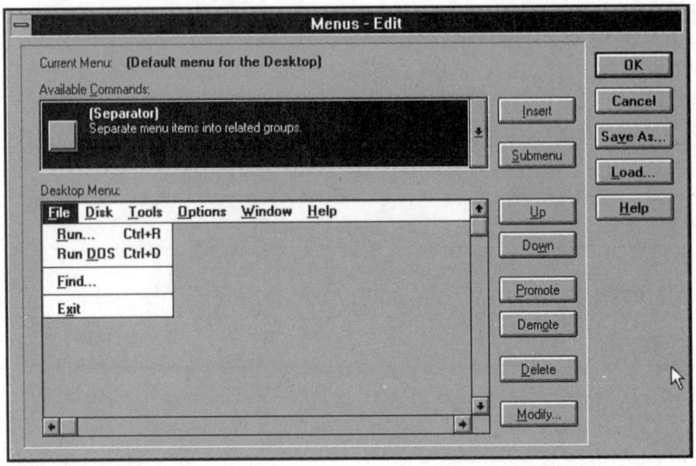

Fig. 12.6
The Menus - Edit dialog box.

The Menus - Edit dialog box contains the elements and commands listed in table 12.2.

Table 12.2 Menus - Edit Dialog Box Elements and Commands

Element/Command	Function
Current Menu	The name of the current menu.
Available **C**ommands	A listing of all the standard Desktop commands you can add to a menu system.

Element/Command	Function
Desktop Menu	Displays the menu structure of the current menu file; items can be dragged to new locations within this structure.
Insert	Places the currently selected command into the menu.
Submenu	Creates a submenu branching off the currently selected menu command.
Up	Moves the selected item up through the Menu list.
Do**w**n	Moves the selected item down through the Menu list.
Promote	Moves the selected menu title or item up one level in the menu hierarchy.
Dem**o**te	Moves the selected menu title or item down one level in the menu hierarchy.
Delete	Deletes the selected item from the menu.
Modify	Edits the current menu name.
OK	Saves the current file and exits the Menus - Edit dialog box.
Cancel	Cancels all operations in progress and exits the Menus - Edit dialog box.
Sa**v**e As	Saves the current menu file under a new file name.
Load	Opens the Load Menu dialog box so that you can load a different MNU file in the Menus - Edit dialog box.
Help	Accesses the on-line Help system.

Tip

Commands from the **W**indow menu do not appear on this list because the **W**indow menu cannot be altered.

The following sections describe how to use the Menus - Edit dialog box to perform specific functions.

Adding New Menu Items

Adding a new menu item is as simple as selecting the command in the Desktop menu where you want the command to appear, choosing an available command, and clicking the **I**nsert button. Assume that you want to add a **L**abel Disk command just above the E**x**it menu item on the Desktop's **F**ile menu. Follow these steps:

1. Scroll through the Available **C**ommands list until you locate the command you want, and then select the command. In this case, select the **L**abel Disk menu item (see fig. 12.7).

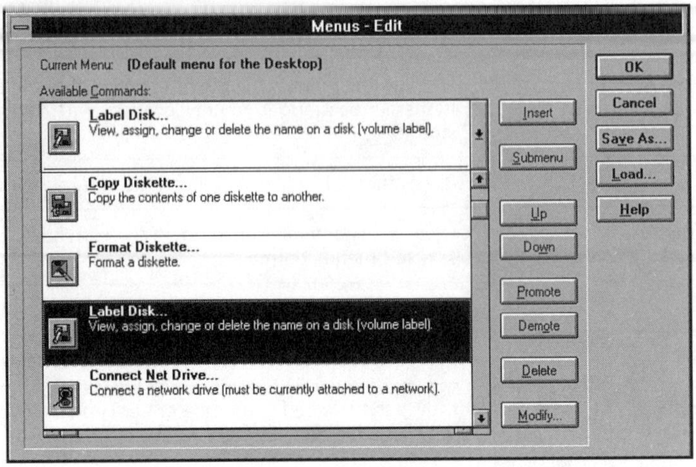

Fig. 12.7 The **L**abel Disk command selected in the Available **C**ommands list.

2. Select the item in the menu so that the new item appears above the selected item. In this case, select the E**x**it menu item on the **F**ile menu.

3. Choose the **I**nsert button. The new menu item is inserted into the menu structure. Figure 12.8 shows a new **L**abel disk command added to the Desktop **F**ile menu.

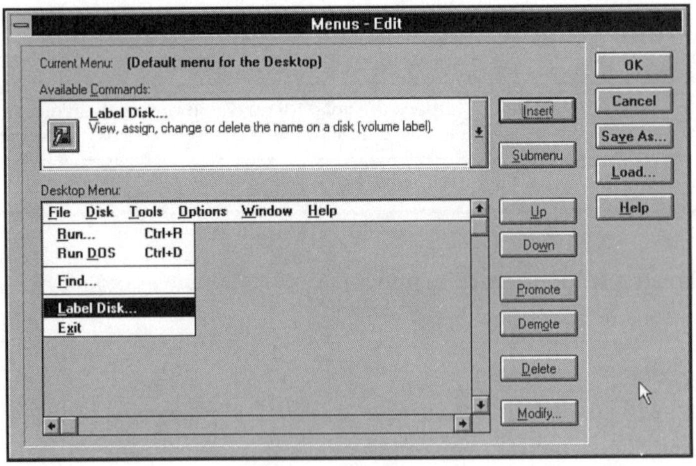

Fig. 12.8 The **L**abel Disk command inserted above the E**x**it command.

Deleting Menu Items

Deleting a menu item is as simple as selecting the item and choosing the **D**elete button. Follow these steps:

1. Select the item for deletion in the menu.
2. Choose the **D**elete button.

Assume, for example, that you want to delete the **L**abel Disk command from the menu structure. Follow these steps:

1. Select the **L**abel Disk command in the **F**ile pull-down menu.
2. Choose the **D**elete button.

Tip

To add a separator line to the menu structure, select the separator line at the top of the Available **C**ommands list and **I**nsert it into the Menu list.

Rearranging Menu Items

You can use either the keyboard or the mouse to rearrange items in the menu structure.

To move items up or down the structure by using the mouse, follow these steps:

1. Select the item you want to move.
2. Choose the **U**p button to move the item up the menu, or choose Do**w**n to move the item down the menu.

You also can move items up and down the menu list by using the keyboard. Follow these steps:

1. Use the up- and down-arrow keys to select the item you want to move.
2. To move an item up in the list, press Alt+U. Repeat this step to move the item up additional levels.
3. To move an item down in the list, press Alt+W. Repeat this step to move the item down additional levels.

Promoting and Demoting Menu Items

You also can promote menu items from the pull-down menu to the menu bar or demote them from the menu bar to a pull-down menu. Follow these steps to promote an item:

1. Select in the menu list the item that you want to promote. For example, select the **F**ind item on the **F**ile menu.

2. Choose the **P**romote button.

Notice in figure 12.9 that the **F**ind option is now in the menu bar following the **F**ile option.

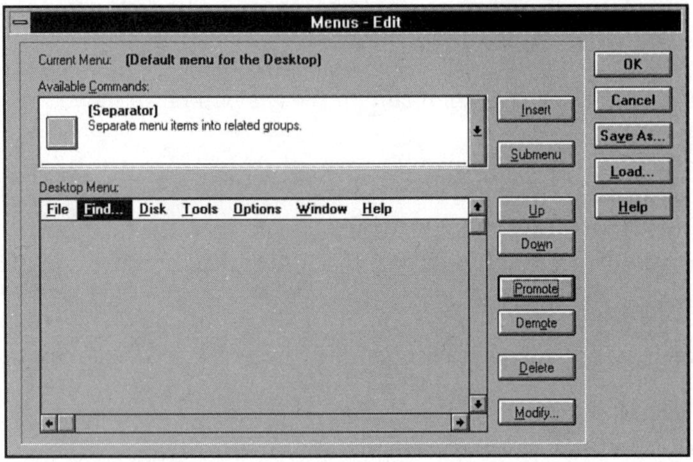

Fig. 12.9
The Find command promoted to menu title status.

To demote an item from the menu bar to a pull-down menu, select the item; then choose Dem**o**te. If you demote the **F**ind item, it goes to the bottom of the **F**ile pull-down menu. You must then use the **U**p or Do**w**n buttons to reposition it in the **F**ile menu.

Creating Custom Menu Items

If you cannot find the right command in the Available **C**ommands list, you can always create a custom menu item. This custom item can be either a menu title or a menu item.

Why would you want to create a custom menu item? You may want to assign a menu slot to your favorite application program. You may even want to make a frequently used document a menu item. By creating custom menu items, you can launch applications, documents—even macros and ScriptMaker scripts—directly from a Norton Desktop menu.

One of the options on the Available **C**ommands list is Custom Item. You can add a Custom Item to the menu bar the same way you add other commands. Follow these steps:

1. Select the place on the menu where you want to insert the Custom Item.

2. Choose Custom Item from the Available **C**ommands list.

3. Choose **I**nsert.

Figure 12.10 shows a Custom Item inserted just above the **F**ind item in the **F**ile menu. After you insert a Custom Item, you must edit it so that it corresponds to a specific command you desire. (More information about editing a Custom Item is provided in the following section.)

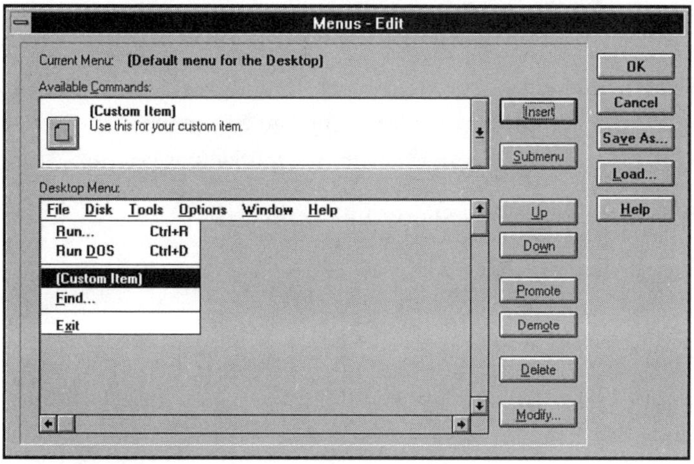

Fig. 12.10
A Custom Item added to the **F**ile menu.

Modifying Menu Items

Use the Menus - Modify Custom Item dialog box to edit the text, underlined letter, and shortcut key of any menu item (see fig. 12.11). Access this dialog box by choosing the **M**odify command button in the Menus - Edit dialog box.

Begin by editing existing text or entering new text in the **T**ext box. This text appears on the menu. Place an ampersand (&) in front of the letter that you want to be underlined; underlined letters are accessible via the keyboard for fast access. The new menu item in figure 12.11, for example, is called *&Custom...*.

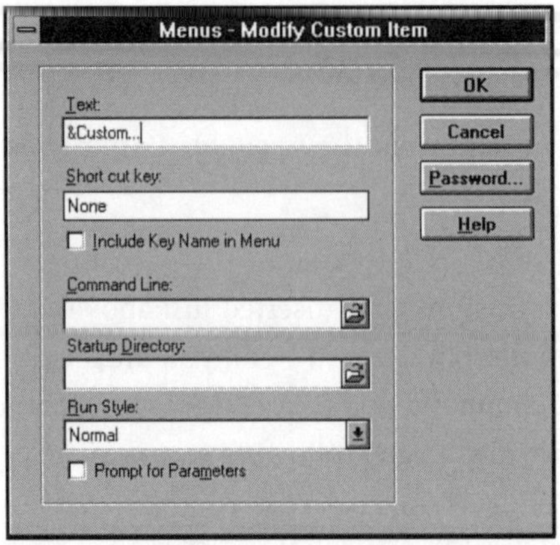

Fig. 12.11 The Menu - Modify Custom Item dialog box.

Tip
Try to keep your menu text as concise as possible. Long menus and menu item names can crowd out other menu items.

Tip
You cannot assign a shortcut key to a menu title, because the underlined item in the title functions as a shortcut key if you press it in combination with the Alt key.

For normal menu items, you can assign a shortcut key. Simply place the cursor in the **S**hort Cut Key box and press the keys. To make Ctrl+C the shortcut key for the **C**ustom command, for example, follow these steps:

1. Place the cursor in the **S**hort Cut Key text box.

2. Press Ctrl+C.

The letters Ctrl+C now appear in the **S**hort Cut Key text box.

If you want to show the shortcut key alongside the menu item listing, select the **I**nclude Key Name in Menu check box.

Creating Cascading Menus

A *cascading menu* is a menu that branches off from a regular menu item. Create a cascading menu by selecting a menu item and then selecting an Available **C**ommand and choosing the **S**ubmenu button. To create a cascading Custom option, follow these steps:

1. Select the **F**ile **C**ustom menu item (added in the earlier example; refer to fig. 12.10).

2. Select the **C**alculator command from the Available **C**ommands list.

3. Choose the **S**ubmenu button.

4. Select the Custom Item option from the Available **C**ommands list.

5. Choose the **S**ubmenu button. You should now have two items cascading from the **F**ile **C**ustom menu item, as shown in figure 12.12.

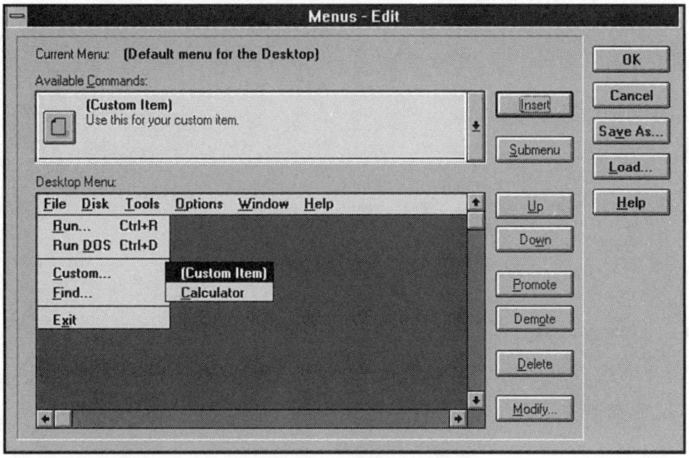

Fig. 12.12
Two items cascading from the **F**ile **C**ustom menu command.

6. Customize the Custom Item menu option to your favorite application. Figure 12.13 shows the Menus - Modify Custom Item dialog box with information about a new command called **K**wikstat. Save the new menu item by choosing OK.

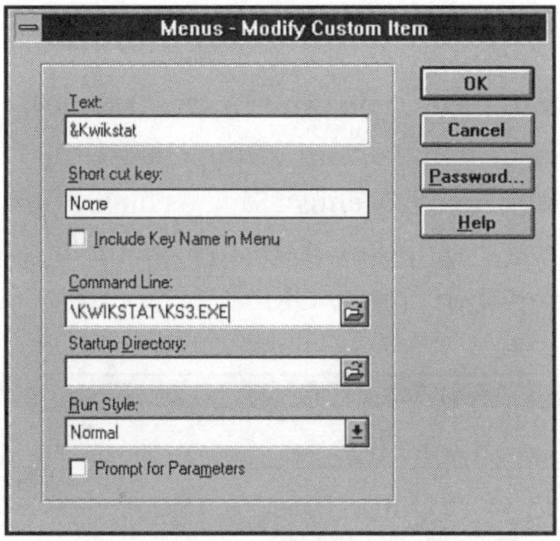

Fig. 12.13
The Menus - Modify Custom Item dialog box, showing the new **K**wikstat command for the **F**ile **C**ustom cascading menu.

Your new cascading menu from the **F**ile **C**ustom option should look similar to the one shown in figure 12.14.

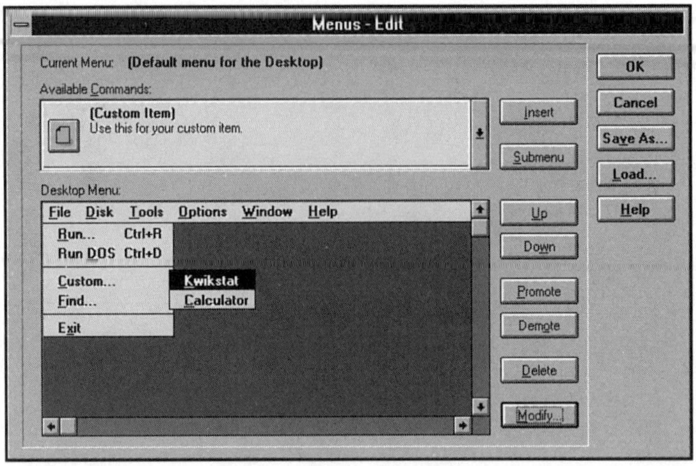

Fig. 12.14 Your new cascading menu items.

> **Note**
>
> If a menu item accesses other menus, the name is followed by ellipses (...) in the Desktop Menu list. You must name the item using this standard.

Saving Your New Menu

After creating a custom menu, you want to save it to disk so that you can use it again. After you create your custom menu, choose the Sa**v**e As button from the Menus - Edit dialog box. A Menus - Save As dialog box appears, as shown in figure 12.15. Enter a description of the new menu in the **N**ew Menu Description text box, and then choose OK.

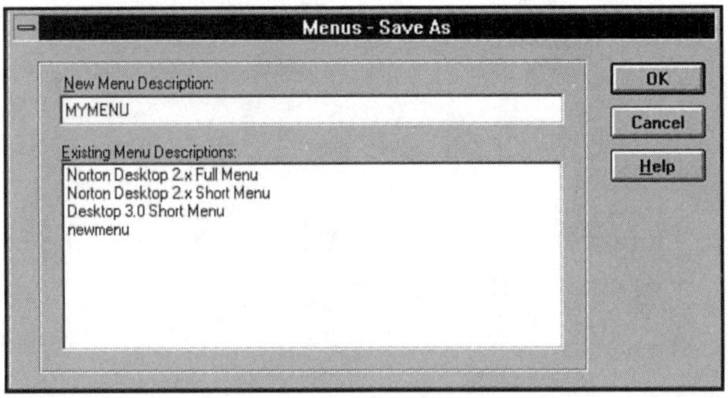

Fig. 12.15 Saving your new menu description.

Instituting Password Protection

If you want to restrict access to a menu item, you can assign a password to the operation in the Menus - Modify Custom Item dialog box. Only users who know the password can choose the item on your system.

To assign a password, follow these steps:

1. Select a menu item. Then choose the **M**odify button, which displays the Menus - Modify Custom Item dialog box.

2. Choose the **P**assword command. The Set Password dialog box appears, as shown in figure 12.16.

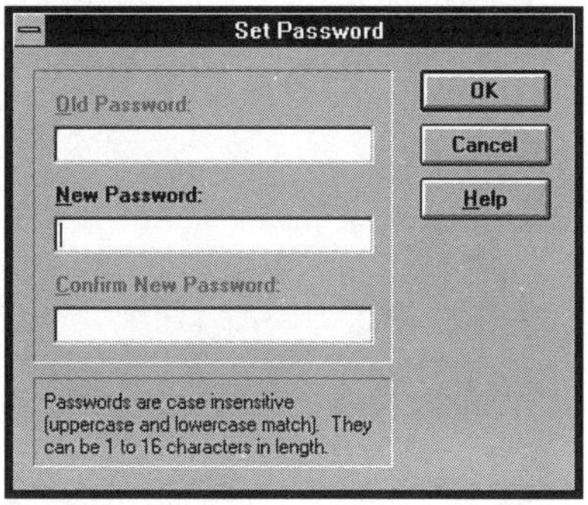

Fig. 12.16
The Set Password dialog box.

3. Enter a password in the **N**ew Password text box. The password can be up to twenty characters long. Enter the same password again in the **C**onfirm New Password text box.

4. Choose OK to confirm the password.

Creating New Menus for Your Computing Needs

The following sections give you some ideas on how to customize your menu system for your particular needs. Use the techniques presented in this chapter to create these menus and customize the menu items as your demands require.

Creating a Basics-Only Menu

The basics-only menu contains only the essentials you need for basic operation. This configuration assumes that all other operations are handled via icons and/or drive windows. The menu bar contains just three menus: **E**ssentials, **W**indow, and **H**elp (see fig. 12.17).

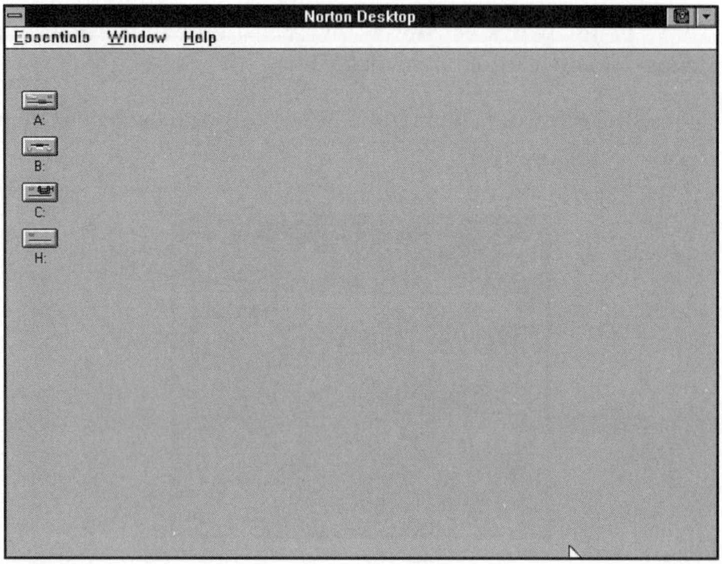

Fig. 12.17
The basics-only menu, containing only three menu items.

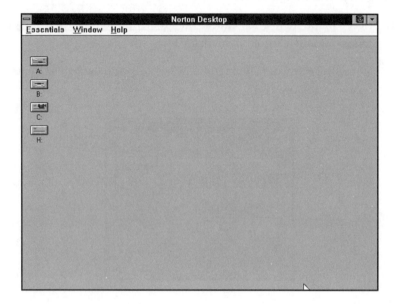

Creating a Quick-and-Easy Menu

The quick-and-easy menu is a variation on the Short menu (see fig. 12.18). The menu bar contains the following menus: **F**ile/Disk Management, **T**ools, **O**ptions, **W**indow, and **H**elp.

Tip
Use this menu with any of the custom icon-based Desktops discussed in Chapter 13, "Creating an Icon-Based Desktop."

Creating an Application-Based Menu

This menu is designed for laptop computer users. The **T**ools menu is replaced by a **P**rograms menu, which contains cascading menus for types of applications (see fig. 12.19). Included on this example menu are custom items for **Q**uicken, **R**ightWriter, E**x**cel, **W**ordPerfect for Windows, **K**wikstat, and Norton Anti**V**irus.

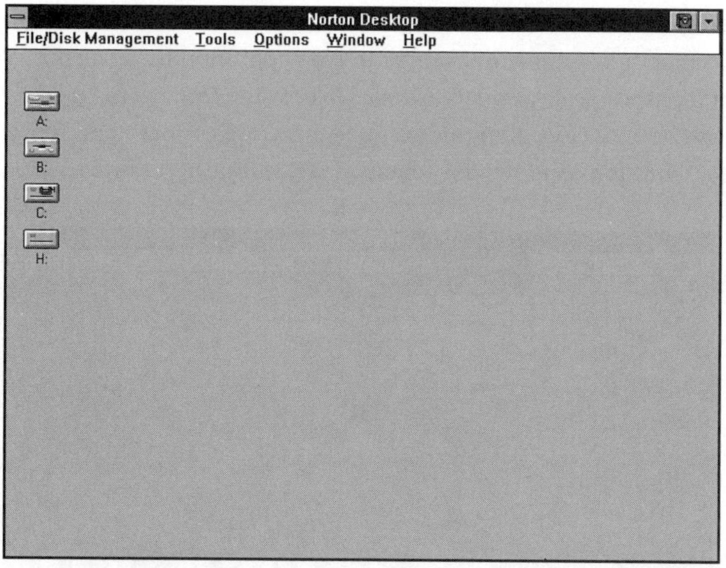

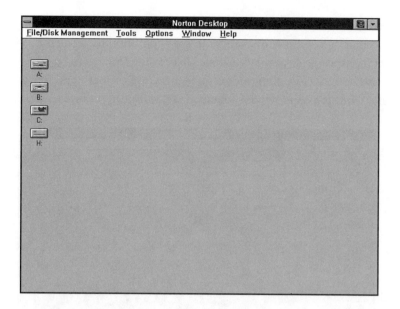

Fig. 12.18
The quick-and-easy menu, containing a modified Short menu.

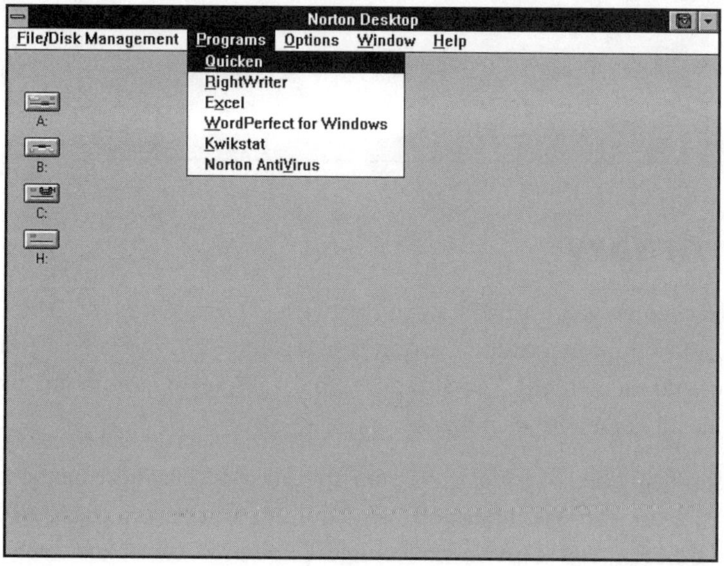

Fig. 12.19
The application-based menu contains application options.

Creating a Document-Based Menu

The document-based menu is similar to the application-based menu, except that specific documents are available on the **D**ocuments menu (see fig. 12.20). Included on this example menu are custom items for specific Word for Windows documents, Excel spreadsheets, and so on.

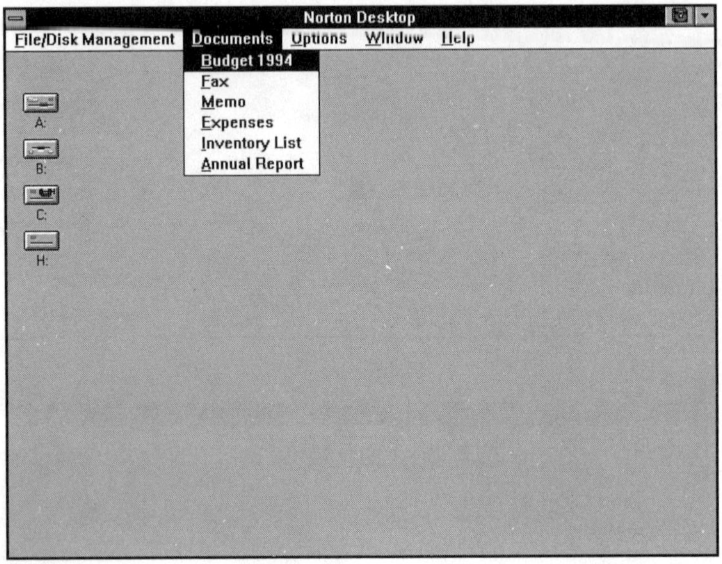

Fig. 12.20
The document-based menu contains document options.

Summary

In this chapter, you learned how to create a menu-based desktop. You learned how to load new menus into Norton Desktop and how to create custom menus and menu items. You also saw some examples of custom menus to provide ideas for your own menus.

If customizing menus is not quite your style, take a look at the next chapter, "Creating an Icon-Based Desktop," which shows you how to create an icon-based Desktop. You learn how to configure and edit Desktop icons, configure an icon-based Desktop, and create a customized Desktop to meet your computing needs.

Chapter 13

Creating an Icon-Based Desktop

In this chapter, you learn to perform the following tasks:

- Configure and edit Desktop icons
- Configure an icon-based Desktop
- Create custom Desktops for your computing needs

As you learned at the start of Chapter 12, "Creating a Menu-Based Desktop," GUI environments usually have two kinds of users—users who prefer to access functions through menus and users who prefer to use icons.

If you prefer pull-down menus, Norton Desktop 3 for Windows offers a menu-based Desktop, which is discussed in Chapter 12. Because menus don't provide customizable, instant access to most functions, however, you may want to investigate icons. This chapter explores how you can use icons to personalize your computing environment and place favorite applications right on the Desktop.

Understanding Norton Desktop Icons

An *icon* is an on-screen symbol that represents a specific file. In Norton Desktop, icons can represent an application, utility, macro, document, or batch file. Icons are often used because they are smaller and easier to arrange on the Desktop than are fully maximized applications (see fig. 13.1).

Icons also are easier to access than are commands in the menu system. To access an item by using menus, you must move the pointer to the menu bar, access the desired menu, and then choose the menu item. If you use icons, you simply double-click an icon. Icons make operations quicker and easier for most users.

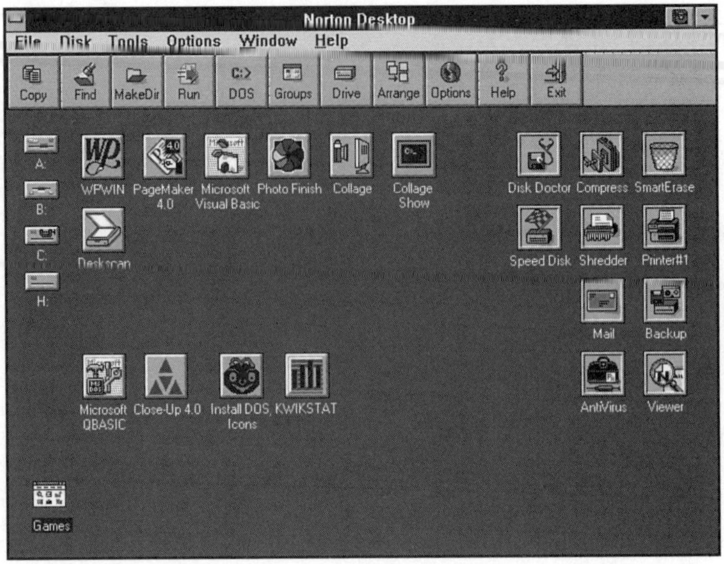

Fig. 13.1
The Norton Desktop contains a number of program and tool icons.

In Norton Desktop, you can place five main icons on the Desktop:

- *Application icons* are icons for currently running applications that are minimized.
- *Desktop icons* represent items that were dragged from another window onto the Desktop, providing instant access to applications and documents.
- *Group icons* represent minimized group windows.
- *Drive icons* enable instant access to drive windows.
- *Tool icons* represent NDW's resident tools, such as SmartErase and Shredder.

You can customize all these icons with custom labels and artwork. You also can place an icon anywhere on the Desktop and then save the Desktop configuration so that the icons always appear in the same place. With a little work, you can manipulate NDW's icons to create an ideal Desktop for your computing needs.

Configuring and Editing Desktop Icons

You can use NDW's Desktop default icons, or you can edit them to create custom icons. Editing an icon is as easy as changing the options in the Properties dialog box or as complex as creating new artwork in the Icon Editor.

Tip
This section focuses on Desktop icons, as they are the icons most often used to customize a Desktop. The other icons, although valuable, are less customizable than Desktop icons.

Using the Properties Command

After you click a Desktop icon, the icon command menu appears (see fig. 13.2). This menu enables you to open and close the icon and also edit the icon's properties.

Choose **P**roperties from the icon command menu to display the Properties dialog box. This dialog box contains four **C**ategories. Use the General category to change the title and command line for the current icon (see fig. 13.3). For example, you can add switches to command lines to start programs under specific parameters.

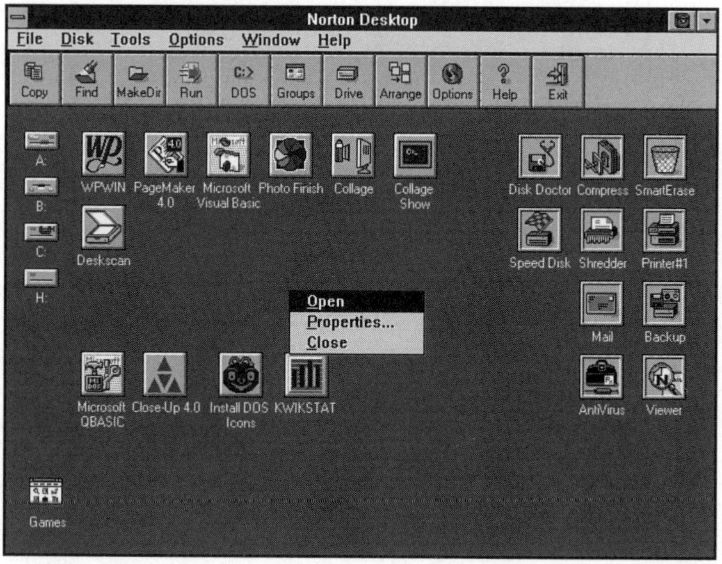

Fig. 13.2
A right mouse click displays the Desktop icon's command menu.

From this dialog box, you also can access the Properties (Advanced) dialog box to specify the start-up directory, description, shortcut key, and run style (see fig. 13.4). Use the Change Icon category to change artwork for the icon (see fig. 13.5). Use the Change Password category to select a password for the icon (see fig. 13.6).

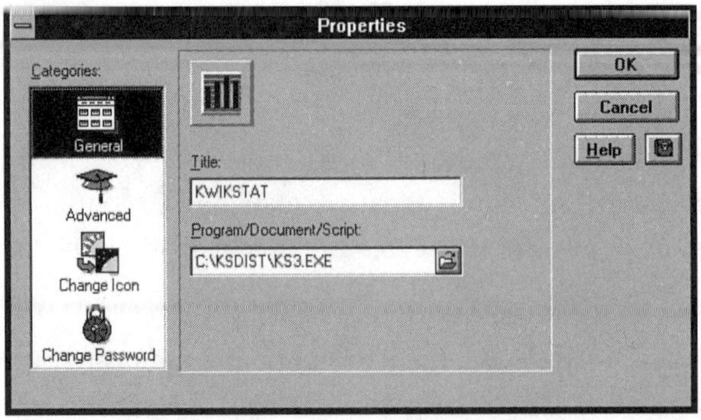

Fig. 13.3
The Properties (General) dialog box enables you to choose the title and program designation for the icon.

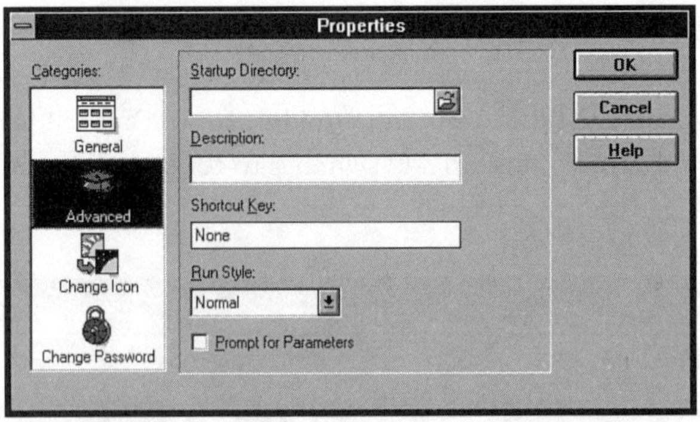

Fig. 13.4
The Properties (Advanced) dialog box enables you to set up advanced options for the icon.

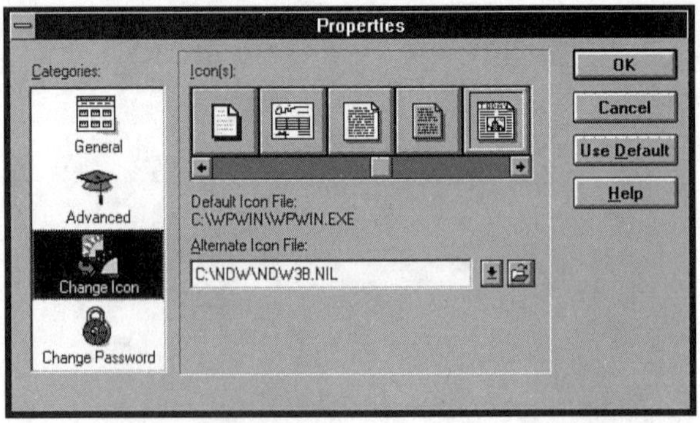

Fig. 13.5
The Properties (Change Icon) dialog box enables you to change the icon currently displayed.

Tip
The Properties dialog box and options are discussed in Chapter 11, "Customizing Norton Desktop's Settings." Refer to Chapter 11 for more details on specific operations.

Assume that you want to edit the WordPerfect for Windows Desktop icon in any of the following ways:

- To change the title.
- To load a file automatically.
- To change the start-up directory.

- To assign a shortcut key.
- To minimize the program on start-up.
- To assign a password so that only you can okay the program's start-up.
- To change the icon artwork.

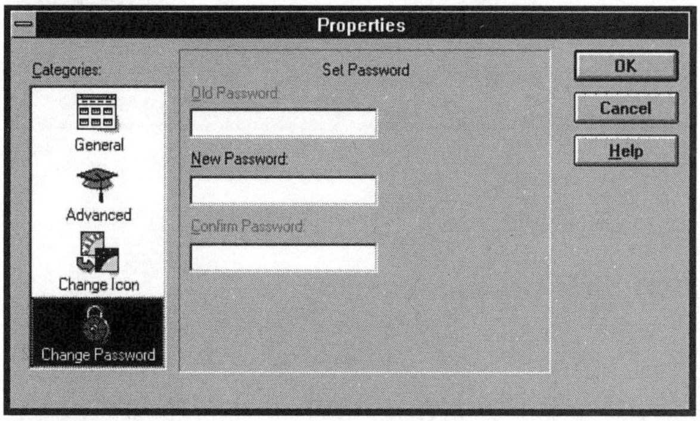

Fig. 13.6
The Properties (Change Password) dialog box enables you to specify password access to the program.

Although such edits may sound daunting, they really are easy if you follow these steps:

1. To display the icon command menu, click the right mouse button after the mouse pointer is on the WordPerfect Desktop icon.
2. Choose the **P**roperties command to display the Properties dialog box.
3. Type the following line in the **T**itle text box:

   WordPerfect Test Document

4. Type the following line in the **P**rogram/Document/Script text box:

   WPWIN.EXE C:\WPWIN\TEXT.SAM

   This command starts the program and loads the file TEXT.SAM, located in the C:\WPWIN directory. Figure 13.7 shows what the Properties (General) dialog box looks like after these changes.

5. Select the Advanced icon in the **C**ategories list to display the Properties (Advanced) dialog box.
6. Type the following line in the **S**tartup Directory text box:

   C:\WPWIN

Tip
For another, faster way of performing steps 1 and 2, hold down the Alt key and double-click the icon.

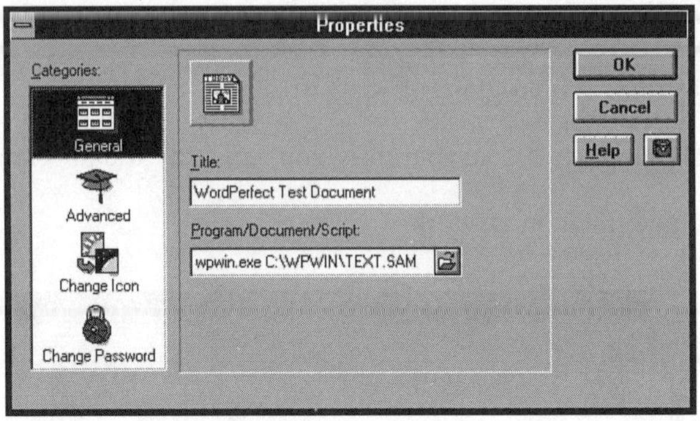

Fig. 13.7
The Properties (General) dialog box, after editing for a WordPerfect document.

7. Type the following line in the **D**escription text box:

   TEST.SAM Document

8. Move the cursor to the Shortcut **K**ey text box, and press Alt+Ctrl+W.

9. Open the **R**un Style drop-down list box, and select Minimized. After these changes, the Properties (Advanced) dialog box looks like the one shown in figure 13.8.

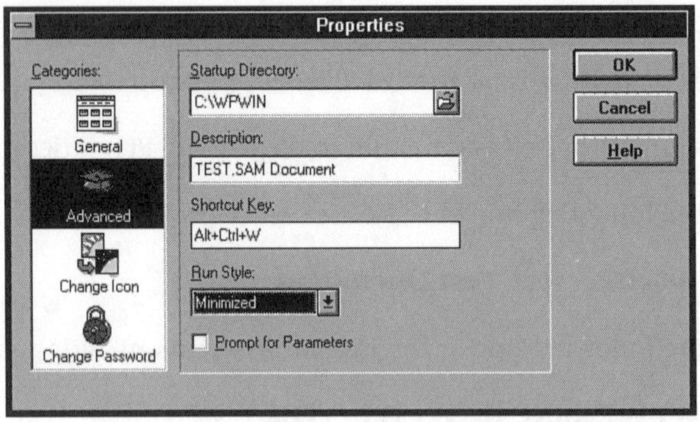

Fig. 13.8
The Properties (Advanced) dialog box, after editing for a WordPerfect document.

10. Select the Change Icon icon in the **C**ategories list to display the Properties (Change Icon) dialog box.

11. Click the Browse open folder icon to search for the NDW3B.NIL file, located in the Norton Desktop directory. Locate and select the file, and then return to the Properties (Change Icon) dialog box. The path and file names appear in the **A**lternate Icon File box, and the icons in the file appear in the **I**con(s) list.

12. Scroll through the **I**con list(s) until you can select the icon shown highlighted in figure 13.9.

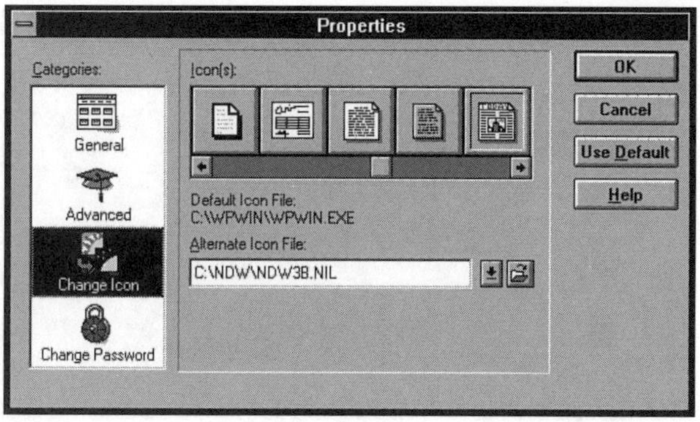

Fig. 13.9
Selecting an icon in the Properties (Change Icon) dialog box.

13. Select the Password icon in the **C**ategories list to display the Properties (Set Password) dialog box.

14. Type the following password in the **N**ew Password text box:

SECRET

As you type each character, asterisks appear. Figure 13.10 shows what the Set Password dialog box looks like after you type this entry.

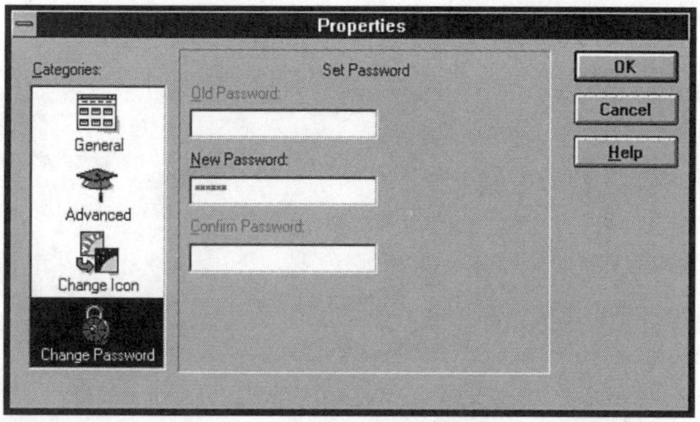

Fig. 13.10
The Properties (Set Password) dialog box after entering a password.

15. Choose the General icon in the **C**ategories list to return to the Properties (General) dialog box. The new icon appears at the top of the dialog box, as shown in figure 13.11. Choose OK to confirm all changes and return to the Desktop.

As you can see in figure 13.12, the WordPerfect Desktop icon now features new artwork and a new label. After you double-click the icon, you are prompted for the password. After you type **SECRET**, WordPerfect starts and loads the TEST.SAM document. Just by making a few simple editing changes to an existing icon by using the **P**roperties command, you create a new Desktop icon.

Fig. 13.11
The Properties (General) dialog box, showing the newly selected icon.

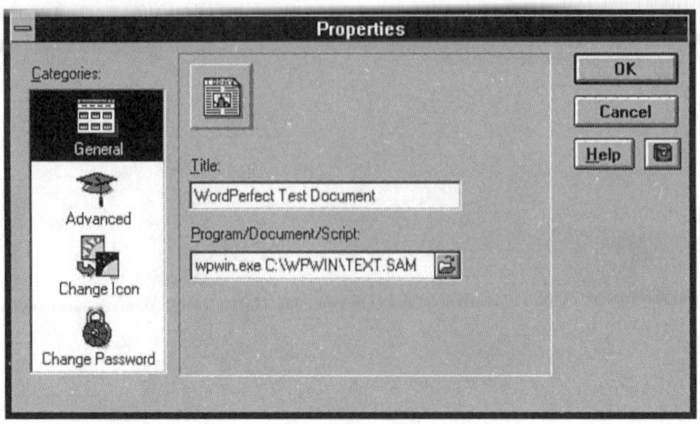

Using Icon Editor

You can make even more extensive changes to an icon's artwork by using the Icon Editor. Choose the **T**ools **I**con Editor command to open the Icon Editor, as shown in figure 13.13.

Fig. 13.12
The new WordPerfect Test Document icon, displayed on the Desktop.

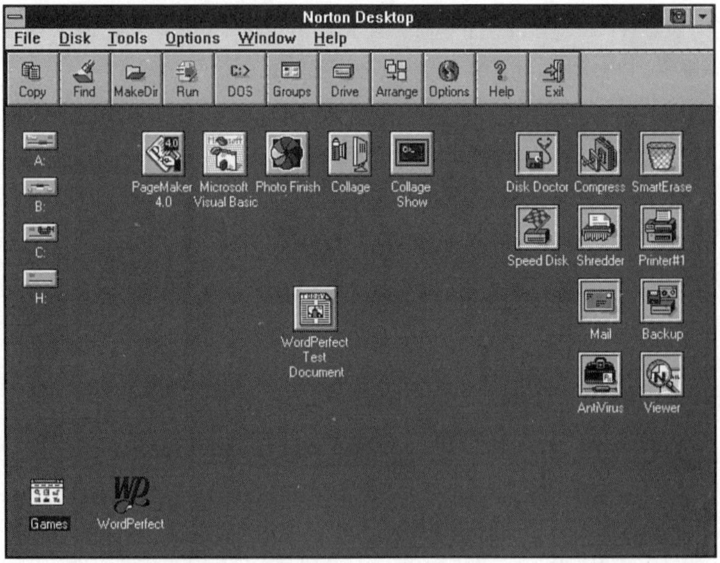

Tip
Icon Editor is discussed in Chapter 17, "Using Icon Editor." See that chapter for more details on specific operations.

Assume that you want to edit the new artwork you earlier assigned to the WordPerfect icon. To edit this artwork, follow these steps:

1. Choose the **T**ools **I**con Editor command to start the Icon Editor.

2. Choose the Icon Editor's **F**ile **O**pen command to display the File Open dialog box, as shown in figure 13.14.

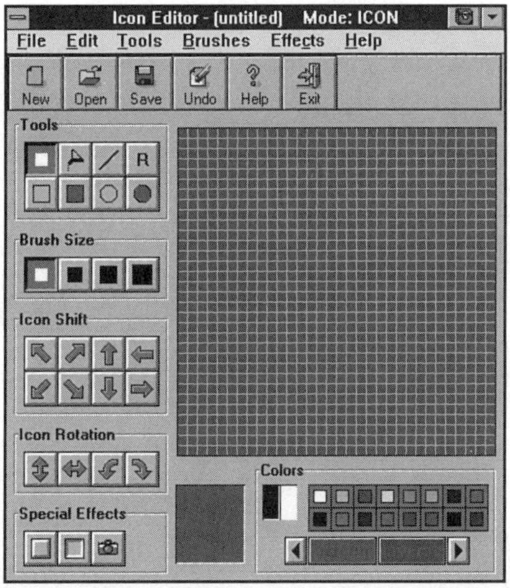

Fig. 13.13
You can use the Icon Editor to create customized icons.

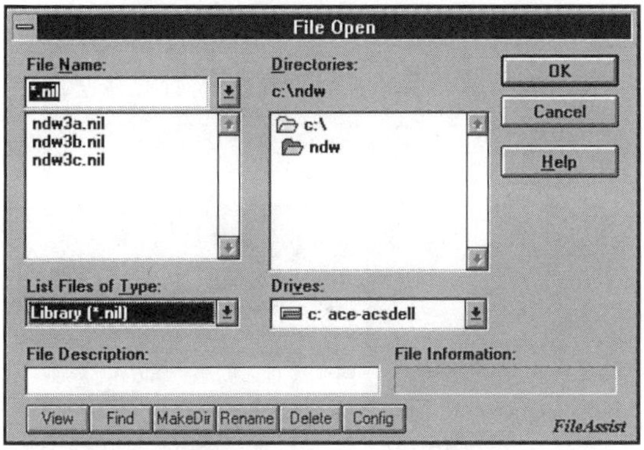

Fig. 13.14
The File Open dialog box enables you to open an icon library.

3. In the List Files of **T**ype drop-down list box, select the Library (*.nil) option to search for NIL files.

4. Select in the File **N**ame scrolling list box the name of the original file containing the icon you want to edit (NDW3B.NIL).

5. After you select the NDW3B.NIL file, choose OK to load the file.

   After the file is loaded in Icon Editor, all the icons in the file appear in a scroll box on the right side of the screen, as shown in figure 13.15.

6. Scroll through the icon list of the Library dialog box until you locate the icon you want.

7. Select the icon, and then click the Modify button. The icon loads in the Icon Editor's Workspace window (see fig. 13.16).

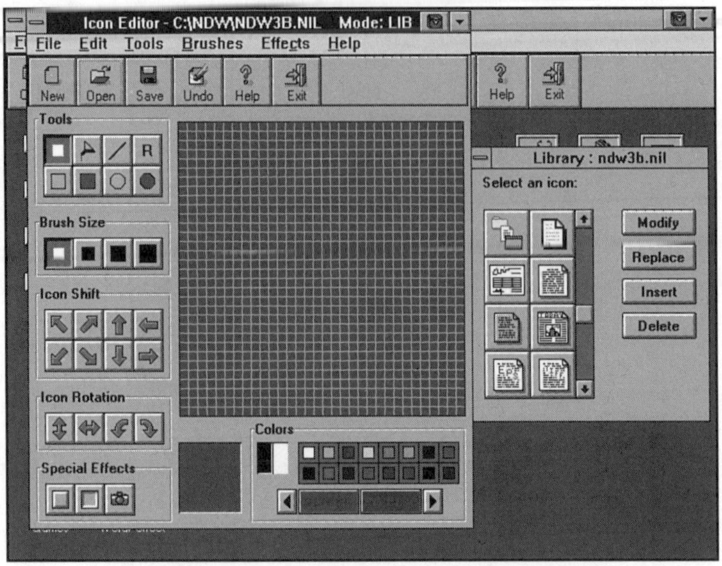

Fig. 13.15
The Icon Editor and Library dialog boxes, with the NDW3B.NIL file loaded.

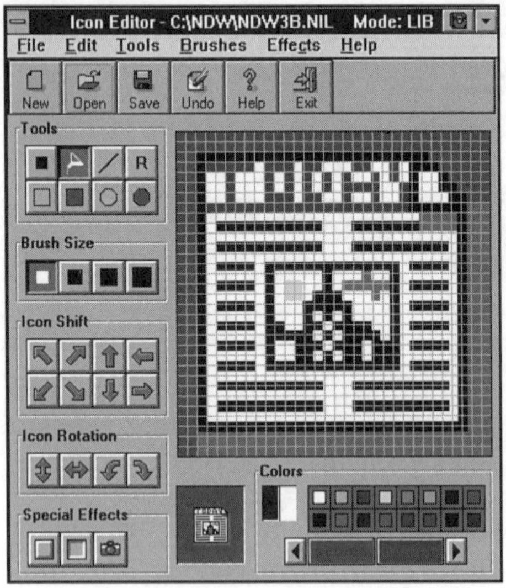

Fig. 13.16
The Today Page icon loaded in the Icon Editor's Workspace window.

8. For this example, select the Icon Editor's Fill tool and the blue color from the Icon Editor's Colors palette. (See Chapter 17 for details of this procedure.)

9. Use the Fill tool to fill the white background with the blue color so that the edited icon appears as shown in the Icon Editor's main Workspace and Icon Selector (the box containing the icon at the bottom of the Editor) in figure 13.17.

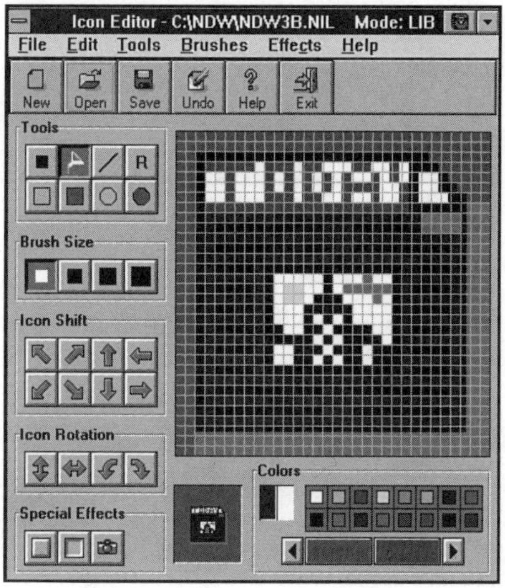

Fig. 13.17
The original white background of the icon is replaced with the blue color by the Icon Editor's Fill tool.

10. After editing is completed, click the Library dialog box's Replace button. The original icon is replaced in the icon list by the edited icon.

11. Choose the Icon Editor's Save tool to save the edited icon file.

12. Choose **F**ile E**x**it to exit the Icon Editor.

Notice that the Desktop icon did not change to reflect the new icon artwork. You first must re-enter the Properties (Choose Icon) dialog box and reselect the revised icon. To do so, follow these steps:

1. Open the Desktop icon's command menu.

2. Choose the **P**roperties command.

3. Select the Change Icon category in the Properties dialog box.

4. Select the edited icon in the **I**con(s) list of the Properties (Change Icon) dialog box, and then choose OK (see fig. 13.18).

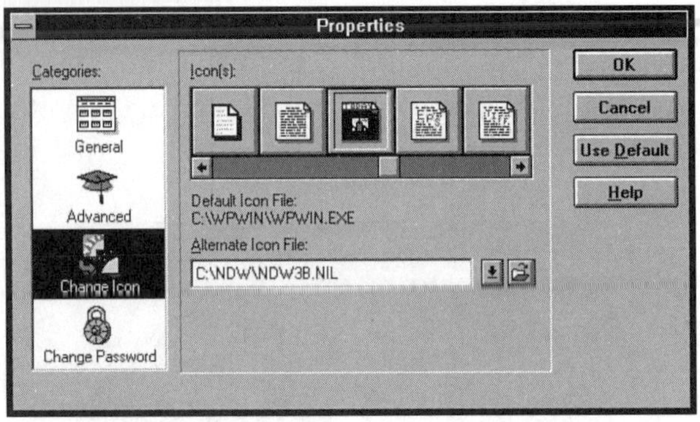

Fig. 13.18
The Properties (Change Icon) dialog box shown, with the edited icon selected.

5. Choose OK to close the Properties dialog box.

   The Desktop icon incorporates the changed icon artwork, as shown in figure 13.19.

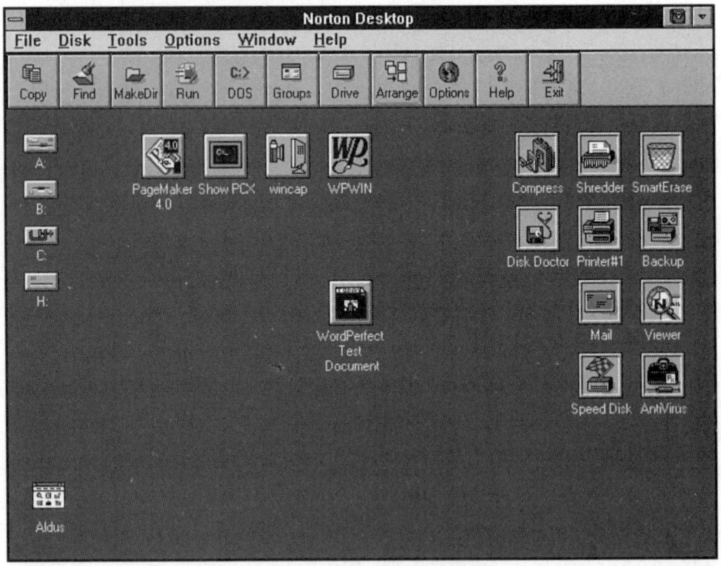

Fig. 13.19
The WordPerfect Test Document icon, with changed artwork displayed on the Desktop.

Configuring an Icon-Based Desktop

Now that you know how to edit specific icons, you are ready to examine how to create an icon-based Desktop. In this section, you learn how to add icons to the Desktop, delete icons from the Desktop, arrange icons on the Desktop, and incorporate Tool icons on the Desktop. You also learn how changing screen resolution affects the look of the Desktop.

Adding Icons to the Desktop

Both ways of creating Desktop icons involve drag-and-drop operations. You can drag a file from a drive window and drop it on the Desktop, or you can drag an icon from a group window and drop it on the Desktop. After files or icons are dropped on the Desktop, Norton Desktop creates a permanent Desktop icon for that item. You then can edit the properties of this icon (to change the label, for example).

To create a Desktop icon by using the drive window, follow these steps:

1. Open a drive window.
2. Select the file you want.
3. Drag the file from the drive window (see fig. 13.20).
4. Drop the file onto the Desktop. A Desktop icon is created, as shown in figure 13.21.

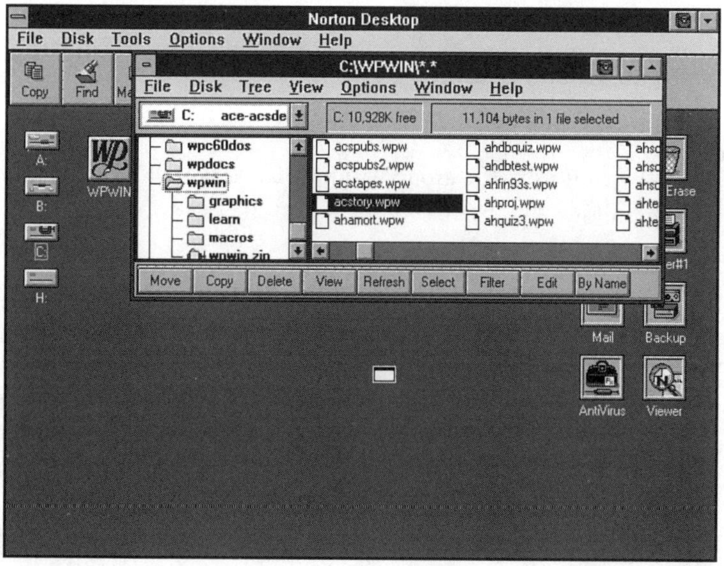

Fig. 13.20
The process of dragging a file from a drive window.

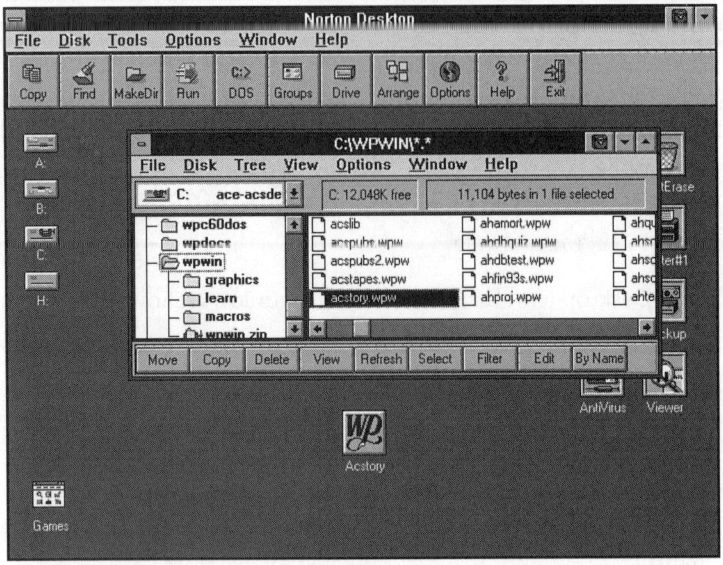

Fig. 13.21
The new WordPerfect document icon shown on the Desktop.

Tip
You can create Desktop icons from just about any executable program or document file. You must associate Document files, however, with an application for them to start correctly.

To create a Desktop icon by using a group window, follow these steps:

1. Open the group window.
2. Select the desired icon (see fig. 13.22).
3. Drag the icon from the group window just as you did the file from the drive window.
4. Drop the icon on the Desktop. A Desktop icon is created.

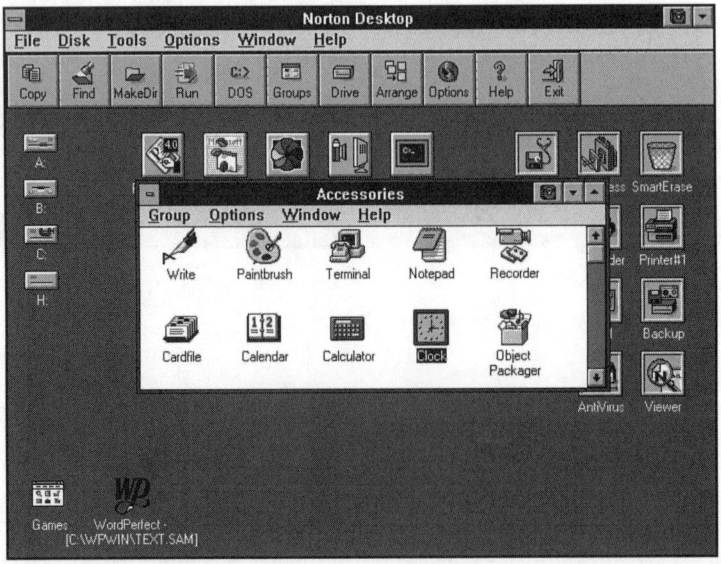

Fig. 13.22
Selecting an icon from a group window to drag to the Desktop.

Removing Icons from the Desktop

You can remove a Desktop icon in either of two ways. Open the icon's command menu, and choose the **C**lose command. The Desktop icon is removed. You also can drag the icon and drop it on the SmartErase tool. The SmartErase program does not actually erase the program from the disk; it only closes the icon on the Desktop.

Arranging Icons on the Desktop

In Norton Desktop 3 for Windows, you can align all Desktop items to an invisible grid. To activate this feature, follow these steps:

1. Choose the **O**ptions **C**ustomize command to display the Control Center dialog box, and then select the Desktop Layout icon in the **C**ategories list to display the Control Center (Desktop Layout) dialog box (see fig. 13.23). From this dialog box, you can choose positions of the Drive icons and toggle the title, menu, and toolbar off and on.

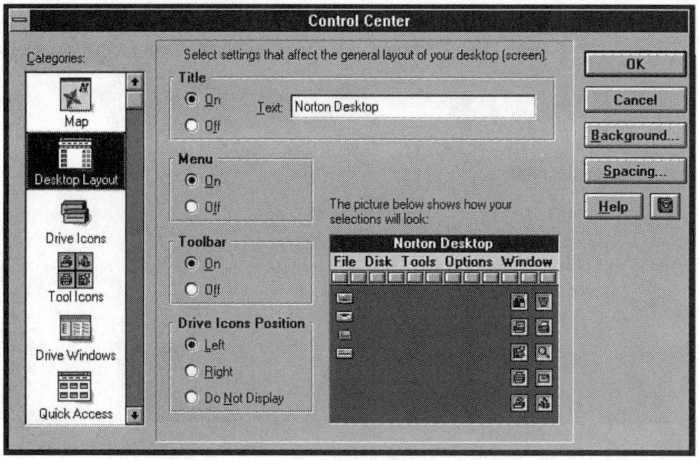

Fig. 13.23
The Control Center (Desktop Layout) dialog box enables you to choose how icons appear on the Desktop.

2. Choose the **S**pacing button to display the Desktop Layout - Grid Spacing dialog box (see fig. 13.24).

3. Select the **A**utomatic Item Alignment check box. You also can change the grid spacing in the Grid Spacing boxes.

4. Choose OK to return to the Control Center (Desktop Layout) dialog box. Choose OK again to return to the Desktop.

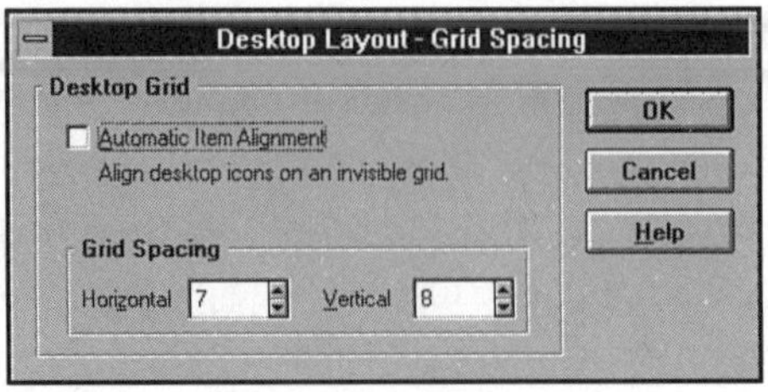

Fig 13.24
The Desktop Layout - Grid Spacing dialog box enables you to specify spacing for icons.

Even with this option activated, you still can move icons around and create a messy Desktop. To align all icons in a neat order, choose the **W**indow A**r**range Desktop Icons command. As figures 13.25 and 13.26 demonstrate, this command cleans up the Desktop.

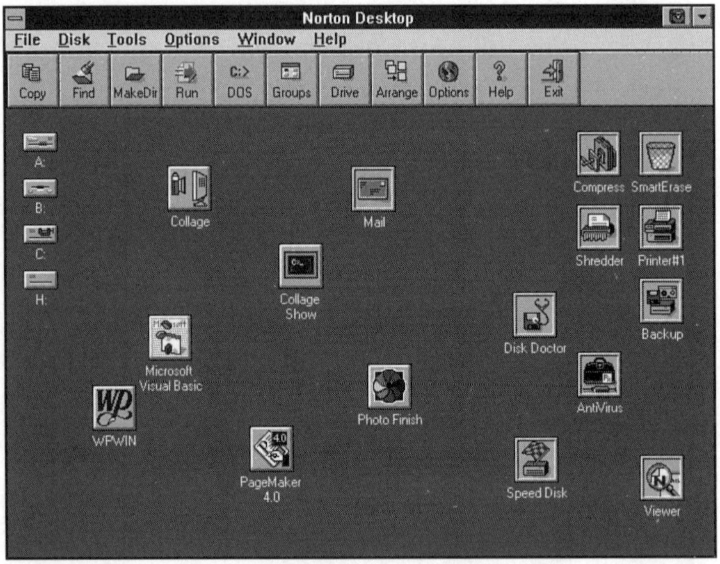

Fig. 13.25
Without planning, you can end up with a Desktop as cluttered as your real desktop.

Using Tool Icons

Norton Desktop enables you to automatically display any of the following ten tool icons:

- Speed Disk
- SmartErase
- Norton Disk Doctor
- Norton Backup
- Norton AntiVirus

- Shredder
- Viewer
- Compression
- Mail
- Printers

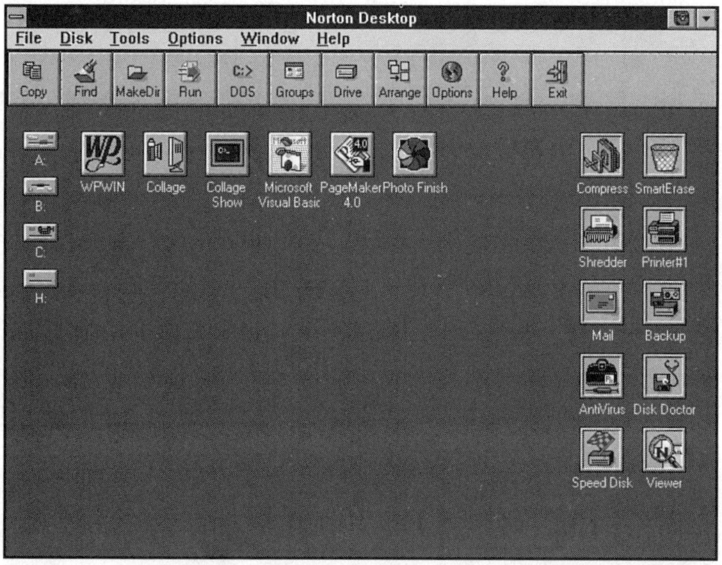

Fig. 13.26
A clean Desktop, courtesy of the **W**indow A**r**range Desktop Icons command.

Simply choose the **O**ptions **C**ustomize command and then select Tool Icons from the **C**ategories list to display the Control Center (Tool Icons) dialog box. Choose in this dialog box the Tool icons you want to automatically appear on the Desktop. Upon Windows start-up, the selected Tool icons appear at the right side of the Desktop.

Note

You also can display all these tools (except Printers) as regular Desktop icons. Just drag and drop the icons from the Norton Desktop Applications group window to the Desktop to create Desktop icons. Notice, however, that some drag-and-drop operations possible with Tool icons are impossible with Desktop icons. You can drop files on the SmartErase Tool icon, for example, to delete them; this operation is impossible with a SmartErase Desktop icon.

Changing Screen Resolution

Tip
Remember to select Save Configuration after making changes!

If you have a high-resolution monitor and video board, you may want to select a higher-resolution driver for the Windows display. The standard VGA driver, for example, displays at 640 x 480 resolution, whereas the SuperVGA driver (included with Windows 3.1) displays at 800 x 600 resolution. This higher resolution means that you can fit more on-screen with SuperVGA, and if you can fit more on-screen, you have room for more icons. Figures 13.27 and 13.28 illustrate the difference that enhanced screen resolution can have on your Desktop.

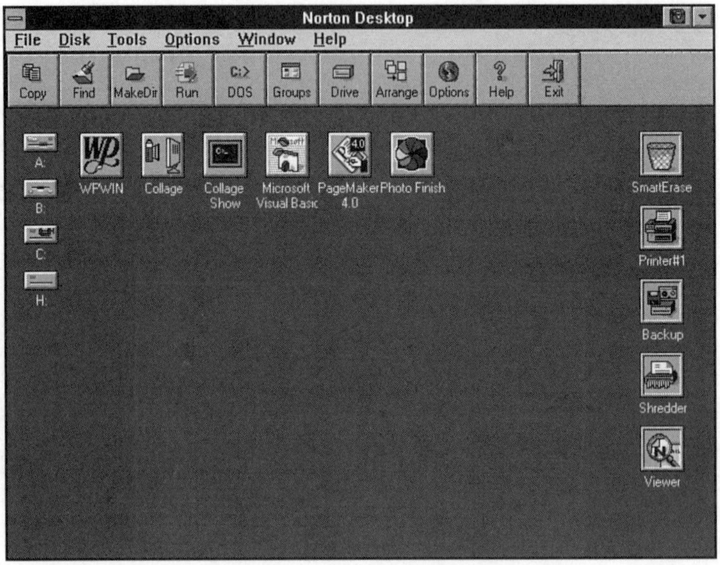

Fig. 13.27
A view of the Norton Desktop at VGA 640 x 480 resolution.

Consult your Windows and video board manuals for instructions on how to change the Windows display drivers by using the Windows Setup utility.

> **Caution**
>
> If you set the monitor to 800 x 600 resolution and rearrange the icons to the outer edges, and then you reset the monitor to 640 x 480 at a later time, many icons on the edges may be located off the screen.

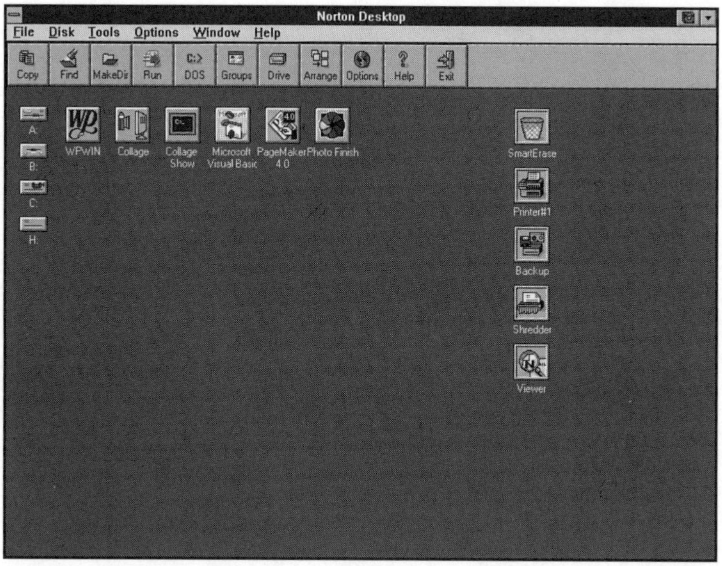

Fig. 13.28
A view of the same Norton Desktop at SuperVGA 800 x 600 resolution.

Creating Custom Desktops for Your Computing Needs

The following sections present sample Desktops that reflect different philosophies on how to configure a Desktop. You can use these examples as templates to create the desktop right for your needs.

> **Note**
>
> Notice that all the Desktops presented use a solid color background. Although you can spruce up the Windows background by using various patterns and wallpapers, complicated backgrounds sometimes interfere with icon visibility. Feel free, however, to experiment with different Windows backgrounds, but make sure that you can see icons (and any text) clearly against the background.

Creating a Drive Window-Based Desktop

The drive window-based Desktop is a clean Desktop (see fig. 13.29). The only icons are the drive windows; all other functions must be accessed through the menus. With this Desktop, you start applications by opening a drive window and double-clicking the file name.

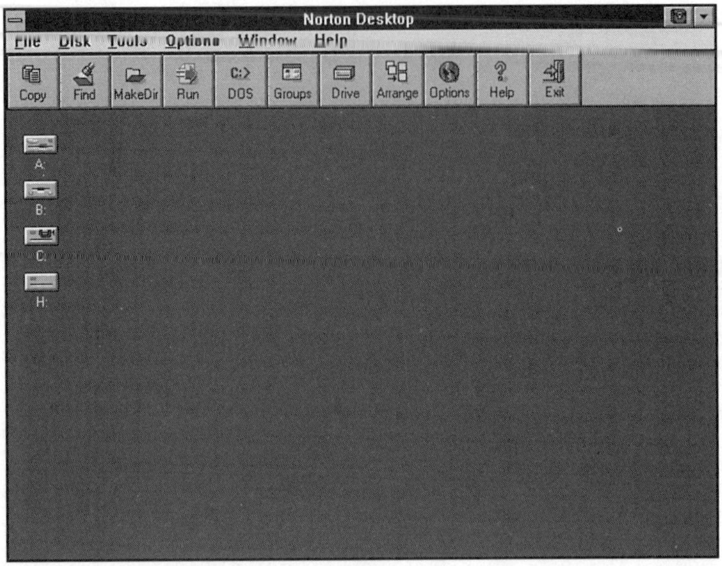

Fig. 13.29
A drive window-based Desktop, containing only Drive icons and no Tool or application icons.

Creating an Application-Based Desktop

The application-based Desktop is filled with icons for specific Windows and DOS applications (see fig. 13.30). By using this Desktop, your favorite applications are just a double-click away.

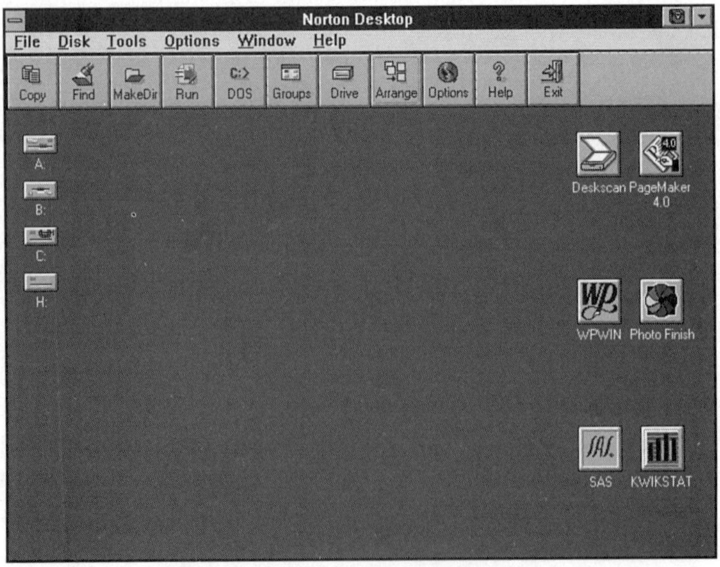

Fig. 13.30
An application-based Desktop, containing only Drive and application icons.

Creating a Document-Based Desktop

Although some users prefer to start applications and then load documents, other users think in terms of starting specific documents. The document-based Desktop addresses those needs with Desktop icons that represent specific documents (see fig. 13.31). (All documents are associated with applications, of course.) Double-clicking these Desktop icons opens the associated applications with the specified document preloaded.

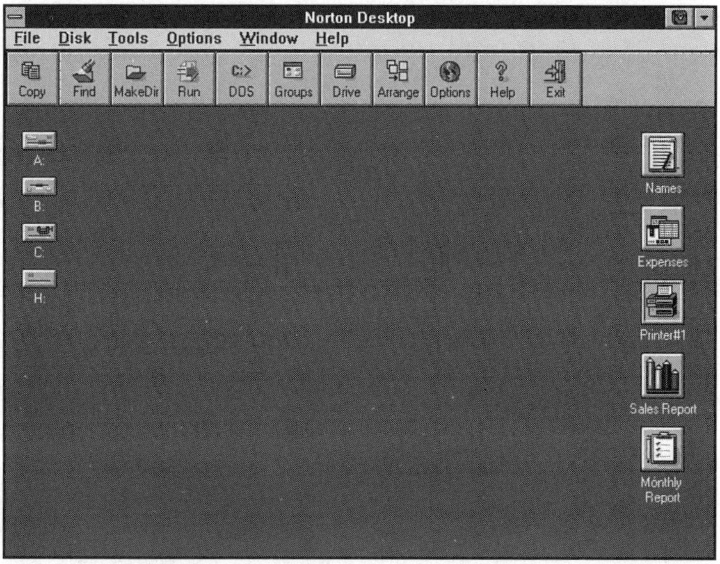

Fig. 13.31
A document-based Desktop, containing only Drive and document icons.

Creating a Utilities-Based Desktop

If you look at the desk in your office, you see that it holds numerous office "utilities," such as a stapler, a notepad, and so on. If you want the computer Desktop to reflect your office desktop, load it up with common Desktop utilities (see fig 13.32). This Desktop includes icons for the Norton Calculator, Desktop Editor, KeyFinder, and other useful tools and utilities.

Creating the Perfect Desktop

All the preceding Desktops have merits. Realistically, however, you may want to combine elements from each Desktop to create your ultimate Desktop. The authors' perfect Desktop includes just the right application icons, a Tools group window in toolbox view, and their most-often used utilities available as Desktop icons (see fig. 13.33). Now is the time for you to experiment and determine what works best for you.

Tip
Design your personal Desktop to suit the way you work, with the programs and utilities that are intuitive for you.

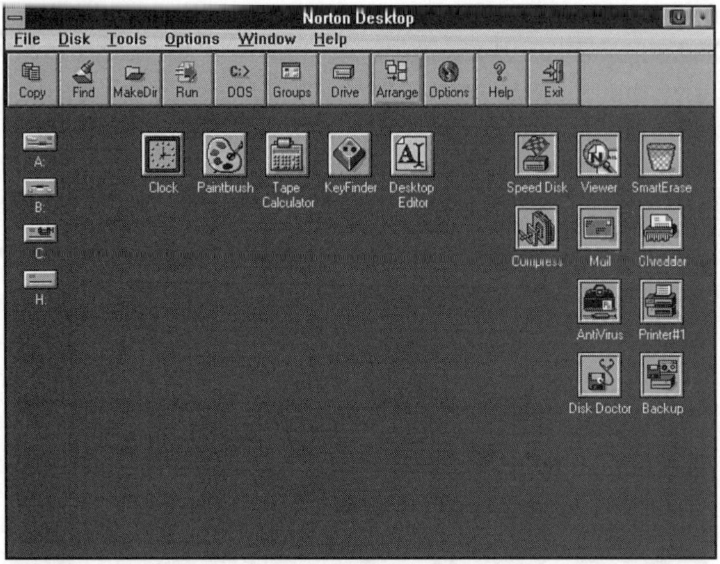

Fig. 13.32
A utilities-based Desktop, containing icons for commonly used utility programs.

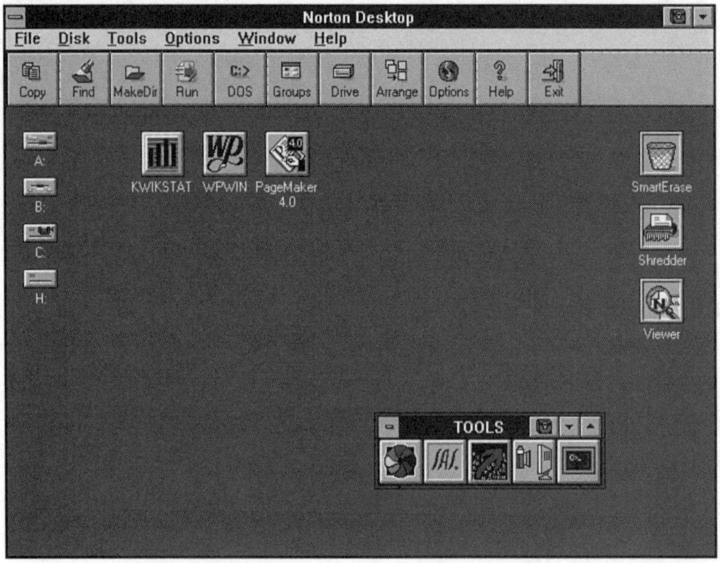

Fig. 13.33
Miller/Elliot's Perfect Desktop.

Summary

This chapter showed you how to use Norton Desktop's icons to create a custom Desktop. You learned how to create Desktop icons and how to edit them. You also were exposed to various sample Desktops and encouraged to create your own personalized Desktop.

Part IV discusses each individual tool and utility of Norton Desktop, with a separate chapter devoted to each.

The first chapter in Part IV is Chapter 14, "Using the Calculators," which discusses the three calculators included with Norton Desktop: the Tape Calculator, the Scientific Calculator, and the Financial Calculator.

Part IV

Using the Norton Desktop Tools and Utilities

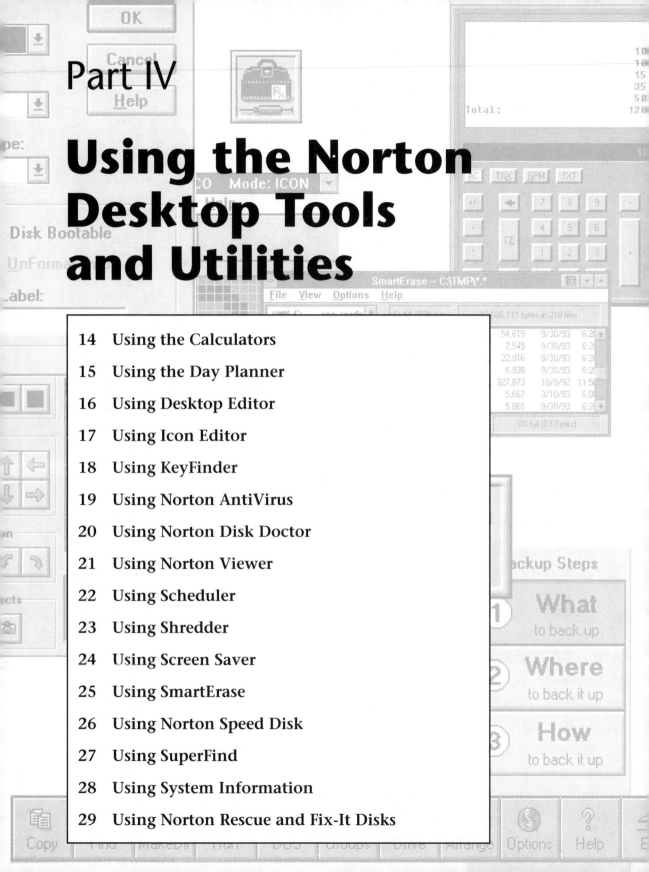

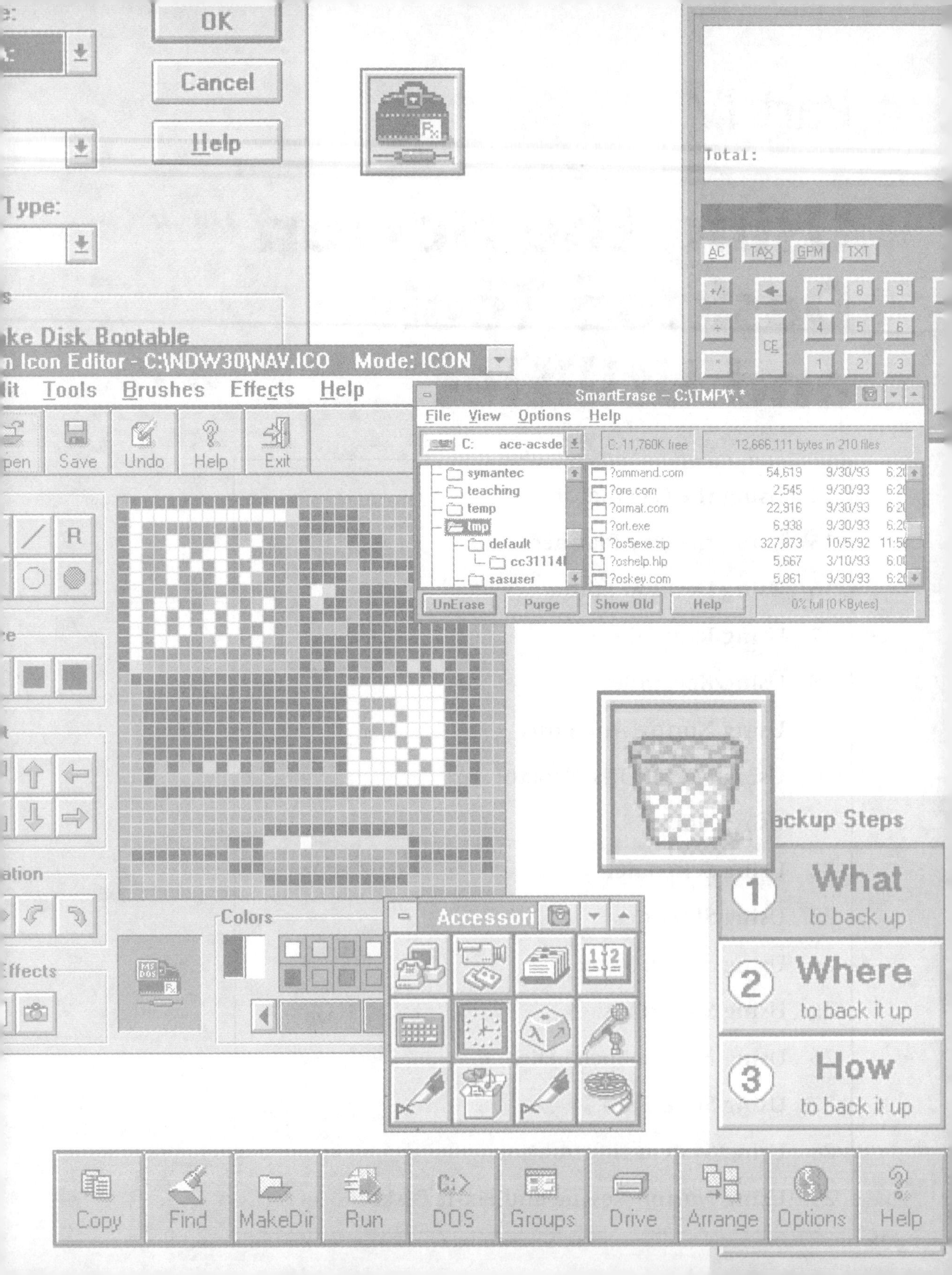
OK
Cancel
Help
Type:
ke Disk Bootable
n Icon Editor - C:\NDW30\NAV.ICO Mode: ICON
lit Tools Brushes Effects Help
pen Save Undo Help Exit
R
Colors
Effects
Total:
AC TAX GPM TXT
7 8 9
4 5 6
1 2 3
CE
SmartErase – C:\TMP*.*
File View Options Help
C: ace-acsde
C: 11,760K free
12,666,111 bytes in 210 files
symantec
teaching
temp
tmp
default
cc31114
sasuser
?ommand.com 54,619 9/30/93
?ore.com 2,545 9/30/93
?ormat.com 22,916 9/30/93
?ort.exe 6,938 9/30/93
?os5exe.zip 327,873 10/5/92
?oshelp.hlp 5,667 3/10/93
?oskey.com 5,861 9/30/93
UnErase Purge Show Old Help
0% full (0 KBytes)
Accessori
ackup Steps
1 What to back up
2 Where to back it up
3 How to back it up
Copy Find MakeDir Run DOS Groups Drive Arrange Options Help

Chapter 14

Using the Calculators

Although those of us older than age 30 remember a time when it was not the case, a calculator is now a standard fixture on the office desktop. Now, thanks to Norton Desktop 3 for Windows, several advanced Windows-based calculators can be a fixture on your Norton Desktop.

In this chapter, you learn to perform the following tasks:

- Understand Norton calculators
- Start the calculators
- Use the Tape Calculator
- Use the Scientific Calculator
- Use the Financial Calculator

Understanding the Calculators

Norton Desktop for Windows includes three on-screen calculators. These calculators are tools for you to use as part of your Windows Desktop. Similar to regular hand-held or desktop calculators, NDW's calculators help you perform quick mathematical operations without resorting to running a full-blown spreadsheet program.

- The *Tape Calculator* is a general calculator with a "tape" memory of previous transactions.
- The *Scientific Calculator* is a specialized calculator for technical operations and uses *Reverse Polish Notation.*
- The *Financial Calculator* is a specialized calculator for financial operations and also uses Reverse Polish Notation.

You can use all three calculators with the numeric keys along the top row of the keyboard, the numeric keypad on the keyboard, or by using the mouse to point and click the on-screen calculator buttons. All three calculators appear at a fixed size on-screen; although they can be minimized to icons, they cannot be maximized to full-screen size.

Note

In addition to NDW's calculators, you still have use of the standard Windows calculator. Although the NDW calculators are fine for specialized tasks (if you need a "tape" backup, for example, or if you are performing complex technical calculations), you may find the standard Windows calculator preferable for most everyday tasks.

Starting the Calculators

Tip
Make any calculator a Desktop icon by dragging the corresponding icon from the Quick Access Group to the Desktop.

You can start the calculators from either the menu system or the Quick Access Group. To start the calculators from the menu system, choose the **T**ools **C**alculator command. The calculator that was last used appears on the Desktop. To switch to one of the other calculators, choose it from the calculator's **C**alculator menu.

Using the Tape Calculator

The Tape Calculator works much the same as most calculators you have used. Perform simple mathematical operations by clicking number and function buttons.

Figure 14.1 shows the Tape Calculator. Notice the large window at the top of the calculator; this *tape window* is the display for the running "tape" of transactions. The "tape" scrolls so that you can review prior transactions. The current data input is shown in the single-line middle window, called the *display window*.

Table 14.1 details the functions available with the Tape calculator.

Table 14.1 Functions Available with the Tape Calculator

Key	Function
+/–	Change sign.
+	Add.
–	Subtract.
*	Multiply.
÷	Divide.

Key	Function
=	Equals.
%	Percent.
<	Backspace (erase last digit).
S	Subtotal.
T	Total.
CE	Clear entry.
C	Clear.
AC	Clear all.
MT	Memory total and clear memory.
MS	Memory subtotal.
M–	Subtract from memory.
M+	Add to memory.
TAX	Calculate sales tax.
GPM	Gross profit margin.
TXT	Switch text mode on or off.

Many of these functions are familiar to you. Some of the functions, however, are unique to the Tape calculator.

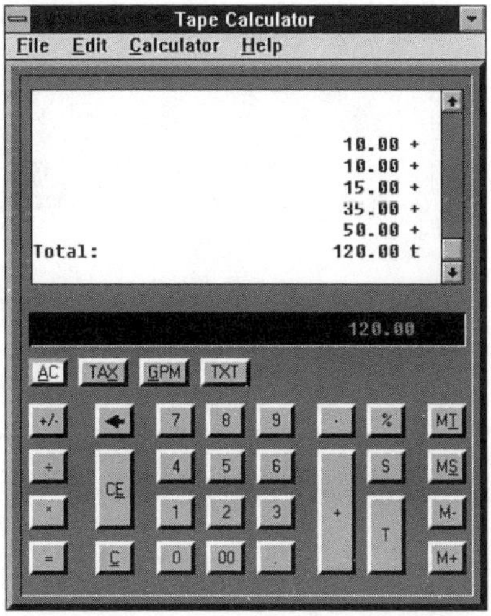

Fig. 14.1
The Tape Calculator enables you to keep a "tape" of your work.

Simple Mathematical Operations

You can choose whether the Tape calculator uses normal input order or Reverse Polish Notation (RPN). RPN on the Tape Calculator works much like an adding machine, as it requires you to enter numbers first and then the operators or functions. The = key works only with multiplication and division; for addition and subtraction, use the T (Total) key.

To add 1 plus 2, for example, you enter the following line:

1 + 2 + T

Normal input (Infix) enables you to enter data as you do on a normal desktop calculator. To add 1 plus 2, for example, you enter the following line:

1 + 2 =

To change computing modes, choose the **F**ile **S**etup command. After the Setup dialog box appears (see fig. 14.2), choose either **R**PN or **I**nfix Computation.

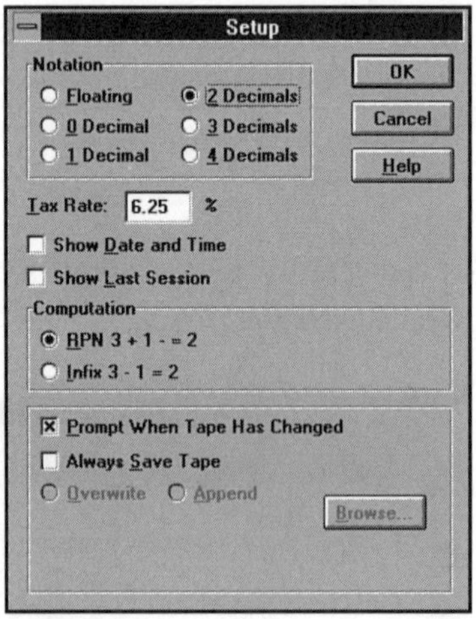

Fig. 14.2
The Tape Calculator Setup dialog box enables you to specify operation options.

The Tape Calculator includes standard memory functions. The M**T** key displays the memory total and clears the memory register. Use this key to clear the memory before beginning new operations. The M**S** key displays the memory contents as a subtotal and does not clear the memory register. Add items to memory by using the M+ key and subtract from the memory total by using the M– key.

The TAX Function

The TAX function enables you to add sales tax to any item. Before you use this function, you must set the tax rate in the calculator's memory. You need to set the tax rate only once, until you need to change the rate again for some reason. Then the Tape Calculator automatically calculates the correct tax rate any time you use the TAX function; you do not need to enter the tax rate every time you perform a calculation.

To set or change the tax rate of the Tape Calculator, follow these steps:

1. Activate the Tape Calculator, and open the Calculator's **F**ile menu.
2. Choose the **S**etup option. The Setup dialog box appears.
3. Choose the appropriate decimal Notation; for most purposes, **2** Decimals works well.
4. Enter the correct **T**ax Rate. Do not enter leading decimal points; for example, for a 6 percent tax rate, enter **6**, and for a 6.25 percent rate, enter **6.25**.
5. Optionally, choose the options to Show **D**ate and Time or Show **L**ast Session.
6. Choose OK to register changes and close the dialog box.

To calculate tax on an item, follow these steps:

1. Enter the selling price.
2. Choose the TA**X** key. The dollar amount of tax appears in the display window.
3. Choose the T key. The tax is added automatically to the selling price.

Tip

The % function works similarly to the TAX function. The % function enables you to set a specific percentage by which the first number is multiplied. Use the syntax **Number * Number % T**.

The GPM Function

The GPM function enables you to calculate gross profit margins. If you know an item's cost and your gross profit margin, the GPM function calculates the target selling price and gross profit dollars. Follow these steps:

1. Enter the unit cost.
2. Choose the **G**PM key.
3. Enter your profit margin.

Do not enter a decimal point; for example, if you want a profit margin of 40 percent, simply enter **40** without a leading decimal point.)

4. Choose the = (equals) key.

The tape window displays the gross profit dollars. The display window displays the target selling price.

The Text Mode

If you select the TXT button, you activate or deactivate the Tape Calculator's Text mode. The Text mode enables you to annotate any data entry. To annotate an entry, follow these steps:

1. Choose the TXT key to activate the Text mode.
2. Type the text from the keyboard.
3. Choose the TXT key to deactivate the Text mode.
4. Enter the numerical data.

Using the Tape

You can save the records of a calculating session by using the "tape" in the Tape Calculator. To save the tape, follow these steps:

1. Open the **F**ile menu.
2. Choose the Save **T**ape As option.
3. Enter a name for the tape file after the Save Tape As dialog box appears, and choose OK to save the file.

Note

Every time you close the Tape calculator, you are asked if you want to save a tape of the session.

You also can send the tape of your session to your printer. To print a tape, follow these steps:

1. Open the **F**ile menu.
2. Choose the **P**rint Tape option. Your printer begins to print the tape.

Using the Scientific Calculator

The Scientific Calculator is a more complex unit than the Tape Calculator (see fig. 14.3). To begin with, it uses Reverse Polish Notation only.

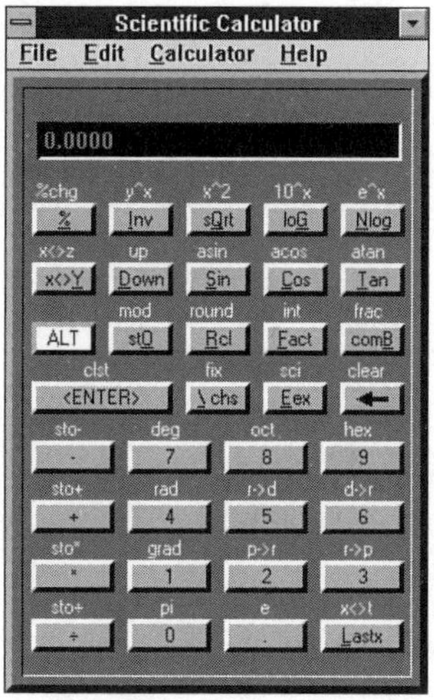

Fig. 14.3
The Scientific Calculator enables you to perform complex scientific calculations.

Dozens of functions for scientific and technical operations are included in the Scientific calculator. Table 14.2 details the available functions.

Table 14.2 Functions Available with the Scientific Calculator

Operator	Operation	Function
%	Percent	Calculates x percent of y.
*	Multiply	Multiplies y by x.
+	Add	Adds y to x.
–	Subtract	Subtracts x from y.
<	Backspace	Deletes last digit.
÷	Divide	Divides y by x.
%chg	Percent change	Calculates percent difference between x and y.
\chs	Change sign	Changes sign of x.

(continues)

Table 14.2 Continued

Operator	Operation	Function
10^x	10 to the x power	Calculates 10 to the x power.
acos	Arc cosine	Calculates arc cosine of x.
ALT	Alternate functions	Enables alternate functions (shown above the normal keys).
asin	Arc sine	Calculates arc sine of x.
atan	Arc tangent	Calculates arc tangent of x.
clear	Clear error	Clears x register.
clst	Clear stack	Clears x, y, z, and t registers.
com**B**	Combinations	Calculates combinations of y, x at a time.
Cos	Cosine	Calculates cosine of x.
d–>r	Degrees to radians	Converts x from degrees to radians.
deg	Degrees	Displays angles as degrees.
Down	Roll stack down	Moves contents of y register to x register, z register to y register, and so on.
e	Euler's constant	Inputs x=Euler's constant (2.718...).
e^x	Natural exponent	Calculates the natural exponent of x.
Eex	Exponential notation	Inputs exponent of 10.
Fact	Factorial	Calculates factorial of x (that is, x!).
fix	Fix decimal places	Displays fixed decimal notation.
frac	Discard integer portion, leaving fraction	Displays fractional portion of x.
grad	Gradients	Uses gradients.
hex	Hexadecimal	Displays integer portion of x in hexadecimal.
int	Truncate fraction, leaving nearest integer	Displays integer portion of x.
Inv	Inverse	Calculates inverse of x (1/x).

Operator	**Operation**	**Function**
Lastx	Last x	Replaces x with previous value of x.
lo**G**	Log	Calculates logarithm of x.
mod	Modulo	Returns modulus of x/y.
Nlog	Natural log	Calculates natural logarithm of x.
oct	Octal	Displays integer portion of x in octal.
p–>r	Polar to rectangular	Converts x, y from polar to rectangular coordinates.
pi	Pi	Inputs pi (3.14159...).
r–>d	Radians to degrees	Converts x from radians to degrees.
r–>p	Rectangular to polar	Converts x,y from rectangular coordinates to polar coordinates.
rad	Radians	Changes display from degrees to radians.
Rcl	Recall from register	Recalls contents of register to x.
round	Round to nearest integer	Rounds x to nearest integer.
sci	Scientific notation	Displays in scientific notation.
Sin	Sine	Calculates sine of x.
s**Q**rt	Square root	Calculates square root of x.
st**O**	Store to register	Stores x to register.
sto*	Multiply to register	Multiplies x by contents of register.
sto+	Add to register	Adds x to contents of register.
sto–	Subtract from register	Subtracts x from contents of register.
sto÷	Divide to register	Divides contents of register by x.
Tan	Tangent	Calculates tangent of x.
up	Roll stacks up	Rolls x register to y register, y register to z register, and so on.
x<>t	Swap x and t	Swaps contents of x and t.

(continues)

Table 14.2 Continued

Operator	Operation	Function
x<>y	Swap x and y	Swaps contents of x and y.
x<>z	Swap x and z	Swaps contents of x and z.
x^2	x squared	Squares x.
y^x	y to the x power	Raises y to the power of x.

As you can see from the table, the Scientific Calculator includes all the functions you would expect from a high-end scientific pocket calculator. Explaining the detailed technical use of each and every function is beyond the intent of this chapter (that could fill a book in itself); if you understand all the terms available, you probably know how to work a calculator such as this anyway.

Using the Financial Calculator

The Financial Calculator operates in a similar fashion to the Scientific Calculator (see fig. 14.4). Like the Scientific Calculator, the Financial Calculator uses Reverse Polish Notation—it also includes many of the same functions contained on the Scientific Calculator. The Financial Calculator has additional functions, however, for various financial and accounting applications, including amortization, depreciation, and discounted cash flow. Several of the functions work with operations available from the **Compute** menu.

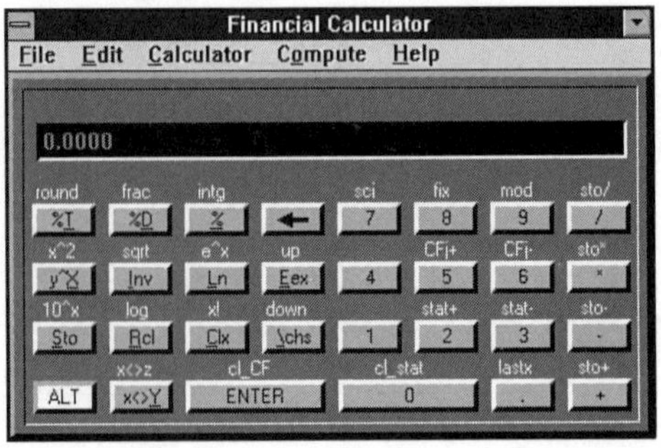

Fig. 14.4
The Financial Calculator contains financial, accounting, and other business calculation features.

Table 14.3 details the functions available from the keypad of the Financial Calculator.

Table 14.3 Functions Available with the Financial Calculator

Operator	Operation	Function
%	Percent	Calculates x percent of y.
*	Multiply	Multiplies z by x.
+	Add	Adds y to x.
–	Subtract	Subtracts x from y.
/	Divide	Divides y by x.
<	Backspace	Deletes last digit.
\chs	Change sign	Changes sign of x.
%**D**	Percent of difference	Calculates the percentage. difference between two numbers.
%**T**	Percent of total	Calculates what percentage one number is of another.
10^x	10 to the x power	Calculates 10 to the x power.
ALT	Alternate functions	Enables alternate functions (shown on top of the normal keys).
CFj+	Add to cash flow	Adds x to the cash flow register.
CFj–	Subtract from cash flow	Subtracts x from the cash flow register (if an inverse of x is present).
cl_CF	Clear cash flow	Clears the cash flow register.
cl_stat	Clear statistics	Clears the statistics register.
Clx	Clear x	Clears value of x.
down	Roll stack down	Moves contents of y register to x register, z register to y register, and so on.
e^x	Natural exponent	Calculates the natural exponent of x.
Eex	Exponential notation	Inputs exponent of x.
fix	Fix decimal places	Displays fixed decimal notation.
frac	Discard integer portion, leaving fraction	Displays fractional portion of x.

(continues)

Table 14.3 Continued

Operator	Operation	Function
intg	Truncate fraction, leaving nearest integer	Displays integer portion of x.
Inv	Inverse	Calculates inverse of x (1/x).
lastx	Last x	Replaces x with previous value of x.
Ln	Natural log	Calculates natural logarithm of x.
log	Log	Calculates logarithm of x.
mod	Modulo	Calculates x/y and displays the remainder (modulus).
Rcl	Recall from register	Recalls contents of register to x.
round	Round to nearest integer	Rounds x to nearest integer.
sci	Scientific notation	Displays in scientific notation.
sqrt	Square root	Calculates square root of x.
stat+	Add to statistics registers	Adds x and y to statistics registers.
stat–	Subtract from statistics registers	Subtracts x and y from statistics registers, when corresponding pairs are present.
Sto	Store to register	Stores x to register.
sto*	Multiply to register	Multiplies x by contents of register.
sto+	Add to register	Adds x to contents of register.
sto –	Subtract from register	Subtracts x from contents of register.
sto/	Divide to register	Divides contents of register by x.
up	Roll stacks up	Rolls x register to y register, y register to z register, and so on.
x!	Factorial	Calculates factorial of x.
x<>**Y**	Swap x and y	Swaps contents of x and y.
x<>z	Swap x and z	Swaps contents of x and z.
x^2	x squared	Squares x.
y^**X**	y to the x power	Raises y to the power of x.

Perhaps the most interesting feature of the Financial Calculator is its capability of performing selected financial calculations without actually using the main calculator. NDW includes separate dialog boxes that enable you to perform seven financial operations simply by filling in the blanks. These operations, accessed from the C**o**mpute menu, are described in the following sections.

Amortization

The Amortization Calculator is a great aid in performing "what if" analyses about loans. You can input the amount you want to pay each month and calculate the size of the loan you can afford. You can input the total amount financed and calculate your monthly payments. You can input both the expected monthly payments and the loan amount and calculate the target interest rate you need.

Choosing the C**o**mpute **A**mortization command displays the Amortization dialog box (see fig. 14.5). This utility enables you to calculate either the principal, periodic payment, or interest rate on a loan. Choose the variable you want to solve, and then fill in data for all other variables. After you select the **C**alculate button, the utility calculates the value of the selected variable, the remaining balance after a specified time period, and the amounts applied to interest and principal.

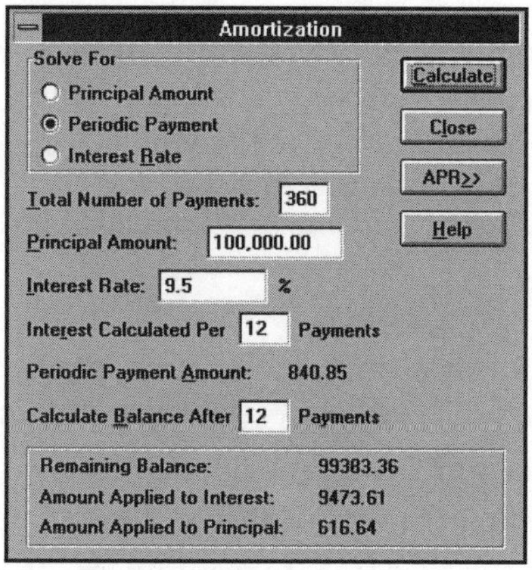

Fig. 14.5
The Amortization dialog box enables you to perform calculations for loan repayment.

The Solve For box contains three options: Pri**n**cipal Amount, Perio**d**ic Payment, and Interest **R**ate. The items below the Solve For box will change according to which of these three options is selected. The variables in a Periodic Payment calculation are as described in the following list:

- *Total Number of Payments.* Input number of total payments for the entire loan. If you have a 30-year loan with 12 monthly payments per year, for example, input **360** in this box.
- ***P**rincipal Amount.* Input the total amount financed.
- ***I**nterest Rate.* Input the interest rate on the loan. If the rate is 9 percent, input **9**. If the rate is 9.5 percent, input **9.5**.
- *Inte**r**est Calculated Per XX Payments.* Input the number of payments per year. If payments are monthly, enter **12**.
- *Periodic Payment **A**mount.* Input the amount of each payment.
- *Calculate **B**alance After XX Payments.* Input the number of months after which you would like to see the balance.

Tip
Choosing the APR option extends the dialog box to display variables for points and other monetary fees and calculates an Annual Percentage Rate based on the total amount of the loan, including principal, interest, and additional fees.

To use the Amortization Calculator, follow these steps:

1. Choose the C**o**mpute **A**mortization command from the Financial Calculator. The Amortization dialog box appears.
2. Choose either Pri**n**cipal Amount, Pe**r**iodic Payment, or Interest **R**ate in the Solve For box.
3. Fill in the other variables, as indicated by empty text boxes.
4. Choose **C**alculate after you make entries in all the boxes. The Solve For variable is calculated, and the Remaining Balance, Amount Applied to Interest, and the Amount Applied to Principal appear.
5. Choose C**l**ose to close the Amortization dialog box.

Bond

Tip
The Bond calculator assumes a standard *par* (sum due on maturity) of $100, a semiannual coupon, and a 365-day year.

A bond is a promise to pay a specified sum on a specified date, plus interest payments at specified intervals in the meantime. The bond may be sold at any time before the maturity date, at a price agreeable to both the issuer and the bondholder. The Bond calculator enables you to calculate the desired Bond Price, based on a desired yield to maturity, or the Bond Yield, based on the original price of the bond.

Choose the C**o**mpute **B**ond command to display the Calculate Bond dialog box (see fig. 14.6).

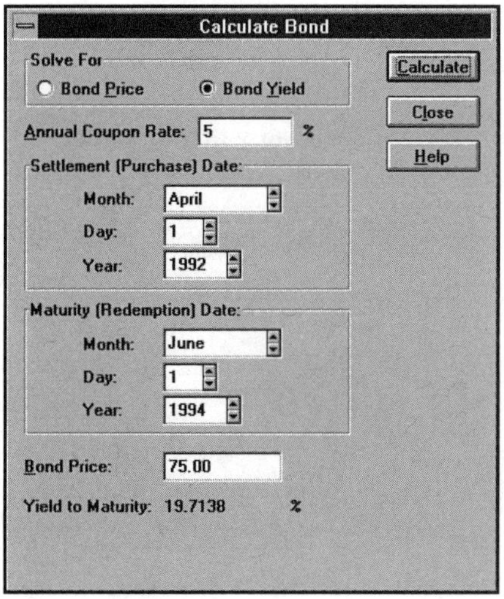

Fig. 14.6
The Calculate Bond dialog box enables you to calculate bond yield or price.

Follow these steps to perform the calculations:

1. Choose the C**o**mpute **B**ond command from the Financial Calculator to access the Calculate Bond dialog box.

2. Choose Bond **Y**ield from the Solve For area.

3. Enter the **A**nnual Coupon Rate of the bond.

4. Enter the Settlement (Purchase) Date of the bond. You can click the up- or down-arrow keys on the Month, Day, and Year increment buttons to select the desired values.

5. Enter the Maturity (Redemption) Date of the bond.

6. Enter the initial **B**ond Price because you are calculating for Bond **Y**ield. (If you are calculating for Bond **P**rice, enter the desired Y**i**eld to Maturity.)

7. Choose the **C**alculate button. The bond calculator solves the missing variable.

8. Choose C**l**ose to close the Calculate Bond dialog box.

Date/Time

This simple financial calculator calculates the exact difference between two dates. The difference can include precise hours and minutes, if you enter them.

To perform date/time calculations, follow these steps:

1. Choose the C**o**mpute **D**ate/Time command from the Financial calculator. The Date/Time dialog box appears, as shown in figure 14.7.

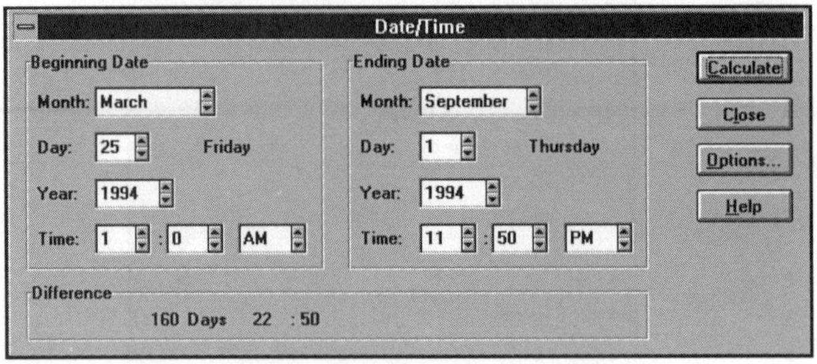

Fig. 14.7
The Date/Time dialog box enables you to calculate the number of days between two dates.

2. Use the increment arrows to set the Month, Day, Year, and Time of the Beginning Date, or type in the values.

3. Use the increment arrows to set the Month, Day, Year, and Time of the Ending Date, or type in the values.

4. Choose **O**ptions if you want to set time to military or if you want to choose between using 30-day months or actual months to perform the calculations.

5. Choose the **C**alculate button. The Difference appears.

6. Choose C**l**ose to close the dialog box.

Depreciation

The Depreciation Calculator enables you to calculate the depreciated value and accumulated value of any depreciable asset. You can choose from three different methods of depreciation: **S**traight-Line, **D**eclining-Balance, and **S**um-of-Years-Digits.

1. Choose the C**o**mpute D**e**preciation command from the Financial Calculator. The Calculate Depreciation dialog box appears (see fig. 14.8).

2. Select the **M**ethod button to display the Method of Depreciation dialog box (see fig. 14.9).

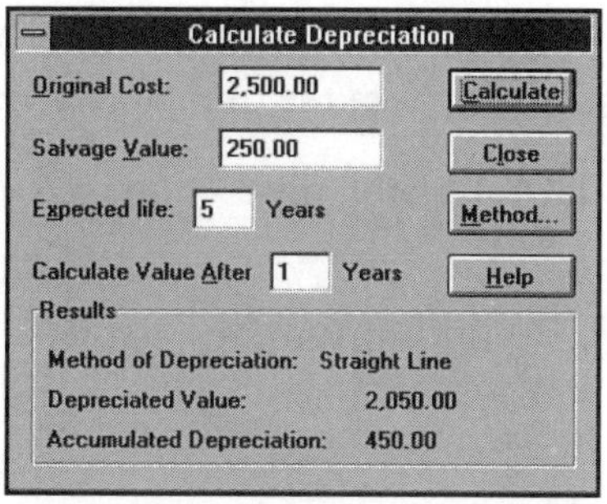

Fig. 14.8
The Calculate Depreciation dialog box enables you to calculate the depreciation of an asset.

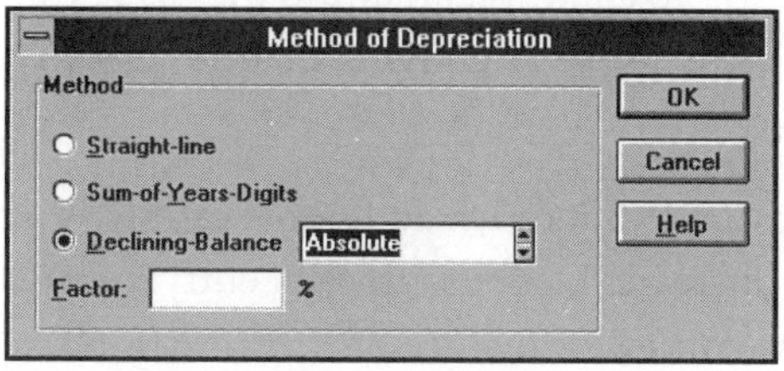

Fig. 14.9
The Method of Depreciation dialog box enables you to select a depreciation method.

3. Choose the preferred Method: **S**traight-Line, Sum-of-**Y**ears-Digits, or **D**eclining-Balance.

4. If you choose **D**eclining-Balance, use the increment arrows to select either Absolute or Straight-Line, and then enter the **F**actor in the text box.

5. Choose OK to close the dialog box and return to the Calculate Depreciation dialog box.

6. Enter the **O**riginal Cost of the asset.

7. Enter the Salvage **V**alue of the asset.

8. Enter the **E**xpected Life of the asset, in years.

9. Enter the time period in the Calculate Value **A**fter *x* Years.

10. Select the **C**alculate button to begin calculation. The Results box displays the Depreciated Value and Accumulated Depreciation after the selected time period.

11. Select C**l**ose to close the Calculate Depreciation dialog box.

Discounted Cash Flow

Norton Desktop enables you to calculate discounted cash flow by using either the net present value or the internal rate of return method.

This operation involves using the main Financial Calculator and the Discounted Cash Flow operation from the C**o**mpute menu. Follow these steps:

1. Start the Financial Calculator; press ALT+cl_CF to clear the cash flow registers.

2. Enter the amount of the initial investment.

   If you have no initial investment, enter **0**. If the cash flow is negative, enter **CHS**.

3. Press ALT+CFj+ to add this amount to the cash flow register. The value 1 appears in the display, signifying that this entry is the first in the cash flow register.

4. Repeat steps 2 and 3 for each additional cash flow amount. The value in the display increases by one with each entry, to reflect the total number of cash flow entries.

5. After you finish entering data, choose the C**o**mpute D**i**scounted Cash Flow command. The Discounted Cash Flow dialog box appears (see fig. 14.10).

   The amounts in the cash flow register appear in the list box.

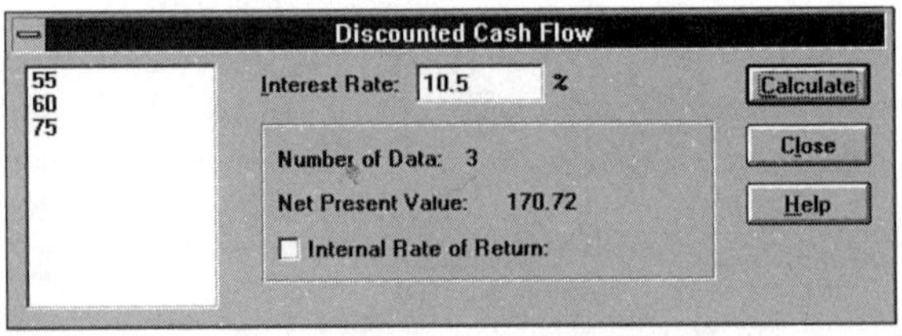

Fig. 14.10
The Discounted Cash Flow dialog box enables you to calculate a net present value on a cash flow.

6. Enter the interest rate in the **I**nterest Rate text box.

7. Choose **C**alculate. The Net Present Value of the cash flow appears. A negative Net Present Value (for example, –32.00) signifies a loss.

8. Select the Internal Rate of Return check box to calculate the internal rate of return, and choose **C**alculate.

Tip
Enter an interest rate that reflects the cash flow time period. If the cash flow occurs over a three-year period, for example, the interest rate entered is the return expected after three years.

Simple Interest

The Simple Interest Calculator enables you to calculate the accrued interest and total principal, plus interest on a simple-interest loan. This utility is ideal for calculating the total outflow on short-term loans, such as 90-day loans at 14.9 percent annual interest. To perform the calculation, follow these steps:

1. Choose the C**o**mpute **S**imple Interest command from the Financial Calculator. The Simple Interest dialog box appears (see fig. 14.11).

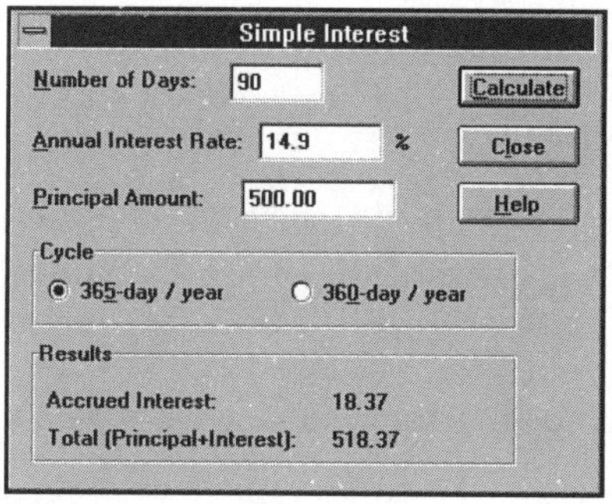

Fig. 14.11
The Simple Interest dialog box enables you to compute simple interest on a principal amount.

2. Enter the **N**umber of Days of the loan.

3. Enter the **A**nnual Interest Rate.

4. Choose either a 36**5**-Day/Year or 36**0**-Day/Year Cycle.

5. Select the **C**alculate button. The Results of the calculation are displayed.

6. Choose C**l**ose to close the Simple Interest dialog box.

Statistics

You can use the Financial calculator to perform various statistical analyses on lists of data pairs. By using the regular Financial Calculator in conjunction with the C**o**mpute S**t**atistics command, you can calculate the following values for both X and Y:

- Average
- Standard Deviation
- Weighted Average
- Summation (total)
- Summation of X (or Y) squared
- Summation of X times Y

To initiate statistical analysis, follow these steps:

1. Clear the statistics registers from the Financial Calculator by choosing Alt+cl_stat on the Financial Calculator.
2. Enter the first Y value.
3. Press Enter.
4. Enter the first X value.
5. Enter ALT+stat+. This step adds the *data pair* to the statistics register. The display shows 1, representing the total number of data pairs entered.
6. Repeat steps 2 through 5 for each new set of data pairs.
7. Choose the C**o**mpute S**t**atistics command. The Statistics dialog box appears, as shown in figure 14.12.

Tip

Choose the **M**ore button to display the full box shown in figure 14.12. This option displays the various summation analyses, hidden while the dialog box is in the Less state.

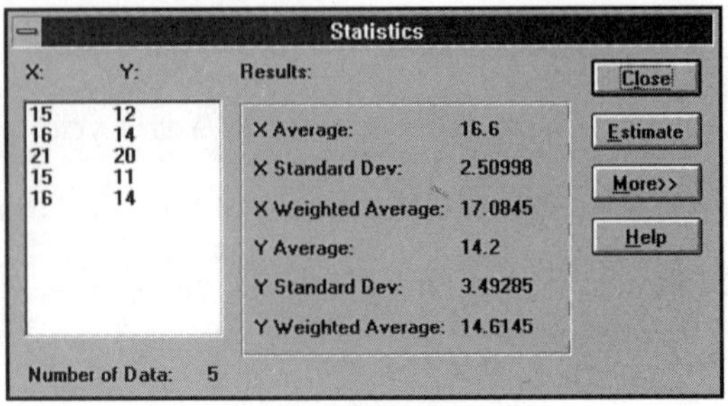

Fig. 14.12
The Statistics dialog box enables you to calculate statistics and linear estimation.

You also can perform linear estimation, calculating an estimated new X value based on a known new Y value, and vice versa. Follow these steps:

1. Choose the **E**stimate option from the Statistics dialog box. The Linear Estimation dialog box displays (see fig. 14.13).
2. Enter a new **Y** value, and choose **C**alculate to calculate a new X value.
3. Enter a new **X** value, and choose **C**alculate to calculate a new Y value.

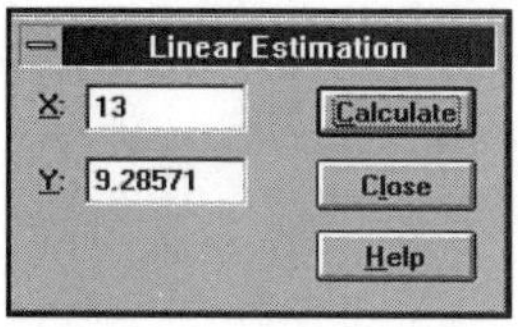

Fig. 14.13
The Linear Estimation dialog box enables you to estimate a Y value from an input X value or vice versa.

Summary

This chapter described the three calculators included with Norton Desktop for Windows. You learned how to use the Tape Calculator, the Scientific Calculator, and the Financial Calculator. You also learned how to perform specific financial analyses, including amortization, bond yield analysis, date/time calculation, depreciation analysis, discounted cash flow analysis, simple interest analysis, and various statistical analyses.

The next chapter, "Using the Day Planner," explains how to start the Day Planner, use the menu bar and Treasure Chests, and work with tags and filters.

Chapter 15

Using the Day Planner

In this chapter, you learn to perform the following tasks:

- Understand the Day Planner
- Start the Day Planner
- Use the Day Planner menu bar
- Work with tags and filters

If you are the type of person who likes to keep close tabs on your schedule, the Day Planner in Norton Desktop 3 for Windows may be the tool designed just for you. Day Planner is a Desktop personal organizer that can be used to keep your schedule, manage your priorities, and keep your phone book.

Understanding Day Planner

Day Planner is like having a personal calendar, a phone book, and a To Do list all rolled up into one. With NDW, your calendar is always a few clicks away. After you are in Day Planner, you see how many features it has to offer. By using Day Planner you can:

- Schedule your appointments for each day, then view your appointment list by day, week, or month.
- Keep your phone book up-to-date. You can also create multiple phone books for personal, professional, and any other use.
- Keep a To Do list current and prioritize your list.
- Arrange the setup of Day Planner to display precisely what you need to see on-screen.
- Use tags to connect people, projects, and assignments to your appointments, tasks, and phone book entries.
- See immediately if you have a scheduling conflict on your calendar.
- Use password protection to protect your information from unauthorized eyes.

In short, Day Planner is a full-featured personal task manager.

Starting Day Planner

You can start Day Planner by choosing the **T**ools **D**ay Planner command. The initial Day Planner screen looks like the example shown in figure 15.1. On this screen, you can see the calendar window at the top, containing a list of events planned for the day, plus a month calendar and a box containing today's date and time. The bottom window contains a To Do List that also contains several items. The first item in the To Do List is checked off, and that entry is displayed in a strike-through font. At the left of the Day Planner screen is a toolbar containing eight of the most commonly used Day Planner commands. At the top of the screen is a menu bar. This chapter describes the use of the command icons on the toolbar and then describes the other commands available in the menu bar.

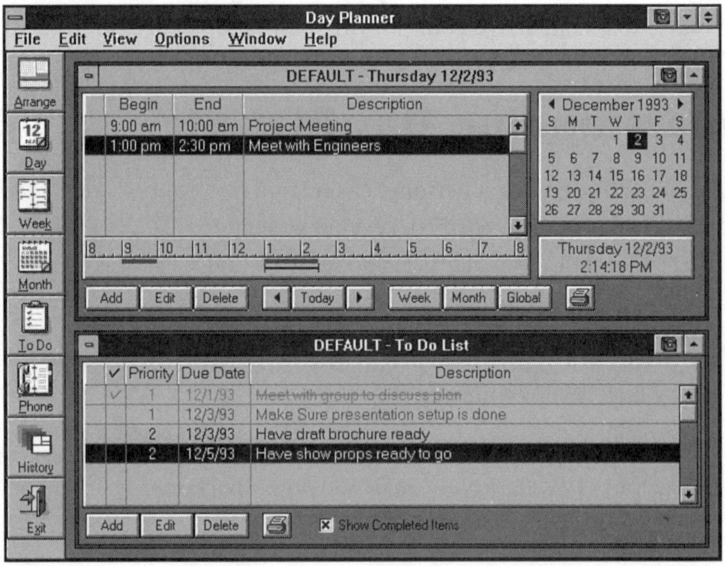

Fig. 15.1
The initial Day Planner screen showing a Calendar, a Task List, and a To Do List.

Arranging Day Planner's Screen

The **A**rrange icon enables you to display your most often used windows in a specified arrangement. After you first begin Day Planner, the Day, Month, Clock, and To Do List windows are displayed. You can change what appears each time you begin Day Planner by choosing and positioning the windows and then choosing **W**indow **A**rrangement, specifying your layout and Arrangement **N**ame in the Arrangement dialog box, and choosing Sa**v**e. From then on, whenever you choose the **A**rrange icon, the screen returns to your preferred arrangement.

Using the Daily Schedule

If you choose the **D**ay toolbar icon, the Daily Appointment List is displayed, as shown in figure 15.2. To enter a new item in the list, click the Add button. An Add Appointment dialog box appears, as shown in figure 15.3. In this dialog box, you can enter a description of the task, the beginning and ending time, the date, and the time that you want an alarm to sound (if you want an alarm to sound). You also can enter notes about the task in the **N**otes section.

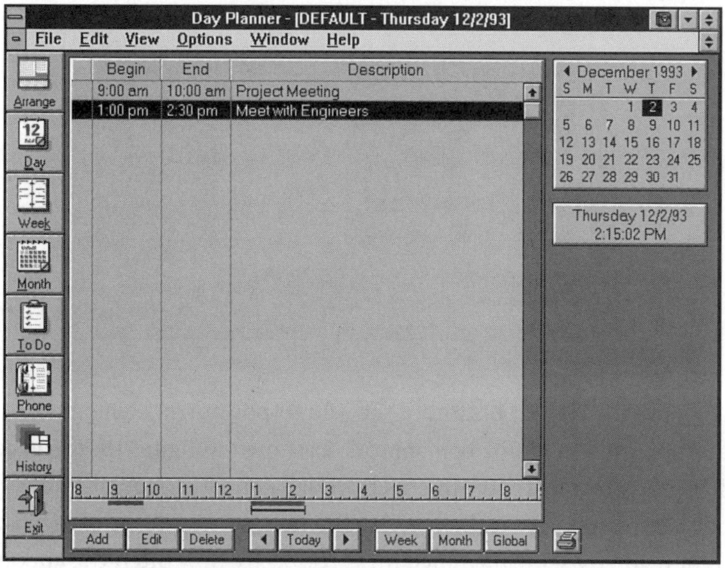

Fig. 15.2
The Daily Task List enables you to review tasks you have entered.

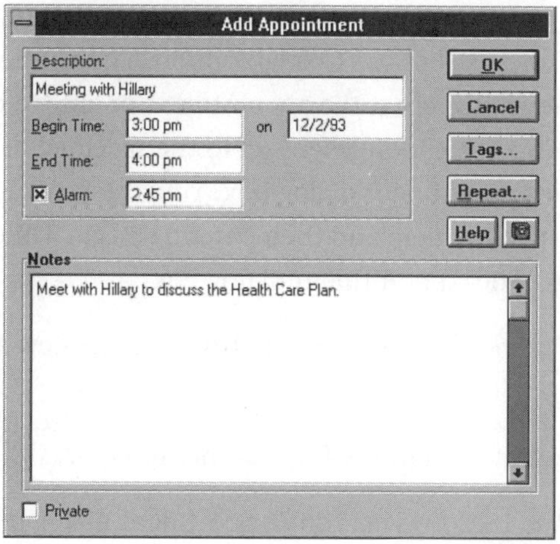

Fig. 15.3
The Add Appointment dialog box enables you to add an appointment to your Task List.

To connect this task to a person or project, choose the **T**ags button. The Assign Tags dialog box appears, as shown in figure 15.4. This dialog box enables you to select a tag to associate with the task. In the Tags **D**efined box is a list of currently defined tags. To place a tag in the Tags For This **I**tem box, select a tag name and then choose **A**dd. If you do not currently have a tag defined for a person or project, enter a new tag name in the Define **N**ew Tag text box. To remove a tag from the Tags For This Item list, select the tag, and then choose **R**emove. To clear all tags from the Tags For This **I**tem list, choose **C**lear. Choose OK to return to the Add Appointment dialog box.

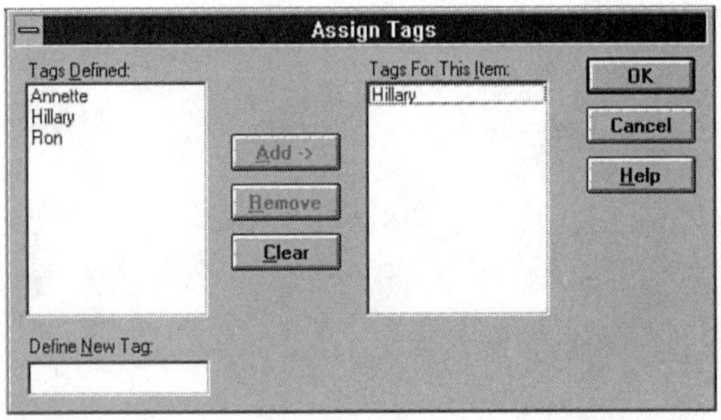

Fig. 15.4
The Assign Tags dialog box enables you to add tags to items.

If you choose the **R**epeat button in the Add Appointments dialog box, the Repeat Appointment dialog box appears, as shown in figure 15.5. You can use this dialog box to add appointments to your calendar at regular intervals without having to re-enter them each time they occur. This is particularly useful for regularly scheduled meetings. To specify how often the appointment should be entered, select a time period from the Repeat Every box. To tell the program how many times to enter the appointment, choose either the **N**umber of Times (Total) or Th**r**ough option. Then either enter the number of times you want to repeat the appointment or enter a date to tell the program to schedule the appointment up to the specified date. Choose OK to return to the Add Appointment dialog box. You also can add a new appointment by clicking a blank field and then entering **B**egin Time, **E**nd Time, and **D**escription in the Add Appointment dialog box.

To use the Day Planner window's Add button to enter new appointments, follow these steps:

1. Choose the **D**ay icon in the Day Planner toolbar.

2. Click the Add button. The Add Appointment dialog box appears.

3. Enter information about the new appointment to add, including a **D**escription, **B**egin Time, **E**nd Time, date, and **A**larm time (if desired). You also can enter any additional notes about the appointment in the **N**otes text box.

4. Optionally, choose the **T**ags button to establish associations between this appointment and people or projects. Choose OK to exit the Assign Tags dialog box.

5. Optionally, choose the **R**epeat button to indicate that the appointment should be repeated at certain intervals. Choose OK to exit the Repeat Appointment dialog box.

6. Choose OK to exit the Add Appointment dialog box and save the information into your Day Planner.

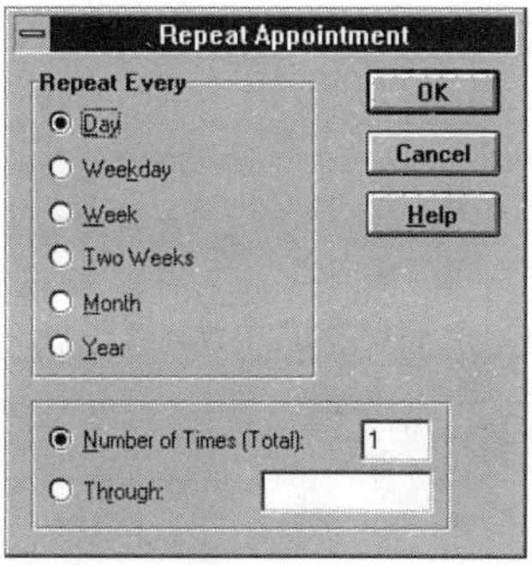

Fig. 15.5
The Repeat Appointment dialog box enables you to easily enter repeating events.

To add appointments without using the Add button, follow these steps:

1. Click an empty **B**egin Time, **E**nd Time, or **D**escription text box.

2. Enter information in the selected text box. Information you enter adds a new appointment to the list.

Tip
You also can add a new appointment by double-clicking the bar chart above the button bar at the bottom of the Day Window.

To edit an existing appointment, highlight the appointment on the list, and then click Edit. A dialog box similar to the Add Appointment dialog box appears, and you can then change any item associated with that appointment. To delete an appointment, highlight the appointment, and then click the Delete button.

To display the task list for today, click the Today button. To move the appointment list forward or backward a day, click the left or right arrow next to the Today button. To select some other day in the current month, click the desired date in the monthly calendar displayed at the upper right of the window.

To switch to a weekly, monthly, or global view, click the appropriate button at the bottom of the window. To print the current task list, click the Printer icon button.

Notice the two lines at the bottom of the appointment list, under the bar that ranges from 8 a.m. to 8 p.m. (refer to fig. 15.6). These green lines show you graphically when appointments are scheduled. If a conflict exists in your schedule, the lines overlap, and the overlap appears in red, telling you that a conflict exists.

Tip
You can edit the **B**egin Time, **E**nd Time, and **D**escription text boxes by selecting the item on the Day list, and then entering the information directly into the field.

Using the Weekly Schedule

If you choose the Wee**k** toolbar icon, the Weekly appointment list appears, as shown in figure 15.6. The weekly view shows your schedule from Monday through Sunday. To add a new task item to a day of the week, click that day, and then click the Add button. Refer to the section "Using the Daily Schedule" for information on adding, editing, or deleting a task.

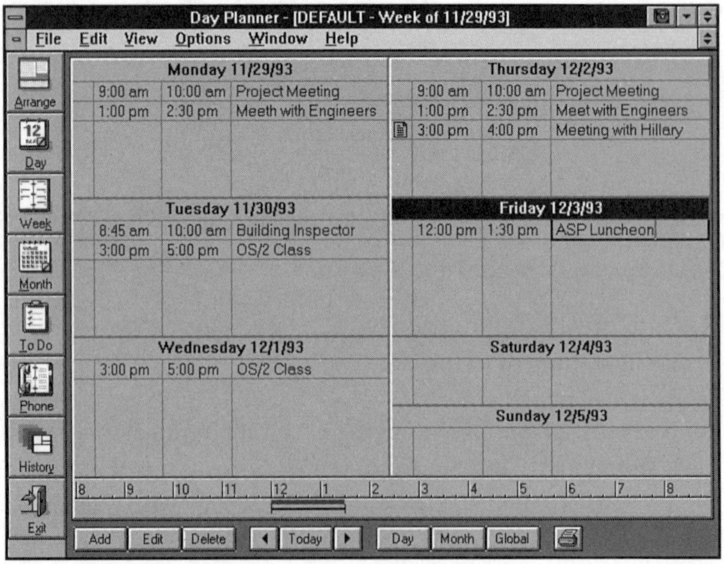

Fig. 15.6
The Weekly Task List Schedule shows the entire week's schedule in one window.

Using the Monthly Task List Schedule

If you choose the **M**onth toolbar icon, the Monthly Task List appears as a monthly calendar, as shown in figure 15.7. The Monthly view shows as many tasks as fits into each day's box. To see a full list for a day, click the day, and then choose the Day view. To add a new task item to a day of the week, click that day, and then click the Add button. Refer to the section "Using the Daily Schedule" for information on adding, editing, or deleting a task.

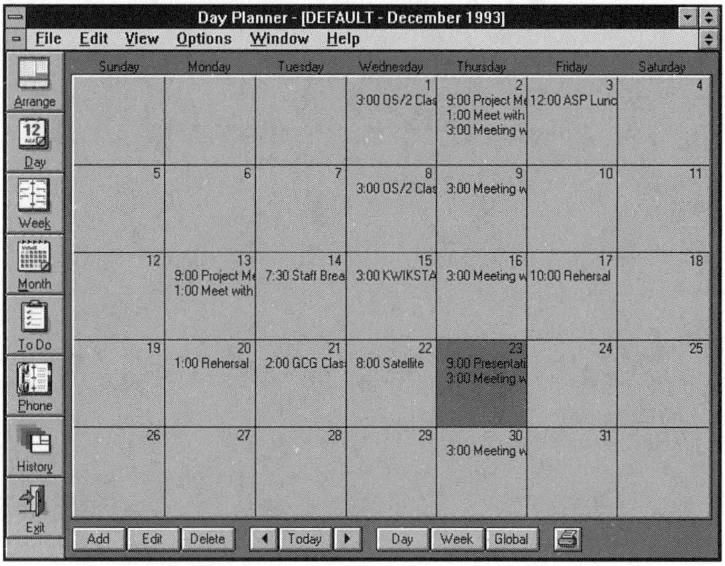

Fig. 15.7
The Monthly Task List Schedule shows an entire month at a time.

Using the To Do List

If you choose the **T**o Do toolbar icon, the To Do List appears, as shown in figure 15.8. This list differs from a daily appointment list in that it does not have a time associated with the task. The To Do List is meant to be a list of prioritized and dated items that you can check off whenever an item is accomplished. Priority 1 items appear in red. Items that have been checked off appear dimmed and struck-out. If you deselect the Show Completed Items check box at the bottom of the window, completed items do not appear on the list.

Adding, editing, and deleting items in the To Do List is similar to performing these tasks in the Appointment Calendar. To add an item to the list, click the Add button. To add a task by using the Add button, follow these steps:

1. Click the Add button on the To Do List window. The Add Task dialog box appears (see fig. 15.9).

2. Enter a **D**escription, choose a **P**riority, enter a D**ue** Date, and (optionally) enter a more extensive description in the **N**otes text box.

3. Optionally, check the Private box if you want to restrict other people from viewing your task entry.

4. Click OK to save the task and add it to your To Do List.

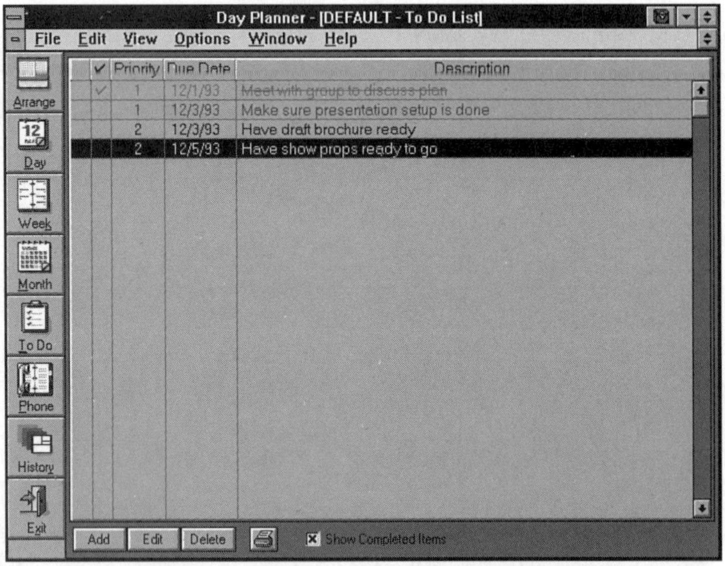

Fig. 15.8
The To Do list enables you to view the task you need to remember to do.

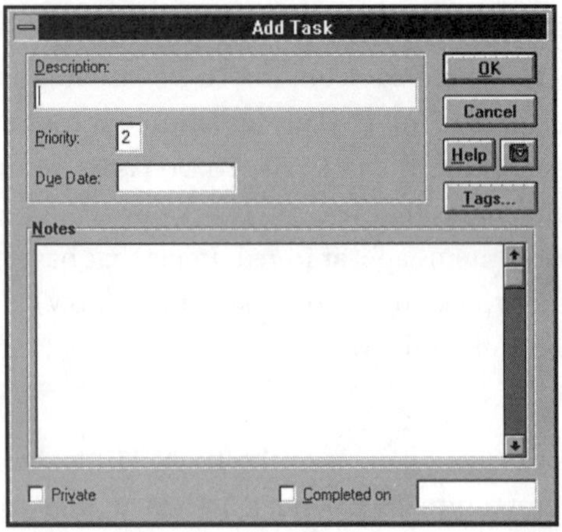

Fig. 15.9
The Add Task dialog box enables you to add a task to the To Do List.

Tip
When entering a date in the D**u**e Date field, you can enter a +7 (for 7 days from now). Day Planner calculates the correct date and places it in the D**u**e Date field.

You also can add a new task by clicking a blank field, and then entering the **P**riority, D**u**e Date, and **D**escription directly onto the Add Task list screen.

Using the Phone Book

When you choose the **P**hone icon on the toolbar, the Day Planner - Phone Book window appears, as shown in figure 15.10. The Phone Book enables you to keep a list of phone numbers and other information for a list of people. Adding, editing, deleting, and printing information is similar to the same procedures for the Appointment Calendar and To Do List.

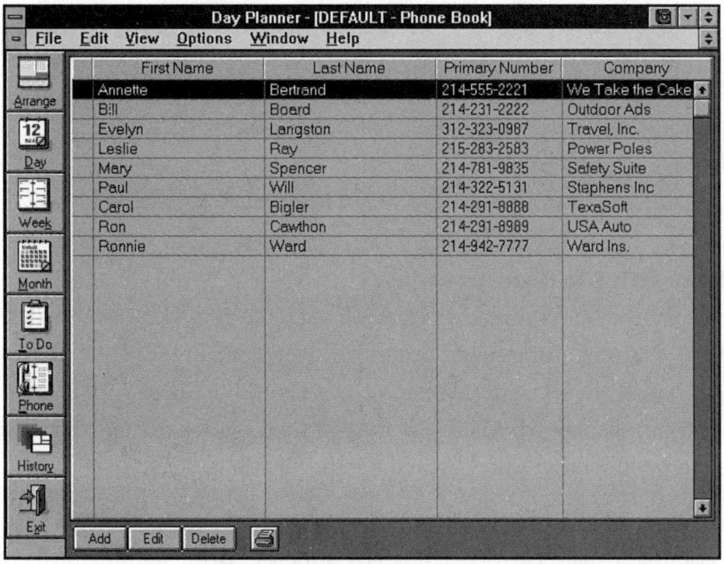

Fig. 15.10
The Day Planner - Phone Book window displays names and phone numbers.

To add a new person to the Phone Book, click the Add button. The Add Phone Book Entry dialog box appears, as shown in figure 15.11. Enter names, phone numbers, addresses, and other information into the dialog box. Choose OK to exit the Add Phone Book Entry dialog box and return to the Phone Book window.

You also can add new entries by clicking a blank field and entering new information, or you can edit current information by clicking a field that currently contains information and entering new information.

The Phone Book window lists the current persons in your phone book. The field on the far left of each name contains a page icon if additional information is listed in the **N**otes field (refer to fig. 15.11). You can cause the list to appear in sorted order by clicking the column name at the top of the list. For example, click Last Name to display the names in last name order.

Tip
If you want to sort the list by the Primary Number column, including area code, make sure that you enter an area code for every phone number.

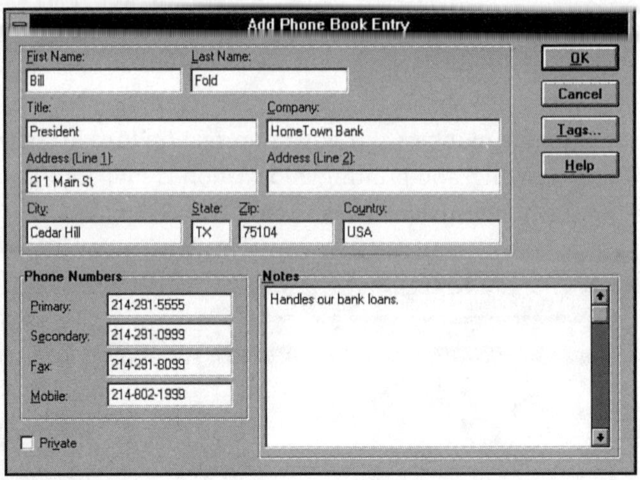

Fig 15.11
The Add Phone Book Entry dialog box enables you to enter a new name in your Phone Book.

Working with File History

The Histor**y** toolbar command is used to see what files you have loaded while using Day Planner and in what order they were loaded. This information can come in handy if you want to switch from file to file. After you load several files, you can display your File History and then open a file by clicking its name. To open a previously opened file, follow these steps:

1. Choose the Histor**y** icon from the toolbar, or choose the **F**ile Histor**y** command. The History dialog box appears, listing all previously opened files.

2. Select the file you want to open.

3. Click OK. The chosen file information appears in your Day Planner.

Exiting Day Planner

To exit the Day Planner, choose the E**x**it toolbar icon or choose the **F**ile **E**xit command from the menu bar. If you access Day Planner information often, you may find it quicker to minimize Day Planner. Then you can double-click the minimized icon to quickly redisplay your calendar.

Using the Day Planner Menu Bar and Treasure Chests

The Day Planner's menu bar contains six menu options: **F**ile, **E**dit, **V**iew, **O**ptions, **W**indow, and **H**elp. The Treasure Chest also appears on the title bar.

The six pull-down menus contain commands you can choose to create, use, and customize your Day Planner. The Treasure Chest contains helpful hints about using Day Planner. Treasure Chests also are located in other Day Planner windows and dialog boxes. Whenever you see a Treasure Chest, click it to display helpful information about the program or dialog box.

The following sections describe the purpose of each of the Day Planner menu bar options.

Using the File Menu

The Day Planner **F**ile menu contains a number of commands used to manage your Day Planner files. The open **F**ile menu is shown in figure 15.12.

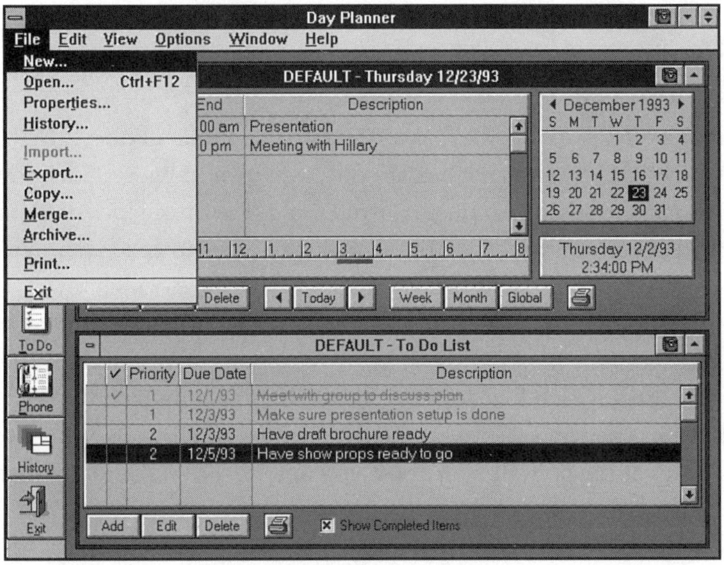

Fig 15.12
The Day Planner **F**ile menu enables you to manage your Day Planner files.

Creating a New File. The **F**ile **N**ew command enables you to create new calendars, Phone Books, or To Do Lists. After you choose this command, the New dialog box appears (see fig. 15.13). Probably the most common new item to create would be a new Phone Book. You may want to create a Personal Phone Book and a Professional Phone Book. To create a new Personal Phone Book, follow these steps:

1. Access the New dialog box by choosing the **F**ile **N**ew command.

2. Enter a name for your Phone Book (such as Personal), choose **P**hone Book as the Type, and specify the directory and file name you want to use to store your Personal Phone Book. If you do not choose a file

name, one is created from your description. For your Personal Phone Book, for example, the information is stored in a file named PERSONAL.P.

3. Click OK to exit back to the main Day Planner window.

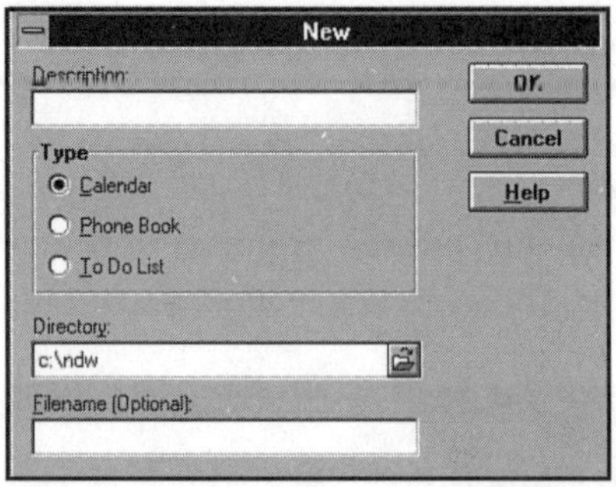

Fig 15.13
The New dialog box enables you to create a new item, such as a Phone Book.

Opening a File. After you choose the **F**ile **O**pen command on the Day Planner window, the Open dialog box appears, as shown in figure 15.14. In this box, you can choose which file to open. Each of the three kinds of files are identified by an icon to the left of the file name. The notepad icon signifies a To Do List, the phone signifies a Phone Book, and the clock signifies your Appointment List. Your original three files are called DEFAULT.T (To Do List), DEFAULT.P (Phone Book), and DEFAULT.A (Appointment List). If you have more than one of each kind of file, you can use this command to specify which file to open and display in the Day Planner window. By using the check boxes at the bottom of the box, you can specify which of the three file types to list.

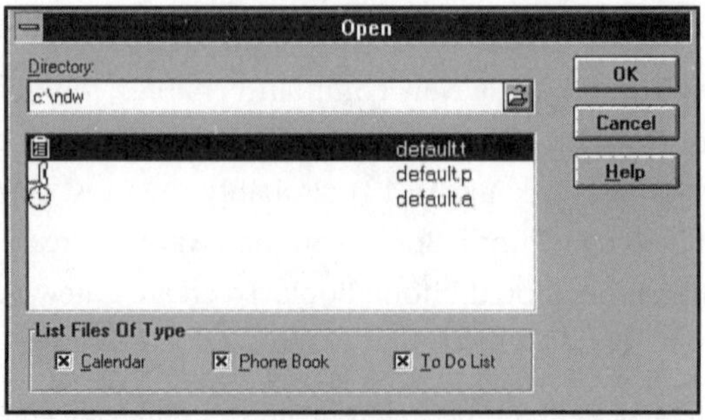

Fig 15.14
The Open dialog box enables you to choose what To Do, Phone Book, and Appointment files to open.

Setting Calendar Properties. To display the Calendar Properties dialog box, choose the **F**ile Proper**t**ies command (see fig. 15.15). This box enables you to enter a **D**escription of your currently opened information file (To Do, Phone, or Appointments file) and choose passwords for **R**estricted and **F**ull Access. If you choose a password, a user cannot access your Day Planner information unless the password is entered.

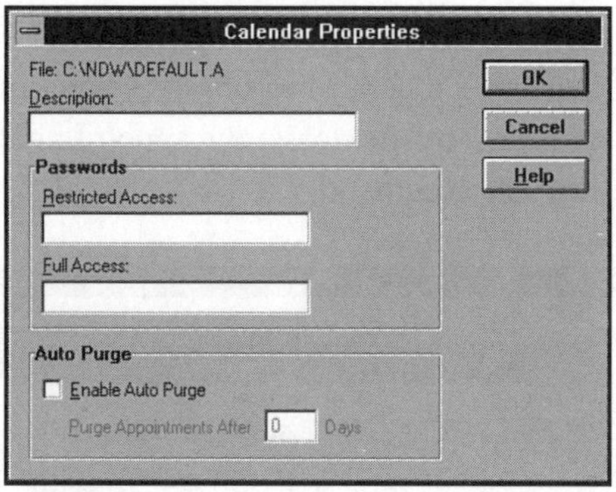

Fig. 15.15
The Properties dialog box enables you to enter a file description and choose a password.

The **E**nable Auto Purge option, if selected, causes the system to delete items that are older than the specified age. Using Auto Purge helps you keep your system uncluttered by old information.

Managing Your Day Planner Files. The **F**ile menu contains several commands to help you manage your Day Planner files. The **H**istory command was discussed earlier, in the section "Working with File History." The **F**ile **I**mport command is used to import phone numbers from Windows Cardfile files. The **F**ile **E**xport command enables you to write information from Day Planner into a text file. You can then print the information or merge it into a word processing or other type of document.

If you have information in a Day Planner file that you want copied, use the **F**ile **C**opy command. The **F**ile **M**erge command enables you to merge information from another Day Planner file into an open file. For example, you may want to combine two Phone Books to create a more comprehensive Phone Book. The **F**ile **A**rchive command enables you to remove completed tasks from your list and store them in another file. This helps you remove clutter from your task list, but enables you to keep the tasks for reference.

The **F**ile **P**rint command enables you to print the information from a Day Planner file. This is helpful, for example, to print a phone book or take a list of tasks or appointments with you when you cannot take your computer.

Use the **F**ile **Ex**it command to exit Day Planner and return to your Desktop.

Using the Day Planner Edit Menu

The Day Planner **E**dit menu contains commands that can be used to edit or manage the information in your Day Planner files (see fig. 15.16). The Cu**t**, **C**opy, and **P**aste commands are used, like in a word processor, to delete, move, and copy pieces of information from one place to another. For example, if you have a meeting that has been moved, you can highlight the appointment, choose **E**dit Cu**t**, then paste the appointment onto a different day by using the **E**dit **P**aste command.

Fig. 15.16
The Day Planner **E**dit menu contains **E**dit command options.

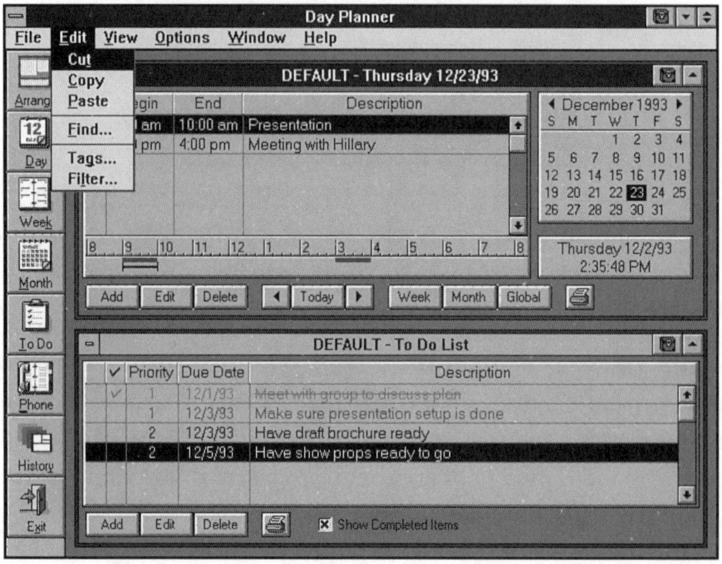

The **E**dit **F**ind command is used to find a search string in your currently opened file. If your Phone Book is displayed in the Day Planner window, for example, the **F**ind command finds an occurrence of a string in your phone list. If your Appointments are displayed, **F**ind locates an occurrence of a string in your appointment list. The Ta**g**s command enables you to create associations among appointments, tasks, and phone numbers. The Fi**l**ter command enables you to select what tasks are displayed. Tags and filters are discussed more fully in the section "Working with Tags and Filters," later in this chapter.

Using the View Menu

The Day Planner **V**iew pull down menu contains seven options. These options correspond to six of the options on the Day Planner toolbar plus an option called **G**lobal (see fig. 15.17). The **A**rrange, **D**ay, **W**eek, **M**onth, **T**o Do List, and **P**hone Book options have been discussed earlier.

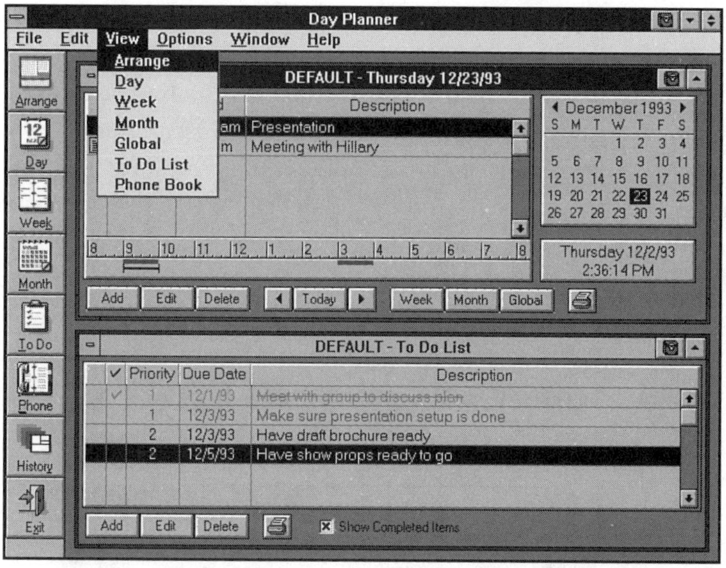

Fig. 15.17
The Day Planner **V**iew menu enables you to select different views of your information.

The **G**lobal option enables you to look at your entire list of appointments. An example of a global list is shown in figure 15.18. The **G**lobal option also is available as an option button on the Appointments List window.

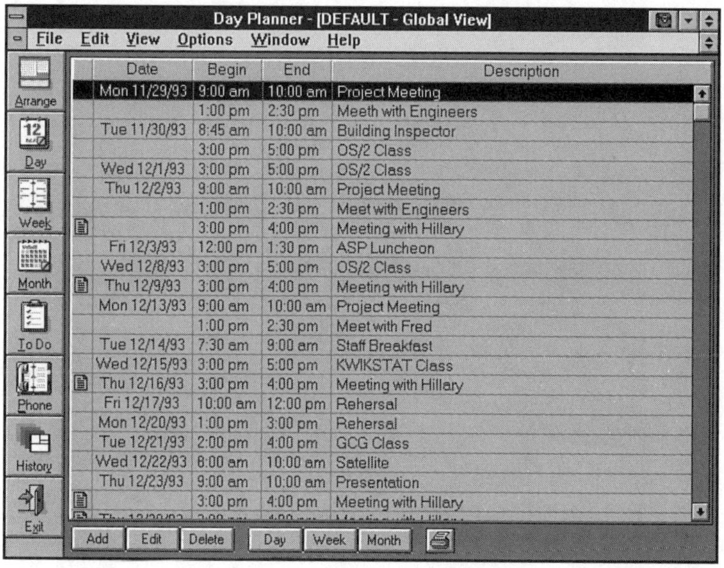

Fig. 15.18
The Global View appointments list displays a list of all current tasks.

Selecting Day Planner Options

The Day Planner **O**ptions menu enables you to choose several customization options for the program. If you choose **O**ptions **C**ustomize, the Customize (Calendar) dialog box appears, as shown in figure 15.19. In this dialog box, you can choose the default number of minutes the program assigns to a meeting if you do not specify an ending time. It also enables you to specify the default lead time that an alarm sounds warning you of an upcoming appointment. At the bottom of the Appointment List window, a bar shows the beginning and ending time for a workday. This is normally set as 8:00 a.m. **t**o 8:00 p.m. You can specify a different range in this dialog box. If you select the Warn About Conflicting Appointments option, a message tells you when you have made appointments that overlap.

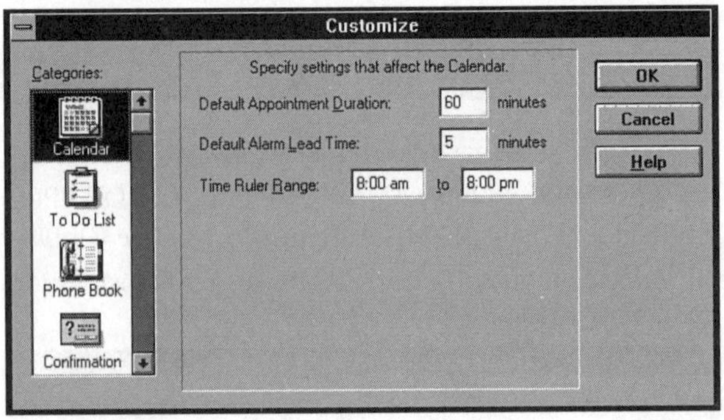

Fig. 15.19
The Customize (Calendar) dialog box enables you to customize your calendar options.

The Customize (To Do List) dialog box enables you to choose the default priority for tasks and enables you to choose to Highlight **U**rgent Items and to display completed tasks in a strike-through font (see fig. 15.20).

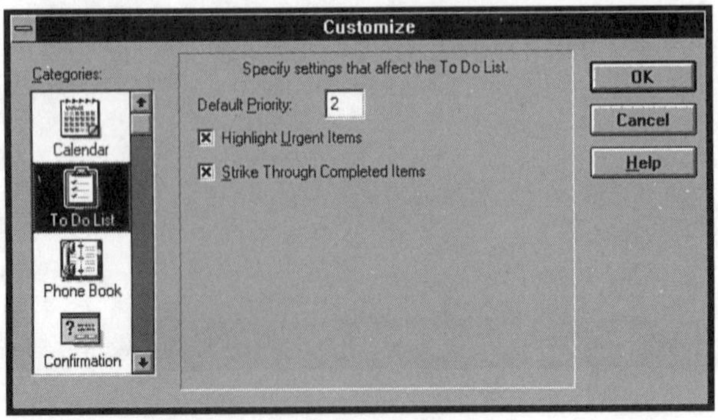

Fig. 15.20
The Customize (To Do List) dialog box enables you to customize your To Do List options.

The Customize (Phone Book) dialog box enables you to specify if you want the list to appear as **L**ast Name First. The Customize (Confirmation) dialog box enables you to choose to Confirm **D**eletions and Confirm **E**xit from the program.

The Customize (Toolbar) dialog box enables you to select a number of items concerning how the toolbar is displayed (see fig. 15.21).

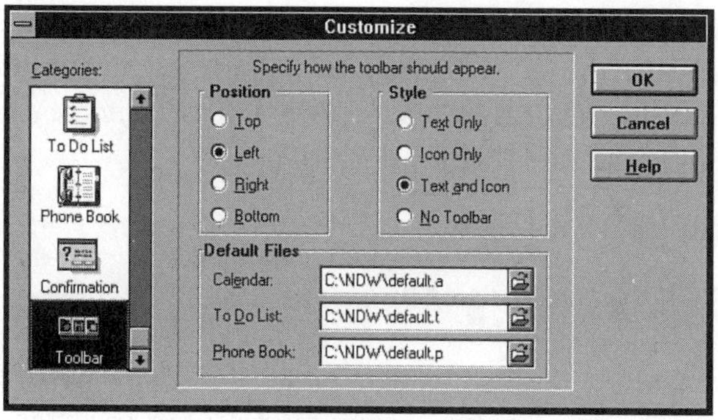

Fig. 15.21
The Customize (Toolbar) dialog box enables you to select how the toolbar is displayed.

In the Position box, you can choose to display the toolbar at the **T**op, **L**eft, **R**ight, or **B**ottom of the window. In the Style box, you can choose to display the toolbar as Te**x**t Only, **I**con Only, Text **a**nd Icon (the default), or **N**o Toolbar. The Default Files box enables you to choose the default names of the Cal**e**ndar, To **D**o List, and **P**hone Book files.

Using the Day Planner Window and Help Menu

The Day Planner **W**indow pull-down menu lists the windows that are currently available. This list includes all views of your Day Planner information, and is essentially the same as the **V**iew pull-down menu list. You can use the **W**indow menu to quickly display your daily, weekly, monthly, or global appointments, your task list, or your Phone Book.

The Day Planner **H**elp menu enables you to display help about Day Planner and to search for specific items about using the program. The Help interface is the same Windows Help system described in Chapter 2, "Getting Up and Running with Norton Desktop for Windows."

Working with Tags and Filters

As you enter an appointment or task in Day Planner, you often want to associate that task with some person—perhaps a person in your Phone Book. In

Day Planner, you can set up associations among tasks, appointments, and phone book entries. To assign tags to appointments, tasks, or phone book entries, follow these steps:

1. Select the task you want to assign by clicking the task's leftmost column.
2. Choose the **E**dit **T**ag command. The Assign Tags dialog box appears.
3. If the tag you want to assign is already in the Tags **D**efined list box, double-click the tag. If the tag is not already assigned, enter the tag name in the Define **N**ew Tag text box, and then choose **A**dd. The tag appears in the Tags For This **I**tem list box.
4. Repeat step 3 if necessary.
5. Click OK to exit the dialog box.

To remove tags from the Tags For This **I**tem list, click the tag name, and then click **R**emove. To clear tags from appointments, tasks, or phone book entries, follow these steps:

1. Select the task you want to clear by clicking the task's leftmost column.
2. Choose the **E**dit Ta**g** command. The Assign Tags dialog box appears.
3. Choose **C**lear to clear the tag from the Tags For This **I**tem list box.
4. Click OK to exit the dialog box.

A filter is used to specify that you want to see only tasks that match some criteria (filter). You can filter your appointments, tasks, and phone book list. To apply a filter to appointments, for example, follow these steps:

1. With your appointment list active, choose the **E**dit Fi**l**ter command. The Filter dialog box appears (see fig. 15.22).
2. Select the desired tag from the Tags **D**efined list box, or define a new tag.
3. Choose **A**dd to add the tag to the Tags in **F**ilter box.
4. Repeat steps 2 and 3 if needed.
5. Click OK to exit the dialog box.

To remove a tag, open the Filter dialog box, highlight the tag to delete, and choose **R**emove.

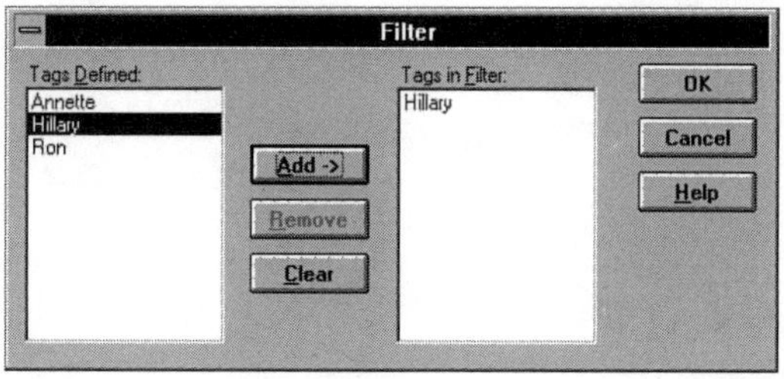

Fig. 15.22
The Filter dialog box enables you to specify the tasks you want to see.

Summary

This chapter detailed how to use NDW's Day Planner. You learned how to enter information into your Appointment Schedule, To Do List, and Phone Book. You also learned how to display, edit, and print information from these lists, how to associate tasks with one another by using tags, and how to limit what information is shown by using a filter.

The next chapter, "Using Desktop Editor," explains how to use the Desktop Editor to edit ASCII text files. You learn how to start the Editor, edit files, and customize the Editor.

Summary

Chapter 16

Using Desktop Editor

16

Sometimes you need to edit small text files, such as the AUTOEXEC.BAT and WIN.INI files. You do not want to use your regular word processor for such tasks; you need something quick and easy—such as NDW's Desktop Editor.

In this chapter, you learn to perform the following tasks:

- Start Desktop Editor
- Use Desktop Editor to edit files
- Customize Desktop Editor

Understanding Desktop Editor

As is the Windows Notepad utility, Desktop Editor is a simple ASCII text editor. Unlike Notepad, however, Desktop Editor includes several unique features that are especially valuable for editing text files.

Desktop Editor is a *line-oriented editor*—that is, it expects lines in text files to be terminated by a carriage return and line feed. After a file is saved in Desktop Editor, each line in the file ends with a carriage return and line feed—even if the line did not end that way before you saved it and you did not specifically modify the file to do so.

Note

Desktop Editor was previously known as the Upper Deck Editor, a Windows-based text editor for programmers. Its original purpose explains some of its unique features and behavior.

The NDW Desktop Editor incorporates the following important features:

- A unique 300-level Undo capability that permits you to "backtrack" through all changes made in an editing session.
- An Autosave function that enables frequent saving of data automatically.

- The capability to cut, copy, and paste to and from the Windows Clipboard.
- The capability to find and replace specified text.
- The capability to find and list all files that contain a specified text pattern.
- A file-comparison function, with either horizontal or vertical split-screen display.
- The capability to record keyboard macros.
- The capability to insert a date/time stamp.
- A word-wrap mode with an adjustable right margin.
- The capability to print the entire document or only selected text.
- The capability to print headers and footers.
- The capability to specify the font for printout.
- The capability to customize function key assignments.
- The capability to customize the position and look of the toolbar.

Note

Desktop Editor also is used, with some modification, as the editor in NDW's ScriptMaker utility.

Starting Desktop Editor

Start Desktop Editor by choosing the **T**ools Deskt**o**p Editor command. The Editor screen resembles the screen of any word processor—totally blank until a file is loaded. After you load a file, its text appears in the Editor's screen ready for editing, as shown in figure 16.1.

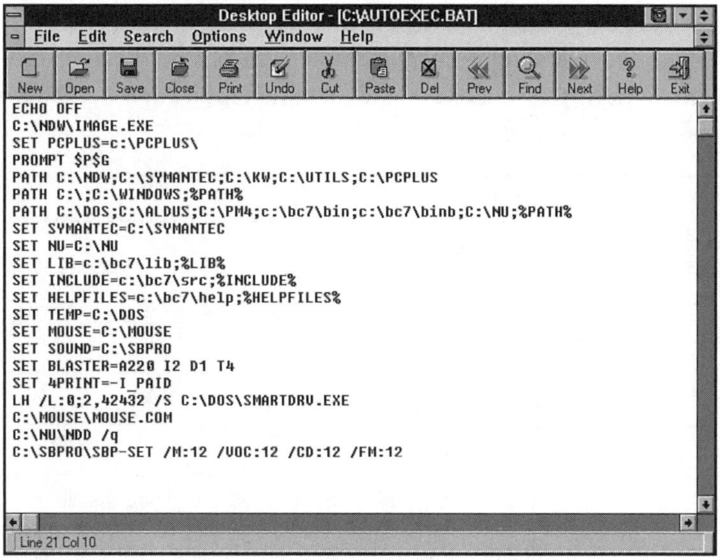

Fig. 16.1
The Desktop Editor window, showing the text of a file ready for editing.

The Editor's menu bar contains the six menu options described in the following table.

Option	Function
File	Displays standard File options, plus options to **I**nsert the contents of another file; Re**v**ert to the saved version of the current file; **W**rite Block, which writes selected text to a separate file; and Compar**e**, which compares the contents of two files.
Edit	Displays standard Edit options, plus **W**ord Wrap and W**r**ap Paragraph options.
Search	**F**inds selected text, **R**eplaces selected text with new text, Finds Files **C**ontaining specific text, and **L**ists Files Containing specific text.
Options	Enables you to choose customized editor options, **T**oolbar status, and **D**ocument Preferences.
Window	Displays standard **W**indow options.
Help	Displays standard **H**elp options.

Below the menu bar is a toolbar containing 14 icons and a textual reference. All these icons are shortcuts to options also available from the menu bar. The position and style of the toolbar can be changed, as discussed in the section

"Customizing the Toolbar," later in this chapter. The toolbar options are as described in the following table. The number of icons on the toolbar depends on the resolution of your monitor and on options you choose when customizing the Desktop Editor.

Icon	Function
New	Creates a new file.
Open	Opens an existing file.
Save	Saves the current file being edited.
Close	Closes the current edit window.
Print	Prints the current file being edited.
Undo	Removes the last change you made in editing the file.
Cut	Removes the selected text in the file and places it in the Clipboard.
Paste	Copies text from the Clipboard into the file at the position of the cursor.
Del	Deletes the currently selected text.
Prev	Searches for the previous occurrence of the last search defined by using the Find option.
Find	Defines text for use in a search.
Next	Finds the next matching text previously specified in a Find.
Help	Displays Help information for the Desktop Editor.
Exit	Exits from the Desktop Editor.

Editing Files by Using Desktop Editor

Simple editing in the Desktop Editor is as easy as using a basic word processor: Open the file you want to edit, edit the text, and then save the file. While editing, you can use search and replace functions and record macros to simplify repetitive tasks. You can even open multiple files simultaneously in separate windows.

Opening and Saving Files in the Desktop Editor

To open a file in the Desktop Editor, follow these steps:

1. Click the Open tool, or choose the **F**ile **O**pen command. The Open File dialog box appears (see fig. 16.2).

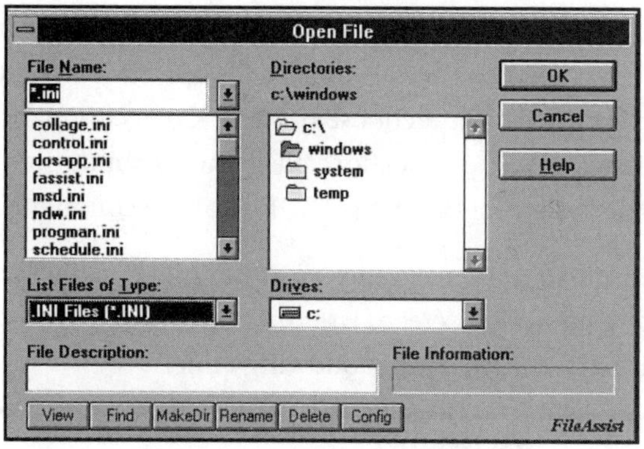

Fig. 16.2
The Open File dialog box enables you to select which file to edit.

2. Use the File **N**ame and **D**irectories list boxes to select the file, or enter a file name in the File **N**ame text box.

3. Choose OK to load the file.

To save a file, click the Save tool or choose the **F**ile **S**ave command. A Save File dialog box, similar to the Open File dialog box shown in figure 16.2, appears, enabling you to enter or choose a name for the file to save.

Notice that the dialog box shown in figure 16.2 is labeled `FileAssist` at the bottom right. This specialized file specification box, although similar to many such boxes used by Windows programs, contains features unique to the Norton Desktop environment. At the bottom of the box, for example, is a File Description text box. When saving a file, you can enter a description in this field. Later, as you browse for files to open and select a file name from the File **N**ame list box, the description for that file is displayed in this text box. The File Information box (to the right of the File Description text box) lists the size of the selected file, as well as the date and time the file was last created or modified. The buttons at the bottom of the dialog box help you perform several useful functions as you open or save a file. If you click the Config button, for example, a Configuration dialog box appears, enabling you to configure FileAssist for the current application. FileAssist dialog boxes are present throughout Desktop tools, whenever you open or save a file.

Editing a File

To edit a file after you open it in the Desktop Editor, simply place the cursor in the text where you want to start editing. You can then insert and delete text just as you do in a regular word processor.

Tip
You can insert the current date and time in your document by positioning your cursor where you want these elements to appear and choosing the **E**dit Time/**D**ate command.

If multiple documents are open at one time, you can cut, copy, and paste text among them just as you can in many other Windows word processors. To cut text, select the text and click the Cut tool or choose the **E**dit Cu**t** command. To copy text, select the text and choose the **E**dit **C**opy command. To paste the cut or copied text in a new location, place the cursor at the insert point, and then click the Paste tool or choose the **E**dit **P**aste command.

If you open multiple files, you can display either one file at a time or multiple files in multiple windows on-screen. Use the **W**indow menu to choose among the options described in the following table.

Option	Function
New Window	Creates a second window for the current file; enables you to view different parts of the same document in different windows.
Cascade	Displays all current documents in cascading windows.
Tile	Displays all current documents in tiled windows.
Arrange Icons	Arranges the icons that represent minimized Editor windows so that they are visible on-screen.
Specific Windows	After you select a specific document, displays it alone in a fully maximized window.

Saving and Closing a File

Tip
Insert other files within your current file by choosing the **F**ile **I**nsert command. An Insert File dialog box appears, from which you can select a file to insert.

To save a file the first time (or to save an existing file under a different name), choose the **F**ile Save **A**s command. After the Save As dialog box appears, type the new name for the document.

To save an existing file, click the Save tool or choose the **F**ile **S**ave command. To save all open files, choose the **F**ile Save A**l**l command.

You also can save selected text in a new file. Simply select the text you want to save; then choose the **F**ile **W**rite Block command, and select the file to which you want to write the text.

To close the current file, click the Close tool or choose the **F**ile **C**lose command. If you did not save the file, you are prompted now to save it.

Tip
At any time, you can cancel all editing changes and revert to the last saved version of the current file by choosing the **F**ile Re**v**ert command.

Using Search and Replace

As you edit a document, you may need to search for specific text or to replace specific text with new text on a global basis. Desktop Editor enables you to do both.

To search for specific text, follow these steps:

1. Click the Find tool or choose the **S**earch **F**ind command. The Find dialog box appears (see fig. 16.3).

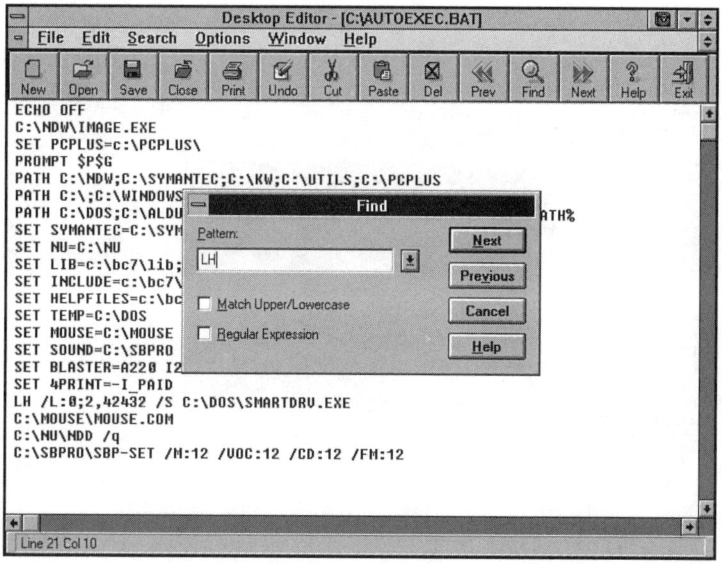

Fig. 16.3
The Find dialog box enables you to specify what text (**P**attern) to find within the file.

2. Type the text you want to find in the **P**attern text box. (Previous search patterns are available from the **P**attern drop-down list.)

3. Determine by selecting the appropriate check box whether you want the search to **M**atch Upper/Lowercase.

4. Determine by selecting the appropriate check box whether you want to search by using a **R**egular Expression; this option turns on the capability to use wild cards (such as * and ?) in searches.

5. Choose the **N**ext button to search for the next occurrence of the search pattern in your text.

Tip

To locate another occurrence of the same text after returning to your document, click the Next tool or choose the **S**earch Find **A**gain command.

6. Choose the Previous button to search backward from the cursor point for the last occurrence of the search pattern in your text.

You can initiate a search-and-replace operation by following these steps:

1. Choose the **S**earch **R**eplace command. The Replace dialog box appears (see fig. 16.4).
2. Type in the **S**earch For text box the text for which you want to search.
3. Type in the **R**eplace With text box the replacement text for the search text.

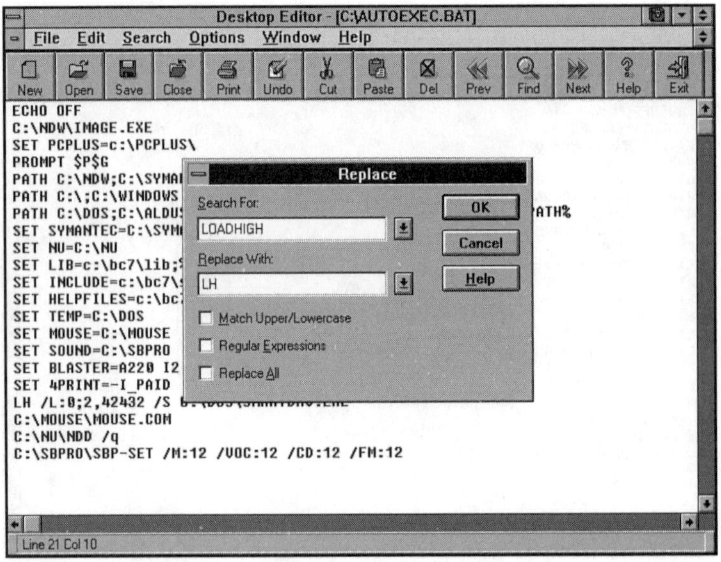

Fig. 16.4
The Replace dialog box enables you to specify that one text string be replaced by another.

4. Select the **M**atch Upper/Lowercase or Regular **E**xpressions check boxes, as necessary. (Refer to steps 3 and 4 of the preceding set of steps.)
5. By default, you must confirm each change. If you know that you want to replace all occurrences without confirmation, you can select the Replace **A**ll option.
6. Choose OK to begin the operation.

You also can search your hard disk for files containing specific text. This search works similarly to the SuperFind utility discussed in Chapter 27, "Using SuperFind."

Caution

This type of search, as opposed to the more comprehensive SuperFind search, works only on a line-by-line basis; the search does not find any patterns spanning more than one line.

To search for files containing specific text, follow these steps:

1. Choose the Desktop Editor's **S**earch Find Files **C**ontaining command. The Find Files Containing dialog box appears (see fig. 16.5).

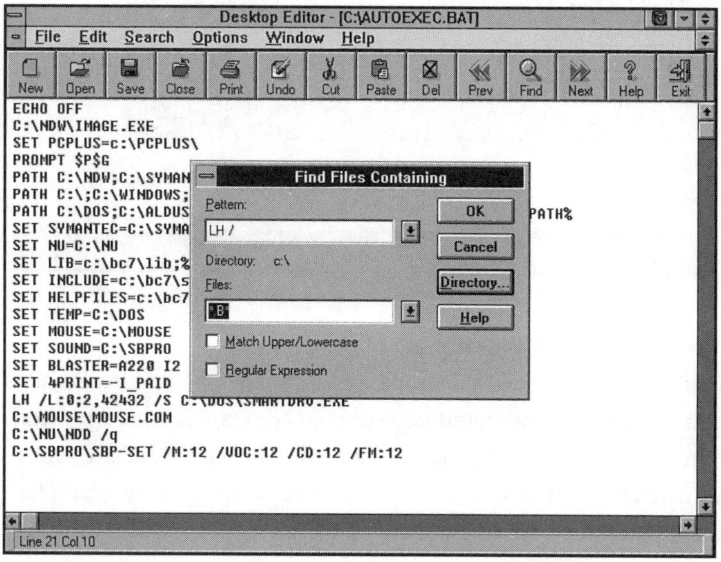

Fig. 16.5
The Find Files Containing dialog box enables you to search for files containing a specific text pattern.

2. Type in the **P**attern text box the text for which you want to search.

3. Select either the **M**atch Upper/Lowercase or **R**egular Expression check boxes, as necessary. (Refer to steps 3 and 4 of the steps for searching for text within a file, earlier in this section.)

4. Choose the **D**irectory button to select the directory through which you want to search. This button accesses a Browse dialog box that enables you to select a specific directory.

5. Type in the **F**iles text box a wild card filter (such as ***.*** to display all files).

6. Choose OK to begin the search.

If the search produces a match, the List Found Files dialog box appears (see fig. 16.6). You then can select files to open and edit.

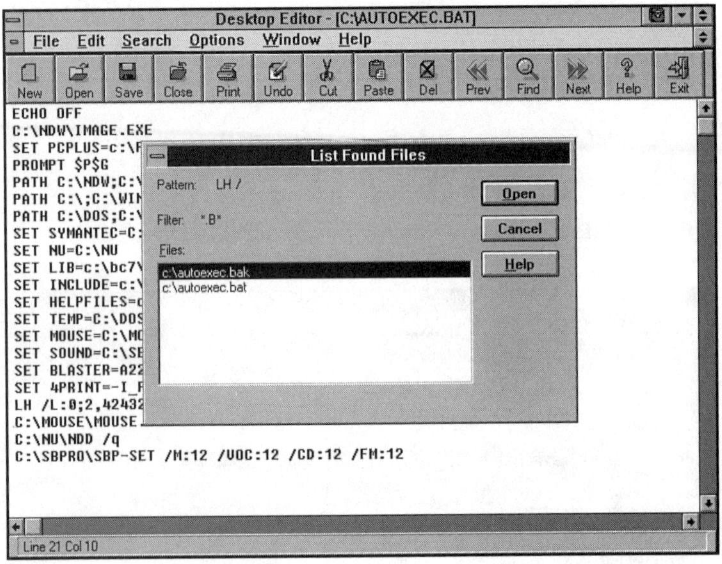

Fig. 16.6
The List Found Files dialog box lists files that contain the pattern specified in the Find Files Containing dialog box.

Comparing Two Documents

> **Tip**
> You can access the List Found Files list at any time by choosing the **S**earch **L**ist Found Files command.

Sometimes you may need to compare two similar documents. Perhaps you are editing one document and you want to compare it with a previous version on disk. You may want to compare your current AUTOEXEC.BAT file with the AUTOEXEC.BAK backup copy, for example, to see what changes you made, or you may want to compare two similar files of programming code. If so, you can use Desktop Editor's Compare feature.

Compare places two documents on-screen, either side-by-side (vertical orientation) or stacked one on top of another (horizontal orientation). After you start the Compare process, Desktop Editor proceeds through the two documents line by line and identifies the first place where the corresponding lines do not match. From that point, Desktop Editor searches for the next place where the two files get back in synch, then searches for the next difference, then searches for the next resynchronization, and so on.

To compare two documents, follow these steps:

1. Choose the **F**ile Compar**e** command. The Compare dialog box appears (see fig. 16.7).

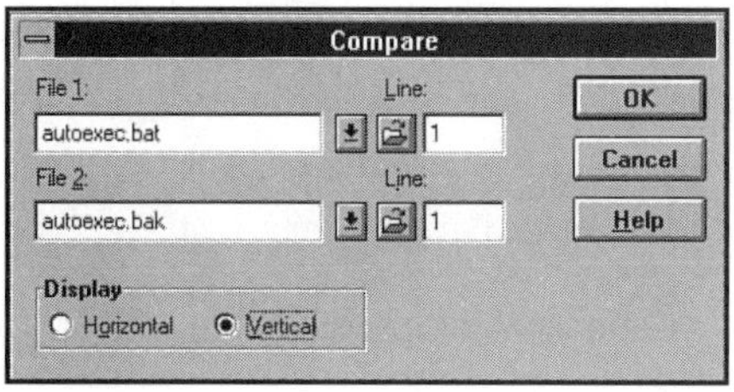

Fig. 16.7
The Compare dialog box enables you to specify two files to compare.

2. Type in the File **1** and File **2** text boxes the names of the two files you want to compare, or select the file names from the drop-down lists. (You also can click the folder icons to browse for files, if necessary.)

3. Choose whether to Display the files in a H**o**rizontal or **V**ertical orientation by selecting the appropriate option button.

4. Choose with what **L**ine (or L**i**ne) to start each file. (The default for each file is line 1.)

5. Choose OK to begin the Compare operation. The two files load into Desktop Editor; text is selected where Compare detects a difference, and a message dialog box appears, informing you of where the files differ (see fig. 16.8).

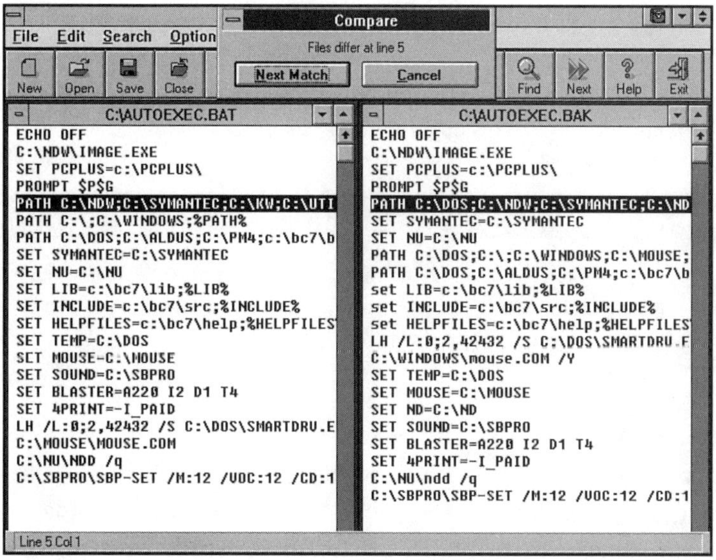

Fig. 16.8
The Compare results of two files, showing where they first differ.

6. Choose the **N**ext Match button in the message dialog box to get the two files back in synch. The Compare message box then indicates that a new match is found, and the matched text is selected. The **N**ext Match button changes to a **N**ext Difference button.
7. Choose the **N**ext Difference button to find the next mismatch.
8. Continue this process until the operation is complete, or choose **C**ancel to cancel the comparison. After you finish the comparison, or choose the **C**ancel button in the Compare message box, the comparison ends.

Recording Keyboard Macros

Even if using a simple text editor such as Desktop Editor, you can often automate repetitive tasks by recording keyboard macros. A macro is simply a computerized recording of keystrokes that you can play back by using a single keystroke.

To record a macro, follow these steps:

1. Choose the **E**dit Record **M**acro command. A REC message appears on the status line while the record operation is in effect.
2. Perform the keystrokes you want recorded.
3. Choose the **E**dit **S**top Recording Macro command.

To play back the macro, choose the **E**dit **P**layback Macro command, or press F8. The recorded keystrokes automatically repeat.

> **Note**
>
> Desktop Editor enables you to record one macro per session. You can record additional macros, but because only one macro remains in memory at any given time, the new macro supersedes the old macro.

Printing a File

Before you can print a file in Desktop Editor, you must choose several options. Begin by choosing the **F**ile Printer Set**u**p command. By using this command, you can choose the printer to which you want to send the output. Then choose the **F**ile Pa**g**e Setup command. This command activates the Page Setup dialog box, as shown in figure 16.9.

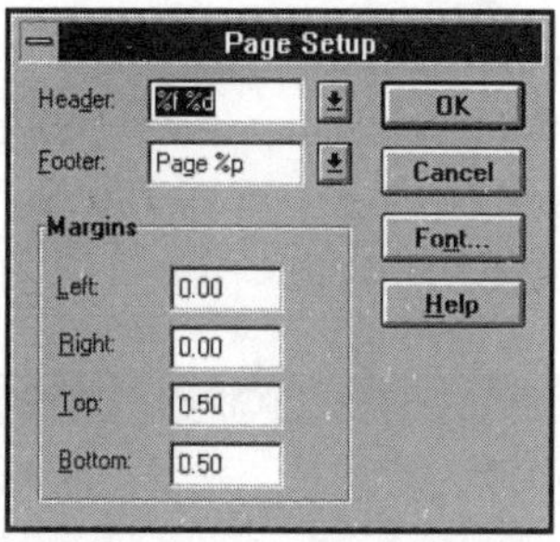

Fig. 16.9
The Page Setup dialog box enables you to specify options for printing pages.

In this dialog box, you can set the options described in the following table.

Option	Function
Hea**d**er	Selects text to display in a header; specifies specific text or uses special sequences to display document variables. Special sequences: *%f* = file name, *%d* = current date and time, *%p* = page number.
Footer	Selects text to display in a footer; specifies specific text or the same special sequences used in headers.
Margins	Specifies the **L**eft, **R**ight, **T**op, and **B**ottom page margins for your printed document.
Fo**n**t	Displays the Printer Font dialog box; enables you to choose font and font size for printouts (see fig. 16.10).

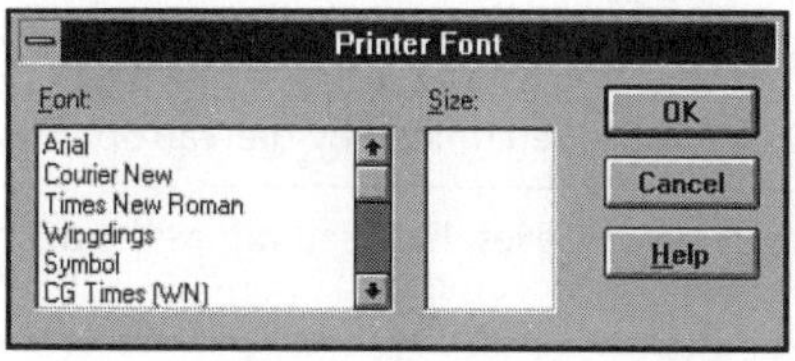

Fig. 16.10
The Printer Font dialog box enables you to choose what font to use for printing a file.

After you set these options, you are ready to begin printing. Initiate printing by choosing the **F**ile **P**rint command; Desktop Editor does the rest and sends the current document to your selected printer.

Customizing Desktop Editor

Three dialog boxes help you configure Desktop Editor to your preferences: the Document Preferences, Editor Preferences, and Key Assignment dialog boxes.

Changing Document Preferences

Access the Document Preferences dialog box by choosing the **O**ptions **D**ocument Preferences command (see fig. 16.11). You can set in this dialog box the options described in the following table.

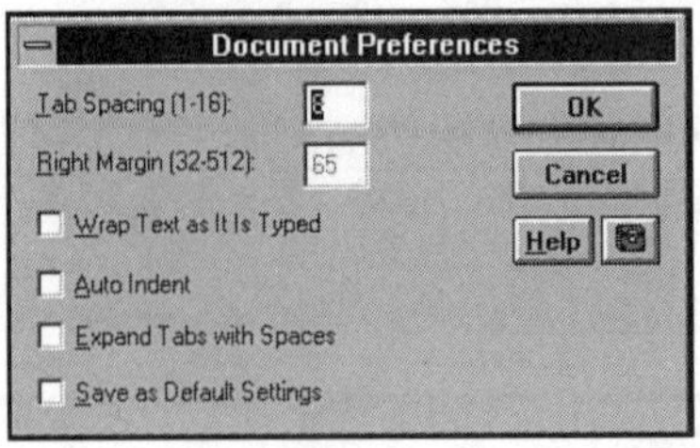

Fig. 16.11
The Document Preferences dialog box enables you to choose options for editing a document.

Option	Function
Tab Spacing	If the **E**xpand Tabs with Spaces check box is selected, determines how many spaces (from 1 to 16) are used for a tab.
Right Margin	Sets the number of characters to the right margin if Word Wrap is enabled.
Wrap Text as It Is Typed	Enables a long line to wrap to create new lines without requiring you to press Enter.
Auto Indent	Positions the cursor in new lines directly below the first nonblank character of the preceding line.
Expand Tabs with Spaces	Inserts a fixed number of spaces in a document after the Tab key is pressed; the number of spaces is determined by the **T**ab Spacing option.
Save as Default Settings	Saves these settings as the default for all new documents.

Customizing Editor Preferences

Choose the **O**ptions **C**ustomize command to access the Customize dialog box. This Customize dialog box enables you to set Editor, Key Assignment, or Toolbar options. Choose from the **C**ategories list at the left of the dialog box which of these three categories you want to set.

Selecting the Editor category preference, as shown in figure 16.12, enables you to set the options described in the following table.

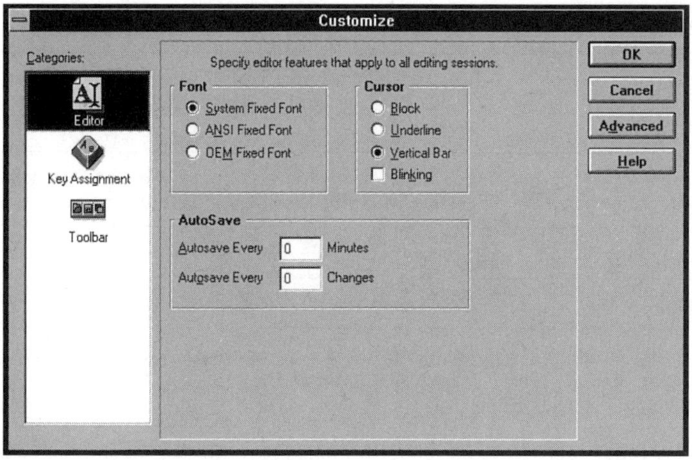

Fig. 16.12
The Customize dialog box with the Editor category selected.

Option	Function
Font	Chooses the font in which to display files on-screen: **S**ystem Fixed Font, A**N**SI Fixed Font, or OE**M** Fixed Font.
Cursor	Chooses shape of the cursor: **B**lock, **U**nderline, or **V**ertical Bar (the normal Windows cursor); selecting or deselecting the Blin**k**ing check box determines whether the cursor blinks.
Autosave Every *X* Minutes	Automatically saves current files at specified time intervals.
Aut**o**save Every *X* Changes	Automatically saves current files after a specified number of changes are made.

To choose among the advanced Customize (Editor) options, choose the A**d**vanced button. An Advanced dialog box appears containing the options described in the following table (see fig. 16.13).

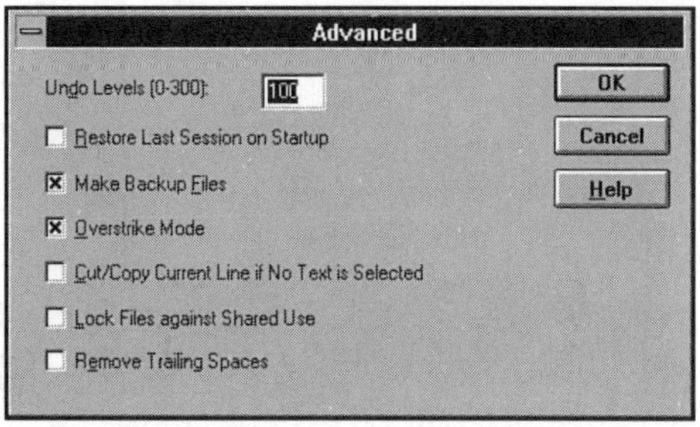

Fig. 16.13
The Advanced dialog box enables you to specify advanced settings for the Editor.

Option	Function
Un**d**o Levels	Chooses number of operations that can be undone by the Undo command; choose from between 0 and 300 levels of undo.
Restore Last Session on Startup	Loads files you were working on at the end of the last session when the new Desktop Editor session begins.
Make Backup **F**iles	Creates backup files (extension BAK) as files are saved.
Overstrike Mode	Determines whether overstrike or insert edit mode is on.
Cut/Copy Current Line if No Text is Selected	Enables Cut and Copy commands to act on current line if no text is selected.
Lock Files against Shared Use	Prevents other applications from accessing files currently loaded in Desktop Editor.
R**e**move Trailing Spaces	Truncates all tabs and spaces after the last nonblank character on a line.

Customizing Key Assignments

The second category in the Customize dialog box is Key Assignment (see fig. 16.14). Use this version of the Customize dialog box to reassign keyboard shortcuts to common operations and to enable menu accelerators and save keyboard preferences to a custom Keyboard Configuration file. You also can use this dialog box to load previously constructed keyboard configuration files.

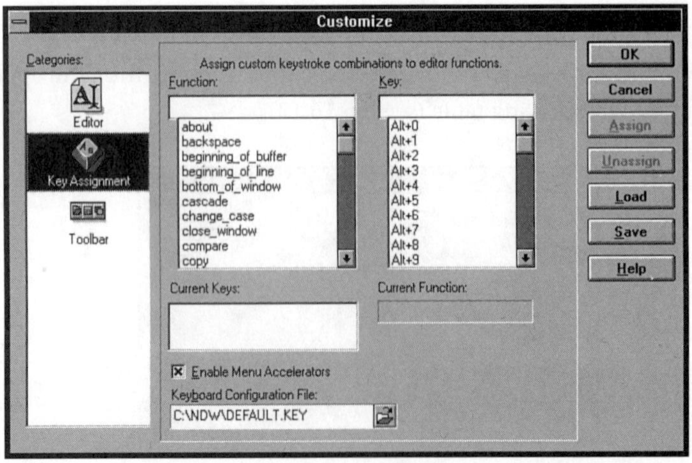

Fig. 16.14
The Customize dialog box with the Key Assignment category selected enables you to select keystroke combinations for Editor functions.

To reassign keyboard shortcuts, simply select a **F**unction from the left scroll box and then select a **K**ey combination from the right scroll box. Choose the **S**ave button to save the assignments to a keyboard configuration file; choose OK to use the assignments for this session only.

Although you can reassign just about any key, most users are content to use Desktop Editor's default key assignments. Desktop Editor's predefined function keys are described in the following table.

Function Key	Function
F1	Help
F2	Save file
Shift+F2	Insert date/time stamp
F3	Open file
F4	Document preferences
Alt+F4	Exit
Ctrl+F4	Close current window
Ctrl+F5	Show all windows
Ctrl+F6	Next window
F7	Begin macro record
F8	Playback macro
Ctrl+F10	Maximize current window

Customizing The Toolbar

The third category in the Customize dialog box is Toolbar (see fig. 16.15). Use this version of the Customize dialog box to choose the position and style of the Editor's toolbar. Initially, the toolbar is located at the top of the screen and is displayed as text only. You can choose for the toolbar to be on the **T**op, **L**eft, **R**ight, or **B**ottom of the screen. You can choose for the toolbar to appear as Te**x**t Only, **I**con Only, Text **a**nd Icon, or **N**o Toolbar. You also can select the Display **S**tatus Bar check box to control whether the status bar is displayed at the bottom of the Editor window. Figure 16.16 shows the Editor with the Text and Icon toolbar located on the right side of the screen.

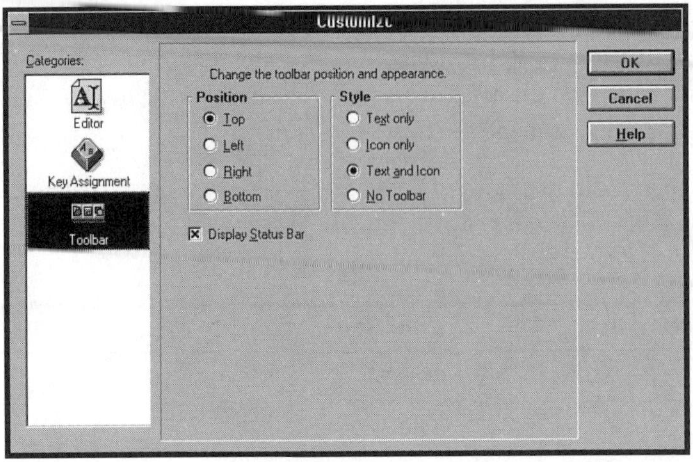

Fig. 16.15
The Customize dialog box with the Toolbar category selected enables you to choose the position and status of the toolbar.

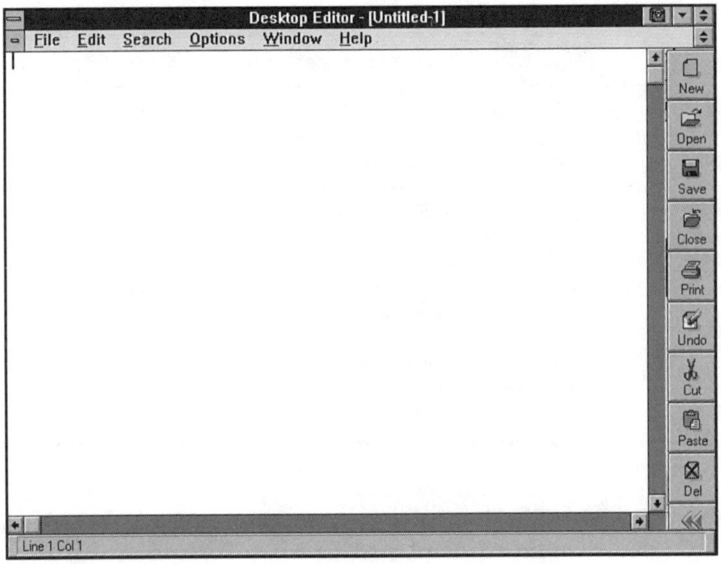

Fig. 16.16
The Desktop Editor screen with the toolbar displayed at the right as text and icons.

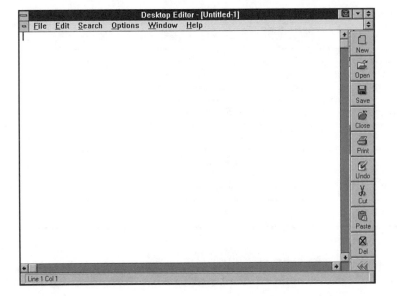

Summary

This chapter discussed NDW's Desktop Editor. In the chapter, you learned how to load, edit, save, and print ASCII text files, such as AUTOEXEC.BAT. You also learned how to configure Desktop Editor to your needs, including assigning new shortcut keys, selecting how the toolbar is displayed, and recording keyboard macros.

The next chapter, "Using Icon Editor," discusses another kind of editor—NDW's Icon Editor. You learn how to start the editor; how to work with icon files, libraries, EXE files, and DLL Files; and how to use the Icon Editor's tools.

Chapter 17

Using Icon Editor

A defining feature of both Windows and Norton Desktop is the use of *icons*. The Windows environment uses icons to symbolize programs, utilities, and documents. Each Windows application comes with its own unique icon. Norton Desktop 3 for Windows also makes extensive use of icons in its toolbars and elsewhere on the Desktop. You can, however, change a program's icon, thanks to the Icon Editor utility included in Norton Desktop.

In this chapter, you learn to perform the following tasks:

- Understand Windows icons and the Icon Editor
- Work with icon files and libraries
- Work with icons in EXE and DLL files
- Use the Icon Editor tools
- Work with colors
- Draw 3-D icons

Understanding Windows Icons and the Icon Editor

The Icon Editor is a Norton Desktop utility that resembles a paint program. Unlike regular paint programs, however, the Icon Editor works only with 32 x 32 pixel images stored in ICO, EXE, DLL, and NIL files—in other words, it paints only icons.

Windows icons are bitmapped images, 32 pixels wide by 32 pixels high. Like other bitmapped images, icons can be edited by paint programs, but most paint programs do not recognize the file types that contain icons.

Icons can be stored in any of the following types of files:

- In individual ICO files.
- As part of a program's EXE file.
- In icon libraries with an NIL extension.
- In Windows dynamic link library files (DLL extensions).

Icons also can be stored in files with ICN extensions. Although the Icon Editor cannot read files in these formats, you can associate icons from these files with Norton Desktop applications and documents.

Tip

The Icon Editor is not just for creating your own icons; you also can edit icons used by Norton Desktop or by other Windows-based programs.

Caution

The Icon Editor can edit only 16-color, 32 x 32 pixel icons. Icons composed at a greater size or color resolution cannot be edited by Icon Editor. Icon Editor also works only with Windows 3.0 or Windows 3.1 EGA and VGA icons. It does not work with Windows 2.x icons or icons at CGA resolution or in monochrome. (A black-and-white icon, however, is not necessarily a monochrome icon; black and white are two of the colors available in the EGA and VGA palettes.)

Why change icons? Maybe you just do not like the standard icon provided for a particular program. Perhaps the colors do not please your eye. Or maybe you need to create an icon for a DOS application that has no icon. Whatever the reason, the Icon Editor is one of the most-used utilities in Norton Desktop. Many users want the power to make their own icons—and the Icon Editor gives them that power.

Remember that the Icon Editor enables you to change existing icons and create new icons. Because the Norton Desktop shell enables you to select any icon to represent any application or document, using the Icon Editor with Norton Desktop is the perfect way to customize the look of your on-screen Desktop quickly and easily.

Note

Norton Desktop enables you to determine which icons appear on the Desktop for a given program or document. Press and hold the Alt key as you double-click the icon you want to change. By using this command, you can associate icons found in any ICO, NIL, DLL, or EXE file to any other file. This procedure, however, affects only the Desktop icon or Group icon; it does not change the preassigned icon that appears while the application or document is minimized on the Desktop. You must use the Icon Editor to alter these preassociated icons in the EXE file itself.

Starting the Icon Editor

You can launch the Icon Editor from the menu system or from the Quick Access Group. To start the Icon Editor from the menu, choose the **T**ools **I**con Editor command.

Figure 17.1 shows the Icon Editor window. Notice that this window cannot be maximized to full-screen size; it can appear only as a minimized window or in icon form.

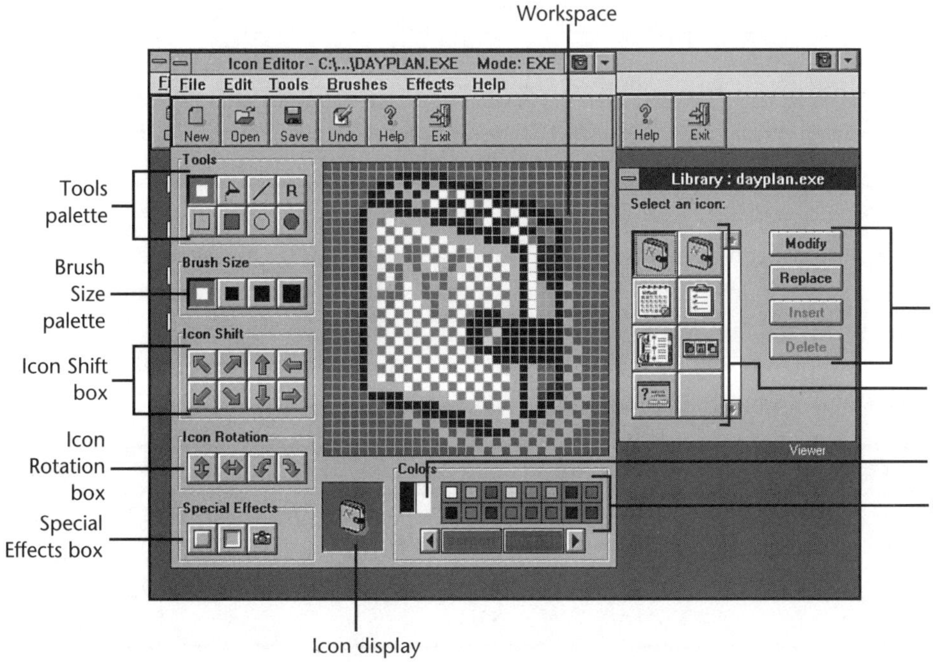

Fig. 17.1
Editing an icon by using the Norton Icon Editor window and the Library Icon Selector.

The Icon Editor window has eight parts, as described in the following table.

Feature	Function
Workspace	Consists of a 32 x 32 grid, in which all editing takes place; displays an enlarged view of the selected icon.
Tools Palette	Contains the eight tools used to edit icons.
Brush Size Palette	Enables you to select four different brush sizes for editing purposes.
Icon Display	Displays, in real size, the icon being edited.

(continues)

(continued)

Feature	Function
Colors Palette	Contains all the available colors for icon editing. The Palette Selector contains two sections: *screen*, which paints the color of whatever background screen is currently active; *inverse*, which paints the color of the inverse of the currently active background screen. Also enables you to assign color to the left or right mouse button. See the section "Working with Colors," later in this chapter.
Icon Shift Box	Moves the icon in the direction of the arrow within the icon workspace.
Icon Rotation Box	Enables you to rotate the icon in the workspace the direction of the arrow.
Special Effect Box	Enables you to select a special 3-D effect for use with the icon.

If you use an icon from a library, another window is simultaneously open: the Library window. A Library window contains all of the icons available in the current file (in this case, in the DAYPLAN.EXE file). It is the window shown at the right of the screen in figure 17.1. This window contains two parts, as described in the following table.

Feature	Function
Library Control Buttons	Loads and unloads icons from the icon library (Modify, Replace, Insert, and Delete).
Icon Selector	Displays all the icons in the current icon file, up to 8 at a time.

The Icon Selector displays all the icons in a given file, up to eight at once. You can scroll through all the icons in a file by using the vertical scroll bar to the right of the eight raised buttons.

The four Library Control buttons enable you to move icons to and from the Workspace and the Icon Selector, as described in the following table.

Button	Function
Modify	Moves an icon from the Icon Selector to the Workspace for editing.
Replace	Replaces the currently selected icon in the Icon Selector with the contents of the Workspace.

Button	Function
Insert	Inserts the contents of the Workspace as an icon into the currently selected file just before the currently selected icon in the Icon Selector.
Delete	Deletes the currently selected icon in the Icon Selector.

Working with Icon Files

Individual icons are stored in files ending with the ICO extension. You can associate ICO files with any application or document on the Desktop. By using the Icon Editor, you can edit existing ICO files or create new ICO files.

To edit an existing ICO file, follow these steps:

1. Open the Icon Editor by choosing **T**ools **I**con Editor.
2. Click the Open tool on the Editor's toolbar, or choose the **F**ile **O**pen command from its menu bar. The File Open dialog box appears (see fig. 17.2).

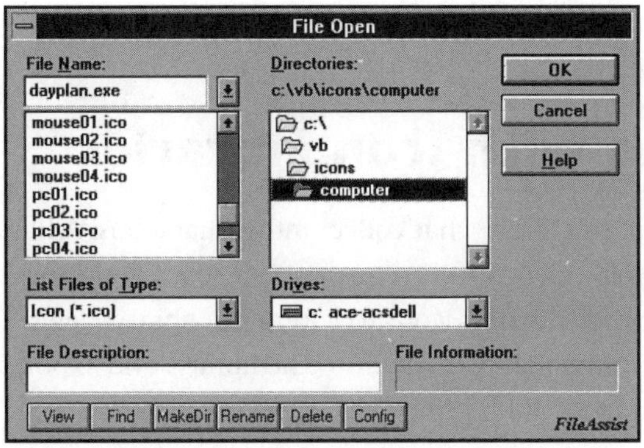

Fig. 17.2
The Icon Editor's File Open dialog box enables you to select which icon to edit.

3. Select Icon (*.ico) in the List Files of **T**ype drop-down list box.
4. Use the **D**irectories and File **N**ame list boxes to locate the file you want to edit.
5. Select the desired file from the File **N**ame list box, and choose OK. The icon you selected is now loaded in the Icon Editor's Workspace and ready for editing.

6. After you finish editing, click the Save tool on the Icon Editor's toolbar to replace the original icon with the edited icon.

To create a new ICO file, follow these steps:

1. Open the Icon Editor, as described in step 1 of the preceding steps, and click the New tool on the Editor's toolbar or choose the **F**ile **N**ew command from its menu bar. The New dialog box appears (see fig. 17.3).

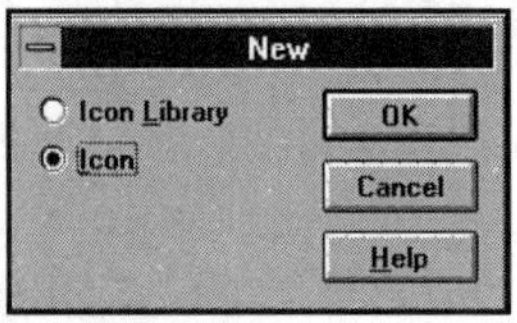

Fig. 17.3
The Icon Editor's New dialog box enables you to create a new icon.

2. Select the **I**con option button, and choose OK. A blank icon is now loaded in the Icon Editor's Workspace, ready for editing.
3. After you finish editing the new icon, click the Save tool to insert the new icon into the Icon Selector. A Save File As dialog box appears.
4. In the File **N**ame text box of this dialog box, type up to an eight-character file name for the icon, and then choose OK.

Tip
You can save a new icon as an ICO file by *exporting* the icon to an ICO file. Simply choose the **F**ile **E**xport Icon command, name the new ICO file, and then click OK.

Working with Icon Libraries

Icon libraries are single files that collect individual icons. A library can include any number of icons—even just a single icon. You can edit individual icons in a library, create new icons to add to the library, delete icons from the library, import individual ICO files into the library, and export icons from the library to individual ICO files.

Icon libraries are useful for dealing with large numbers of icons. Norton Desktop 3 for Windows includes one such large icon library in the file labelled NDW.NIL.

Creating Manageable Icon Libraries

Try to limit your icon libraries to a manageable size. Nothing is more annoying than having to scroll through a library of more than 100 icons to find the one icon you really need. You may want to create separate icon library files for collections of similar icons. You can, for example, create an icon library filled exclusively with icons for DOS applications or an icon library filled exclusively with icons for games. Creating easily identifiable icon libraries makes finding that one icon you want easier if you have hundreds on your hard disk.

To edit an existing icon library, follow these steps:

1. With the Icon Editor open, click the Open tool or choose the **F**ile **O**pen command. The File Open dialog box appears (refer to fig. 17.2).
2. Select Library (*.nil) from the List of Files **T**ype drop-down list box.
3. Use the **D**irectories and File **N**ame list boxes to locate the file you want to edit.
4. Select the desired file, and choose OK. The icons in the library you selected are now loaded in the Icon Selector.
5. Perform your editing operations.
6. Click the Save tool or choose the **F**ile **S**ave command to save the edited icon library.

To create a new icon library, follow these steps:

1. With the Icon Editor open, click the New tool or choose the **F**ile **N**ew command. The New dialog box appears (refer to fig. 17.3).
2. Select the Icon **L**ibrary option button. A blank Workspace appears, along with an empty Icon Selector. A Library window also appears (similar to the one shown in fig. 17.1).
3. Create a new icon by using the tools in the Icon Editor's Tools palette.
4. After you finish creating the new icon, place it in the Icon Selector by clicking the Insert button in the Library window.
5. Click the Save tool, or choose the **F**ile Save **A**s command. The Save As dialog box appears.

6. In the File **N**ame text box, type up to an eight-character file name for the icon, and then choose OK.

To delete an icon from an icon library, follow these steps:

1. Open the icon library, as described in steps 1-4 of the first set of steps in this section, and select the icon you want to delete from the Library window Icon Selector.

2. Choose the Delete button in the Library window.

To import an existing ICO file into an icon library, follow these steps:

1. Open the icon library, and select the position in the Icon Selector where you want to place the new icon.

2. Choose the **F**ile **I**mport Icon command. The File Import Icon dialog box appears (see fig. 17.4).

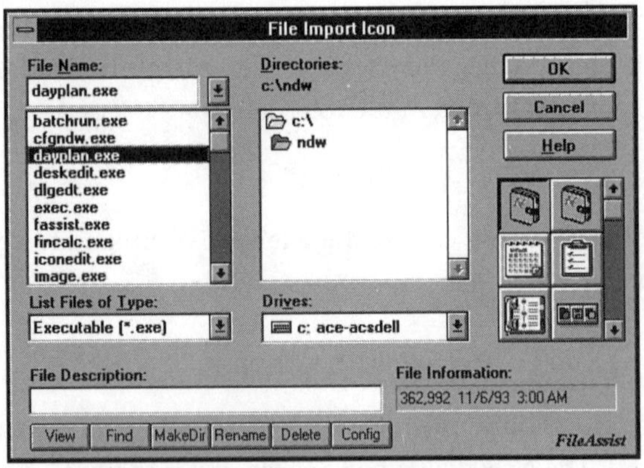

Fig. 17.4
The File Import Icon dialog box enables you to import an icon into an existing icon library.

3. Select Icon (*.ico) in the List Files of **T**ype drop-down list in the File Import Icon dialog box.

4. Use the **D**irectories and File **N**ame list boxes to locate the file you want to import.

5. Select the desired file, and choose OK. The icon is displayed in the Icon Editor.

6. Select the Insert button in the Library window to insert the new icon into the Icon Selector.

Note

You can import icons from other icon library NIL files or from application EXE files. To import a single icon from a file containing multiple icons, you must select the desired icon from the Import Icon dialog box's scrolling Icons list.

To export an icon from an icon library into an individual ICO file, follow these steps:

1. With the icon you want to export currently displayed in the Icon Editor Workspace, choose the **F**ile **E**xport Icon command. The Export Icon dialog box appears.

2. In the File **N**ame text box, type up to an eight-character file name for the new icon file.

3. Choose OK to create the new ICO file.

Working with Icons in EXE Files

Executable files are program files ending with an EXE extension. Executable files for Windows programs almost always include preassigned icons for the application. These icons appear after the program is loaded into a program group, dragged onto the Norton Desktop, or minimized to icon form.

Some EXE files contain more than one icon. In that respect, EXE files resemble NIL-format icon libraries. The Windows 3.1 file PROGMAN.EXE, for example, contains more than a dozen high-quality icons that are used by the Windows Program Manager and other Windows applications.

Note

After you edit an icon in an EXE file, the edited icon replaces the existing version. This new version automatically appears if the application is minimized on the Desktop. The new version does not change, however, in program groups or as a Desktop icon. You must use the **P**roperties command to place the new icon in a program group.

Warning

Use caution if you replace or edit icons in EXE or DLL files. Make sure that you do not try to change a file that is currently running under Windows—whether an application, a Windows system file, or one of NDW's application or system files. The results could be unpredictable at best and, at worst, may crash your system.

To edit an icon in an EXE file, follow these steps:

1. With the Icon Editor open, click the Open tool or choose the **F**ile **O**pen command. The File Open dialog box appears (refer to fig. 17.2).

2. In the List Files of **T**ype drop-down list box, select Executable (*.exe).

3. Use the **D**irectories and File **N**ame list boxes to locate the file you want to edit.

4. Select the file you want to edit, and choose OK. The icon you selected is now loaded in the Icon Selector.

5. Click the Modify button in the Library window to load the icon into the Workspace for editing.

6. After you finish editing the icon, click the Replace button in the Library window to replace the original icon with the edited icon.

7. Click the Save tool or choose the **F**ile **S**ave command to save the edited icon to the original EXE file.

Caution

You can only edit icons in EXE files; you cannot add new icons to the file or delete existing icons.

Tip

Windows 3.1 includes a special DLL file full of useful icons. Look for the MORICONS DLL file in the WINDOWS directory.

Working with Icons in DLL Files

Dynamic Link Library (DLL) files link data from one Windows application to another. A majority of Windows applications use DLL files as a way of communicating with other Windows applications—or with Windows itself. Many DLL files include one or more icons.

Warning

Previous warnings regarding editing icons in EXE files also apply if you edit icons in DLL files. The results could be unpredictable at best and, at worst, may crash your system.

To edit an icon in an DLL file, follow these steps:

1. With the Icon Editor open, click the Open tool or choose the File **O**pen command. The File Open dialog box appears (refer to fig. 17.2).
2. Select DLL in the List Files of **T**ype drop-down list box.
3. Use the **D**irectories and File **N**ame list boxes to locate the file you want to edit.
4. Select the file from the File **N**ame list box, and choose OK. The icon you selected is now loaded in the Icon Selector.
5. Select the Modify button in the Library window to load the icon into the Workspace for editing.
6. After you finish editing, select the Replace button in the Library window to replace the original icon with the edited icon.
7. Click the Save tool or choose the **F**ile **S**ave command to save the edited icon to the original DLL file.

Using the Icon Editor Tools

You can use eight drawing tools (Brush Style) to edit and draw icons. Figure 17.5 displays these eight tools, which are described in detail in the following table.

Tool	Function
Brush tool	Select and move this tool across areas of the Workspace to paint either individual pixels by clicking them with the left or right mouse button or to paint entire areas by dragging the mouse across pixels while you hold the left or right mouse button. The brush size is determined by the Brush Size palette.

(continues)

(continued)

Tool	Function
Filler tool	Select, point, and click with this tool to fill an area with the selected color.
Line tool	Select this tool, point to where you want the beginning of a line to appear, click and hold the left mouse button, and drag the pointer until the line is the correct length; lines can be drawn in any direction.
Replacer tool	Select this tool and point to an area where you want to replace the chosen color with a new color, and click.
Rectangle tool	Select this tool, point to where you want the corner of a rectangle to appear, click and hold the left button, and drag the pointer until the rectangle is the size you want.
Filled Rectangle tool	Works the same as the Rectangle tool, except that the inside of the rectangle is filled with color by clicking the right mouse button.
Circle tool	Similar to the Rectangle tool. Select the tool, click one "corner" of the circle, and drag the pointer while holding the left mouse button until the ellipse is the correct size. Notice that the ellipse does not appear on-screen during the drawing process; during drawing, a rectangle appears that represents the area to be occupied by the ellipse.
Filled Circle tool	Works the same as the Circle tool, except the inside of the ellipse is filled with color by clicking the right mouse button.

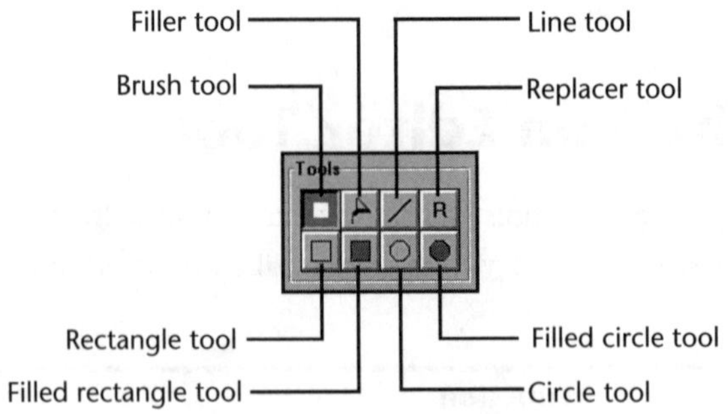

Fig. 17.5
The Icon Editor's drawing tools enable you to edit or create original icons.

If you are editing an existing icon, the most common tools to use are the Brush, Filler, and Replacer. These tools enable you to change the colors of existing icons easily.

If creating a new icon, you use some combination of all the tools. Starting with "big picture" tools (such as the Rectangle, Circle, and Line tools) to draw the rough outlines of your icon is the best course; then use the "detail" tools (such as the Brush and Filler) to fine-tune the image. You find you often must work pixel by pixel to get the right look for your icon.

While using the various tools, you can select one of four different "brush" sizes. The Brush Size palette consists of four buttons with squares of varying sizes. These squares represent, respectively, a single pixel brush, a 2 x 2 pixel brush, a 3 x 3 pixel brush, and a 4 x 4 pixel brush. These brush sizes affect the size of the Brush and Replacer tools as well as the thickness of the lines drawn by using the Line, Circle, and Rectangle tools.

Tip
You can undo any editing mistakes by clicking the Undo tool or choosing the **E**dit **U**nDo command.

As you work in the Workspace, your progress is mirrored in the Icon Viewer. The Icon Viewer shows you what your icon looks like at actual size; this feature is extremely useful—because what looks good as a big icon often does not look good as a small one.

Note

Because you are dealing with bitmapped images, some objects may appear to have rough or jagged edges; some lines may appear not to be completely straight. This is most apparent in the Workspace, because the icon is enlarged many times its normal size. If you observe the icon in the Icon Display, you see that the jagged edges tend to smooth themselves out at the normal, smaller icon size.

Tip
Be careful while drawing words in an icon. The letters often end up so small that they are unreadable. Use the Icon Viewer to check the results of your lettering as you progress.

Working with Colors

You can assign colors to both the left and the right mouse buttons. To assign colors to mouse buttons, follow these steps:

1. Move the mouse pointer to the desired color in the Colors palette for the left mouse button.

2. Click the left mouse button. The selected color appears on the left side of the Color Assignment box.

3. Move the pointer to the desired color in the Colors palette for the right mouse button.

4. Click the right mouse button. The selected color appears on the right side of the Color Assignment box.

The Color Palette displays all 16 colors available with Icon Editor. You also can draw in the *screen color* and the *inverse color*.

The screen color always represents the current background color of your screen. If an area in your icon is colored with the screen color, it appears blue if the background color of your screen is blue or red if the background color of your screen is red. The inverse color is always the correct contrasting color to the screen color. This color changes with the color of your background, just as the screen color does.

You can think of the screen color as a *transparent* color, because it "disappears" into the background color of your Desktop. If you color the background of an icon by using the screen color, for example, and then draw a red dot in the middle of the icon, the only thing you see after you minimize the icon on your Desktop is the red dot.

You can assign the screen or inverse colors to a mouse button the same way you assign other colors. The *screen* button represents the screen color, and the *inverse* button represents the inverse color. The Screen and Inverse Color Selectors appear just below the Colors palette in figure 17.1.

Note

You can select different sample screen background colors so that you can see how your icon works with different color combinations. Clicking the arrow buttons next to the screen and inverse buttons cycles the screen background through all available colors. The different colors are reflected in the Icon Display.

The Replacer tool is an interesting tool for quick color editing. Essentially, this tool enables you to replace all instances of a given color with a different color. You can choose to replace all green areas with blue areas, for example, by using the Replacer tool. Dragging this tool over a green area changes it to blue; dragging it over areas of any other color has no effect.

Notice that the new color is assigned to the button used, while the color to be replaced is the color assigned to the other mouse button. If you assign red to the left button and green to the right button, for example, you can change all green to red by using the left mouse button.

The best way to learn how to draw and color icons is to play around with the tools. This experimentation helps you discover fairly quickly what does and does not work. You also may want to load some icons you like from various applications to examine which techniques produce various results.

Drawing 3-D Icons

You can easily draw an icon with a 3-D look by using the Special Effects tools. The 3-D effect is caused by dark and light lines lending a sense of perspective to a flat drawing. Essentially, all raised items cast a shadow, which can be represented by a black line (on the shadowed side) and a white line (on the side reflecting light). Inset items have a shadow cast on the inside of the border; again, dark and light lines represent shadows and light.

The Special Effects box contains two 3-D buttons. The icon with the raised effect is similar to the Desktop "button" icons in Norton Desktop.

Drawing Raised and Inset Button Icons

To draw a raised or inset icon, start with a blank Workspace and follow these steps:

1. Use the Filler tool to fill the entire Workspace with your choice of color.

2. Click the raised or inset Special Effects icon.

A raised icon is shown in figure 17.6, and an inset icon is shown in figure 17.7.

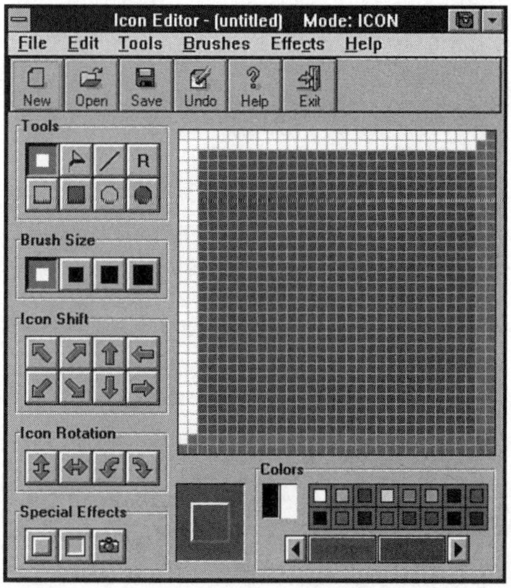

Fig. 17.6
The Norton Desktop Icon Editor screen, showing a raised icon.

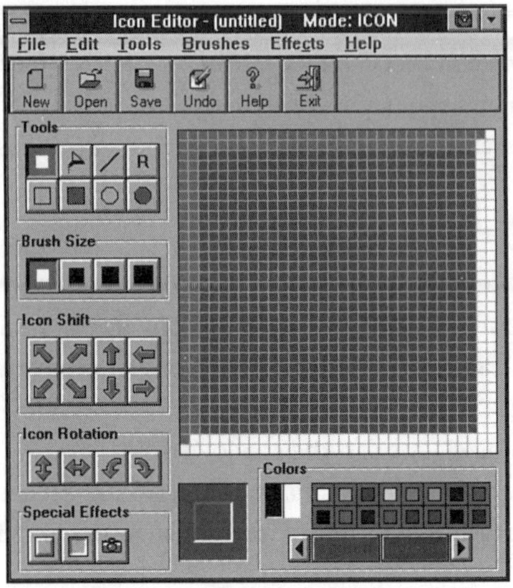

Fig. 17.7
The Norton Desktop Icon Editor screen, showing an inset icon.

Using the Camera Special Effects Tool

The third icon in the Special Effects tool is the Camera tool. By using this tool, you can "take a picture" of anything on-screen. This is particularly useful if you want to capture a current icon and easily modify it.

To use the Camera tool, follow these steps:

1. Make sure that the item you want to capture is displayed on-screen. You can move Norton Editor screen to one side if necessary by dragging it like a window screen. Make sure that you have a blank Workspace.

2. Click the Camera Special Effects icon. A message dialog box appears, asking if you want to minimize the Icon Editor. Choose **Y**es if the item you want to capture is behind the editor. An open square box cursor appears somewhere near the middle of the screen.

3. Move the square box so that it covers the item you want to capture. In figure 17.8, for example, the box covers the Word Perfect icon. The picture that is covered appears in the Workspace and Icon Display areas.

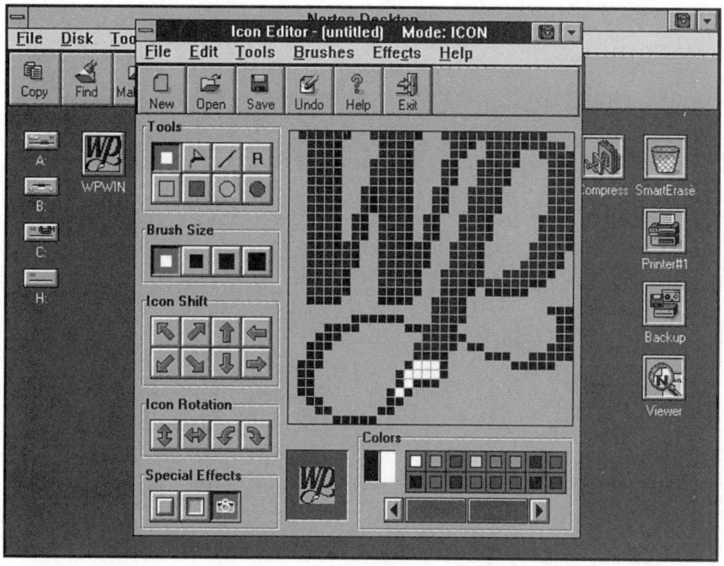

Fig. 17.8
Capturing an existing icon from the Desktop by using the Camera tool in the Norton Icon Editor.

4. Click the left mouse button after you are satisfied with the image displayed in the Workspace; the image is copied into the Workspace. You can then edit the image by using the other Icon Editor tools.

After you edit your new icon, choose the Save option to display a Save As dialog box to save the icon.

Summary

This chapter showed you how to use the Icon Editor to edit existing icons and create new icons. You learned how to import and export various types of files and how to use all the Icon Editor tools. You also learned how to create 3-D icons, including both raised and inset icons, and how to capture images from the screen.

The next chapter shows you how to use KeyFinder to add nonstandard characters to your documents and to display characters for common fonts and compares the Norton Keyfinder to the Windows Character Map.

Chapter 18

Using KeyFinder

KeyFinder is a tool that displays all the characters available in a given font. You can use KeyFinder to identify the keystrokes necessary to enter special characters or even to create those characters for insertion in your text. KeyFinder is very similar to the Character Map tool in Windows 3.1, but with some additional features.

In this chapter, you learn to perform the following tasks:

- Understand fonts and characters
- Start KeyFinder
- Examine the KeyFinder window
- Insert KeyFinder characters in your document
- Use KeyFinder character tables for common fonts
- Compare KeyFinder and the Windows Character Map

Understanding Fonts and Characters

A *font family* is a complete collection of letters, numbers, regular characters, and special characters with a consistent typeface. Font families have identifiable names, such as Helvetica, Arial, Times Roman, and GillSans. You use different font families for different needs; desktop publishers often keep a variety of fonts at their disposal.

The KeyFinder tool displays built-in Windows fonts, including TrueType fonts, as well as third-party fonts such as the fonts used in Adobe Type Manager (ATM). KeyFinder displays all available characters for all font families installed on your system. Each font family can have up to 256 possible characters, which correspond to 256 specific ASCII character codes, but not all font families support all 256 possible characters.

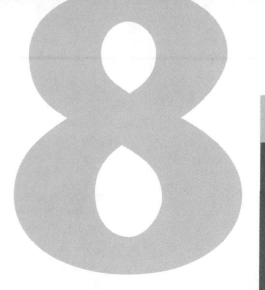

KeyFinder displays both regular and special characters. Regular characters correspond to specific keys on the keyboard. Special characters do not have specific key assignments, but they are available if you press special key combinations.

Using Scalable Fonts

TrueType is a new feature in Windows 3.1 that enables you to display and print scalable fonts on any computer system. TrueType works similarly to Adobe Type Manager (ATM) and other third-party scalable font packages. *Scalable fonts* are fonts that can be displayed and printed in a variety of sizes, although only a font master is stored on your hard disk. Unlike scalable fonts, traditional fonts require that a sample of the font at each desired size be stored on your hard disk. Scalable *font masters* take up little disk space and are "scaled" to create fonts at a variety of sizes. Scalable fonts such as TrueType and ATM give you increased font and size variety while using less disk space than do traditional fonts.

Note

Special characters, such as the ", Γ, Π, and ¢ symbols, add professionalism to your documents. Different special characters are available in different font families. (See the KeyFinder character tables for common fonts that appear later in this chapter.)

You access many special characters by holding down the Alt key and pressing a series of four numbers on the numeric keypad. You can enter the © symbol, for example, in many font families by using the Alt+0169 key combination.

Note

You must use the numeric keypad with the NumLock key activated to enter codes for special characters. You cannot use the number keys at the top of the keyboard to access special characters.

You undoubtedly will have difficulty remembering all the key combinations for all the special characters in all the available font families. KeyFinder, therefore, is a useful tool in helping you locate the key combinations for various special characters quickly and easily.

Starting KeyFinder

You can start KeyFinder from either the menu system or Quick Access. To access KeyFinder from the menu, choose the **T**ools **K**eyFinder command. (See Chapter 8, "Launching Files with Norton Desktop," for more information about Quick Access.)

> **Note**
>
> Because KeyFinder is such a useful utility, you may even want to create a permanent Desktop icon for it or add it to NDW's Launch List. See Chapter 13, "Creating an Icon-Based Desktop," for information on creating a Desktop icon or Chapter 8, "Launching Files with Norton Desktop," for information on using the Launch List.

Examining the KeyFinder Window

Figure 18.1 shows the default KeyFinder window. Notice that KeyFinder cannot be maximized to full-screen size; it appears only as a minimized window or in icon form.

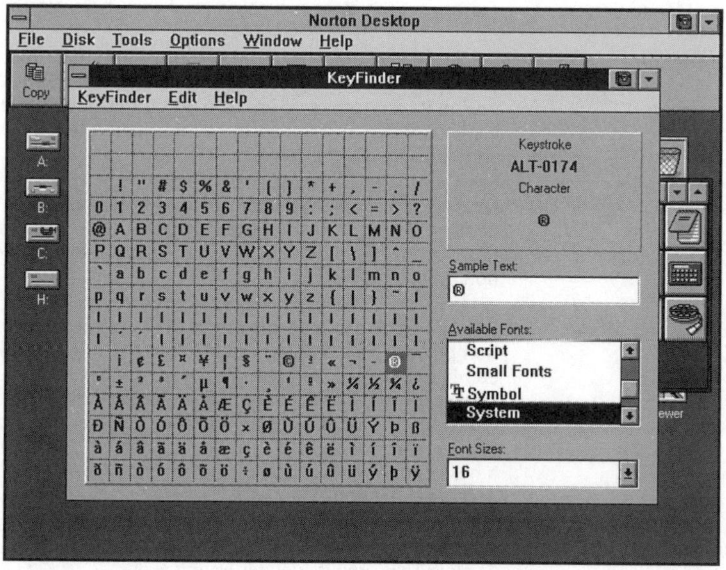

Fig. 18.1
The KeyFinder window, displaying all the characters used in the System font as well as the keystroke combination for a sample character.

The parts of the KeyFinder window are as described in the following table.

Window Part	Function
Character Table	Displays all the available characters in the selected font family.
Keystroke Information box	Displays the selected character from the Character Table and the keystroke combination you use to create the character.
Sample Text box	Text box used to enter characters you want to cut and paste into other Windows applications.
Available Fonts List	Scrolling list box that displays all available font families in your system; the selected font is highlighted.
Font Sizes list	Scrolling drop-down list box that displays all the available type sizes for the selected font family.

The KeyFinder window also offers several available menu options that affect the appearance of the displayed information. Open the **K**eyFinder menu to access these options, as described in the following table.

Option	Function
Swap **O**rientation	Transposes the rows and columns of the Character Table.
Real Font **S**ize	Displays the characters in the Keystroke Information box at the actual size selected in the **F**ont Sizes list; the default setting for this option is on; turning off this option selects a standard size for the Keystroke Information box display and hides the **F**ont Sizes list.
Show **A**SCII	Displays the actual ASCII control codes, such as CR for carriage return, instead of the normal keystroke combination, for the first 32 characters in the Keystroke Information box.
Programmer **M**ode	Displays additional information in the Keystroke Information box of specific value to programmers: the keystroke combination, the character displayed, the decimal equivalent for the character, the hex equivalent of the character, the octal equivalent of the character, the type of font selected, and the font family selected; also displays a hex number grid on the outside of the Character Table and hides the **F**ont Sizes list.
Sample **T**ext	Turned on or off (as a toggle), displays or hides the **S**ample Text box; its default option is on.
E**x**it	Exit KeyFinder.

Typically, you use KeyFinder to search for a specific character in your current font family. You may, for example, be using the Arial TrueType font while typing a document in WordPerfect for Windows and want to insert the copyright character (©). To do so, follow these steps:

1. With your cursor at the point in your document at which you want to insert the copyright character, minimize your document and choose the Desktop's **T**ools **K**eyFinder command to access KeyFinder.

2. Scroll through the **A**vailable Fonts list until Arial is highlighted.

3. Select the © character in the Character Table. Notice that the Keystroke Information box now displays the keystroke Alt+0169 for this character.

4. Close the KeyFinder by choosing **K**eyFinder E**x**it to return to your WordPerfect document, and then press Alt+0169 to insert the copyright character.

Inserting KeyFinder Characters in Your Document

You also can copy characters directly from KeyFinder's **S**ample Text box into your document. This operation saves you the effort of keying in characters and removes the opportunity for you to forget the keystroke combination—or type it erroneously.

To use the preceding example and copy the KeyFinder copyright character into your document, follow these steps:

1. While editing a document (in WordPerfect for Windows, for example), minimize your document and then choose the Desktop's **T**ools **K**eyFinder command to access KeyFinder.

2. Scroll through the **A**vailable Fonts list until Arial is highlighted.

3. Locate the © character in the Character Table.

4. Double-click the © character in the Character Table. A copy of the character appears in the **S**ample Text box. (You can select more than one character this way, placing each character one after the other in the Sample Text box.)

5. Select the text in the **S**ample Text box.

6. Choose the KeyFinder's **E**dit **C**opy command or press Shift+Ins to copy the selected text in the **S**ample Text box into the Windows Clipboard.

7. Close or minimize the KeyFinder and restore your open document in your WordPerfect Windows application.

8. Place the cursor at the location in the document where you want to insert the character.

9. Choose the application's **E**dit **P**aste command or press Ctrl+Ins to insert the KeyFinder character in your document.

Note

You must have the same font selected in your application as in KeyFinder for the Paste procedure to work correctly. What you actually insert in your document is a key combination. Because key combinations can represent different characters in different font families, pasting a Symbol font character into an Arial font document, for example, gives you results that are different from what you intended. Notice that you can always change the font of the inserted character in your application after you insert the character.

Using KeyFinder Character Tables for Common Fonts

Figures 18.2 through 18.4 display KeyFinder Character Tables for three common font families. These tables give you an idea of the special characters available in these fonts.

Comparing KeyFinder and Character Map

Windows 3.1 includes a tool called Character Map (see fig. 18.5). This tool is similar to NDW's KeyFinder tool. Both tools display characters for available font families. You can use both tools to copy characters directly to other Windows applications. Character Map, however, lacks some functions inherent in KeyFinder.

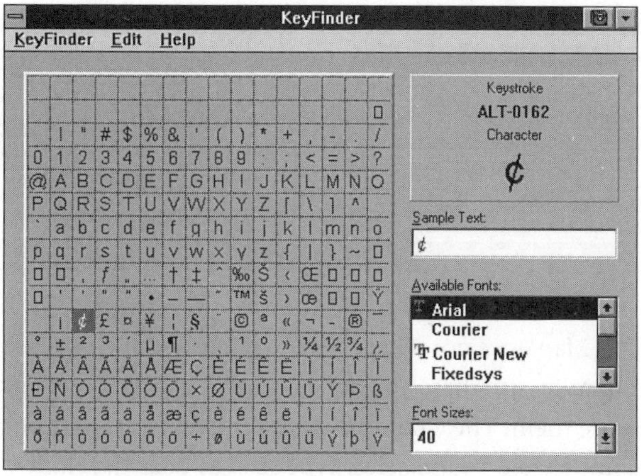

Fig. 18.2
The KeyFinder window displaying all the characters for the Arial TrueType font.

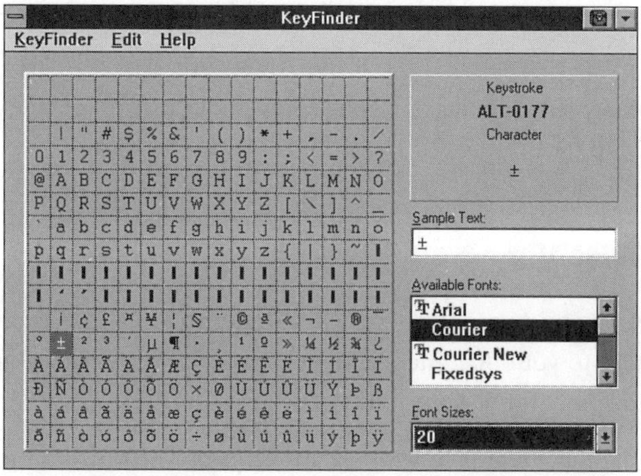

Fig. 18.3
The KeyFinder window displaying all the characters for the Courier font.

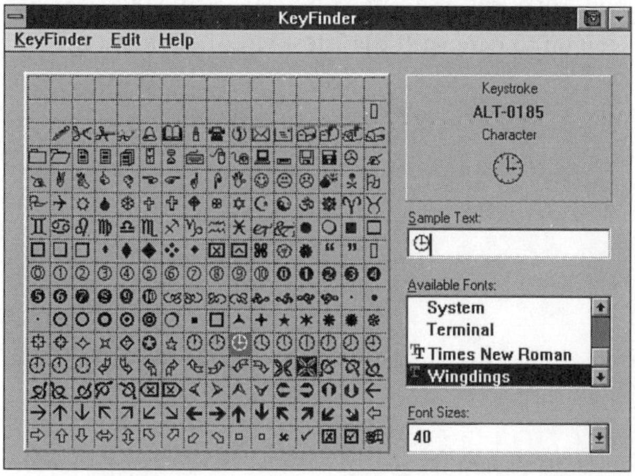

Fig. 18.4
The KeyFinder window displaying all the characters for the Wingdings TrueType font.

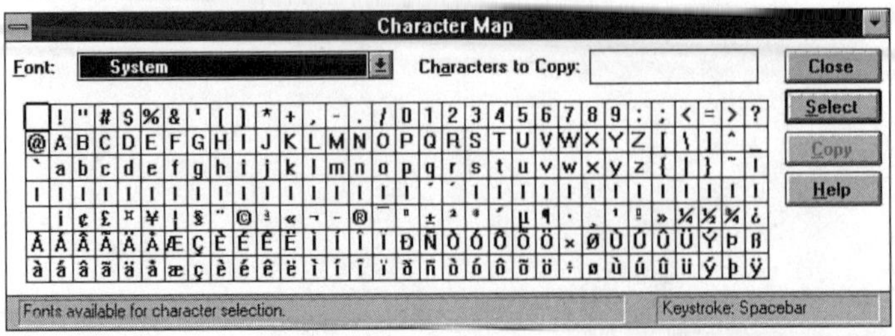

Fig. 18.5
The Windows 3.1 Character Map window, displaying characters for the System font.

The Character Map does not display the first 32 special characters. Although not all font families use these characters, some, such as the Windows Terminal font, do use them. The Character Map displays characters only at a fixed size; it does not enable you to select type sizes as does KeyFinder. Finally, the Character Map does not display the detailed information available in KeyFinder's Programmer Mode, which may be a concern for more technical users.

For these reasons, you may want to use KeyFinder instead of the Windows 3.1 Character Map tool.

Summary

This chapter showed you how to use KeyFinder to locate special characters and add them to your documents. The chapter also provided samples of KeyFinder displays for various font types.

The next chapter explains how to use the Norton AntiVirus to protect your system from potentially destructive computer viruses. You learn how to launch Norton AntiVirus, use Virus Intercept, scan your disks, inoculate your disks, and keep up to date with the latest virus information.

Chapter 19

Using Norton AntiVirus

On March 6, 1992, the feared Michelangelo *computer virus* was supposed to strike. With massive worldwide media attention, nothing quite so significant ever had seemed to hit the PC world. On every nightly news show, in every newspaper, around every office water cooler, computer experts and novices alike were talking about viruses, lost data, and unrecoverable system failures. The threat heightened the awareness for a need to guard against dangers, such as Michelangelo, Stoned, Joshi, Jerusalem-B, and who knows how many other rogue programs that seemed to threaten the very fabric of personal and business computing.

The fact that Michelangelo was far less pervasive than feared and caused very little damage does not mitigate the importance of the message that was heard during the weeks leading up to March 6. Computer viruses are real, and they cause real damage. You must protect your system from the danger they pose—or run the risk of catastrophic system failure and data loss.

In this chapter, you learn to perform the following tasks:

- Understand Norton AntiVirus
- Launch and configure Norton AntiVirus
- Use Virus Intercept
- Use AntiVirus
- Keep Norton AntiVirus up-to-date
- Schedule virus checking
- Inoculate and uninoculate a file

Understanding Computer Viruses

A computer virus is similar to a biological virus. Both invade your system (computer or human) and replicate themselves. Viruses can be destructive, such as the AIDS virus, or annoying, such as the common cold virus. You want to protect yourself from viruses and effect a cure if you become infected.

A computer virus is actually a computer program that places copies of itself in other programs on your system. Most viruses do not infect data files, invading only executable and system files. Although many viruses merely display an annoying message on your screen after some trigger event, others actually destroy programs or system information.

Literally thousands of different viruses have been forced on the computing world. Most viruses are of one of two types: *program-infecting viruses* or *system-infecting viruses*. Many of these viruses are "stealthlike" in nature; they conceal themselves from observation and defend against removal.

Program-Infecting Viruses

Program-infecting viruses infect executable program files, including programs with the EXE, COM, SYS, OVL, and DRV extensions. Some viruses damage these files permanently by overwriting pieces of the program's code. Other, more insidious viruses actually attach themselves to the program's code, enabling the program to continue functioning while the virus courses its way through other files by using your system's memory as the conduit.

Fortunately, most program-infecting viruses can be removed without causing damage to your original program files. Few program-infecting viruses cause damage to your disk's system areas, alleviating the need to totally reformat your disk to remove the virus.

System-Infecting Viruses

System-infecting viruses are the real threats to the operation of your computer system. These viruses infect or replace the *master boot program* and/or the *boot sector program* that are necessary for your computer to start correctly after you first turn on the computer. Viruses of this type can actually prevent your system from starting or prevent you from accessing information on your hard disk.

These viruses cannot be removed simply by erasing files. Special programs, such as Norton AntiVirus, are necessary to remove them and restore your system to working order. In the worst of cases, you must completely reformat your hard disk to eradicate the virus, with the possibility of losing valuable data in the process.

Understanding Norton AntiVirus

Norton AntiVirus detects more than 2,300 known viruses of both the program-infecting and system-infecting types. Norton AntiVirus also is capable of eliminating these viruses from your system. In addition, Norton AntiVirus constantly monitors your system to detect currently unknown viruses.

Norton AntiVirus maintains a *virus definition table* that identifies numerous known viruses. This table constantly is updated by Symantec; you can contact them to receive up-to-date listings that include newly discovered viruses. Norton AntiVirus uses this table to check files for known viruses. If the program identifies a known virus, it alerts you and prompts you for action.

But how do you protect yourself against new viruses that are not yet identified in the definition table? Norton AntiVirus provides this protection by *inoculating* your disks. Inoculation is a fancy word for a simple process. Norton AntiVirus examines all your program files and writes data regarding their sizes in an *inoculation file*. Each time you use these program files, Norton AntiVirus compares their current file size with the file size information stored in the inoculation file. If the file sizes are different, the files are likely to be infected with a new and unknown virus; the program alerts you and prompts you for action.

Launching and Configuring Norton AntiVirus

The Norton AntiVirus program is accessible through normal NDW launch methods. If you opt to install Norton AntiVirus as a Desktop tool, you can simply double-click the Norton AntiVirus Tool icon. Otherwise, launch the program from the menu system by choosing the **T**ools Norton Anti**V**irus command.

After Norton AntiVirus loads, you are presented with the main Norton AntiVirus window, as shown in figure 19.1. This dialog box determines what disks are scanned. You can choose to scan All **F**loppy disks, **A**ll Hard Drives, or **N**etwork Drives. The drives currently selected to be scanned are listed at the bottom left of the dialog box and are highlighted in the **D**rives box. You also can select or deselect drives to scan by choosing them individually from the **D**rives list box. To scan the selected drives, using all the current settings, choose the S**c**an Now button. Before you scan, however, you may want to select from a number of scan options.

You can configure various aspects of Norton AntiVirus by accessing the **O**ptions icon. Here you can set preferences for Scanner, Auto-Protect, Alerts, Activity Log, Exclusions, Inoculation, Password, and General settings.

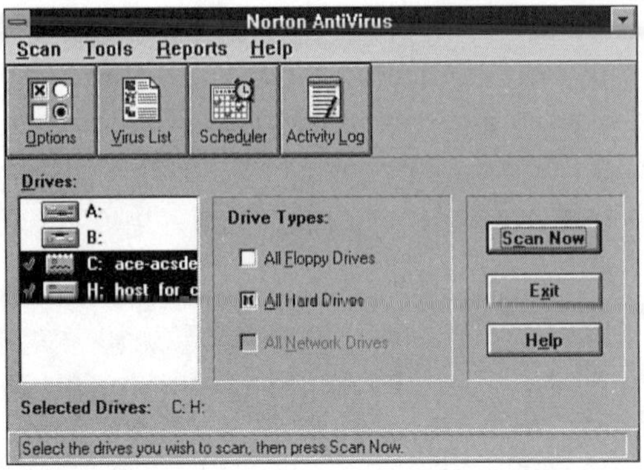

Fig. 19.1
The Norton AntiVirus window enables you to check your disk for virus infestation.

Choosing Scanner Options

To configure Norton AntiVirus, choose the **O**ptions icon and the Scanner category. The Options - Scanner Settings dialog box appears (see fig. 19.2). In this dialog box, you can select what areas of your computer's memory, disk areas, and program files (including compressed files) to scan. If you choose to scan **P**rogram Files Only, you can select the Pro**g**ram Files button and specify the extensions of all program files to scan. These normally include program files with extensions EXE, COM, OVL, SYS, and other command extensions.

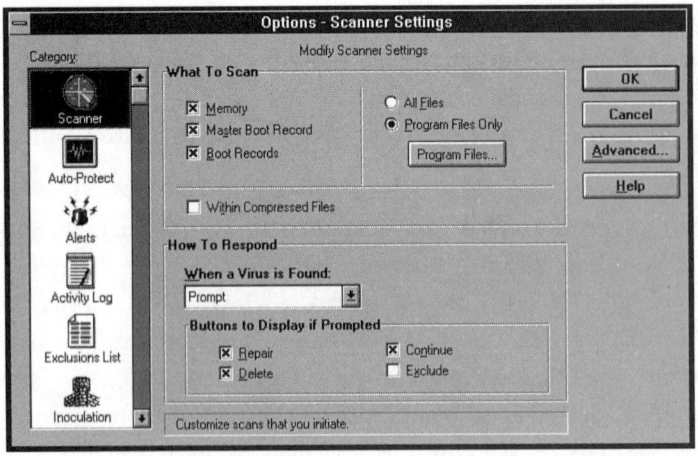

Fig. 19.2
The Options - Scanner Settings dialog box enables you to specify what to scan and how to respond.

You also can customize how you want the program to respond if a virus is found. Your choices on the **W**hen a Virus Is Found list are Prompt, Notify Only, Repair Automatically, Delete Automatically, and Halt Computer.

If you are prompted that a virus has been located, you can select among the options presented to you. These are **R**epair, **D**elete, Co**n**tinue, and E**x**clude.

The **R**epair option enables the program to attempt to repair the damage caused by the virus; the **D**elete option causes the program to delete the offending file. The Co**n**tinue option enables the program to continue scanning without any changes, and the E**x**clude option tells the program to exclude the offending file from further scan checks.

The **A**dvanced Scanner button enables you to choose additional options, including network scanning options, specifying whether you want scanning to be stopped and other options.

Choosing Auto-Protect Options

From the Options window, choose the Auto-Protect icon from the Categor**y** list to display the Options - Auto-Protect Settings dialog box (see fig. 19.3). The Auto-Protect options enable you to specify how AntiVirus monitors your computer for possible infection. The Scan A File When options enable you to specify when a file is scanned; you can choose any combination of the three options: when a file is **R**un, Ope**n**ed, or Cr**e**ated.

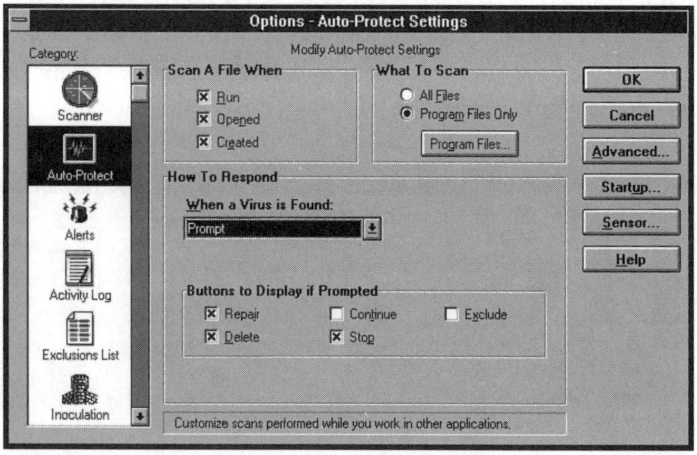

Fig. 19.3
The Options - Auto-Protect Settings dialog box enables you to choose automatic protection options.

The What to Scan box enables you to specify what files to scan. You can choose either to scan All **F**iles or Progra**m** Files Only. If you choose Progra**m** Files Only, you can click the Pro**g**ram Files button and specify what kind of program files are to be checked.

The How To Respond box contains options that are similar to the options found in figure 19.2 and are explained in the preceding section. The only new option is Sto**p**. If you choose this option, it causes the program to stop scanning.

If you choose the **A**dvanced button, you can choose additional Auto-Protect options, including specifying checks for viruslike activities such as the initiation of a low-level format or writing to disk *boot records*.

If you select the Start**u**p button, you can choose the items to be scanned after you start up. You can choose what areas of memory and system files to scan and specify a bypass key that enables you to bypass the scanning process.

If you choose the **S**ensor button, you can choose whether or not the program uses special sensing techniques to detect unknown viruses and specify what actions to take if a suspected virus is found.

Choosing Alerts Settings

From the Options window, you can choose the Alerts icon from the Categor**y** list to display the Alerts Settings dialog box (see fig. 19.4). In this dialog box, you can select the **D**isplay Alert Message check box to specify an alert message that appears in a text box on-screen. The **A**udible Alert option causes a sound to be played if an alert is given. The **R**emove Alert Dialog After option enables you to specify that the alert be removed from the screen after the specified number of seconds. If the computer is running unattended, you may not want the program to stop, but to detect and delete any infection and continue with the program.

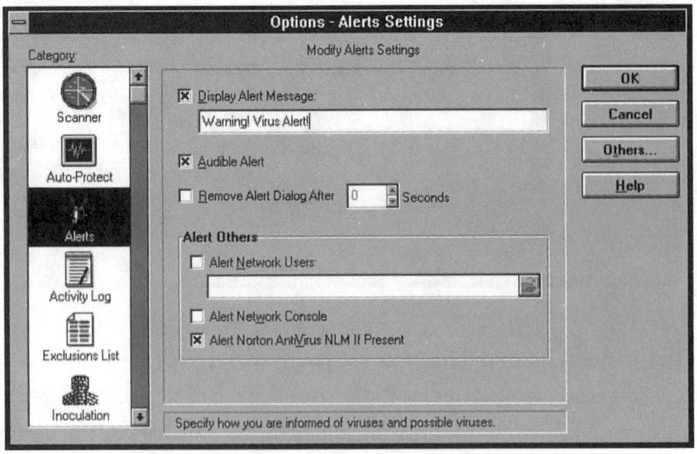

Fig 19.4
The Options - Alerts Settings dialog box enables you to specify alert warnings.

The Alert Others box enables you to choose to Alert **N**etwork Users if a virus is found. The Alert Net**w**ork Console option causes a message to be sent to the computer specified as the network console. The Alert Norton Anti**V**irus

NLM If Present option causes a message to be sent to your NAV **N**etware **L**oadable **M**odule, if present, which may be configured to page your MIS staff.

Modify Activity Log Settings

From the Options window, you can choose the Activity Log icon from the Categor**y** list to display the Options - Activity Log Settings dialog box (see fig. 19.5).

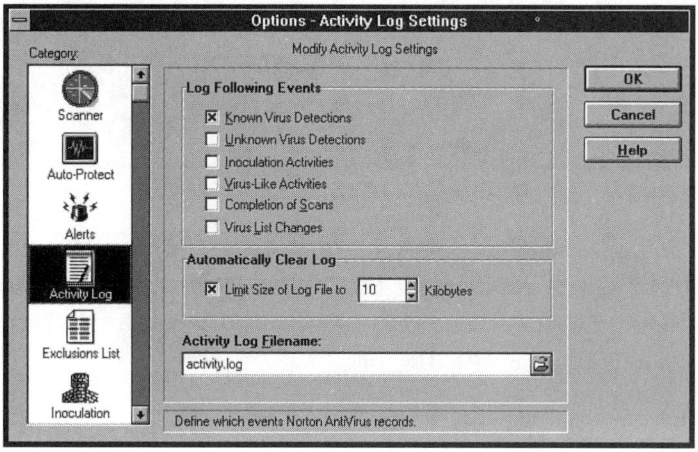

Fig. 19.5
The Options - Activity Log Settings dialog box enables you to select which events are logged.

The Log Following Events box enables you to choose what events, as they occur, are entered into the activity log. The Automatically Clear Log box enables you to specify when the Activity Log file clears. If this option is selected, the log is cleared after it reaches the specified file size. The Activity Log **F**ilename text box enables you to enter the name of the log file. You can use the default name, ACTIVITY.LOG, or enter a new name.

Modify Exclusion List Settings

From the Options window, you can choose the Exclusions List icon from the Category list to display the Options - Exclusions List Settings dialog box (see fig. 19.6).

The **I**tems box enables you to enter file specifications for files that you want to exclude (under certain circumstances) from being checked for viruses. By default, the files listed are CONFIG.SYS and *.VI?. As listed in the Exclusions for \Config.sys box, the reasons for excluding checks for this file include Unknown Virus Detection and Inoculation Detection.

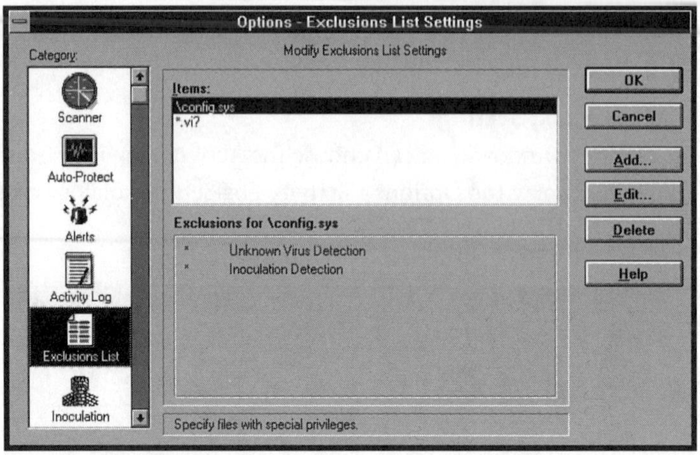

Fig. 19.6
The Options - Exclusions List Settings dialog box enables you to choose what files are excluded from scans.

You can choose to add new exclusion items by selecting the **A**dd button or edit a current item by choosing the **E**dit button. For both **A**dd and **E**dit, you can specify the file specification (such as *.VI?) and choose from a list of exclusions. This list encompasses the following exclusions:

Known Virus Detection

Unknown Virus Detection

I**n**oculation Detection

Low-Level Format of Hard Disk

Write to **H**ard Disk Boot Records

Write to **F**loppy Disk Boot Records

Write to **P**rogram Files

Read-Only Attribute Changes

For example, you may have a program that writes to its own program file (possibly to save setup changes). The AntiVirus program may detect that as virus activity. You could prevent the detection by specifying that this program be excluded from checking writes to program files.

Modify Inoculation Settings

From the Options window, you can choose the Inoculation icon from the Categor**y** list to display the Options - Inoculation Settings dialog box (see fig. 19.7).

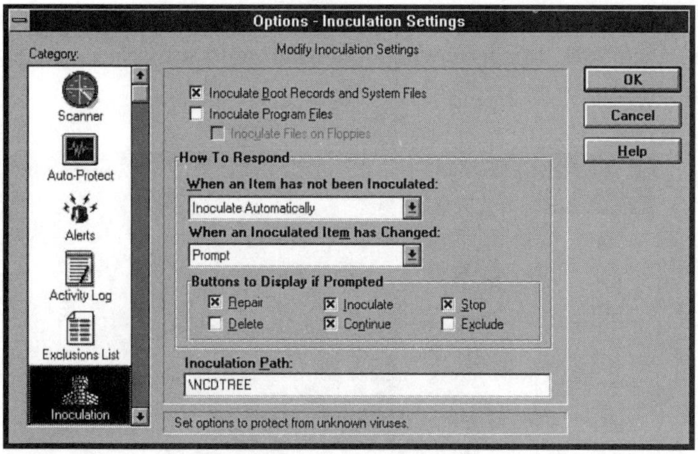

Fig. 19.7
The Options - Inoculation Settings dialog box enables you to choose what files to inoculate.

From this dialog box, you can choose to have the program Inoculate **B**oot Records and System Files and/or choose to Inoculate Program **F**iles, optionally including files on floppies.

The How to Respond box enables you to specify what happens if an item specified in these check boxes has not been inoculated. The choices in the drop-down list box are Prompt, Inoculate Automatically, Notify Only, and Deny Access.

The When an Inoculated Ite**m** has Changed drop-down list box contains the choices Prompt, Notify Only, and Deny Access.

The Buttons to Display if Prompted box enables you to choose what buttons activate if the inoculation alert box is displayed. These options are described in the sections for the Scanner and Auto-Protect options.

Modify Password and General Settings

From the Options window, you can choose the Password icon from the Cate**gory** list to display the Options - Password Settings dialog box (see fig. 19.8).

This dialog box enables you to specify passwords to protect your Norton AntiVirus settings. After these passwords are set, only people with access to your password can change your AntiVirus settings. This gives you added protection against an unauthorized user changing your settings and possibly causing an infection.

Choose the General icon from the Categor**y** list to display the Options-General Settings dialog box (see fig. 19.9). This box enables you to specify if a file is backed up as it is repaired and to specify what file extensions are used for the backup file. You also can choose whether to scan high memory while scanning memory.

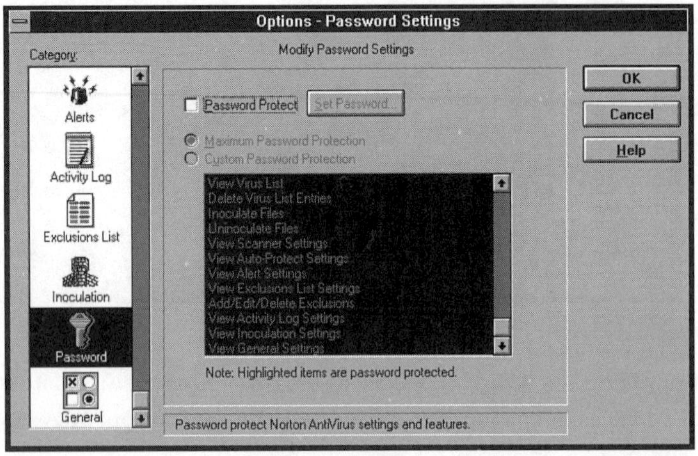

Fig. 19.8
The Options - Password Settings dialog box enables you to password protect AntiVirus settings.

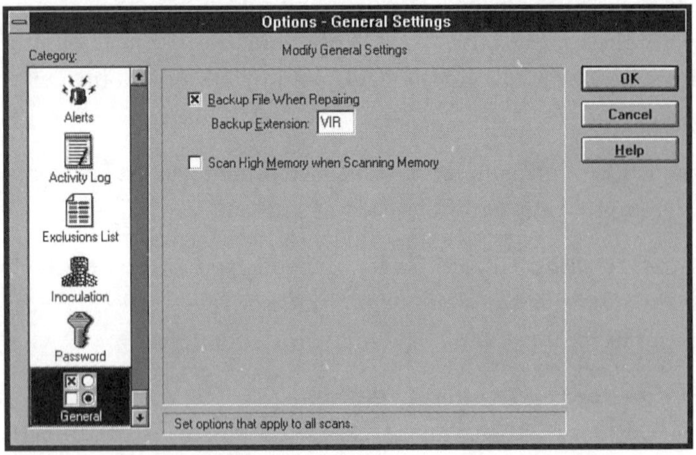

Fig. 19.9
The Options - General Settings dialog box enables you to choose general AntiVirus settings.

Using Virus Intercept

Virus Intercept, if loaded in system memory, constantly monitors your system for viruses. Virus Intercept functions as the front line in the defense against foreign intruders, ever vigilant against viruses invading your system.

Virus Intercept checks for both known and unknown viruses. To check for known viruses, Virus Intercept refers to the virus definition table. To check for unknown viruses, Virus Intercept first inoculates a file and then, whenever that file is accessed, checks the file against the stored inoculation data. If the file has changed, you are alerted to the possibility that an unknown virus has infected the file in question. Inoculation is done only on boot record and SYS files by default. NAVTSR also checks for viruslike code if enabled (this also is disabled by default).

The first time you run an application, Virus Intercept calculates inoculation data for that application and stores it in the inoculation file. Whenever that application runs, Virus Intercept checks the inoculation data to verify that the application's code has not changed. If the code has changed, a virus possibly has infected the program, and Virus Intercept alerts you to that fact.

As you install NDW, a special command line is inserted in your system's CONFIG.SYS file. The following line loads the Virus Intercept program in memory as a device driver:

```
DEVICE=C:\NDW\NAVTSR.EXE
```

In your WIN.INI file, the following lines are added:

```
Load=c:\NDW\NAVTSRW.EXE"
"WIN.INI
Load=NAVWTSR.EXE"
```

The program stays in memory all the time, checking your files for any virus defined in the program's virus definition list. Whenever you start your system, copy a file, copy a disk, or start an application, Virus Intercept is working.

Tip
If your CONFIG.SYS file does not include this line, use an ASCII text editor, such as NDW's Desktop Editor, to add the line.

If the utility finds an infected file, the utility displays an alert and stops whatever operation your computer is executing at the time of detection. You should then launch Norton AntiVirus. After the infected file is identified, you can repair or delete the file.

Virus Intercept is a passive program; after it is loaded, you do not have to do a thing to make it work. The program works automatically in the background, making its presence known only if a possible virus is detected. If you soon forget about Virus Intercept, everything is working normally.

Caution

Virus Intercept cannot scan for viruses under certain circumstances: by using the DOS DISKCOPY command, copying files with LapLink or other similar types of products, by using Norton Commander's Commander Link, downloading files with a modem, or by using file compression programs. (Virus Intercept cannot check compressed files.) As soon as you use one of these methods to add new files to your disks, you should scan them by using NAV.

Using AntiVirus

Norton AntiVirus scans files for viruses and then gives you the option of repairing the file (if the file is repairable) or deleting the file. By using Anti-Virus, you can scan complete disks, specific directories, or individual files for possible viruses.

Scanning for Viruses

NAV scans for known viruses—viruses defined on the virus information table. NAV also can scan for unknown viruses (like Virus Intercept does) if the **U**nknown Virus Detection option is enabled. If AntiVirus finds a virus, you have the option of repairing the infected file (if possible) or deleting the infected file.

To scan a drive for viruses, follow these steps:

1. Select the AntiVirus icon from the Desktop.
2. Select the drive(s) you want to scan. You can select specific drives from the **D**rives box or specific Drive Types (All **F**loppy Drives, **A**ll Hard Drives, or All **N**etwork Drives).
3. Choose S**c**an Now to begin scanning.

To scan a directory for viruses, follow these steps:

1. Choose the **S**can **D**irectory command. The Scan Directory dialog box appears (see fig. 19.10).
2. Select the drive and directory you want to scan.
3. Choose OK to begin scanning.

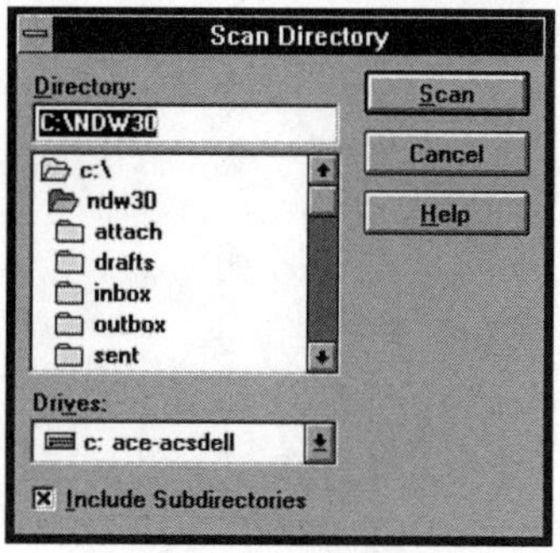

Fig. 19.10
The Scan Directory dialog box enables you to choose a directory to scan.

To scan a specific file for viruses, follow these steps:

1. Choose the **S**can **F**ile command. The Scan File dialog box appears (see fig. 19.11).

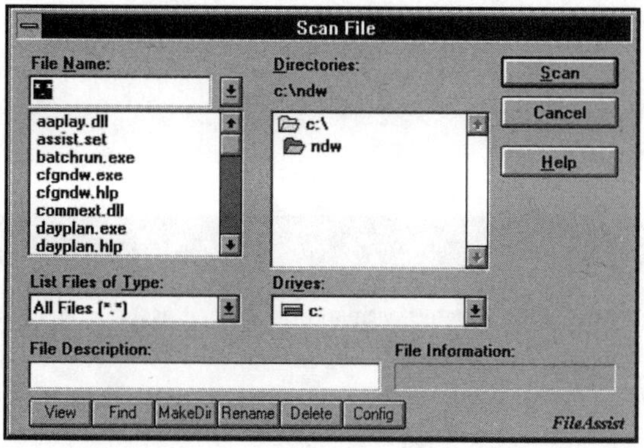

Fig. 19.11
The Scan File dialog box enables you to choose a file to scan.

2. Select the file you want to scan.

3. Choose OK to begin scanning.

Tip
Use the **S**can **F**ile command to check new files you copy to your system, such as files downloaded from on-line bulletin board systems.

As AntiVirus checks your disk, the program displays the Scan Results dialog box (see fig. 19.12). If AntiVirus detects a file that is infected with a known virus, the program displays the name of the infected file and its identified virus. If other viruses are identified, their names are added to the list. The Scan Results dialog box also enables you to repair, delete, or reinoculate the scanned areas.

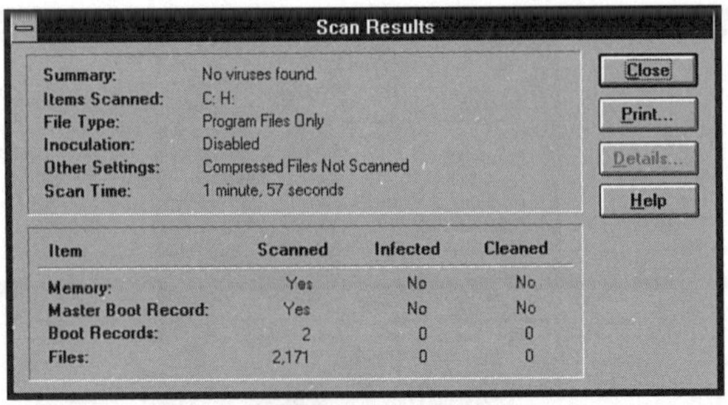

Fig. 19.12
The Scan Results dialog box reports on items scanned and viruses found.

Note

If AntiVirus identifies a mismatch between known file size (stored in the inoculation file) and current file size, the program displays the message `This file may contain a strain of an unknown virus`. This message does not always mean that the file is infected. The message can occur if the file has changed since the original inoculation, through no fault of a virus. If you believe the message occurred for this reason, you should reinoculate the offending file.

Note

If you really do have a file infected with an unknown virus, you can choose to attempt to repair the file or delete it.

Removing Viruses from Your System

You can use two techniques to remove a virus from your system: instruct AntiVirus to attempt to repair the offending file or delete the file. Both options are available from the Scan Results dialog box, depending on what options you choose to be active in the Options dialog boxes described earlier.

Note

You cannot repair all infected files. An infected file is repairable only if the virus has not permanently overwritten any part of the file. If a repaired file does not operate correctly, the repair was unsuccessful and you need to delete the file and reload a new copy from the original program disks.

To repair an infected file, follow these steps:

1. From the Scan Results dialog box, select the file to repair.
2. Choose the **R**epair command.
3. From the Repair Files dialog box, click the Repair button to remove the virus. Alternatively, you can click the Repair All button to remove viruses from the rest of the files in the Scan Results dialog box.

Tip
If the Repair button in the Repair Files dialog box is grayed, the selected file is irreparable. You must delete this file.

To delete an infected file, follow these steps:

1. From the Scan Results dialog box, select the file to delete.
2. Choose the **D**elete command.
3. From the Delete Files dialog box, click the Delete button to delete the selected file. Alternatively, you can click the Delete **A**ll button to delete all infected files listed in the Scan Results dialog box.

Tip
If you must delete a program file, you can recopy the file to your hard disk from your original program disks—assuming, of course, that you kept your original disks.

Repairing Damage to Your Disk's System Area

Some particularly destructive viruses cause damage to the *system area* on your hard disk. These viruses can cause your system not to boot or cause you to lose access to data on your disk. If you are comfortable with advanced technical matters, methods exist to recover from this type of damage.

> **Warning**
>
> Do not attempt to repair virus infection if you are not sure how to do it. The following procedures may require the assistance of technical support personnel.

One type of damage affects your hard disk's partition table. Damage to the partition table is repairable by Norton AntiVirus only if the original partition table information was copied by the virus to a known location. If not, the partition table must be repaired manually.

A partition table virus can be removed manually by using the DOS version of Norton Disk Doctor, located on the Fix-It disks. Follow these steps:

1. Insert a clean, write-protected, bootable DOS diskette in drive A.
2. Reboot your computer.

> **Caution**
>
> The version of DOS on the disk must be exactly the same version as the version on your hard disk.

3. Remove the disk, and replace it with the Norton Fix-It disks.
4. At the A: prompt, type the following line:

    NDD C: /REBUILD

This command recreates your hard disk's Master Boot Program and partition table.

You also can remove a virus manually without Norton Disk Doctor. Follow these steps:

1. Insert a clean, write-protected, bootable DOS disk in drive A.
2. Reboot your computer.

> **Caution**
>
> The version of DOS on the floppy disk must be exactly the same version as the version on your hard disk.

3. By using either the DOS BACKUP command or a DOS version of Norton Backup, back up all data on your hard disk.
4. After the backup is complete, perform a Destructive low-level format.
5. Partition the drive by using the DOS FDISK command.
6. Format the drive by using the DOS FORMAT command.
7. Restore the backed up data.

Another type of system damage occurs to your hard disk's boot sector. To repair boot sector damage, follow these steps:

1. Insert a clean, write-protected, bootable DOS disk in drive A.
2. Reboot your computer.

Caution

The version of DOS on the floppy disk must be exactly the same version as the version on your hard disk.

3. At the A: prompt, type the following line:

C:[*path*]SYS C:

The SYS command automatically rebuilds the hard disk's boot sector.

Keeping Norton AntiVirus Up to Date

To keep your system free of virus attacks, you want to keep your list of known viruses as current as possible. You can display your current list of viruses by choosing the **T**ool **V**irus List option (see fig. 19.13). From this list, you can see what viruses are currently known to your program. If you want to know something about a specific virus, you can highlight that virus name and choose the **I**nfo button. A brief description of the virus and what it does is displayed.

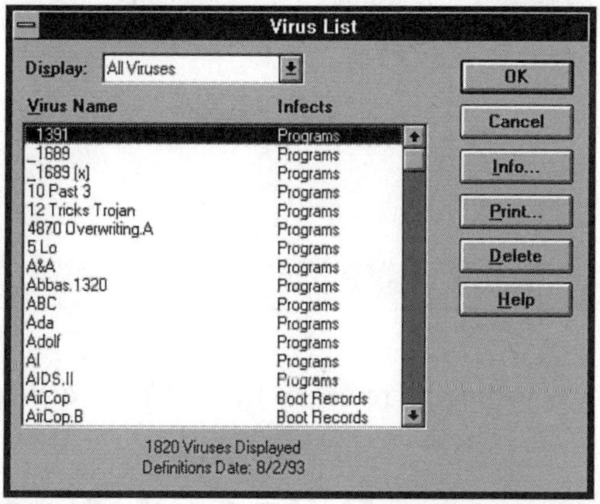

Fig. 19.13
The Virus List dialog box lists all viruses currently known to the NAV program.

Note

You can obtain new virus definitions through various on-line bulletin board services, such as the Symantec BBS and the Symantec forum on CompuServe, through the Symantec Faxline, and through Symantec's virus definitions update disk service. See your NDW package for more information on these services.

Scheduling Virus Checking

By using the Desktop Scheduler, you can select a time for virus checking to be performed on a regular basis. The Scheduler is described in detail in Chapter 22, "Using Scheduler." To schedule a weekly scan of your disks, for example, you can choose the **T**ools **S**cheduler option from the Norton AntiVirus menu bar or choose the Scheduler icon. This accesses the Scheduler screen (see fig. 19.14). In the Scheduler, you can choose to **A**dd an event and then specify the event as a Virus Scan, weekly, at a specific time. You then see an entry similar to the one in figure 19.14 on the Scheduler screen.

To schedule a weekly scan, follow these steps:

1. Choose the **T**ools **S**cheduler option. The Scheduler dialog box appears (see fig. 19.14).

2. Specify a description, specify the program NAVW.EXE as the command to run, and specify a frequency, day of week, and time.

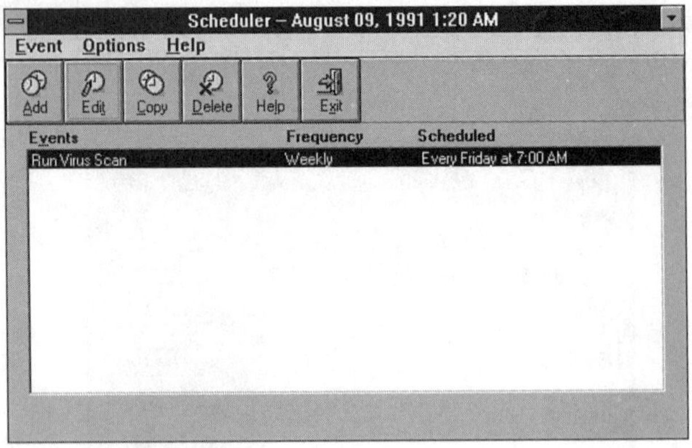

Fig. 19.14
The Scheduler dialog box enables you to schedule periodic virus scans.

3. Minimize the Scheduler to return to the AntiVirus dialog box.

Inoculating and Uninoculating a File

As Virus Intercept monitors your hard disk, the program saves information about original file size in an *inoculation file*. This file contains information about the original size of a file so that the program can detect whether a file's size has changed. The inoculation file is continually growing, because new data is added to old data every time you copy, add, and delete files.

The inoculation file may grow so big that you want to uninoculate your drive (which removes the inoculation file) and then reinoculate your files, creating a new, up-to-date inoculation file.

To inoculate a file, follow these steps:

1. Choose the **T**ools **I**noculation command. The Inoculation dialog box appears (see fig. 19.15).

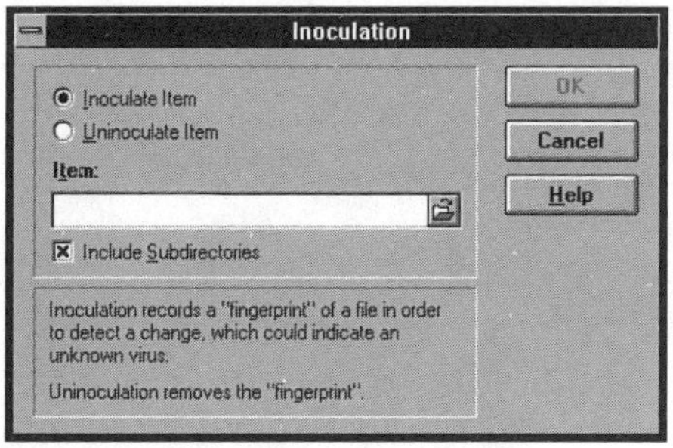

Fig. 19.15
The Inoculation dialog box enables you to specify a file to inoculate or uninoculate.

2. Enter in the I**t**em text box the name of the file you want to inoculate, or use the Browse list to select a file.

3. Choose OK.

You may uninoculate a file the same way by choosing the **U**ninoculate option button.

Summary

This chapter conveyed important information about protecting your system from dangerous computer viruses. You learned about different types of computer viruses and how they affect your system. You also learned how to identify and repair infected files. The message is simple: Use Norton AntiVirus. You cannot be too safe.

The next chapter, "Using Norton Disk Doctor," conveys additional information about disk damage—this time about identifying and repairing physical disk damage by using Norton Disk Doctor. In that chapter, you learn to run the Norton Disk Doctor, repair damaged disks, and run NDD automatically.

Summary

Chapter 20

Using Norton Disk Doctor

Preventive maintenance is a good practice, especially in dealing with computer systems. Norton Disk Doctor for Windows provides a way to perform preventive maintenance on your hard disk in the form of a "checkup" that can identify potential problems before they happen.

Understanding Norton Disk Doctor

Norton Disk Doctor for Windows performs six separate tests on your disks and warns you if it finds errors. You can repair problems directly from the Norton Disk Doctor for Windows or by using the DOS version of Norton Disk Doctor included as part of the Fix-It Disks. (See Chapter 29, "Using Norton Fix-It and Rescue Disks," for a complete discussion of all the utilities on the Fix-It Disks.)

Although enclosed inside your computer so that they are not visible to the user, hard disks are actual physical items. They are, therefore, subject to wear and tear and often contain flaws or develop defects. You need not be concerned, however, unless the defects affect the operation of the disk.

Most disks contain a small number of defects that often do not affect how the disk works. Up to one percent of a disk's surface can contain defects and still remain acceptable to most disk manufacturers, because the bad areas of the disk are located, marked, and sectioned off from use as the disk is formatted.

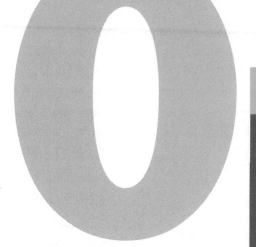

Problems occur if defects arise after the disk is formatted—during the wear and tear of everyday use. Changes in temperature, excessive humidity, cigarette smoke, environmental pollution, age, and rough handling can damage disks. If a formatted disk develops flaws, the disk may produce diminished performance, lost data, and complete system failure.

You can identify and repair these catastrophes before they happen by running Norton Disk Doctor.

If you notice a slowdown in your hard disk's performance, run Disk Doctor. If you have trouble saving files to or reading files from your hard disk, run Disk Doctor. If you have trouble running applications, run Disk Doctor. If you have difficulty accessing your hard disk and starting your system, run Disk Doctor. Better yet, run Disk Doctor *before* you experience any of these symptoms; it can alert you to any developing problems before they affect your system's operation.

Note

The Speed Disk tool also helps if you are experiencing slow access. However, Speed Disk only rearranges the files on your disk, and does not provide the repair capabilities of the Disk Doctor. The best procedure is to run Disk Doctor first and then run Speed Disk.

Note

Develop a schedule for checking your hard disk. Plan to run Norton Disk Doctor for Windows on a regular basis, perhaps once a week, to determine if problems are developing. If the Disk Doctor discovers defects, run the DOS version Norton Disk Doctor (included on the Fix-It Disk) to repair the damage. Depending on the size of your hard disk and the options you choose, a Disk Doctor quick check usually only takes a minute or two. With more thorough testing options chosen, Disk Doctor can take more than an hour to run.

Running Norton Disk Doctor for Windows

You can access Norton Disk Doctor for Windows in several ways.

To access Disk Doctor from the main menu, choose the **T**ools Norton **D**isk Doctor command. Or choose the Disk Doctor icon from the Desktop. After Disk Doctor starts up, the window shown in figure 20.1 appears.

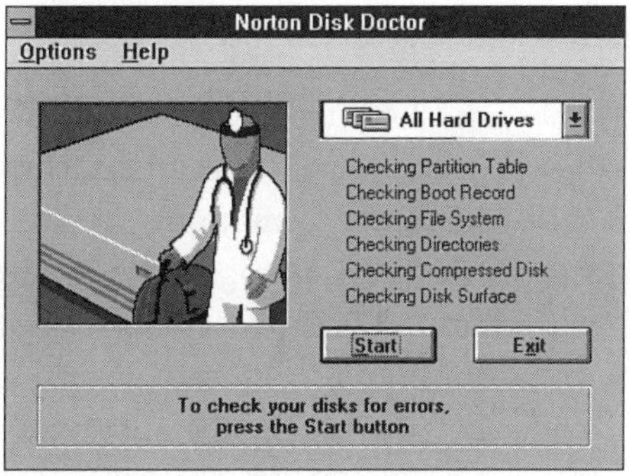

Fig. 20.1
The Norton Disk Doctor for Windows initial options window.

From the initial Disk Doctor window, you can choose which single hard drive or floppy drive to check, or you can choose to check all hard drives present on your system.

From the Disk Doctor **O**ptions menu, choose **T**est Preferences. These preferences include **A**nimation and **D**isk Surface Testing options. If you choose **A**nimation, pictures of a doctor checking your disk appear on-screen during the test. Animation slows the program a little, so if speed is critical, turn animation off.

If you choose **D**isk Surface Testing, the selected disk's surface is thoroughly tested during the Disk Doctor's examination. This extensive test takes a great deal of time, so you may want to perform this test only occasionally. After you choose the drive to check, choose the **S**tart button to begin the diagnosis.

Disk Doctor automatically tests the following six areas:

- *Checking Partition Table.* This test verifies that your partition table is intact. A partition table shows the operating system how to find the individual partitions on the hard disk. If the partition table is damaged, the operating system is unable to access the hard disk. Partition table errors are very serious.

- *Checking Boot Record.* This test examines your disk's boot record. The boot record contains information about disk characteristics used by the operating system, such as size, number of sectors, cluster size, and layout. A damaged boot record can cause the operating system to lose access to specific files.

- *Checking File System.* This test examines the file allocation table (FAT). The FAT contains information that enables the operating system to find all the sectors belonging to individual files. If the FAT is damaged, the operating system can lose access to specific files.

- *Checking Directories.* The Checking Directories test checks the directory structure and the file structure and looks for lost clusters. The directory structure shows the operating system how to find specific files on the disk. If the directory structure is damaged, the operating system can lose access to entire directories. Disk Doctor compares each file's directory information with its FAT information for agreement. *Lost clusters* are parts of the disk that contain data but are not linked to specific files. In most cases lost clusters represent "abandoned" data that can be deleted.

- *Checking Compressed Disk.* If you are using a compression program such as Stacker or MS-DOS 6.2's DoubleSpace, the Disk Doctor checks the reliability of the data on the compressed drive. Figure 20.2 shows an information screen that appears before Disk Doctor begins its test on the compressed drive. You can choose to skip this test if you are sure that the compressed drive is okay.

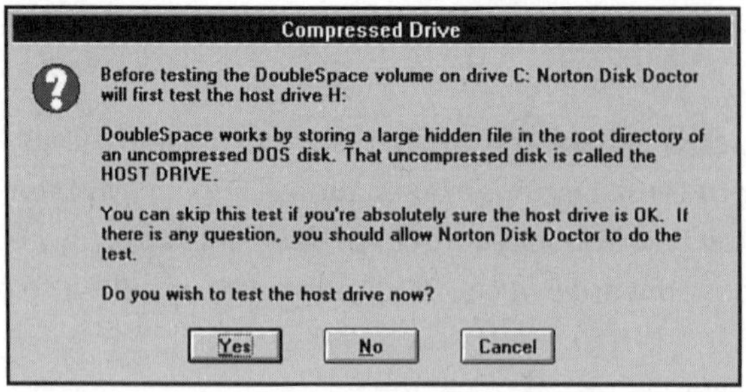

Fig. 20.2
A Norton Disk Doctor information dialog box for testing a compressed drive.

- *Checking Disk Surface.* If you choose this option, Disk Doctor extensively tests the surface of your hard disk, making sure that all areas of the disk can reliably read and write data.

If Disk Doctor finds a problem during the diagnosis, it displays a dialog box explaining the problem and asking if you want to fix it.

> **Warning**
>
> If Disk Doctor locates a problem, fix the problem immediately. The longer you wait before fixing a problem, the greater is the probability of losing valuable data.

After Disk Doctor finishes all its tests, it displays a brief summary of its findings (see fig. 20.3). You also can choose to display a more detailed report by clicking the **D**etails button. The **D**etails button accesses a more extensive report listed in a scrolling dialog box, as shown in figure 20.4. You can send this report to your printer by choosing the **P**rint button, save it to a disk file by choosing the **S**ave button, or send it in a mail message.

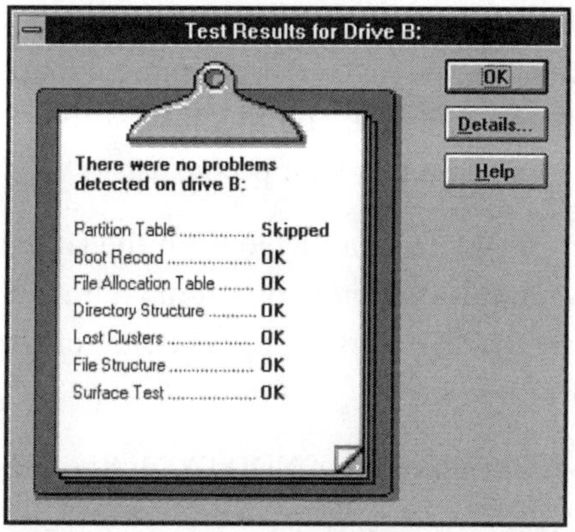

Fig. 20.3
A Norton Disk Doctor for Windows Test Results dialog box showing a summary report.

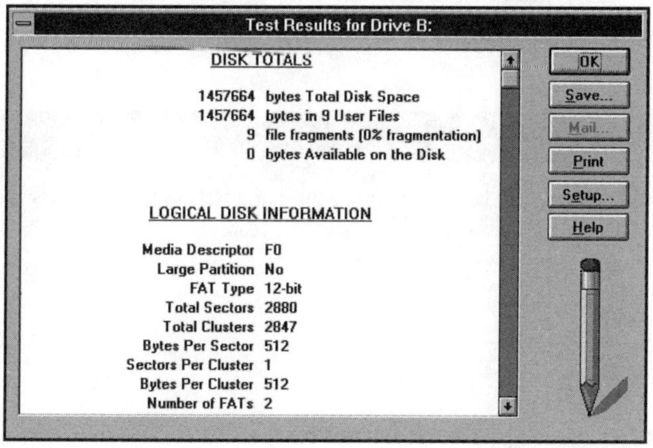

Fig. 20.4
A Norton Disk Doctor for Windows Test Results dialog box showing a detailed report.

After you close the summary or report dialog box, the main Disk Doctor window reappears. You then can choose to analyze another drive by choosing it from the drop-down list box and choosing **S**tart, or you can exit Disk Doctor by choosing the E**x**it button.

Norton Disk Doctor can be a lifesaver if you have serious disk problems. You should run Norton Disk Doctor for Windows on a regular basis. Repairing a hard disk by using Disk Doctor is much easier than trying to recover lost information after a hard disk failure.

Repairing Damaged Disks by Using the Fix-It Disks

Tip
If you cannot access Windows, you can still use the DOS version of Norton Disk Doctor to fix disk problems.

The Fix-It disks (discussed in Chapter 29, "Using Norton Fix-It and Rescue Disks") include a DOS version of Norton Disk Doctor. Storing the program on the separate Fix-It disks enables you to fix problems that result in a complete hard disk failure. If you cannot even reboot your computer, you can use your Rescue disk to boot your computer and then use Norton Disk Doctor on the Fix-It disks to diagnose and repair your problems.

The version of Norton Disk Doctor included on the Fix-It disks must be run from DOS. If your computer will not boot from your hard drive, first boot it by using your Rescue Disk. To start the DOS version of Disk Doctor from the DOS prompt, follow these steps:

1. Place the Fix-It disk containing NDD.EXE into drive A, type **A:**, and press Enter.

2. Type **NDD**, and press Enter. The Disk Doctor opening screen appears. Figure 20.5 shows the initial Disk Doctor screen.

Note

The DOS version of Disk Doctor conducts the same tests as the Windows version.

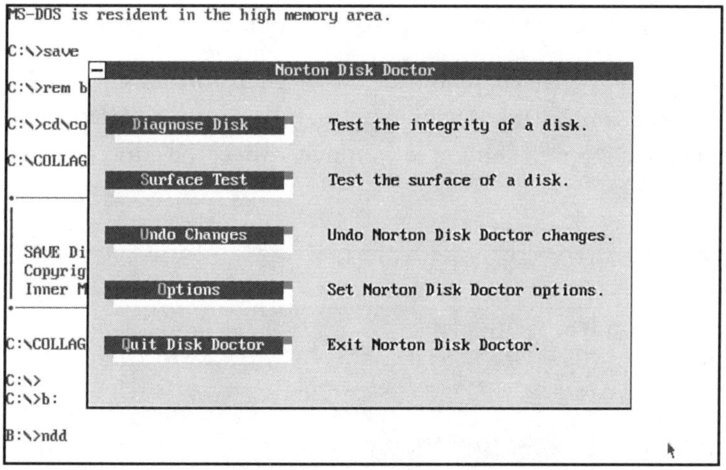

Fig. 20.5
The initial DOS version of Norton Disk Doctor's opening dialog box.

Norton Disk Doctor enables you to diagnose your disk and fix any identified errors in one simple operation. After you start the tests, Disk Doctor reports errors and enables you to fix the errors immediately. To begin the testing process, follow these steps:

1. With Disk Doctor running, choose **D**iagnose Disk from the Norton Disk Doctor dialog box (refer to fig. 20.5).

2. A Select Drives to Diagnose dialog box appears, as shown in figure 20.6. Select the drives to diagnose. Notice that Disk Doctor can analyze more than one drive at one time.

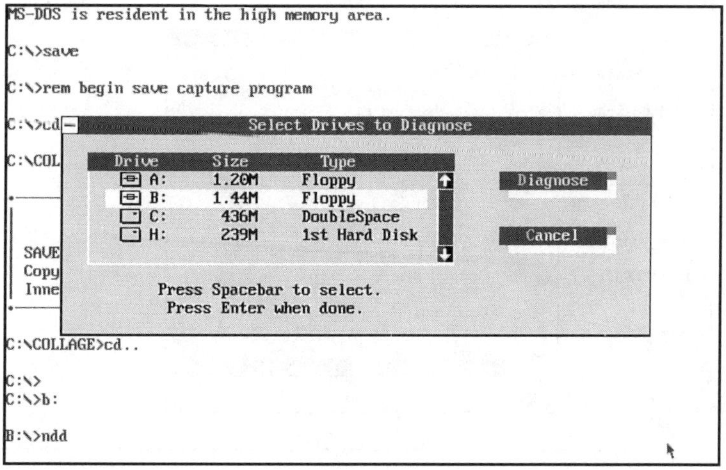

Fig. 20.6
The DOS Norton Disk Doctor Select Drives to Diagnose dialog box enables you to choose which drives to test.

3. Choose the **D**iagnose button. Disk Doctor begins the analysis.

4. If errors are detected, follow the on-screen instructions. Figure 20.7 shows a sample Disk Doctor message. If an error is detected, you often are given the option to continue, correct the error, or cancel the test.

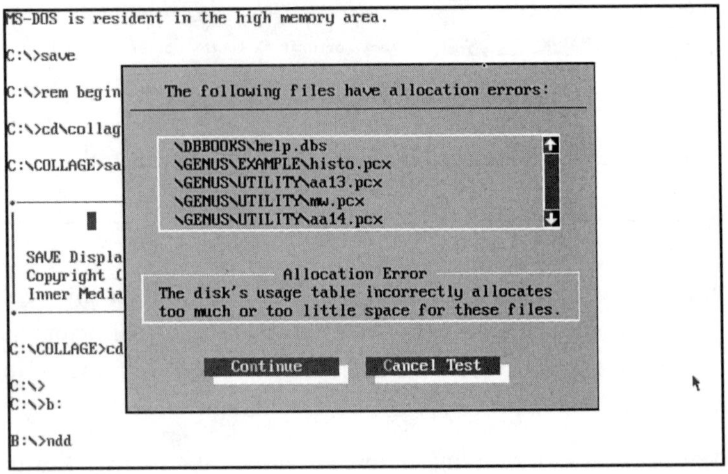

Fig. 20.7 A DOS Norton Disk Doctor message telling you about an error found while diagnosing a disk.

After the Diagnosis if complete, the Surface Test or Decompression Test screen appears, depending on whether your disk is compressed. Figure 20.8 shows the Decompression Test dialog box.

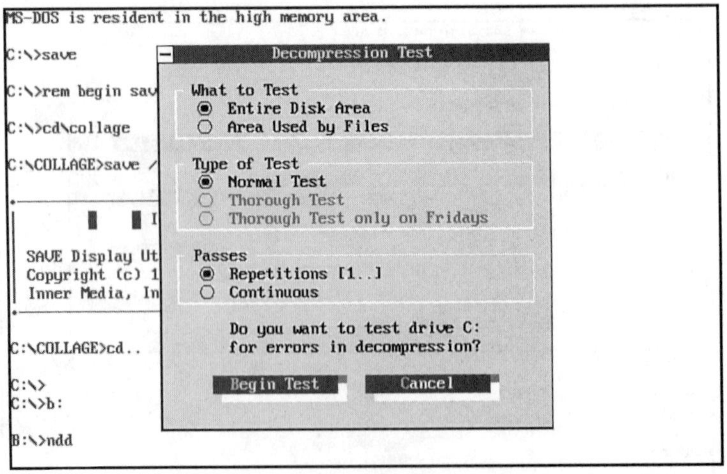

Fig. 20.8 The DOS Norton Disk Doctor Decompression Test (Surface Test) dialog box.

5. Choose the options you want from the list that follows these steps.

6. Choose the **B**egin Test button to start the analysis of the physical disk surface.

   After the tests are completed, a Summary screen appears as shown in figure 20.9.

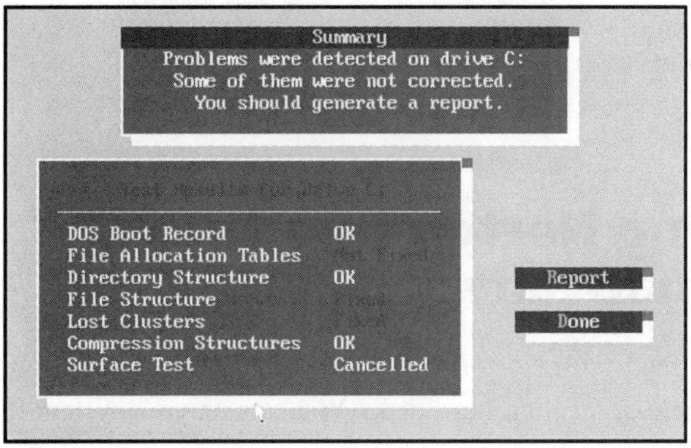

Fig. 20.9
Following the disk tests, the DOS Norton Disk Doctor summary report is displayed.

7. Choose the **R**eport button to generate a more detailed report of the results. This report is similar to the report shown in figure 20.4.

The Decompression Test or Surface Test dialog box enables you to set various testing options. These options are as described in the following list:

- *What to Test.* You can choose either Entire Disk Area or Area Used by Files. The Entire Disk Area test option tests all parts of the disk for bad areas. The Area Used by Files test option tests only the area occupied by existing files. The Entire Disk Area option is slower, but more thorough.

- *Type of Test.* The Normal Test type is a fast, cursory test of the disk. The Thorough Test type is a longer, more thorough test. The Thorough Test Only On Fridays causes the Thorough Test to be performed if the current system date is a Friday; otherwise, a Normal Test occurs.

- *Passes.* This option enables you to choose the number of passes of your disk that Disk Doctor makes during testing. Choosing 1 Repetition is usually sufficient. On rare occasions, you may want to perform additional or Continuous passes for an extremely thorough stress test of your disk.

Note

Norton Disk Doctor enables you to UnDo any changes you make with the program. To utilize this option, you first must create an UnDo file after you encounter a disk error. After the Create Undo File dialog box is displayed, you can choose **C**reate Undo File, **S**kip Undo File or E**x**it. If you choose to create an undo file, Disk Doctor creates a file called NDDUNDO.DAT, which contains all your disk changes. To UnDo changes, simply choose the Undo Changes button from the opening screen and then follow the on-screen instructions. Disk Doctor locates the NDDUNDO.DAT file and returns the disk to its initial state for the current editing session.

Running Norton Disk Doctor Automatically

Some users like to run Norton Disk Doctor daily for a frequent and regular periodic diagnosis of their hard disks. You can set your system to run Norton Disk Doctor for Windows automatically every time you start Windows, or you can set the DOS version of Norton Disk Doctor to run every time you restart your computer system.

Loading Norton Disk Doctor for Windows Automatically

To run Disk Doctor for Windows whenever you run Windows, simply drag the Norton Disk Doctor icon or file and drop it in NDW's Startup Group. The next time you launch Windows, the opening screen is automatically Norton Disk Doctor for Windows. You then can perform diagnostic tests or exit to Norton Desktop.

Loading Norton Disk Doctor for DOS Automatically

You can run the DOS version of Norton Disk Doctor by a command line operation by typing in certain commands and switches from the DOS prompt. Disk Doctor then loads and performs specific operations automatically. You can add a Disk Doctor command line to your AUTOEXEC.BAT file to run Disk Doctor whenever you start your system.

Tip

Add NDDW to your Startup group by adding at its command line the /Q switch and any drive letters to check (for example, NDDW c: d: /Q). NDDW runs as soon as Windows starts up and exits if no problems are found.

Note

This option works only if you install the DOS Disk Doctor from the Fix-It Disk in a directory on your hard drive.

The following table outlines the command-line switches available for both the Windows and DOS Disk Doctor.

Switch	Function
/C	Specifies a complete test.
/Q	Specifies all tests excluding the surface tests.
/R[A]:*pathname*	Writes (R) or appends (A) a report of the tests to the named path and file.
/X:*drives*	Excludes drives from testing.
/REBUILD	Rebuilds a destroyed DOS disk.
/UNDELETE	Undeletes a previously skipped DOS partition.

The syntax you use for the Disk Doctor command line is as follows:

NDD drive: switches

You must add this line to the end of your AUTOEXEC.BAT file by using an ASCII text editor, such as NDW's Desktop Editor.

To run Disk Doctor and perform a complete test on drive C, for example, add the following line to the AUTOEXEC.BAT file:

NDD C: /C

To run Disk Doctor and perform all tests except surface tests on all drives except drive D, add the following line to the AUTOEXEC.BAT file:

NDD /X:D: /Q

Tip
You may need to specify the entire path of the NDD command. If Norton Disk Doctor for DOS is installed in the NORTON directory on drive C, for example, you may need to enter **C:\NORTON\NDD** at the command line.

Summary

Checking your disks for physical wear and having the capability to repair damage that does occur is important. This chapter showed you how to use Norton Disk Doctor for Windows to check your disks for potential physical damage and how to use the DOS version of Norton Disk Doctor on the Fix-It disks to repair damaged disks.

The next chapter shows you how to view the contents of files with the Norton Viewer. You will learn how to launch the Viewer, select default and current viewers, select viewer options, and display a number of file types.

Chapter 21

Using Norton Viewer

You may, on occasion, want to view the contents of more than one file side by side. You may be examining several Excel worksheets at one time, for example, or you may be searching for the perfect icon among several icon files. Norton Desktop 3 for Windows offers the perfect tool for these situations: the Norton Viewer.

One of the useful features of NDW is that you can see the contents of your files without needing to actually start the corresponding applications. You can view files while using Norton drive windows, or you can use the Norton Viewer tool to view multiple files at one time.

In this chapter you learn to perform the following tasks:

- Understand Norton Viewer
- Use the viewing options

Understanding Norton Viewer

Norton Viewer is a tool that enables you to view the contents of a single file or of multiple files. You can view files of different formats in tiled or cascading windows on-screen. (See table 21.1 for a list of the file formats supported by Norton Viewer.) You can load files for viewing from within the Viewer, or you can drag and drop files from a drive window onto the Viewer Tool icon.

Note

A file viewer also is available as a part of each drive window. See Chapter 5, "Using the Drive Windows," for more information.

Table 21.1 File Formats Supported by Norton Viewer

Viewer Name	Formats
Autocad	Autocad graphics files.
Compressed Archives	ZIP, PAK, ARC, ZOO, LZH packed files; notice that the Viewer displays a list of the files contained in each compressed file.
CompuServe GIF	GIF graphics files.
CorelDRAW!	CorelDRAW! CDR graphics files.
dBASE	DBF dBASE files.
Documents & Text	TXT, DOC, SAM, BAT, INI, SYS, WPS files from popular word processors, including Microsoft Word, Word for Windows, Ami Pro, and WordPerfect.
Hex Dump	Any binary hexadecimal files.
Lotus 1-2-3	WK1, WK3, WKT, WKQ, WKS, WQ1 spreadsheet files from Lotus and Quattro applications.
Micrografx Designer	Micrografx DRW graphics files.
Micrografx Draw	Micrografx PIC graphics files.
Microsoft Excel	XLS, XLW, XLA, XLM spreadsheet files.
OLE	OLE objects.
Paintbrush	PCX graphics files.
Paradox	Paradox DB database files.
Programs	EXE, DLL, PRS, DSP, NSS, OVL, OVR, OV1, OV2, OV3, OV4, COM executable files.
TIFF	TIF gray scale and color graphics files.
Timeline	Spreadsheet files.
Windows Metafile	Windows WMF graphics files.
Windows Bitmaps	BMP graphics files.
Windows Icons	ICO, ICL, IC, NIL, DLL, EXE files containing icons.
WordPerfect Clipart	WPG WordPerfect graphics files.
WordPerfect Image	WPG WordPerfect graphics files.

Launching Norton Viewer

To launch the Viewer with a preselected file loaded, follow these steps:

1. From an open drive window, select one or more files to view.
2. Drag the files from the drive window, and drop them on the Viewer Tool icon.

To start Norton Viewer as a stand-alone application, you can use one of the following methods:

- Double-click the Viewer Tool icon.
- Open the Norton Desktop group, and double-click the Viewer icon.

After Viewer is launched, follow these steps to select files for viewing:

1. Choose the Norton Viewer **O**pen tool from the toolbar, or choose the **F**ile **O**pen command from the menu bar. The Open File dialog box appears (see fig. 21.1).

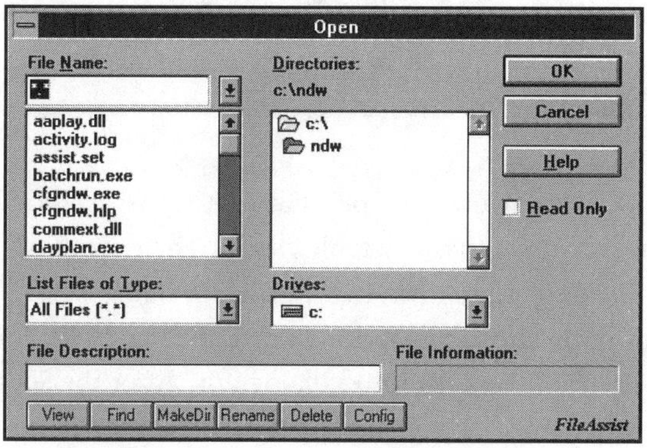

Fig. 21.1
The Norton Viewer Open File dialog box enables you to open a file to view.

2. Select a file for viewing from the File **N**ame and **D**irectories lists.
3. Choose OK to load the file into the Viewer.

Selecting Default and Current Viewers

Table 21.1 indicates that Norton Viewer actually contains multiple viewers. Each viewer is capable of reading different types of files. The Norton Viewer program automatically reads the file extension to determine its type, cross-matches the extension with the extension assignments in the NDW.INI file, and then loads the appropriate viewer for that file type.

Confusion can occur if the same file type can be read by different viewers. EXE files, for example, can be read by both the Programs viewer and the Windows Icons viewer. The NDW.INI file associates EXE files with the Programs viewer; if you load an EXE file, the Programs viewer also is loaded automatically.

If Viewer does assign the wrong viewer to a particular file, however, you can change viewers. With a file loaded, choose the **O**ptions **C**ustomize command, and then select the Set Default Viewer category from the **C**ategories list of the Customize dialog box. The Set Default Viewer version of the Customize dialog box appears, which enables you to choose a default viewer (see fig. 21.2). You then can view icons in an EXE file, for example, by changing the viewer from Programs to Windows Icons.

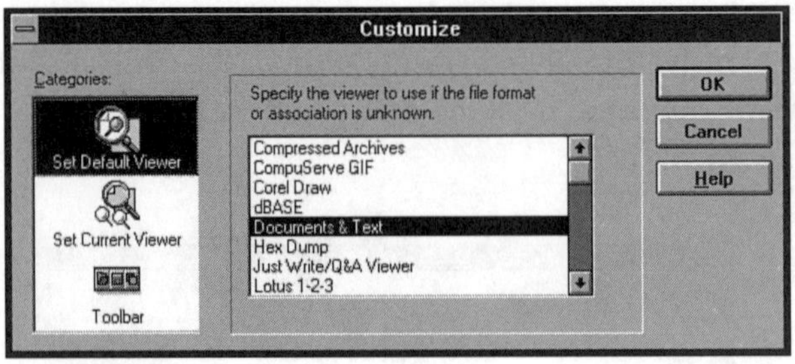

Fig. 21.2
The Set Default Viewer version of the Customize dialog box enables you to choose what viewer is normally used.

If Viewer cannot recognize a file type (that is, if no association exists in the NDW.INI file), it defaults to the default viewer. The default viewer is the Documents & Text viewer, shown highlighted in figure 21.2. You can change the default viewer by choosing **O**ptions **C**ustomize and selecting the Set Default Viewer option of the Customize dialog box. After the Set Default Viewer version of the Customize dialog box appears, select the viewer you want from the list, and choose OK.

You also can choose to customize the location and look of the Viewer's toolbar from the **O**ptions **C**ustomize dialog box.

Using the Viewing Options

You can customize your use of the Norton Viewer to meet your needs in any situation by using the flexible viewing options that Viewer provides. You can choose how to display multiple files, automatically resize graphics files to fit the viewer window, search for specific characters in a text file, or enhance the file you are viewing by changing its font.

Displaying Multiple Files

Because you can load multiple files into Viewer, you can choose how you want the multiple files displayed. These options are as described in the following list:

- *Display one file at a time.* Either maximize an individual view window, or select the file you want from the list in the **W**indow menu. Figure 21.3 shows a Viewer window displaying a single file.

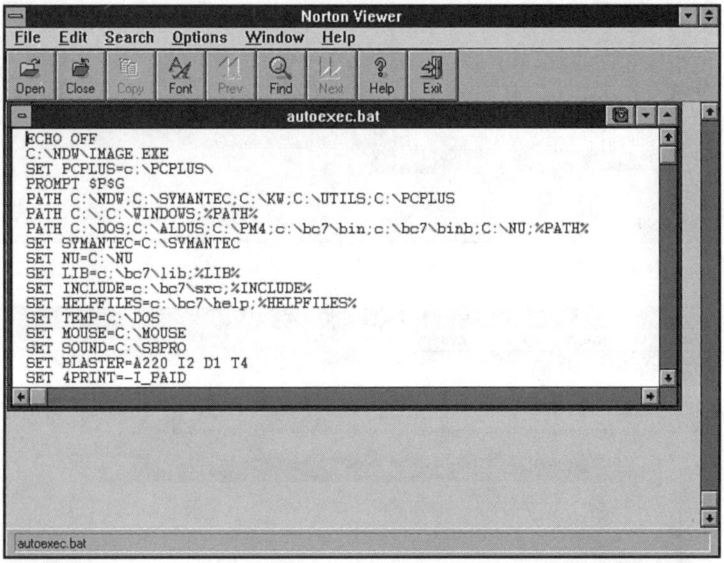

Fig. 21.3
The Viewer can be used to display the contents of a single file.

- *Random display of multiple files.* Size the individual view windows yourself. They may not be perfectly neat, but they can appear however you want them. Figure 21.4 shows a Viewer window with multiple view windows sized and placed randomly.

- *Cascading windows.* Choose the **C**ascade option from the **W**indow menu. Figure 21.5 shows a Viewer window with cascading view windows.

- *Tiled windows.* Choose the **T**ile option from the **W**indow menu. Figure 21.6 shows a Viewer window with tiled view windows.

- *Minimized windows.* Choose the minimize button to minimize view windows to provide more room in the Viewer for maximized windows. Notice in figure 21.7 the different icons for different types of files.

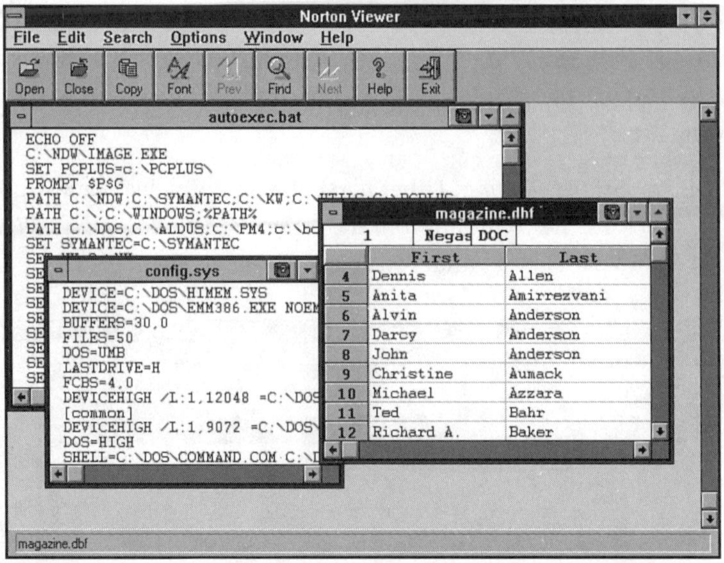

Fig. 21.4
A Viewer display of randomly sized and placed multiple files.

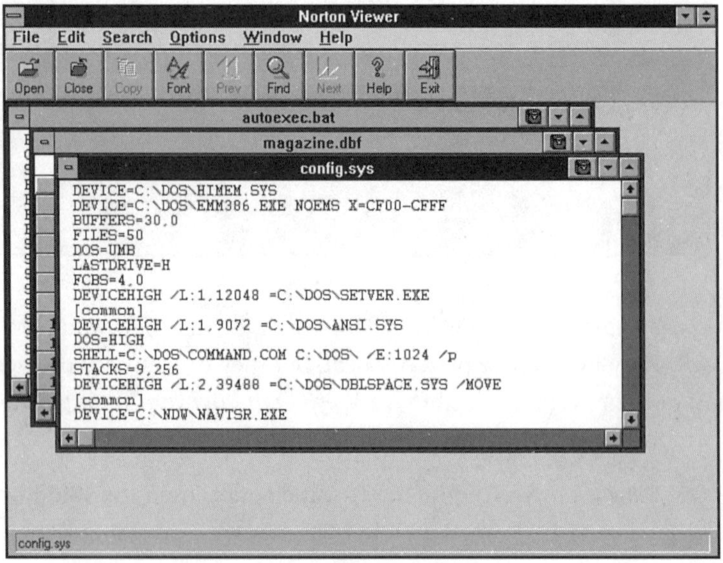

Fig. 21.5
A Viewer display of files shown in cascading view windows.

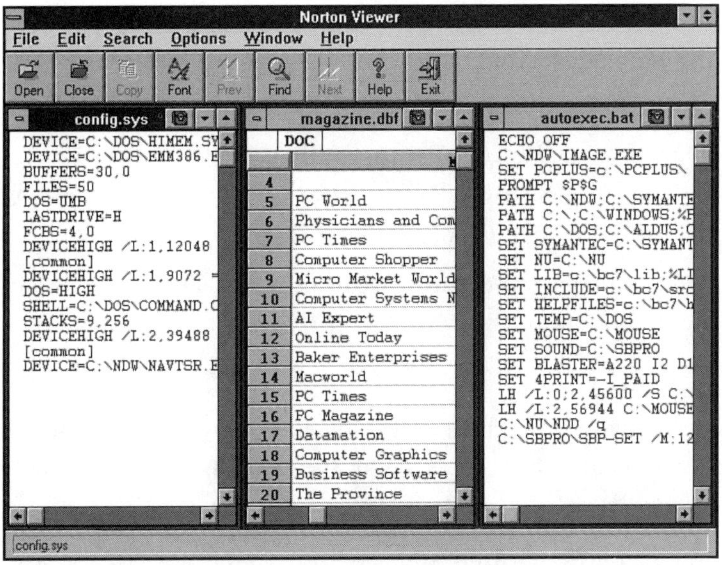

Fig. 21.6
A Viewer display of files shown in tiled view windows.

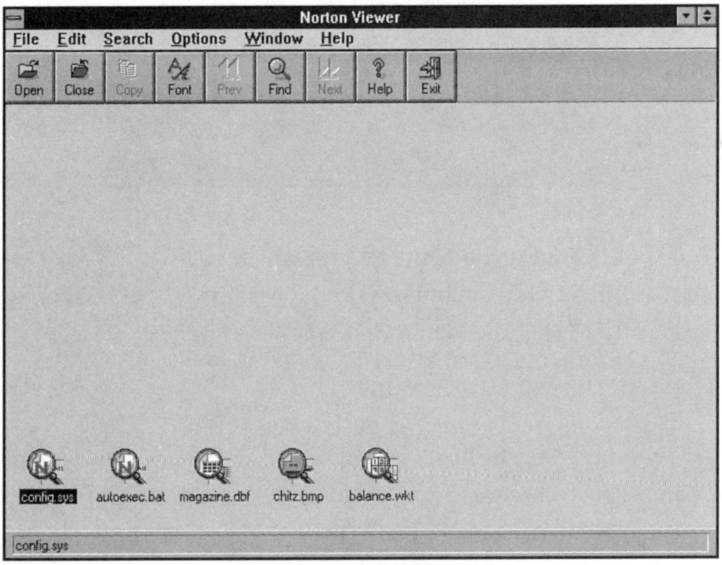

Fig. 21.7
A Desktop containing several files minimized in the Viewer to icons, showing how different file types have different Viewer icons.

Viewing Graphics Files

If you are viewing bitmapped graphics files, Viewer provides several options to enhance your viewing. By using your mouse, you can enlarge, reduce, and zoom in on selected areas of the graphic images. These options are as described in the following list:

- Size an image to fit the window size by double-clicking the image with the left mouse button.
- Size a window to the image size by clicking the image with the right mouse button. A menu appears, enabling you to copy the image to the Windows Clipboard, size the frame to fit the image, size the image to fit the frame, or open the Set Current Viewer dialog box.
- Zoom in on an area of the image by using the mouse to draw a box around the area.

Viewing Text Files

If you are viewing a document or text file, Viewer enables you to search for specific characters or text. To search for specific text while in the Viewer, follow these steps:

1. Choose the **S**earch **F**ind command. The Find dialog box appears (see fig. 21.8).

Fig. 21.8
The Norton Viewer's Find dialog box enables you to find specific text in the file being viewed.

2. Type in the **F**ind text box the text for which you want to search, and choose whether to match upper- and lowercase text by selecting or leaving deselected the **M**atch Upper/Lowercase check box.
3. Choose OK to begin the search.

If you are viewing a spreadsheet or database, you can search for specific text or you can instruct Viewer to *Goto* specific cells or fields. Searching a spreadsheet or database file for specific text is exactly like searching a text document, except that you can specify where in the file to begin the search. Moving to a specific cell or field, however, is different.

Note

Viewer automatically detects the type of file in which you are searching and displays the appropriate dialog box.

To move to a specific cell or field, follow these steps:

1. Choose the **S**earch **G**oto command. The Goto dialog box appears (see fig. 21.9).

2. Choose the **C**olumn and **R**ow you want to view.

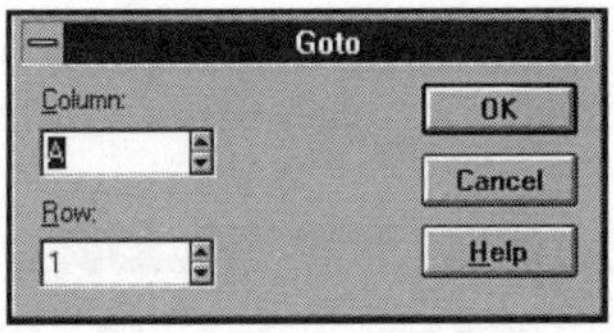

Fig. 21.9
The Norton Viewer Goto dialog box enables you to choose a location to view in a spreadsheet.

3. Choose OK to display the area of the spreadsheet around the specified cell or field.

Selecting Display Fonts

Different users have different preferences; you may prefer to see more text in smaller type while viewing a file, while another user might prefer to read larger type, leaving less of the file visible on-screen. Fortunately, NDW enables you to customize the font used in the Norton Viewer windows.

To change the fonts for Norton Viewer, follow these steps:

1. Choose the Font tool bar command. The Font dialog box appears (see fig. 21.10).

2. Select the Font, Font Style (Regular, Italic, Bold, or Bold Italic), and Size you want.

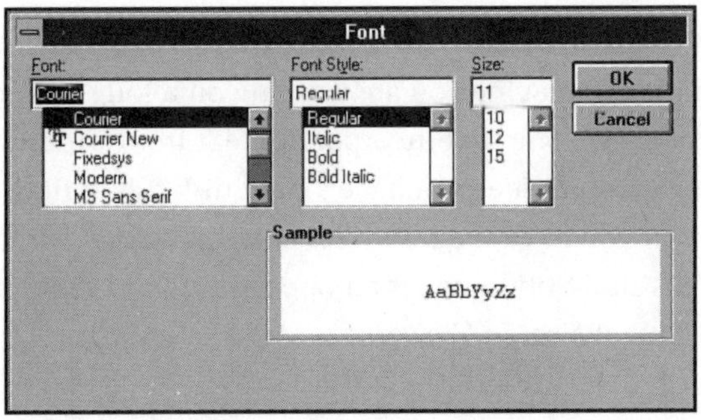

Fig. 21.10
The Norton Viewer Font dialog box enables you to choose what font to use while displaying a file's contents.

3. Choose OK to close the dialog box and implement the new fonts.

> **Note**
>
> If more than one window is open in Norton Viewer, you can specify different fonts for each window by choosing each window individually and clicking the Font toolbar icon. Notice that the last font setting is used as the default font for each subsequent view window opened.

Figure 21.11 shows three text files, each using a different display font.

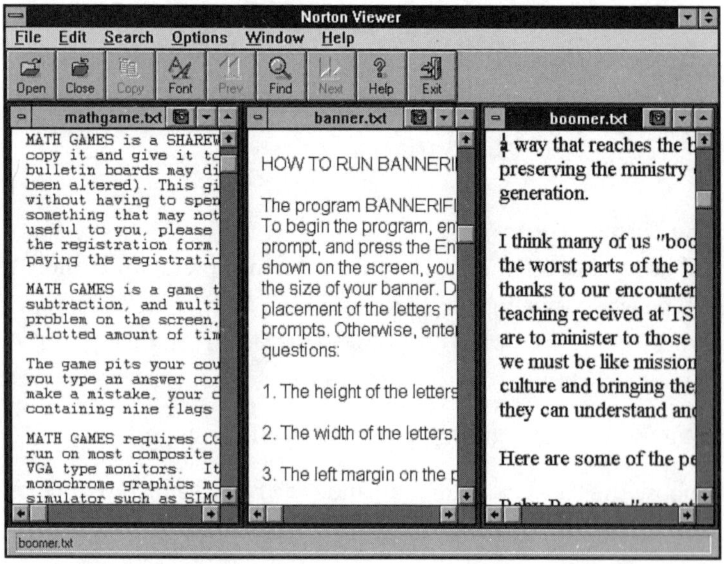

Fig. 21.11
Three text files with different display fonts—Courier, Ariel, and Times Roman fonts in point sizes of 10, 12, and 14.

Using a Norton Viewer Example

The following example demonstrates how you can apply Norton Viewer in everyday operations. Imagine you are working on a long report in your Windows word processor—one that incorporates text from various text files and graphics from a graphics file. You have a hard disk full of files, and you want to make sure that you have the right files at hand before you load them into your report. This situation provides an opportunity to use the multiple-file viewing capability of Norton Viewer.

Suppose that all your text files are in a single directory. You know that the files have the TXT extension. You can begin the search process by loading all the possible files into Viewer and then choosing the right files.

To search for files by using the Norton Viewer, follow these steps:

1. Open a drive window and scroll to the directory that contains the files.
2. Select the possible files and drag and drop them onto the Norton Viewer Tool icon (see fig. 21.12).

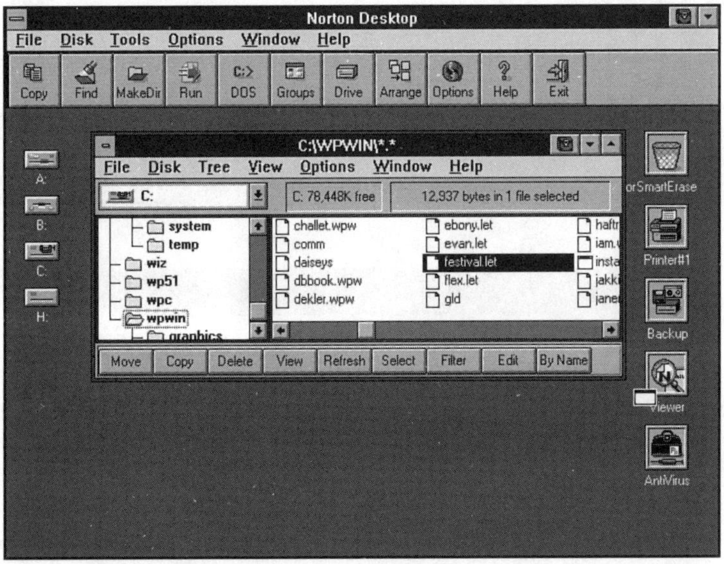

Fig. 21.12
The process of dragging and dropping files from a drive window onto the Norton Viewer Tool icon.

Norton Viewer launches and cascades the windows for the selected files (the default arrangement), as shown in figure 21.13.

3. To confirm that a specific graphics file is the right file for your report, choose the **F**ile **O**pen command in Norton Viewer to locate and load the graphics file, using the same method as you used to load the text files. The graphics file is added to the front of the cascading windows.
4. To see all the files that are loaded in the Viewer at one time, choose the **W**indow **T**ile command to tile the windows.

Fig. 21.13
Selected text files loaded into Norton Viewer, shown in a cascading display.

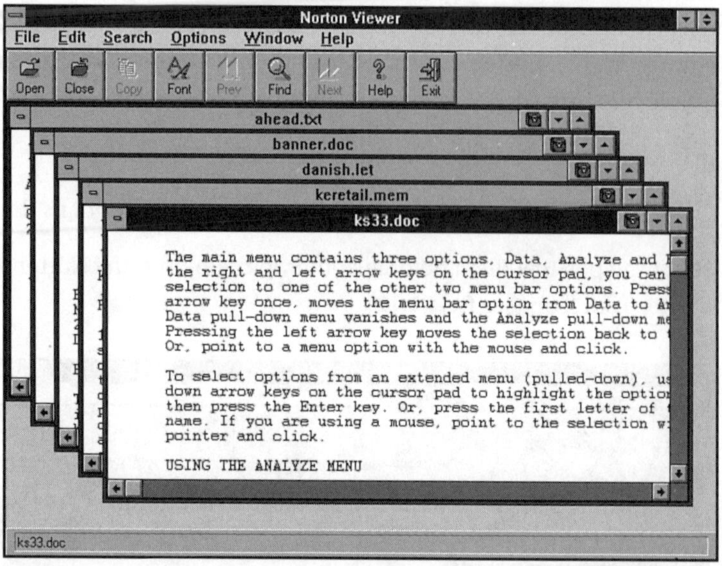

Note

The tile mode is a better choice than the cascade mode if you want to view several files at one time.

5. Maximize Viewer to full-screen size. Figure 21.14 shows the result.

Fig. 21.14
All loaded files displayed in tile view, with Norton Viewer maximized to full-screen size.

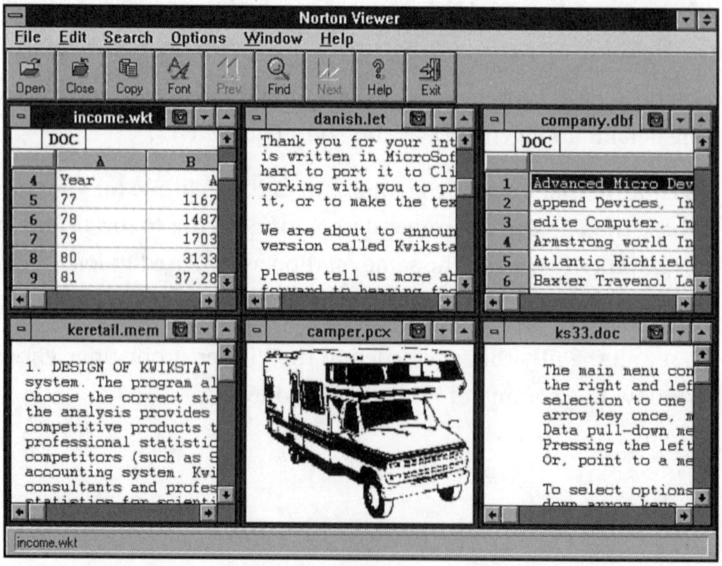

Summary

This chapter showed you how to view different types of files with the Norton Viewer. You learned how to load files into the Viewer and how to view different types of text and graphics files. You also learned how to configure Norton Viewer, including selecting different viewers and different types of views.

The next chapter, "Using Scheduler," shows you how to use the Scheduler utility to notify you of specific events on your personal and business calendar. You learn how to schedule events, use an automatic backup, and run Scheduler automatically.

Chapter 22

Using Scheduler

No one has a perfect memory. From the dawn of time, humans have searched for ways to remind them of important events. Thanks to Norton Desktop 3 for Windows, you can use your computer to remind you of important events. NDW includes a special utility called Scheduler, which enables you to program your computer much like you would your video cassette recorder.

In this chapter, you learn to perform the following tasks:

- Understand Scheduler
- Start Scheduler
- Schedule events
- Use Automatic Backup
- Run Scheduler automatically

Understanding Scheduler

Scheduler is a simple utility, included with NDW, that functions much like an automated timer or alarm clock. Each operation you program into Scheduler is called an *event*. You can schedule *program events*, which run programs at specified times, or *message events*, which display on-screen messages at specified times.

Basic Scheduler operation is much like setting the timer on a VCR. Begin by setting the day and time you want to activate Scheduler. Next, tell Scheduler whether you want the programmed operation to run hourly, daily, weekly, and so on. Finally, you choose whether you want Scheduler to alert you via an on-screen message (which you dictate) or to run a specific Windows or DOS program. After you confirm your programming, Scheduler works in the background, waking up to alert you or to automatically run a program at the predetermined time.

Starting Scheduler

You can start Scheduler from either the menu or the Quick Access Group. To start Scheduler from the menu, choose the **T**ools Schedu**l**er command. You also can choose the Scheduler icon from the Desktop.

> **Note**
>
> If, during NDW's installation, you choose to run the daily backup event automatically, Scheduler launches every time you start Windows and Norton Desktop. If the Scheduler icon appears in the lower-left corner of your Desktop, simply double-click the icon to open the Scheduler window.

Figure 22.1 displays the Scheduler window. Notice that this window cannot be maximized to full-screen size; it appears only as the window shown in figure 22.1 or in icon form.

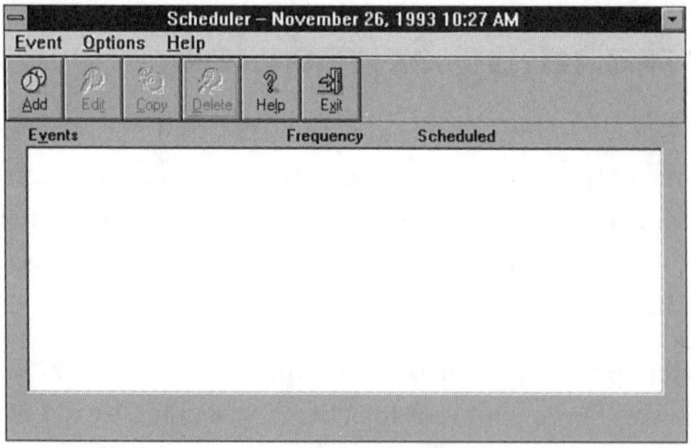

Fig. 22.1
The Scheduler window enables you to manage tasks in your schedule.

The E**v**ents list box lists all events currently programmed into Scheduler, displaying the name of the event, the event's frequency, and the scheduled time of the event. Add new events by choosing the **A**dd button; remove older events by choosing the **D**elete button.

The Scheduler **O**ptions menu contains an option to **H**ide When Iconized that instructs NDW not to display an icon for Scheduler if Scheduler is in icon form. This option is useful if you like to run Scheduler totally in the background, without taking up valuable Desktop space. The Load With **W**indows option instructs NDW to automatically launch Scheduler whenever Windows and Norton Desktop are loaded.

Scheduling Events

You can easily add and remove events in Scheduler. You can even edit existing events or copy existing events to create new events.

Adding Program Events

Add events to Scheduler by choosing the **A**dd option from the Scheduler window to display the Add Event dialog box. The options displayed in the Add Event dialog box depend on the current selection in the Ty**p**e of Event drop-down list box. The events you can choose are Display Message, Run Program, Scan for Viruses, Backup System, and Run Disk Doctor. To schedule a new program event, follow these steps:

1. Click the **A**dd icon in the Scheduler window to display the Add Event dialog box (see fig. 22.2).

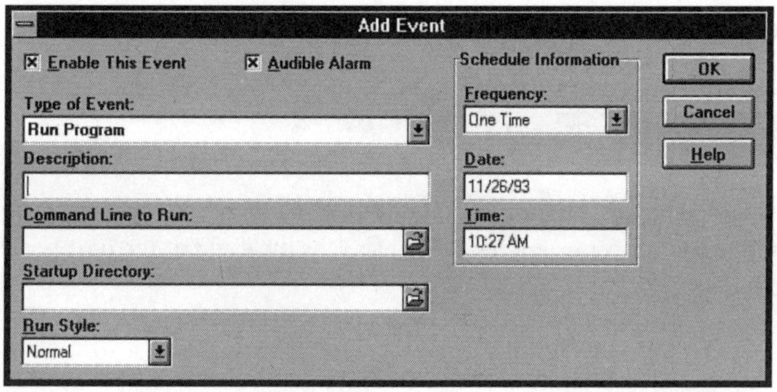

Fig. 22.2
The Scheduler Add Event dialog box, displaying options for a Run Program event.

2. From the Ty**p**e of Event drop-down list, select the Run Program option.
3. Type a description of the event in the Descr**i**ption text box.
4. Type the command line of the program you want to run in the C**o**mmand Line to Run text box, or use the folder icon to browse for the program command. Make sure that you include complete drive and directory information. If necessary, enter the name of the start-up directory in the **S**tartup Directory text box.
5. Choose the frequency to run this event by using the **F**requency drop-down list box. You can choose among One Time, Hourly, Daily, Week Days (Monday through Friday only), Weekly, or Monthly.

Tip
With the cursor in the C**o**mmand Line to Run text box, you can click the open file button to search for specific program files by using the Browse dialog box. After you select a specific file, its complete drive and directory path information is inserted in the text box.

6. Enter the starting date and time in the **D**ate and **T**ime text boxes; make sure that you remember to designate a.m. or p.m.

7. If you choose the Weekly option, enter the day of the week the event is to occur.

   If you choose the One Time or Monthly option, specify the date the event is to occur.

   If you choose the One Time option, indicate the **D**ate and **T**ime the event is to occur.

8. If you are launching a Windows program to run in the background while other operations are running in the foreground, choose Run Minimized from the **R**un Style pull-down list box.

9. Choose OK to confirm the scheduled event.

At the selected time, Scheduler activates and runs the selected program.

Note

If the event Scheduler cannot run your event at the given time—if your computer is turned off, for example—Scheduler runs the event at the next possible opportunity.

Note

Scheduler can run both Windows and DOS applications. Scheduler automatically runs programs with EXE, COM, and BAT file extensions. It also launches applications that you preloaded with selected document files if the selected files have an extension associated with a recognized application.

Adding New Message Events

To schedule a new message event, follow these steps:

1. Choose the **A**dd icon in the Scheduler window to display the Add Event dialog box.

2. Choose the Display Message option from the Ty**p**e of Event drop-down list.

3. Type a description of the event in the Descr**i**ption text box.

   A Messa**g**e to Display text box appears in the dialog box instead of the C**o**mmand Line to Run text box.

4. Type the message you want displayed in the Messa**g**e to Display text box. Notice that the text box automatically scrolls as you enter long messages.

5. Choose the frequency to run this event, using the **F**requency drop-down list box. You can choose from One Time, Hourly, Daily, Week Days (Monday through Friday only), Weekly, or Monthly.

6. Enter the **D**ate and **T**ime for the starting time you want; make sure that you remember to designate a.m. or p.m.

7. If you choose the Weekly option, indicate which day of the week the event is to occur.

   If you choose the One Time or Monthly option, indicate the specific date the event is to occur.

   If you choose the One Time option, indicate the Month and Year the event is to occur.

8. Choose OK to confirm the scheduled event.

At the selected time, Scheduler activates and displays the message in an Event Notification dialog box (see fig. 22.3).

Fig. 22.3
A Norton Scheduler Event Notification dialog box.

Removing Scheduled Events

One Time events are automatically deleted after they run. You also can remove other scheduled events by following these steps:

1. Select the event in the E**v**ents list box in the Scheduler window.

2. Choose the **D**elete icon.

Editing Scheduled Events

You can edit any scheduled event that has been entered. To edit an event, follow these steps:

1. Select the event to edit from the E**v**ents list box in the Scheduler window.

2. Choose the Edi**t** icon. The Edit Event dialog box appears.

3. Make whatever changes are necessary in the Edit Event dialog box.

> **Note**
>
> The Edit Event dialog box is identical to the Add Event dialog box.

4. Choose OK to confirm your changes.

Copying Scheduled Events To Create New Events

You also can create new events based on existing events. To accomplish this task, edit an existing event, making whatever changes are necessary, and then copy the edited event as a new event. To create a new event based on an existing event, follow these steps:

1. Select the event to copy from the E**v**ents list box.

2. Choose the **C**opy icon. The Copy Event dialog box appears.

3. Make whatever changes are necessary in the Copy Event dialog box.

> **Note**
>
> The Copy Event dialog box is identical to the Add Event and Edit Event dialog boxes.

4. Choose OK to confirm the new event.

Scheduling a Sample Program Event

Running Speed Disk, for example, on a regular basis is a good practice. For this example, create a program event that runs Speed Disk weekly on Friday at 4 p.m. (a little before quitting time).

Begin by opening the main Scheduler window and then follow these steps:

1. Choose the **A**dd icon to display the Add Event dialog box.

2. Choose the Run Program option from the Ty**p**e of Event drop-down list.

3. Type the following in the Descr**i**ption text box:

   Weekly Speed Disk Optimization

4. Click the open folder icon to the right of the C**o**mmand Line to Run text box to display the File To Launch dialog box (see fig. 22.4).

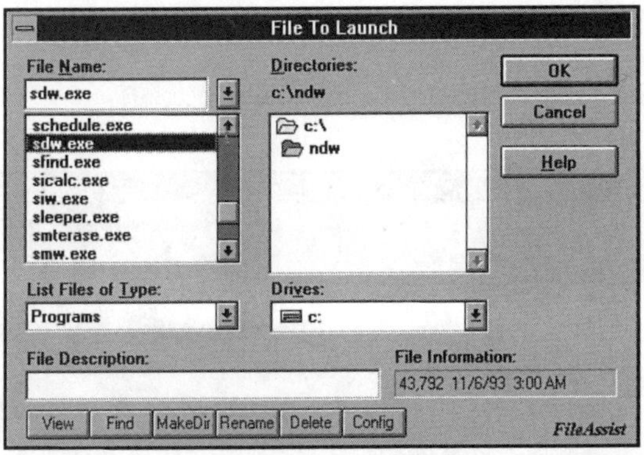

Fig. 22.4
The File To Launch dialog box enables you to search for the SDW.EXE file.

5. Select the file SDW.EXE in the File **N**ame list box.

6. Choose OK to place the file in the C**o**mmand Line to Run box (see fig. 22.5).

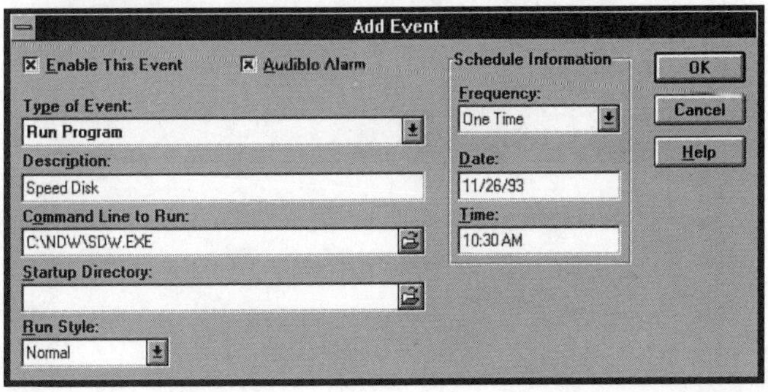

Fig. 22.5
The SDW.EXE command line loaded in the C**o**mmand Line to Run box.

7. From the **F**requency drop-down list, choose the Weekly option (see fig. 22.6).

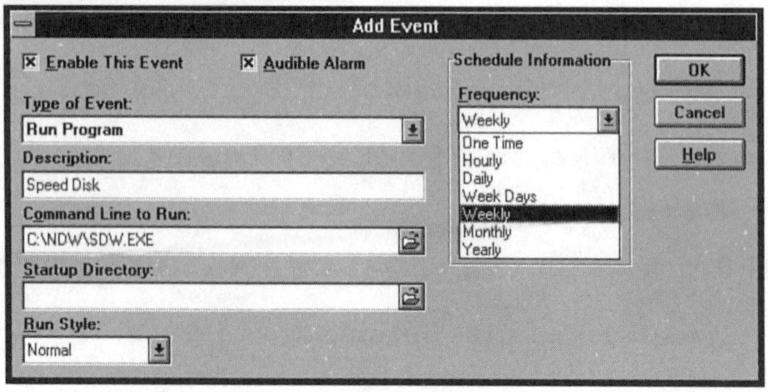

Fig. 22.6 Choosing the Weekly **F**requency option in the Add Event dialog box.

8. Choose Friday from the **D**ay of Week drop-down list.
9. Enter **4:00 PM** in the **T**ime text box.

   Figure 22.7 shows the completed dialog box.

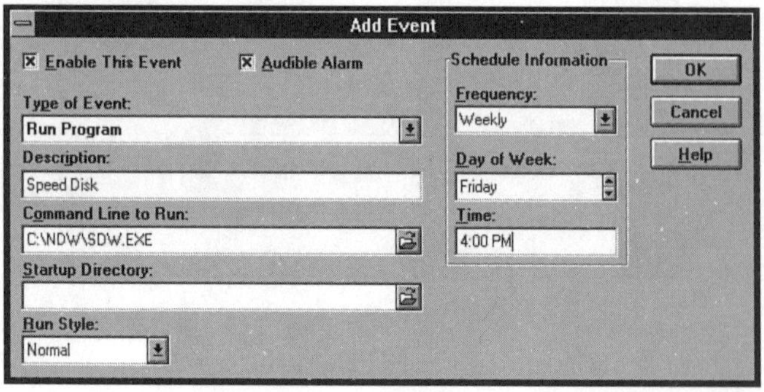

Fig. 22.7 The completed Add Event dialog box for running Speed Disk on a weekly basis.

10. Choose OK to add the event to the Scheduler Events list (see fig. 22.8).

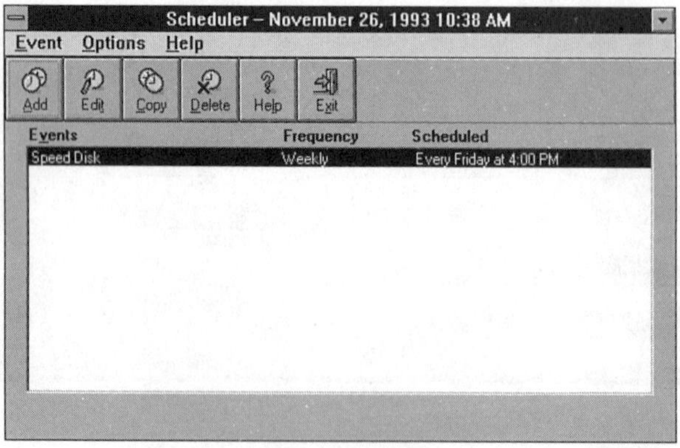

Fig. 22.8 The weekly Speed Disk event added to the Scheduler Events list.

Scheduling a Sample Message Event

Suppose that you have a regular staff meeting every Wednesday afternoon at 3 p.m. You want Scheduler to alert you to the meeting every week.

Begin by opening the main Scheduler window, and then follow these steps:

1. Choose the **A**dd icon to display the Add Event dialog box.

2. Choose the Display Message option from the Ty**p**e of Event drop-down list, and type the following line in the Descr**i**ption text box:

   Weekly Staff Meeting

3. Type the following line in the Messa**g**e to Display text box:

   It's 3:00. Time to go to the weekly staff meeting. Don't be late!

   Figure 22.9 displays the Add Event dialog box as it appears so far.

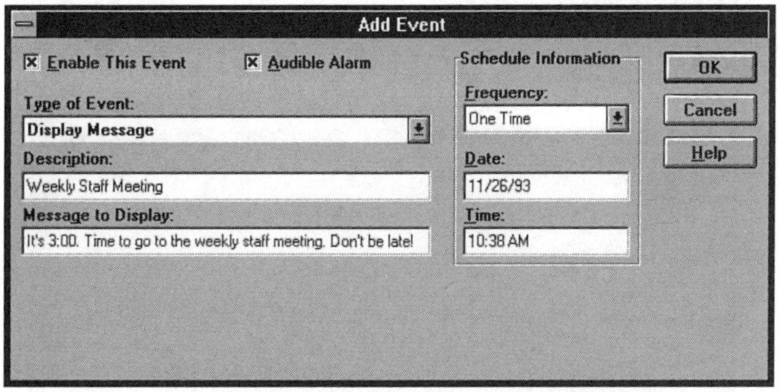

Fig. 22.9
The Add Event dialog box with Description and Message event added.

4. From the **F**requency drop-down list, choose the Weekly option (see fig. 22.10).

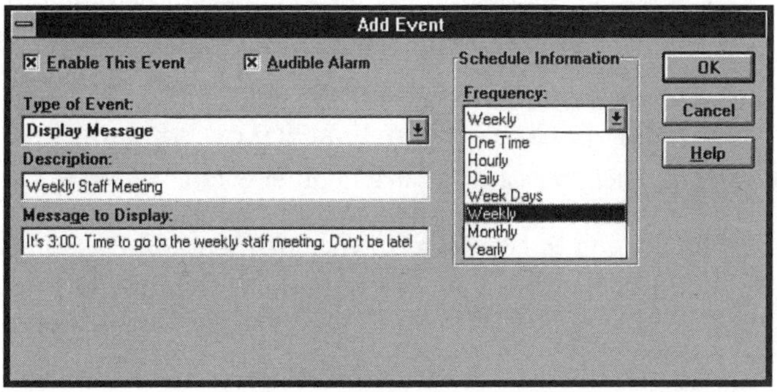

Fig. 22.10
The Add Event dialog box **F**requency options for a Display Message event.

5. Enter the **T**ime as **3:00 PM** and the **D**ay of Week as **Wednesday**.

   Figure 22.11 shows the completed dialog box.

. 22.11
he completed Add Event dialog box for a Display Message event.

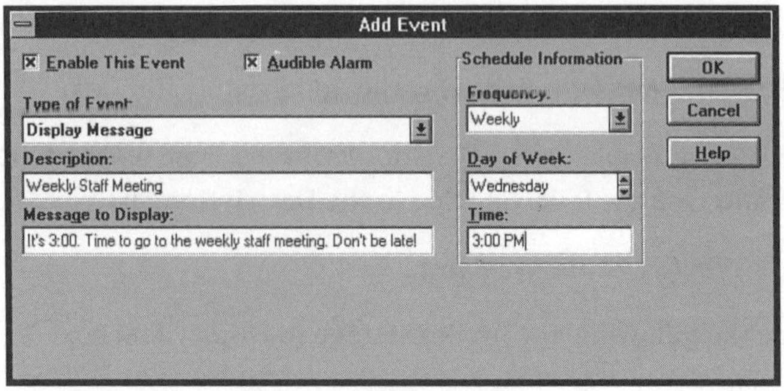

6. Choose OK to add the event to the Scheduler Events list (see fig. 22.12).

Fig. 22.12
The Weekly Staff Meeting event added to the Scheduler Events list.

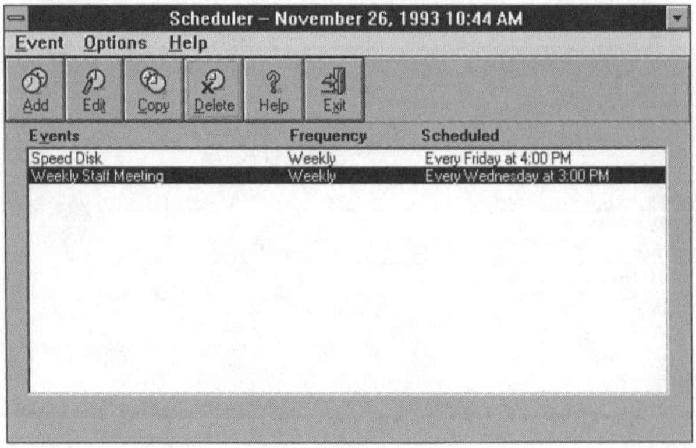

Using Automatic Backup

Automatic Backup is a preprogrammed Scheduler event designed to automatically run a preset Norton Backup for Windows backup routine. The NDW Installation program gave you the option of running Automatic Backup automatically; if you did not choose this option, you can still program Scheduler to run Automatic Backup as a normal Scheduler event.

As described in Chapter 9, "Backing Up Files with Norton Backup for Windows," Automatic Backup is an event that launches Norton Backup every weekday at 4 p.m., using the ASSIST.SET setup file. This file instructs Norton Backup to run a Full backup on day one and Incremental backups on the remaining days. If you want to program this event, do nothing more than launch Scheduler; this event then runs automatically at 4 p.m. each weekday.

If you want to change the time of the backup, you can edit the event by using the Edit Event dialog box. To delete this event from Scheduler, simply choose the Automatic Backup event, and click the **D**elete button.

Note

Remember that, even though this process is described as an automatic backup, you still need to take the backup disks in and out of your PC. Automatic Backup is not too effective if you are not around to help. If you prefer, you can create a new event that displays a message reminding you to back up your hard disk. Simply use the **C**opy option to create a new message event based on the original Automatic Backup event parameters. If you are performing a tape backup, you must make sure that a tape is in your tape drive before the scheduled event takes place.

Running Scheduler Automatically

If you want to run periodic events automatically—the same event scheduled either daily, weekly, or monthly—make sure that Scheduler automatically launches whenever Windows and Norton Desktop are loaded. This precaution saves you from having to remember to launch the program that helps you remember to do things.

Tip
Because Scheduler cannot run any events if Scheduler itself is not running, do not close Scheduler if you have events scheduled. The safest procedure is to run Scheduler automatically whenever you launch Windows and Norton Desktop.

You can choose one of the following two methods to launch Scheduler automatically:

- Check the Load with **W**indows option in the Scheduler **O**ptions menu.
- Drag and drop the Scheduler icon or program file on the AutoStart group icon.

Either method ensures that Scheduler launches automatically whenever Windows and Norton Desktop are loaded.

Note

Loading Scheduler automatically serves a second useful Desktop function. Because Scheduler's Desktop icon functions as an analog clock with Scheduler running in the background, you now have a handy reminder of the current time on your Desktop. This feature, however, works only if you did not check the **H**ide When Iconized option in the Scheduler window.

Summary

This chapter detailed NDW's Scheduler utility. You learned how to use Scheduler automatically to remind you of events and to run selected programs. You also learned about the Automatic Backup program and how to run Scheduler automatically.

The next chapter, "Using Shredder," shows you how to use Shredder to totally eliminate unwanted files from your hard disk.

Chapter 23

Using Shredder

Thanks to sophisticated data recovery utilities, such as NDW's SmartErase, you can easily recover files that have been erased from your disks. Sometimes, however, you want to permanently erase sensitive files and do not want anyone to unerase them. Norton Desktop 3 for Windows enables you to do this by using its Shredder utility.

In this chapter, you learn to perform the following tasks:

- Configure Shredder
- Shred confidential files

Learning about Shredder

Shredder is a special NDW utility that permanently deletes files from your hard disk. Files deleted by Shredder cannot be recovered by UnErase or any similar utility.

To understand how Shredder works, you must first understand how you normally delete files. If you delete a file by using the DOS DELETE or ERASE commands (or by using similar commands in Windows and Norton Desktop), DOS does not actually remove the file from your disk. Instead, DOS marks the directory entry for the file as available for reuse. Even though the file name no longer appears on your directory list, the file's data remains intact on your hard disk until DOS writes new data over the marked data. Only the first letter of the file's name is changed, telling DOS that the file's space can be reused. Because the data is still on the disk, however, utilities such as UnErase can find and recover the file by remarking the data as a normal file.

This method of deleting files normally works just fine. You may encounter situations, however, in which you do not want anyone to accidentally or purposefully recover data you delete. If you have such confidential data, you can use Shredder to forever remove the data from prying eyes.

Shredder works by completely *overwriting* the data you want to delete. By default, Shredder overwrites the data area with a series of zeros. You also can configure Shredder to overwrite the data with any pattern of three characters of your choice or to shred the data in accordance with U.S. Department of Defense standards. Shredder can even overwrite complete directories.

Configuring Shredder

Configuring Shredder is a simple procedure. To configure it for your system, follow these steps:

1. Choose the **O**ptions **C**ustomize command, or click the Options toolbar icon. The Control Center dialog box appears on the screen.

2. Click the Shredder icon in the **C**ategories list of the Control Center dialog box. The Control Center dialog box changes to offer Shredder configuration options (see fig. 23.1).

Fig. 23.1
The Control Center dialog box containing Shredder configuration options.

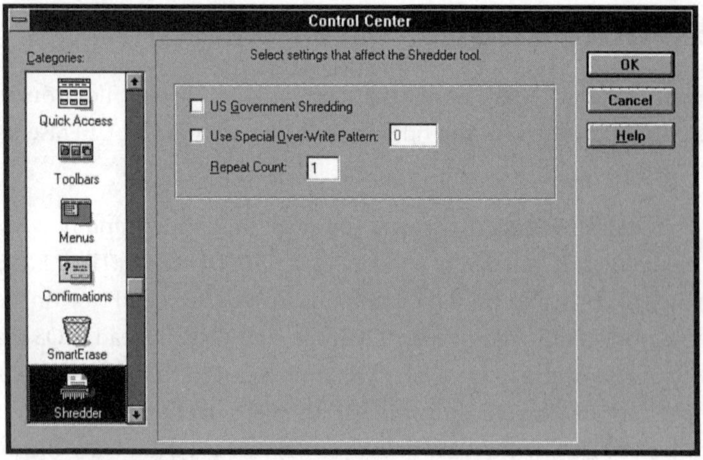

3. Select the US **G**overnment Shredding check box to delete data according to U.S. Department of Defense standards, as described later in this section.

4. Select the Use Special **O**ver-Write Pattern check box and type the new character set into the text box to use an overwrite pattern other than 0 for normal shredding.

5. Specify the number of times you want the data overwritten by typing that value in the **R**epeat Count text box.

6. Click OK or press Enter to confirm the configuration.

Normal shredding is a relatively fast and simple procedure and does not require additional configuration. The US **G**overnment Shredding option, however, is different.

The U.S. Department of Defense standard for data deletion (DOD 5220.22M) requires the program to perform the following multiple-pass procedure each time it deletes a file:

Pass one: Overwrite the data with 0s.

Pass two: Overwrite the data with 1s.

Pass three: Overwrite the data with 0s.

Pass four: Overwrite the data with 1s.

Pass five: Overwrite the data with 0s.

Pass six: Overwrite the data with 1s.

Pass seven: Overwrite the data with a different value; Shredder uses 246 as the default value.

Verification: Verify that the last write contains the specified values.

Each pass means that the data area of the file is overwritten with a value (either 0 or 1 in this case). The multiple passes are used because even as new data is written magnetically to the disk, overwriting the existing file, some residual signal from the previous data may remain that could be recovered. Making seven passes over the data virtually assures that the original data is obliterated.

Because of this multiple-step procedure, which Shredder follows exactly, the US **G**overnment Shredding option takes considerably longer than does standard shredding. As you can imagine, however, this method does provide the most secure data deletion possible.

Shredding Confidential Files

NDW provides two ways to shred data. The simpler method is to drag files onto the Shredder Tool icon. The other method involves actually accessing Shredder and specifying the files to shred.

To shred files by using the Shredder Tool icon, you must have configured Norton Desktop to include a Shredder Tool icon on the Desktop. (See Chapter 11 for information on customizing the Desktop.) Follow these steps to use the Shredder Tool icon to shred files:

1. Open a drive window, and select the files or directories you want to shred (see fig. 23.2).

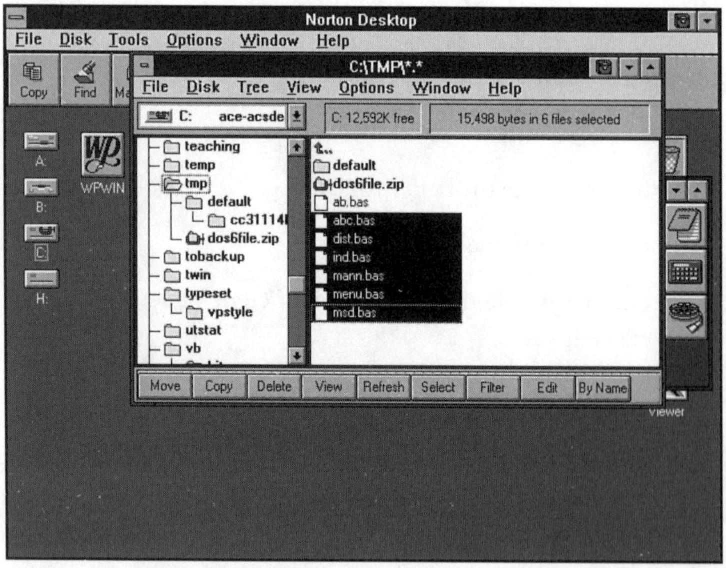

Fig. 23.2
Several files in a drive window selected for dragging and dropping onto the Desktop's Shredder Tool icon.

Tip
If you do not have a Shredder Tool icon on your Desktop, select the files you want to shred from a drive window and then choose **T**ools S**h**redder.

2. Drag the selected files and/or directories onto the Shredder Tool icon. A confirmation dialog box appears.

3. Choose OK to confirm each file's shredding after the confirmation dialog box appears.

To shred files by using the Shredder utility, follow these steps:

1. Choose the **T**ools S**h**redder command from the Desktop menu bar. The Shred dialog box appears (see fig. 23.3).

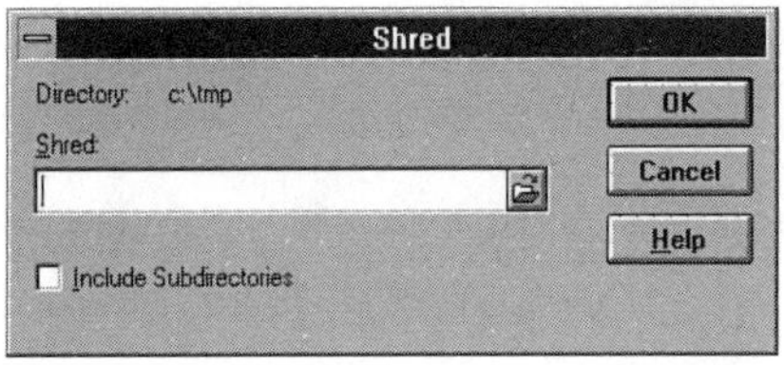

Fig. 23.3
The Shred dialog box enables you to specify what files to shred.

2. Type in the **S**hred text box the name of the file or directory you want to shred.
3. Select the **I**nclude Subdirectories check box to include all subdirectories under a selected directory in your shredding operation.
4. Choose OK to begin shredding the specified file or files.

Tip
Use the Browse button at the end of the **S**hred text box to pick files and/or directories from a standard Browse dialog box.

> **Warning**
>
> Remember that data deleted by using Shredder is *permanently* overwritten and not recoverable by UnErase or any other utility. Make sure that you really want to delete this data before you choose the **S**hredder option.

Check whether the files are actually shredded by trying to undelete them in the UnErase dialog box. If the files are shredded, they no longer contain any information and therefore cannot be recovered (see fig. 23.4).

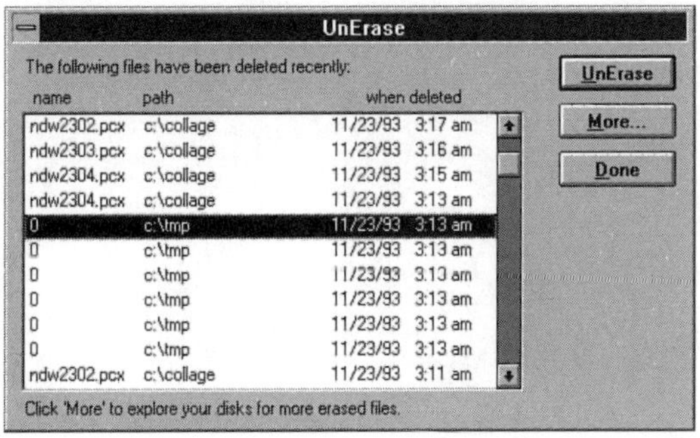

Fig. 23.4
The **U**nErase test for shredded files shows that shredded files no longer contain any information.

Summary

This chapter taught you how to permanently delete data from your hard disk by using the Shredder utility. You learned how to shred files directly in

Shredder and how to drag and drop files onto the Shredder Tool icon. You also learned how to configure Shredder for your own personal needs.

Chapter 24, "Using Screen Saver," shows you how to put your computer "to sleep" by using NDW's Screen Saver utility.

Chapter 24

Using Screen Saver

In this chapter you learn to perform the following tasks:

- Understand Screen Saver
- Configure Screen Saver
- Display sample Screen Saver images

If you leave your computer unattended for extended periods of time, the static screen image can actually "burn" itself into the phosphors of your computer monitor's screen. To protect your screen from this "burn in," NDW provides Screen Saver, a screen saver utility that displays a series of constantly changing screen images.

Understanding Screen Saver

Screen savers are popular Windows accessories. Stand-alone programs, such as After Dark and Intermission, are so popular that Symantec was inspired to add a Screen Saver utility to NDW. (Microsoft was similarly inspired and added a screen saver module to Windows 3.1.)

Why are screen savers so popular? One reason is that they are useful. Screen savers really do protect your monitor from phosphor burn-in. Screen savers also can serve as security tools, because you can choose to keep the main screen inaccessible until the user enters a confidential password.

Screen savers also are fun. By choosing among numerous colorful, animated, humorous screen saver images, users have discovered a small way to enliven and personalize their computing experience.

NDW's Screen Saver utility comes with a variety of different images to protect your screen from burn-in. You can choose among a number of options for each Screen Saver image, as well as general options for Screen Saver itself.

Note

In NDW 3, you can use even Windows screen saver modules or modules from third-party programs (such as After Dark and Intermission) with the Screen Saver utility.

You can start Screen Saver just as you do any other application, or you can configure it to start automatically as Windows and Norton Desktop are loaded. Screen Saver activates after certain predefined conditions are met. Normally, you set a time limit for computer inactivity, after which Screen Saver activates and displays the preset image. You may, for example, set Screen Saver to activate after five minutes of inactivity. After five minutes go by, during which no keys are pressed or mouse movements detected, Screen Saver activates.

Note

Unlike some screen savers, the Norton Screen Saver operates even if you run a DOS program from the Desktop.

You also can activate Screen Saver by moving the pointer to a preset "sleep now" corner. This corner, set up in Screen Saver's Preferences dialog box, is an area of your screen that puts your computer to sleep if you place the mouse pointer there.

You can deactivate Screen Saver and return to normal system operation either by moving the mouse or by pressing any key on the keyboard. You also can configure Screen Saver to deactivate only after a preset password is entered.

Configuring Screen Saver

The options available for Screen Saver are simple and easy to understand. You must open the main Screen Saver window to access Screen Saver's options; you can access the Screen Saver window from the menu system or from the Quick Access Group. To access the Screen Saver window from the menu system, choose the Desktop's **T**ools **S**creen Saver command.

After you open Screen Saver, the initial Screen Saver window appears, as shown in figure 24.1. Notice that this window cannot be maximized to full-screen size; it can appear only as a minimized window or in icon form.

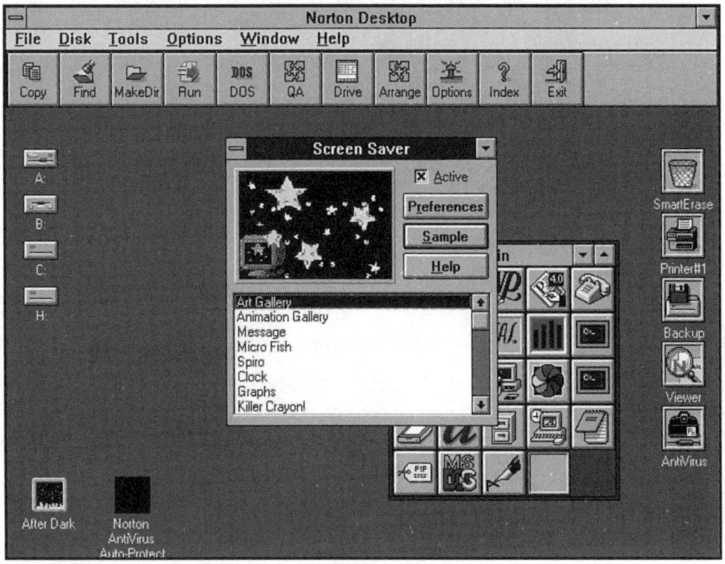

Fig. 24.1
The Norton Desktop for Windows initial Screen Saver window.

The bottom part of the window contains a scroll box listing all available screen saver images for Screen Saver. The **A**ctive check box at the top right controls whether Screen Saver is ready to activate. Choosing the **S**ample button displays the currently selected saver from this list.

Note

Screen saver images from other programs are identified as such in the Screen Saver scroll box. The names of images from After Dark, for example, are preceded by (AD) in the screen saver list.

Selecting Screen Saver's Preferences

If you choose the P**r**eferences button in the Screen Saver initial window, the Screen Saver's Preferences dialog box appears, as shown in figure 24.2.

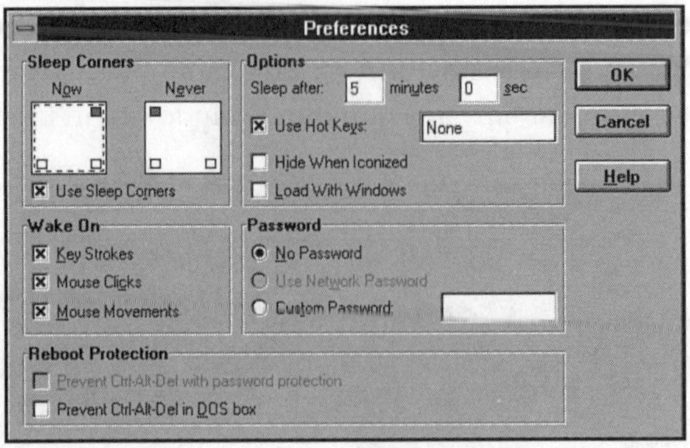

Fig. 24.2
The Screen Saver's Preferences dialog box enables you to choose how and when a screen saver is displayed.

This dialog box enables you to set the following preferences:

- *Sleep Corners: Now.* Selects the corner to which you can move the mouse pointer to activate Screen Saver immediately.

- *Sleep Corners: Never.* Selects a corner to which you can move the mouse pointer so that Screen Saver does not activate no matter what the length of system inactivity.

- *Use Sleep Corners.* Turns on or off the selected Now and Never Sleep Corners.

- *Sleep After X Minutes X Sec.* (The *X*s represent the number of minutes and seconds entered in these text boxes.) Instructs Screen Saver to activate after a selected amount of inactivity. Type the minutes and seconds of inactivity you want in their respective text boxes.

- *Use Hot Keys.* Enables your use of a hot key combination to activate Screen Saver immediately. Type in the text box to the right of the option's check box the keystrokes for a hot key combination.

- *Hide When Iconized.* Instructs NDW not to display the Screen Saver icon if Screen Saver is iconized. This option frees up valuable Desktop space if you install Screen Saver as a permanent background application. Selecting this option is recommended.

- *Load With Windows.* Instructs NDW to load Screen Saver automatically as Windows and Norton Desktop are loaded. Selecting this option is recommended.

- *Wake On: **K**ey Strokes.* Enables you to restore the screen by pressing any key.
- *Wake On: Mouse Cli**c**ks.* Enables you to restore the screen by clicking either mouse button.
- *Wake On: **M**ouse Movements.* Enables you to restore the screen by moving the mouse.
- ***N**o Password.* Disables the use of a password with Screen Saver.
- *Use Net**w**ork Password.* If you are connected to a Novell network, requires you to enter your network password to deactivate Screen Saver.
- *Cus**t**om Password.* Requires you to enter a custom password of up to nine characters in the Cus**t**om Password text box to deactivate Screen Saver.

Warning

Be cautious about using a password to activate Screen Saver. If you forget your password, you cannot "wake up" your system. The only way out of this situation is to reboot your computer, with the potential loss of any changes made to unsaved documents and applications. You should use a Screen Saver password only in cases of extreme security.

Note

If Screen Saver is in your StartUp group and you forget the password, even rebooting does not help much; every time your computer is idle, the machine becomes inactive/useless. You need to uninstall and then reinstall NDW or edit your WIN.INI file to set the SLEEPER.EXE command of the LOAD= statement.

- *Reboot Protection: **P**revent Ctrl-Alt-Delete with Password Protection.* Forces the user to enter the correct password before performing a warm boot of the system.
- *Reboot Protection: Prevent Ctrl-Alt-Delete in **D**OS Box.* Prevents the user from performing a warm boot of the system in a DOS box.

Click OK to save the choices you make in the Preferences dialog box.

Selecting and Configuring a Screen Saver Image

To select a screen saver image for Screen Saver to display, follow these steps:

1. With the Screen Saver initial window open, scroll through the screen saver scroll box until the screen saver you want is selected.

2. Select the **A**ctive check box to activate Screen Saver (if it is not already selected).

3. Minimize the Screen Saver window.

> **Caution**
>
> Do not close the Screen Saver window. Screen Saver cannot be activated after it is closed; it can be activated only if it is minimized.

After you select a screen saver image and choose the **S**ample button, the middle of the Screen Saver window displays the options for that particular screen saver. Options often include size and speed, as well as other settings unique to that particular image. You set these options by using scroll bars, check boxes, text boxes, buttons, and increment arrows.

> **Note**
>
> If you use AfterDark 2.0 or a later version with Screen Saver, individual AfterDark modules do not appear in Screen Saver's scroll box. You must select the AfterDark Runner, which then loads AfterDark and enables you to select AfterDark screen savers.

Sample Screen Saver Images

Screen Saver comes complete with a variety of screen saver images. NDW 3 includes the following images:

- *Art Gallery.* Art Gallery blanks the screen and displays a series of line drawings; unlike Animation Gallery, these drawings are static. You can select the speed of the drawings as they float across the screen, as well as the color of the drawings (see fig. 24.3).

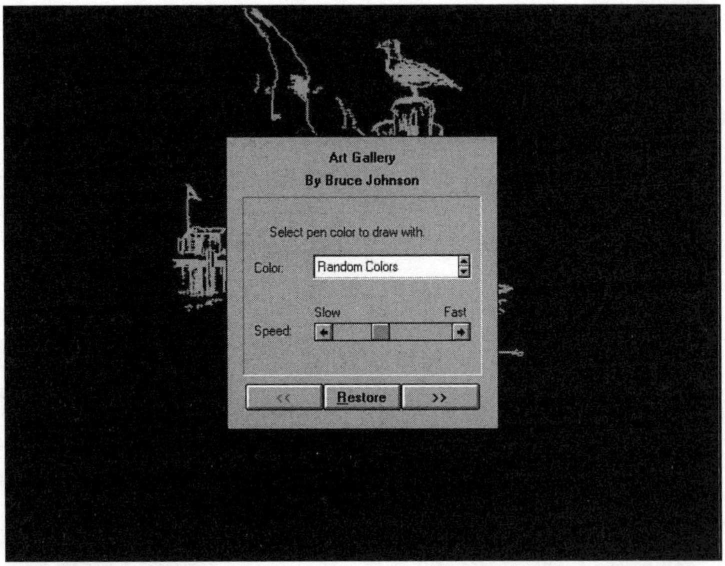

Fig. 24.3
The Art Gallery screen saver.

- *Animation Gallery*. Animation Gallery blanks the screen and displays a series of animated line drawings, such as an ostrich or elephant strutting across the screen. You can choose the color of the drawing and choose to have the drawing appear Small, Medium, or Large sized (see fig. 24.4).

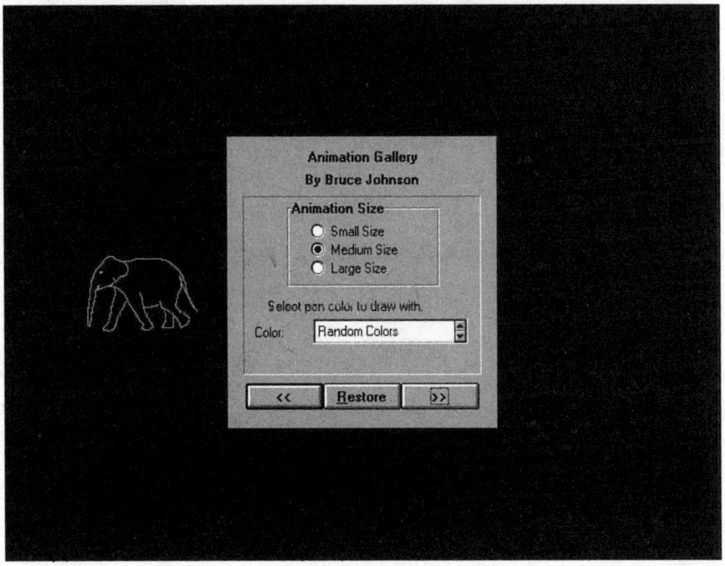

Fig. 24.4
The Animation Gallery screen saver.

- *Message.* This screen saver displays a message of your choice on-screen. You can select the font, point size, type style (boldface, italic, and so on), as well as the color of the message. You can choose how and where the message appears on-screen and how fast the message moves around the screen. You even can choose to have the message appear as a banner trailing an on-screen airplane, as a "billboard" on a balloon or a blimp (see fig. 24.5), or as a stand-alone scrolling or flashing message.

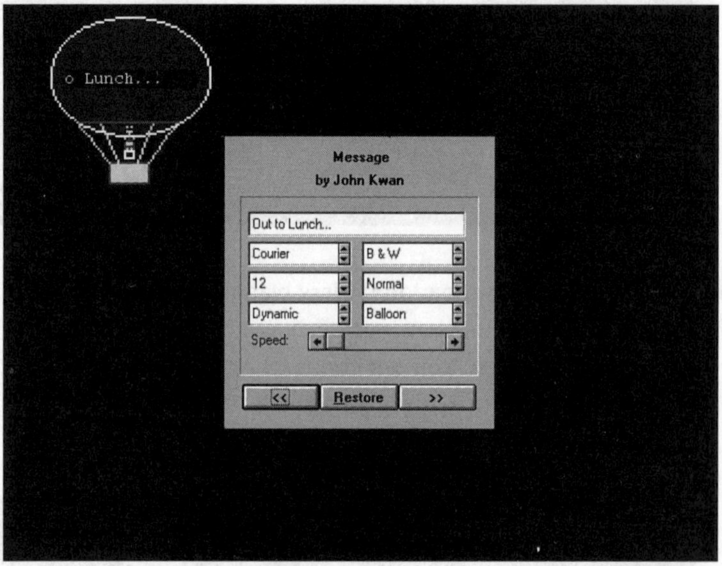

Fig. 24.5
The Message screen saver.

- *Micro Fish.* This screen saver creates a computerized aquarium on your PC screen, complete with an assortment of colorful computer-generated fish (see fig. 24.6). You can select the number of fish to display at any one time, as well as their speed.

- *Spiro.* Spiro works much like the old SpiroGraph toy, creating random symmetrical line images (see fig. 24.7). You can choose to display up to 16 simultaneous spiros and have them centered or intersecting.

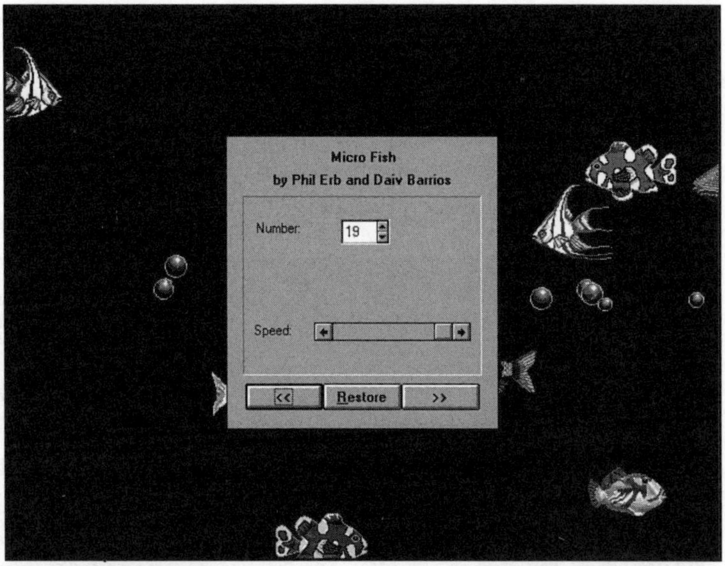

Fig. 24.6
The Micro Fish screen saver.

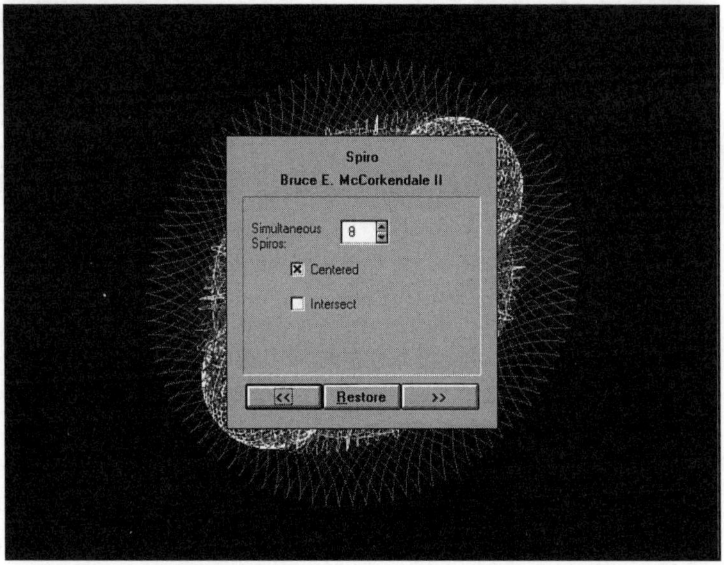

Fig. 24.7
The Spiro screen saver.

- *Clock.* This screen saver displays a functioning clock on screen (see fig. 24.8). You can select among analog or 12-hour and 24-hour digital clocks. Options include displaying seconds (or the second hand on the analog clock), selecting the size and color of the clock, selecting whether the clock floats, flashes, or scrolls horizontally or vertically. You also can set the speed of the clock's movement.

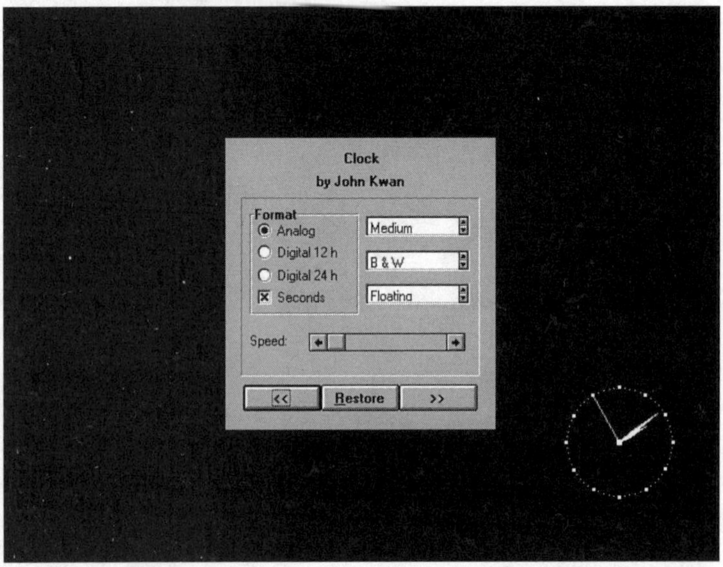

Fig. 24.8
The Clock screen saver.

- *Graphs.* Graphs displays a graph of a parabolic figure (see fig. 24.9). You can control the color or choose random colors for this saver.

- *Killer Crayon!* Killer Crayon! is more than just a screen saver—it is a game. You control a red crayon, and you must trace a path on-screen that forces the other crayons—up to four at a time—to box themselves in (see fig. 24.10). After a crayon runs into its own trail (or the trail from other crayons), it melts. You get five crayons, and scoring is based on the speed at which you melt your opponents. Killer Crayon! starts in a demo mode so that it really does function as a screen saver. To play, click the Play the Game button to start a new game, and use the arrow keys to change your crayon's direction.

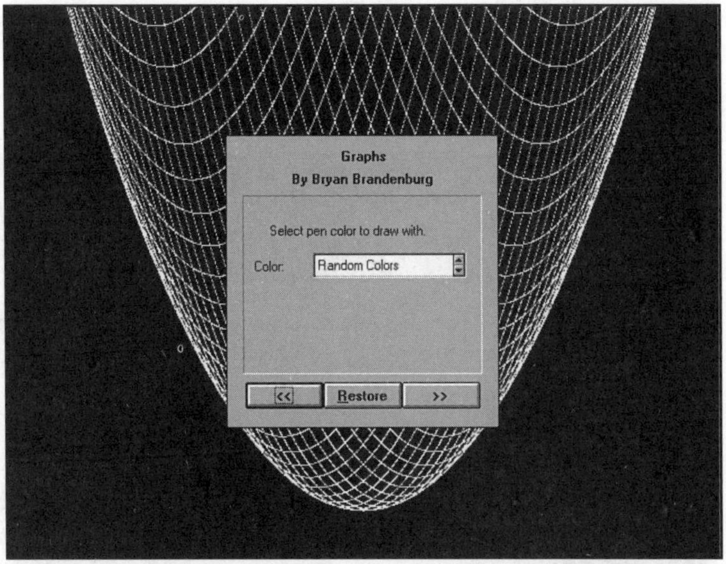

Fig. 24.9
The Graphs screen saver.

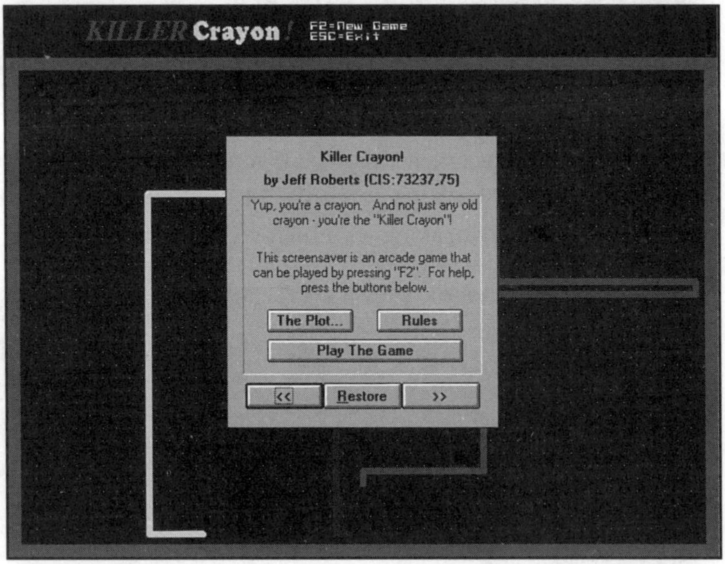

Fig. 24.10
The Killer Crayon! screen saver.

- *Tornados*. This screen saver blanks your screen and displays a series of speeding, whirling tornados (see fig. 24.11). You can choose from one to 16 tornados, as well as their speed.

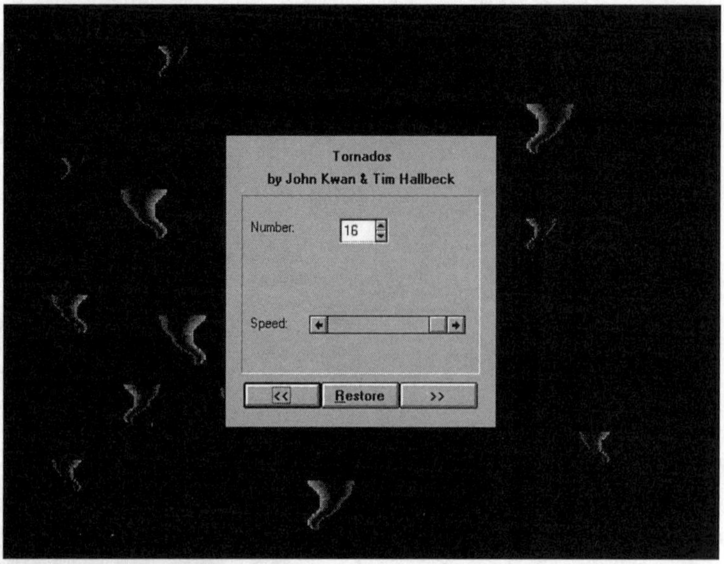

Fig. 24.11
The Tornados screen saver.

- *Staring Eyes*. This screen saver blacks out your screen and then displays from 1 to 16 sets of staring eyes (see fig. 24.12). You can choose the number of pairs of eyes, along with their speed of movement.

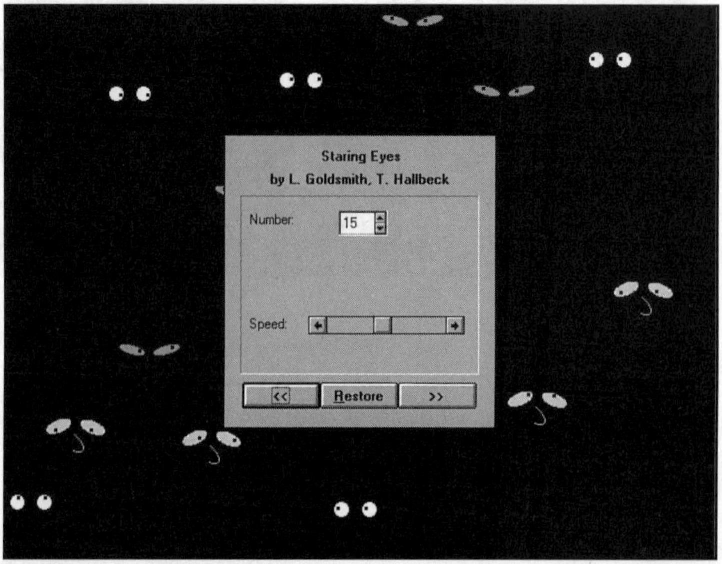

Fig. 24.12
The Staring Eyes screen saver.

- *Spotlight.* This screen saver blacks out your screen and then displays a spotlight that shines through the darkness to reveal some of the hidden areas of your screen (see fig. 24.13). You can choose from one to four separate spotlights, along with their size and speed.

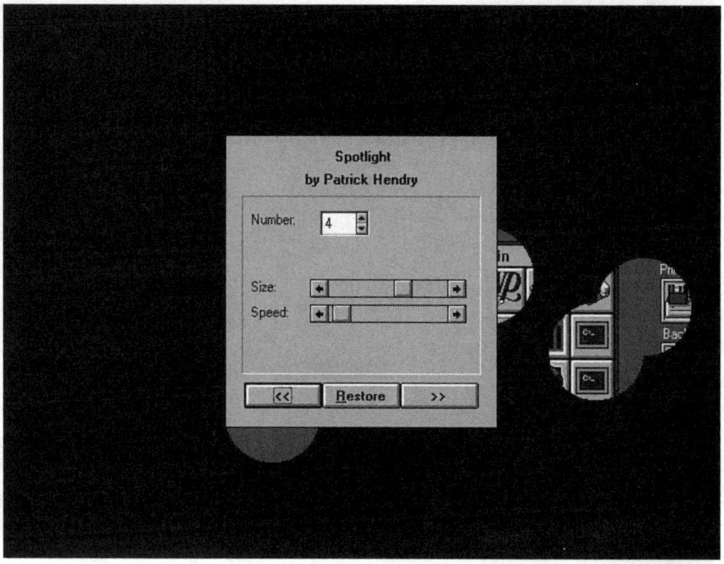

Fig. 24.13
The Spotlight screen saver.

- *Rotation.* The Rotation screen saver displays a group of rotating, three-dimensional wire-frame objects (see fig. 24.14). You can choose how many objects to display and how fast they move. You also can choose different combinations of sizes and shapes.

- *Screen Shuffle.* Screen Shuffle turns your screen into a giant sliding-piece puzzle. This screen saver cuts your screen into a series of squares and then shuffles them around (see fig. 24.15). You can choose the size of the squares and the speed of the shuffle.

- *Trivia.* Trivia blanks the screen and displays a series of trivia questions and answers (see fig. 24.8). You can control the speed at which new word balloons appear.

- *Triquetrous Lights.* This screen saver blanks the screen and displays an explosion that breaks into a series of fragments (see fig. 24.17). You can choose from 16 to 64 fragments per explosion, the speed of the fragments' movement, and whether to display jumbo and/or shaded fragments.

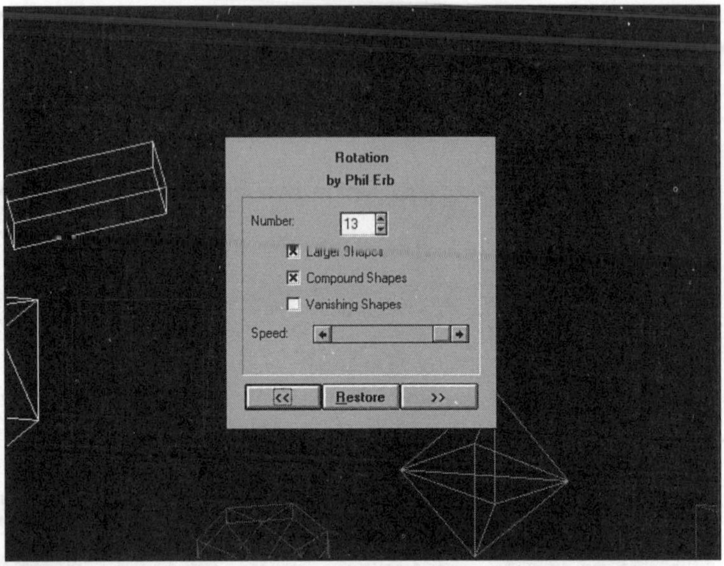

Fig. 24.14
The Rotation screen saver.

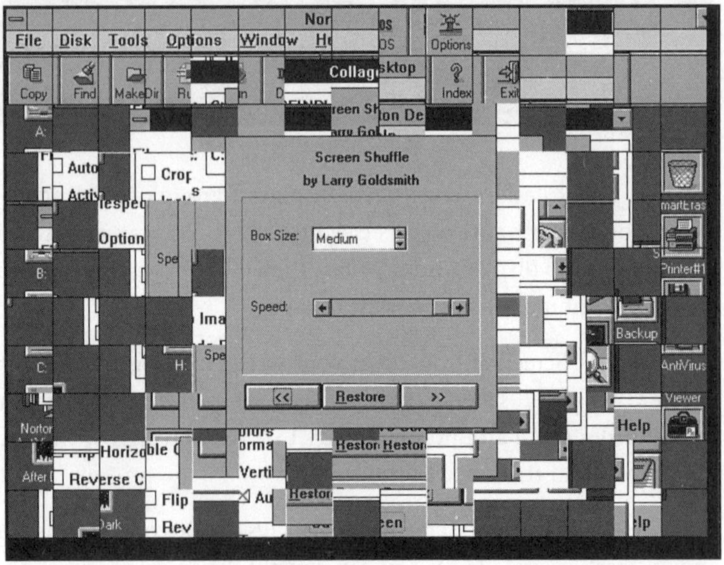

Fig. 24.15
The Screen Shuffle screen saver.

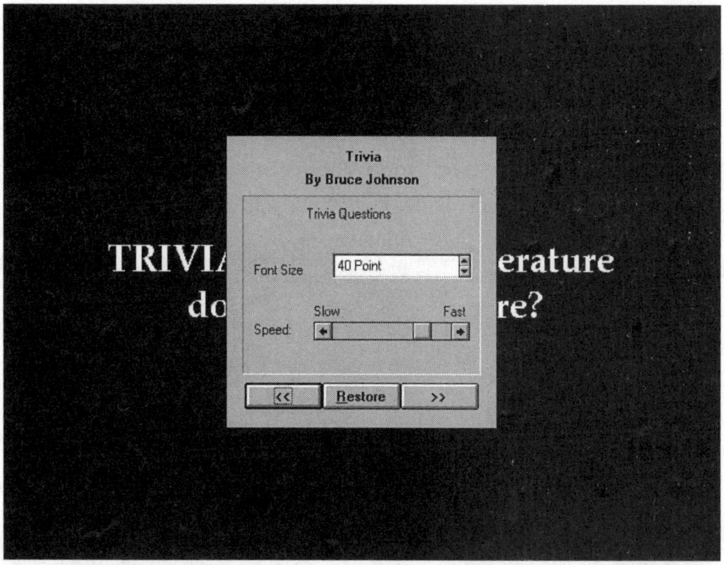

Fig. 24.16
The Trivia screen saver.

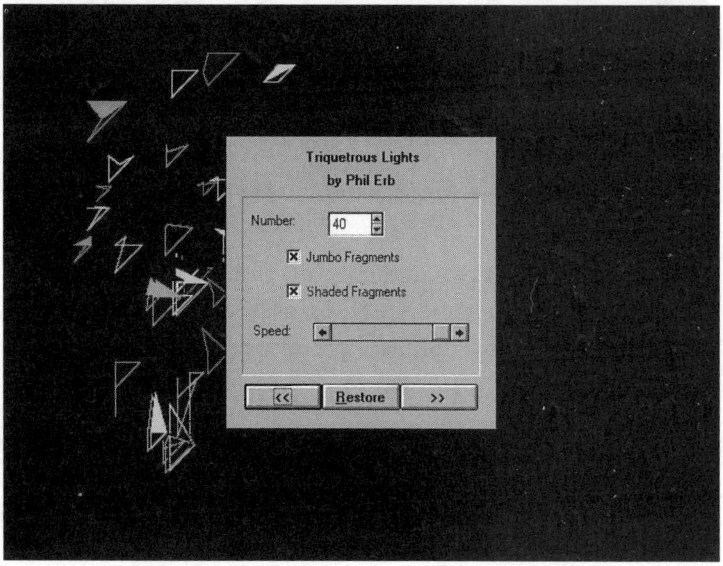

Fig. 24.17
The Triquetrous Lights screen saver.

■ *Fading Away.* This screen saver "fades" the screen to black (see fig. 24.18). You can select from Random Pixel Fading (in which the screen appears to slowly disintegrate) or Horizontal or Vertical Scanning (in which the screen disappears one horizontal or vertical line at a time). You also can set the screen to Restore After Blanking, which reverses the fade process and selects the speed at which the fade occurs.

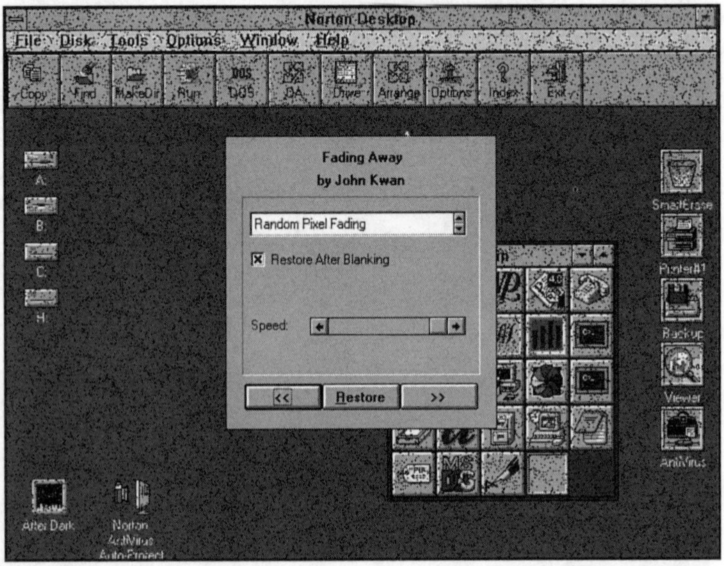

Fig. 24.18
The Fading Away screen saver.

■ *Space Voyage.* Put yourself at the viewport of a warp-speed starship with the Space Voyage screen saver. This screen saver displays a field of stars that simulates the effect of high-speed space travel. You can select the speed of travel (see fig. 24.19).

■ *Bouncing Lines Example.* This screen saver consists of one or two horizontal lines that bounce back and forth between the top and bottom of the screen (see fig. 24.20). You can select either one or two lines and set the speed for the lines' movements.

■ *Starless Night.* The Starless Night screen saver is just a black screen. No options are available with this screen saver.

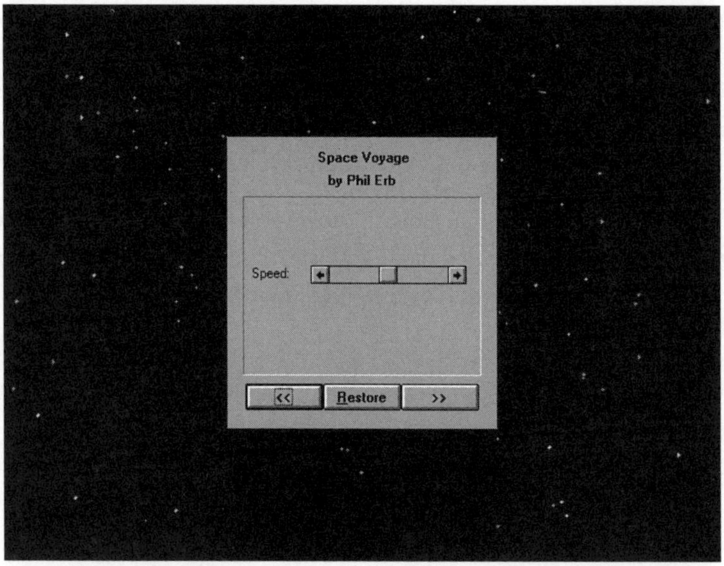

Fig. 24.19
The Space Voyage screen saver.

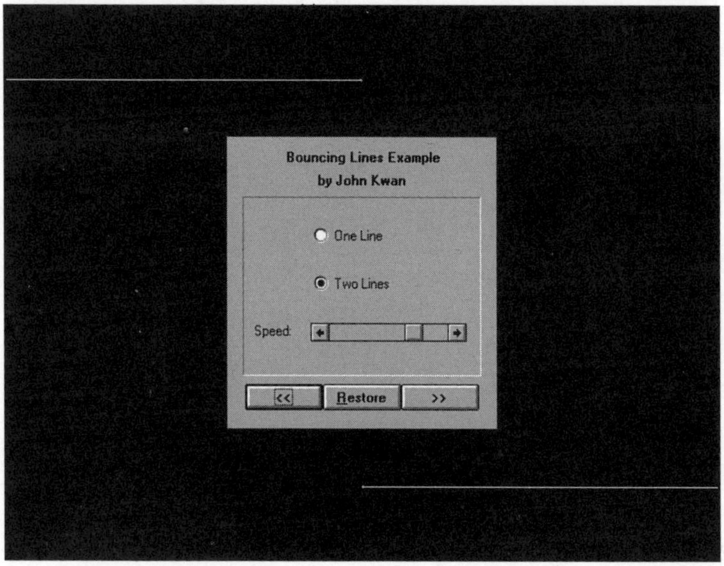

Fig. 24.20
The Bouncing Lines Example screen saver.

Summary

This chapter showed you how to activate and configure Screen Saver and provided examples of all Screen Saver screen saver images. Now you know how to "put your computer to sleep"—and save your screen in the process.

The next chapter, "Using SmartErase," shows you how to use SmartErase to recover any accidentally erased data. You learn how to configure SmartErase and how to erase and recover files by using SmartErase.

Chapter 25

Using SmartErase

In this chapter, you learn to perform the following tasks:

- Understand SmartErase and SmartCan
- Erase files by using SmartErase
- Recover deleted files by using SmartErase
- Use an example of SmartErase's UnErase capabilities

In Chapter 23, "Using Shredder," you learned how DOS normally deletes files: "Deleted" files themselves are not deleted, but are hidden and marked so that their data can be overwritten by other data. If the data is overwritten, it cannot be recovered. If the data is not yet overwritten, it can be recovered by using SmartErase, a tool that creates a "buffer" that protects recently deleted files from being overwritten.

Understanding SmartErase and SmartCan

SmartErase is an NDW tool that stores the contents of recently deleted files to an area of your disk that is reserved to protect these files. This area is actually a hidden directory on your disk, so it does not appear on directory listings. Files are stored in this protected areas of your disk for a specified length of time, during which SmartErase quickly and easily can restore these files to their previous status.

SmartErase is actually just the visible portion of a two-program utility; it works with a DOS-based terminate-and-stay-resident (TSR) program called SmartCan. SmartCan loads via a command in your AUTOEXEC.BAT file and remains in memory, tracking any and all deleted files. If you are familiar with the Norton Utilities programs, you may recognize that SmartErase is a combination of the Norton Utilities programs SmartCan and UnErase.

Tip
Because SmartCan is a DOS-based TSR, it protects all deleted files, including those files deleted from DOS while Windows is not even running.

SmartCan intercepts commands to delete files, instead transferring the file information to a hidden subdirectory named SMARTCAN. By moving and hiding the files to be deleted, the data in these files is protected from being overwritten for a specified period of time. After this time period ends, SmartCan releases the deleted file's data area for reuse by other files, in effect starting the normal deletion process.

Warning

SmartCan can hold files only while disk space is available. (You are limited to available hard disk space or a predefined amount of space that you select when you configure SmartErase.) If you run out of disk space, SmartCan permits files in the SmartCan area to be overwritten, even though the specified period of time may not have elapsed. Files are overwritten on a first-in-first-out basis.

Tip
If you attempt to make space on your disk by deleting files in the SmartCan area while the TSR is active, those files are deleted and restored in SmartCan; you must purge them instead.

Files that are moved to the SmartCan area are hidden from normal view. By activating SmartErase, however, you can view these hidden files and easily restore them to active condition. You also can use SmartErase to "purge" old files from the SmartCan area.

If SmartErase cannot find the deleted files by using the SmartCan information, it turns to information created by Norton Desktop's Image program. Image loads when your system loads and keeps a backup copy of your disk's critical areas. SmartErase also can use the Image data to recover deleted files.

If neither SmartCan nor Image can help SmartErase recover files, SmartErase uses the DOS 5.0 or DOS 6.0 Mirror feature. Mirror works similarly to Image, creating a copy of your disk's critical areas.

Occasionally, none of these methods is successful in unerasing deleted files. In these cases, you may need to use the DOS-based UnErase utility located on the Norton Fix-It disks. See Chapter 29, "Using Norton Fix-It and Rescue Disks," for more details on this and other Fix-It disk utilities.

If UnErase does not work, you may need to restore a copy of the deleted file from your most recent backup disk set. See Chapter 10, "Restoring Files with Norton Backup and the Fix-It Disk," for more information on restoring backed-up data.

Configuring SmartErase

All configuration for the SmartErase tool is done via the Control Center (SmartErase) customization dialog box, as shown in figure 25.1. To display the Control Center (SmartErase) dialog box, choose the **O**ptions **C**ustomize command, and select SmartErase from the **C**ategories list.

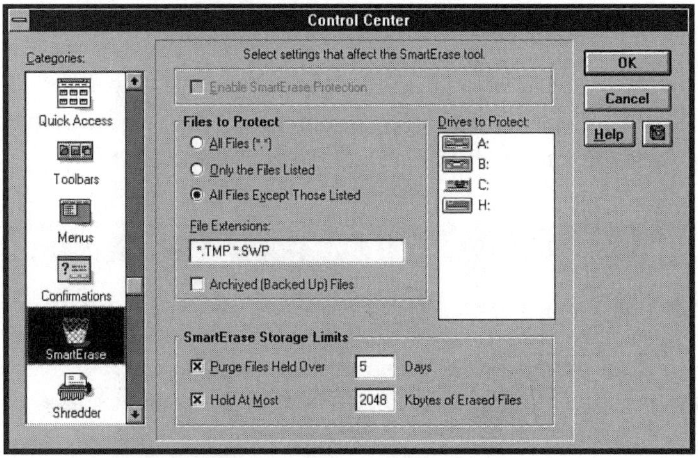

Fig. 25.1
The Control Center (SmartErase) customization dialog box.

The following table describes the four main items available in the Control Center (SmartErase) dialog box.

Option	Function
Enable SmartErase Protection	Turns on SmartCan.
Files to Protect	Selects the kinds of files to protect.
SmartErase Storage Limits	Determines the length of time files are protected and/or the amount of disk space allocated for the SmartCan area.
Drives to Protect	Selects the drives that receive SmartCan protection.

Activating SmartCan

SmartCan is not active unless the following command line appears in your AUTOEXEC.BAT file. Make sure that a space appears before each / in the command.

```
SMARTCAN /ON /SKIPHIGH
```

As you install NDW, this line is added to your AUTOEXEC.BAT file automatically if you select this option during installation. This command line loads the SmartCan TSR (the SMARTCAN part of the command line) and turns it on (the /ON switch in the command line). If, for some reason, this line is not visible in your AUTOEXEC.BAT file, the **E**nable SmartCan option is grayed out in the Control Center (SmartErase) dialog box. You must add this line to your AUTOEXEC.BAT file and then choose the **E**nable SmartCan option to activate SmartCan.

To deactivate SmartCan, change the /ON switch to /OFF. If you deselect the **E**nable SmartCan option, the switch automatically changes to /OFF. You also can edit the command line manually in the AUTOEXEC.BAT file.

Choosing Not To Use SmartCan

Many users prefer not to use SmartCan. Because the SmartCan TSR uses valuable system memory and the SmartCan area takes up valuable disk space, many users believe that the tradeoff between use of system resources and additional protection from accidental file deletion is unacceptable. These users find that SmartErase does such a good job of recovering files that it provides enough protection without enabling SmartCan. Turning off SmartCan does not completely remove it from memory. To fully remove SmartCan, delete the entire command line. Because NDW looks for SmartCan on startup, however, erasing this line can cause you to receive a message every time you start Norton Desktop informing you that file deletions are not protected. To disable this message in the future, select the check box option to disable the message that appears in the message dialog box.

Selecting Files To Protect

This section of the SmartErase customization dialog box provides the options described in the following table.

Option	Function
All Files (*.*)	Saves all deleted files, no matter what the file name or extension.
Only the Files Listed	Enables you to save only those file types listed in the File Extensions text box.
All files E**x**cept Those Listed	Enables you to save all files except those file types listed in the **F**ile Extensions text box.
Archived (Backed Up) Files	Provides protection only for files that have not been backed up or have changed since the last backup.

The simplest option is to provide protection for all files. This option, however, uses the most disk space in the SmartCan area. You may want to limit the types of files you protect to conserve valuable disk space.

Enter data in the **F**ile Extensions text box by using the * wild card character, followed by the XXX extension. You must leave one space between each file name. To save all DOC, XLS, and SAM files, for example, enter the following line:

***.DOC *.XLS *.SAM**

Note

Many programs produce new temporary or backup files every time you use them. A proliferation of automatically protected TMP and BAK files can quickly fill the disk space allocated for the SmartCan area. You may want to include files with these extensions in the list of files not to protect with SmartCan.

Selecting SmartErase Storage Limits

SmartErase holds files in the SmartCan area for a specified number of days or until files exceed the available disk space or a selected amount of disk space.

Selecting the **P**urge Files Held Over *X* Days option enables you to tell SmartErase how long to protect files. The default setting is five days. To change this setting, select the option's check box and enter a new numerical value in its text box.

Selecting the Hold at **M**ost *X* Kbytes of Erased Files option enables you to tell SmartErase how much disk space to allocate to file protection. If this option is not selected, the SmartCan area grows as large as the free disk space you have available. This practice is seldom advisable; you should, instead, define a fixed amount of space to allocate to the SmartCan area—select the check box and enter a new numerical value in the text box.

Warning

Setting too small a number for the SmartCan area size limits the amount of protection provided by SmartCan. The area must be large enough to hold whatever files you need to protect.

Erasing Files by Using SmartErase

If you install the SmartErase Tool icon on your desktop, you easily can erase files. Simply follow these steps:

1. With a drive window open, select the file(s) you want to delete.
2. Using the mouse, drag the selected file(s) from the drive window and drop them onto the SmartErase Tool icon.
3. After you are prompted to confirm the deletion, choose **Y**es.

Note

SmartCan protects deleted files, no matter how you delete them. To provide SmartCan protection, you do not need to use SmartErase to delete files. As long as SmartCan is loaded, any file you delete is protected in the SmartCan area.

Recovering Deleted Files by Using SmartErase

By Using SmartErase, you can easily recover recently deleted files. If the SmartErase Tool icon is visible on your Desktop, simply double-click the icon to run SmartErase. You also can start this part of SmartErase by choosing the **T**ools **U**nErase command. The UnErase list of recently erased files appears (see fig. 25.2). This window lists the names of files that have been recently erased and that are known to SmartErase.

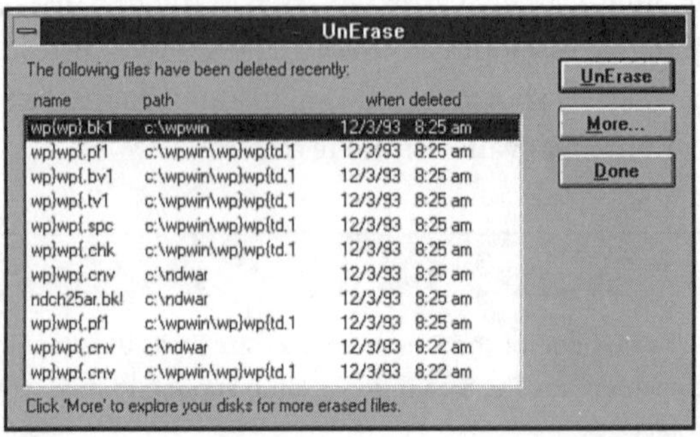

Fig. 25.2
An UnErase dialog box listing recently erased files.

To search for more erased files on disk, click the **M**ore button. A SmartErase drive window appears (see fig. 25.3).

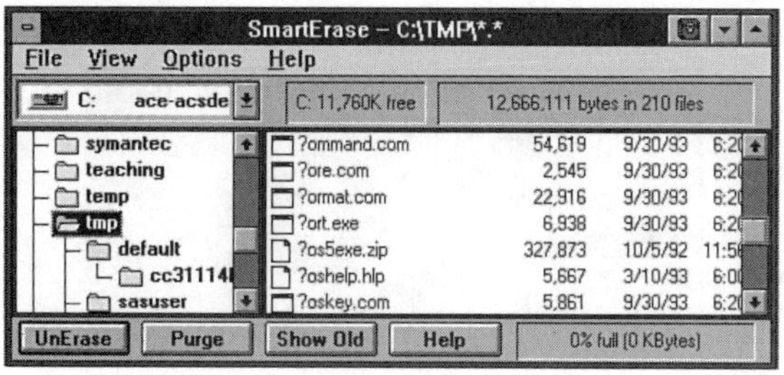

Fig. 25.3
The SmartErase drive window, showing recently erased files.

This window is similar to other NDW drive windows, with the exception of a button bar with four buttons at the bottom of the screen, a status area, and the file pane displaying erased files instead of normal files.

The four buttons at the bottom of the window perform the functions described in the following table.

Button	Function
UnErase	Initiates the unerase procedure for files selected in the drive window.
Purge	Permanently deletes all protected files from the SmartCan area.
Show Old	Displays information on all deleted files in the selected directory, including duplicate entries and entries that were deleted far in the past; toggles to a Hide Old button.
Help	Displays the Help screens for SmartErase.

To recover a recently deleted file, follow these steps:

1. Choose **T**ools **U**nErase from the Desktop menu bar. The last 11 files deleted are listed. If the file you want to unerase is not in the list, click the **M**ore button to display a list of additional deleted files.

2. Scroll through the list to select the directory that contains the file you want to recover.

3. Highlight the name of the file you want to recover.

4. Click the UnErase button.

   If the file was not protected by SmartCan, the file name appears with a question mark as its first character. After you click the UnErase button, a dialog box appears that prompts you for the first letter of the file name (see fig. 25.4). Type the first letter of the file name, and choose OK to begin the UnErase operation.

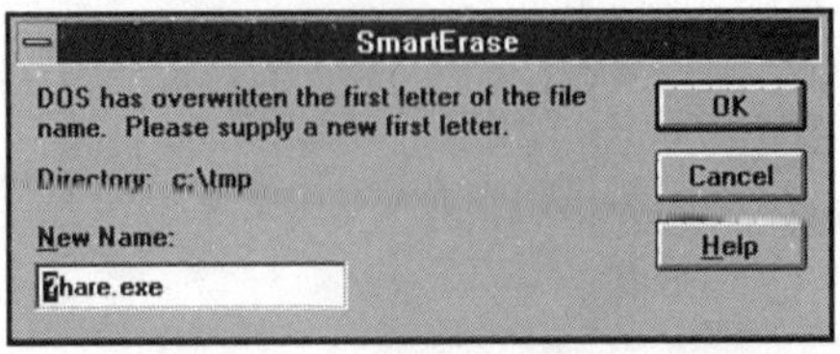

Fig. 25.4
The SmartErase dialog box that appears if the first character of the file name is missing.

Note

SmartErase automatically opens to the directory from which you last deleted a file.

Tip
Files that cannot be recovered by using SmartErase can sometimes be manually unerased by using the UnErase utility in Symantec's Norton Utilities program.

If the file has not been overwritten, SmartErase automatically recovers the file. If, however, the file has been overwritten, the apparently recovered file may be damaged and unusable. Remember that SmartErase can work only on data that has not been overwritten.

Using an Example of SmartErase's UnErase Capabilities

Suppose that you accidentally deleted an important file, DONTKILL.TXT, from your DATA directory. You can put your knowledge of SmartErase to use in recovering the file.

Begin by launching SmartErase. After the UnErase window appears, it displays a list of recently erased files, as shown in figure 25.5. Select the DONTKILL.TXT file, and click the **U**nErase button to recover the file.

You can open a normal drive window to confirm that the file has been restored. Figure 25.6 shows the file DONTKILL.TXT completely restored.

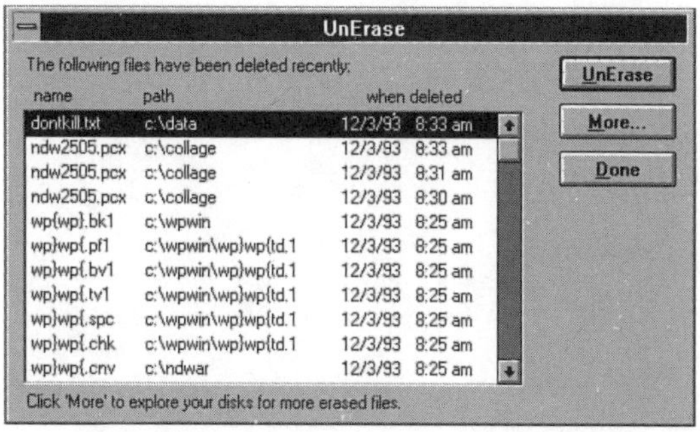

Fig. 25.5
The UnErase window, with the DONTKILL.TXT file highlighted.

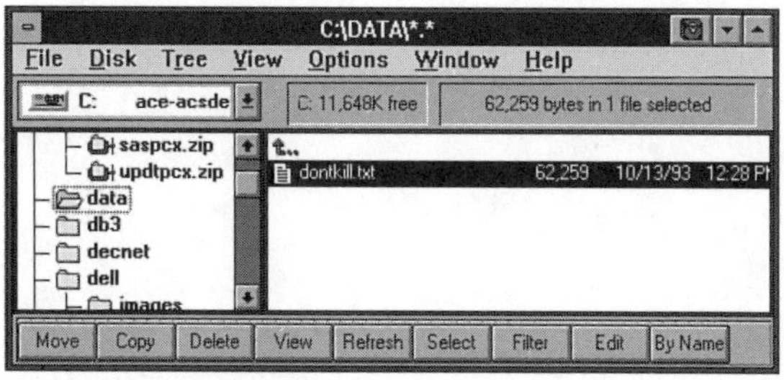

Fig. 25.6
An open drive window confirming the DONTKILL.TXT file recovery.

> **Note**
>
> If you delete a file, DOS replaces the first character of the file name on your disk with the ACSII character number 229 (the Greek letter sigma). DOS does not immediately overwrite the file's information on the disk. The ASCII 229 character, however, tells DOS that the file and the space the file occupied are now free to be used by other files. If you are running SmartCan, it protects the deleted file's area from being overwritten, thus enabling SmartErase to recover that file's contents.

Summary

This chapter showed you how to protect and recover data by using the SmartErase tool and the SmartCan utility. You learned how SmartErase and SmartCan work, how to configure SmartErase, how to erase files by using SmartErase, and how to recover deleted files by using SmartErase.

In the next chapter, "Using Speed Disk," you learn how to use the Speed Disk utility to optimize your hard drive without leaving Windows. You will learn how to run the Speed Disk program, how to choose optimization methods, and how to select Speed Disk configuration options.

Chapter 26

Using Norton Speed Disk

Your hard disk is constantly changing. Old data is erased and new data is written to empty areas of your disk virtually every minute your PC is in use. All this constant shuffling of data scrambles whatever neat, orderly arrangement the data may originally occupy. In fact, the more you use your PC, the more your data is likely to become scrambled.

In this chapter, you learn to perform the following tasks:

- Start speed disk
- Choose optimization methods
- Select other configuration options

Having scrambled data on your system is not an ideal situation. If data is spread at random across your entire hard disk, your computer takes longer to locate specific data. The read-write heads of your hard disk may need to travel back and forth across the entire hard disk surface several times to locate all the data in a particular file. To minimize the time required to locate data on your hard disk, therefore, that data needs to be contiguously arranged.

For this reason, Symantec includes the Speed Disk optimization utility as part of Norton Desktop 3 for Windows. Using Speed Disk speeds up the performance of your hard disk—often quite noticeably.

Speed Disk belongs to the category of utilities referred to as *disk optimizers* or *defragmenters*. (Norton uses the term *unfragment*, which means the same as *defragment*.) Speed Disk optimizes your hard disk by defragmenting data that is fragmented nonsequentially. In essence, Speed Disk takes all the data on your hard disk and rearranges it so that all related data is contiguous.

To defragment your hard disk, Speed Disk reads data into memory in small chunks, moves other data out of the way, and then rewrites the data to disk in a predetermined order. This disk optimization is one of the easiest methods you can use to improve the performance of your computer system and is well worth the time to perform on a regular basis.

Starting Speed Disk

You can start Speed Disk by clicking the Speed Disk icon, if it is located on the Desktop, or by choosing **T**ools Sp**e**ed Disk.

As Speed Disk loads, it first tests your system memory. Then the utility displays the Optimize Drive dialog box, which instructs you to select the drive you want to optimize, as shown in figure 26.1. Click a Drive icon in the dialog box to select or deselect it for optimization. If a check mark appears to the left of a Drive icon, that drive is selected.

Fig. 26.1
The Optimize Drive dialog box enables you to choose drives to optimize.

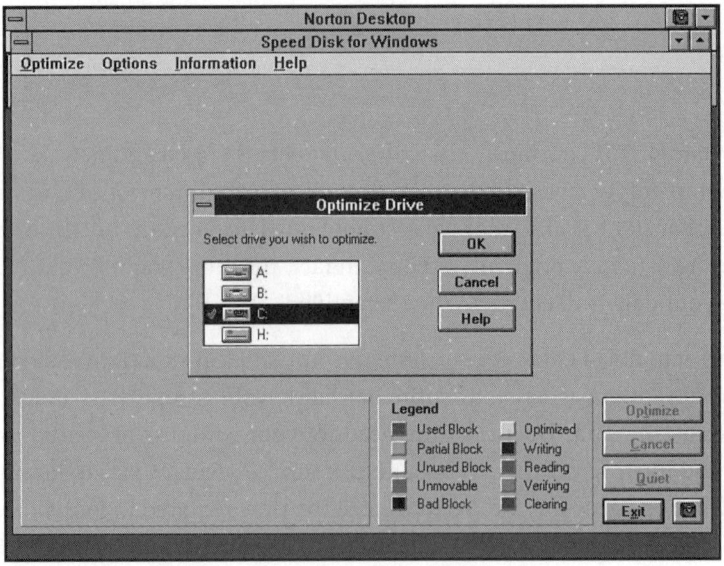

After you select the drive to optimize and click OK, Speed Disk reads and analyzes the disk information for the selected disk and then displays the Recommendation dialog box, as shown in figure 26.2. This dialog box tells you what percentage of disk space is not fragmented and offers a recommendation as to what type of optimization method to use. You can accept Speed Disk's recommendation by choosing the **O**ptimize button, or you can use a different type of optimization by choosing one of the other option buttons at the bottom of the dialog box. If you click the Cancel button, the main Speed Disk for Windows screen appears, and you can choose other options from the **O**ptimize, O**p**tions, **I**nformation, or **H**elp menus.

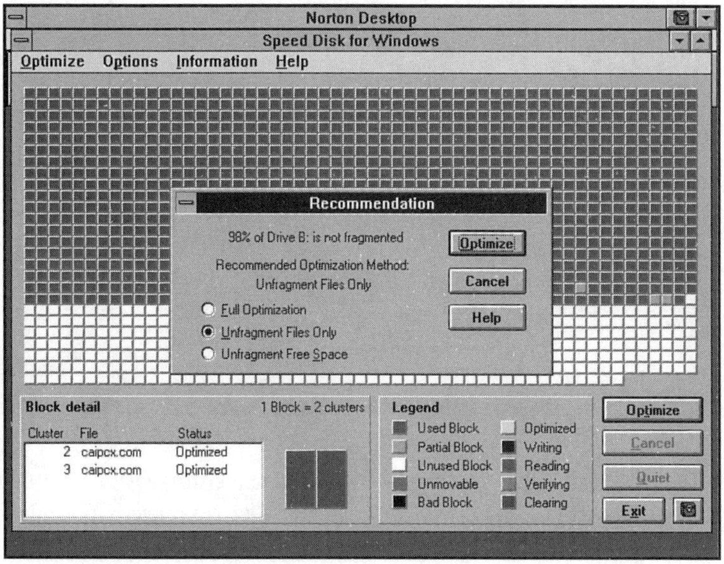

Fig. 26.2
The Speed Disk Recommendation dialog box tells you which optimization method is considered by NDW as the best one to use.

The main Speed Disk screen, shown in the background of figure 26.2, displays a visual representation of your hard disk. Each block represents a group of clusters, as shown in the Legend in the lower-right section of the screen. The Legend also tells you what different types of blocks represent; for example, one color in a block (gray) represents an unmovable block. The lower-left section of the screen displays Block Details that tell you how many blocks are in a cluster and describes the status of clusters.

From the **I**nformation menu of the main Speed Disk screen, you can choose to display **D**isk Statistics for the drive scheduled to be optimized. This report gives you additional information about your hard or floppy disk (or whatever drive you are checking). A sample Statistics for Drive B: report dialog box is shown in figure 26.3. The more fragmented are the files, the more you need to defragment your hard disk.

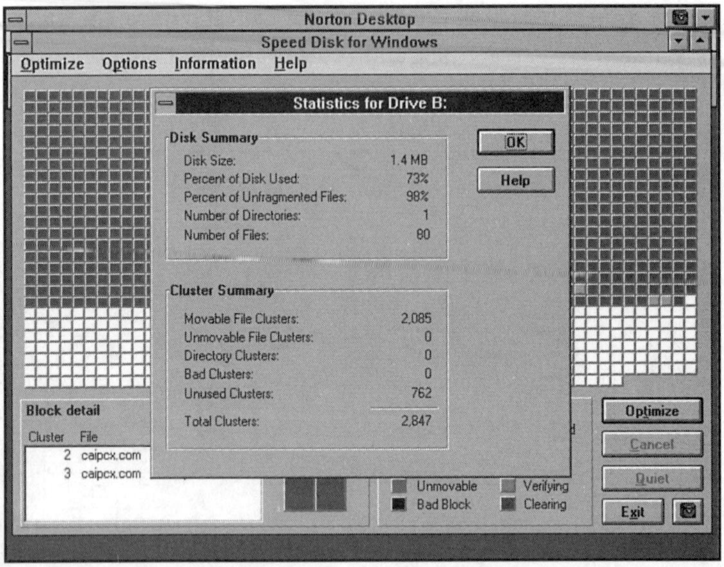

Fig. 26.3
A sample Statistics for Drive B: dialog box displays disk summary information.

Notice that you can generate two reports from the **I**nformation menu. The two options available on this menu are described in the following table.

Option	Function
Disk Statistics	Displays a complete readout of vital disk statistics, including disk size, percentage of disk used, and percentage of defragmented files.
Show Unmovable Files	Specifies any files you do not want moved from their current positions, such as files protected by some copy-protection schemes.

Choosing Optimization Methods

Tip
Establish a routine to use different optimization methods at different times. Run **U**nfragment Files Only weekly, for example, and **F**ull Optimization monthly or if you detect a drop in system performance.

Usually, you want to follow Speed Disk's optimization recommendation. If you want more control over how files are arranged on your disk, however, you can configure Speed Disk to perform different types of optimization.

The three different types of possible optimizations vary in their effectiveness, as described in the following list:

- *Full Optimization.* This method fully optimizes your disk, without changing the directory placement.

- *Unfragment Files Only*. This method is not a full optimization; it defragments only files, sometimes leaving holes on your disk and sometimes not defragmenting very large files. This method performs the fastest optimization, but the results are not as noticeable as are those of the full optimization method.

- *Unfragment Free **S**pace*. This method does not defragment files, but rather moves files around to fill in empty disk space, leaving all unused disk space at the end of the disk.

To choose an optimization method, follow these steps:

1. Open the Speed Disk for Windows' **O**ptimize menu, and choose **M**ethod. The Optimization Method dialog box appears, as shown in figure 26.4.

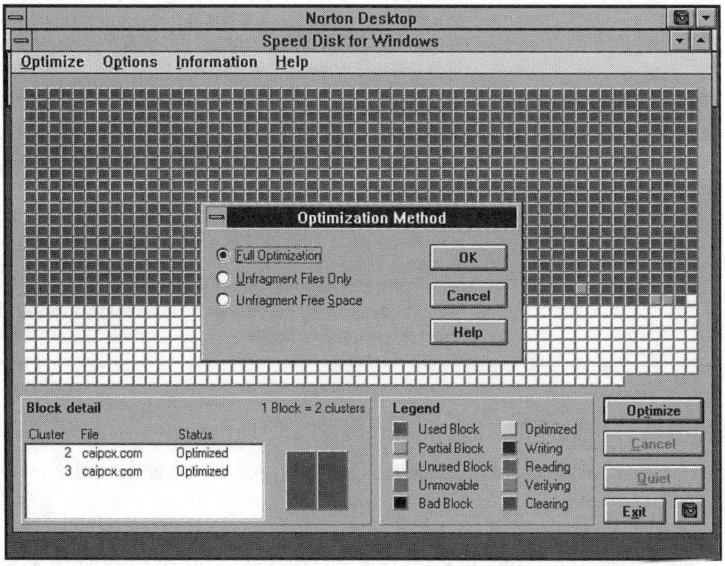

Fig. 26.4
The Optimization Method dialog box enables you to choose which optimization method to use.

2. Choose the option button for the method of optimization you want to use: **F**ull Optimization, **U**nfragment Files Only, or Unfragment Free **S**pace.

3. Choose OK to confirm the optimization method and close the dialog box.

Selecting Other Configuration Options

Several other configuration options are accessible through the Speed Disk O**p**tions menu. These options fine-tune the results of the Speed Disk operations and also affect how fast Speed Disk works. The more complex your configuration, the longer Speed Disk takes to run.

The choices available from the O**p**tions menu are described in the following table.

Option	Function
Verify Write	Specifies that Speed Disk performs additional verification on each area of the disk to make sure that the data is written to disk correctly. This option slows down the optimization process and is generally not necessary. You may want to use it, however, if your hard disk is older and somewhat unreliable.
Wipe Free Space	This option specifies that, as data is moved from one place on disk, freeing up that space, the old data is wiped from the disk so that it cannot be recovered. This security measure is needed only if you must protect the data on your disk from being read by unauthorized persons.
Block Map (or Bar **M**ap)	Specifies how the progress map appears on the Speed Disk progress screen: either as blocks or bars.
Set Sound	Specifies if progress for the disk optimization is accompanied by sound. This option is useful only if your computer has a sound card, such as SoundBlaster. You can choose to enable sound and choose a sound file (either a MID or WAV sound file).

After you set the optimization method and any other custom configurations, you can begin the disk optimization. The full process is as described in the following steps:

1. Begin Speed Disk by clicking the Speed Disk icon or choosing **T**ools Sp**e**ed Disk. The Speed Disk main screen appears with the Optimize Drive dialog box displayed (refer to fig. 26.1).

2. Choose from the list of drives in the Optimize Drive dialog box which drive you want to optimize, and click OK. The Recommendation dialog box appears (refer to fig. 26.2).

3. Choose the **O**ptimize button to accept the recommendation and proceed with the optimization, or select the option button for the method of optimization you want to implement and then choose **O**ptimize to begin the optimization process.

After optimization begins, the *disk map* begins to change on-screen. The disk map consists of the squares covering the upper portion of the Speed Disk for Windows window. Blocks on the map change colors according to the Legend at the bottom of the window, showing you what is happening during the optimization. Speed Disk starts to read information from certain sectors into memory and then to write that information into other sectors. This process is represented by colored blocks shuffling around the disk map. In the same area that contains the Block detail, a progress bar appears, displaying the progress of the optimization.

Tip
You can change the colors of the disk map by double-clicking the color in the legend that you want to change.

Warning

Never turn off your PC while Speed Disk is running. This practice can damage files and possibly make your hard disk unreadable.

After optimization is complete, a dialog box informs you that Speed Disk is finished condensing files. You then can either optimize another drive or exit Speed Disk. After you exit Speed Disk, rebooting your PC is the recommended procedure. The next time you use your PC, your disk is organized, and the performance of your hard disk should be improved.

Summary

This chapter explained how to optimize hard disk performance by using Speed Disk. After a period of use, your disk is likely to become fragmented, causing access time to slow. Using Speed Disk on a regular basis can help you optimize your use of your computer.

The next chapter shows you how to locate specific files by using SuperFind. You learn how to specify file search options, search for files by file specification, and search for files with specified text.

Chapter 27

Using SuperFind

As hard disks get bigger and the information stored on them becomes more voluminous, finding specific pieces of data becomes more difficult. You may have dozens of directories and subdirectories, each containing dozens or even hundreds of files. Given the eight-character file name restraint of DOS, file names provide an extremely difficult way to determine the contents of each of the literally thousands of files that can reside on your hard disk. How do you find exactly what you seek? The answer is simple—use SuperFind.

In this chapter, you learn to perform the following tasks:

- Understand SuperFind
- Start SuperFind
- Search for files by using SuperFind
- Create SuperFind batch files

Understanding SuperFind

SuperFind is a very useful utility included with NDW that enables you to locate specific files. You can search for files by file type or for files containing specific text. You can search for files on your entire system, only on selected drives, or only in selected directories and subdirectories. You can even search for files created during a certain time period or for files that meet certain size restrictions. In short, SuperFind enables you to find just about anything on your system through just about any method.

As SuperFind conducts its search, it displays all files it finds in a special SuperFind drive window. In this window, as in other NDW drive windows, you can move, copy, delete, print, drag and drop, or view the selected files.

Note

Because SuperFind conducts its search in the background, you can continue operating other applications while the SuperFind search is in progress.

Starting SuperFind

SuperFind can be started by clicking the Find Icon. After SuperFind is started, the SuperFind window appears, as shown in figure 27.1. Notice that this window cannot be maximized to full-screen size; it can appear only as a minimized window or in icon form.

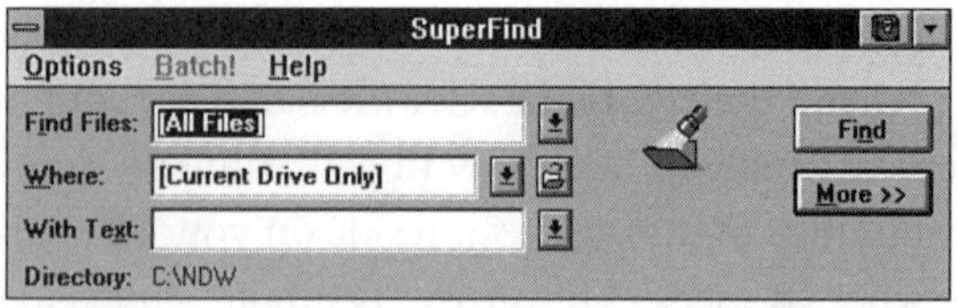

Fig. 27.1
The Desktop standard SuperFind window enables you to specify search options.

If you choose the **M**ore button in the SuperFind window, the window expands to include additional search criteria (see fig. 27.2). The expanded window displays a **L**ess button that you can use to hide the additional criteria by returning to the original SuperFind window. The expanded window includes options to specify searches by date, time, file size, and file attribute.

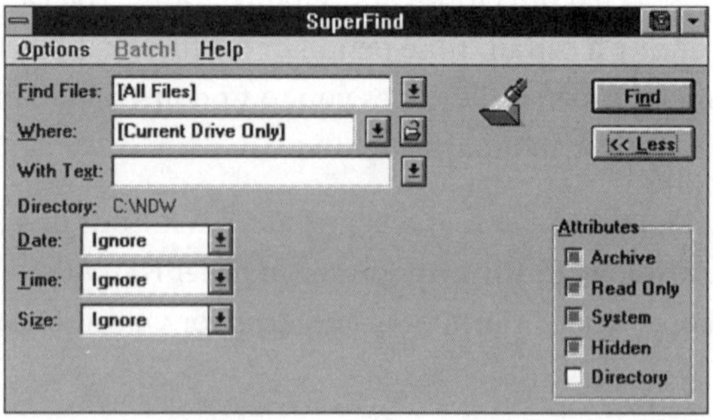

Fig. 27.2
The expanded SuperFind window enables you to specify search by date, time, file size, or file attribute.

Searching for Files by Using SuperFind

The four basic steps involved in a SuperFind search are as follows:

1. Specify the types of files for which to search.
2. Specify where to search.
3. Specify criteria to be used in the search (date range, file size, text strings, and so on).
4. Begin the search by choosing the Fi**n**d option.

You can use SuperFind's built-in search criteria for all these options, or you can define your own criteria.

Searching by Using SuperFind's File Sets

The F**i**nd Files drop-down list box displays six predefined file sets. A file set is a set of files for which to search, as defined by the file extensions. The following table outlines the predefined file sets included with SuperFind.

File Set	Search
All Files	Searches for all files by using the *.* wild card.
All Files Except Programs	Searches for files by using the *.* wild card, excluding files with EXE, COM, and BAT extensions.
Database Files	Searches for dBASE and Q&A database files by using the DBI and DTF extensions.
Documents	Searches for text files by using the DOC, TXT, and WRI extensions.
Programs	Searches for executable files by using the EXE, COM, and BAT extensions.
Spreadsheet Files	Searches for 1-2-3 and Excel spreadsheet files by using the WK?, WQ?, and XLS extensions.

These predefined file sets may be enough for your needs, or you may want to edit them or create new file sets. If you edit or create new file sets, you can choose a name for the file set, as well as extensions to include or exclude from the search.

Note

A minus sign precedes extensions to exclude from the search.

You also can enter a one-time file set in the Find Files text box by following these steps:

1. Move your cursor to the F**i**nd Files text box.
2. Delete the current file set description.
3. Type in a new file set description by using wild cards and file extensions.
4. Choose the Fi**n**d button to begin a search based on these temporary criteria.

To permanently edit an existing file set, follow these steps:

1. Choose the **O**ptions Search **S**ets command. The Search Sets dialog box appears (see fig. 27.3).

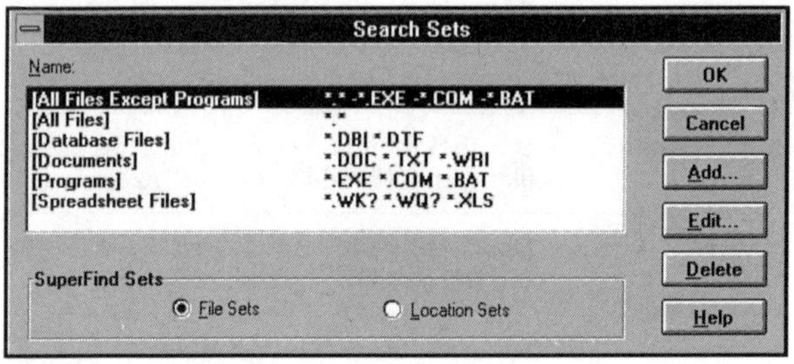

Fig. 27.3
The Search Sets dialog box enables you to choose a search by file type.

2. Choose the **F**ile Sets option button.
3. Choose from the **N**ame list the file set you want to edit.
4. Choose the **E**dit button. The Edit File Set dialog box appears (see fig. 27.4).

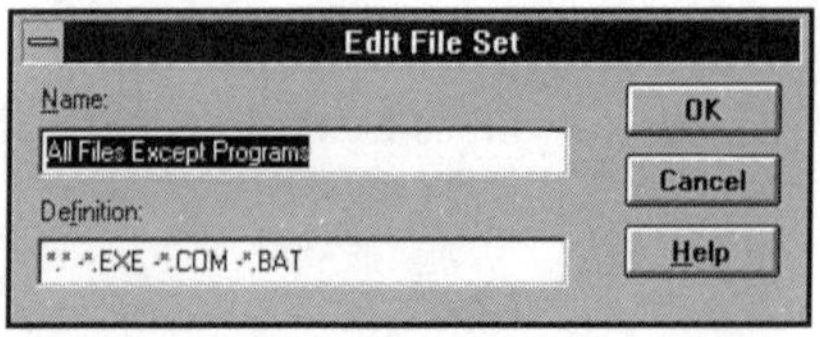

Fig. 27.4
The Edit File Set dialog box enables you to edit file sets.

5. To edit the file set name, type new text in the **N**ame text box.
6. To edit the file types for which to search, type new or changed extensions in the De**f**inition text box. Leave one space between each definition, precede each extension with the * wild card (as in *.COM), and precede all files to exclude with a minus sign.
7. Choose OK to close the Edit File Set dialog box.
8. Choose OK again to close the Search Sets dialog box.

The edited file set now appears after you open the F**i**nd Files list box in the SuperFind window.

To add a new file set, follow these steps:

1. Choose the **O**ptions Search **S**ets command. The Search Sets dialog box appears.
2. Choose the **F**ile Sets option button.
3. Choose the **A**dd button. The Add File Set dialog box appears (see fig. 27.5).

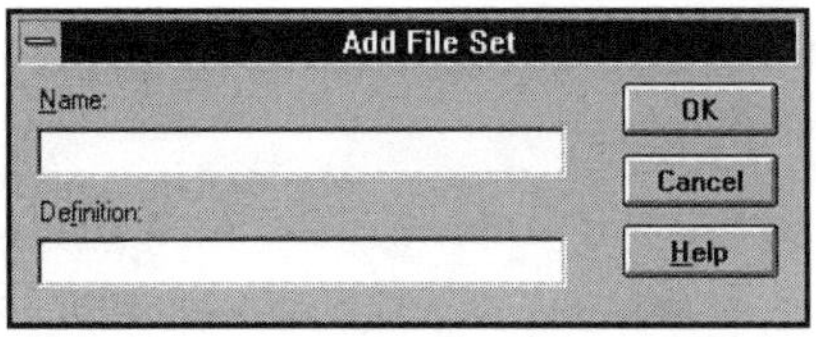

Fig. 27.5
The Add File Set dialog box.

4. Type a name for the file set in the **N**ame text box.
5. Enter in the De**f**inition text box the file type or types you want to include or exclude in your search.
6. Choose OK to close the Add File Set dialog box.
7. Choose OK again to close the Search Sets dialog box.

The new file set now appears after you open the F**i**nd Files list box in the SuperFind window.

Tip
If the file set list becomes too long, you also can delete file sets. Simply select the file set to delete in the Search Sets dialog box, and click the **D**elete button.

Searching by Using SuperFind's Location Sets

A location set is much like a file set, except that a location set specifies certain directories or drives for a search. SuperFind comes with nine predefined location sets, as described in the following list.

- All Drives Except Floppies
- All Drives
- Current Dir and Subdirs
- Current Directory Only
- Current Drive Only
- Floppy Drives Only
- Local Hard Drives Only
- Network Drives Only
- Path

As with file sets, you can type temporary definitions into the **W**here text box (generally useful for specifying particular directories to search), you can edit existing location sets, you can add new location sets, and you can delete existing location sets.

Adding new location sets is a simple procedure. A new location set might consist of a directory or set of directories in which you store particular types of files, for example. To add a new location set, follow these steps:

1. Choose the **O**ptions Search **S**ets command. The Search Sets dialog box appears.
2. Choose the **L**ocation Sets option.
3. Choose the **A**dd option. The Add Location Set dialog box appears (see fig. 27.6).
4. Type a name for this location set in the **N**ame text box.
5. Type a directory path or multiple directory paths in the De**f**inition text box. Separate each directory path with a space.

   You also can click the Directory button to display the Select Directory to Search dialog box, which is kind of a mini-Browse box. After you select a directory from this box and click the OK button, the selected directory path appears in the Definition text box. Only a single directory can be selected by using this method; you must manually type any multiple directories.

6. Choose OK to close the Add Location Set dialog box.
7. Choose OK again to close the Search Sets dialog box.

The new location set appears in the **W**here drop-down list box in the SuperFind window.

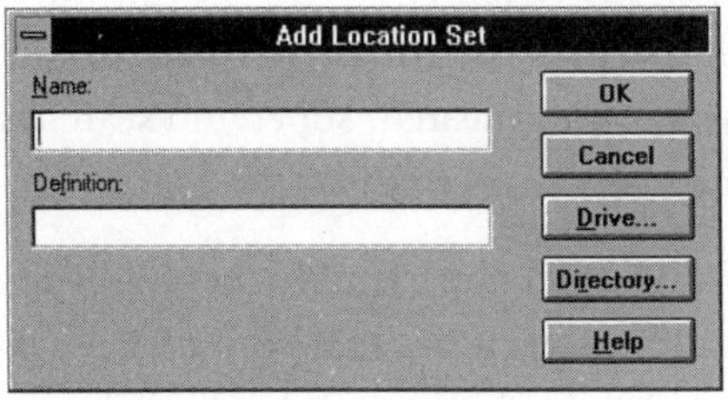

Fig. 27.6
The Add Location Set dialog box.

Searching by Using SuperFind's Search Criteria

SuperFind enables you to search by several other criteria. After you expand the SuperFind window by clicking the **M**ore button, additional criteria appear, as described in the following table.

Criteria	Search
Date	Searches for files by using specified date criteria: on date, not on date, before date, before or on date, after date, after or at date, between date and date, not between date and date.
Time	Searches for files by using specified time criteria: on time, not on time, before time, before or on time, after time, after or at time, between time and time, not between time and time.
Size	Searches for files by using specified size criteria: less than size, greater than size, between size and size, not between size and size.
Attributes	Searches for files according to attributes: archive, read only, system, hidden, or directory.

You can set the Date, Time, and Size criteria by accessing the appropriate list box and choosing the criteria. After you choose criteria, a text box appears to the right of the list box. The **D**ate and **T**ime text boxes are preformatted;

all you need to do is enter the appropriate date and time. The Si**z**e text box requires you to enter the appropriate size in kilobytes. If you choose one of the between criteria, two text boxes appear, as in between 10:00 a.m. and 10:00 p.m.

The Attributes criteria are three-way check boxes. Selecting the check boxes changes their state. An empty box specifies a search for files with that attribute turned off. A checked box specifies a search for files with that attribute turned on. A grayed box means a search with the attribute ignored.

Searching for Specific Text

You can instruct SuperFind to look not only for specific types of files, but also for files that contain specific text strings. Simply type in the With Te**x**t box the text for which you want to search. SuperFind searches for files that contain that text and meet all other criteria.

You can, for example, instruct SuperFind to look for Documents in the Current Directory and Subdirectories that contain the text *Norton Desktop*. Choose the Fi**n**d button to begin the search; all files matching these criteria appear in a SuperFind drive window.

Using Other SuperFind Options

You can switch on and off the other options available with SuperFind on the pull-down **O**ptions menu, as described in the following table.

Option	Search
Match Upper/Lowercase	Searches for text, performing an exact uppercase/ lowercase match.
OEM	If you are searching for text created by DOS, run on the OEM Text option, because DOS uses the OEM character set. Otherwise, turn off OEM so Superfind will use the ANSI character set in the search.
Animation	Turns on or off the animated icon displayed while SuperFind is conducting a search.
Running Man	Uses the animated "running man" icon instead of the default "question mark" icon.
Reuse Drive Window	Reuses a single drive window for multiple searches (the alternative is to create a new drive window for each new search).
Exclusive Search	Forces Windows to allot SuperFind exclusive resources to speed up a search (disables the capability to search in the background).
Minimized Search	Minimizes SuperFind to an icon during its search.

Using Sample SuperFind Searches

Now that you know all about SuperFind's options and search criteria, you can try some sample searches. The next three figures show the criteria and options needed to search for specific types of files.

The SuperFind window in figure 27.7 searches for all documents on the current drive that contain the text *Norton Desktop*. The window in figure 27.8 searches for all backup files (extension BAK) on the current drive created after November 20, 1993. The window in figure 27.9 searches for all large spreadsheet files (larger than 250K) in the C:\NDW directory.

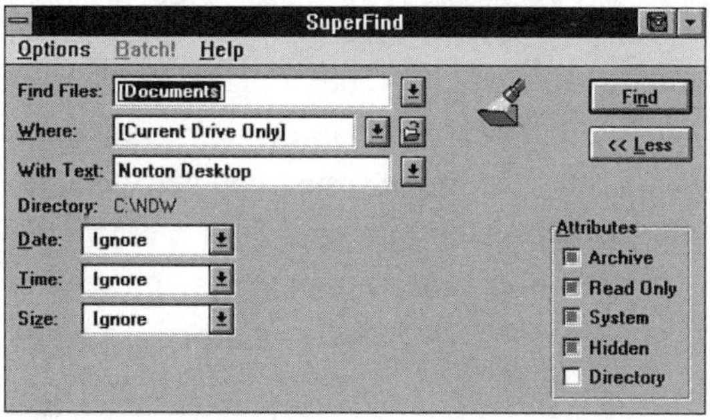

Fig. 27.7
Search criteria for documents containing the text *Norton Desktop*.

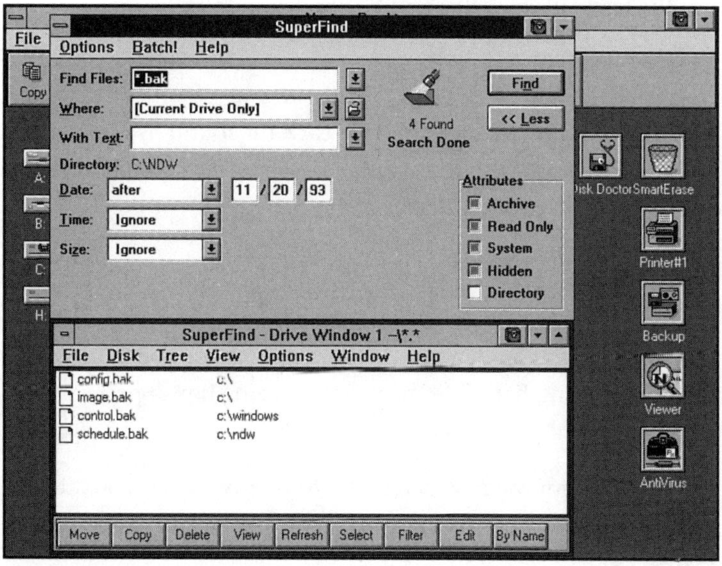

Fig. 27.8
Search criteria for backup files created after November 20, 1993.

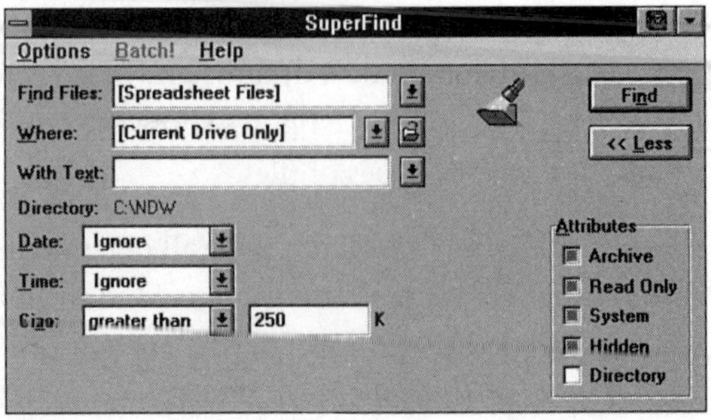

Fig. 27.9
Search criteria using the Si**z**e option to specify large spreadsheet files.

Creating SuperFind Batch Files

After SuperFind finds a group of files and displays the file names in a drive window, you can use the **B**atch! command on the menu bar to perform batch operations on each of the files in the group. You may rename all the selected files to share a different file extension, for example, or you may copy them all to another drive or directory. You can even elect to print all the files—just by using the **B**atch! command.

The **B**atch! command actually creates an executable batch file (with a BAT extension) based on your input. The following line is a sample batch file command to copy all files with an EXT extension to drive A:

COPY C:*.EXT A:

The batch file contains separate lines for each file found by SuperFind. Creating a batch file to work with these files is much faster than performing individual operations on each particular file in the group.

Using the Batch! Command

To use the **B**atch! command, follow these steps:

1. After a search is completed, choose the **B**atch! option from the SuperFind menu bar. The Create Batch dialog box appears (see fig. 27.10).

2. Type a name for the new batch file in the Sa**v**e As text box. Make sure the file has a BAT extension.

3. To insert a command, such as COPY, before each file name, type the command in the **I**nsert Before Filename text box.

4. To insert commands or instructions after each file name, type the instructions in the **A**ppend After Filename text box.

5. To include the full path for each file selected, select the **F**ull Path check box.

6. To insert spaces around each file name, select the **S**paces Around Filename check box.

7. To insert the word CALL at the start of each line (necessary if the command in the Before text box is a batch file), select the **C**ALL Each Command check box.

8. To add a line containing the DOS PAUSE command between each line in the output file, select the **P**AUSE After Each Command check box.

9. Choose OK to save this batch file.

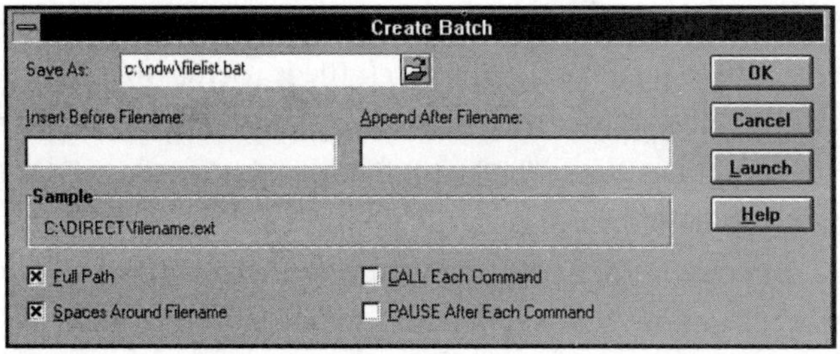

Fig. 27.10
The Create Batch dialog box enables you to perform batch operations on groups of files.

You can run batch files directly from the Create Batch dialog box by selecting the **L**aunch button. You also can run batch files from the DOS prompt by typing the batch file name or from Windows by accessing the **F**ile menu, choosing the **R**un option, and typing the batch file name.

Using Sample SuperFind Batch Files

To help you better understand what **B**atch! files can do, three sample **B**atch! files follow. Each of these files performs a common task, and each is very easy to complete.

Note

You can use any standard DOS commands to create these batch files.

- *COPYFILE.BAT*. Figure 27.11 shows the Create Batch dialog box for a batch file designed to copy all selected files from hard disk drive C to floppy disk drive A. The batch file uses the standard DOS COPY command before each file name and the destination drive A after each file name. The full path for each file name is specified in this and the other two sample batch files.

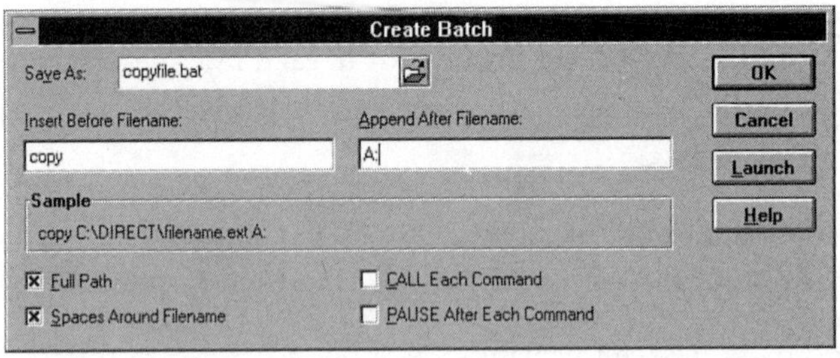

Fig. 27.11
Create Batch dialog box for COPYFILE.BAT, used to copy selected files.

- *RENFILE.BAT*. This batch file renames all selected files with an ARC extension (see fig. 27.12). This batch file is useful when you want to mark older files so that they do not appear in file find boxes in your Windows applications. The batch file uses the standard DOS REN (rename) command before each file name, and the destination extension *.ARC after each file name (the wild card instructs DOS to reuse the existing file name while appending the new extension).

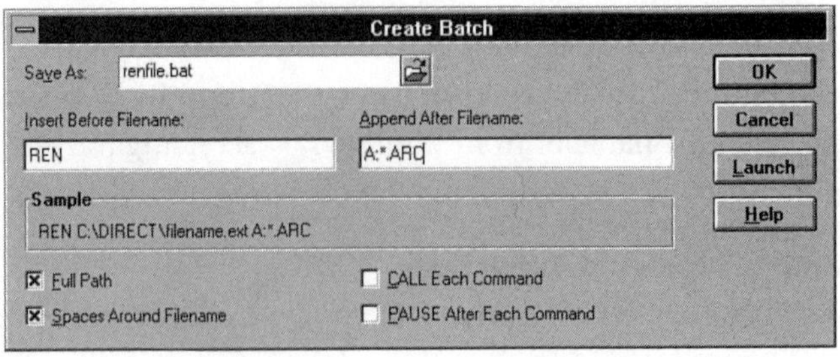

Fig. 27.12
Create Batch dialog box for RENFILE.BAT, used to rename selected files.

- *PRNFILE.BAT*. This batch file sends all selected files to the printer. (This batch file works well only with text files.) The batch file uses the standard DOS COPY command before each file name and the PRN destination device after each file name (see fig. 27.13).

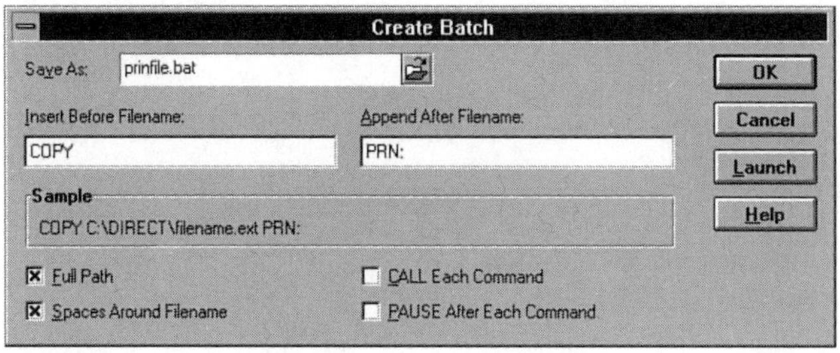

Fig. 27.13 Create Batch dialog box for PRNFILE.BAT, used to print selected files.

Summary

In this chapter, you learned how to search for files by using SuperFind. You learned how to configure SuperFind to search for specific types of files and how to define SuperFind's search criteria. You also learned how to use the **B**atch! command to create batch files that act on groups of files that have been located with SuperFind.

In the next chapter, "Using System Information," you learn more about your system by using the System Information tool. You learn how to use the System Information tool and how to display, read, and print system reports.

Chapter 28

Using System Information

How does a computer user find out all the numbers associated with his system's performance? NDW comes to the rescue with a handy utility called System Information.

In this chapter, you learn to perform the following tasks:

- Understand System Information
- Start System Information
- Understand System Information reports

Understanding System Information

System Information is a utility that displays detailed reports about your computer system, including information on disk drives, memory, peripherals, and even benchmark comparisons of your system versus other types of systems. (The benchmark comparison tells you how your system stacks up against the competition.)

More important, however, System Information provides you the basic facts about your computer system that you need if you ever experience problems with your hardware or software, need to call a technical support line, or want to add peripherals or upgrade your system. For the advanced user, System Information also can help you track down system irregularities and fine-tune your system for better performance.

Starting System Information

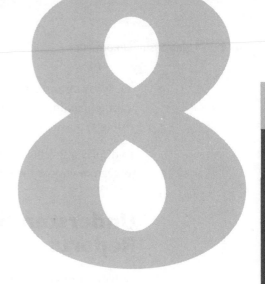

You can launch System Information by using the Desktop menus or from the Desktop Applications group. To start System Information from the menu system, for example, choose the **T**ools S**y**stem Info command. Notice that the System Information window that appears is a sizeable window; you may want to maximize it to full-screen size to make as much of each report as visible as possible.

To display a specific report, click an icon on the System Information's toolbar, or choose the report's name from the **S**ummary pull-down menu.

Understanding System Information Reports

System Information provides 11 separate reports. These reports tell you just about everything you need to know about your system. You can print any report by opening the System Information's **F**ile menu and choosing the **P**rint Report option. You also can save any report to disk for future reference by opening the System Information's **F**ile menu and choosing the **S**ave Report option.

The System Summary

The System Summary lists basic information about various parts of your system, including the computer itself, disk drives, memory, and your operating system (see fig. 28.1). If someone asks what kind of system you have (microprocessor, CPU speed, memory, and so on), this report is the one you want to consult.

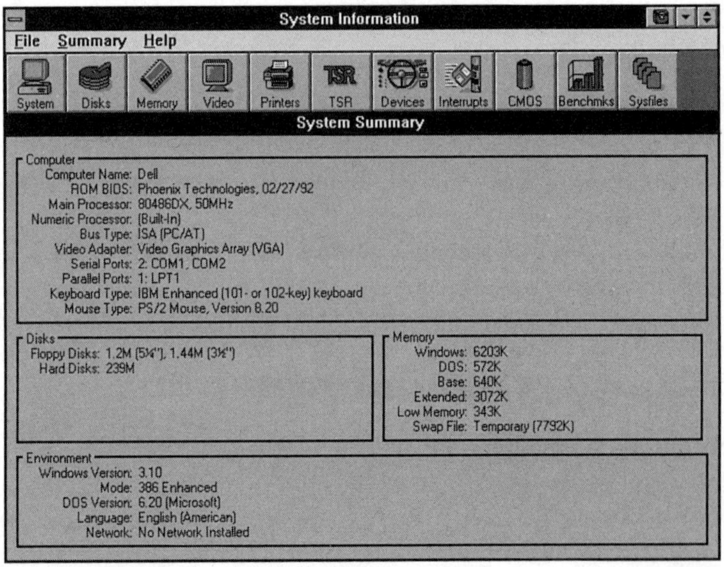

Fig. 28.1
NDW's System Summary report, describing information about your computer system.

The Disk Summary

The initial window of the Disk Summary report is the All Drive Summary (see fig. 28.2). This window displays basic information about the size and unused space available for each fixed drive in your system. (This report excludes floppy disk drives.)

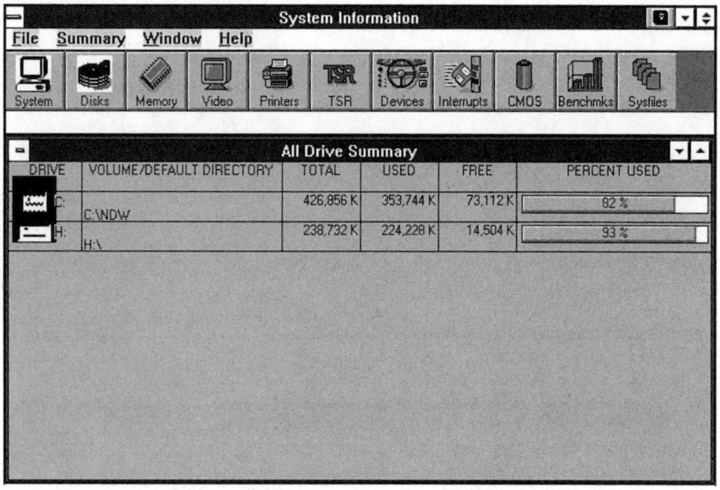

Fig. 28.2
The Disk Summary report's All Drive Summary window provides information about drive usage.

If you double-click an individual Drive icon in this report, a second window appears (see fig. 28.3). The Drive Summary window displays more detailed information about the selected drive.

The Windows Memory Summary

The opening screen of the Windows Memory Summary report is a graphical depiction of the Windows memory used by fonts, device drivers, system libraries, and applications (see fig. 28.4). Each bar displays both discardable and nondiscardable memory. (Discardable memory can be reused; non-discardable memory contains information that must remain in memory at all times.) This window also displays total memory, memory in use, and memory available.

If you click any of the bars in these graphs, additional windows appear. These windows, as shown in figures 28.5, 28.6, 28.7, and 28.8, display more detailed information about these particular items in memory.

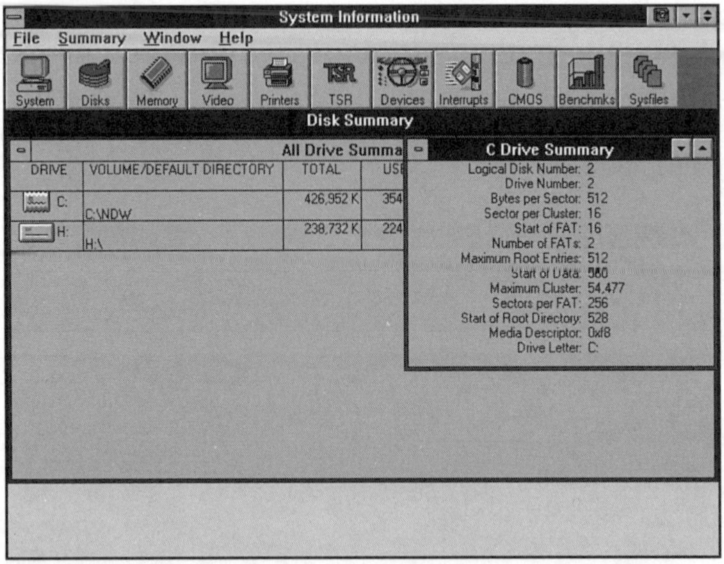

Fig. 28.3
The Drive Summary window, showing a summary report on drive C.

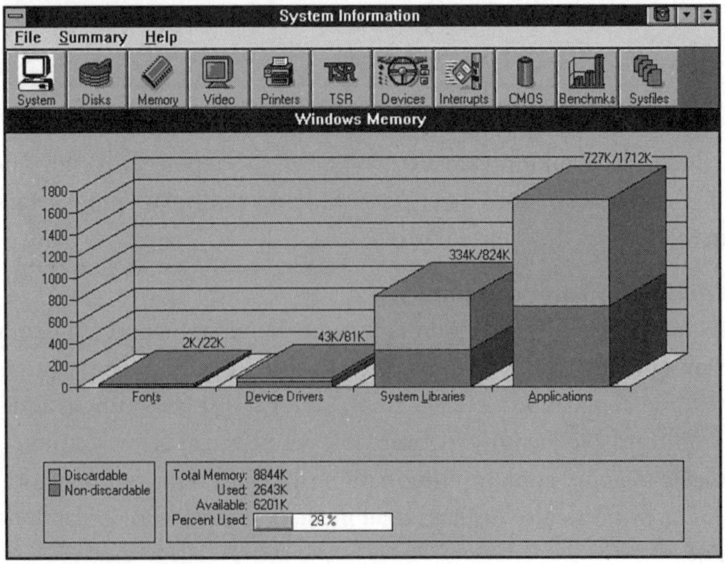

Fig. 28.4
The Windows Memory Summary report displays a graphical memory usage chart.

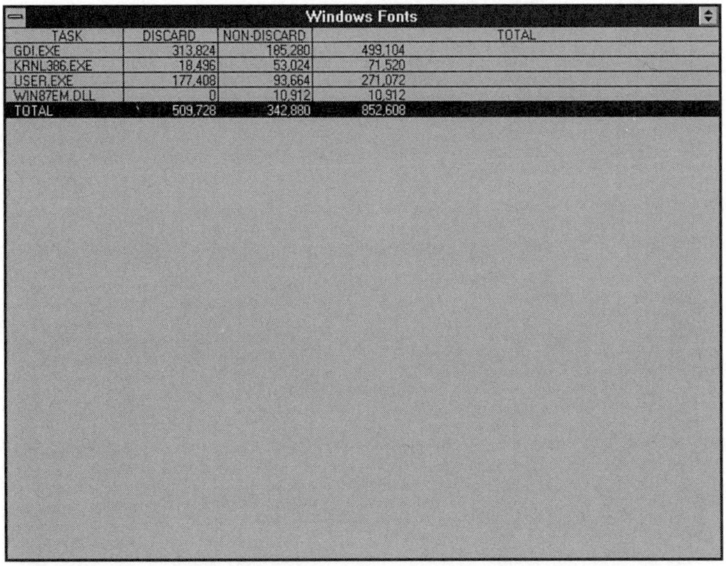

Windows Fonts

TASK	DISCARD	NON-DISCARD	TOTAL
GDI.EXE	313,824	185,280	499,104
KRNL386.EXE	18,496	53,024	71,520
USER.EXE	177,408	93,664	271,072
WIN87EM.DLL	0	10,912	10,912
TOTAL	509,728	342,880	852,608

Fig. 28.5
The Windows Fonts window, listing the font files available in Windows.

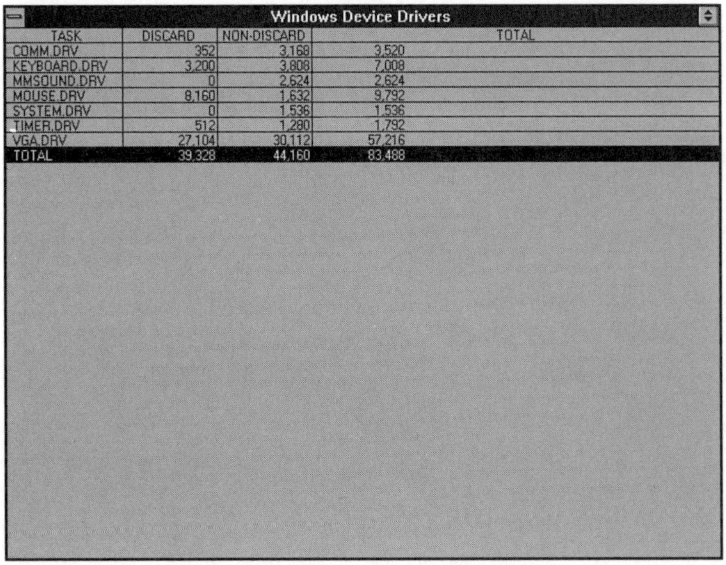

Windows Device Drivers

TASK	DISCARD	NON-DISCARD	TOTAL
COMM.DRV	352	3,168	3,520
KEYBOARD.DRV	3,200	3,808	7,008
MMSOUND.DRV	0	2,624	2,624
MOUSE.DRV	8,160	1,632	9,792
SYSTEM.DRV	0	1,536	1,536
TIMER.DRV	512	1,280	1,792
VGA.DRV	27,104	30,112	57,216
TOTAL	39,328	44,160	83,488

Fig. 28.6
The Windows Device Drivers window, listing the available Windows device drivers.

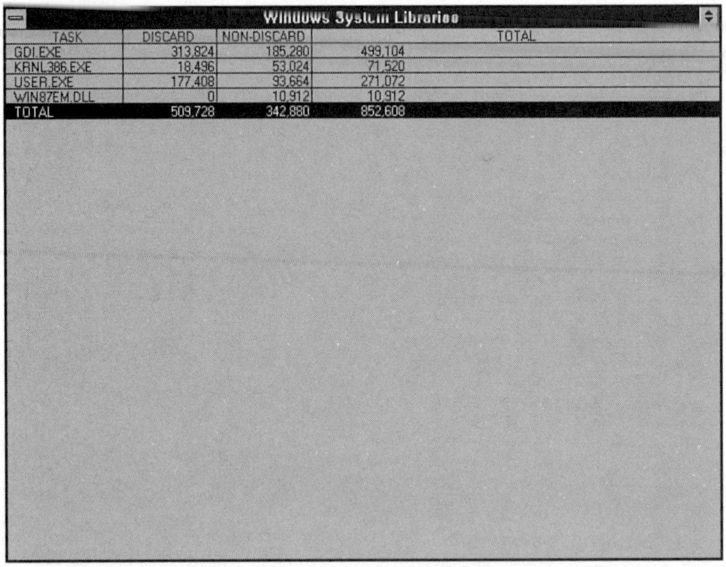

Windows System Libraries

TASK	DISCARD	NON-DISCARD	TOTAL
GDI.EXE	313,824	185,280	499,104
KRNL386.EXE	18,496	53,024	71,520
USER.EXE	177,408	93,664	271,072
WIN87EM.DLL	0	10,912	10,912
TOTAL	509,728	342,880	852,608

Fig. 28.7
The Windows System Libraries window, listing Windows system libraries.

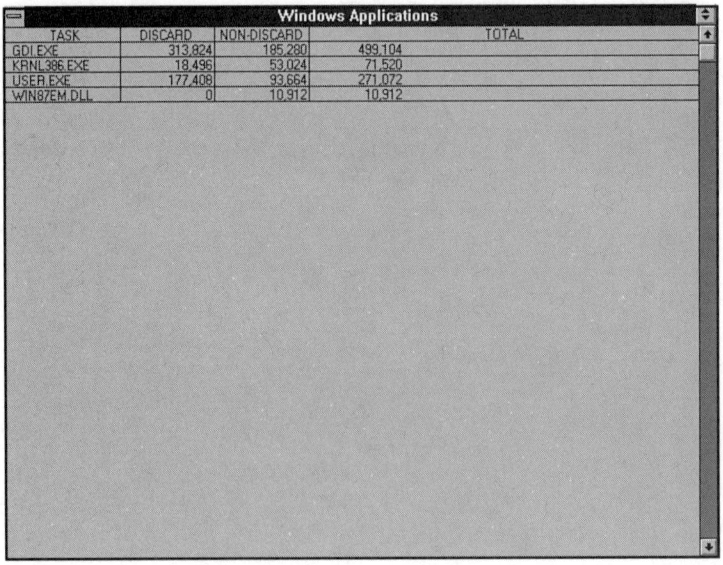

Windows Applications

TASK	DISCARD	NON-DISCARD	TOTAL
GDI.EXE	313,824	185,280	499,104
KRNL386.EXE	18,496	53,024	71,520
USER.EXE	177,408	93,664	271,072
WIN87EM.DLL	0	10,912	10,912

Fig. 28.8
The Windows Applications window, listing available Windows applications files.

The Display Summary

The Display Summary report provides information about your system's video display (see fig. 28.9). Included are data about your video adapter and driver, display characteristics, and display capabilities.

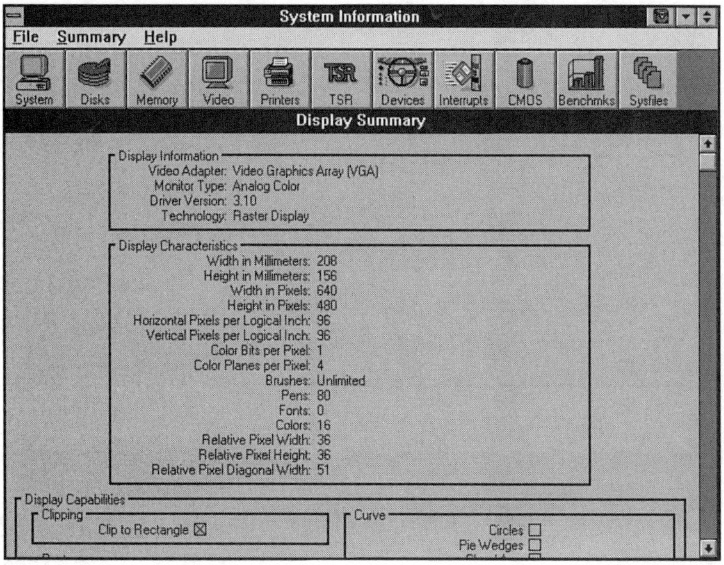

Fig. 28.9
The Display Summary report shows information about the display currently used.

The Printer Summary

The Printer Summary report uses the same criteria used in the Display Summary, but applies it to your currently active printer (see fig. 28.10).

The TSR Summary

The TSR Summary displays information about all terminate-and-stay-resident (TSR) programs loaded in your system's memory before you loaded Windows (see fig. 28.11). Included are programs such as COMMAND.COM and the DOS system area.

The DOS Device Driver Summary

The DOS Device Driver Summary report lists all DOS device drivers that are currently in your system's memory, along with their memory addresses (see fig. 28.12).

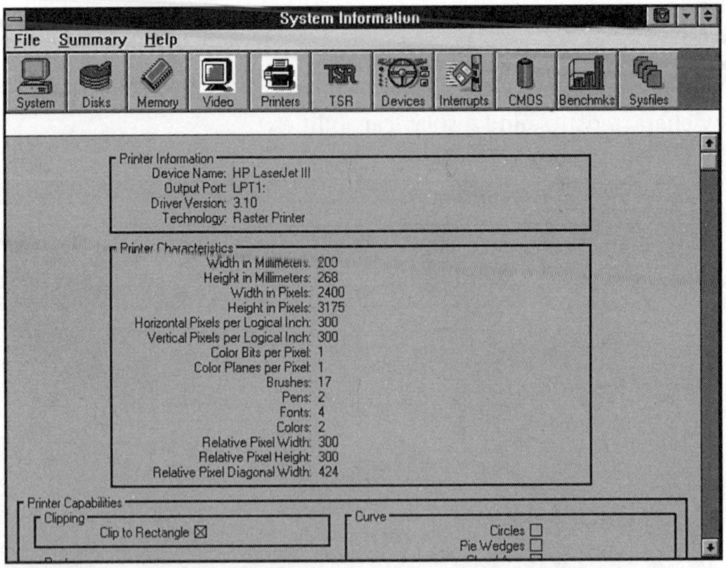

Fig. 28.10
The Printer Summary report displays information about available printers on your system.

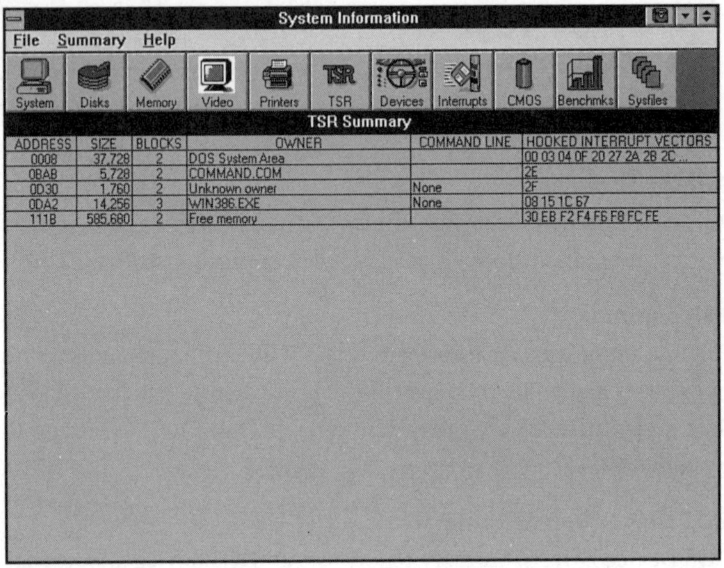

Fig. 28.11
The TSR Summary report lists TSR programs in your system's memory.

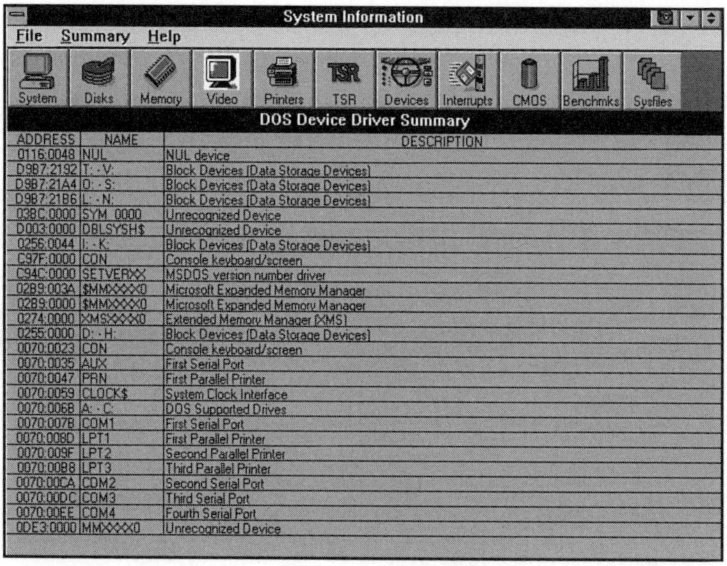

Fig. 28.12
The DOS Device Driver Summary report lists device drivers currently in your system's memory.

The Real Mode Interrupt Summary

The Real Mode Interrupt Summary report lists the real-mode addresses of all software interrupts (see fig. 28.13). This information is important to system-level programmers who need to know which TSR programs and device drivers are intercepting interrupts.

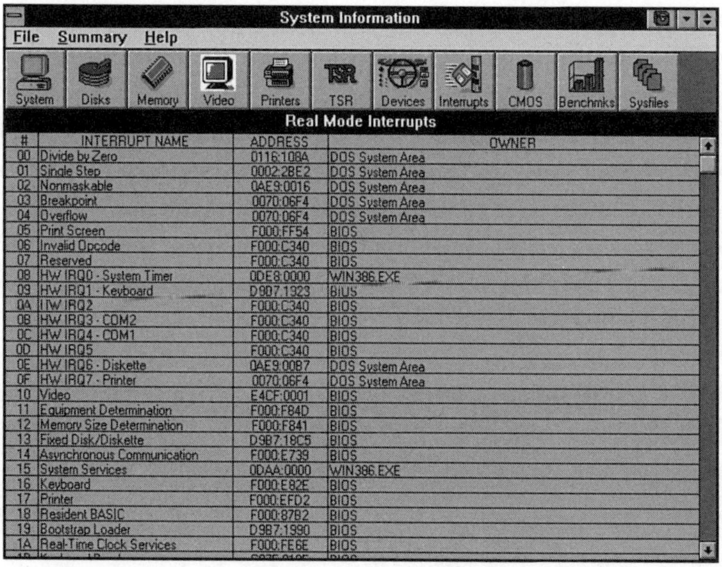

Fig. 28.13
The System Information Real Mode Interrupts report.

The CMOS Summary

Most PCs use a battery-powered CMOS chip to store essential information necessary for your system to function. This report lists the information contained on the CMOS chip and tells you the condition of the battery (see fig. 28.14).

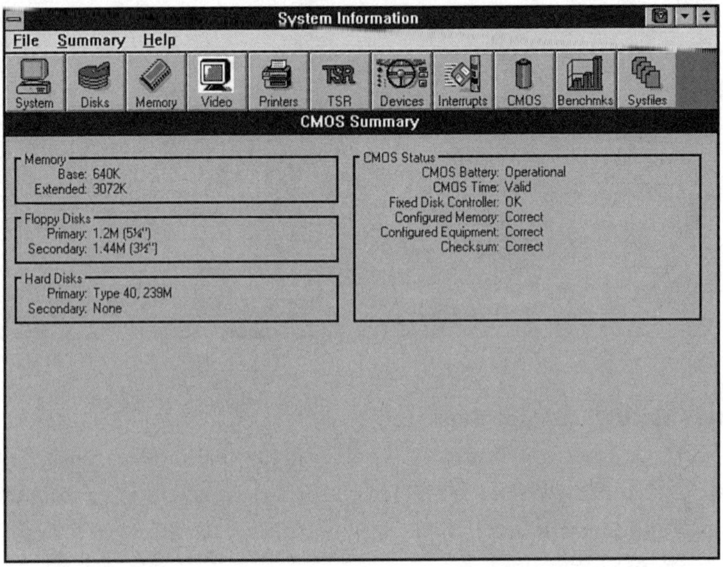

Fig. 28.14
The CMOS Summary report shows the status of your system's CMOS settings.

The Processor Benchmark Tests

The Processor Benchmark Tests report is fun. System Information tests the speed of your CPU and displays a bar chart that compares your CPU's performance to that of an IBM XT computer (an 8088 PC is used as the base system for comparisons), an IBM AT computer (the original 80286 PC), and a Compaq33 computer (a fast 33-MHz 80386 PC). As you can see in figure 28.15, the IBM AT runs 4.4 times faster than the IBM XT; the Compaq33 runs 34.7 times faster than the IBM XT; and the test 80486/50 runs 108.2 times faster than the IBM XT.

Note

External factors, such as moving your mouse (which takes some processor power), can affect the numbers listed in this report.

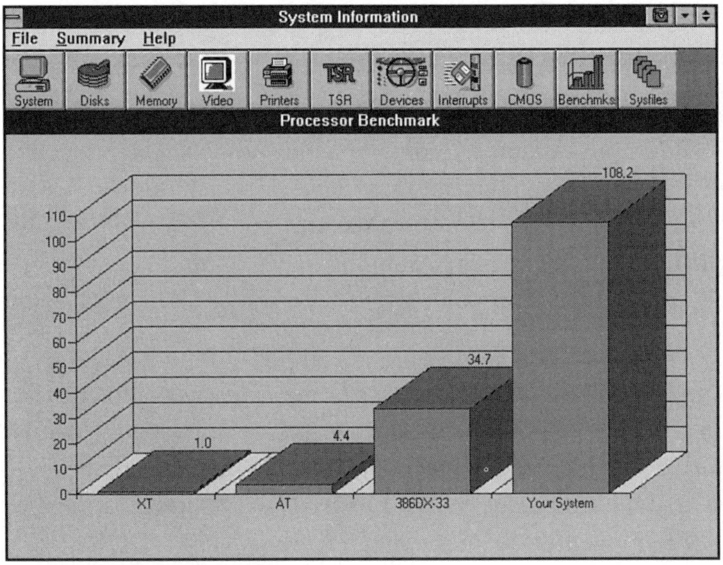

Fig. 28.15
The Processor Benchmark report displays a graph comparing your computer to others.

The Network Disk Information Listing

If you are attached to a network that Norton Desktop recognizes, you can produce reports about your network disks. Figure 28.16 shows the Network Information Overview window.

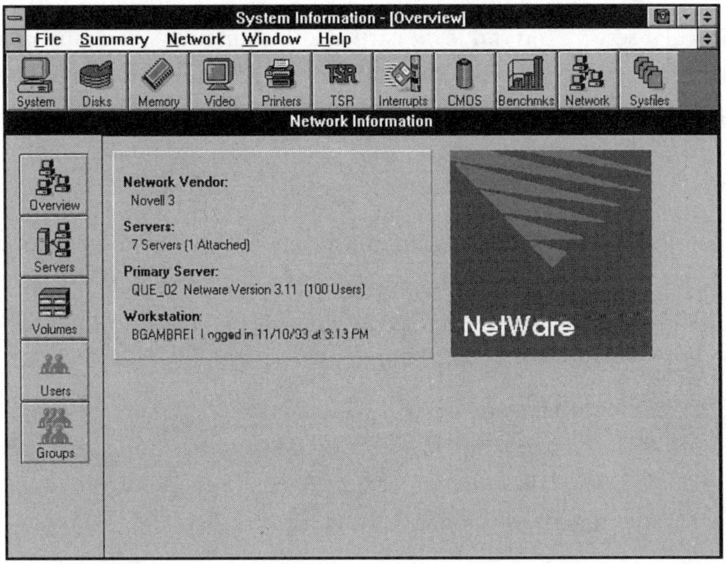

Fig. 28.16
The Network Information report displays information about your system's current network connection.

Notice that attaching your computer to a network adds a Network tool to the toolbar across the top of the System Information window and also adds the **N**etwork menu to the menu bar.

The window in this example informs you that your computer is attached to a Novell 3 network. Seven servers are available, of which this computer is attached to only one (QUE_02), which has 100 total network ports. With the five different windows available from the Network Information window's toolbar, this utility can prove an invaluable resource for network users and administrators.

By using the toolbar down the left side of the screen, you also can view information about each server on the network. This information includes the Netware version used, the number of users supported, the number of users logged in, the number of *volumes* (or hard drives) the server can support, plus additional information about the specific server.

Clicking the Volumes tool from the left-side toolbar displays a window containing information about each volume or drive on a specified network server. This window includes information about the number of directories, the total amount of memory, the number of bytes per sector, the number of sectors per block, and the total free space on the drive.

Clicking the Users tool from the left-side toolbar displays a list of all users on a particular server. You can learn particular information about any user by clicking that particular user's name in the list—Login Name, Login Date, and to which particular groups the user belongs. You can view information about all users, only logged-in users, or only users logged into multiple network servers.

Finally, clicking the Groups tool from the left-side toolbar display enables you to look up information on groups of users. This tool is particularly valuable for viewing the membership of groups. Again, you can view all users or only those users who are logged in.

The Startup Files Listing

The Startup Files report simply lists the contents of five important start-up files, each in a separate window (see fig. 28.17). The files listed in this window are as described in the following list:

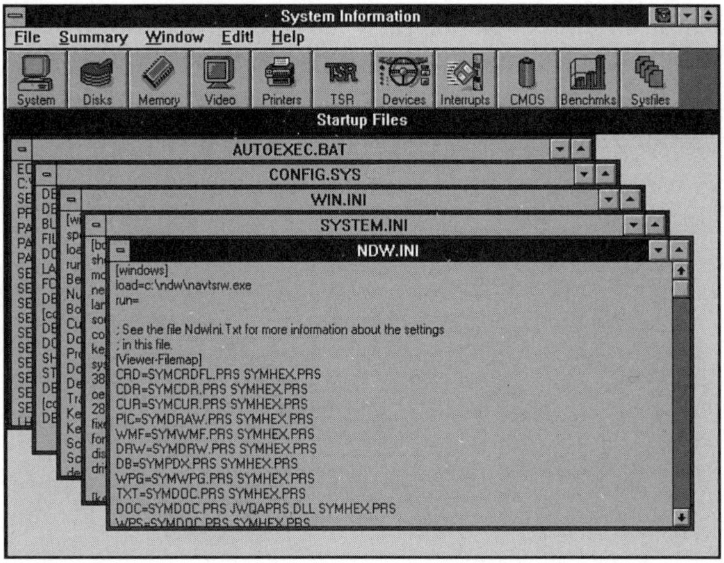

Fig. 28.17
The Startup Files listing displays the contents of several start-up files for DOS and Windows.

- *AUTOEXEC.BAT.* An important batch file read just before DOS turns over control of your system to you. Commands in this file can set your path, change the standard DOS prompt, and install TSR programs.

- *CONFIG.SYS.* The first file read after your system is powered up. Commands in this file install device drivers that control aspects of your system.

- *WIN.INI.* A lengthy file that lists configuration options for Windows and many Windows programs.

- *SYSTEM.INI.* An important file that lists configuration options for many lower-level Windows functions.

- *NDW.INI.* The start-up file for Norton Desktop 3 for Windows and its tools and utilities.

Tip
To edit any of these files, activate the file's window and choose the **T**ool **T**ext Editor command. This command starts the Desktop Editor with the selected file loaded and ready for editing.

Summary

This chapter showed you all you need to know about the System Information utility and all the reports the utility produces. Now you can compare the performances of your friends' and neighbors' systems with yours.

The next chapter, "Using Norton Fix-It and Rescue Disks," discusses the valuable DOS-based utilities on the Norton Fix-It Disks. You learn how to use the Fit It disks and run the DOS version of Norton Disk Doctor, UnErase, UnFormat, and the Emergency Restore Disk.

29

Chapter 29

Using Norton Rescue and Fix-It Disks

The Norton Rescue disk and Fix-It disks contain important utilities that may be invaluable in an emergency. The Rescue disk contains important system information that you can use to restore your computer if you have problems with your settings or disk drive or if your start-up files are damaged. The Fix-It disks contain several DOS-based utilities that can help you recover your hard disk and restore backed up files. Keep your Rescue disk and the Fix-It disks (or copies of the disks) in a safe, accessible place in case you are ever confronted with a hard disk catastrophe.

In this chapter, you learn to perform the following tasks:

- Use the Rescue disk
- Use the Fix-It disks
- Use Speed Disk
- Use UnErase
- Use UnFormat
- Use Emergency Restore

Caution

If you did not create a Rescue disk during the installation of the program, create one now by using the Create Rescue Disk utility in the Norton Desktop Quick Access Group. The Norton Fix-It disks are the last two disks of the original disk set that came with the Norton Desktop for Windows program.

Understanding the Rescue and Fix-It Disks

Although some programs on the Rescue and Fix-It disks are the same, you use the disks for somewhat different purposes. The Rescue disk is primarily used to help restore lost settings on your computer, and the Fix-It disks are used primarily to help recover from virus infections, restore backup files if you cannot access Norton Backup for Windows, and recover your hard disk from logical read and write problems.

The following utilities are included on the Rescue disk:

- *Rescue.* Enables you to restore your hard disk's setup configuration, including the partition tables, boot records, and CMOS values.
- *UnFormat.* If you accidentally format the hard disk, you can use UnFormat to undo the damage.
- *UnErase.* Like SmartErase, UnErase can recover erased files. It sometimes can recover files that SmartErase cannot recover.
- *Norton Disk Doctor.* A DOS-based version of the Norton Disk Doctor for Windows program.

The Rescue disk is a bootable disk that you can use even if your hard disk does not work. The Rescue disk also includes copies of your hard disk's AUTOEXEC.BAT (named AUTOEXEC.SAV) and CONFIG.SYS (named CONFIG.SAV) files.

The following DOS utilities are included on the Fix-It disks:

- DOS version of *Norton Disk Doctor* (*NDD.EXE*). The same as on the Rescue disk.
- DOS version of *Speed Disk* (*SPEEDISK.EXE*). A disk optimizer; run Speed Disk to make a hard disk run faster.
- DOS version of *UnErase* (*UNERASE.EXE*). The same as on the Rescue disk.
- DOS version of *UnFormat* (*UNFORMAT.EXE*). The same as on the Rescue disk.
- DOS version of *Norton AntiVirus* (*NAV.EXE*). Helps you clean virus infections from your hard disk.
- DOS *Norton Backup Restore* (*NRESTORE.EXE*). Restores backed up files if you cannot run Norton Backup for Windows. See Chapter 10, "Restoring Files with Norton Backup and the Fix-It Disk," for more detailed information.
- *Norton Recovery Install* (*NRINST.EXE*). Installs Fix-It disk DOS programs to your hard disk.
- *Norton Emergency Rescue Program* (*RESCUE.EXE*). Enables you to replace CMOS settings on your computer.

Note

The utilities on the Fix-It disks are so valuable that you may want to copy them permanently to your hard disk rather than running them from the Fix-It disks each time. The recommended practice is to copy all files on the Fix-It disks to a separate directory on the hard disk for easier access. You may place them, for example, in a directory named \NTOOLS. You still should keep the original Fix-It disks in a safe place in case of catastrophic hard disk failure.

Using the Rescue Disk

Occasionally, your hard disk may become unbootable or lose some of its information about your computer's setup. This situation can be caused by your battery going dead, a virus infection, or some other software or hardware failure. The Rescue disk often can restore these settings and make your computer run again.

Using the Rescue Disk To Unformat Your Disk

If your hard disk has been accidentally reformatted, all files that existed on the disk are seemingly gone. However, you can use the UnFormat program to attempt to recover this information by taking the following steps:

1. Place the Rescue disk in drive A, and boot your computer.

2. Run the UnFormat program to unformat the hard disk. See the section "Using UnFormat," later in this chapter.

Using Rescue To Unerase Critical Files

If erased, some files on your hard disk can make your computer unbootable or can make Windows unavailable. The files COMMAND.COM, AUTOEXEC.BAT, and CONFIG.SYS in the root directory are essential when you boot your computer. The Files WIN.EXE, WIN.INI, and SYSTEM.INI are among the essential files necessary to run Windows.

If you erase critical files on your hard disk and cannot access SmartErase from Windows, you can use the UnErase program on the Rescue disk to recover these files by following these steps:

1. Place the Rescue disk in drive A, and boot your computer.

2. Run the UnErase program to unerase critical files on your hard disk. See the section "Using UnErase," later in this chapter.

Using the Rescue Disk To Solve Disk Access Problems

Occasionally, your hard disk may become unaccessible or unbootable because important setup information does not load. If your hard disk was not reformatted, but cannot be accessed or is having read and write problems, follow these steps:

1. Place the Rescue disk in your drive A and boot your computer.
2. Use the Norton Disk Doctor to analyze and attempt to recover your hard disk.

Like Norton Disk Doctor for Windows, this DOS version of Norton Disk Doctor runs numerous diagnostic tests on the hard disk and warns you of existing or pending problems. NDD also enables you to repair certain physical faults. Run Disk Doctor if you cannot access windows (to run NDDW) and you have trouble accessing a disk, if you have problems while trying to run applications, if disk access time mysteriously slows, if the computer does not boot, or if other unexplainable problems occur.

Using the Rescue Disk To Restore Important Settings

If the Norton Disk Doctor is unable to recover your disk, run the Rescue program by following these steps:

1. Boot the computer by using the Rescue disk, if you have not already done so.
2. After the computer boots, type **RESCUE** at the DOS prompt, and press Enter. The Rescue Disk menu appears (see fig. 29.1).

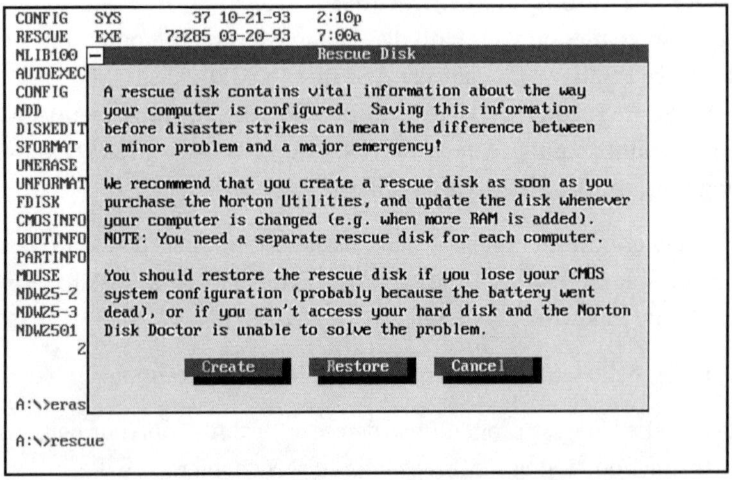

Fig. 29.1
The Rescue Disk menu enables you to create a rescue disk or restore information to your computer.

3. From the menu, choose **R**estore. The Restore Rescue Information dialog box appears (see fig. 29.2). On this menu, you can choose what information to restore—CMOS information, Boot Records, or Partition Tables. The following table describes when to choose each of these items.

Option	Description
CMOS	Choose if your computer has lost information because of a battery failure.
Boot Records	Choose if your computer does not boot or if you cannot access your disk.
Partition Tables	Choose if your hard disk has lost partition information.

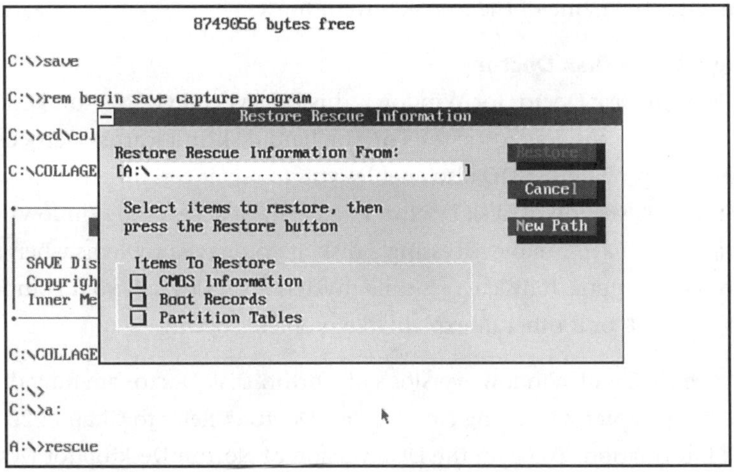

Fig. 29.2
The Restore Rescue Information dialog box enables you to choose what information to restore.

If you are unsure what problem has occurred, restore all three items.

Tip
If you change information on your hard disk, such as your AUTOEXEC.BAT or CONFIG.SYS, you may want to re-create your Rescue disk so that it is current.

Caution

If your hardware changes at any time, make sure that you create a new Rescue disk. Using an old Rescue disk from an old hardware setup can damage your system.

Using the Fix-It Disks

The Fix-It disks are primarily for use when your computer is bootable but you cannot access your Windows program for some reason. The Fix-It disks contain DOS versions of important Norton tools that can help solve disk problems. Some of the same programs exist on the Fix-It disks and the Rescue disk, and which disk you use does not matter. The following sections describe how to use the DOS-based utilities on your Fix-It disks.

You can run these tools either from your hard disk or from a floppy disk. If you are running the tool from your hard disk's DOS prompt, first change to the directory containing the tools by using the CD command. To change to the \NTOOLS subdirectory, for example, type the following line at the DOS prompt, and then press Enter:

CD \NTOOLS

Then enter the name of the tool you want to use.

Using Norton Disk Doctor

Like Norton Disk Doctor for Windows, this DOS version of Norton Disk Doctor runs numerous diagnostic tests on the hard disk and warns of any existing or pending problems. NDD also enables you to repair certain physical faults. Run the DOS version of Disk Doctor if you cannot access the Windows version and you have trouble accessing a disk, if you have problems when trying to run applications, if disk access time mysteriously slows, if your computer does not boot, or if other unexplainable problems occur.

Both the DOS and Windows versions of Norton Disk Doctor are fully discussed in Chapter 20, "Using Norton Disk Doctor." Refer to Chapter 20 for more information. To begin the DOS version of Norton Desktop for DOS, type **NDD** at the DOS prompt, and press Enter.

Using Speed Disk

Your hard disk is constantly changing. Old data is erased and new data is written to empty areas of your disk virtually every minute a PC is in use. This constant shuffling of data scrambles any neat, orderly arrangement the data once may have occupied. The more you use a PC, the more the data is likely to be scrambled.

If you need to optimize your hard disk but cannot access the Windows version of Speed Disk, use the DOS version included on your Fix-It disks. The program runs essentially the same as described in Chapter 26, "Using Speed Disk." To begin the DOS version of Speed Disk, type **SPEEDISK** at the DOS prompt, and press Enter.

Using UnErase

In Chapter 25, "Using SmartErase," you learned how to use SmartCan to create a trash can for recently deleted files and how to recover files by using SmartErase. If SmartErase cannot completely recover deleted files, however, you must rely on UnErase, which you can find on the Fix-It disks.

UnErase is a DOS-based utility program on the Norton Fix-It disks. You *must* run UnErase from the DOS prompt.

UnErase is quite similar to the unerase portion of SmartErase. If the files you want to recover are not yet overwritten, UnErase's automatic function works like SmartErase's unerase function. UnErase goes beyond SmartErase, however, in its capability to manually reconstruct files that are only partially overwritten.

UnErase's manual reconstruction attempts to recover a file on a cluster-by-cluster basis. Because clusters often are fragmented across an entire hard disk, this experience can be time-consuming. Think of a hard disk as a giant jigsaw puzzle—UnErase must find and assemble all the right pieces in the right order.

Manual recovery is the choice of last resort and recommended only for advanced users. If done right, you can recover otherwise unrecoverable data. If done wrong, you end up with a scrambled mass of data passing itself off as a file. Use manual UnErase only if absolutely necessary—and with caution.

Tip
Always try to recover files automatically before attempting manual reconstruction. If automatic recovery is unsuccessful, use manual recovery.

Starting UnErase

To start UnErase, you must exit Windows, insert the desired Fix-It disk, and then follow these steps:

1. Change to the floppy disk drive that contains the Fix-It disk. If the Fix-it disk is in drive A, for example, type **A:** and press Enter.

2. At the DOS prompt, type **UNERASE** and press Enter. The main UnErase screen appears (see fig. 29.3).

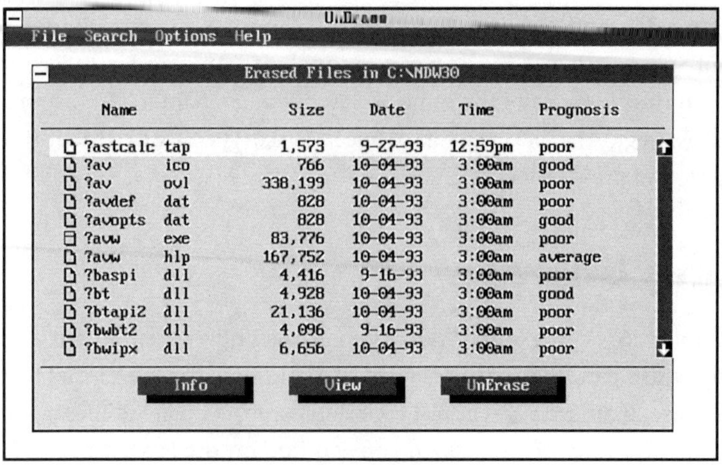

Fig. 29.3
The main UnErase screen, showing files that are candidates to be unerased.

Automatically Recovering Deleted Files

Recovering deleted files by using the UnErase automatic function is identical to using the unerase function in SmartErase.

Tip
Use SmartErase to automatically unerase files while in Windows. You need to use the DOS-based automatic UnErase only if SmartErase doesn't do the job; UnErase is a more powerful—and more complicated—utility.

To unerase files, follow these general steps:

1. Identify the deleted file you want to unerase.

2. Choose the UnErase option.

3. Fill in the missing first character of the file name, if required.

4. Initiate the unerase procedure.

You navigate through the directories in UnErase as you do in a Norton drive window. You also can instruct UnErase to display all deleted files on your hard disk by opening the **F**ile menu and choosing the View **A**ll Directories option.

The file list of deleted files displays a Prognosis column. Files with an excellent prognosis can be unerased automatically; files with a poor prognosis must be unerased manually.

Manually Recovering Deleted Files

You must manually recover files if automatic UnErase or SmartErase is unsuccessful. The procedure to recover files manually is complex and not guaranteed to work in all situations. Remember that overwritten data cannot be recovered no matter what method you use.

To use manual UnErase, follow these steps:

1. Open the **F**ile menu and choose the **M**anual UnErase option. The Manual UnErase window appears.

2. After you are prompted to do so, type the missing first character of the file name.

3. Choose the Add Clusters option. The Add Clusters dialog box appears.

4. Choose the All Clusters option. The manual UnErase window reappears.

5. Use the View File option to view the contents of the file being recovered. If the file is complete, choose the Save option. If the file is not complete, choose the Add Clusters option to return to the Add Clusters dialog box. From here you can add the Next Probable Cluster, use the Data Search option to search for clusters that contain key text, or enter a Cluster Number directly.

6. After you finish the recovery process, choose the Save option in the Manual UnErase window.

Step 5 is the critical step. You may need to switch between the Manual UnErase window and the Add Clusters dialog box several times to effect a complete recovery, alternately viewing the file and searching for clusters to add to the file. You also may need to delete clusters that do not belong in the file; just highlight the cluster in the Added Clusters List in the Manual UnErase window, and then press Del. You also can rearrange clusters by dragging them to new positions within the Added Clusters List. As you can see, Manual UnErase is not a process for the timid.

Using UnFormat

UnFormat enables you to recover an entire hard disk that was reformatted or damaged. Like UnErase, UnFormat is a DOS-based utility that needs exclusive access to the hard disk to function correctly; you cannot run UnFormat in Windows.

To understand how UnFormat works, you first must understand what happens when a disk is formatted. The DOS FORMAT command wipes clean the system area of your hard disk but does not overwrite the actual data present in the data area of the disk. The system area contains the root directory, the boot record, and the File Allocation Table (FAT), which *point* to files in the data area. After a disk is formatted, therefore, the system area reports no data present, although data still may exist in the data area of the disk.

Note

UnFormat usually works only on fixed disks, not on floppy disks. Until DOS version 5, the standard DOS FORMAT command erased all data on a floppy disk, making unformatting impossible. If you use NDW's Format Diskette command or the FORMAT command of DOS version 5 or later, however, you can perform a Safe Format on floppy disks, which can be unformatted.

UnFormat works much like UnErase, hooking up data not overwritten with the appropriate pointing systems. UnFormat begins by looking for the IMAGE.DAT file, created by the Image program installed with NDW. The IMAGE.DAT file contains a snapshot of a hard disk system area before it was cleared or damaged. If UnFormat locates IMAGE.DAT, it can re-create the lost or damaged system area and reconnect the system area to the data area.

If UnFormat does not find IMAGE.DAT, it tries to reconstruct the system area by using the data in the data area. This attack is like building an index to a book by moving through the contents of the book word-by-word—a long, tedious process, but it works most of the time.

Starting UnFormat

To start UnFormat, you must exit Windows and insert the desired Fix-It disk and follow these steps:

1. Change to the floppy disk drive that contains the Fix-It disk. If the Fix-It Disk is in drive A, for example, type **A:** and press Enter.

2. At the DOS prompt, type **UNFORMAT** and press Enter.

Recovering a Disk by Using UnFormat

After you choose the drive you want to unformat, a dialog box appears that asks if you used IMAGE.EXE or MIRROR.COM to save recovery information (see fig. 29.4). *Always* answer **Y**es in this dialog box. UnFormat searches for the IMAGE.DAT file. If UnFormat doesn't find the file, you must rebuild the system area manually.

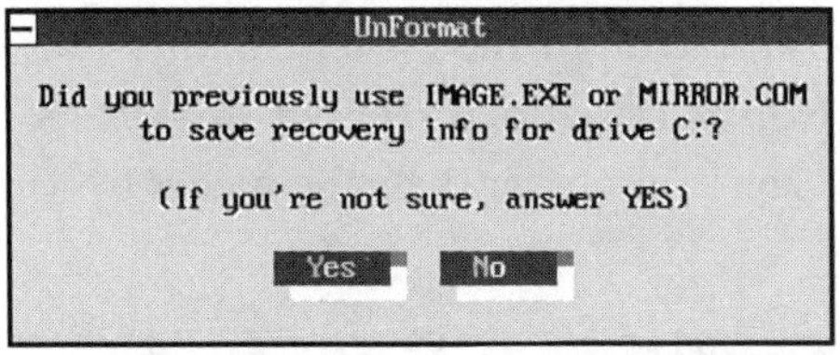

Fig. 29.4
The UnFormat dialog box asking if IMAGE or MIRROR was previously used.

To use the IMAGE.DAT file to unformat a disk, follow these steps:

1. After the dialog box in figure 29.4 appears, choose **Y**es. A dialog box appears and asks if you are sure that you want to unformat the selected disk.

2. Choose **Y**es. If the IMAGE.DAT file is found, a dialog box appears that displays the last time the file was updated. You are given the choice of using the most recent version of IMAGE.DAT or the previous version.

3. If you accidentally reformatted your disk, choose the most recent version. If, however, the disk was damaged or corrupted by a virus, use the previous version of the file to restore your disk to the condition before the damage occurred. A prompt warns you that restoring the disk overwrites any current data.

4. Choose Yes.

5. After you are given the option of performing a full or partial restoration, choose the Full option. UnFormat begins the recovery and displays a progress map.

After the recovery is complete, a message advises you to run Norton Disk Doctor. Exit UnFormat and run the DOS version of Disk Doctor.

Note

Running Norton Disk Doctor is a precautionary procedure in case any physical damage to your disk remains.

If no IMAGE.DAT file is found, UnFormat recovers your disk by reading all information in the data area. The downside to this manual recovery is that UnFormat doesn't know how to label directories and assigns arbitrary names

(DIR0, DIR1, DIR2, and so on), which you then must rename by using drive windows in Norton Desktop. UnFormat also deletes all file names in the root directory. You can recover these file names by using UnErase.

Using Emergency Restore

Emergency Restore is a DOS-based subset of Norton Backup that enables you to restore backed-up files without starting Norton Backup for Windows. Use the Emergency Restore if you cannot use the Norton Desktop Backup for Windows version of the program. See Chapter 10, "Restoring Files with Norton Backup and the Fix-It Disks," for detailed information on this valuable utility.

Summary

This chapter explained the important utilities on the Norton Rescue and Fix-It disks. You learned how to recover lost PC settings; how to recover deleted files by using UnErase; and how to regain use of accidentally formatted disks by using UnFormat. (Remember always to keep a copy of the Rescue and Fix-It disks close at hand; you also may want to keep copies of the programs from the Fix-It disks on your hard disk.)

Part V discusses Norton Desktop's new ScriptMaker utility. The following chapter, "Learning ScriptMaker Basics," shows you the basics of this powerful utility.

Part V

Using ScriptMaker

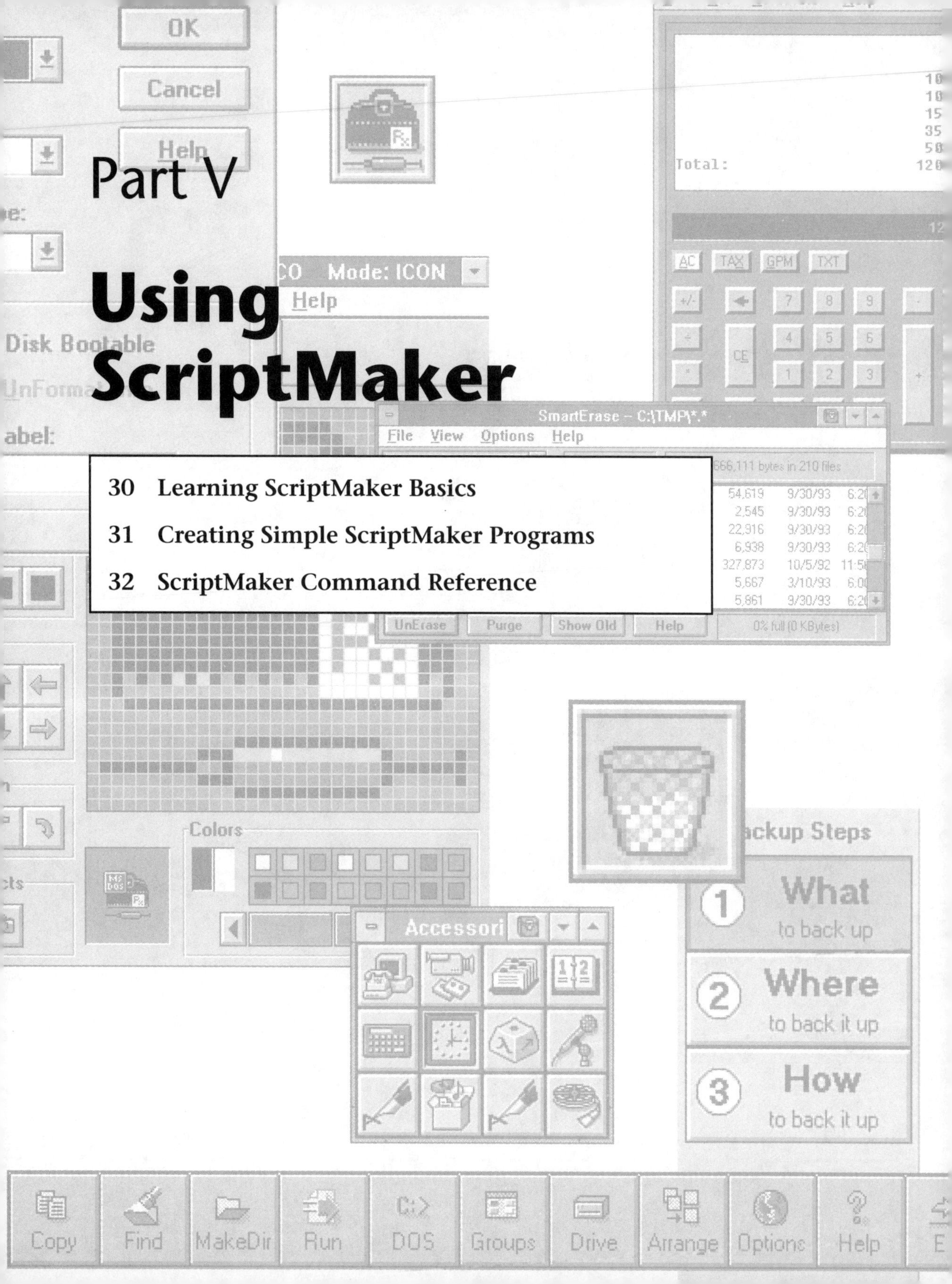

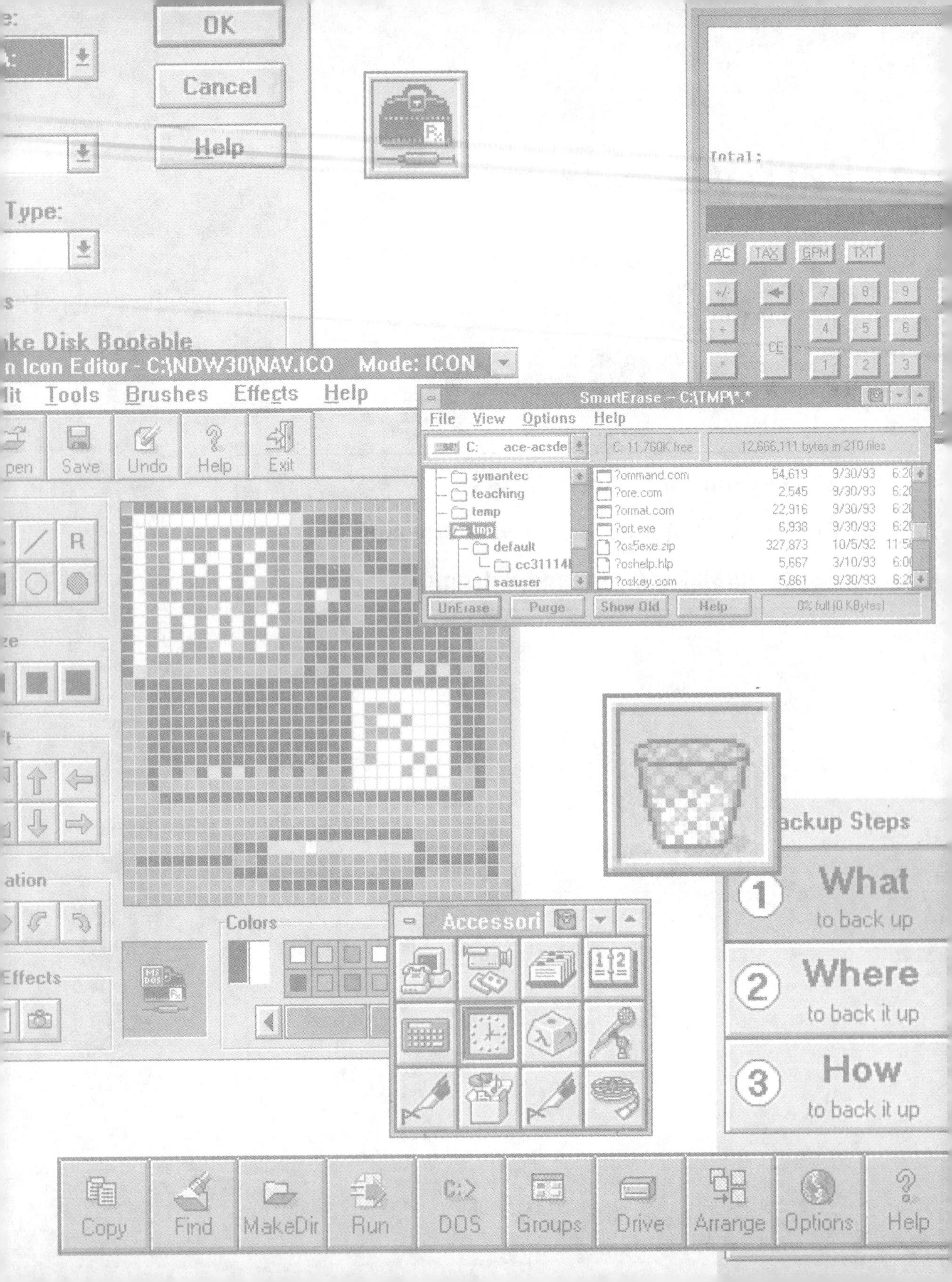

OK
Cancel
Help
Type:
ake Disk Bootable
Total:
AC
TAX
GPM
TXT
n Icon Editor - C:\NDW30\NAV.ICO Mode: ICON
lit Tools Brushes Effects Help
pen Save Undo Help Exit
Colors
ation
Effects
SmartErase – C:\TMP*.*
File View Options Help
C: ace-acsde
C: 11,760K free
12,666,111 bytes in 210 files
symantec
teaching
temp
tmp
default
cc31114
sasuser
?ommand.com 54,619 9/30/93
?ore.com 2,545 9/30/93
?ormat.com 22,916 9/30/93
?ort.exe 6,938 9/30/93
?os5exe.zip 327,873 10/5/92
?oshelp.hlp 5,667 3/10/93
?oskey.com 5,861 9/30/93
UnErase
Purge
Show Old
Help
0% full (0 KBytes)
Accessori
ackup Steps
1 What to back up
2 Where to back it up
3 How to back it up
Copy
Find
MakeDir
Run
DOS
Groups
Drive
Arrange
Options
Help

Chapter 30

Learning ScriptMaker Basics

In this chapter, you learn to perform the following tasks:

- Understand ScriptMaker programs
- Understand ScriptMaker
- Understand the ScriptMaker language
- Use the Macro Recorder with ScriptMaker
- Use the Dialog Editor

In the DOS environment, users have long been accustomed to creating *batch files* to automate their work. DOS batch files string a series of commands together into a single file, which can then be executed like a regular program. Unfortunately, no Windows equivalent of a batch file has been included in Windows.

Norton Desktop 3 for Windows, however, includes a program called *ScriptMaker* that enables you to create programs for the Windows environment. ScriptMaker comes with its own language based on the Visual Basic standard, comprised of a series of commands and functions that can perform Windows operations automatically. If you string together a series of these commands, you create a program.

ScriptMaker program files can be edited by using any ASCII text editor; ScriptMaker, however, includes its own editing environment (based on NDW's Desktop Editor), which comes complete with an on-line reference of ScriptMaker commands. Creating a ScriptMaker program is as easy as writing a few lines of "code" and then compiling and saving the file. Norton Desktop can then run these programs just as it can any other application.

Note

Previous versions of Norton Desktop for Windows included a program enabling you to create your own batch procedures. This program was called Batch Builder. NDW version 3.0 introduces a different program, ScriptMaker, which uses a Visual Basic-type language to enable you to write Windows procedures and programs.

Understanding ScriptMaker Programs

ScriptMaker *programs* are made up of a series of *command lines*; the commands combine to form a single executable file that can be started just like a regular program. Each line in a program executes a single command or operation. After you start a program, each of the commands is executed, line by line.

The Norton Desktop program language, ScriptMaker, consists of more than 300 separate functions and commands based on the commonly known Visual Basic language. The commands enable you to do everything from arranging icons and displaying message boxes to modifying INI files and establishing DDE links. You use whichever functions and commands are necessary to achieve the results you seek.

ScriptMaker files are actually ASCII text files. You can read, edit, or create a program by using any ASCII text editor, including NDW's Desktop Editor or the Windows Notepad. As you look at a program, you can read it just as you do any system file. After the files are compiled, they become EXE files and can be run just as can any other Windows program file.

Why would you want to use these programs? Simply, to increase your productivity. Any time you need to perform a complex task more than once, you should consider automating that task by using a ScriptMaker program. Programs eliminate the need to type multiple lines of complex commands or perform complicated mouse or keyboard operations. Programs simplify your Windows computing.

Understanding ScriptMaker

ScriptMaker is nothing more than a tool you can use to create Windows programs. Although you can create program code by using any ASCII text editor, ScriptMaker is more than just a text editor; it includes a number of features designed to make creating and editing ScriptMaker files easier, and it includes the capability to compile the program code into an executable file.

Open ScriptMaker by choosing the **T**ools Sc**r**iptMaker command. The ScriptMaker editing window appears, as shown in figure 30.1.

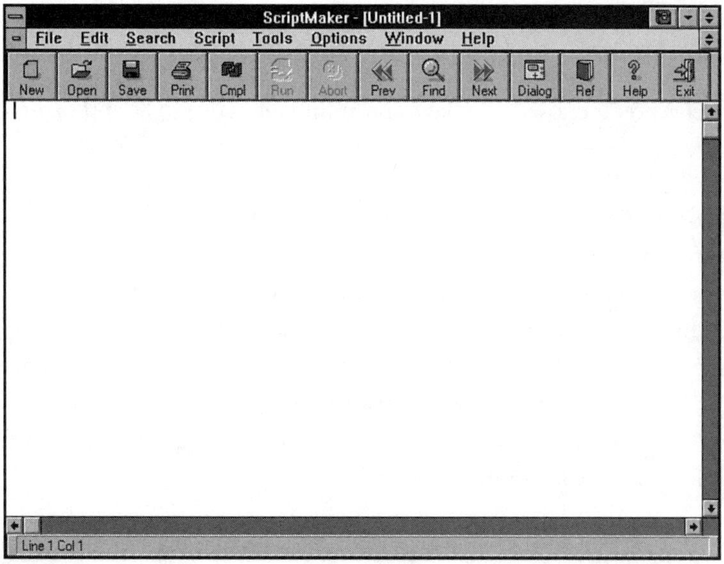

Fig. 30.1
The ScriptMaker editing window enables you to write ScriptMaker programs.

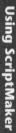

The ScriptMaker editor is essentially the Desktop Editor utility with some ScriptMaker specific features added. The items on the **F**ile, **E**dit, **S**earch, **O**ptions, **W**indow, and **H**elp menus are all identical to the same menus in Desktop Editor. In fact, except for ScriptMaker-specific functions, the ScriptMaker editor operates identically to the Desktop Editor. (Refer to Chapter 16,"Using Desktop Editor," for more information on Desktop Editor functions.)

The script-specific features are located on the **T**ools and S**c**ript menus. The four options on the Sc**r**ipt menu are as described in the following list:

- ***C****ompile*. Turns the ScriptMaker program code into an executable file. Reports if any errors in the program code are found.
- ***R****un*. Runs a compiled program.
- ***A****bort*. Cancels a running program.
- *Save* ***E****xe*. Saves the compile code as an EXE program.

The three options on the **T**ools menu are as described in the following list:

- ***R****ecorder*. Turns on the Macro recorder, enabling you to capture commands to be placed into a program. Recording a Macro is covered later in this chapter.

- *Dialog Editor*. Enables you to build a dialog box that can then be placed into a script.
- *Reference*. If chosen, displays an on-line reference to ScriptMaker commands.

Displaying Commands and Functions by Using the Reference Dialog Box

One of the most useful functions of ScriptMaker is its capability to display an on-screen reference to ScriptMaker commands. To activate the on-screen reference, click the Ref icon on the toolbar or select the **T**ools Re**f**erence command. The Reference dialog box appears (see fig. 30.2). Notice that you cannot minimize or maximize this window, and it always appears on top of other Norton Desktop windows.

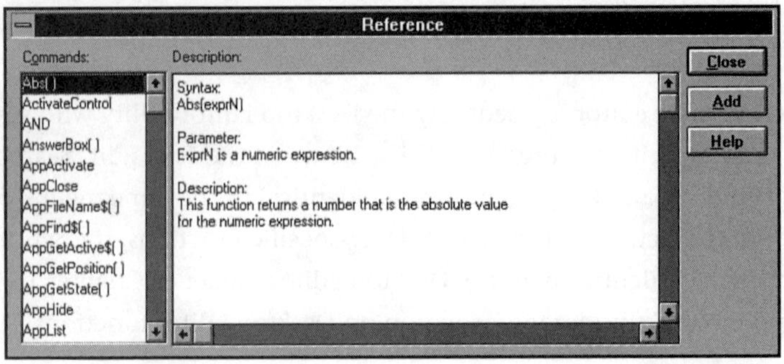

Fig. 30.2
The Reference dialog box enables you to look up the meanings of ScriptMaker commands.

The Reference dialog box is divided into two parts. The scrolling C**o**mmands list displays all commands available in the ScriptMaker language. The Description box displays information about the selected command. Included in this information is the command itself, a brief description of what the command does, the correct syntax for the command, and a brief example of the command in use.

You also can use the Reference dialog box to paste commands directly into your ScriptMaker files. This feature is discussed after the following section.

Tip
Keep the Reference dialog box on-screen as you work with ScriptMaker as an invaluable tool for finding the right command for your programs.

Creating and Editing a Script

Creating a ScriptMaker file is as easy as typing commands in a text file line by line. To demonstrate, you can create a simple three-line program. This file displays a message box on-screen and waits for the user to choose OK.

In the ScriptMaker window, as shown in figure 30.3, enter the lines of code necessary to create the following simple program:

```
Sub Main()
    MsgBox "Press OK to Close",0,"Test Message"
End Sub
```

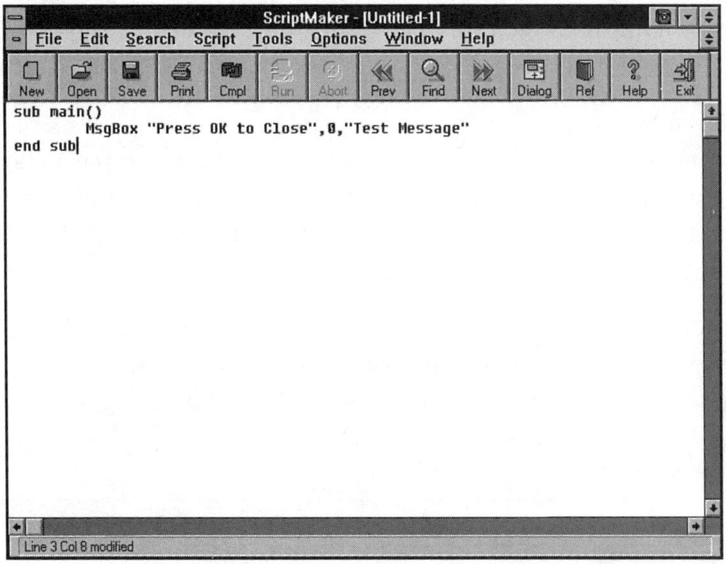

Fig. 30.3
A simple three-line program entered in the ScriptMaker window.

This three line program executes the message box command (`MsgBox`). This command creates a message box that displays a message until the user clicks the OK button. You define both the message and the title of the message box.

All programs begin with the statement `Sub Main()` and end with `End Sub`. The text following the `MsgBox` command consists of *parameters*. In this case, the first parameter (`"Press OK to Close"`) creates the text that appears in the message box. The `0` indicates what kind of message box is to appear. In this case, the message box is a box containing only one option, an OK button. The third parameter (`"Test Message"`) creates the title for the message box.

Note

See Chapter 32, "ScriptMaker Command and Function Reference," for a complete listing of ScriptMaker commands and functions.

Pasting Functions and Commands from the Reference Dialog Box

In addition to typing functions and commands into the ScriptMaker editing window, you also can paste them into the window from the Reference dialog box. Using the preceding example, you switch to the Reference dialog box, scroll down the C**o**mmands list to highlight the `MsgBox` command, and then choose the **A**dd button. ScriptMaker automatically adds the word `MsgBox` to the current line in the edit window, leaving the cursor at the end of the line so that you can type in whatever parameters you want to give the command.

Testing a Script

How do you know whether your program works? The easiest way to find out is to test it. To test the file, click the Cmpl icon on the toolbar or select the S**c**ript **C**ompile command. ScriptMaker goes through the file line by line and runs each command and function, alerting you if it finds any errors.

In the case of the sample file, you have only one line to execute. If no errors are found, a message tells you that the compile was successful. To run the program, click the Run icon or choose S**c**ript **R**un. The message dialog box shown in figure 30.4 appears on-screen.

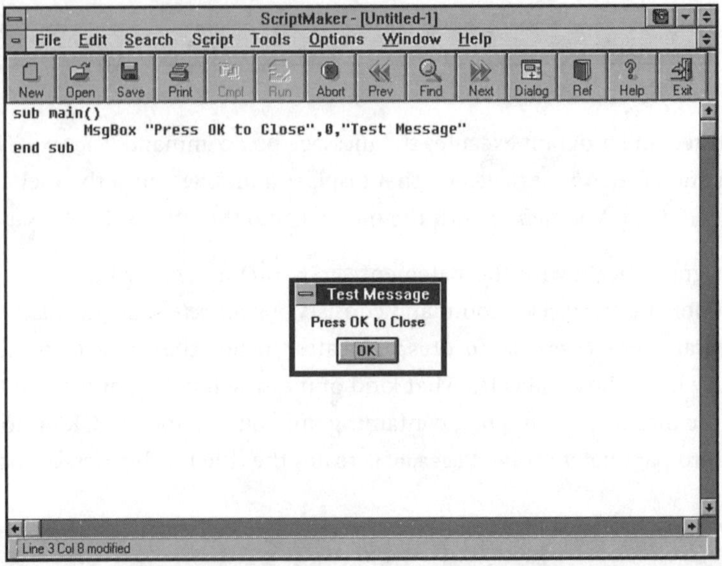

Fig. 30.4
The Test Message dialog box displays a message from your first program.

Saving a ScriptMaker File

If you are certain that your file is working correctly, save the program code as a file. Select the **F**ile Save **A**s command to assign a new file name for the file;

save the file with an SM (sample) extension. Save this sample file under the following name:

TEST1.SM

If you are resaving an existing file, choose the **F**ile **S**ave command or click the Save icon on the toolbar.

You also can save your script as compiled code and as an executable file by choosing S**c**ript **S**ave Code (save as an SMC file) and S**c**ript Save **E**XE (save as an EXE file). You can save the program as compiled code or as an executable file only after you successfully compile the program. Compile and save the sample program as TEST1.EXE.

Printing a ScriptMaker Program

You may want to create a printout of your program so that you can analyze it away from your computer. To print a copy of the file, choose the **F**ile **P**rint command, or click the Print icon on the toolbar.

Running a ScriptMaker Program

After your file is complete, compiled, and saved as an EXE file, you can run it the same as you run any other application: You can double-click its name in a drive window, create a Desktop icon, or use the **F**ile **R**un command. As with any application, you also can assign the file to the Launch List via the Launch Manager.

For this example, select the **F**ile **R**un command. After you are prompted for the file name, enter **TEST1.EXE**, and choose OK.

This example is very simple, but it introduces you to basic ScriptMaker operations. The following section introduces you to the essentials of the ScriptMaker language.

Understanding the ScriptMaker Language

The ScriptMaker language is a programming language—or a foreign language, for that matter. To use it correctly, you must know what all its words mean and how to use them correctly. You must know both definitions and syntax. After you master this knowledge, you can create wonderfully complex programs to automate a wide variety of Windows operations. If you know something about the BASIC language or Visual Basic, you should find the ScriptMaker language fairly simple to use.

The ScriptMaker language includes the following components: *variables, operators, commands,* and *comments.* Each line in a program is composed of one or more of these components. The following sections explain what these components are and how they are used.

Understanding Variables

A *variable* is an item used to store variable information. Just as you used *x* as a common variable in high-school algebra equations, ScriptMaker uses variables to receive information returned from specific commands and functions. A variable may be assigned either integers or strings by using the equal sign (=), as shown in the following example:

```
x = 400
a$ = "This is a test."
```

The variable `x` holds the numeric value 400 and the variable `a$` holds the string value `"This is a test."`

Before a variable can be used to hold a value, it must be *declared.* The following script line declares the variable `x` as a numeric variable at the same time the value `400` is assigned to the variable name:

```
x = 400
```

The preferred programming practice is to declare variable types before using them. The `Dim` statement is used to declare variables. The following statements, for example, declare the two variables `x` and `a$`:

```
Dim x
Dim a$
```

The variable `x` is numeric and the variable `a$` is declared a string variable because of the appended dollar sign ($). The restrictions on variable names are as described in the following list:

- They must begin with a letter.
- They can contain only letters, digits, or underscores (_).
- They cannot exceed 255 characters in length.
- They cannot be a *reserved word.*

Note

A reserved word is any word that is used as a command or function. A list of commands and functions appears in Chapter 32, "ScriptMaker Command and Function Reference."

Understanding Constants

A *constant* is a piece of data that is not changeable. A constant can be an *integer* (a whole number, positive or negative, on which mathematical operations can be performed) or a *string* (a series of characters enclosed within quotation marks).

One of the most common examples of a constant is a *text string*. In the example earlier in this chapter, you entered the text string `"Press OK to Close"` as a parameter for the `Message` command. This string of characters, enclosed in quotation marks, is a constant. More formally, a constant is defined toward the beginning of a script by using the keyword `Const`. The following lines, for example, are two constant declarations:

```
Const cDataBasename = "C:\MYDATA.DB"
Const cTHOUSAND = 1000
```

The constant `cDataBasename` is a string constant, because the variables assigned to it are a string. The constant `cTHOUSAND` is numeric. These two constants can now be used in the script. Constants are never declared inside procedures or functions.

Understanding Operators

Operators are items that cause operations to be performed, normally on integers. The plus and minus signs (+ and -), for example, are operators that cause addition and subtraction operations to be performed. The following statements, for example, result in the variable `x` containing the value `400`, the variable `y` containing the value `500`, and the variable `z` containing the value `2`:

```
x = 400
y = x + 100
z = x /200
```

Table 30.1 lists the operators available with the ScriptMaker language.

Table 30.1 ScriptMaker Operators

Operator	Operation
+	Addition
-	Subtraction
*	Multiplication
^	Raise a number to a power
/	Division
\	Division
MOD	Modulo
=	Equals
>	Greater than
>=	Greater than or equal to
<	Less than
<>	Not equal
<=	Less than or equal to
AND	Logical AND
NOT	Logical NOT
OR	Logical OR
XOR	Logical XOR

Understanding Commands

Commands are at the heart of the ScriptMaker language. They can be categorized into four basic types: *functions*, *subroutines*, *constructs*, and *operators*. Operators were covered in the preceding section. All the ScriptMaker commands are described in Chapter 32, "ScriptMaker Command and Function Reference."

Functions are used in ScriptMaker to enter or return values and perform operations in programs. The function `val`, for example, can be used to convert a string to a number, as in the following line:

```
a = val("123")
```

In this case, the input into the function is the string `"123"`. The function `val` transforms the input `"123"` into a number `123` and assigns that number to the variable `a`. Notice that this function has string input and a value output. From the list in Chapter 32, you can easily identify functions because the name is followed by parentheses `()`. In a script, a function always appears to the right side of an equal sign (=).

Subroutines execute processes. They do not return a value as does a function. The command `BEEP`, for example, causes your computer's speaker to sound a beep. The `MsgBox` command used earlier (not to be confused with the `MsgBox()` function) is a subroutine. Three parameters were passed to the subroutine, and the subroutine used that information to display a message.

Constructs (or *logical constructs*) are used to decide a course of action within the program. Perhaps the most commonly used construct is the `if...then...else...end` if construct, as shown in the following example:

```
If answer = 1 then
   MsgBox "You answered 1",0,"Message"
else
   MsgBox "You did not answer 1",0,"Message"
end if
```


The "action" taken in this example is determined by the value of the variable answer. Other commonly used *flow-control constructs* are `For...Next` and `While...Wend`. See Chapter 32 for more information about flow control, and choose the Ref icon on the ScriptMaker toolbar for the specific syntax and usage of these constructs.

Understanding Comments

Comments are nonexecutable lines added to ScriptMaker files for descriptive purposes. A comment line starts with a single quote (') or with the keyword `REM`. Any information after the single quote is regarded as a comment, as in the following examples:

```
' This is a comment
REM This is a comment
```

For multiple comment lines, using `/*` and `*/` is often preferable to using `'` or `REM`, as in the following example:

```
/* This is a beginning line of a multi-line comment.
   The comment can go on for several lines.
   Finally, the next line ends the comment.
*/
```

Tip
Use comments in your programs to notate your procedures for future reference.

Understanding Syntax

You cannot operate ScriptMaker unless you know the correct syntax. *Syntax* is the set of rules that governs the use of a function or command. Each function and command has its own specific syntax that must be used for that function or command to execute correctly.

In addition, functions and subroutines require parameters for correct operation. A *parameter* is additional information that is supplied to a function or to another program.

The syntax for functions specifies that parameters be enclosed in parentheses and separated (*delimited*) by commas. A parameter can be a string, in which case it must be enclosed by quotation marks, or a variable. Variable parameters are not enclosed in quotation marks.

Functions that return a value are preceded by a variable name and an equal sign (=), as shown in the following example:

```
answer=MsgBox("Would you like to proceed?",35,"A Question, Please")
```

This syntax indicates that the response returned by the `MsgBox()` function is to be placed into the response variable. The next time response is used, it is equal to the value returned by the `MsgBox()` function.

Note

ScriptMaker uses both a `MsgBox` subroutine and a `MsgBox()` function. The `MsgBox()` function is denoted by a pair of parentheses, whereas the `MsgBox` subroutine does not have these parentheses.

Subroutines do not return a value and stand alone on a line. The following line, for example, executes the `MsgBox` subroutine:

```
MsgBox "This is a message!",0,"A Message Box"
```

Notice that the `MsgBox` subroutine also contains three parameters, but it does not return a value. Some commands—such as `BEEP`, for example—do not require parameters.

Chapter 31, "Creating Simple ScriptMaker Programs," contains a number of example ScriptMaker programs. You can use those programs, plus the example ScriptMaker program included with Norton Desktop 3 for Windows, to learn more about how these commands are used. Two other tools that can help you program your script are the Macro Recorder and the Dialog Editor. These two tools are described in the following sections.

Note

Strings are always enclosed in quotation marks. Variables are not enclosed in quotation marks. If a variable returns a string into a variable identifier, the variable is not enclosed in quotes. Any time that information is enclosed in quotes, it is used as a string, exactly as the information appears in the quotation marks.

Using the Macro Recorder with ScriptMaker

Figuring out exactly what commands cause tasks to operate in your Windows environment may prove difficult for you. To help you create the script related to Windows or Norton Desktop commands, ScriptMaker includes a *Macro Recorder*. This recorder records your keystrokes or selections within windows and turns them into ScriptMaker commands. You can save a series of commands into a script and then cause the script to mimic the tasks you performed while the recorder was on.

To begin recording, choose the **T**ools **R**ecorder command from the ScriptMaker menu. The Record Macro dialog box appears, as shown in figure 30.5. In this dialog box, you can specify what you want recorded. By default, **H**igh Level BASIC Statements, **K**eyboard, and **M**ouse Relative To **S**creen are selected. The options available in this dialog box are as described in the following table.

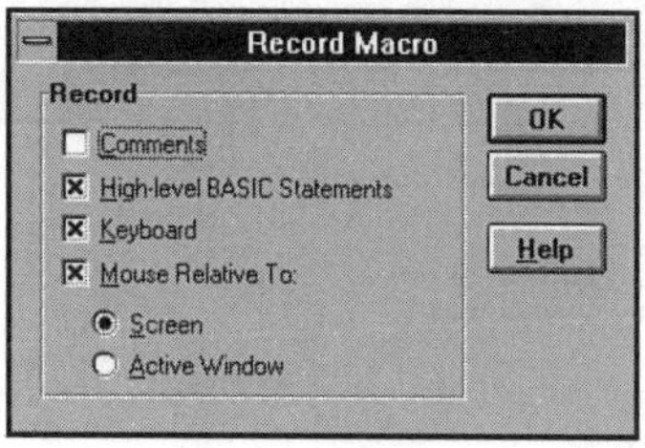

Fig. 30.5
The Record Macro dialog Box enables you to record keystrokes and commands.

Option	Meaning
Comments	Comments are recorded.
High-Level BASIC Statements	Tasks are recorded as BASIC Statements that can be used in ScriptMaker.

(continues)

V

Using ScriptMaker

(continued)

Option	Meaning
Keyboard	All keyboard keystrokes are recorded.
Mouse Relative To	All mouse movements are recorded relative to either the **S**creen or to the currently **A**ctive Window.

Choose OK to begin recording. A small control panel appears at the top left of the screen, enabling you to specify for the recording to stop, continue, or pause. After you finish recording, choose Stop. The Stop Recorder dialog box appears, as shown in figure 30.6. You can choose to insert the recorded command at the current cursor position in ScriptMaker, place it into the Windows Clipboard, or insert the command as the main routine.

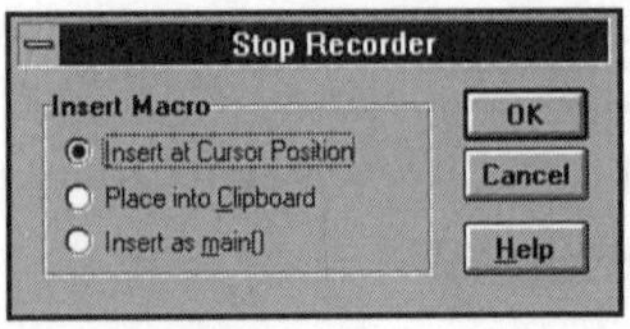

Fig. 30.6
The Stop Record dialog box enables you to choose how to save the recorded information.

Figure 30.7 shows the result of recorded commands that switch to the Norton Desktop and enter the command to turn the toolbar off and on. These simple commands can be compiled and saved to create a program that turns your toolbar off or on. (The comments at the top of the program were entered later.)

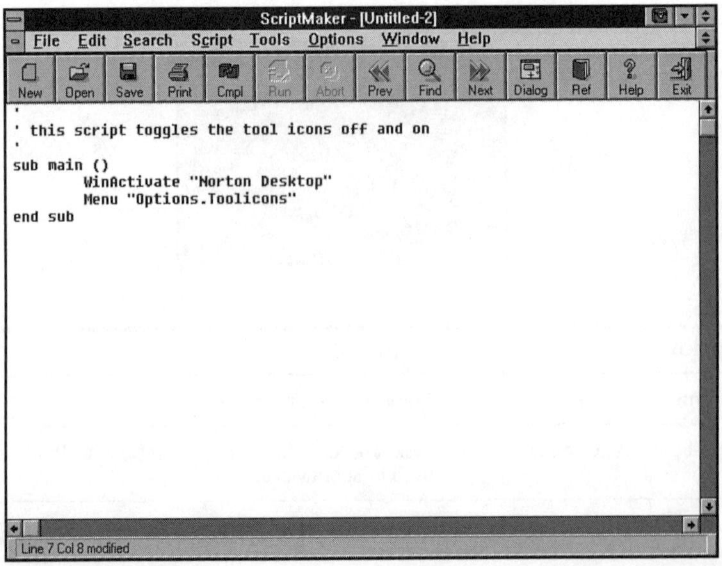

Fig. 30.7
A ScriptMaker program designed as a toggle to turn your toolbar off and on.

Using the Dialog Editor

Although ScriptMaker has all the commands necessary for you to program a Windows dialog box, an easier way to do so is to create a dialog box by using the Dialog Editor. This editor enables you to draw on-screen all the components of a dialog box, and then it turns that picture into ScriptMaker commands you can incorporate into a script.

To start the Dialog Editor, choose **T**ools **D**ialog Editor from the ScriptMaker menu bar. The initial Dialog Editor screen appears, as shown in figure 30.8. This window contains the beginnings of a dialog box called Untitled.

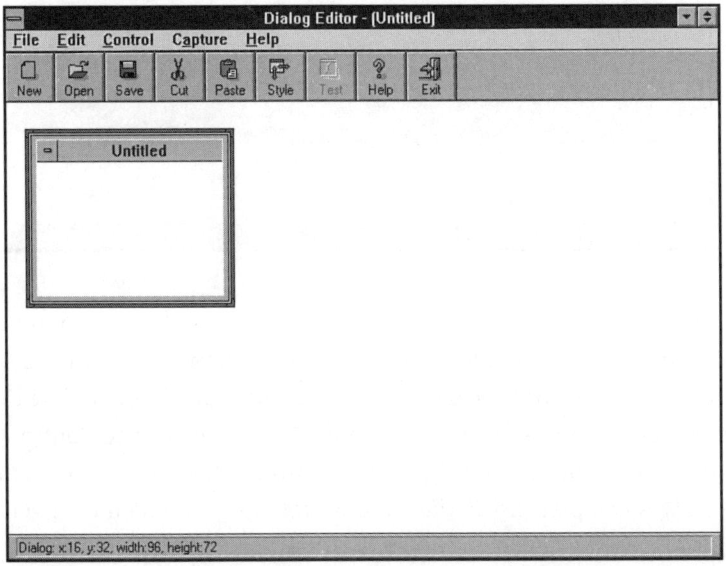

Fig. 30.8
The Initial Dialog Editor window enables you to create a dialog box.

Note

You also can begin Dialog editor from the Desktop window by clicking the Dialog Editor icon.

The following sections show you by example how to use the Dialog Editor to create a dialog box.

Designing a Dialog Box by Using the Dialog Editor

Resize the Untitled dialog box to the size you want by using your mouse, just as you resize any window. Make it about the size of the dialog box shown in figure 30.9. Double-click the dialog box, and you are prompted to enter dialog box information. Enter **Help Desk** in the **T**ext field, and then choose OK. The title for the dialog box changes to Help Desk.

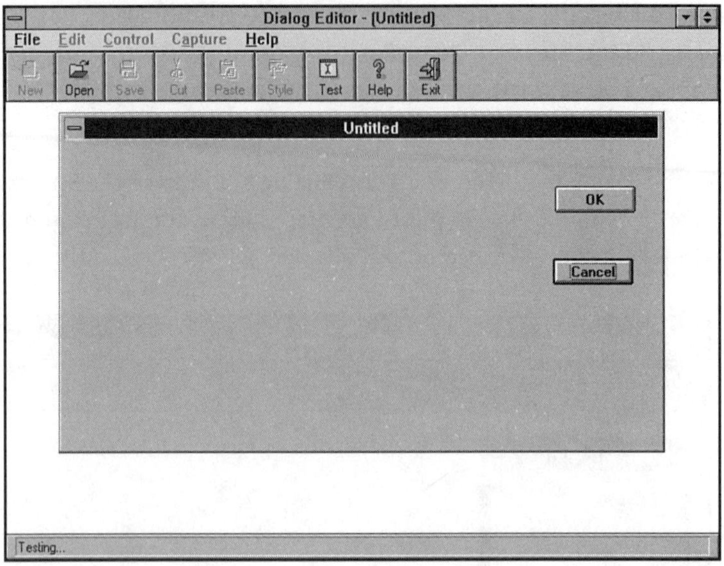

Fig. 30.9
Resizing the Untitled dialog box and adding the OK and Cancel buttons to the newly created dialog box.

Open the **C**ontrol menu, and choose the O**K** Button option. The outline of a button appears on-screen. Move the button to the upper left of the screen and click once to deposit the OK button. (You also can click and drag the button to get it to a precise location.) In the same way, use the **C**ontrol C**a**ncel Button command to place the Cancel button in the box, as shown in figure 30.9. A complete list of the options on the **C**ontrol menu is given in table 30.2.

To place a text box in the dialog box, choose **C**ontrol **E**dit. An Edit Me text box appears on-screen. Position it as shown in figure 30.10, and then size the box to match the size of the one in the figure. In the same way, place a list box on-screen by choosing **C**ontrol **L**ist Box, and place a check box by choosing **C**ontrol **C**heck box so that the dialog box now resembles the one shown in figure 30.10.

Using the components described in table 30.2, make the final Help Desk dialog box resemble the one shown in figure 30.11.

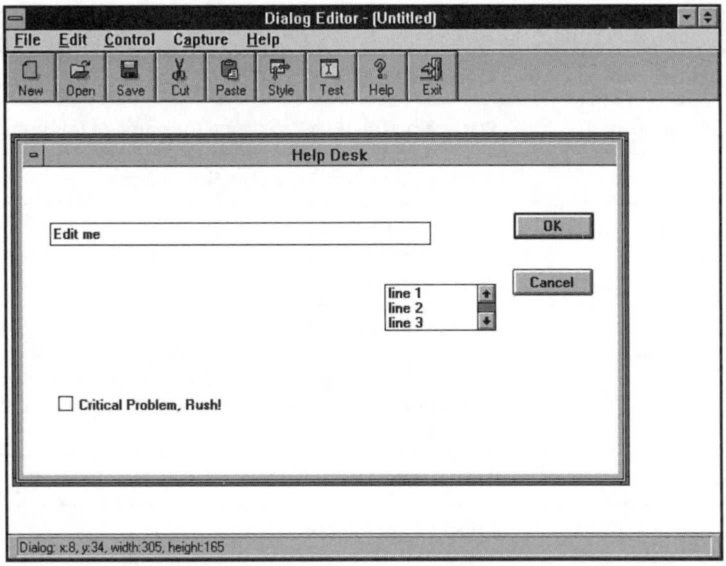

Fig. 30.10
Several components placed in the Help Desk dialog box—a text box, a list box, a check box, and command buttons.

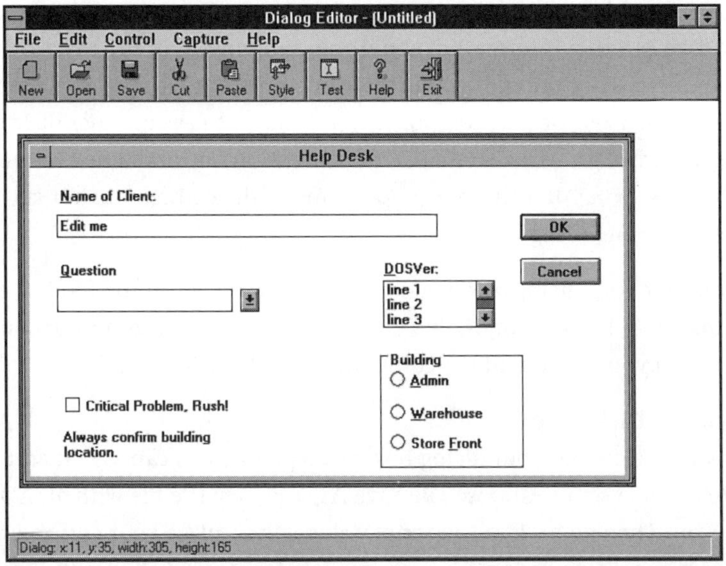

Fig. 30.11
The finished Help Desk dialog box.

Table 30.2 Dialog Editor Control Options

Option	Comments
O**K** Button	Places an OK Button.
C**a**ncel Button	Places a Cancel Button.

(continues)

Table 30.2 Continued

Option	Comments
Push Button	Places a button. You can define the name of this button.
Option Button	Places an option button. (See **G**roup Box.)
Check Box	Places a check box.
Static Text	Places text in the box.
Edit	Places a text box.
Group Box	Defines a group box. You may commonly first define a group box and then define several Option buttons inside this box.
List Box	Creates a list box.
Co**m**bo Box	Creates a combo box.

After you double-click a component, a dialog box appears, enabling you to enter titles or other information about the component. In the `text$` field of a component description, if you include an ampersand (`&`) before a character, it defines a *hot key* for that component, just like hot keys in other dialog boxes. For example, the `text$` label for the Option button named Admin was entered as `&Admin`. After the label appears in the dialog box, the hot key is underlined (refer to fig. 30.11).

You can test your dialog box by choosing the Test icon on the toolbar, by pressing F2, or by choosing **E**dit **T**est Dialog. The dialog box appears on-screen, and you can test all the components of the box.

Saving the Dialog Box

After you decide that your dialog box is acceptable, you can save it and incorporate it into a script. Choose **F**ile Save **A**s, and save the file with an ADG extension. Then go back to the ScriptMaker editor, place your cursor where you want the dialog code placed, choose **F**ile **I**nsert, and choose the name of the dialog box file. The code for the dialog box is copied into the ScriptMaker editor, as shown in figure 30.12.

For an example of how to incorporate this dialog box into a script, see the Help Desk example in Chapter 31, "Creating Simple ScriptMaker Programs."

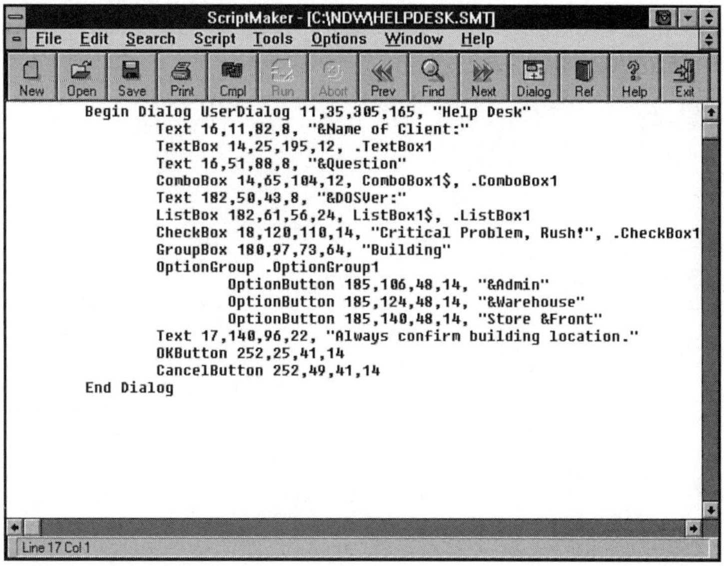

Fig. 30.12
The ScriptMaker code for the dialog box created in the Dialog Editor.

Capturing a Dialog Box

An easier way to create a dialog box than drawing it in the Editor is to capture an existing dialog box. To capture a dialog box, first open a program containing a dialog box you want to capture. Then, in another window, open the Dialog editor. Choose **C**apture and then choose either Capture in **P**lace or Capture from **B**ack.

The Capture in **P**lace option means that the dialog is currently visible onscreen. The Capture from **B**ack option moves the Dialog Editor into the background so that you can capture a dialog box that is behind it. After you choose one of these options, a fishhook-shaped pointer appears. Move the hook until it is on top of the dialog box you want to capture, and then click the mouse. Return to the Dialog Editor, and click the Paste button. The dialog box you captured is now in the Dialog Editor. You can now edit the dialog box, save it, and incorporate it into your own script.

Summary

This chapter introduced you to the basics of ScriptMaker and the ScriptMaker language. You learned how to create, edit, save, and run a ScriptMaker file. You also learned about ScriptMaker's functions and commands, as well as how to use the Macro Recorder and Dialog Editor.

Chapter 31, "Creating Simple ScriptMaker Programs," introduces you to several sample ScriptMaker programs.

Chapter 31

Creating Simple ScriptMaker Programs

Sometimes the best way to learn about a program is by actually doing something with it. This chapter, therefore, presents several sample ScriptMaker programs. Each program performs a useful function and also teaches you a little about the ScriptMaker language. Each program includes commentary about why things are being done the way they are so that you can see for yourself how ScriptMaker works. And these programs are just to get you started. You can modify these programs for your particular needs or use them as templates for completely new programs of your own design.

Note

The Batch Runner program found in Norton Desktop for Windows version 2.0 has been replaced by the ScriptMaker in version 3. This change follows Microsoft's decision to make all its Windows programs contain a standard Visual Basic macro language. Because it is based on the Visual Basic standard, ScriptMaker conforms to this trend.

Display Simple Message Program

This example is a very simple program that displays a message and then waits for the user to choose OK (see fig. 31.1).

Fig. 31.1
A message box displaying the message `This is my first program!`

To see the script in action, you must type it, compile it, and run it. Follow these steps to create and run this program:

1. Open ScriptMaker from the Desktop by choosing **T**ools Sc**r**iptMaker. (ScriptMaker menus are described in Chapter 30, "Learning ScriptMaker Basics.")

2. Type the following lines:

```
Sub Main( )
        MsgBox "This is my first program!"
End Sub
```

The ScriptMaker window should look like the one shown in figure 31.2.

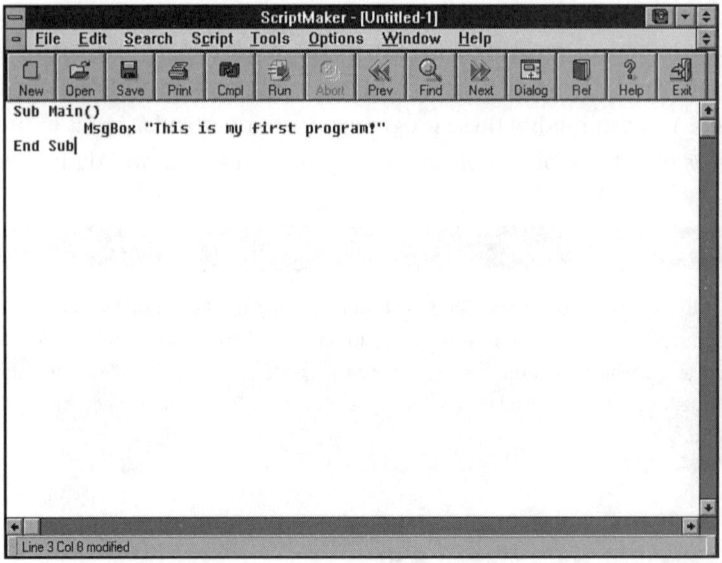

Fig. 31.2
The ScriptMaker window containing your first program.

3. Choose Sc**r**ipt **C**ompile, or click the Cmpl icon. A message appears telling you whether the compile is successful. If an error is reported, check how you typed the information, making sure that everything is exactly as described in step 2, and then compile again.

4. After the compile is successful, choose the S**c**ript **R**un option, or click the Run icon. Your message appears on-screen, as shown in figure 31.1.

You may want to save your script to a file in case you want to use it again. To save the script, choose the **F**ile Save **A**s option. Save the file as MYFIRST.SM. To run this script outside the ScriptMaker window, you must save the program as an executable file by following these steps:

1. Choose the S**c**ript Save **E**xe option. A Save Exe As box appears, as shown in figure 31.3.

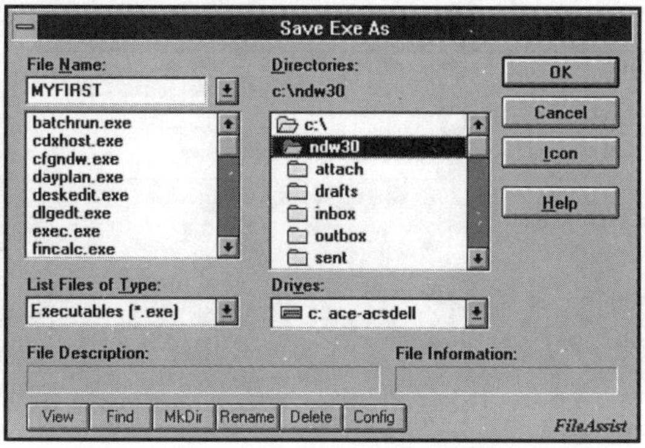

Fig. 31.3
The Save Exe As dialog box enables you to save a ScriptMaker program.

2. Enter the name you want to give this program. You must enter a DOS compatible file name of up to eight characters. For example, enter the name **MYFIRST**. The program is saved as MYFIRST.EXE.

3. Click OK.

The program is now saved as an executable file. To run this program, follow these steps:

1. Exit Scriptmaker.

2. From the Desktop, open a drive window for the drive on which you saved your executable script, as shown in figure 31.4.

3. Double-click the file name MYFIRST.EXE. The program runs, and the message is displayed.

You also can create a Desktop icon from the executable file. To do so, click and drag the file MYFIRST.EXE from the drive window to the Desktop. A ScriptMaker icon appears, as shown in figure 31.5. You can then run the program by double-clicking the icon. You can change the icon and its name by using the techniques described in Chapter 13, "Creating an Icon-Based Desktop," in the sections "Using the Properties Command" and "Using Icon Editor."

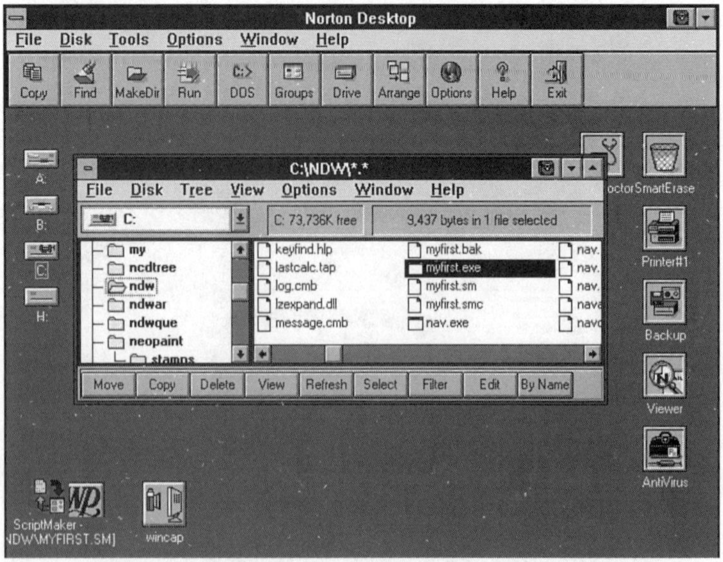

Fig. 31.4
A drive window containing the executable program MYFIRST.EXE.

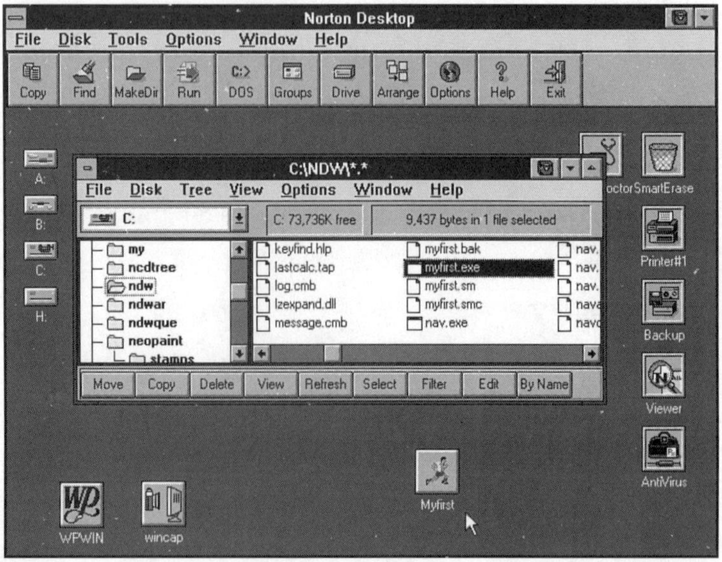

Fig. 31.5
Desktop showing the Script File Icon for MYFIRST.EXE.

Ask for Confirmation Program

This is another simple program; it demonstrates the use of **Y**es and **N**o buttons in dialog boxes. In the following example, the `MsgBox()` function displays a message box that requires you to choose **Y**es, **N**o, or Cancel. The number returned is sent to the variable `answer`.

```
answer=MsgBox("Would you like to proceed?",
35,"A Question, Please")
```

The first string in the `MsgBox()` function is what appears in the message box; the second item (`35`) is a code telling the function what kind of message box to display. For example, the `35` is a code consisting of 3+32, where 3 tells the `MsgBox()` function to display **Y**es, **N**o, and Cancel options and 32 tells it to display the question mark (`?`) logo in the message box. The third parameter in the function is the name of the message box.

> **Note**
>
> You can readily display the parameters for `MsgBox()` or any other ScriptMaker command by clicking Ref (Reference) and choosing the command name from the displayed list.

The `answer` variable contains a number indicating how the user responded. In this case, the three possibilities are as follows:

2 means Cancel was chosen.

6 means **Y**es was chosen.

7 means **N**o was chosen.

These codes are found in the reference for `MsgBox()`. The completed program is as shown in the following example:

```
Sub Main()
   answer=MsgBox("Would you like to proceed?",35,"A Question,
Please")
     if answer=7 then ' indicates No was pressed
        MsgBox "You pressed the No button."
     elseif answer = 6 then
        MsgBox "You pressed the Yes button."
     elseif answer = 2 then
        MsgBox "You pressed Cancel."
     end if
End Sub
```

If you run this program, the message box shown in figure 31.6 appears. Notice the question mark logo that appears in the message box. If you choose the **N**o button, the message in figure 31.7 appears. You could, of course, place more meaningful code in response to a **Y**es, **N**o, or Cancel answer.

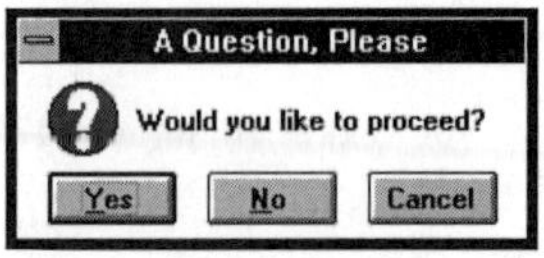

Fig. 31.6
The A Question, Please dialog box with **Y**es, **N**o, and Cancel options.

Fig 31.7
The **N**o response message box.

Copy a File Script

This example is a more complex script that copies a file from any disk to any destination on your computer. Standard file selection boxes ask the user which file to copy and where to copy the file.

Note

Lines that begin with a single quote (') are comment lines. Information on these lines is to document what is happening in the script. This information does not affect how the script actually operates.

A script to perform a file copy is shown in the following example:

```
Sub Main()
     answer=MsgBox("This procedure will copy a file.
     Would you like to proceed?",36,"Copy a File")
     if answer=6 then ' answer was yes, Okay to proceed
          '
          ' first locate the file to be copied
          '
          file2copy$=OpenFileName$("Choose file to
          Copy","All Files:*.*" )
          '
          ' then locate the destination for the file
          ' SaveFileName will warn you if the file exists
          '
          where2copy$=SaveFileName$("Copy Destination","All
          Files:*.*" )
          '
          ' finally, copy the file to its destination
          ' but only if a destination was given
          '
```

```
            if where2copy$<>"" then
               FileCopy file2copy$,where2copy$,FALSE
            else
               MsgBox "No file copied",48,"Copy Message"
               end
            end if
        end if
        MsgBox "Thank you and goodbye.",0, "End of Copy Script"
    end sub
```

The first message box (`MsgBox()`) is similar to the previous example. It explains what is about to happen and asks whether you want to proceed. The code `36` means that the box is a **Y**es, **N**o box with a question mark logo. The message box returns a numeric value into the variable named `answer` (see fig. 31.8).

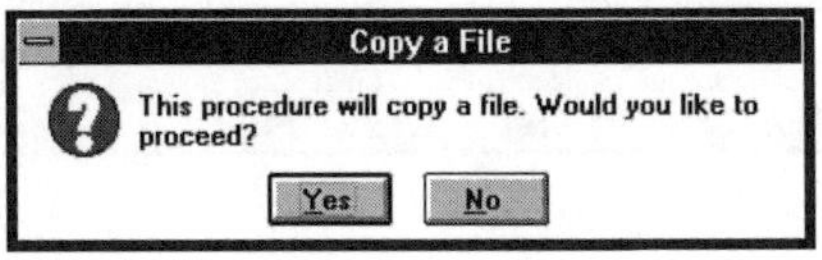

Fig. 31.8
The Copy a File message box.

If the variable `answer` equals `6`, the answer is yes, so the copy proceeds. If `answer` is anything else, the answer is no, so the script ends with the `Thank you and goodbye.` message.

If the copy proceeds, the `OpenFileName$` function is performed. This function displays a standard file list box and enables the user to choose or enter the name of the file to be copied. The file name specified is stored in a variable named `file2copy$` (see fig. 31.9).

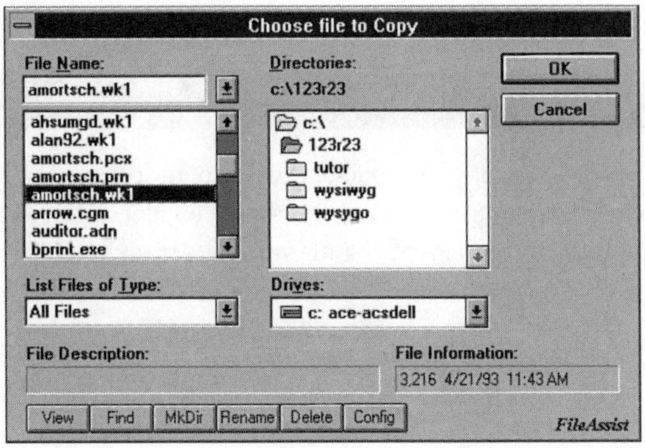

Fig. 31.9
The Choose File To Copy dialog box.

The `SaveFileName` function is very similar and enables the user to enter the name of the file to be saved, including choosing a destination on a different drive or directory. If the file to be saved already exists, a warning automatically appears asking if it is all right to overwrite the existing file. If you answer **Y**es, the copy proceeds. If you answer **N**o to the overwrite question or cancel the list box, the variable `where2copy$` is blank (see fig. 31.10).

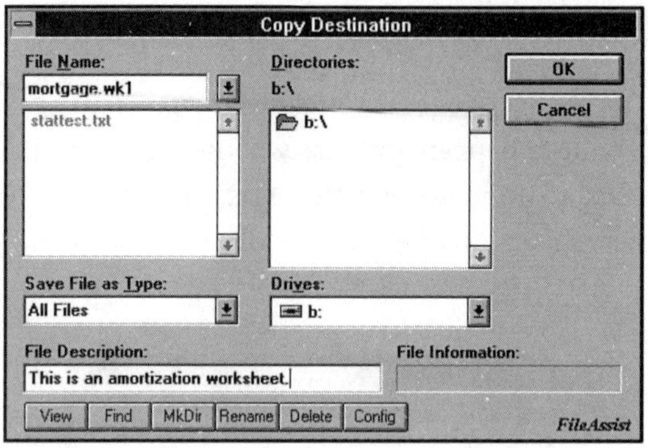

Fig. 31.10
The Copy Destination dialog box.

If the variable `where2copy$` is not blank, the `FileCopy` command is acted on. The `FileCopy` command copies the file called `file2copy$` to the destination called `where2copy$`. After the copy operation is finished, a message appears telling you that the copy file script is ended (see fig. 31.11). If the variable `where2copy$` is blank, a message tells you that no file was copied, and the script ends then.

Fig. 31.11
The End of Copy Script message box.

> **Note**
>
> You could probably think of some additional ways to make this script better. As an exercise, you may add another `If` statement that determines whether the variable `file2copy$` is blank or contains `*.*`. If the variable is blank, you may want to end the script or ask the question again. If the variable contains `*.*`, you may want to ask the user whether he really wants to copy all files to the destination.

Change Wallpaper Script

This batch file enables the user to change Windows wallpaper, to define whether the wallpaper appears as tiled or centered, or to choose no wallpaper.

```
Sub Main()
     ' define a carriage return line feed
     crlf$=chr$(13) + chr$(10)
     '
     ' Tell the user what the program does
     '
     a$ = "This procedure lets you choose wallpaper."+crlf$
     a$ = a$ + "Or, choose cancel for no wallpaper."
     answer=MsgBox(a$,33,"Select a Wallpaper")
     '
     ' if answer = 2 then cancel was pressed
     '
     if answer = 2 then
          DesktopSetWallpaper "", true
          end
     end if
     '
     ' otherwise, continue to choose a wallpaper
     ' get the system windows directory name
     '
     wdir$ = SystemWindowsDirectory$( )
     ChDir wdir$
paper$ = OpenFileName$("Wallpapers","Wallpapers (*.bmp):*.bmp" )
     '
     'if no paper chosen, set to null
     '
     if paper$ = "" then
          DesktopSetWallpaper "", true
          end
     end if
     '
     'do you want the paper tiled or centered?
     '
a$="You have chosen the wallpaper named "+paper$ + "." + crlf$
     a$ = a$ + "Do you want the wallpaper tiled?"
     answer = msgbox(a$,36,"Tiled or Centered")
     if answer = 6 then
          DesktopSetWallpaper paper$,TRUE
     else
          DesktopSetWallpaper paper$,FALSE
     end if
end sub
```

In this script, the variable `crlf$` is defined as the carriage return line feed command. This variable is handy for use in message boxes, as shown later in the script. For this script, an introductory message appears, as shown in

V

Using ScriptMaker

figure 31.12. If the user chooses to cancel, the `DesktopSetWallpaper` command is set to null (`"" = nothing`), which causes the system to use no wallpaper, and the script ends.

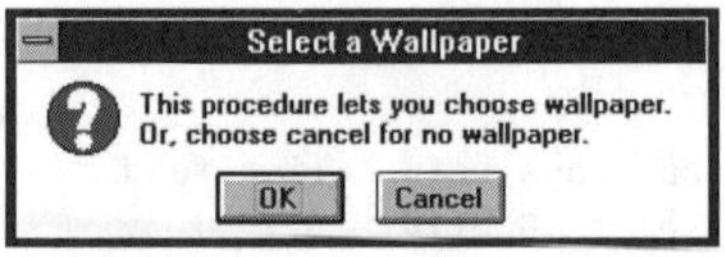

Fig. 31.12
The Select a Wallpaper dialog box enables you to choose a wallpaper.

If the user continues, a dialog box appears, enabling you to choose a wallpaper (*.BMP) file, as shown in figure 31.13. If the user chooses Cancel, no wallpaper is used, and the program ends. If a wallpaper is chosen, the user is asked whether the wallpaper should be tiled or centered. Then the appropriate `DesktopSetWallpaper` command is used to carry out the selections, and the program ends.

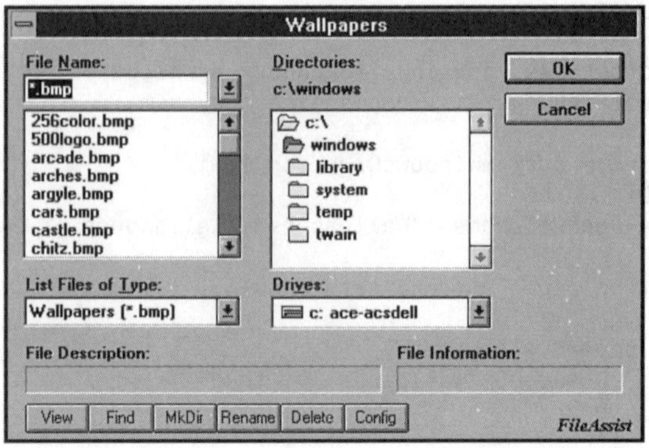

Fig. 31.13
The Wallpapers dialog box enables you to choose a BMP file.

Help Desk Dialog Box Example

This example brings together a number of ScriptMaker capabilities. It illustrates how you can design your own dialog box to match your particular needs. This Help Desk script enables you to enter information about someone in an organization who has a computer question or problem.

```
sub main()
'
'Define all variables to use in the dialog box
'
CRLF$=Chr$(13)+chr$(10)
Dim IsRush$
IsRush="&Critical Problem, Rush!"
dim DOSVer$ (1 to 9)
DOSVer$(1)="DOS 1.x"
```

```
DOSVer$(2) ="DOS 2.x"
DOSVer$(3) ="DOS 3.x"
DOSVer$(4) ="DOS 4.x"
DOSVer$(5) = "DOS 5.x"
DOSVer$(6) = "MSDOS 6.0"
DOSVer$(7) = "PCDOS 6.1"
DOSVer$(8) = "DRDOS X.X"
DOSVer$(9) = "Other or N.A."
dim ProbType$ (1 to 6)
ProbType$(1)="Hardware Problem"
ProbType$(2)="Software Problem"
ProbType$(3)="Network Problem"
ProbType$(4)="What Software to Buy"
ProbType$(5)="What Hardware to Buy"
ProbType$(6)="Inquiry about a Class"
dim Building$ (1 to 3)
Building$(1)="Administration"
Building$(2) ="Warehouse"
Building$(3)="Store Front"
' Design a dialog box
Begin Dialog MyDialog 13,32,272,156,"Help Desk"
     Text 6,5,78,8,"&Name of Client:"
     TextBox 6,17,209,12,.ClientName
     Text 6,37,43,8, "&Question Type:"
     ComboBox 6,49,120,44, ProbType, .question
     Text 142,37,69,8, "&DOSVer:"
     ListBox 142,49,73,32,DOSVer,.whatdos
     CheckBox 6,107,83,14, IsRush, .Rush
     GroupBox 142,90,75,61, "Building"
     OptionGroup .Building
        OptionButton 147,103,48,14, "&Admin"
        OptionButton 147,118,48,14, "&Warehouse"
        OptionButton 147,133,48,14, "Store &Front"
     Text 6,126,104,26,"Always confirm building location."
     OKButton 227,16,41,14
     CancelButton 227,40,41,14
end Dialog
'
'Display the results
'
dim HelpTask as MyDialog
HelpTask.ClientName = "Caller Name"
HelpTask.Building = 1
dim Button_Number%
Button_Number = dialog (HelpTask)
if Button_Number <>0 then
   a$="Client name: "+HelpTask.ClientName+CRLF$+CRLF$
   a$= a$+"Question type: "+HelpTask.Question+CRLF$+CRLF$
   a$= a$+"Operating System:
"+DOSVER$(HelpTask.whatDOS)+CRLF$+CRLF$
   a$= a$+"Building: "+building$(HelpTask.Building+1)+CRLF$+CRLF$
   a$= a$+"Rush code is: "+str$(HelpTask.Rush)
   MsgBox a$,0,"Help Desk Task"
end if

End sub
```

The script begins by defining the values of variables that are used in the program. The `CRLF$` variable contains the ASCII codes for a carriage return, line feed—a code useful for message boxes. The `IsRush$` variable contains a string that is used in the dialog box. The arrays `DOSVer$`, `ProbType$` contain information that is used in list boxes, and `Building$` contains information that is used in the final report.

The `Begin Dialog` command is the start of the code that defines the contents of the dialog box that appears on-screen. This description continues through the command line `End Dialog`. Between these two lines are a number of commands that define the appearance of the dialog box. The `Text` commands tell where to place a line of text. The `Textbox` command tells where to place a longer string of text.

A `ComboBox` enables the user to enter a problem type or to choose a standard problem type from the array called `ProbType`. A `Listbox` enables the user to choose an item from the array called `DOSVer`. A `Checkbox` is used to choose a `Rush` option. A `GroupBox` is used to display three building `OptionButton` choices. Finally, an `OKButton` and a `CancelButton` are defined. After the program runs, the dialog box that results looks like the one shown in figure 31.14.

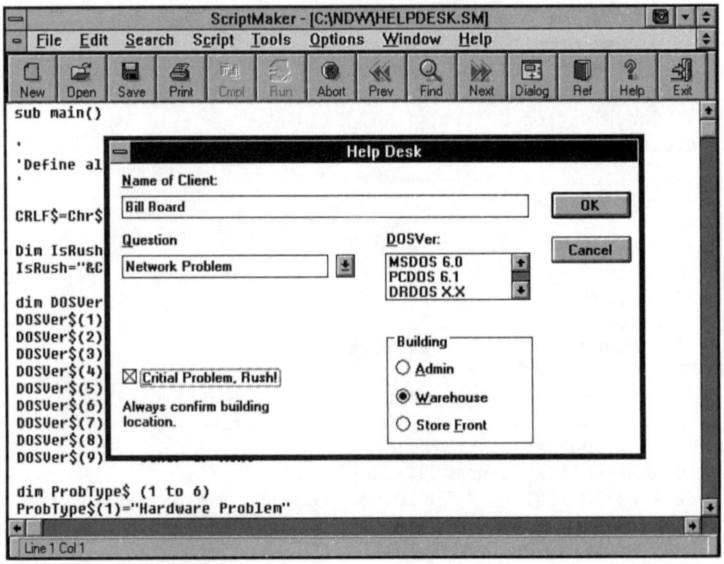

Fig. 31.14
The Help Desk dialog box you created.

After the definition of the dialog box, a variable named `HelpTask` is defined as `MyDialog`. Notice that `MyDialog` is the name of the dialog box. The following line returns the value of the `optionbutton` (either OK or Cancel):

```
Button_Number = dialog(HelpTask)
```

If the value of `Button_Number` is not 0, a message box called Help Desk Task appears, summarizing all the options chosen in the dialog box, as shown in figure 31.15.

Tip
As an exercise, you can create a Print option for the dialog box so that information is not only displayed on-screen, but also sent to your printer.

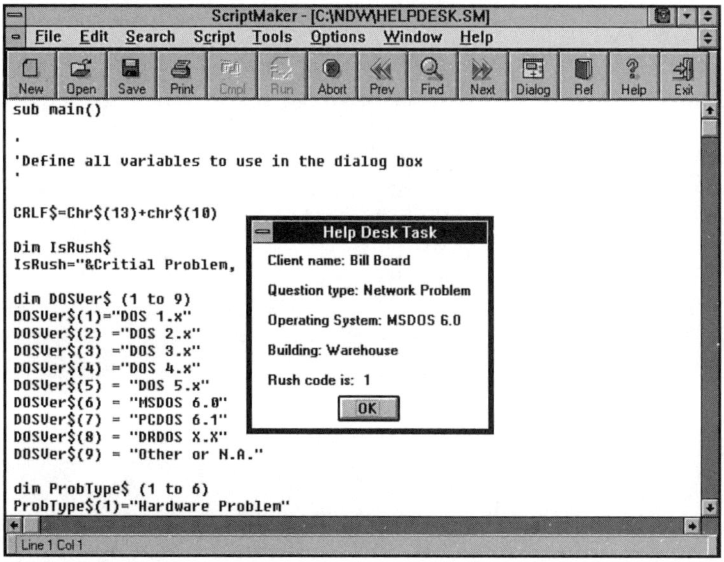

Fig. 31.15
The Help Desk Task message box.

Summary

This chapter introduced you to four different ScriptMaker files. Through these examples, you learned various ScriptMaker functions and techniques.

The final chapter, "ScriptMaker Command and Function Reference," is an extensive reference to ScriptMaker commands and functions.

Chapter 32

ScriptMaker Command Reference

The ScriptMaker language contains more than 300 commands and functions. It would take a book at least this size to fully document them all. Fortunately, if you know what command you want to use, you can quickly look it up through ScriptMaker's Ref (Reference) icon on the toolbar. The on-line **H**elp menu also provides references to commands, including a description of the command's syntax and examples of use. Many of these commands operate just like commands in the BASIC or Visual Basic languages.

This chapter provides you a quick way to find the specific command for what you need to do.

The lists that follow are broken down alphabetically by type and then alphabetically within type.

Note

The following ScriptMaker commands covered in this chapter include both functions and subroutines. Functions are denoted by a () after the command's name, whereas subroutines do not include parentheses.

Array Commands

`ArrayDims()`	Finds the dimension of an array.
`ArraySort()`	Sorts a one-dimensional array.
`Dim`	Declares an array.
`LBound()`	Determines lower bound for an array.
`UBound()`	Determines upper bound for an array.
`Option Base`	Sets lower bound for an array.
`ReDim`	Redimensions size of an array.

Clipboard Commands

`Clipboard$`	Sets the textual contents of the Clipboard.
`Clipboard$()`	Retrieves the contents of the Clipboard.
`ClipboardClear`	Clears the contents of the Clipboard.
`Snapshot`	Saves a snapshot of the screen to the Clipboard.

Conversion Commands

`Asc()`	Converts character to ASCII value.
`CDbl()`	Converts to double precision.
`CInt()`	Converts number to integer.
`CLng()`	Converts number to long integer.
`CSng()`	Converts number to single precision.
`Chr$()`	Converts ASCII value to a string.
`CStr()`	Converts a decimal value to a string.
`Hex$()`	Converts a decimal value to Hexadecimal.

Oct$()	Converts a decimal value to an Octal value.
Str$()	Converts a decimal value to a string.
Val()	Converts a string to a number.

Date and Time Commands

Date$	Sets the current date.
Date$()	Gets the current date.
DateSerial()	Gets the serial representation of a numeric date.
DateValue()	Gets the numeric representation of a serial date.
Day()	Gets the day value from a serial date.
Hour()	Gets the hour value from a serial time.
Minute()	Gets the minute value from a serial time.
Month()	Gets the month value from a serial date.
Second()	Gets the second value from a serial date.
Weekend()	Gets weekend indicator from a serial date.
Year()	Gets year value from a serial date.
Now()	Gets the serial representation of the current date and time.
Time$	Sets the current time.
Time$()	Gets the current time.
Timer()	Gets the number of seconds since midnight.
TimeValue()	Gets the serial representation of a time.

Desktop Commands

DesktopCascade	Cascades nonminimized windows.
DesktopSetColors	Changes the system colors.

(continues)

(continued)

`DesktopSetWallpaper`	Changes the wallpaper.
`DesktopTile`	Tiles nonminimized windows.

Dialog Commands (Predefined, Built-In)

`AnswerBox()`	Asks the user to select a button.
`AskBox$()`	Gets a typed response from the user.
`InputBox$()`	Gets input from the user.
`AskPassword$()`	Gets a password from the user.
`MsgBox`	Displays a message.
`MsgBox()`	Displays a message with input.
`MsgClose`	Closes a message box.
`MsgOpen`	Opens a message box.
`MsgSetText`	Sets the message in the text box.
`MsgSet Thermometer`	Sets the thermometer.
`OpenFileName$()`	Gets a file name by using the common Open dialog box.
`PopupMenu()`	Displays a list of choices in a popup box.
`SelectBox()`	Displays a list of choices in a select box.
`SaveFileName$()`	Gets a file name by using the common File Save dialog box.

Dialog Commands (User Defined)

`Begin Dialog…End Dialog`	Creates a user-defined dialog.
`CancelButton`	Creates a cancel button.
`CheckBox`	Creates a check box.

ComboBox	Creates a combo box.
GroupBox	Creates a group box.
ListBox	Creates a list box.
OKButton	Creates an OK button.
OptionButton	Creates an option button.
OptionGroup	Creates an option group.
PushButton	Creates a push button.
Text	Creates a text dialog box.
TextBox	Creates a text box.
Dialog	Displays a user defined dialog.
Dialog()	Displays a user defined dialog with inputs.

Manipulating Other Applications' Dialog Components

ActivateControl	Activates a component.
ButtonEnabled()	Determines if a button is enabled.
CheckBoxEnabled()	Determines if a check box is enabled.
ComboBoxEnabled()	Determines if a combo box is enabled.
EditEnabled()	Determines if an edit box is enabled.
ListBoxEnabled()	Determines if a list box is enabled.
OptionEnabled()	Determines if an option box is enabled.
ButtonExist()	Determines if a button exists.
CheckboxExist()	Determines if a check box exists.
ComboBoxExist()	Determines if a combo box exists.
EditExist()	Determines if an edit box exists.
ListboxExist()	Determines if a list box exists.
OptionExist()	Determines if an option box exists.

(continues)

(continued)

GetCheckBox()	Determines the state of a check box.
GetComboBoxItem$()	Gets the text of an item from a combo box.
GetComboBoxItemCount()	Determines the number of items in a combo box.
GetEditText$()	Gets the current contents of a text box.
GetListBoxItem$()	Gets the text of an item from the list box.
GetListBoxItemCount()	Determines the number of items in a list box.
GetOption()	Determines if an option button is set.
SelectButton	Selects a button.
SelectComboBoxItem	Selects a combination box item.
SelectListBoxItem	Selects a list box item.
SetCheckBox	Sets the state of a check box.
SetEditText	Sets the contents of a text box.
SetOption	Sets an option button.

Dynamic Data Exchange (DDE) Commands

DDEExecute	Sends a command to a server application.
DDEInitiate()	Initiates a DDE conversation.
DDEPoke	Sends data to a server application.
DDERequest()	Requests data from a server application.
DDETerminate	Terminates a DDE conversation.
DDETerminateAll	Terminates all DDE conversations.
DDETimeOut	Sets a time limit for a DDE conversation.

Environment Commands

`Environ$()`	Determines the value of an environment variable.
`MCI()`	Sends a command to the Media Control Interface.
`SystemRestart`	Restarts Windows.
`ReadINI$()`	Determines the value of an entry in an INI file.
`ReadINISection`	Reads all the entries in a section of an INI file.
`SystemFreeMemory()`	Gets information about free memory.
`SystemFreeResources()`	Gets information about free resources.
`SystemTotalMemory()`	Gets information about total memory.
`SystemWindowsDirectory$()`	Gets information about Windows directory.
`SystemWindowsVersion$()`	Gets Windows version number.
`SystemMouseTrails`	Turns mouse trails off or on.
`WriteINI`	Writes an entry to an INI file.

Error Trapping Commands

`Erl()`	Gets error-status data.
`Err`	Sets the current error value.
`Err()`	Gets the current error value.
`Error`	Simulates the occurrence of an error.
`Error$()`	Gets the error message for an error.
`On Error...Resume`	Defines how to handle an error.

File I/O Commands

`ChDir`	Changes the current directory.
`ChDrive`	Changes the current drive.
`Close`	Closes currently opened files.
`Reset`	Resets an open file.
`CurDir$()`	Gets the current directory.
`Dir$`	Gets a list of files on disk.
`FileList`	Fills an array with file names.
`FileDirs()`	Gets a file name that matches a specification.
`DiskDrives`	Gets a list of valid drives.
`DiskFree()`	Gets amount of free space on a drive.
`EOF()`	Detects the end of a file.
`FileAttr()`	Determines the opened mode of a file.
`FileDateTime`	Gets a file's date and timestamp information.
`FileExists()`	Determines if a file exists.
`FileLen()`	Determines the length of a file.
`LOF()`	Gets the length of a file.
`FileParse$()`	Parses a file name and breaks it into parts.
`FileType()`	Determines a file's type.
`FreeFile()`	Gets an available file number.
`GetAttr()`	Determines file attributes.
`Input#`	Inputs information from a file.
`Input$()`	Inputs from a file.
`Line Input#`	Inputs complete line at a time from a file.
`Kill`	Erases a file.
`Loc()`	Determines the position of the file pointer.
`Seek()`	Locates the file pointer.
`MkDir`	Makes a directory.

`Name...As`	Renames a file on disk.
`Open`	Opens a file for input or output.
`Print#`	Prints to a file.
`Write#`	Writes to a file.
`RmDir`	Removes a directory from disk.
`Seek`	Moves the file pointer.
`SetAttr`	Sets a file's attributes.

Flow Control Commands

`Do...Loop`	Programs control loop.
`For...Next`	Programs control loop.
`While...Wend`	Programs control loop.
`End`	Exits the program.
`Stop`	Stops the program's execution.
`Exclusive`	Prevents other applications from starting.
`Exit Do`	Exits a `Do...Loop`.
`Exit For`	Exits a `For...Next` loop.
`GoSub...Return`	Beginning and end of a subroutine.
`GoTo`	Branches to a label.
`On Error`	Defines branch when an error is encountered.
`If...Then...Else...End If`	Decision command based on expression evaluation.
`Select Case...End Select`	Decision command based on the value of a variable.
`Sleep`	Pauses the program for a specified time.

Function and Subroutine Commands

`Call`	Calls a subroutine.
`Declare`	Declares an external routine reference.
`Exit Function`	Exits a function.
`Exit Sub`	Exits a subroutine.
`Function...End Function`	Beginning and end of a function.
`Sub...End Sub`	Beginning and end of a subroutine.

Keyboard and Mouse Playback Commands

`DoKeys`	Sends keystrokes to an application.
`QueKeyDn`	Places a key press into an event que.
`QueKeys`	Places keystrokes into an event que.
`QueKeyUp`	Places a key up event into the event que.
`SendKeys`	Sends specified keys to the active application.
`QueEmpty`	Empties the event que.
`QueFlush`	Flushes the event que.
`QueSetRelativeWindow`	Sets subsequent mouse movements relative to a specified window.
`QueMouseClick`	Generates a mouse click.
`QueMouseDblClick`	Generates a mouse double-click.
`QueMouseDblDn`	Places a double down mouse event in the event que.
`QueMouseDn`	Shifts mouse pointer down.
`QueMouseMove`	Defines a mouse move.
`QueMouseUp`	Shifts mouse pointer up.

Mathematical Commands

`Abs()`	Absolute value.
`Atn()`	Arc tangent.
`Cos()`	Cosine.
`Sin()`	Sine.
`Tan()`	Tangent.
`Exp()`	Exponentiation—a number raised to a power.
`Fix()`	Extracts the integer part of a number.
`Int()`	Converts a number to an integer.s
`Log()`	Natural logarithm.
`Random()`	Generates a random number.
`Randomize`	Randomizes the random number generator.
`Rnd()`	Selects a random number from 0 to 1.
`Sgn()`	Determines the sign of a number.
`Sqr()`	Square root.

Menu Commands

`Menu`	Selects a menu item.
`MenuItemChecked()`	Determines if a menu item is checked.
`MenuItemEnabled()`	Determines if a menu item is enabled.
`MenuItemExits()`	Determines if a menu item exists.

Other Commands

'	Comment.
/* ... */	Comment.
Rem	Comment.
Beep	Sounds a beep.
Command$	Gets command line arguments.
DoEvents	Processes pending events before continuing.
Shell()	Runs another program.

Expression Operators

*	Multiply.
+	Add.
-	Subtract.
/	Divide.
\	Integer divide.
MOD	Finds module.
^	Raises to a power.
<	Comparison, less than.
<=	Comparison, less than or equal to.
<>	Comparison, not equal to.
=	Comparison, equal to.
>	Comparison, greater than.
>=	Comparison, greater than or equal to.
AND	Logical AND operator.
NOT	Logical NOT operator.
OR	Logical OR operator.
XOR	Logical XOR operator.

Printer Commands

`PrinterGetOrientation()`	Determines printer's page orientation.
`PrinterSetOrientation`	Sets the printer's orientation.
`PrintFile()`	Prints a file.

ScriptMaker Environment Commands

`ScriptMakerHomeDir$()`	Determines Scriptmaker's home directory.
`ScriptMakerOS()`	Determines the host operating system.
`ScriptMakerVersion$()`	Determines the ScriptMaker version.

String Commands

`+`	Concatenates operator.
`InStr()`	Substring locator.
`Item$()`	Parses the text.
`ItemCount()`	Gets number of items.
`Line$()`	Gets a group of lines.
`LineCount()`	Gets number of lines.
`Word$`	Gets a word or sequence of words.
`WordCount()`	Gets number of words.
`LCase$()`	Converts a string to lowercase.
`Left$()`	Extracts leftmost characters.
`Len()`	Gets length of a string.
`LTrim()`	Trims blanks off left side of a string.
`Mid$`	Replaces a substring in a string.
`Mid$()`	Extracts a substring from a string.

(continues)

(continued)

`Null()`	Gets a null string.
`Right$()`	Extracts the rightmost characters.
`Rtrim$()`	Trims blanks off right side of a string.
`Space$()`	Gets a string of all spaces.
`String$()`	Gets a string of repeating characters.
`UCase$()`	Converts a string to uppercase.

Variables and Constants

`Deftype`	Sets a default data type.
`Dim`	Declares variables.
`Const`	Declares constants.
`Let`	Assigns a value to a variable.

Viewport Window Commands

`Print`	Outputs text to a viewport.
`ViewportClear`	Clears a viewport.
`ViewportClose`	Closes a viewport.
`ViewportOpen`	Opens a viewport.

Windows Commands

`AppActivate`	Activates a window.
`WinActivate`	Activates a window.
`AppClose`	Closes a window.
`WinClose`	Closes a window.

`AppFileName$()`	Determines the executable file name associated with an application window.
`AppFind$`	Determines the complete name of a window.
`AppGetActive$()`	Determines the name of the active window.
`AppGetPosition`	Determines the position of the active window.
`AppGetState()`	Determines the maximized, minimized, or restored state of a window.
`AppHide`	Hides a window.
`AppList`	Gets a list of the top-level applications.
`WinList`	Gets a list of the top-level windows.
`AppMaximize`	Maximizes the application window.
`AppMinimize`	Minimizes the application window.
`AppRestore`	Restores the application window.
`AppSetState`	Sets the state of the application.
`WinMaximize`	Maximizes specified window.
`WinMinimize`	Minimizes specified window.
`WinRestore`	Restores specified window.
`AppMove`	Moves a window.
`WinMove`	Moves a window.
`AppShow`	Shows a window.
`AppSize`	Sizes a window.
`WinSize`	Resizes a window to a specified size.
`AppType()`	Determines the platform on which an application runs.
`HLine`	Scrolls the window horizontally by line.
`HPage`	Scrolls the window horizontally by page.
`HScroll`	Sets scroll bar on horizontal scroll bar.
`VLine`	Scrolls the window vertically.
`VPage`	Scrolls the window vertically by page.
`VScroll`	Sets scroll bar on vertical scroll bar.
`WinFind()`	Determines the handle of a window.

Part VI

Appendixes

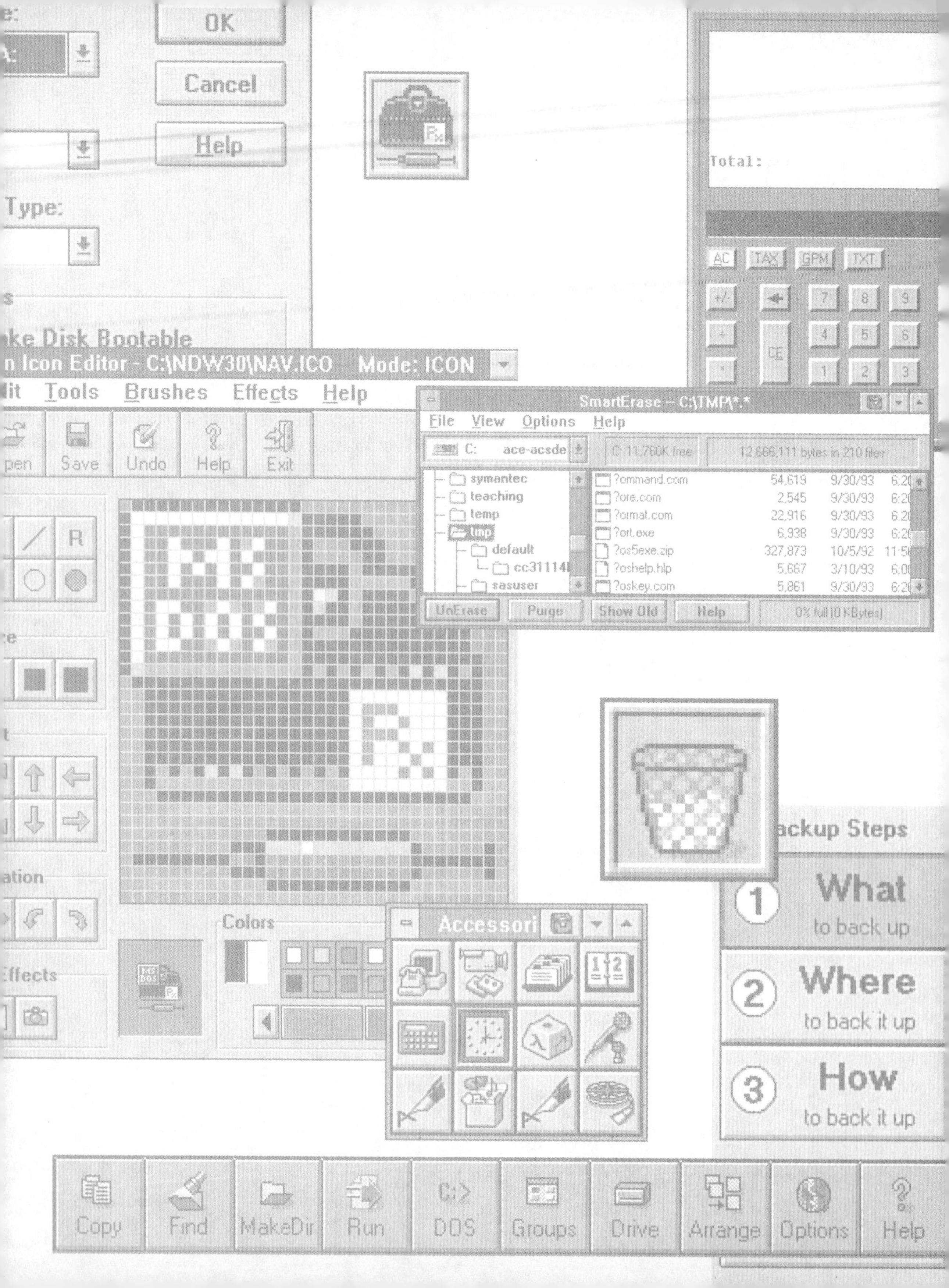
OK
Cancel
Help
Type:
ke Disk Bootable
Total:
AC TAX GPM TXT
n Icon Editor - C:\NDW30\NAV.ICO Mode: ICON
lit Tools Brushes Effects Help
pen Save Undo Help Exit
SmartErase – C:\TMP*.*
File View Options Help
C: ace-acsde
C: 11,760K free
12,666,111 bytes in 210 files
symantec
teaching
temp
tmp
default
cc31114
sasuser
?ommand.com 54,619 9/30/93
?ore.com 2,545 9/30/93
?ormat.com 22,916 9/30/93
?ort.exe 6,938 9/30/93
?os5exe.zip 327,873 10/5/92
?oshelp.hlp 5,667 3/10/93
?oskey.com 5,861 9/30/93
UnErase Purge Show Old Help
0% full (0 KBytes)
ation
Effects
Colors
Accessori
ackup Steps
1 What to back up
2 Where to back it up
3 How to back it up
Copy Find MakeDir Run DOS Groups Drive Arrange Options Help

Appendix A

Installing Norton Desktop for Windows

Installing Norton Desktop 3 for Windows is as simple as running the INSTALL.EXE program supplied on the NDW Installation disk and then following the instructions that appear on-screen. If that statement seems *too* simple — or if you find the concept of "running programs" intimidating — just follow these steps:

1. With your computer running, insert the NDW Program Disk #1 into the appropriate floppy disk drive. On most machines, the 5 1/4-inch drive is referred to as drive A, and the 3 1/2-inch drive is drive B. (If your only floppy disk drive is a single 3 1/2-inch drive, that drive name is probably drive A.)

Note

You can install NDW directly from the DOS prompt or from within Windows.

2. If Windows is not running, make sure that you are at the DOS prompt. Type the name of your floppy disk drive, followed by **INSTALL**, and then press Enter. If you inserted the Install disk into drive A, for example, type **A:INSTALL** and then press Enter.

   If Windows is running, open the Program Manager's **F**ile menu and choose the **R**un command. After the Run dialog box appears, type the name of the floppy disk drive, followed by **INSTALL**, in the **C**ommand Line text box. If you inserted the Install disk into drive A, for example, type **A:INSTALL**. Click the OK button.

3. Several seconds after the NDW installation begins, a screen appears, prompting you to register your copy of Norton Desktop (see fig. A.1). Type your name in the **N**ame text box, and press Tab to move to the second text box (or click the box with the mouse). Enter your company name in the **C**ompany text box. Click OK, or press Enter to proceed.

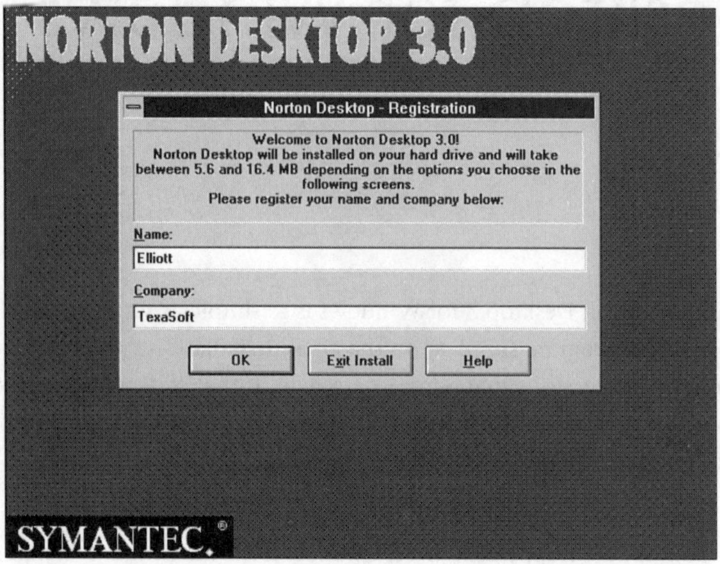

Fig. A.1
The Norton Desktop Registration Screen enables you to personalize your Desktop program.

Note

You must fill in both boxes or NDW does not proceed with the installation. If you are using NDW for personal use, type **None**, **Home**, or something similar in the second text box.

The Norton Desktop 3.0 Install Type Selection dialog box now appears on-screen (see fig. A.2). This dialog box enables you to choose among the following three installation options:

- *Automatic Install.* This is the recommended option. It enables you to install Norton Desktop for Windows by using the default options. This installation requires 17.2M free disk space.

- *Interactive Install.* This install option is essentially the same as Automatic Install, but you are given more control over the various installation options.

- *Custom Install*. This option enables you to choose which Norton Desktop modules to install. If you do not want to install all components of the program or if you do not have enough room on your hard disk, choose this option.

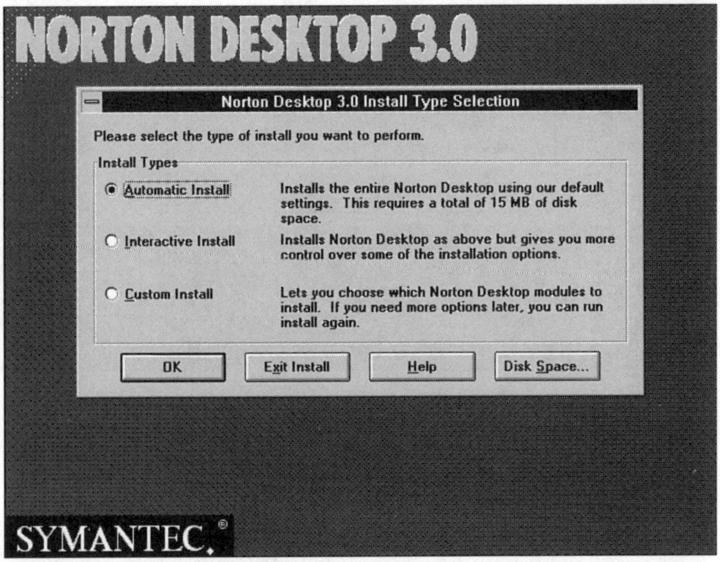

Fig. A.2
The Norton Desktop 3.0 Install Type Selection dialog box enables you to choose what install type to use.

> **Note**
>
> NDW's Install program does not assume that you install version 3 over a previous version; Install, therefore, does not take into account the disk space used by a previous NDW version — even if you instruct it to install itself in the same directory the previous version occupies. You may receive `Insufficient disk space` messages even though sufficient disk space actually is available, because Install is overwriting the previous version.

4. To install all applications (recommended), simply click OK or press Enter. The **A**utomatic Install option is already selected by default. The Select Installation Path dialog box appears (see fig. A.3).

   To install only a subset of the available applications, choose the **C**ustom Install button. A list of applications you can install is displayed. Choose which applications you want to install.

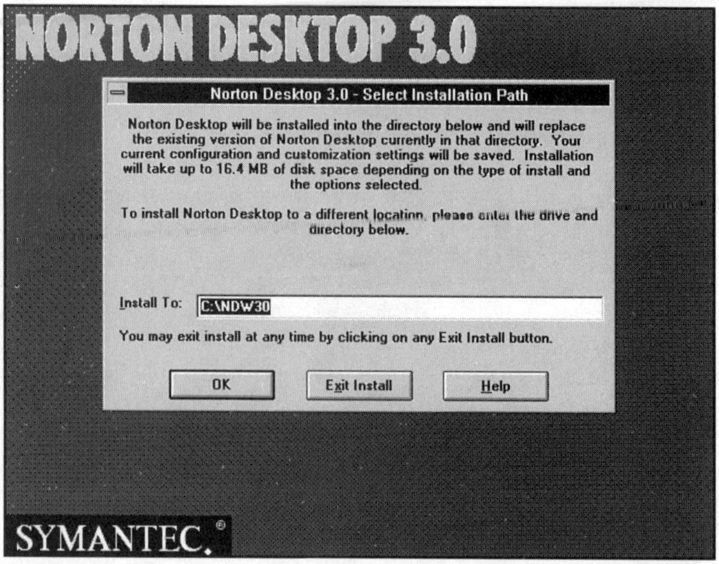

Fig. A.3
The Select Installation Path dialog box enables you to choose where the program is installed.

The Select Installation Path dialog box enables you to choose the name of the directory in which the program is installed. (By default, this directory is \NDW30.)

5. To install NDW in the default \NDW30 directory, choose OK; otherwise, enter a new directory name in the **I**nstall To text box, and then choose OK.

Before the program is actually installed, Norton scans your disk for viruses (see fig. A.4). This scan is to prevent your system from infecting other files. The scan may take several minutes, depending on the size of your hard disk.

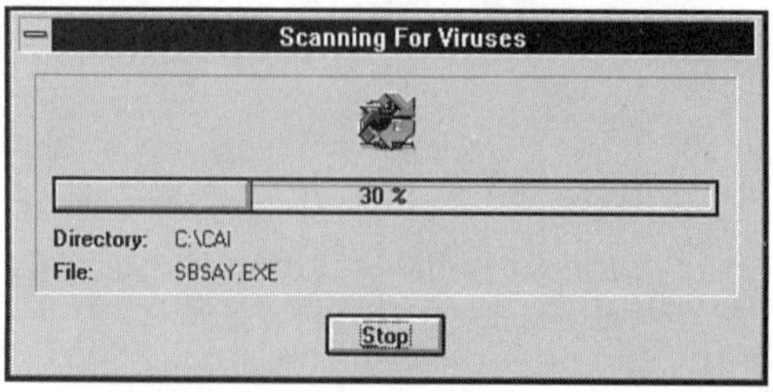

Fig. A.4
The Scanning for Viruses information dialog box.

After the virus scan is complete, the installation program begins copying files to your hard disk (see fig. A.5). Several important messages appear on-screen during installation, such as reminders to send in your registration card and information about features of the program.

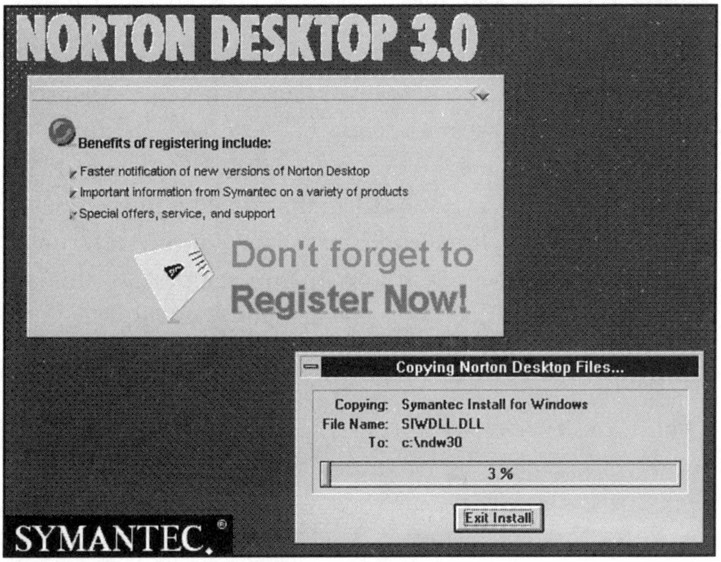

Fig. A.5
The initial display that appears on-screen while the installation program copies the NDW files to your hard disk.

After the information from the first disk is copied to your hard disk, the program prompts you to enter disk number 2, as shown in figure A.6.

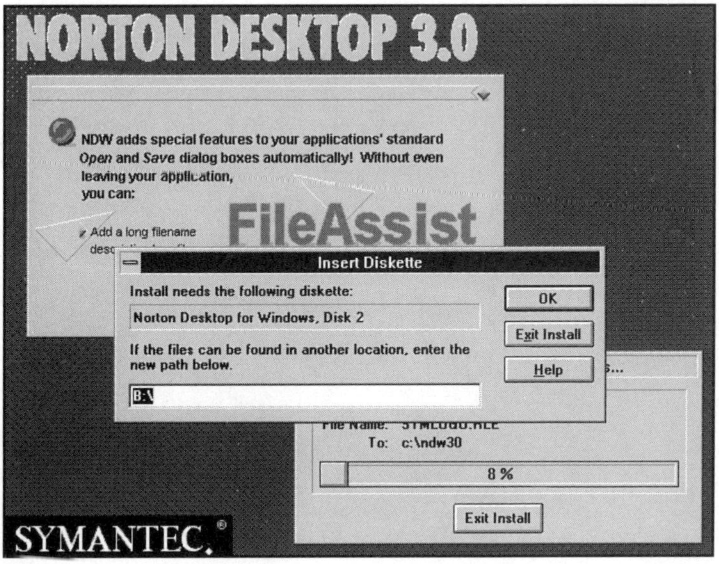

Fig. A.6
The Insert Diskette dialog box prompts you to insert an installation disk.

6. Remove the current disk in the drive, place the requested disk in the drive, and choose OK. You are prompted for all the disks needed during the installation process. After all files are copied, you are asked if you want to make the Norton Desktop the default Windows desktop.

7. Answer **Y**es if you want the Norton Desktop to appear each time you begin Windows. Install now asks if you want to create a Rescue Disk.

8. Answer **Y**es to create a Rescue disk to help you recover your computer hard disk in case it becomes damaged. *Creating a rescue disk is highly recommended.* To create this disk, you need a blank floppy disk. You are prompted to place the blank disk in the disk drive. If you do not create a rescue disk during installation, make sure that you create one later by choosing the Rescue Disk program from the Desktop utilities. (See Chapter 29, "Using Norton Fix-It and Rescue Disks.")

   Finally, you are asked if you want to restart Windows.

9. Choose **Y**es. After Windows comes back up, you see the Norton Desktop (if you chose this option in step 7).

After you install Norton Desktop for Windows as your default desktop, it appears on-screen every time you begin Windows. You are now ready to use Norton Desktop 3 for Windows.

Appendix B

New Features in Norton Desktop for Windows

Version 3 of Norton Desktop for Windows, although retaining the same basic features of version 2.2, represents a significant improvement over that earlier release. If you own either version 1.0 or 2.0 of the program and have not yet upgraded, read this section to examine the changes among these versions. The enhancements should encourage you to upgrade as soon as possible

This third generation of Norton Desktop for Windows makes learning, using, and customizing your Desktop easier than ever. In creating this new version, Symantec focused on how people actually work with Windows and tailored the changes to the program to meet those needs.

New and improved tools in version 3 make the Desktop more of a time-saving tool than ever before. The new *Day Planner* tool integrates an Appointment Calendar, a To Do List, and a Phone Book. *FileAssist* enables you to manage files from within other applications and also enables you to use longer file name descriptions.

In version 3, most of Desktop's customization options are centered in a central program called the *Control Center*. By using a graphical "control panel," you can choose configurations for all program options. The Control Center even shows you exactly how the changes affect the look of your Desktop. Graphical toolbars used throughout the program are completely configurable.

The new *drag-and-drop* features in version 3 enable you to drag multiple items from drive and group windows onto the Desktop. You also can connect DOS directories to Windows Program Groups.

The *Norton Viewer* has long been a popular part of Norton Desktop, and now the Viewer has even more capabilities. More than 100 file formats are now supported in the Viewer. It also supports the Windows Clipboard's copy and paste operations, and OLE 2.0 embedded objects. The Viewer is compatible with popular viewer plug-in packages and enables you to view the contents of files contained inside files compressed by the PKZIP 2.0 format.

Norton programs have long been known for their data efficiency, protection, and recovery features, and NDW 3 does not fail you here either. An improved *Speed Disk* program enables you to optimize your hard disk without leaving Windows. It also supports compressed drives (such as those created by Stacker or DoubleSpace) and optimizes very large hard drives. One of Norton's flagship programs, the *Disk Doctor*, can now diagnose and repair your disks under Windows—including compressed drives and large hard disks.

Other new protection features include added features in *Norton Backup* that support tape sharing and offer support for QIC 4/80 and SCSI devices. Backup also provides DES encryption; Netware bindary, rights, and trustee; and is operated from an easier "1-2-3 GO" interface. *Norton AntiVirus* now detects more than 2,300 known viruses and is capable even of detecting unknown viruses. The Desktop *Rescue Disk* provides you with a bootable disk containing these and other rescue programs that can be used in an emergency if your computer no longer can be booted from your hard disk.

Norton Desktop 3 for Windows has extensive *Novell NetWare support*. It contains unerase support for NetWare salvage and supports Filter files in the File Manager by Netware attribute; file search based on NetWare owner; AntiVirus NLM; and Backup NetWare bindary, rights, and trustee. A network menuing administration package also is available.

The improvement in Desktop's *Help system* includes a graphical QuickHelp, an on-line tutorial, and a new feature called the *Treasure Chest*. The Treasure Chest contains tips and shortcuts about the use of the program and can be a valuable tool in helping you become a power Desktop user.

The Batch Builder and Macro systems in version 2.0 have been replaced by a tool called *ScriptMaker*. This tool is a Visual Basic-like script language in which you can write simple to extensive programs while taking advantage of Desktop's unique features.

As an added bonus, even with all its new features, Norton Desktop 3 for Windows is even faster than the previous versions.

Index

Symbols

A

D

M

N

Q

R

S

T

U

V

W

X-Y-Z

Complete Computer Coverage

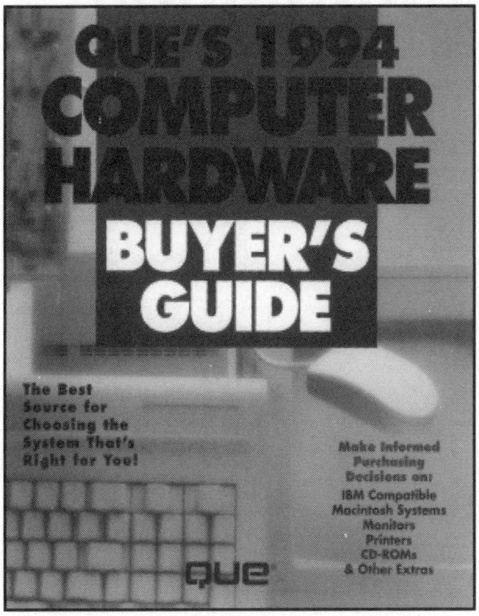

Que's 1994 Computer Hardware Buyer's Guide

Que Development Group

This absolute must-have guide packed with comparisons, recommendations, and tips for asking all the right questions familiarizes the reader with terms they will need to know. This book offers a complete analysis of both hardware and software products, and it's loaded with charts and tables of product comparisons.

IBM-compatibles, Apple, & Macintosh

$16.95 USA

1-56529-281-2, 480 pp., 8 x 10

Que's Computer User's Dictionary, 4th Edition

Bryan Pfaffenberger

This compact, practical reference contains hundreds of definitions, explanations, examples, and illustrations on topics from programming to desktop publishing. You can master the "language" of computers and learn how to make your personal computer more efficient and more powerful. Filled with tips and cautions, *Que's Computer User's Dictionary* is the perfect resource for anyone who uses a computer.

IBM, Macintosh, Apple, & Programming

$12.95 USA

1-56529-604-4, 650 pp., $4^{3}/_{4}$ x 8

que

To Order, Call: (800) 428-5331

I Hate Computers—But Que Makes It Easy!

I Hate WordPerfect 6
Elden Nelson
Version 6.0 for DOS
$16.95 USA, 480 pp.
ISBN: 1-56529-361-4

I Hate Windows
Gordon Macomb
Version 3.1
$16.95 USA, 300 pp.
ISBN: 1-56529-214-6

I Hate 1-2-3
Patrick Burns
Through Release 3.4
$16.95 USA, 300 pp.
ISBN: 1-56529-253-7

I Hate Buying a Computer
Jim Felici
Covers General Hardware
$16.95 USA, 256 pp.
ISBN: 1-56529-278-2

I Hate DOS
Bryan Pfaffenberger
Version 6.0
$16.95 USA, 300 pp.
ISBN: 1-56529-215-4

I Hate Excel 5
Patrick Burns
Version 5 for Windows
$16.95 USA, 352 pp.
ISBN: 1-56529-532-3

I Hate PC's
Bryan Pfaffenberger
Covers IBM PCs Compatibles
$16.95 USA, 300 pp.
ISBN: 1-56529-254-5

I Hate Word for Windows
Suzanne Weixel
Version 6.0 for Windows
$16.95 USA, 480 pp.
ISBN: 1-56529-616-8

To Order, Call: (800) 428-5331
OR (317) 581-3500

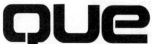